MAD
★ AS ★
HELL

JACK W. GERMOND AND JULES WITCOVER

MAD ★ AS ★ HELL

Revolt at the Ballot Box, 1992

WARNER BOOKS

A Time Warner Company

Warner Books, Inc., 1271 Avenue of the Americas, New York, NY 10020

W A Time Warner Company

Printed in the United States of America

First Printing: July 1993

10   9   8   7   6   5   4   3   2   1

Library of Congress Cataloging-in-Publication Data

Germond, Jack.
    Mad as hell : revolt at the ballot box, 1992 / Jack Germond, Jules
Witcover.
        p.   cm.
    Includes index.
    ISBN 0-446-51650-3
    1. Presidents—United States—Election—1992.   2. United States—
Politics and government—1989–1993.   I. Witcover, Jules.
II. Title.
E884.G47   1993
324.973'098—dc20   92-50533
                                                                CIP

Book design by H. Roberts

In memory of Paul Tully

I hold it, that a little rebellion, now and then,
is a good thing, and as necessary in the political
world as storms in the physical.
—*Thomas Jefferson; letter to James Madison*
January 30, 1787

ACKNOWLEDGMENTS

If the presidential campaign of 1992 differed in any significant manner from others in recent years, it was in the hunger of voters for straight answers from the candidates and in the innovative ways that hunger was expressed, and was responded to by those candidates.

While campaigning in traditional ways through the primaries and then in the general election, the candidates also capitalized on the new enterprise and technologies in television to reach out more directly and personally to voters, often in contexts in which the voters could reach back to them. At the same time, thousands of voters labored in behalf of an independent candidate who shunned the traditional route. And behind these innovations and direct candidate contact, a small army of campaign professionals continued as in past years to shape the political tactics and strategies of the candidates.

In seeking here to provide a reliable account of the circumstances, events and voters' frame of mind that brought about the election of Bill Clinton, we have tried to meld all these elements through personal observation on the campaign trail and then in extensive post-election interviewing. Having witnessed the candidates' use of the new opportunities to communicate directly during the primaries and general election, and talking to voters as they did so, we then interviewed nearly a hundred of the key political figures who helped direct the various campaigns. Among those to whom we are indebted for their observations either during or after the campaign are:

President Clinton, for interviews along the way and in the Oval Office after his inauguration; also, Roger Ailes, former Representative John B. Anderson, Clifford Arnebeck, Paul Begala, Charles Black, Mark Bohannon, Gloria Borger, Janet Brown, Jerry Brown, Ron Brown, John Brummett, Patrick Buchanan, Iris Jacobson Burnett, Patrick Caddell, Dan Carol, James Carville, James Cicconi, Pat Clancy, Governor Mario Cuomo, Richard Darman, Don Devine, Tom Edsall, Mort Engelberg, Mike Foudy, Ed Fouhy, Jack Gargan, Mark Gearan, Bob Goodwin, Joe Grandmaison, Stan Greenberg, Frank Greer, Mandy Grunwald, Marisa Hall, Mark Halperin, Senator Tom Harkin, Sharon Holman, John Jay Hooker, Jesse Jackson, Ed Jesser, Hamilton Jordan, Dennis Kanin, Mickey Kantor, David Keene, Senator Bob Kerrey, Larry King, Tim Kraft, Marcia Kramer, Bill Kristol, Lionel Kunst; also, James Lake, Al LaPierre, Tom Luce, John Marino, John Mashek, Mary Matalin, Richard Moe, Clay Mulford, Dee Dee Myers, Tom Oliphant, Andy Paven, Ross Perot, Nancy Sanders Peterson, James Pinkerton, Victoria Radd, Tom Rath, Cokie Roberts, Senator Jay Rockefeller, Ed Rollins, Steve Rosenthal, Sal Russo, John Seigenthaler, Carole Simpson, John Solomon, James Squires, Fred Steeper, George Stephanopoulos, Orson Swindle, Bob Teeter, David Tell, Ginny Terzano, Alice Travis, former Senator Paul Tsongas, Paul Tully, Kimberly Usry, Denton Walthall, Paul West, Paul Weyrich, Governor L. Douglas Wilder, David Wilhelm, Carter Wilkie, Curtis Wilkie, Richard Winger, Senator Harris Wofford, James Wooten.

TABLE OF CONTENTS

BLOWING THE WHISTLE

In the early evening of October 18, the night before the three candidates for the presidency of the United States—George Bush, Bill Clinton and Ross Perot—were to hold their second debate of the 1992 campaign, the telephone rang in a farmhouse eighteen miles north of Richmond, Virginia. Kimberly Usry, a twenty-eight-year-old single woman who had only recently been laid off from her job as a marketing director for a traffic-control company, picked up the phone.

The caller was a representative of the famed Gallup polling organization. He started asking her questions about the approaching election, including whether she planned to vote for the reelection of President Bush.

"Not in hell!" she shot back, according to her recollection.

The caller then asked whether she had made up her mind between Clinton and Perot. She told him she had not, and so he put her down as "undecided" (!)—and invited her to the debate the following night at the University of Richmond.

Kim Usry accepted with enthusiasm, particularly because she was told she would be part of a small audience that would have the unprecedented opportunity to ask the candidates a question directly. Over the next twenty-four hours, she weighed the possibilities, appreciating that she might have the one-in-a-million chance to confront a present or future president with the one issue she most had on her mind.

The next afternoon, Kim Usry arrived at a holding room for invited guests at the university, and after a time she and the other 208 Richmond-area "undecideds" selected in the Gallup phone survey were marched into the auditorium of the Robbins Center. They were seated in a wide semicircle and Carole Simpson of ABC News, chosen to be the moderator, greeted them, going through a sort of warm-up. She asked them for sample questions—specifically not the ones they intended to ask the candidates if called upon—to get a sense of what subjects they would raise, and to impress on them the seriousness of their responsibility. When one woman attempted to show Simpson a question she had written, to ask her if she thought it was a good one, the moderator told her flatly that she didn't want to see or hear it.

The first presidential debate, at Washington University in St. Louis four nights earlier, had the customary format of a moderator and press panel, and the result had been a relatively traditional affair. Going in, the president was trailing the Arkansas governor by ten or more percentage points in most of the polls and his strategists were looking for him to close the gap with a strong and aggressive showing.

So George Bush went on the attack, criticizing Clinton for having protested against the Vietnam war twenty-three years earlier when he was a student in England, insisting "it's wrong to demonstrate against your own country or organize demonstrations against your own country on foreign soil." Several days earlier, when Bush first made the charge, Clinton had countercharged that the president was questioning his patriotism in the manner of Senator Joseph R. McCarthy of Wisconsin, the infamous communist witch-hunter of the 1950s. In the first debate, Clinton hit back in the same way again, noting that in the 1950s the president's own father, Senator Prescott Bush of Connecticut, "was right to stand up to Joe McCarthy. You were wrong to attack my patriotism. I was opposed to the war, but I love my country," he said, glaring at the president.

Kim Usry had watched that first debate and that exchange on television, and she hadn't liked what she saw and heard. So when the second debate started, she was primed to get something off her chest. After the first two questions and answers, concerning foreign trade and the federal deficit, she signaled to a young woman standing next to her on the aisle who was holding a microphone, then jumped up and was recognized by the moderator.

"I'd like to address all the candidates with this question," she said. "The amount of time the candidates have spent in this campaign trashing their opponents' character and the programs is depressingly large. Why can't your discussions and proposals reflect the genuine complexity and the difficulty of the issues, to try to build a consensus around the best aspects of all proposals?"

Simpson turned to the candidates. "Who wants to take that one?" then bluntly adding: "Mr. Perot, you have an answer for everything, don't you? Go right ahead, sir."

The Texas billionaire only recently had rejoined the fray after having pulled out of the presidential race in mid-July before he had properly gotten in. He brushed aside the moderator's put-down and agreed with the questioner. "And I have said again and again and again, let's get off the mud wrestling," he lectured, "let's get off personalities, and let's talk about jobs, health care, crime, the things that concern the American people. . . ."

Next, Simpson invited the president to respond. Instead, he went right back on the attack. "I believe that character is a part of being president. I think you have to look at it. . . . You know, nobody likes who shot John, but I think the first negative campaign [sic] run in this election was by Governor Clinton, and I'm not going to sit there and be a punching bag. I'm going to stand up and say, 'Hey, listen, here's my side of it.' "

The incumbent went on like that, raising the mention of his father by Clinton in the first debate and trailing off into a maudlin reminiscence of him: "I remember something my dad told me. I was eighteen years old going to Penn Station to go on into the navy, and he said, 'Write your mother,' which I faithfully did. He said, 'Serve your country.' My father was an honor, duty and country man. And he said, 'Tell the truth.' And I've tried to do that in public life, all through it. That says something about character."

In the next breath, though, he was attacking again: "My argument with Governor Clinton—you can call it mud wrestling, but I think it's fair to put it in focus—is I am deeply troubled by someone who demonstrates and organizes demonstrations in a foreign land when his country's at war. Probably a lot of kids here disagree with me. But that's what I feel. That's what I feel passionately about. I'm thinking about Ross Perot's running mate [retired Admiral James B. Stockdale, a former Vietnam prisoner of war] sitting in the jail. How would he feel about it? But maybe that's generational. I don't know."

Now it was Clinton's turn. Facing Kim Usry directly, he spoke to her as if they were the only two people in the room: "Let me say first of all to you that I believe so strongly in the question you asked that I suggested this format tonight. . . . I've been disturbed by the tone and the tenor of this campaign. . . . So I'm not going to take up your time tonight [defending himself against Bush's charges], but let me just say this. We'll have a debate in four days and we can talk about this character thing again. . . . Here's my point. I'm not interested in his [Bush's] character. I want to change the character of the presidency—"

Carole Simpson interjected that before the debate started she had asked the guests "how they felt about the tenor of the campaign." She turned to the audience: "Would you like to let them know what you thought about that when I said, 'Are you pleased with how the campaign's been going?' " The audience shouted back: "No!" Whereupon she invited someone else to talk about it.

Denton Walthall, a thirty-seven-year-old father of two with his dark hair tied in a ponytail, stepped up to the microphone. He too had been called by a Gallup representative, had declared himself to be undecided and was invited to attend the debate.

In advance, Walthall had dutifully prepared about a dozen issue-oriented questions. But driving to the university hours before the debate, he recalled later, he spotted a handmade sign held up along the road. It bore the international prohibition sign—a red circle with a red diagonal slash across it—and the words: NO UNEMPLOYMENT—NO CRIME—NO HOMELESSNESS. These were the basic issues, he said to himself, that the candidates should be addressing.

Driving on, Walthall remembered watching the televised debate among the vice presidential candidates with his six-year-old son, Nicholas, two nights earlier. When Democratic nominee Albert Gore, Jr., made reference to a television report critical of the Bush administration, Vice President Dan Quayle had interrupted, observing: "Senator, don't always believe what you see on television." The boy turned to his father and asked: "Daddy, what can you believe on TV?" And with all the charges back and forth, Walthall thought, it was no wonder his son didn't know what to believe.

The handmade sign, Walthall said later, and his son's question got him to thinking as he approached the university. Why couldn't the politicians forget about the personal stuff and address real needs? He decided to ignore his prepared list of questions and ask one that really got to what was on his mind about the campaign. And when Kim Usry asked the candidates point-blank to stop "trashing" each other, he recalled, "I said, 'Amen, sister.' "

The answers they had given to Usry, especially Bush's, Walthall said later, really set him off. "I had heard the whole thing in 1988," he said. "Willie Horton, the pledge of allegiance, Boston harbor. It was the same thing all over again. I thought, 'Does this man have to stoop to all this to be reelected?' I said [to myself], 'The hell with it.' "

A bit nervous but determined, Walthall stood up and began:

"Forgive the notes here, but I'm shy on camera. The focus of my work as a domestic mediator is meeting the needs of the children that I work with, by way of their parents, not the wants of their parents. And I ask the three of you, how can we, as symbolically the children of the future president, expect the two of you, the three of you, to meet our needs, the needs in housing and in crime and you name it, as opposed to the wants of your political spin doctors and your political parties?"

Simpson tried to help him. "So your question is?" she asked. Walthall pressed on, and finally got to it. "Can we focus on the issues and not the personalities and the mud?" he asked earnestly. "I think there's a need. If we could take a poll here with the folks from Gallup perhaps, I think there's a real need here to focus at this point on the needs."

Clinton responded at once. "I agree with him," he said. Then Bush: "Let's do it. Let's talk about programs for children."

Walthall was getting more emotional. "Could we cross our hearts?" he inquired plaintively. "It sounds silly here, but could we make a commitment? You know, we're not under oath at this point, but could you make a commitment to the citizens of the United States to meet our needs, and we have many, and not yours again?''

Immediately Bush hedged. ''I think it depends how you define it,'' he said. ''I mean, I think in general let's talk about these issues, let's talk about the programs. But in the presidency a lot goes into it. Caring goes into it. That's not particularly specific. Strength goes into it. That's not specific. Standing up against aggression. That's not specific in terms of a program. This is what a president has to do. So in principle, though, I'll take your point and think we ought to discuss child care or whatever else it is.''

Perot jumped in. ''Just no hedges, no ifs, ands and buts,'' he snapped. ''I'll take the pledge because I know the American people want to talk about issues and not tabloid journalism. So I'll take the pledge and will stay on the issues.''

Clinton had the last word, and again he spoke it directly to the questioner: ''I worked twelve years very hard as a governor on the real problems of real people. I'm just as sick as you are by having to wake up and figure out how to defend myself every day. I never thought I'd ever be involved in anything like this.''

Anything like this. To the jobless woman from the rural Virginia farmhouse and the father with the ponytail, that was what the presidential campaign of 1992 had come down to: a sickening display of name-calling and personal attacks, all in the guise of the issue of ''character.'' In the end, Kim Usry voted for Perot, Denton Walthall for Clinton.

Shortly after the election, Roger Ailes, the media specialist for the Bush campaign in 1988 who saw only spot duty as a debate coach for Bush in 1992, told us he was convinced that Walthall had been a sort of ''plant,'' in the sense that his physical appearance alone gave away the likelihood that he would ask a hostile question, and so he was called upon. Commenting on Simpson's warming-up of the questioners by inquiring about their areas of interest, Ailes said: ''When you preinterview, you pretty well know what the question is going to be. That's a trick I've used with studio audiences for twenty-five years. You can pinpoint with ninety percent accuracy what they're gonna ask. If you find a forty-year-old guy with a ponytail who is working with kids, you know damn well what kind of question he's gonna ask.''

Charles Black, a chief Bush strategist, agreed. He recalled standing in the back of the hall while Simpson was warming up the audience and eliciting from the audience what kinds of questions were going to be asked, telling participants, he said, "what was or wasn't a good question." As far as he was concerned, Black said later, "Carole Simpson was screening questions [and] rehearsing the voters. She was doing a dry run, jumping in with follow-up questions, changing the subject." He became so concerned, Black said, that he phoned Bob Teeter, the Bush campaign chairman, in Bush's hotel suite and told him to prepare the president for anything—including hostile questions.

Black insisted later, to Simpson's firm denials, that "she was groomed on who to call on. . . . She knew that guy, I'm convinced, the guy with the ponytail who stood up and said we don't want any negative campaigning, we hope you folks will not say anything bad about each other. It had a chilling effect on everybody's going on the attack. . . . Bush got two good hits in on Clinton in the first ten minutes and then he never got any more. And he was right. The tone and the environment were such that he would have gotten booed, which is the worst thing that can happen to you in a TV setting like that."

Another Bush insider who played a key role in the debate negotiations and in preparing Bush, and was also present for the warm-up, was even stronger in his criticism of Simpson. She had voters read their questions, he said, and then told them whether they were too long or not sufficiently focused. "She said what were good subjects," he said. "She was not interested in patsies, she was trying to make good television." Beyond that, he said, "she built a group spirit. She started specifying that 'we don't want to be negative,' and built a group spirit around that."

None of this criticism, however, squared with the fact that Carole Simpson was not a free agent in choosing the questioners. Ed Fouhy, producer of the debates for the Commission on Presidential Debates, was in direct telephone communication with Simpson from the control booth throughout the debate. At the start he instructed her specifically which person to call on first, and thereafter either specified individuals or which sections of the audience to go to, so that the television cameras under his direction could be properly focused, assuring a seamless flow in the picture and sound that went out to the home audience.

With Simpson facing the candidates and her back to the audience most of the time, she was in no position to go hunting for specific people to call on, according to Janet Brown, director of the debates commission, who was sitting in the booth next to Fouhy and heard him instruct Simpson on who was to be recognized next. Simpson had her hands full allocating time fairly among the candidates and keeping the flow of the debate going, Brown said later.

Walthall flatly denied he was a plant or had been rehearsed. Reflecting on his question, he allowed that "it was really silly when I said 'cross our hearts,' but I was serious in what I meant." After the debate, he went home and turned on his television set to unwind. "The first thing I see," he recalled, "was one of Bush's anti-Clinton ads, the one with Clinton on the cover of *Time* [as a photo negative, the use of which prompted the magazine to sue the Bush campaign]. I thought, 'Here's this shit again. This guy hasn't made a commitment and we can pretty much expect this the rest of the way.' "

It was true enough. The president had made no explicit commitment to stop attacking Clinton on the "character" issue. But something happened that night in Richmond, and the back-to-back questions of Kim Usry and Denton Walthall had a lot to do with it. "It set him off his game," Jim Lake, the Bush campaign's communications director, said later. For the rest of the debate, Bush skipped direct references to Clinton's "character."

Ailes later acknowledged that the scolding on negative campaigning from Kim Usry and Denton Walthall had stopped the president in his tracks. "It moved him to go to his natural instincts, which was to be a nice guy," Ailes said. Teeter said later that Bush himself confided that the format "did not lend itself to a tough attack. . . . He couldn't do what we all had been telling him was the objective. . . . We wanted a debate that was more confrontational" between Bush and Clinton.

But that, David Wilhelm, the Clinton campaign manager, said later, was where the Bush campaign had made its greatest miscalculation, and why the Richmond debate was, as he put it, "the most dramatic crystallization of a mind-set that existed throughout the campaign, and it was something the Bush people never really understood.

"Bush kept trying to make the campaign about Clinton, and the American people wanted the campaign to be about them—their problems, their hopes, their dreams, their economy," Wilhelm said. "When we were at our best we kept talking about that, the things that mattered in the average voter's life. And when George Bush tried to make the campaign be about something other than that—Bill Clinton's draft record, or trip to the Soviet Union—people reacted very negatively. And when that fellow with the ponytail stood up and said essentially, 'Hey, make this about my problems,' it really crystallized the failure of the Bush strategy. If there was one moment that did it, that was it.''

In that same second debate in Richmond, another questioner perhaps underscored even more the gap between Bush and the average voter. Marisa Hall, a twenty-five-year-old single woman, was concerned that the candidates were out of touch with the trials that everyday people like herself were facing in the recession. There was a lot of talk from them about how the mushrooming national debt was undermining the nation's well-being, but she wasn't getting a sense of what it meant in terms of the individual.

"How has the national debt personally affected each of your lives?'' she asked. "And if it hasn't, how can you honestly find a cure for the economic problems of the common people if you have no experience in what's ailing them?''

Perot quickly responded that the national debt ''caused me to disrupt my private life and my business to get involved in this activity. That's how much I care about it.'' He noted that ''I came from a very modest background'' and that ''as lucky as I've been,'' he owed it to the country's children and his own to try to do something about the sick economy.

Simpson then turned to the president.

"Well,'' he said, ''I think the national debt affects everybody.''

"You personally,'' Simpson said, trying to nail him down in behalf of the questioner.

Bush seemed confused. "Obviously it has a lot to do with interest rates,'' he offered.

Simpson interjected again: "She's saying 'You personally. You on a personal basis. How has it affected you . . . personally?' ''

Bush: "I'm sure it has. I love my grandchildren. . . . I want to think that they're going to be able to afford an education. I think that that's an important part of being a parent. If the question—maybe I—get it wrong.''

Looking at Marisa Hall, the president asked her: "Are you suggesting that if somebody has means, that the national debt doesn't affect them? . . . I'm not sure I get—help me with the question and I'll try to answer it.''

''Well,'' the woman said, ''I've had friends that have been laid off from jobs. . . . I know people who cannot afford to pay the mortgage on their homes, their car payment. I have personal problems with the national debt. But how has it affected you, and if you have no experience in it, how can you help us, if you don't know what we're feeling?''

Bush still seemed puzzled. Simpson stepped in again. ''I think she means,'' she said, ''more the recession—the economic problems today the country is facing, rather than the deficit.''

The president finally got the idea—in his fashion. ''Well, listen,'' he said, ''you ought to be in the White House for a day and hear what I hear and see what I see, and read the mail I read and touch the people that I touch from time to time.''

Bush went on to tell how he had gone to the Lomax AME church outside Washington, a black congregation, ''and I read in the bulletin about teenage pregnancies, about the difficulties families are having to make ends meet. I talk to parents. I mean, you've got to care. Everybody cares if people aren't doing well.''

He was sounding very defensive now. ''But I don't think it's fair to say, 'You haven't had cancer, therefore you don't know what it's like.' I don't think it's fair to say, you know, whatever it is, that if you haven't been hit by it personally—. But everybody's affected by the debt because of the tremendous interest that goes into paying on that debt, everything's more expensive. Everything comes out of your pocket and my pocket. So that's it. But I think in terms of the recession, of course you feel it when you're president of the United States. And that's why I'm trying to do something about it by stimulating the export . . . investing more, better education systems.''

Listening to Bush at such times was like listening to a phonograph record with the needle skipping. ''Thank you,'' he said to Marisa Hall at last. ''I'm glad you clarified it.'' In the Clinton holding room nearby where the Democratic nominee's chief strategists were watching, television adviser Mandy Grunwald recalled, ''We all looked at each other. It was almost sad.''

Now it was Clinton's turn. He raised up off the stool against which he was leaning and strolled toward the woman. According to one aide who took part in Clinton's debate preparations, Clinton was told at the time that "the audience was his friend, he should go to the audience" if he was so moved, and he did. In the debate prep, Grunwald remembered, Clinton had asked: "How far can I go without losing the camera?" Now he walked as far as the previously calculated spot, then said to his questioner: "Tell me how it's affected you again. . . . You know people who've lost their jobs and lost their homes?"

"Well, yeah, uh-huh," she replied, somewhat taken aback by Clinton's direct approach. But he was just getting warmed up. Standing only a few feet from her, he didn't talk about learning about other people's troubles by reading about them on a church bulletin board.

"I've been governor of a small state for twelve years," he said. "I'll tell you how it's affected me. Every year Congress and the president sign laws that make us do more things and give us less money to do it with. I see people in my state, middle-class people—their taxes have gone up in Washington and their services have gone down, while the wealthy have gotten tax cuts.

"I've seen what's happened in the last four years when—in my state, when people lose their jobs there's a good chance I'll know them by their names. When a factory closes, I know the people who ran it. When the businesses go bankrupt, I know them.

"And I've been out here for thirteen months meeting in meetings just like this ever since October [1991], with people like you all over America—people that have lost their jobs, lost their livelihood, lost their health insurance. What I want you to understand is the national debt is not the only cause of that. It is because America has not invested in its people. It is because we have not grown. It is because we've had twelve years of trickle-down economics. We've gone from first to twelfth in the world in wages. We've had four years where we've produced no private sector jobs. Most people are working harder for less money than they were making ten years ago.

"It is because we are in the grip of a failed economic theory. And this decision you're about to make better be about what kind of economic theory you want. But just people saying I'm going to fix it [isn't enough] . . . what are we going to do? I think [what] we have to do is invest in American jobs, American education, control American health care costs and bring the American people together again."

Around this time, a television camera caught Bush looking at his wristwatch, and the shot was flashed to the millions and millions of Americans watching at home. The immediate impression to many was that he was getting impatient with the whole business and was wishing for the debate to be over. Later, aides insisted that the president was checking his watch because it seemed to him that his opponents were talking beyond the time allocated for each answer, as reached in the pre-debate negotiations.

If that was so, it was another example of the proper, rules-abiding George Bush being tripped up by his own rigid adherence to agreements made. Twelve years earlier in another famous presidential debate in Nashua, New Hampshire, Bush had agreed to a two-man debate with Ronald Reagan. When Reagan unexpectedly invited the other Republicans running for the nomination to join them, Bush sat stiffly and unyieldingly, enabling Reagan to make him look the poor sport. But Bush's position was that an agreement had been made, and gentlemen didn't break agreements. And here was another agreement being broken.

Later, Marisa Hall assessed the three responses. "Perot answered the question correctly," she said. "President Bush never answered it. It kind of upset me. He started talking about going to that black church, then he started talking about his grandchildren." As for Clinton, she said, "a lot of people were saying his answer had been rehearsed, but what he said made me feel good. And when he came toward me, I liked that." On election day, she voted for Clinton.

To point to a single question and answer in one debate as a revelation of Bush's political vulnerability would be unfair if it were not so typical of a seeming incomprehension of what average voters were feeling and saying all through the campaign year. Comparing the fears of a jobless worker unable to pay his house mortgage with the concern of a wealthy man about whether his grandchildren will be properly educated was ludicrous on its face.

In the Clinton holding room, the Democratic nominee's chief aides and strategists were whooping it up. When he walked over to Hall, who had just confused Bush with a simple question, and demonstrated at once that he understood, Clinton press secretary Dee Dee Myers said later, "that was probably the most memorable moment for the hundred million people who tuned in to the debates, because the contrast was so stark. Perot was having a good debate but no one was thinking about him as a real president. People out there were tuning in because Perot was good theater and because they were going to pick a president between the other two. That was the moment that most clearly distinguished them and I said, 'The campaign is over. George Bush is dead. He just killed himself.' We couldn't get to the press room fast enough [to start "spinning" reporters with that conclusion]."

Mickey Kantor, the campaign chairman, agreed. As soon as Bush said, "in effect, 'I don't get it,' " Kantor said later, "we knew that was it, because we knew what Bill Clinton would do. . . . It was vintage Bill Clinton, and over his shoulder, that was when Bush looked at his watch. Now, did that win the whole campaign? No. But was it symbolic of everything the American people were concerned about? Absolutely. . . . First, somebody says, 'Quit throwing mud, and then Bill Clinton connects and George Bush doesn't. It gave us exactly what we wanted. I mean, I would have been happy then if we'd have shut off [the campaign], say, 'No more debates, that's the end. We're gonna stop campaigning,' and make that the end. That would have been the last image I would have wanted in the campaign."

When Clinton came into the holding room afterward to an "ecstatic" welcome, one of those present said, it was clear he knew he had done well, but because he had not seen how Bush looked, and what the dynamic of the whole debate was coming over a television set, he didn't realize at first just how well. The staff did not keep him guessing.

Later, after the election, Clinton told us in an interview in the Oval Office: "I'd like to tell you that I grasped the event, and the significance of it, at the time, but I didn't. But when I heard [President Bush] talking to that woman [Marisa Hall], I knew that she was asking him a different question than he was answering. I did know that.

"You know, it's not easy to listen to people anytime. It's a lot easier to be a good talker than a good listener. But in that format, with all that pressure, with one hundred million people watching, it's probably even harder to be a good listener. And one thing I thought about going into that debate was that these are real people; it doesn't matter whether they're for Bush or for Perot or for me, these are people who are out there living with the consequences of America today, and I have to listen to them. And I'm going to try to respond to them. I can give my speech, but respond to them.

"I really thought about it a lot, about the format, about how it was going to be different going in. . . . If we're having a debate and there's a press panel, and you ask me a question, one of your tough questions, it's a perilous question, I have to answer it. But if I have a minute and a half, I can answer it in thirty seconds then put my minute spin on it. With those people who were out there, I felt I had a lot less room to do that. . . . I saw the American people sort of screaming for me to pay attention to them and listen to them. So I knew I had done well with the questions because I listened to them and I watched them, and I had thought about them. But I had no idea it would have the impact on the voters that it apparently did."

For all the admonitions in Richmond against personal attacks, four nights later in the third presidential debate at Michigan State University in East Lansing, Bush was at it again. He began talking again about Clinton, about "this pattern that has plagued him . . . about trying to have it both ways on all these issues"—Bush on the campaign trail had been calling it "waffling." Clinton started coming back at him, then stopped. "I could run this string out a long time," he said, "but remember this, Jim [Lehrer, the moderator]. Those 209 Americans last Thursday night in Richmond told us they wanted us to stop talking about each other and start talking about Americans and their problems and their promise, and I think we ought to get back to that. I'll be glad to answer any question you have, but this election ought to be about the American people."

Several minutes later, though, Bush raised "this question about trust" again, repeating that "there's a pattern by Governor Clinton of saying one thing to please one group, and then trying to please another group," and that "that pattern is a dangerous thing to suggest would work for the Oval Office."

Clinton was right back with his friends from the Richmond debate. "I really can't believe Mr. Bush is still trying to make trust an issue," he said, "after 'read my lips' [his reneged-on no-new-taxes pledge in 1988] and [his promise of] 15 million new jobs and embracing what he called voodoo economics, and embracing an export enhancement program for farms he threatened to veto, and going all around the country giving out money in programs he once opposed.'' The president indeed had made those promises in the campaign and had been spreading government largesse of all sorts in states where he needed political help.

"But the main thing,'' Clinton intoned, "is he still didn't get it, from what he said the other night to that fine woman on our program, the 209 people in Richmond. They don't want us talking about each other. They want us to talk about the problems of this country.''

In the remaining two weeks of the campaign, the governor of Arkansas never stopped reminding voters, as he dashed frenetically around the country by bus and jet plane, about the questions asked that night at the University of Richmond by the unemployed woman, the father with the ponytail and the voter concerned about how the "national debt'' affected the candidates. Clinton deftly cast the three of them as the voice of America, crying out in protest against the demeaning of the nation's political process by an incumbent president who insisted on talking about personal matters instead of the serious problems facing the country, and didn't "get it'' when asked how those problems touched him.

In a large sense, it was not a miscasting. Kim Usry, Denton Walthall and Marisa Hall did indeed express the public revulsion against negative campaigning, particularly when it was focused on matters of personal behavior and lifestyle, in a presidential election year in which millions of Americans were out of work or in fear of being so, or were without health care insurance or in fear of losing it.

Only four years earlier, American voters had looked on benignly or simply looked away as the same George Bush had resorted to the same sorts of negative campaign tactics to destroy the campaign of Democratic presidential nominee Michael S. Dukakis. Then, in 1988, it was Willie Horton, the furloughed murderer from Massachusetts—the black furloughed murderer—who raped a white woman in Maryland; the Dukakis veto of a state bill requiring teachers to lead the pledge of allegiance in their public school classrooms; the condemnation of pollution in Boston Harbor that Dukakis was attempting to clean up; the demonizing of the American Civil Liberties Union, to which Dukakis belonged.

This time around, however, the voters—given voice by the Kim Usrys, the Denton Walthalls and the Marisa Halls—had had a bellyful. They were, in one of the ever-whining George Bush's favorite phrases, "sick and tired" of the name-calling and the finger-pointing. They wanted the issues that had reduced the quality of their lives discussed and debated in the campaign. Like Howard Beale, the unbalanced television anchorman in the 1970s hit film *Network* and his aroused audience of fed-up Americans, they were proclaiming: "We're mad as hell and we're not going to take it anymore!"

They did not, as in the movie, throw open their windows, lean out and fill the night air with that declamation of their dismay. Instead, they trooped to the polls on Election Day, November 3, and voted in record numbers and in percentages not attained since John F. Kennedy narrowly defeated Richard M. Nixon for the presidency more than three decades earlier. And in place of the fictional Howard Beale, they had the real-life Ross Perot rallying them with basically the same message of discontent, impatience and resolve to take their country back.

In the movie, the character of the crazed television anchorman, played by British actor Peter Finch, met an untimely end, but in real life Perot managed to survive after bizarre behavior that made the comparison with the film character not entirely exaggerated.

The prime survivor of the whole fictionlike saga of the 1992 presidential campaign, however, was Bill Clinton, who correctly gauged the bubbling discontent with the tenor of the campaign process in the country and deftly nurtured it into the political weapon that drove George Bush from the White House.

There was, to be sure, much more involved than rebellion against negative campaigning in the defeat of a president who less than two years earlier had attained higher popularity ratings than any previous occupant of the White House in American history. In the ensuing period, a deep recession gripped the nation and held it fast, as the president first denied its severity, then denied its longevity, then prematurely proclaimed its end.

Bush, who had zestfully plunged into foreign policy challenges, capping them with a most impressive mobilization of world leaders behind his determined and successful effort to turn back Iraqi strongman Saddam Hussein's invasion of Kuwait, seemed strangely detached when he had to turn his attentions to the economic woes at home.

Part of it, his friends said, was the man's natural optimism—his sunny view that things would always get better, would always turn out for the best. It was an optimism born of the experience of a favored lifetime of family wealth and position, and sheltered from the experiences and hardships of all those who were not similarly favored. He always said he cared about others' problems, but the social and cultural gulf between himself—born into aristocracy, educated at the best and most prestigious schools and launched into business and politics by family money and connections—and the man in the street was immense. Never was that more apparent than in the stammering way he grappled with Marisa Hall's question about the "national debt."

The popular cliché about Bush throughout the campaign—embraced and spread at every opportunity by the Clinton campaign—was that "George Bush doesn't get it." Democrats never ceased telling voters that he didn't "get it" about the existence, depth and duration of the recession; about the hardships of daily life for people whose lifestyle was light years removed from his own.

When they scanned the newspapers while standing in unemployment lines or checking the want ads, they would see pictures of the president riding in a golf cart or on his boat at Kennebunkport, Maine. On the evening television news they would see him repeatedly at play when they were trying to find work, or fearful of losing the work they had. And when they read about how Bush had gone into a supermarket and didn't know what the price scanner at the checkout counter was all about, the incident only confirmed for millions that "George Bush just doesn't get it" when it came to the trials of their everyday lives.

On the other hand, Perot for all his wealth was a walking man-in-the-street, and every sentence and sound bite he uttered established that identity. (In explaining himself, he would tell his listeners "I can't sound-bite it for you"—and then do precisely that.)

As for Clinton, he knew what it took to persuade voters that he understood the condition of their lives. In a town-meeting exchange with voters one early morning in Winston-Salem, North Carolina, in the final days of the campaign—an event televised on the *CBS Morning News* show—a mother and part-time hospital worker named Debbie Gilbert tested Clinton on his knowledge of life at the level of the average American.

"Governor," she said, "I just have a hard time believing that many politicians today, who claim that they want to help ease the burden on the average American, can really do that, because I don't believe that politicians know what it's like to be in the shoes of the average American family. I want to know if you know how much it costs to buy a pound of hamburger, a pair of blue jeans, a tank of gas and visit the doctor's office.''

Clinton replied without hesitation. "Well, gasoline is about $1.20, depending on what kind of gasoline it is," he said. "Hamburger meat's a little over a dollar. A gallon of milk's two dollars. A loaf of bread's about a dollar now. . . . What it costs to go to the doctor depends on doctor visits. I know doctors that still do visits for fifteen dollars.'' When that one drew laughter, he added: "I do, but not many.'' He continued: "Blue jeans run anywhere from $18 to $50, depending on what kind you get.''

When the questioner rated Clinton's answers as "pretty good,'' he explained why he was able to be so readily responsive. "One of the virtues about being governor of a small state—both of my opponents have made fun of that,'' he said, "is that the people know me and I know them. And every now and then my wife and I just get out and go to the grocery store and just talk to people in the grocery store, and walk up and down the aisles and listen.''

A few days later, in a speech in Southgate, Michigan, the president, commenting on Clinton's knowledge of prices, demonstrated that he too knew what one common household item cost. But in giving the price of milk at "$2.70, say,'' he failed to indicate what quantity he was talking about—quart, half gallon or gallon, as if reciting a figure that had been handed to him by his staff.

To the end of the campaign, Bush pounded away at the idea that the ultimate issue on which voters should decide how to cast their ballots was personal trust. Did they have confidence that the individual they would vote for could be counted on to do what he said he would do? Clinton, he said repeatedly, was a "waffler'' who first said one thing, then another. But didn't he himself say "read my lips, no new taxes'' and then agree to impose them?

Still, Bush had established himself as a recognized world leader—even *the* world leader—in the preparations for and implementation of the Persian Gulf War. And the whole Communist bloc in Central and Eastern Europe had collapsed on his watch. In the aftermath of those triumphs,

Bush's popularity had reached or surpassed 90 percent in the most reputable public opinion polls.

How, in the course of less than two years, did George Bush fall so far that a reelection that had once seemed a certainty now appeared to be in such jeopardy? It had all begun so promisingly, so joyously, on that January day in 1989 when he took the oath of office at the Capitol and pledged to keep the Reagan Revolution on its path, and "to make kinder the face of the nation and gentler the face of the world."

CHAPTER 2

BETRAYING THE REVOLUTION

Well before George Bush became president of the United States, many conservatives in the Republican Party had held deep reservations about him as a true believer. He had, after all, once favored the position that abortion was a matter of a woman's choice. And who could forget his labeling of the sainted Ronald Reagan's plan for economic growth—tax cuts plus increased defense spending equals a balanced budget—as "voodoo economics" in the 1980 GOP primary campaign?

But once Reagan had—reluctantly—accepted him as his running mate that year, Bush had embraced Reaganomics and all other aspects of the Reagan Revolution as his own. That's the way it always was with George Bush; he might be wishy-washy in getting around to taking a position, but once he took it, he took it categorically. And he accepted as an article of political faith that when a presidential nominee chooses you as his vice presidential sidekick, you owe him total loyalty.

That complete commitment to the man who had given his political career a lease on life did not, however, satisfy some on the party's far right. "Bush never had one hundred percent confidence from card-carrying conservatives because he did not come out of the conservative movement like Reagan did," recalled Charles Black, the key conservative Republican consultant who eventually served in Bush's campaign. "And having run against Reagan and having some policy differences with him back in the '80 campaign, he just never achieved their full trust."

Bush's fealty to Reagan not only failed to convince some conservatives of his trustworthiness but also often led to ridicule of him from their ranks. Conservative columnist George Will, who in 1980 demonstrated an interesting character trait of his own by secretly helping to coach Reagan for a debate with Jimmy Carter and then extravagantly praising his performance afterward on television, once called Bush a "lapdog."

But Bush also had important friends on the right, and none was more influential in winning conservative support for him than Lee Atwater, the young protégé of Senator Strom Thurmond of South Carolina who rose rapidly in party ranks by dint of his keen sense of Southern and conservative politics and an instinct for the political jugular. Tapped to be Bush's 1988 campaign manager (and stand-in for James A. Baker III, Bush's closest political friend, then hiding out as Reagan's secretary of the treasury), Atwater as early as 1985 deftly started reintroducing Bush to the conservative community as a totally dependable convert to the true faith.

Exhibit A was Bush's appearance as featured speaker at a dinner in memory of William Loeb, the late, vitriolic publisher of the ultraconservative *Manchester Union Leader* who in his time had called Bush a "hypocrite" and worse in print. In these and other transparent panderings to the right, Atwater was able to garner enough right-wing support for Bush to scuttle the hopes of then Representative Jack Kemp and other presidential hopefuls on the right, and establish him as the logical heir to the Reagan Revolution. Once Bush clinched the Republican nomination in 1988, the choice in the general election—Bush or liberal Democrat Michael S. Dukakis—was an easy one for conservatives.

It was especially so after Bush's acceptance speech in New Orleans, in which the presidential nominee addressed in the most categorical terms the one issue that was, for many conservatives, dearest to their hearts. Contrasting himself with Democratic presidential nominee Dukakis, Bush drew thunderous cheers and applause with these words:

"I'm the one who will not raise taxes. My opponent now says he'll raise them as a last resort, or a third resort. But when a politician talks like that, you know that's one resort he'll be checking into. My opponent won't rule out raising taxes. But I will. And the Congress will push me to raise taxes and I'll say, 'No.' And they'll push, and I'll say, 'No.' And they'll push again, and I'll say to them: 'Read my lips: no new taxes!' "

It was, by all odds, the most memorable line in the acceptance speech, and the one that, more than any other, helped sway wary conservatives. Ronald Reagan could not have delivered it better (and would have had little reason, having agreed by some counts to thirteen tax increases in his eight years in the Oval Office). At the time Bush delivered the lines, some campaign aides—especially his future budget director, Richard Darman—raised warning signals that it could come back to haunt him, considering the mushrooming federal deficit problem. But other political advisers like Atwater, media expert Roger Ailes and speechwriter Peggy Noonan insisted that he say something decisive and dramatic that would help bring him out of the shadow of eight years as Reagan's pliant vice president.

"It was the one issue that unified the right and didn't antagonize anybody else," according to James Pinkerton, a Reagan and Bush White House aide influential in policy matters. So Bush rehearsed the punch line, in the style of a Clint Eastwood tough-guy movie, and delivered it with the required bluster to banish lingering memories of the "wimp image" that had haunted him for so long.

The emphatic manner in which Bush made the no-new-taxes pledge was particularly effective among conservatives because he had always been considered somewhat shaky on the issue that to them was at the core of their philosophy of smaller and less intrusive government. Some of them remembered how, after Democratic presidential nominee Walter F. Mondale had stated flatly in his 1984 acceptance speech that he would raise taxes, Bush had muddled the Republican response with ambiguous answers that had to be contradicted by Reagan himself.

Reagan in a news conference after the 1984 Democratic convention said he had "no plans for a tax increase," but added that if, "after all our best efforts" at cutting costs the budget still was not balanced, "you would have to look at the tax structure" to meet government expenses.

Shortly afterward, in a radio talk from Santa Barbara, he said that as long as he was president there would be no increase in "individual income taxes." That remark raised questions about whether he would accept some other kind of tax.

When Bush, then his vice president, was asked about it, he repeated what Reagan had said, specifically that if "revenues don't add up and you're still in deficit" after cutting costs to the bone, "then he will consider revenue increases." His reply was just different enough to generate questions about whether there was a split between Reagan and his vice president on this critical issue of the campaign.

Bush at the time was scheduled to have lunch with Reagan at the president's ranch in Santa Barbara. When he got there the two men were bombarded with questions about tax policy. Going in for lunch, Reagan said flatly that "we have no plans for, nor will I allow any plans for, a tax increase." But afterward, Bush came out and in response to questions acknowledged that it was always possible that conditions might "change dramatically," and that accordingly "any president would keep his options open."

The resultant confusion irked Bush no end, and he dismissed inquiring reporters with one of his more famous and sillier Bushisms: "No more nit-picking. Zippity doo-dah! Now it's off to the races." It was left to Reagan to finally put the mini-controversy to rest. "My opponent," he said of Mondale, "has spent his political life supporting more taxes and more spending. For him, raising taxes is a first resort. For me, it is a last resort."

In 1986, as Bush was revving up for his own presidential bid, he caused more consternation among some conservatives when he declined to sign a no-new-taxes pledge being circulated by Grover Norquist, head of Americans for Tax Reform. At least two other candidates for the 1988 Republican presidential nomination, former Governor Pierre S. (Pete) du Pont of Delaware and Kemp, signed it along with about 140 members of Congress. Norquist kept pressing Bush, and a compromise was worked out in early 1987 whereby Bush agreed to sign a letter to a prominent Republican conservative, Representative Robert Dornan of California, that incorporated the exact language of the Norquist pledge. Norquist promptly had a million copies of the letter printed and circulated among conservatives.

In a fateful irony, it was this same pledge that du Pont handed to Senator Bob Dole in a debate among the GOP candidates in New Hampshire in the 1988 presidential primary. Dole declined to sign it, a refusal that later was credited with contributing to his pivotal loss there to Bush. Coupled with a stinging eleventh-hour Bush television ad accusing Dole of "straddling" the tax issue, the very pledge that Bush himself would not sign became a principal tool in his own nomination and election. Some wondered later what might have happened had du Pont turned to Bush instead of to Dole with his challenge to sign the pledge.

Still, ideologues whether on the right or the left have long memories, and many of those on the right remained suspicious of the Yankee-born transplant to Texas. When Bush in his 1988 acceptance speech promised a "kinder, gentler" nation, there was some griping on the right about it. Recalling the phrase later, Don Devine, a prominent right-wing consultant, asked: "Kinder, gentler than what? Obviously Reagan. It was a slap at Reagan from day one." Apparently overlooked was the fact that the new president pointedly began the speech by hailing his predecessor and political benefactor as "a man here who has earned a lasting place in our hearts and in our history." Bush went on, though, to promise "a new engagement in the lives of others—a new activism, hands-on and involved, that gets the job done." To those who chose to see this pledge too as a not-so-subtle slap at the notoriously hands-off Reagan in the day-to-day operations of government, hackles again were raised.

When Bush moved into the White House and not surprisingly began to put individuals of his own choosing into key administration positions, the griping continued. Old Reaganites growled that they were not being treated with proper sensitivity in the mechanics of transition, and they increasingly viewed Bush more as usurper than legitimate heir to the Reagan legacy.

"Almost from day one, there was a disenchantment with the manner in which the Bush team replaced Reagan people with Bush people," Jim Lake, the 1992 Bush campaign communications director, recalled after the 1992 election. "Not so much that they did it, but there was a sort of cavalier and arrogant, inconsiderate methodology that was not universal but frequent. A lot of people were handled with short shrift. It was sort of, 'Who am I, the enemy? I'm not the enemy, we've been here together.'

There was a disappointment at the us-and-them, enemy sort of approach.'' But, Lake added, ''that was inside-the-Beltway stuff. I don't think anybody outside knew, much less cared, about that.''

Bill Kristol, Vice President Quayle's chief of staff and an important conservative voice within the new administration, agreed about the snubs to the Reagan people. ''In the transition,'' he recalled, ''a lot of Bushies were saying, 'We're not going to be like Reagan,' which was foolish. . . . There were too many background comments like, 'Bush isn't like Reagan. He stays awake at meetings.' . . . A bad taste was left in a lot of Reaganites' mouths from the campaign through the transition that was unnecessary and unwise. On the other hand, that stuff could have been fixed with a little outreach and stroking.''

One complaint grew out of expectations that Bush would essentially be a caretaker over a continued Reagan administration, which obviously was what many conservatives hoped for. ''Republicans saw him in a historical context as the guy who would fill the Truman role,'' said David Keene, head of the American Conservative Union. ''He'd be the consolidator of the change. Roosevelt had Truman; Reagan would have Bush. In fact, Bush never saw himself that way. Immediately, he began to separate himself from the Reagan administration. He didn't see himself or project himself as sort of carrying on what had been done. It had to be something new, and if you were going to do something new, there had to be something wrong with what came before.''

Kristol viewed it all as a matter of poor communications. ''George Bush got a bum rap from conservatives,'' he said later, ''but on the other hand it was a failure of this administration to be unable to get credit from conservatives for the things we did that were continuing on the path Reagan laid out. We failed to explain on areas where we felt we had to diverge. Reagan was able to get away with all kinds of divergences from pure conservative principles. He somehow had a credibility and reserve of goodwill that George Bush didn't have.''

In an obvious effort to fill that void, as well as to reward a faithful lieutenant, Bush installed Atwater as Republican national chairman, from which post Atwater functioned not only as a fielder of complaints from the right wing but also as an interpreter of the right's political concerns to the president. ''The first year, 1989, was a good year for Bush,'' Paul

Weyrich, head of the Free Congress Foundation and one of the more influential voices on the Republican right, said later, "because Atwater stopped a lot of the nonsense" to which conservatives objected.

Nevertheless, Lake said, "there was a developing unease that there was no vision that Bush was trying to realize. . . . There were some people who felt that he needed to have some direction, rather than just coming in and attending to the day-to-day business that was going on, dealing with what came across your desk." And although Bush in the beginning was drawing such rave reviews from the public that his popularity in the polls was exceeding that of Reagan himself at his strongest, the conservatives missed few opportunities to snipe at him. This was especially so if anything occurred to raise suspicions about the sanctity of his no-new-taxes pledge.

Their confidence on the issue seemed at first to be reinforced even by the one Bush cabinet member the conservatives suspected most of being a closet tax-and-spender—Darman, just nominated to be director of the Office of Management and Budget. In his confirmation hearings, he informed the Senate Government Affairs Committee that neither he nor the new president had any intention of playing games with the no-new-taxes promise, such as asking for them under some euphemism such as "revenue enhancement." He himself would apply the old "duck test," Darman said: If it looks like a duck, walks like a duck and quacks like a duck, it's a duck. "If it looks like a tax, it's a tax," he testified, adding with a grin: "Ducks are off the table."

Less than two weeks after Bush was sworn in, however, word came from Secretary of the Treasury Nicholas Brady, an old Bush chum, that the new administration was considering requiring savings and loan and commercial bank depositors to pay a fee for the privilege of lending their money to said institutions. Congress, and conservatives especially, raised the roof. Bush quickly proclaimed that the notion was merely an "option" that hadn't even reached his desk. Many on the party's right who intended to take Bush up on his offer to read his lips, however, were wondering whether those lips were forming the word "maybe." By Darman's terms, this suggested S&L and bank "fee" sure looked and sounded like a duck to them.

Even before Bush was sworn in as president, however, he had demonstrated how firmly committed he intended to be to the no-new-taxes pledge. As candidate and president-elect, he rejected the work of a bipartisan National Economic Commission created specifically to give both parties political cover on any tax increases. Once he took office, he dodged the tax-increase bullet in his first year—fired at him, insiders said later, by Darman. Bush negotiated agreement with congressional leaders on a budget that specified savings that by all odds were unrealistic. It included $5.3 billion in new "revenues" that the administration optimistically said would result from its proposed lowering of the capital gains tax, which was not likely to happen (although, surprisingly, it did pass in the House as sixty-four Democrats knuckled under).

There was some sentiment in the White House that if the president got through one year without new taxes he could then get away with saying he had fulfilled his campaign pledge. Darman, according to one insider, pressed this case, arguing that if the president wanted to accomplish anything at all on the domestic front "you had to fix the budget deficit, and you couldn't do it without some kind of tax. You would be tied down to the deck."

Ed Rollins, the manager of the 1984 Reagan reelection campaign, recalled later a dinner early in the Bush administration at which Darman and Bob Teeter, the Detroit pollster who later was to become the Bush campaign chairman, discussed how long the Bush administration would have to hold to the no-tax pledge, and when it could be broken.

"I said, 'You guys are nuts, you can't break it,' " Rollins recalled. " 'You've got to basically try and make it through this term without breaking it, and certainly through the congressional elections.' " Rollins at the time was director of the National Republican Congressional Committee in charge of electing GOP House members. Most of his candidates, he said, had also taken the no-tax pledge and breaking it would be poison to their election chances.

Darman's apparent willingness to have Bush break the no-tax pledge did not prevail, however, against the political advice of most others, including Atwater, that going back on it would be political suicide. Meanwhile conservatives, while placated on the tax issue, found grounds to complain on other fronts.

In March, when the Senate rejected Bush's nomination of former Senator John Tower to be his secretary of defense, critics on the right charged that he had mismanaged the affair. And they griped when he agreed to a deal with Democrats on humanitarian aid only to the contras in Nicaragua.

In June, when the Beijing regime brutally suppressed pro-democracy forces demonstrating in Tiananmen Square, they scored Bush for failing to take stronger action. And when, after announcing there would be no high-level dialogue with China's leaders until they ended their repressive posture, he sent top aides Brent Scowcroft and Lawrence Eagleburger to Beijing to schmooze with them, the far right hit the roof.

In October, the conservatives groused about the administration's failure to seize on an attempted coup against Panamanian dictator Manuel Noriega to get rid of him. And when Bush held a very conciliatory summit meeting with Soviet President Mikhail Gorbachev at Malta, warnings were sounded on the party's right that the Cold War really wasn't over. Conservatives chided the president for accepting Gorbachev's word that the Soviet Union was no longer shipping arms to Nicaragua and leftist guerrillas in El Salvador.

In late December, however, the Bush-ordered invasion of Panama that ended in Noriega's surrender won the president favor on the right. And throughout that first year Atwater, from his post as party chairman, served effectively as the chief protector of Bush's political interests in dealing with the party's conservative base. He engineered such gestures to the right as a special presidential news conference at which Bush announced his support for a constitutional amendment banning flag-burning, and a visit to the memorial across the Potomac that depicts American troops raising the flag on Iwo Jima in World War II.

By the start of 1990, Bush's approval rating in the *Washington Post/ ABC News* poll had reached 79 percent, the highest figure attained by any first-year president since the end of that war. It topped the 77 percent achieved by John F. Kennedy after his first year in office. Remarkably, 74 percent of black voters and 66 percent of Democrats gave him favorable marks in the same survey. One Republican of presidential ambitions, Pete du Pont, who had been holding dinners with conservatives around the country with the thought of running against Bush in 1992, was so spooked by his numbers in the polls that he backed off.

Through all this, the problem of a rapidly increasing federal deficit born of the Reagan policies of borrow and spend hovered over the general sense of national well-being. In July of 1989, Alan Greenspan, chairman of the Federal Reserve Board, had warned that a slowing economy could slip into recession. But he added that with a careful monetary policy it was possible to avoid "an unnecessary and destructive recession." At the time, unemployment was at a politically acceptable 5.2 percent and steady.

Nevertheless, some of the political hands were worried. One night in August, Jim Lake, Charlie Black and Bob Teeter had dinner at the Jefferson Hotel in Washington and together they outlined a prospective speech to suggest to the president. It expressed his awareness of the economic condition, the need for adjustments in the changed world picture and what he intended to do about it. The next day Teeter presented it to Bush, informing him of the concerns expressed the night before that he needed to let the American people know he was on top of the situation. Bush agreed, but the speech never happened. Darman and White House chief of staff John Sununu, convinced that talk of recession was unwarranted, "talked him out of it," Lake said later.

But as the new year of 1990 began, more warning signs were flashing. Labor Department statistics showed that 98,000 manufacturing jobs had been lost in 1989, and producer prices had gone up 4.8 percent. Major banks began to drop their prime lending rates to counter what appeared to be an economic slowdown, reflected in a growth rate of only 0.5 percent in the gross national product for the final quarter of 1989 (later revised to 1.1). Bush's new budget of $1.23 trillion included many cuts previously proposed by Reagan and rejected by Congress, and was based on economic assumptions deemed far too optimistic by the Congressional Budget Office and numerous independent economists. Democrats who had swallowed the budgetary gimmicks in Bush's first year vowed not to go along a second time.

Conservatives complained about priorities in the Bush budget, but on key litmus-test issues he was in lockstep with them. When a civil rights bill aimed at strengthening laws against job discrimination was introduced, the Bush administration dismissed it as a "quota bill" and said it would introduce an alternative of its own that would not result in racial quotas in the workplace. And Bush continued to advocate a reduction in capital gains tax rates, a conservative favorite.

Atwater regularly reassured Republicans on the right that they had a good friend in George Bush—at the same time counseling the president on what he had to do to keep this important part of his political base happy. But in early March, the party chairman collapsed while giving a speech and was diagnosed as having a slow-growing tumor on his brain. His health quickly deteriorated and the president was denied his most astute hands-on political adviser, particularly in dealing with the most restive conservatives. Filling the void, eagerly, was Sununu, the former New Hampshire governor whose self-confidence in his own political skills, and arrogance in applying them, knew no bounds.

It was at this juncture, according to Weyrich, that Bush began to get into trouble with conservatives. Whenever issues had come up touching on their sensitivities including talk of a possible tax increase, Weyrich said later, Atwater was there to say to Bush: "Okay, you're the president. But do you really want to do this? Because if you do, you're gonna have problems with your base." With Atwater gone, Weyrich said, "I think the lack of that, arguing in political terms, really was the beginning of the problem. There was nobody over there who understood politics, including Sununu. He understood it, but he didn't argue it as effectively as Lee did."

As leading Democrats in Congress fretted over the growing deficit and pressed for action to reduce it, the right flank of the Republican Party remembered Bush's acceptance speech invitation of "Read my lips: no new taxes!" and reassured themselves that on this one most critical issue they had a man in the White House they could count on. Even though Bush was now faced with the prospect of brutal automatic budget cuts under the Gramm-Rudman "sequester" law, he had been so categorical in that pledge that it seemed inconceivable that he would go back on it.

Democratic congressional leaders, for their part, had vowed that while they recognized the need for new taxes to make a meaningful dent in the deficit, they were not going to take the rap for it politically. If there were to be new taxes, they wanted the president signed on with them. It seemed an impossible impasse, but when House Ways and Means Committee chairman Dan Rostenkowski, Mr. Taxes in the House, came up with a new plan in March to attack the deficit by freezing most spending and raising income tax rates, the White House was surprisingly, if tentatively, receptive. The no-new-taxes pledge continued to hang over Bush's head, but if it could be made to appear that he was forced into breaking it by the Democrats after drawn-out resistance, maybe . . .

Presidential press secretary Marlin Fitzwater called Rostenkowski's proposal "serious and thoughtful" and said it "gives us a basis for discussion." But at a news conference the next day, Bush said flatly that he would not support a tax increase, or for that matter a freeze on Social Security benefits. At the same time, he added, "I don't want to appear totally inflexible." House Speaker Thomas S. Foley was wary. No deal including a tax increase, he reiterated, was "politically and governmentally possible without the prior approval of the president." He called Bush's response "foggy" and "confusing."

When Congress in early May summarily dismissed Bush's budget proposal—the Republicans didn't even bother submitting it to a vote—and the House passed one of its own, the ball was in Bush's court. He responded by calling congressional leaders of both parties to the White House for negotiations on a deficit-reduction package that could win bipartisan support. After ninety minutes in the president's private quarters, Senate Majority Leader George Mitchell came out and told reporters that further budget discussions would be "without preconditions." And Foley added: "The presumption is that everything is on the table."

Did that mean taxes, too, in spite of "Read my lips"? Senate Minority Leader Dole said: "I don't know how you can have discussions otherwise." And House Minority Leader Robert Michel added: "I don't know how you make these figures match without doing some on revenues." But Bush had said categorically, "no new taxes." The next day Fitzwater reported that Bush had not discussed taxes "because his philosophy on this issue is quite well known."

Still, Republican conservatives began to get nervous. They knew that one of the president's principal economic advisers, budget director Darman, had been instrumental in 1982, when he was at the White House, in getting Reagan to sign on to the largest tax increase in history, and they suspected he was at it again, pressuring Bush to agree to new taxes. Three days after the White House meeting, nineteen House Republicans sent the president a letter reminding him of his no-new-taxes pledge, pressing him to keep it and urging him to step up efforts to gain a cut in the capital gains tax rate. Also, eight GOP candidates for the Senate wrote Bush and urged him to "reject any budget agreement which violates your pledge of no new taxes." They knew how much it meant to their own election chances.

Sununu, the conservatives' principal ally in the White House, or so they thought, sought to mollify them by saying in effect that the absence of preconditions meant only that the Democrats were free to propose tax increases, but they would be rejected. "We're allowing them to bring their good arguments for taxes to the table," he said. ". . . It is their prerogative to put them on the table and it's our prerogative to say no. And I emphasize the no." The Democratic leaders howled, and Fitzwater was sent out by Bush to reiterate that there would be "no preconditions to the talks." The conservatives became even more nervous, even though public opinion still opposed new taxes. An early May poll by NBC News and *The Wall Street Journal* found that 57 percent of those surveyed said Bush should stick to his read-my-lips pledge.

From the start of what soon came to be called the budget "summit" talks, it was clear that the Democratic congressional leaders were not going to let the president, having called them in to face the growing deficit crisis, simply pass the ball to them. They haggled over the true size of the deficit and insisted that Bush, at the height of his popularity, take the lead in coping with it.

For a time, the president tried to argue, on weak ground, that it was Congress's responsibility to lead the way. When, he said, some Democratic leaders told him, "You should go first," he replied: "Wait a minute. Who appropriates all the money, where's the revenue, who's got the obligation under the Constitution to raise the revenue? So let's not talk about who's going first." The problem with that argument was that the Constitution, under Article II, Section 3, stipulated that it was the president who was supposed to "go first" in laying out a legislative agenda, by providing "the Congress Information of the State of the Union, and recommend to their Consideration such Measures as he shall judge necessary and expedient. . . ."

House Majority Leader Richard Gephardt ridiculed Bush's contention. "It's the first time in this century we've seen a president want to give power to the Congress," he cracked. "The president is wrong if he thinks the budget is more our responsibility than his." When Darman produced a deficit-reduction plan limited essentially to spending cuts in domestic programs, the Democrats told the administration to get serious.

On the morning of June 26, George Bush finally did—to the shock of conservatives everywhere. In a two-hour breakfast meeting at the White

House, Speaker Foley informed the president that unless he was willing to agree that no effective deficit-reduction package could be hammered out without including some tax increases, the Democrats were going to walk away. Foley said he wanted something in writing so that the negotiations could go forward with the public clearly understanding that the effort was truly bipartisan. The Democrats were not about to go out on a limb and have Bush saw it off behind them. Bush, realizing he had come to the end of the line in his efforts to shunt the responsibility onto the Democratic-controlled Congress, finally agreed.

"Okay, well, let's do it," Bush said, according to Mitchell, in a manner that suggested to the Senate majority leader that the Republicans present—the president, Sununu, Darman and Brady—had already discussed the matter and were prepared to swallow the medicine. Bush asked Darman and Sununu to draft a statement and the two aides went into an adjoining room. They came out with a three-sentence joint statement for Bush and the congressional leaders written in the third person—an obvious dodge to give the president cover, and grounds to say later that he had been dragooned into the deal.

After reading the statement, Mitchell asked for an opportunity to caucus with Foley and Gephardt, and the three went into another room with the Darman-Sununu draft. They quickly agreed that Bush had to make the statement himself, and in the first-person singular. Mitchell jotted down the changes on the draft and the Democrats returned to the room. Bush looked at the changes, agreed to them and handed the draft to Darman to revise accordingly.

Instead of holding a news conference to disclose this critical development, however, Bush ordered the statement simply released, low key, to the press. Sununu came out of the meeting room and handed it to Jim Cicconi, an aide, as Fitzwater read it over his shoulder.

"You know what this means," the press secretary said to Sununu. "This means no more 'read my lips.' "

"No it doesn't," Sununu snapped. "Just put it out, word for word."

Fitzwater took the statement and tacked it up on the bulletin board in the White House press room—a sort of stealth missive delivered in the fashion of a hand grenade rolled under a door. This is what Bush's statement said:

"It is clear to me that both the size of the deficit problem and the need for a package that can be enacted require all of the following: entitlement and mandatory program reform, tax revenue increases, growth incentives, discretionary spending reductions, orderly reductions in defense expenditures and budget process reform, to assure that any bipartisan agreement is enforceable and that the deficit problem is brought under responsible control. The bipartisan leadership agrees with me on these points. The budget negotiations will resume promptly with a view toward reaching substantive agreement as quickly as possible.''

The statement was almost identical to the first draft except for putting it directly in Bush's mouth. The Democrats, according to Mitchell later, had considered balking at the phrase ''tax revenue increases'' instead of simply ''tax increases'' out of concern that the Republicans would contend that it really didn't mean what it clearly meant—that the president was breaking his Clint Eastwood–like pledge. But the Democrats decided that the Republicans would try to do that anyway, so they didn't insist on the change.

The Democrats were right. When word quickly got out, shocked conservatives on Capitol Hill squirmed and squealed. ''He very explicitly didn't say 'raise taxes,' '' House Minority Whip Newt Gingrich lamely observed. ''He said 'seek new revenues.' '' But Darman's duck had come waddling out of the White House press room, quacking the news unmistakably: if you read George Bush's lips now, he was saying, ''New taxes after all.'' In short order, Republican Representative Robert S. Walker of Pennsylvania, a zealous witch doctor in the mysteries of voodoo economics, dashed off a letter to Bush and got eighty-nine House GOP colleagues to sign it, saying they were ''stunned by your announcement'' and informing him that a tax increase was ''unacceptable.''

Fitzwater at first tried to claim that the statement didn't say what it clearly did about ''tax revenue increases.'' All the president was saying, he insisted, was that ''everything is on the table'' for discussion. Asked whether Bush was breaking his no-new-taxes pledge, Fitzwater dodged. Well, a reporter asked, did he think Bush would have been elected in 1988 had he not made the pledge, and instead had said new taxes would be needed (as 1984 Democratic nominee Mondale did to his later regret)? The president, Fitzwater offered, ''said the right thing then and he's saying the right thing now.''

Another reporter asked: Was this ''the sound of concrete cracking'' about Bush's feet? "This is the sound of a foundation being laid," the press secretary replied. Bush, nailed in the Rose Garden by reporters, said only that "I'll let the statement speak for itself." To conservatives, it did just that, and they were enraged at what they had just heard.

It was, Ed Rollins said later, "probably the most serious violation of any political pledge anybody has ever made." Jim Lake had foreseen the likely fallout. "I can remember having a conversation with Charlie Black in the period when they were talking about it," Lake recalled. "I said, 'Charlie, this is outrageous. If you're gonna go do this, you'd better lay a predicate out here. You'd better lay a foundation.' But nobody did it. From the very beginning of the administration . . . there seemed to be no real awareness that communications—about ideas, where you were going, what you were doing, why you were doing it—was important. . . . They never really understood the essential need, at the level of the presidency, that the president must convey to the American people his thoughts of where he's taking the country."

"There was a belief," Weyrich said later, "because the '88 election was really defined on that one issue, so clearly more than on any other issue, that Bush could never possibly go back on that, because it would be politically fatal. And so the assumption was that he would understand that, and that sort of thing wouldn't happen. There was genuine shock that the administration repudiated it, and repudiated it in the way that they did. There was no real explanation of this and there was no real apology—'I was forced into it' type of thing. There was no excuse."

The broken promise on taxes, political adviser Mary Matalin said later, had negative ramifications for Bush far beyond the tax issue. He had always had, she said, "a high honesty quotient" in the polls and this episode "really cut against his credibility, big time." From then on, she said, even when the administration scored achievements "nobody believed it. Or else they'd say something like, 'Why are you just doing it now? Why are you doing that in an election year?' "

That problem, Matalin said, preceded Bush's breaking of the no-tax pledge and went to "the minimal if not nonexistent political communications out of the White House" under Sununu, particularly after the death of Atwater, when Sununu seized all political decision-making for himself. That was why, she said, in her opinion, "John Sununu contributed more than any other single human being to the downfall of this presidency."

Bush himself, Black said later, "realized he was taking a big political risk, that he was putting a big chunk of his political capital on the table." If so, then why was the word put out in such a cavalier fashion? "It wasn't planned, it was just ad hoc," Black said. Well, he was asked, wasn't there a political person in the room? Black paused, then said: "Sununu." Another insider suggested that Darman, wanting the no-tax pledge abandoned all along, "snookered Sununu."

In a news conference three days after the posting of the Bush capitulation in the White House press room, the president was asked whether he could blame people for questioning whether he had really meant his no-new-taxes pledge. "I can understand people saying that," he replied. "I think it's wrong. I'm presented with new facts. I'm doing like Lincoln did, think anew" (a reference to Lincoln urging Congress in 1862 to "think anew" about the issue of slavery). Bush noted that Reagan before him had said he would not raise taxes but did so in 1982 when faced with new circumstances. "I've got to see the country go forward, and I've got to take the heat," he said. "And I think in the final analysis the American people will understand that."

The president would not, however, be drawn into a discussion about specific taxes, saying only that the negotiators were "free to discuss a wide array of options, including tax increases." And when Bob Dole in a television interview said Bush wasn't going to accept a budget deal that included increased taxes, the president authorized an aide to reiterate that "everything is up for discussion."

Meanwhile, Bush continued to take other actions favored by the conservatives, such as vetoing a bill requiring employers to grant unpaid leave to parents for births, adoptions and medical emergencies at home. But such issues were blocked from the radar screens of those on the party's right who had based their faith and support of George Bush on one position above all others: "Read my lips: no new taxes!" Black observed later: "Once they thought he had broken faith, it was easier to nit-pick things."

Had Bush not made the pledge so emphatically, so categorically, so defiantly, the faithful might not have been so jolted, and angry, about his cave-in. George Bush, though, had a way of going too far with tough-guy rhetoric, perhaps to make up for his personal courtliness and solicitousness that earlier had earned him the denigrating label of "wimp." In just one example, when he was clearly on his way to defeat for the 1980 Republican presidential nomination at the hands of Reagan, we asked him whether he was persevering in pursuit of the vice presidential nomination. His reply was: "Take Sherman and cube it." Translation: Even General William Tecumseh Sherman's famous statement that if nominated for president he would not run and if elected he would not serve was not strong enough to express Bush's rejection of the idea. Yet when Reagan asked him to be his running mate, he snapped up the offer in a split second—apparently without a thought that his earlier categorical statement would in retrospect seem utterly deceptive and dishonest.

The same, apparently, was so about his willingness to go back on his famously graphic invitation to the nation's voters to listen to what he was saying about taxes and take him at his word. With conservatives especially, "he put all his chips on the no-tax pledge," Bill Kristol said later. "It was not so much breaking it, but the way he broke it, the almost cavalier way he announced it; his clear failure, and the failure of those around him, to see what it meant in terms of his personal word, especially with the conservative Republicans. It seemed to reveal, perhaps somewhat unfairly, that there was no core of belief there.

"People understand that you can make pledges and you've got to break them, and there were ways to explain why he was doing what he was doing," Kristol said. "He didn't seem to acknowledge the extent to which he personally put his credibility on the line by breaking it. . . . It was a matter of, 'He doesn't stand for anything.' "

In all this, the guiding hand of Dick Darman was seen by conservatives long convinced that he was out to scuttle the no-new-taxes pledge. Convinced that the deficit problem had to be addressed in a more direct and forceful way, one critic on the right inside the White House suggested, Darman had created "a crisis atmosphere" that would force the president's hand. "Darman made a strong case that earlier budget estimates had been overtaken by events—the economy, the S&L bailout and so on—and the deficit would be significantly higher than expected," this critic recalled.

Also implied was the notion that Darman had struck a deal with the Democratic leaders on a tax increase in advance of the fateful White

House meeting. It was Darman's style, this insider said, to never take part in a meeting that he had not already stacked in his favor. In fact, he said, Darman would rebuke associates for failing to do likewise.

For his part, Darman had looked upon the read-my-lips bravado as a mistake from the start and, according to others in the speechwriting and review process, regularly knocked out any reference to it in speeches coming out of the White House. He liked to cite polls indicating that most voters thought taxes would have to go up to deal with the deficit, and relished the notion of negotiations with the Democratic congressional leaders or, as some of his critics were suggesting, collusion with them to strike a truly effective deficit-reduction deal including deeper spending cuts along with tax increases.

Darman also was known to believe that Bush in breaking the no-tax pledge did not suffer in the polls for that act in itself, but in his failure to explain why he had done it. Reagan (at the urging of Darman and James Baker) had accepted a tax package totaling substantially more than provided in the Bush budget deal and survived because, one veteran of the Reagan White House said, he "sold it as the greatest thing since sliced bread, and then changed the subject."

As the budget negotiations went forward, however, something was happening halfway around the world that would refocus Bush's attentions, and those of all Americans, from the perfidy of his broken pledge on taxes. On August 2, 1990, Iraqi forces invaded the tiny but oil-rich state of Kuwait. George Bush, whose whole experience in public life had groomed him to play on the international rather than the domestic stage, almost gratefully turned his eyes and his energies toward the Persian Gulf, with dramatic ramifications for the country, and for his own political fortunes.

CHAPTER 3

MIRAGE IN
THE DESERT

When Saddam Hussein made his audacious plunge into neighboring Kuwait, he caught President Bush by complete surprise. For months, the president had been courting the Iraqi dictator, extending favorable conditions for the import of American heavy machinery of various sorts in the hope, as Bush put it later, of "bringing him into the family of nations" in a peaceful Middle East.

The president's ambassador in Baghdad, April Glaspie, had even told Saddam in an interview that later earned Bush intensive criticism that the Bush administration had "no position" on a longtime oil and border dispute between Iraq and Kuwait. That comment, the critics said, amounted to an invitation to Saddam to do whatever he wanted in the matter, and what he wanted—and did—was roll into Kuwait in force, seize the kingdom and drive the Kuwaiti royal family into exile.

Bush angrily called the action "naked aggression" but at first indicated that American military intervention was not being considered. Later the same day, however, his anger turned to determination to undo the deed when British Prime Minister Margaret Thatcher, one of his closest allies in the international community, pressed him at a meeting in Aspen, Colorado, to respond with force. "We're not ruling any options in," he said afterward, "but we're not ruling any options out." He quickly signed executive orders for a firm trade embargo against Iraq and the freezing of all Iraqi and Kuwaiti assets in the United States.

Only a few years earlier, such a move might have triggered a superpower confrontation with Iraq's strongest ally, the Soviet Union. But the erosion of Communism there and throughout Central and Eastern Europe—for which Bush unabashedly took much credit—had created a new world climate almost overnight. Now, Secretary of State James Baker and Soviet Foreign Minister Eduard A. Shevardnadze stood in the Moscow airport after a meeting and jointly condemned "the brutal and illegal invasion of Kuwait." Baker observed that "we might have been in earlier days viewing this very tragic action through an East-West prism." Instead, the two ranking diplomats announced "the unusual step of jointly calling upon the rest of the international community to join with us in an international cutoff of all arms supplies to Iraq."

Within days, the United Nations Security Council voted to impose a broad trade embargo against the invader. Saddam Hussein responded by annexing Kuwait. Oil prices shot up. Bush, who had immediately ordered an American aircraft carrier group to steam from the Indian Ocean to the Arabian Sea at the entrance to the Persian Gulf, now dispatched American troops to Saudi Arabia to let Saddam know he would encounter U.S. might if he attempted to subject that country, and its oil-rich fields vital to American interests, to a similar fate.

Thus began Operation Desert Shield, and what proved to be the diplomatic triumph of the Bush administration. Over the next five months, Bush in a most impressive display of international leadership persuaded most of the rest of the world, notably including the Soviet Union, to join in an unprecedented coalition through the United Nations to pressure Saddam to back off, or face military consequences. The American president demonstrated a toughness and resolve that astonished his political detractors at home and earned respect and support abroad, from London to Moscow and Tokyo.

From the start, Bush seemed almost eager for confrontation and a showdown. In informing Congress of his plans to impose severe sanctions against Iraq, he spoke categorically with the self-assurance of a Wild West gunslinger. "Iraq will not be permitted to annex Kuwait," he said. "That's not a threat or a boast. That's just the way it's going to be. . . . I cannot predict how long it will take to convince Iraq to withdraw from Kuwait. Sanctions will take time to have their full intended effect. We will continue to review all options with our allies. But let it be clear: we will not let this aggression stand."

This tough-talking, resolute George Bush struck a chord with the American people, so long frustrated by the years of Middle East hostage-taking and never-ending intrigues. Until now, his second year in the Oval Office had been marked by a slipping popularity at home, from a near-record 79 percent at the start of 1990 to 65 percent in July, according to *Washington Post*/ABC News polls. The conservative reaction to his broken pledge on taxes and discouraging economic statistics, including an unemployment rate of 5.5 percent in July, the highest monthly jobless climb in more than four years, had begun to take the bloom off his first-year acclaim.

But military crisis and the sending of American troops to danger zones almost always guarantee public approval for the national leader, and that was the case now. As he called up segments of the nation's military reserve forces, Bush's favorable ratings started to climb again. His political advisers were aware, however, that much depended on a swift resolution of the crisis. Ever since the sinkhole of the Vietnam War, Americans were wary of military adventures that might drag on indefinitely—the Vietnam Syndrome, some called the reluctance to use American forces to police trouble spots.

Among those skeptical about U.S. military involvement in the Middle East were many conservatives such as Patrick Buchanan, the controversial newspaper columnist and television commentator who had established himself after stints in the Nixon and Reagan administrations as one of the most popular voices on the Republican Party's far right. While smarting over Bush's broken no-new-taxes pledge, they took heart in his continued loyalty to another of their litmus-test issues—opposition to proposed civil rights legislation seeking to bar job discrimination. The conservatives viewed Democratic proposals as requiring racial quotas in hiring—although the legislation specified that quotas were not to be applied. When the Democratic bill passed Congress in early August, Bush made clear that he remained opposed, and eventually he vetoed it on grounds it would "introduce the destructive force of quotas" in the workplace. His veto was sustained by the margin of one vote in the Senate, and conservatives reserved final judgment on the president who they felt had betrayed them on taxes.

That sense of betrayal had endured throughout lengthy and contentious negotiations between the administration and the Democratic congressional leadership to forge an effective deficit reduction plan. With an eye on the Republican congressional critics of his broken pledge, Bush threatened to veto any spending bill passed by Congress that exceeded his own budget requests, although Congress continued to vote less money for most items than the president asked for. He berated congressional Democrats for endangering "the economic well-being of this country" by not achieving a budget deal.

At the end of September, a five-year deficit-reduction plan finally was agreed upon. At a Rose Garden ceremony, Bush accepted the result philosophically, and somewhat apologetically. "Sometimes you don't get it the way you want," he said, "and this is such a time for me. . . . But it's time we put the interests of the United States of America here and get this deficit under control." He then went on national television to build public support for the plan. "Tell your congressmen and senators you support this deficit-reduction agreement," he said. "If they are Republicans, urge them to stand with the president. If they are Democrats, urge them to stand with their congressional leaders."

Having thus put his prestige squarely on the line—and pointedly reminded conservatives once again of his broken pledge on taxes—Bush personally lobbied House Republicans in the White House and by telephone. He was stunned three days later when the House soundly rejected the plan, with right-wing Republicans noisily basking in I-told-you-sos. "The president gave away the crown jewel of his campaign promise to bring the Democrats to the table," said conservative California Representative Duncan Hunter. "That was 'no new taxes.' The president was extorted." At the same time, Democrats rebelled against new excise taxes that they said would fall unfairly on lower-and middle-income Americans.

Bush quickly raised the ante by himself rejecting a stopgap spending measure, technically closing the government's coffers and precipitating a shutdown of certain government functions. Because the action took place over a long Columbus Day weekend, tourists in Washington seeking to visit closed federal monuments and museums bore the brunt, but the image conveyed of a government at a standstill did not help the president's own image.

After new stopgap legislation was passed and accepted by Bush extending federal borrowing and spending authority, Congress went back to the task of writing an acceptable deficit-reduction bill. Bush, to the further chagrin of conservatives and others in his own party, told a news conference he would accept a boost in income tax rates on wealthier Americans—a demand by Democrats arguing for tax ''fairness''—if they would accept the cut in capital gains tax rates that he wanted. But a delegation of Republican senators promptly called on him denouncing such a deal, and Bush backed off.

As the White House and congressional leaders continued to wrangle, the president found himself under attack from Republicans and Democrats alike. He added insult of his party's conservatives to the earlier injury of breaking his ''read my lips'' pledge when, while he was jogging in the rain in St. Petersburg, Florida, a reporter shouted to him: ''Are you ready to throw in the towel on capital gains?'' Bush disdainfully snapped back: ''Read my hips!'' and kept on jogging. The wiseacre remark resonated through the conservative community even more than his original Clint Eastwood takeoff itself.

Bill Kristol, Quayle's chief of staff, later called it ''cavalier . . . a terrible sort of signal'' to conservatives and voters generally. ''It was a matter of, 'He doesn't stand for anything,' '' Kristol said. And Paul Weyrich observed: ''It suggested contempt for those of us who had taken him seriously. That was a serious mistake that was then masked over by the Gulf.'' He told the White House chief of staff and others in the administration, Weyrich said, ''that as soon as the Gulf business wears off, Bush is going to be right back where he started to go right after the budget deal [in June], which was way, way down.''

After much further maneuvering, agreement finally was struck on a plan that would provide $140 billion in taxes to reduce the federal deficit by $40 billion in the first year and just under $500 billion over five years. In the process, however, the political price to Bush became even more evident. Ed Rollins at the National Republican Congressional Committee wrote a memo advising GOP congressional candidates to distance themselves from Bush on the budget and deficit-reduction issue if they hoped to be elected.

Rollins, leading the Republican effort to elect more House members, had persuaded almost all the candidates to take the pledge against new taxes themselves, he said later, "because with Bush it was the one significant thing we still had to differentiate us from the Democrats, particularly in the post–Cold War period. So I yelled and screamed inside, and eventually outside, over how serious it was." When more than 100 members voted against the deficit-reduction package Bush had signed on to, Rollins said, "candidates became terribly confused, so I was advised by the Republican leadership [in the House] to give them some guidance." He drafted the memo and, as he routinely did, gave it to the congressional committee chairman, Representative Guy Vander Jagt of Michigan (defeated in 1992), to sign it. Vander Jagt, a close friend of the president, "knew what was going to happen," Rollins said later, and asked him: "Would you sign this one?" Rollins agreed.

In dispensing this advice, Rollins was doing no more than realistically assessing the political impact of Bush's broken pledge on taxes. "But the president just went batshit," Rollins recalled. "I became the focal point." But he was receiving polls from around the country that showed, three weeks before the midterm elections, "that twenty-five incumbents were going down. So what I basically had to do was dump all the challengers and just go save [incumbent] members."

Bush demanded privately that Rollins be fired. "Sununu accused me of leading the House Republicans in revolt against the president's tax plan, which was absurd," Rollins said later. "They [Bush's aides] kept saying, 'You're cooking your numbers, it's all false.' " But Rollins was acting on the basis of data from leading Republican pollsters. "I have great respect for this president," he said then, "but my job is to help House Republicans survive. I have to give the best political advice I can and, in this case, it's to run away from the budget package."

In the end, Rollins said, "I took the rap for the whole frustration of the House Republicans." But he refused to step aside under pressure and stayed on for several months thereafter. "In post-election polls in '90," he recalled, "the anger that Republicans had toward the president for breaking the tax pledge [resulted in] one of the lowest turnouts of Republicans in history in the congressional races in 1990."

One Republican congressman seeking reelection, Peter Smith of Vermont, demonstrated the severity of Bush's troubles on the budget issue by noting to his own constituents in introducing the president at a Burlington rally that he had disagreed with him on the broken no-tax pledge. Later the same day, Bush went over to Manchester, New Hampshire, to speak in behalf of another Republican congressman, Robert C. Smith. When he got there he was greeted by the congressman's wife, who informed the president that her husband had to stay in Washington to vote—on a routine appropriations bill. Such was the presumed strength of George Bush's political coattails at this point.

A *Washington Post*/ABC News poll published on October 19 charted his slide. From the 79 percent job approval recorded at the start of the year, it was now down to 56 percent, after a brief boost resulting from his dispatch of American troops to the Middle East upon the Iraqi invasion of Kuwait. Those who said they disapproved of the way he was doing his job had doubled, from 20 percent to 40. Even support of his stationing of American troops in the Persian Gulf region until Iraq got out of Kuwait had dropped from 75 percent to 60. And most significant to political professionals, 79 percent in the same survey said they believed the country was "pretty seriously off on the wrong track," while only 19 percent said they thought it was going in the right direction. The figures marked the lowest confidence rating found in a major poll since 1974, during the Watergate affair. Still, there was little talk about the president's presumed bid for reelection in 1992 being in any jeopardy, and no Democrats were stepping forward to challenge him.

In the off-year congressional elections in November, the Republicans lost one Senate and eight House seats in what was widely seen as a rebuff to Bush for the whole tax and budget fiasco. Losing Republicans blamed his abandonment of his no-new-taxes pledge. Shortly afterward, Bush in effect told party conservatives that he had learned his lesson. Warning that the Democrats would seek further tax increases in the next Congress, he promised: "They're going to do it over my dead veto, or live veto, or something like that. . . . It ain't gonna happen, I'll guarantee you that."

Sununu, Bush's arrogant and contemptuous chief of staff, was even more pointed in describing what the attitude of the Bush White House was going to be from then on. Speaking to the Conservative Leadership Conference in Washington and boasting of how Bush had tamed Democratic spending proclivities in the budget deal, Sununu proclaimed: "There's not another single piece of legislation that needs to be passed in the next two years for this president. In fact, if Congress wants to come together, adjourn and leave, it's all right with us. We don't need them."

With the elections behind him, Bush was in fact able to give his full attention to the continuing crisis in the Middle East. In the months leading up to those elections, he had assured the American people that the military buildup was purely defensive. But now, with Saddam showing no signs of abandoning Kuwait, he authorized what was clearly a switch to establishing a powerful offensive capability in the Persian Gulf region. It called for nearly doubling the U.S. force commitment to 400,000 troops by early 1991 to make certain, Bush said, that the United Nations coalition against Iraq that he was skillfully building "has an adequate offensive military option."

The clear message was that if Saddam Hussein continued to defy the U.N. resolutions calling on him to withdraw from Kuwait, he would face expulsion. "I have not ruled out the use of force at all," Bush said, "and I think that's evident by what we're doing today." He expressed the hope that sanctions already in place would do the job "within a two-month period" but added that the United States had the authority to use force without further U.N. approval if it came to that.

Bush's hard-nosed attitude began to cause concern among many in Congress who either did not favor use of force against the Iraqi strongman or were fearful that once again an American president would lead the country into a shooting war without meeting the constitutional requirement that Congress, not the executive, shall declare war. Some called for a request from Bush to make such a declaration if he intended to go on the offensive, and the president promised to consult with Congress— unless unforeseen circumstances dictated otherwise.

It was reported, however, that in a bipartisan meeting with congressional leaders, Bush pulled a copy of the Constitution from his pocket, said he knew it said Congress had the power to declare war, then added: "It also says that I'm the commander in chief." Critics of the use of force, including such usually disparate figures as Pat Buchanan and Vietnam War critic George McGovern, took note.

Meanwhile, the Bush administration sought various rationales to justify the force buildup and the possible use of it. The president himself defended his actions on high moral grounds, saying the stakes were not the Gulf's rich oil supplies but traditional American opposition to aggression against small and helpless nations.

Jim Baker, however, usually the suavest of diplomats since laying aside the political hat he wore as Bush's 1988 campaign boss, put the matter in more political terms for Americans at home watching the unemployment rate steadily rise. Saying he wanted to bring the discussion "down to the level of the average American citizen," Baker observed that "if you want to sum it up in one word, it's jobs. Because an economic recession worldwide, caused by the control of one nation—one dictator, if you will—of the West's economic lifeline, will result in the loss of jobs for American citizens."

The validity of that concern was underlined by the Federal Reserve Board, which twice in three weeks lowered interest rates as a means to head off what many economists were now saying looked like a recession in the making. The Federal Reserve chairman, Alan Greenspan, danced around the use of that dread word, acknowledging that the economy had gone into a "meaningful downturn" in October but insisting it wasn't clear whether it was heading for a recession. He blamed rising oil prices as a result of the invasion of Kuwait, uncertainty in the Gulf situation and tighter credit by lending institutions. And, with limited optimism, he observed that "the world out there, when you look at the hard data, is not in as bad shape as it feels."

Soon after, however, the government's index of leading economic indicators was found to have fallen 1.2 percent in October, a drop for a fourth straight month. When the index fell for three months in a row, it was usually regarded as a sign that recession had set in. In October, the average factory workweek dropped, deliveries of goods from suppliers fell off, raw material prices, stock prices and new building permits all declined.

What was going on might have been only a "downturn" to Greenspan, but to workers getting pink slips, it was a lot more than that. And when the Labor Department's November unemployment figures were in—267,000 fewer payroll jobs and the jobless rate up to 5.9 percent, the highest in three years—the Federal Reserve lowered interest rates again to ease what Greenspan called a "credit crunch" resulting from anti-inflation policies by the Fed.

The next set of economic indicators out in late December showed a further drop, with manufacturers' orders for new consumer goods dipping sharply and new orders for durable goods nosediving 10.5 percent, tying a record slide. Nearly everybody was talking recession now—that is, everybody but the president and his administration. He was almost totally occupied now with the situation in the Middle East—and its ramifications in Congress.

With Saddam Hussein showing no signs of yielding in the face of the economic embargo imposed on him by members of the U.N. coalition crafted by Bush, the U.N. Security Council in late November, with American prodding, had specifically authorized the use of force against Iraq if its troops were not pulled out of Kuwait by January 15, 1991.

The action followed a Thanksgiving visit by Bush to American troops in Saudi Arabia during which he branded the Iraqi leader ''a classic bully who thinks he can get away with kicking sand in the face of the world.'' Hinting at imminent action, he told the troops that ''we are not here on some exercise. This is a real-world situation. And we are not walking away until the invader is out of Kuwait. That may be where you come in.''

As tension mounted, Bush decided to send Baker to Baghdad to ''go the extra mile for peace'' and to try to convince Saddam Hussein that he meant business. After several delays, Baker met Iraqi Foreign Minister Tariq Aziz in Geneva only five days before the U.N. deadline and resolved nothing. Congress meanwhile was stirring over the prospect that the president seemed about to take the country into a shooting war without congressional authorization. Democratic Senators Tom Harkin of Iowa and Brock Adams of Washington demanded full debate on a resolution prohibiting Bush from using force in the Gulf without explicit authorization from Congress.

When Senate Majority Leader George Mitchell agreed to a debate, Bush dispatched his own request for an authorizing resolution—the first such request from an American president in seventeen years, since President Lyndon B. Johnson's bid for the Gulf of Tonkin resolution that gave him a free hand in Vietnam in 1974. For three days, heated debate ensued in the Senate and House, culminating in a largely partisan vote of support for Bush. The Senate approved by only five votes, the House by sixty-seven. Four days later, with the United Nations deadline passed, the United States was at war.

In the early morning of January 16, Operation Desert Shield became

Operation Desert Storm. American air power began a swift and unmerciful pounding of Baghdad and other targets in Iraq in a devastating display of state-of-the-art military technology. With satellite television bringing the sounds and views of war into millions of American homes, including displays of remarkably accurate air strikes and inflated initial claims of pinpoint destruction of enemy targets, a mood of national exhilaration swept the country.

Domestic woes for the time being were shunted aside, although the unemployment rate was now up to 6.1 percent, as the American people rallied behind their fighting men and women—and the bold and forceful commander in chief who had engineered this impressive response to the Iraqi tyrant he had compared in his more inflammatory moments with Adolf Hitler. A *Washington Post*/ABC News poll two days after the unleashing of American air power gave Bush a job approval rating of 79 percent.

By the time of his annual State of the Union address, thirteen days after the start of the air attacks, Bush was greeted on Capitol Hill in the manner of a conquering hero. He gave over a good portion of the speech to acclaiming the success of the war effort and the justice of the cause. "What is at stake is more than one small country," he said. "It is a big idea—a new world order where diverse nations are drawn together in common cause to achieve the universal aspirations of mankind: peace and security, freedom and the rule of law. Such is a world worthy of our struggle, and worthy of our children's future." Gone for the moment was Baker's justification for going to war in the oil-rich Middle East—protecting American jobs.

On the domestic front, Bush offered little more in the speech than his old recycled ideas spurned by the Democratic Congress in his first two years in office, including his tireless call for a cut in capital gains tax rates. But with Saddam Hussein to kick around, he could give short shrift to the developing economic slide at home and not worry much about approval ratings. Besides, in mid-February his Council of Economic Advisers in its annual report projected a swift recovery from the recession the Bush administration would not yet acknowledge was holding sway.

"This temporary interruption in America's economic growth," Bush told Congress in his economic report, "does not signal a decline in the basic long-term vitality of the U.S. economy." And with a war on, the Democrats felt obliged to mute their criticisms of problems at home while

Americans were risking their lives in a foreign land. Typical was the comment of Democratic Senator Paul Sarbanes of Maryland: "The difficulty I'm having is the almost sanguine attitude about the unemployment situation." The jobless rate had now reached 6.2 percent with 232,000 payroll jobs lost in January.

On the night of February 23, American and U.N. coalition ground troops were sent into Iraq, and a brilliant encircling movement masterminded by the American commander, General H. Norman Schwarzkopf, drove the Iraqi army to its knees in 100 hours. For the first time in a truly major military engagement since American armed forces were withdrawn from Vietnam in 1975 and American diplomats were driven from the besieged American embassy in Saigon, Americans found cause to exult over a military victory.

There had been, to be sure, Grenada under Reagan and Panama under Bush, but they were modest conquests compared to the hammering of the defiant Saddam Hussein and his huge Iraqi military machine, identified by U.S. intelligence to be "the world's fourth-largest fighting force."

Americans at home gave in first to relief and then to wild celebration, with the president rebounding even higher from the political doldrums that had beset him in his second White House year. In another *Washington Post*/ABC News poll, 90 percent of Americans surveyed approved of his handling of the war. A *New York Times*/CBS News poll put his job approval at 87 percent, the highest recorded since the June 1945 rating for Truman at the time of the German surrender in World War II. A *USA Today* survey was even better: 91 percent job approval.

On March 6, wild cheers and applause greeted Bush from both sides of the aisle when he reported to a joint session of Congress and the nation over network television that his New World Order—that unfortunate label used earlier by Hitler to describe his own vision—had passed its first test. American forces in the Gulf, Bush proclaimed, "set out to confront an enemy abroad, and in the process, they transformed a nation at home."

With the newfound domestic unity resulting from the success of the war, Bush said, "our first priority is to get this economy rolling again. The fear and uncertainty caused by the Gulf crisis were understandable. But now that the war is over, oil prices are down, interest rates are down and confidence is rightly coming back. Americans can move forward to lend, spend and invest in this, the strongest economy on earth." He told

Congress "we must bring the same sense of self-discipline, that same sense of urgency, to the way we meet challenges here at home."

When it came to specifics, however, Bush selected two areas of domestic legislation that hardly went to the heart of the economic situation—crime and transportation. "If our forces could win the ground war in 100 hours," he said, "then surely the Congress can pass this legislation in 100 days."

In the meantime, Bush invited the country to stage a prolonged celebration of the victory in the Gulf—a seemingly innocuous gesture that nevertheless would guarantee a continued spotlight on his great achievement in advance of his expected reelection bid in 1992. "Tonight," he told the nation, "I ask every community in this country to make this coming Fourth of July a day of special celebration for our returning troops. They may have missed Thanksgiving and Christmas, but I can tell you this: for them and for their families, we can make this a holiday they'll never forget."

Over the next four months, Americans took the president up on his proposal. As Iraqi forces withdrew from Kuwait and American troops began to come home, the scene on the homefront was like no other since the end of World War II. Welcoming parades blossomed in big cities and small towns across the nation, complete with yellow ribbons that had come to mark the long wait for American hostages held in Iran. And through it all, George Bush rode a wave of public approval that smothered any thought that he might encounter a serious threat to reelection the following year.

"The conservatives who were looking at it, like Pete du Pont, who came very close [to running]," Paul Weyrich recalled later, "got mesmerized by the polls. I told Pete, 'Don't be fooled by these polls. This is patriotism. We were in a war and people support the president during a war. It has nothing whatsoever to do with what the reality is going to be after we get out of this situation.' "

Du Pont had been holding private meetings with conservative leaders around the country for more than a year to sound out how much support a challenge to Bush would have among them. "He was very serious," Weyrich observed later. "He realized that as a former small-state governor who had been out of office for a number of years, that his real chance to do something was to take on Bush and beat him; that in all probability that come 1996, if Bush was reelected, you'd have all kinds of people like [Secretary of Defense Richard] Cheney and Quayle, and if Bush was defeated, then you would have other people from Dole to [Senator Phil] Gramm to [Reagan education secretary and Bush drug czar] Bill Bennett and other folks like that who would be in there. And measured up against them, he would have difficulty in terms of how long he had been out of office, and all that.''

But while the country, and Bush, were reveling in the success of Desert Storm, the economy was still failing to respond. The index of leading economic indicators fell for a sixth straight month and the unemployment rate jumped from 6.2 percent to 6.5 percent, marking the greatest increase in a single month in five years, with another 290,000 salaried jobs lost. A month later, the jobless rate climbed again, to 6.8 percent.

Even so, Michael J. Boskin, chairman of Bush's Council of Economic Advisers, remained bullish. ''Many of the preconditions for recovery are falling into place,'' he insisted. ''Consumer confidence has rebounded, oil prices are back down to prewar levels, inventories are lean, the money supply has rebounded.'' None of this, though, was bringing much joy to men and women in the unemployment office lines. Neither did the report in May that the Big Three auto makers—General Motors, Ford and Chrysler—all reported major losses in the first quarter of 1991, totaling $1.86 billion.

Some of Bush's political advisers were getting nervous. ''Inside the Beltway,'' Lake said later, ''there was a developing unease that there was no vision that Bush was trying to realize, trying to move toward. The war, and the handling of the war, the breakdown of Communism and the whole East bloc failure caused people to forget about the economy. So it never really got full-blown, this unease.''

In a short time, however, Bush's foreign policy luster was being smudged by Saddam Hussein's continued reign of terror in Iraq against Kurds and other persecuted dissident elements of the population, and by the decline of Soviet President Mikhail Gorbachev, in whom Bush had invested his support in that turbulent and disintegrating empire.

Also, second-guessing on the Bush administration's posture toward Iraq in advance of the invasion of Kuwait was intensifying. American Ambassador April Glaspie denied before a congressional committee that she had in effect given Saddam Hussein a green light by telling him in a

July meeting that "we have no opinion on the Arab-Arab conflicts, like your border disagreement with Kuwait," as she had been quoted in a transcript released thereafter by him.

Glaspie testified that the "so-called transcript" was an edited piece of "disinformation" and that she had told the Iraqi leader in no uncertain terms that the United States would not tolerate an invasion of Kuwait. Moreover, she said, Saddam "wanted me to inform President Bush that he would not solve his problems with Kuwait by violence—period." If there was an American mistake in the dealings with him, she said, it was in not realizing "he was stupid" in discounting her warning. But critics found that hard to swallow.

Added to all this was a developing mini-scandal within the Bush White House. Reports surfaced that the imperious Sununu had routinely been using military aircraft and other government transportation for personal and partisan political activities in violation of ethical standards. At first the White House defended him on grounds that he had to be in constant communication with the president, but as details of his trips became known, including ski vacations and trips to his dentist and a rarestamp auction, pressures built for his removal.

Although Bush regarded Sununu as a valuable aide, his general boorishness and abrupt treatment of political friends and foes alike in Washington left him with few other defenders. One of the cardinal rules of life in the capital city is that he who fails to build goodwill in good times will have none in reserve to support him in times of trouble, and that rule applied in spades to Sununu.

On top of all this, Bush—and the country at large—experienced a scare in early May when the president suffered acute fatigue and shortness of breath while jogging at Camp David, the presidential retreat in the mountains of western Maryland. His doctor sent him off to the Bethesda Naval Hospital after detecting an irregular heartbeat in the sixty-six-year-old chief executive. At Bethesda, doctors found no heart damage but put him on drugs to slow his heartbeat—even as that of the collective nation quickened as the public considered the possible consequences: the ascendancy of Vice President Dan Quayle to the presidency.

That prospect had hung over the country ever since Quayle took his oath of office in January 1989. His own two years in the vice presidency had done little to assuage the concerns about his qualifications that had greeted his surprise choice by Bush to be his running mate on the 1988 Republican national ticket.

Quayle had, in fact, become America's national joke—the favorite butt of gags on the late-night television talk shows and the subject of endless ridicule not only from Democrats but among many members of his own party as well. His penchant for malapropisms, coupled with the look and recreational preferences of the young rich-kid stereotype, made him hard to take seriously by those who did not share his strong conservative views and almost worshipful attitude toward the man who had put him in constitutional line for the presidency.

Polls taken days after the president was stricken with what now was diagnosed as Graves' disease, a thyroid condition treatable with medication, were not reassuring about Quayle's ability to instill confidence in the public in a succession crisis. *Time* magazine found that 67 percent of those surveyed said they would not consider voting for Quayle for president in 1996, to only 19 percent who said they would. A *Washington Post*/ABC News poll found that 57 percent said they believed him not qualified to take over the presidency, and 54 percent said Bush should choose a different running mate for 1992.

Overshadowed by the president's illness and the speculation about Quayle were some modest signs of economic improvement at last. The nation's unemployment rate had dropped slightly in April, from 6.8 percent to 6.6, leading Boskin to declare the figures "good news" but cautioning at the same time that "you always want to see it confirmed over a span of time, not just for one month, particularly where there are some questions about the quality of the data over the past several months." The caution was well placed, in light of the fact that the economy lost 124,000 payroll jobs in the same month.

Economic indicators continued to improve slightly by June, leading Federal Reserve Board chairman Greenspan to declare that the economy appeared to have hit bottom in the second quarter just ending. But he hedged on how soon he thought the economy would start expanding.

On another front, conservatives took heart from Bush's negative response to passage again by the Democratic-controlled House of a revised civil rights bill aimed at discrimination in the workplace. Once again the president denounced it as a "quota bill" although this version, too, explicitly said quotas would be illegal. With his special elegance for language, he told a West Point commencement audience: "You can't put a sign on a pig and call it a horse."

Bush also regained some favor with his party's right wing when the Supreme Court's first and only black member, Associate Justice Thurgood Marshall, the eighty-two-year-old veteran of the nation's greatest civil rights battles, announced his retirement after twenty-four years on the bench. Bush quickly nominated another black jurist, forty-three-year-old Clarence Thomas of the U.S. Court of Appeals for the District of Columbia, to fill the vacancy. Thomas was regarded as one of the most conservative judges in the federal judiciary but not among the most scholarly. The move was seen widely as a further effort to move the Court rightward in keeping with a development conspicuously advanced by the appointments of Ronald Reagan.

The composition of the Court was of critical interest to all those on both sides of the running debate over national policy toward abortion. Opponents looked upon Thomas as insurance that the Court would overturn the landmark *Roe* v. *Wade* decision that had established the legality of abortion. Abortion rights activists saw Thomas's appointment as the likely death knell of that decision, and both sides threw themselves into the fight over his Senate confirmation.

Bush added fuel to the debate by insisting in introducing Thomas as his choice that he had "kept my word to the American people and to the Senate by picking the best man for the job on the merits," not on the fact that he was black. Critics scoffed at the notion that there was no better choice available and that race had nothing to do with the nomination. The American Bar Association gave Thomas a cool rating of "qualified" with not one member of the review committee rating him "well qualified." Bush also insisted he had never asked Thomas how he stood on *Roe* v. *Wade,* and Thomas in his confirmation hearings astonished his Senate interrogators by insisting that in all his years in law school and on the bench he had never discussed the historic and highly controversial decision with anyone!

A measure of Thomas's standing within the largely liberal black political community was the fact that most leading black organizations came out in opposition to his nomination or remained neutral. In the end, however, it was opposition from another major voting block—the women of America— that most indelibly marked the confirmation hearings of Thomas.

As the Senate Judiciary Committee was about to send the nomination to the full Senate without a recommendation on confirmation, a former aide to Thomas, Anita Hill, a tenured law professor at the University of Oklahoma, came forward and accused him of sexual harassment when she had worked for him at the Department of Education and later at the Equal Employment Opportunity Commission, from 1981 to 1983. Over one dramatic, widely viewed television weekend of Senate committee hearings, all hell broke loose in Washington.

Hill, who is black, faced extensive and at times abusive interrogation from the Judiciary Committee panel of eight white males who also heard flat denials from Thomas and his allegation that he himself was being victimized by the committee because of his race. Defenders of both Hill and Thomas testified, often emotionally, as character witnesses, and in the end Thomas was confirmed by a fifty-two to forty-eight vote, the closest confirmation of a Supreme Court justice in this century.

Women voters who supported abortion rights, already hostile to Bush, watched the proceeding with increasing bitterness toward the Judiciary Committee, Thomas and the man who had nominated him as the "best-qualified" person to fill the shoes of the almost deified Thurgood Marshall. *Roe v. Wade* certainly appeared to be down the drain. It was, abortion rights defenders feared, only a matter of time now when the challenge to it would come before this conservatively reinforced Supreme Court.

This intensifying concern, and deep resentment at the spectacle of the all-male Judiciary Committee in the virtually all-male (ninety-eight out of 100) Senate club treating Anita Hill as if she were a guilty party, had political ramifications beyond the Supreme Court or any of its rulings. Women's political groups rallied to start correcting the gender imbalance in Congress, fielding female candidates in record numbers for the House and Senate. Of 106 women who eventually ran for House seats in 1992, forty-eight won, as did six of eleven who had captured their party's Senate nominations in what was widely called "The Year of the Woman."

As the Clarence Thomas matter was developing over the summer, the bubble had burst on the brief period of economic optimism. The Labor Department's monthly reports on unemployment out in June and July found the figure had gone up again to 6.9 percent for May and then 7 percent for June, the highest of the Bush presidency. Democrats in Congress called on the president to extend the eligibility period for unemployment compensation beyond the twenty-six weeks then provided. Both Houses quickly passed enabling legislation over Republican opposition and sent it to the White House.

But while the Democrats watched the jobless figure, White House economists were looking elsewhere for signs of recovery. When the Commerce Department reported a modest 0.4 percent rise in the gross national product for the second quarter, Boskin insisted that the figure "further indicates that the recession appears to have ended in the spring and a recovery has begun."

Bush, recognizing the political impact of the jobless benefits extension, signed the legislation but then declined to make a fiscal emergency declaration required to release the funds. He had signed the bill, he explained, because doing so "at least demonstrates that I am concerned" about the high unemployment, but then added "I won't bust the budget" by spending the $5.8 billion involved. He again called for a capital gains tax cut, decried by the Democrats as another windfall for the rich, as the best way to "create jobs almost instantly." (Later in the session, Congress passed another jobless benefits bill requiring the spending of the necessary money, and Bush vetoed it. The Democratic Senate's bid to override the veto failed by two votes.)

It was now late August. The last of the Desert Storm victory parades was over and the bloom of that great Bush military success was fading. The president was being obliged to fight his battles on the domestic front that had not been nearly so hospitable to him. In a way, one Bush insider said later, "Desert Storm set a new standard of performance for Bush, and had a perverse effect. If he could do that, he could fix other problems if he applied himself."

On the foreign policy front, Bush watched in a detached fashion as the Communist bloc continued to crumble, culminating in a failed coup of party hard-liners to topple his old friend Gorbachev, the rise of Boris Yeltsin, president of the Russian Republic, and Gorbachev's resignation from the Soviet Communist Party, effectively ending its power after seventy-four years.

Within days, the Soviet Congress of People's Deputies, prodded by Gorbachev with Yeltsin in support, voted to cede major powers to the various republics. Bush, pressed at home to recognize the independence of the Baltic republics of Lithuania, Estonia and Latvia, did so only four days before the new Soviet provisional government under Gorbachev recognized them as independent states.

Bush's reaction to the collapse of Soviet Communism, and to the coup that attempted to oust Gorbachev, was remarkably cautious and even timid at first. His first impulse at the time of the attempted coup was to make the best of it. He limited himself to describing the move against Gorbachev as "disturbing" and "extra-constitutional," and said his "gut instinct" about the most visible coup leader, Soviet Vice President Gennady Yanayev, was that "he has a certain commitment to reform." Boris Yeltsin had to prod him into being more straightforwardly critical of the brief, renegade regime.

For all the turmoil in the Soviet Union and the nagging recession at home, Bush declined to be shaken from his routine. He continued to get away whenever possible to his summer home in Kennebunkport, where he played tennis and golf and sailed his favorite cigarette boat. Some political aides were concerned at the image projected by the nation's chief executive commenting on foreign and domestic matters of great moment from his golf cart, but Bush was not going to be denied his intensive recreational habits by such things.

At the insistence of his political advisers, he reluctantly agreed to a meeting with them at Camp David in August 1991 to discuss the outlook for his reelection campaign in 1992. Had Lee Atwater still been around, the political types were certain, the Bush reelection campaign would have been in shape long since. But Atwater's death in March after his long, debilitating illness left no one who was quite so persuasive with Bush on matters of political mechanics.

"We nagged him, and nagged and nagged, a whole bunch of us," Jim Lake, his eventual campaign communications director, said later. " 'When are you going to get started? When are you going to get started?' But he wouldn't budge." The Camp David meeting, Lake said, "was his way of throwing a bone to the guys who were nagging at him."

The meeting, Lake and others reported afterward, turned out to be more a social event than anything else, just to keep the politicos happy. With the presidential election year now only about five months off, they needed to start raising money and making plans for Bush's reelection, and they pressed him to start talking about what he intended to do to right the economy. "It was clear he didn't get it that day," Lake recalled. "He couldn't quite comprehend the urgency." He clearly wanted to put all that political stuff off for as long as he could, and focus on governing—and preferably in the foreign policy realm. He finally agreed to a start-up on fund-raising, but little else.

"His view was," said one of those at the meeting, "you govern. You shouldn't be whoring around doing something as sleazy as politics. But at the time he was riding high and didn't expect to have [a] primary [challenge]."

"George Bush," Lake said, "believes that the president of the United States, whoever he is, must be the leader of the free world; that only the United States and its leader has the moral authority, the economic base and the respect and admiration of enough of the world to really make a difference. And that is really where the president can really make a difference, and that's where it really counts—if our children don't have to fight wars, we don't have to spend our treasure, and if we're not constantly shedding blood someplace.

"I have no doubt," Lake said, "that he wanted to put off the campaign because he wanted to govern. Nothing happened in August—or in September or October or November, until December—because he really felt he wanted to be the president, and to govern. This politics stuff, that's not really what's important. Governing is important."

By the same token, Lake said, Bush was convinced, "coming from that generation of presidents," that his success in the Gulf War and other aspects of foreign policy would insulate him from serious opposition for a second term. "If you go off and end up with the kind of approval ratings he did out of an extraordinarily successful Mideast engagement, there's no possible way for any challenger to make any marks."

Others mentioned at the Camp David meeting, Mary Matalin recalled, that there was going to have to be a domestic agenda for the reelection campaign and that the president could not simply rely on his first-term foreign policy accomplishments. At the same time, she said, there was confidence that "if we could point to all the foreign policy accomplishments, we could not only accentuate the positives but focus on leadership" as an overriding issue to which the voters would respond.

Campaign chairman Bob Teeter told Bush around this time, Lake said, that because of the economy his reelection was not a sure thing, "and that the president ought to go out and talk about the economy before the campaign began, and [present] a plan for the future on the economy."

Teeter knew, and Darman shared the view, that there was a new aspect to the downturn, and that was business "downsizing." Large numbers of white-collar workers were losing their jobs and, unlike blue-collar workers who were laid off in slack periods and hired back on when things got better, they were not going to get their jobs back. They were workers who were highly leveraged with house mortgages and kids in college or college loans still to pay off. Such factors, Teeter said later, generated "tremendous apprehension about the future" among them, many of whom were Republicans or Reagan Democrats, the blue-collar and middle-income suburban white voters lured away from their traditional party by the Great Communicator and retained by Bush in 1988.

Bush recognized, and said in many conversations with aides, that the economy was not coming back, but he didn't want any massive remedial program that would worsen the deficit morass. And internally Sununu and Darman were arguing that the best way to deal with the economy was to do nothing, because it was going to improve. The president's annual State of the Union message in January, they insisted, would be time enough to lay out what his economic plans were.

That view coincided with Bush's own preference to keep politics, and any aggressive domestic action, on the back burner in favor of playing on the grander foreign policy field. Many political insiders, frustrated by Bush's failure first to adequately explain his rationale for breaking the no-new-taxes pledge and then to talk about the slipping economy, feared trouble ahead. But administration economists kept insisting things were getting better. A rise of 2.4 percent in the gross national product in the third quarter, the Commerce Department subsequently reported in late October, indicated recovery, they said. "Certainly the first few months of the recovery were stronger than the last couple of months," Boskin said, "but the recovery is continuing."

The campaign political group did meet regularly through the fall—Sununu, Teeter, Charlie Black, Craig Fuller [Bush's chief of staff as vice president], Bill Kristol and others—and the subject repeatedly came up about the need for the president to send an economic package to Congress before the State of the Union speech. But there was no agreement on what it ought to contain, or whether it made sense to send something up that would be slapped down by the Democrats. The so-called fairness issue haunted Bush political aides, knowing that any legislation approved by the Democrats was likely to contain higher taxes on the wealthy, which Bush was just as likely to veto.

"The problem was," one in attendance at those meetings said later: " 'What can we get passed?' " If the Democrats did tack on a "millionaires' surtax," this insider, a political adviser, recalled arguing, "I said, 'Screw it. If they put the thing on it, sign it.' Hell, it was political. I don't know about the economic side, but that wasn't my role. Nobody would disagree with the political urgency of doing something, but the debate would be, 'Well, maybe it's worse to send something up there that they won't pass, or they give us something we had to veto.' "

Among those pushing hardest in or out of the official Bush circle for an economic growth package were the old Reagan loyalists—Kristol, Bill Bennett, Jack Kemp, House Minority Whip Newt Gingrich and White House aide Jim Pinkerton—who met regularly in what one called "a floating crap game" to try to get the president to embrace their recommendations. There were discussions about having Bush keep Congress in session to act on a growth package, Kristol recalled, "so at least we could say, 'We're trying to fix it, but the Democrats won't let us' . . . but the bottom line was, it never happened. . . . Once the budget deal kicked in, that became the most effective argument internally against those economic growth measures. The budget deal ended up tying our own hands. Darman's response was that it also tied the hands of the Democratic Congress. They couldn't push through a lot of spending."

Kristol recalled later speaking at an annual meeting of Michigan Republicans at Mackinac Island at which he warned that a clear majority of Americans "think the country is on the wrong track. We Republicans have got to be on the right side of the wrong track." But spokesmen for the Bush campaign at the same meeting, he said, gave assurances that everything was proceeding satisfactorily.

On the political front in what the politicians called this off-off-year of 1991, there wasn't much action to occupy those on the Republican side. The only event of some passing interest was a special Senate election in Pennsylvania for a vacant Republican seat that seemed secure for the party. But by the time that election was over, it would send political reverberations reaching far beyond the borders of the Keystone State.

C H A P T E R   4

WARNING ROCKET

When a small plane collided with a helicopter over Philadelphia in April of 1991, sending Senator H. John Heinz III of Pennsylvania to his death, the crash had major, unforeseen ramifications for the presidential politics of 1992. The immediate conventional wisdom was that his replacement in the Senate surely would be another Republican, Attorney General Dick Thornburgh. He had served as governor of the state from 1979 through 1986 and had left office with high approval ratings based on his success in reducing the state payroll and cutting taxes. Equally important, it was widely thought, he would have the blessing of his then exceedingly popular boss, the president of the United States, and Thornburgh's election would be seen in part as a confirmation of Bush's popularity as his own reelection campaign approached.

To be sure, the Democratic governor, Robert P. Casey, would choose an interim successor to Heinz to serve for six months or so until a special election could be held in November. But Democrats had not elected a senator from Pennsylvania since Joe Clark in 1962 and there was no obvious candidate with either statewide name recognition or political base. Casey seemed to confirm this speculation by casting around for a candidate, discussing the appointment with various elected officials and offering it to, among others, former Mayor William Green of Philadelphia and Lee A. Iacocca, the chairman of the Chrysler Corporation and a native of Allentown, Pennsylvania, both of whom turned him down. No one, it seemed, wanted the questionable honor of a Senate seat when the prospect was an uphill campaign against an opponent as formidable as Dick Thornburgh.

As a result, Governor Casey was obliged to turn to an old friend and political ally, Harris L. Wofford, the sixty-five-year-old secretary of labor and industry in Casey's cabinet and a man who had never run for anything since losing an election in junior high school.

Unsurprisingly, there was obvious hubris among the Republicans when Wofford was chosen. Ron Kaufman, the deputy director of the White House political office, told Paul West of *The Baltimore Sun* that the appointment "makes our job a ton easier now." The selection of Wofford, he added, "makes no sense politically. He's out of the political loop. He's not well known. He's from the east"—meaning the Philadelphia area rather than the Pittsburgh area, a supposed burden because the state's other senator, Republican Arlen Specter, was also a Philadelphian.

Thornburgh himself, presiding at the Justice Department, quickly signaled his intention to run, but also to delay as long as possible making an official entry into the campaign. There was no reason to allow some nobody the benefit of a long campaign in which to build his name recognition. Thornburgh would continue as attorney general through the late spring and most of the summer, at which point the Republican state central committee could be convened to ratify his nomination.

Thornburgh's optimism seemed justified. Wofford had been standing in the background shadows of the Democratic Party for thirty years, since the 1960 campaign of John F. Kennedy. Then, Wofford won his fifteen minutes of attention as the adviser who had urged JFK to make a supportive telephone call to Coretta Scott King when Martin Luther King, Jr., was arrested and jailed in Georgia. The gesture was credited with evoking a heavier and more monolithic turnout among black voters than expected.

Wofford had served as an assistant for civil rights to President Kennedy and as associate director of the Peace Corps. He left the federal government in 1966 to be president of the State University of New York College at Old Westbury and then later served as president of Bryn Mawr College for eight years. He practiced law in Philadelphia before returning to active politics as Democratic Party state chairman when Casey, with whom he had practiced in Washington during the 1950s, became the nominee for governor in 1986. When Casey went to Harrisburg, Wofford went along as secretary of labor and industry.

He was considered intelligent and personable, a man with a wide range of intellectual interests and experience but not the kind of person who would make a strong candidate himself. Perhaps because of his academic experience as a law professor as well as administrator, he was always being described as "tweedy," although corduroys were more his style. And his background and personality raised obvious questions about his suitability for the stump in a state with as much devotion to red-meat politics as Pennsylvania. He was, the consensus went, a 1960s liberal running in an era in which liberalism was very much out of fashion.

Thornburgh's history in politics was much more conventional. He had been a federal prosecutor in Pittsburgh, then had gone to Washington during the Gerald Ford administration to be assistant attorney general in charge of the Criminal Division of the Justice Department. Using that appointment as a springboard, he had returned to Pennsylvania to win the governorship in 1978 as a conventionally moderate Eastern Republican. Because he was opposed by a conservative Democrat, Peter Flaherty, he won a majority of the black vote and far more labor support than any Republican in the state except Specter had enjoyed.

Three months into his first term in Harrisburg, Thornburgh was confronted with the dangerous accident at the nuclear power plant at Three Mile Island, a crisis he handled with reassuring calm and competence. It won him widespread approbation from his constituents and, in the mysterious way American politics works, immediately placed him on the lists of those in the coming generation of Republicans with national potential. And that speculation was reinforced when, after the two terms the state constitution allowed a Pennsylvania governor, he returned to Washington to become attorney general as the replacement for the discredited Edwin Meese. Thornburgh was charged by then President Reagan with restoring the reputation of the Justice Department for competence and probity.

But Thornburgh's political persona had undergone some changes along the way. Although he originally was counted as a moderate Republican, he became increasingly conservative as a defender of Reagan and his economic and social policies in the early 1980s. He put his days as a supporter of the American Civil Liberties Union and as a member of Planned Parenthood behind him as he adopted strong positions against crime and against abortion rights. As attorney general he seemed to go out of his way to find conservative positions to espouse and to pick fights with the press that had always given him high marks. The prevalent view in Washington, one shared by some of his longtime political allies, was that Thornburgh was positioning himself for a place on some future Republican national ticket; he understood that it was essential to rid himself of any lingering identification as a linear descendant of that most infamous—in the eyes of the Reaganites—of Eastern Republicans, the late Nelson A. Rockefeller.

Even as governor, Thornburgh's move to the right had cost him something politically. Running for a second term in 1982, he was the odds-on favorite but defeated a throwaway Democratic opponent, an obscure congressman named Allen Ertel, by less than two percentage points, catching political professionals in both parties by surprise. Running against Thornburgh nine years later, Wofford recalled how Thornburgh had "squeaked through" in 1982, and the Democrat took some encouragement from that bit of history.

"I awakened the next morning after the election," Wofford said later, "and realized that if Allen Ertel, a rather colorless candidate with no money, had had some money, and if we all hadn't given up on him, he would have beaten Thornburgh then. It was that Thornburgh wasn't that well liked in the state. He had made a lot of enemies with labor, with blacks, with a whole range of people."

By the time Thornburgh left after that second term, however, his approval ratings had climbed above 70 percent on the strength of his success in reducing taxes and the state payroll, and leaving a substantial surplus in the state treasury. But Wofford remembered the Ertel race and drew comfort from what it suggested about Thornburgh's hold on the Pennsylvania electorate. Moreover, he convinced himself, as long-shot neophyte candidates are inclined to do in such circumstances, that his four and a half years as secretary of labor and industry had given him "more of a network than most people recognized" that would be helpful in a campaign. And, anyway, he conceded, he was "congenitally optimistic."

That optimism was quickly tested. Wofford's campaign took a benchmark poll and found him running 47 percent behind Thornburgh—a finding so discouraging that Wofford and his advisers could only hope that there would be no early public poll with similar figures. That hope dissolved within two weeks when a poll commissioned by a Pittsburgh newspaper found essentially the same gap—in this case, 44 points. But another survey by Michael Donilon, a Washington poll-taker, in July found some evidence that Wofford was not a totally hopeless case. Beyond that, not incidentally, it produced what may have been the first evidence that the electorate of 1991 and 1992 might be a different dish of tea.

The survey used a standard technique to measure potential. First it matched Thornburgh and Wofford and found that almost no one knew the first thing about this Democratic state cabinet official who had been appointed to the Senate two months earlier. Only 12 percent of the respondents had a "favorable" impression of Wofford and only 6 percent an "unfavorable" impression. Thornburgh's figures, by contrast, were 60 percent and 16 percent. Unsurprisingly, the matchup showed Thornburgh with 65 percent, Wofford with 21.

Then the poll-takers offered descriptions of the two candidates designed to elicit a more informed response. With any responsible professional, the goal in using this technique is to present the two candidates in language fair to both in terms of their assets as candidates. Some pollsters, however, have been known to tailor the descriptions to get the "right" answers to encourage a potential candidate.

In this case, Wofford was described this way:

"Harris Wofford says the rich get too many breaks in America, while working families keep falling farther behind. That's why Wofford supports a plan that would cut taxes on the average middle income family by more than six hundred dollars and would raise taxes on rich people who make over one hundred and thirty thousand dollars a year. Wofford also supports creating a national health insurance system because he says that's the only way that every working family will get affordable and available health care. Wofford has also introduced a bill that will make it easier for middle income families to get college loans for their children."

Republican Thornburgh was described this way:

"Dick Thornburgh says we need to fight for traditional American values again in this country. That's why, as governor, he cut taxes, removed thousands of people from the welfare rolls and left the state a two hundred million dollar budget surplus. And as attorney general he has been fighting alongside George Bush to get the nation's toughest crime law—one that will provide the death penalty for drug kingpins. Thornburgh has also been leading the fight against racial quotas—opposing the 1991 Civil Rights bill because he says it is a racial quota bill that forces employers to hire unqualified people based on the color of their skin."

Asked now how they would vote, the poll respondents turned things almost upside down: Wofford 45 percent, Thornburgh 42.

In itself, a survey such as this one is not enough to tell a campaign manager how his candidate is likely to fare. There are far too many imponderables—the way the two candidates perform, the issues that develop during the campaign, gaffes by one candidate or another and simply the visceral responses voters have to the cut of a candidate's jib. But this data did suggest to Wofford's managers that voters were far more focused on their own economic concerns than on social issues; that Thornburgh's successes as governor were not necessarily a free ticket to the Senate, and that his position as a close ally of President Bush was not necessarily a compelling asset, even though the same survey gave Bush an approval rating of 69 percent.

These managers were a pair of Southern boys named James Carville and Paul Begala, who soon would gain as much celebrity status as politics gives to noncandidates, by virtue of what they would do in Pennsylvania and shortly afterward on the national campaign scene. Carville, from Louisiana Cajun country, was a fast-talking, colorful, irreverent political pro with a knack for sighting and exploiting opponents' vulnerabilities and his own clients' strengths. He recruited Begala, his younger, feisty sidekick, from a Texas college campus and the two had run winning campaigns around the country, including those of Governor Casey and Democratic Senator Frank Lautenberg of New Jersey.

The poll findings buoyed Carville. "At that point," Carville said, "I think we knew then we had a live wire."

That information in the Democrats' hands also suggested that the

Republican candidate might be making serious strategic errors in behaving as a regal figure from Washington, delaying his decision on when he wanted the coronation to take place, and in relying on his connections to the president. Despite the lingering popularity Bush enjoyed from the war in the Persian Gulf, the poll respondents said, by 59 to 26 percent, that the country was "off on the wrong track" rather than "headed in the right direction." Political professionals hold that a "wrong track" number over 50 percent is always cause for concern for incumbents, and one close to 60 percent is an alarm bell.

Thornburgh added to the perception of himself as a latter-day Cincinnatus returning to his home as its savior. He stalled through the summer on making his candidacy official and continued to serve as the nation's chief law enforcement officer, brushing off editorialists' complaints against an attorney general raising money for a Senate campaign while still holding office. "His behavior and he himself hammered the nail in [the fact] that he was a high-powered Washington insider," Wofford recalled long afterward.

Thornburgh then handed Wofford an irresistible opening. In his August speech officially declaring his candidacy, he made a point of saying how he had "walked the corridors of power" in Washington. Somebody faxed the speech to Carville and Begala, and when Begala started reading it, Carville said later, "he said, 'I can't believe it! Look at what this guy's saying!' And he read it out [loud]. I said, 'Oh, no! He didn't say that!' Just about that time we were having this conversation about running against Washington. So immediately I tracked [Wofford] down."

"James got me on the radio phone two minutes after Thornburgh had said it," Wofford said. "He said, 'I think, Senator, you should go right out in front of City Hall [in Philadelphia] and give them your pitch that you want to turn Washington inside out, turn out the insiders.' " Wofford followed Carville's advice and, as he put it, "we got right in all the original stories . . . saying it's the people in the corridors of power who let us down. Let's turn them out."

The campaign did not turn around magically on the strength of that one Thornburgh gaffe and Wofford's quick exploitation of it. That may happen in the movies, but not in the real-world politics of a Senate campaign to which voters are not paying very close attention until the final weeks, if then. But it did define the structure of the campaign. On the one side, there was Thornburgh using his position, résumé and connections in high places as his prime credentials while attacking Wofford on his connections to Governor Casey, whose own fiscal problems had driven his approval rating down below 30 percent. On the other, there was Wofford defining Thornburgh as part of the establishment responsible for things being on the wrong track, and insisting the real issues were the availability of jobs, health insurance and educational opportunity.

Wofford focused narrowly on the middle class. On education, he would tell his audiences that the rich go to Princeton, the poor get Pell federal grants and the middle class gets nothing. On health care, the message was that the poor get Medicaid, the rich go to the Mayo Clinic and the middle class gets squeezed. One particularly memorable commercial on health insurance showed Wofford arguing: "If criminals have the right to a lawyer, I think working Americans should have the right to a doctor. That's why I'm fighting for national health insurance in the Senate."

Wofford had another serious problem to overcome—a lack of money such as any candidate suffers when he or she is forty points behind and portrayed in the press as a certain loser. Campaign manager Begala knew that the only solution lay in showing some movement that would counter that image, and that the only way to do that in this case was to throw the long bomb. Thus, around Labor Day, he decided to invest everything the campaign had on hand—about $250,000, a modest war chest in a state as large as Pennsylvania—in television advertising. "We spent every penny of it," he recalled. "We started moving right away"—and, not incidentally, attracting enough money to stay on the air for the rest of the campaign. "We never went dark after that," he said.

But the important thing about the signs of life in the Wofford campaign was that they gave Carville and Begala an argument to take to the Democratic Senatorial Campaign Committee in Washington in an appeal for its maximum funding, $980,000. Wofford's agents and some of his Senate allies began an intense campaign to get the money from the DSCC, by no means a certainty because the committee's chairman, Senator Charles H. Robb of Virginia, was opposed. The committee, Robb pointed out, had disbursed only $6 million to all Democratic Senate candidates in the 1990 election and now a single candidate in a special race was asking for one sixth as much just for himself. How could Robb explain that to those senators running in 1992 and in need of help from the DSCC?

Senate Majority Leader George Mitchell of Maine was sympathetic to Wofford but unwilling to pressure Robb. He had held the same job himself at one time, he said, and he wasn't about to "emasculate" the current chairman. There was, however, precedent for getting the committee to vote on the request rather than simply leaving the decision to the chairman, and the Wofford campaign pressed even harder for such a vote. "I probably threatened to douse myself in kerosene," consultant Carville recalled.

Begala was convinced the case was valid. "From June on," he said, "I was absolutely certain we could win the race. . . . We thought if the damned party doesn't stand with us now when we have a chance to change the whole dynamics of the political landscape, then fuck it, we don't deserve to have a party."

When the committee met to see the polling data and the commercials and hear the campaign plans, the key man proved to be Senator Lloyd Bentsen of Texas, the 1988 vice presidential nominee and one of the party's most influential elder statesmen. Making the case like a lawyer in court, Bentsen conceded that although the committee had "a fiduciary obligation" to other senators who would be running in 1992, "this is an investment we ought to make."

Bentsen had no sooner finished than Senator Tom Daschle of South Dakota, one of the Democrats in the 1992 group, took the floor. "I'm running in 1992," he told his colleagues, "and the best thing you can do to help me win in South Dakota is to help this man win in Pennsylvania because . . . right now there's a guy with some money thinking about running against me. But if Wofford wins, he goes away, and that will be happening all across the country."

The committee voted to give Wofford half the money as quickly as possible and deliver the rest later if the campaign continued to show promise. "The most unheralded event of the political season was when the DSCC went out and borrowed half a million dollars and gave it to Wofford," Carville said. From that point on, the trend line for Wofford rose steadily for the rest of the campaign, as Thornburgh's sank.

To the surprise of most, including Carville and Begala, Wofford proved to be a fast learner as a candidate and particularly adept at making thirty-second television commercials. Two leading Washington consultants, Robert Shrum and David Doak, portrayed him not first in terms of his connections to JFK or the Peace Corps, but instead as someone fighting on issues. The usual biographical commercials were delayed until the final days of the campaign at a time Thornburgh, his lead melting away, was floundering for a footing. Wofford, Carville recalled, "was a great candidate to camera."

Wofford also proved to be a candidate willing to accept the discipline of sticking to the central message of his candidacy despite a confessed tendency "to get off on one of my other long-term interests" and end up talking to a reporter from *The Washington Post* about Gandhi rather than health care. "James really helped me understand how you can only get through on a few things in a mass campaign and if you care about winning, you can only focus on those things," Wofford said. It was a lesson that Carville soon would bring to the 1992 presidential campaign with emphatic results—and media attention.

Wofford's candidacy seemed to pick up steam after a debate in mid-October in which he was widely judged as the winner. "I guess I really sensed a surge of support around the state," he recalled. But Wofford also knew that the response of campaign audiences can be deceiving. He had been in that John Kennedy campaign in 1960, after all, when huge crowds persuaded the Democrats and much of the press that Kennedy was on the way to a landslide but, in fact, won by a whisker.

So there was reason for caution, even if—as it appeared—Thornburgh's campaign was being compromised by one miscalculation after another. After weeks of attacking Wofford's demand for national health insurance, for example, the Republican candidate suddenly showed up to be photographed visiting patients in a hospital and offering his own plan for health care. It was a clear admission that the relentless Wofford focus on the economic issues and the middle class was paying a political dividend.

Wofford broke "the discipline of the message" only once, late in the campaign, when he suddenly made a public connection between his race and the presidential campaign to follow in the next twelve months. The campaign strategy had been to avoid mentioning the president at all. "Bush was not an issue," Carville said. "We never said Bush because

Bush was still popular.'' But, entering a labor rally in Washington, Pennsylvania, nine days before the election, Wofford was stopped by a man who told him: ''Senator, your election is going to mark the first day of the end of the Bush administration.''

Wofford liked the sound of it. ''I think I knew in my head, I'd been told a thousand times that Bush is very, very popular and you must never make this a referendum on Bush,'' he recalled, but when he began his speech to the union crowd he repeated what the man had told him, adding: ''Let me tell you, we can make that [come] true.'' The crowd loved it, and the press seized on the fresh story—Wofford making the election a referendum on Bush.

Back at campaign headquarters, Carville said, ''we went berserk.'' Wofford was subjected to a barrage of advice—from his campaign consultants, his sons, his staff, political allies like Representative John Murtha.

''All of them told me you can't ever say anything like that again,'' Wofford said—which, he added, gave him even more pleasure when he could say election night that his victory was indeed the end of the Bush administration. He defeated Thornburgh with 55 percent of the vote, a comfortable margin by any reckoning. ''The way it turned out, it was very smart,'' Carville said. ''[But] we were so hot with the health care thing and anti-Washington stuff we didn't want to step on our own story.''

After the election, the view grew that Wofford had won it largely by emphasizing the health care issue, and there is no question it played a major role in his success. Thornburgh played into that view with his belated attempt to build his own credentials on the health question, but it was clearly too late—and reinforced the notion that the Republican candidate was struggling for a way to neutralize the Democrat everyone had laughed away only six months earlier.

But the Wofford campaign was not just about health care by any means; the Democratic candidate never really offered a detailed plan of his own. The campaign was about the frustrations the voters felt at being so powerless in the face of the ineffectuality of the government in Washington. ''It was just about the middle class getting squeezed and government being unresponsive, and health care being illustrative to it,'' Carville said later.

Nor was it possible to sort out just how much of the triumph could be traced to the health care issue and how much to Thornburgh's failures as a candidate. "It's like when the crop comes, you say, 'How much is the rain and how much is the soil?' " said Carville, the Louisianian with a fondness for metaphor. "You can't have a crop without either one. We had fertile soil but Thornburgh gave us a good rain."

After the fact, at least, Begala could see a significant inference to be drawn from the campaign—that in this case "the mythology of the Dukakis lesson was wrong."

"The point is not to respond every time you're attacked," he said. "You know what Patton said—the purpose of war is not to die for your country, it's to make the other son of a bitch die for his country. The purpose of a campaign is not to respond to every attack, it's to make the other son of a bitch respond to your attacks. So that means finding the terrain that is more salient to your voters."

In Wofford's case, this meant ignoring almost all of the Republican attacks on social issues—gun control, pornography, abortion rights—to focus on the issues that the poll in July had identified. "We tried to make it all about the economy and all about Washington," Begala said. "You could tell that's where people's heads were." Again, the experience of the Wofford race on sticking to a winning message would have particular pertinence to what was about to follow on the national political scene, with George Bush seeking reelection.

The Republican response to the news from Pennsylvania was clouded by the conviction in party circles that Thornburgh had run such a wretched campaign. Charlie Black recalled seeing the results in terms of the argument the political people in the Bush camp were making to the White House. "It just reinforced what we were trying to say, that there was a great deal of unrest and disquiet out there and that we were on the wrong track politically because of the economy," he said later.

"It was important because, without the bad economic feeling and the unrest in the land, Wofford would have had no chance. Thornburgh still should have beat him, but the discontent among the voters aimed at Republicans gave Wofford the opening and Wofford went through it. Yeah, I saw some lessons in it but I didn't see a lesson that said, 'Oh, hell, this is the end of the world' or anything because Thornburgh still could have won if he'd done half the stuff he was advised to do."

The Republican strategists also questioned whether Pennsylvania was the kind of laboratory situation from which they could draw many conclusions. It was a state that was always closely contested and, more to the point, one they could afford to lose without any feeling that their base was in jeopardy. "We didn't take it lightly but we also didn't take it as directly analogous to the Bush political situation," said Black.

In the immediate aftermath of the election, Mary Matalin, then political director of the Republican National Committee, was blaming the outcome on the inadequacies of Thornburgh's campaign. But, she said later, "we knew it was bigger than Thornburgh not running a good race." Still, few if any Republican professionals were prepared to see the Wofford triumph as any genuine threat to a president who still had approval ratings in the 60 percent–plus area. "I don't remember anyone being cognizant of that, the harbinger of things to come," Matalin said.

But there were exceptions. Thomas Rath, a New Hampshire lawyer and Republican activist heavily involved in the Bush campaign for the presidential primary in his state, was clearly alarmed. "We have just seen the most enormous red flag in political history," he told *The Wall Street Journal*. "The 1992 presidential campaign has just turned from a cakewalk into a 12-month version of World Wide Wrestling."

The special election in Pennsylvania was not the only warning signal that the White House was receiving just then. Through the summer and fall, as the "wrong track" numbers inched up toward 70 percent, the president was coming under increasing criticism, and not only from Democrats, for not paying enough attention to business—especially domestic policy business. He always seemed to be playing golf or riding around in his cigarette boat at Kennebunkport when bad economic news surfaced. Or, if he wasn't there, he was off on another foreign trip, appearing on television with François Mitterand or John Major, talking about international affairs, rather than with Dan Rostenkowski or Bob Dole, doing business on the economy. Moreover, both Bush and his chief of staff, John Sununu, were showing signs of being rattled by the criticism.

The day before the special election—and also the day before Bush was to leave for Rome and The Hague for two international conferences— the Democratic National Committee pulled a political stunt that paid remarkable dividends. It unveiled a black T-shirt modeled on the ones rock music groups sell to fans to celebrate their world tours. The back carried the legend THE ANYWHERE BUT AMERICA TOUR and listed all the foreign ports of call the president had visited or was scheduled to visit. The message on the front read: GEORGE BUSH WENT TO ROME AND ALL I GOT WAS THIS LOUSY RECESSION.

The shirt was the brainchild of Dan Carol, the young director of research for the DNC, which had been coming up with similar gimmicks. Another was a "Hall of Shame" report purporting to list one hundred ethical lapses by Bush administration officials or Bush family members. It was compiled over the long months of trying to find a way to bring down to size a president with approval ratings that had reached unprecedented heights earlier the same year. "We wanted to do something to highlight all his trips abroad," Carol recalled. And after toying around with such ideas as organizing rallies in Rome, New York, or Rome, Georgia, to call attention to the president's neglect of the folks back home, the T-shirt became the weapon of choice. "What was his weak point and how could we exploit it?" said Carol.

The Democratic operative thought he was on the right track with the T-shirts when, before they were officially put on sale, he wore one to a barbecue restaurant in suburban Virginia called Red, Hot and Blue. The place had been partly owned by the late Lee Atwater when he was chairman of the Republican National Committee and was considered a gathering place for conservative yuppies. Several patrons, Carol said, stopped him to comment on the shirt and ask where he got it. He was sure he had a winner when California Representative Vic Fazio displayed one of the shirts on the floor of the House of Representatives and the story made the television network news programs.

But the man who sold the T-shirts for the Democrats was George Bush. He couldn't seem to let the gimmick go by unremarked, mentioning the "silly" shirts repeatedly over the next few weeks, beginning with his flight to Rome the morning after the election. Chatting with reporters aboard Air Force One en route to the NATO summit, the president was asked if he was "feeling the heat a little bit" because of the way the Democrats had been "pouring it on you for all this foreign travel."

"No, I see they are doing it, but I don't worry about that," Bush replied. "You know, I read the T-shirts and kind of the little gimmicks on the floor of the Congress. It's getting to be the silly season. . . . The only thing that worries me is being out of town when these people are doing crazy things.'' But a day or so later, with other international leaders standing at his side in Rome, he insisted his travel schedule was not going to be dictated by ''people holding up a silly T-shirt.''

Then, back home attending a Republican fund-raiser in St. Louis, he continued to display his preoccupation. ''The liberals in Congress go and hold their press conferences, sell their funny little T-shirts and sabotage the initiatives that the American people want,'' he complained. ''And I'm getting sick and tired of it.''

Bush's inability to ignore the T-shirts was a business bonanza for Carol's office at the DNC, where interns were being pressed into service taking orders and dealing with suppliers. ''This was like a Junior Achievement program,'' Carol recalled. In the end, the DNC sold some 15,000 shirts, first for $10 each and later for $15, and cleared $100,000 to be used in the campaign to prevent the reelection of George Bush.

But most intriguing about the episode of the T-shirts was evidence that the Democrats clearly had hit a nerve in the White House on the whole matter of Bush's travel abroad—and his consequent neglect of economic problems at home. On the night Harris Wofford defeated Dick Thornburgh, two things happened there.

Chief of staff Sununu, presiding over the weekly political meeting of White House and Republican National Committee staffs, provided them with facts and figures on presidential travel to refute the accusations—''Ron Brown's cheap shots,'' Sununu called them, referring to the Democratic national chairman—that the President was spending an inordinate amount of time abroad. That was to be the spin over the next few days.

But later that night when Mary Matalin was trying the spin on Ann Devroy, a White House reporter for *The Washington Post*, she learned that even while she was getting her marching orders, the White House was announcing that Bush's scheduled trip to Japan and the Far East had been postponed, ostensibly because the president didn't think it prudent to be out of the capital when Congress was winding down its session.

The confluence of events—Harris Wofford's triumph in Pennsylvania and a Bush White House obviously so shaken by the criticism of excessive travel abroad that a major overseas trip was being scrubbed— sent waves of hope through the Democratic Party. ''You could see the country was moving Democratic,'' said Carville. ''You could just feel it underneath there.''

Others in the party may not have been as immediately optimistic. But they were buoyed by Wofford's self-effacing assessment of his own success: ''I was just lucky to be the messenger of a message that was there.'' That message, with significance for the presidential election just ahead, was clear: voters long accused of apathy were mad enough about unmet domestic needs and Washington's aloofness that they could be persuaded to take action at the ballot box.

For three years, even the notion that there might be any such message that could be used effectively against George Bush had seemed to be something no Democrat dared to accept. Now it was a notion that could not—and would not—be ignored.

C H A P T E R 5

RUNNING FOR
COVER

For the Democratic Party, the aftertaste of the 1988 presidential election was bitter and persistent. Losing an election is always disheartening under any circumstances but losing an election that may have been won—as Michael Dukakis may have won—was the foulest of political fates. At the very least, the Democrats were obliged to live with the divisions of their postmortems. Had Dukakis lost solely because of his own ineffectual campaign? Or was the loss the ultimate proof of a more fundamental reality—that conventional Democratic liberalism simply would not sell? Did anyone care about the future of a party that now had lost five out of the last six presidential elections?

Meanwhile, George Bush flourished in the White House, despite all the reservations about him on his own party's far right. He was not a politician held in awe by his rivals, as Ronald Reagan had been when he came to office in 1981, and he had little power to intimidate his opposition, even as demoralized as the Democrats were in 1989. But the unemployment rate was down to 4.9 percent, the lowest since 1973, and the press was gushing about the avuncular style of the new president who loved golf and horseshoes, cooked hamburgers, played with his grandchildren, held frequent press conferences and sometimes even jogged with reporters. His embarrassing defeat in the Senate's rejection of John Tower to be secretary of defense was offset by Democratic embarrassments of their own in 1989. The speaker of the House, Jim Wright, was forced out of Congress after an ethics investigation. Then the House majority leader, Tony Coelho, decided it would be prudent to follow suit after questions were raised about his business associations. They were succeeded by Thomas Foley as speaker and Richard Gephardt as majority leader, neither of whom offered a similar partisan edge.

Even before these troubles in Congress, the Democrats suffered through an unpleasant chapter in the choice of a new chairman of the Democratic National Committee. By any reckoning, Ronald H. Brown had credentials as good or better than any of his rivals for the chairmanship. But he had been associated with Senator Edward M. Kennedy, having served on his Senate and 1980 campaign staffs. Even worse, Brown had been the 1988 convention manager for Jesse Jackson. He was not just a liberal Washington insider but a black man, and Southern party leaders and others of a conservative bent resisted stubbornly. Then he began to enlist the support of the heaviest of the Democratic heavyweights and two of the winter book favorites for 1992, Senator Bill Bradley of New Jersey and Governor Mario Cuomo of New York. Brown was elected, but the contest had exposed an ugly fault line within the party.

All of this was fodder for those who had allied themselves with the Democratic Leadership Council, an organization that had been created in 1985 in response to the defeat suffered by the party behind another liberal, former Vice President Walter Mondale. The DLC originally was intended to be a direct counterweight to the Democratic National Committee, a place for Democrats to play on the national stage without being identified as ''national Democrats''—a label that in the South and parts of the West meant ''soft-headed liberals.'' The group originally had been denigrated as ''a little white boys' club'' because so few of its early members were either women or blacks. But by 1989 it had broadened its membership beyond such conservative Democrats as Senators Sam Nunn of Georgia and Charles Robb of Virginia to include more people like Gephardt and the youthful governor of Arkansas, Bill Clinton, who were considered determined moderates.

For the most devoutly liberal politicians like Cuomo and Jackson, the DLC was still a foreign body—Jackson derided the organization as "Democrats for the Leisure Class"—but at least some of the early stigma had been erased. And the DLC was solidifying its position as a permanent and respectable element of the Democratic Party, with serious studies of national problems and sometimes unconventional but interesting ideas about how to deal with them.

The first sign of political life for the Democrats in 1989 came in the elections of two governors that November, Jim Florio to succeed a popular Republican, Tom Kean, in New Jersey, and L. Douglas Wilder to succeed Gerald Baliles in Virginia, making him the first black to win a state governorship in an election since Reconstruction. But even these successes were somewhat tarnished by the fact that Florio and Wilder defeated Republican candidates, Representative James Courter in New Jersey and former state Attorney General Marshall Coleman in Virginia, whose campaigns were distinguished largely by their ineptitude.

In each case, the winning Democrats solidified their positions by taking early and strong stands for abortion rights in the wake of the Supreme Court's decision in the Missouri case that summer, which seemed to open the way to a full-scale attack in the near future on *Roe* v. *Wade*. When both Courter and Coleman tried to waffle on the issue, they paid the price of offending both sides and convincing no one. In Wilder's case in particular, it appeared that his aggressive action to control the agenda on the abortion rights question was responsible for causing enough defections among Republican women to provide his paper-thin margin of victory.

In any case, through much of 1989 domestic political maneuvering was obscured by events of far greater magnitude around the world. The transformation of the Soviet Union and Eastern Europe and the uprising at Tiananmen Square in China were clearly changes of far more interest to Americans than the tribulations of the defeated and dispirited Democratic Party. There were, nonetheless, signs of weaknesses in President Bush that might have given the Democrats reason to be encouraged about their future.

Bush appeared remarkably slow to grasp either the national excitement about the changes in Europe or the national anger directed at the Chinese government for its brutal repression of the demonstrators for democracy. At the very least, it seemed the president had a tin ear when it came to hearing his constituents. His willingness to kowtow to the Chinese, in particular, showed a national leader totally out of touch with the people he was leading.

But, as Ronald Reagan had done with the invasion of Grenada, Bush satisfied the most atavistic appetites of Americans with his invasion of Panama and seizure of Noriega to stand trial on drug charges. In January of 1990, with Bush's approval rating at 79 percent, if there was any ground for Democratic optimism about the prospects of defeating Bush in 1992, it was well disguised.

Even the Republican president's willingness to abandon his pledge of "no new taxes" later that spring was not seen as an undiluted benefit to the Democrats because, after all, many of them too had signed on to the tax package. And when Bush's approval rating slipped to 56 percent in mid-October, apparently in reaction to his broken promise on taxes, by this time he was involved in the confrontation with Saddam Hussein and ordering more troops into Saudi Arabia. It was hardly a propitious time for the Democrats to begin plotting their campaigns to unseat him.

There was, however, one bright spot for the Democrats in 1990. In the midterm elections, they captured the governorships of two of the largest and most critical states—Texas, where Ann Richards defeated Republican Clayton Williams, and Florida, where former Senator Lawton Chiles unseated Republican incumbent Bob Martinez. In both cases, though, close examination led to the conclusion that the Democratic success had as much to do with the weaknesses of the Republican candidates as with any change in national political directions. And, whatever their value as indicators of better things ahead, the glow of those successes was soon lost in the national preoccupation with the dramatic confrontation in the Persian Gulf, and the debate over whether Iraq should be attacked.

Ordinarily the potential candidates for 1992 would have begun to show themselves by now, first in the 1990 campaign itself, then immediately after the first of the year by "moving around"—showing themselves at party events, particularly in states with early primaries and caucuses, and by taking an increasingly prominent role on issues in Washington. Over the previous twenty years, the marathon campaign had become a staple for either party out of power, largely because of the way candidates get their money. Candidates without a national identification and following needed as much time as possible to build recognition worth a few points in a Gallup poll. That recognition in turn could be used as a credential to raise seed money to finance the kind of public activity that would drive those numbers up a little higher, and make it easier to raise more money.

Moreover, under the public financing system for presidential elections established in the 1974 federal election law, all contributions obtained during the year before the election year—in this case, 1991—were eligible for federal matching once a candidate qualified, by raising $5,000 or more in amounts of $250 or less in each of twenty states.

Since it was a rule of thumb that a candidate needed to raise $10 million or so to compete in the primaries, it was necessary to raise roughly half of that in the advance year. Not many candidates met that standard, and there were many examples of campaigns failing because they fell too far short and ran out of money too early in the primary season. That very thing had happened, for example, to Dick Gephardt in the contest for the Democratic nomination in 1988. So it was prudent to start as early as possible.

The long campaign served another purpose for the challengers and particularly those making their first entry into presidential politics. It gave them time to get the kinks out of their operations—and themselves—a few months before everyone was watching closely for gaffes. Those first-time candidates always seemed to underestimate the rigors of a presidential campaign and the hazards along the way and needed the time to get their sea legs. But when 1991 rolled around, President Bush had the country caught up in a war in the Persian Gulf and, the politicians reasoned quite sensibly, the last thing that would appeal to American voters would be the spectacle of partisan rivals trying to climb up his back. Once the fighting started in earnest in mid-January, there was a de facto moratorium on presidential politics that lasted for several months.

When the war ended as such an unqualified success in the eyes of most Americans, there seemed even less reason to believe the president could be challenged successfully. So the Democrats remained essentially cowed through the spring. There were, however, some stirrings on the fringes. Governor Wilder was testing the water, but few political professionals believed the country was ready for a black candidate. George McGovern also was talking about still another campaign, but the market for the 1972 nominee seemed even more limited.

Early in May the first announced candidate appeared. Former Senator Paul Tsongas of Massachusetts declared in his hometown of Lowell for the Democratic presidential nomination. But Tsongas seemed almost equally unlikely. In two terms in the House of Representatives and one in the Senate, Tsongas had won a reputation as a thoughtful and capable legislator. But he had been forced to retire in 1984 after his single senatorial term because he was suffering from cancer, an illness he now reported to have been cured. And his absence from the political scene had inhibited him in building the kind of political credentials prospective presidential candidates need. Finally, after Michael Dukakis, the demand for "another Greek from Massachusetts" was certainly limited.

There was no mystery about who ought to make up the Democratic field. There were at least three candidates from the 1988 campaign who might logically be expected to compete—Jesse Jackson, Senator Albert Gore, Jr., of Tennessee and House Majority Leader Gephardt. And there were five or six others who had signaled that they were interested in the presidency and were considered potentially serious players in the 1992 field: Bradley, Cuomo, Senate Majority Leader George Mitchell, Senator Sam Nunn of Georgia and perhaps Senator John D. (Jay) Rockefeller IV of West Virginia and Senator Lloyd Bentsen of Texas, the 1988 vice presidential nominee.

But most of them seemed to be telegraphing a preference to protect their political viability for 1996 rather than take the fall in 1992 against a candidate who seemed as unassailable as the George Bush of early 1991. They all had some other reason to offer. Gore was concerned about spending more time with his family in the aftermath of an accident in which his son was seriously injured. Bradley had experienced a close call in his own reelection campaign in New Jersey in 1990 and took it as a message to tend to business in the Senate for another term. Cuomo kept telling everyone that "I have no plans and no plans to make plans." But, in the pragmatic world of big-league politics, the rational inference was that the 1992 campaign looked like a loser.

There was some inspired speculation about several other Democrats—Clinton, Senator Tom Harkin of Iowa and Senator Bob Kerrey of
Nebraska. But they were considered second-line candidates at best, and
little apparent reason for party leaders to be bullish about their prospects
for 1992. Ron Brown kept telling anyone who would listen that there
eventually would be a strong field and that the president was more vulnerable than was generally realized. ''I continue to believe,'' he said in
March, ''that the basic issues of the 1992 campaign are going to be bread-
and-butter, domestic issues . . . and the president has no domestic policy
whatsoever.'' But Brown's protestations were widely written off as the
predictable and obligatory bravado of an out-of-power party chairman.

The first reason for any optimism came on May 7, 1991, when
Rockefeller made a speech to a DLC meeting in Cleveland and then
almost off-handedly told reporters who caught him backstage that he just
might run after all. ''The door is open,'' he said. ''I'm looking.''

The possibility of a Rockefeller candidacy was intriguing for several
reasons. He was, in contrast to Tsongas or Wilder, a politician with some
long-term capital to risk. At fifty-three, he could afford to wait for more
auspicious circumstances, so the thought that he might not play it cozy
like so many of his fellow Democrats obviously suggested he didn't
consider Bush invulnerable. Beyond that, Rockefeller seemed to be a
potential candidate who would not exacerbate the divisions between liberals and conservatives in the party. Although his record in two terms as
governor of West Virginia and now seven years in the Senate had been
conventionally liberal, he was seen first not as a ''liberal'' but as a
''celebrity'' and a rich one at that.

Rockefeller had never made any secret of his personal contempt for
Bush, whom he saw as, like himself, a man who had been born to
privilege, but who, unlike himself, had never been serious about using
his opportunity to help those in less fortunate circumstances. ''Early on
I saw Bush as a phony,'' he said later. ''I developed a true disdain for
him. . . .'' For Bush, he said, ''the presidency was a trophy'' rather than
an opportunity. At the time he opened the door in Cleveland, Rockefeller's
anger had been stoked by White House pressure exerted against Republicans on two commissions he was heading—one on medical care and one
on children.

Rockefeller was nothing if not serious about the issues. In his first term in the Senate he had, as he put it, "buried myself" in issues primarily of concern to his constituents in West Virginia. He was conscious of the fact he was the first sitting governor of the state ever elected to the Senate and that he made it with only 51.8 percent of the vote despite a huge outlay of his personal fortune to finance his campaign. But in 1990, "blessed by a weak opponent," he had captured 69 percent of the vote. Now he felt liberated to lead commissions dealing with national problems and even to begin thinking about the presidency in a serious way.

Less than two weeks later Rockefeller was off to see what his potential might be in the New Hampshire primary still nine months in the future, and the reception he received and his own performance were at least mildly encouraging. At this embryonic stage of his campaign he was by no means a polished candidate with a practiced talent for delivering sound bites to the television cameras; on the contrary, he had a tendency to talk too long in too much detail about the issues—the problems of health care and children, for example—he considered most pressing. But he was, nonetheless, a man with an easy charm and a sometimes acerbic wit supporting the celebrity of simply being a Rockefeller.

His earnestness on issues was much like that his uncle Nelson Aldrich Rockefeller had displayed as a neophyte candidate for governor of New York way back in the 1950s. And, like his uncle, he found he enjoyed the campaigning. Riding around the back roads in New Hampshire, he told a reporter, "I've just become engrossed in this thing, in the intricacy of the process." Rockefeller also was finding the voters in New Hampshire more interested in the issues than he had expected. "People want to listen to people who are totally serious about what's going on in this country, which is not much," he said.

The signs of interest among New Hampshire Democrats, long accustomed to being courted over two or three years, were obvious. When the party's state chairman, Chris Spirou, held the annual Jefferson-Jackson Day dinner in May, it attracted a crowd of 450 to hear Tsongas and George Mitchell, compared to only sixty-eight people who had attended two years earlier. "It's happening," Spirou crowed, "it's happening."

The following morning about forty of the most active of the party activists crowded into the oceanfront home of Joe Grandmaison in Rye to meet Rockefeller and to give him a straightforward message: the economic situation is serious and we are sick and tired of the silence from Democratic leaders in Washington, when they should be fixing the blame on George Bush and the Republican Party. Grandmaison, a former party chairman and gubernatorial candidate with twenty years of activist history in the state, put it this way: "It's been more a sense of frustration that nobody [in Washington] has been saying anything." Joe Keefe, a lawyer and former congressional candidate, added: "It's got to the point where it's embarrassing."

There were, nonetheless, a few signs of life, in terms of both the mechanics and the message that would be important if the Democrats were to have any realistic chance of winning in 1992. For one thing, the relationship between the DNC and DLC had eased considerably. The so-called conservative group had come to include more Democrats almost all the way across the spectrum and to be viewed as more a forum for new ideas than a rival power center. And Brown had shown himself to be relentlessly optimistic in even the worst of times—"I always thought George Bush was a loser," he explained later—and an effective spokesman for the party, largely erasing the earlier reservations among Southern party leaders. Indeed, some state party chairmen from the South who had been most implacably opposed to his election had become close allies and even boosters.

Brown was determined to make the DNC a factor in the presidential campaign and he assigned the task to political director Paul Tully, a professional of prodigious appetites for food and drink and equally prodigious political insights. Under Tully's direction, the DNC had produced plans to lay the groundwork for the general election campaign no matter who was nominated—to have a strategic approach and some of the mechanics in place by the time a nominee was chosen, rather than beginning from scratch the day after the nominating convention. Tully's product included detailed plans for general election targeting that showed how the Democrats could win a national election despite all the recent history to the contrary.

In essence, it took as a base the states Dukakis had carried in 1988 and then identified the most closely contested states that Dukakis had lost in which the demographics also made it clear there were enough "persuadable" voters—essentially swing voters—to reverse the result in 1992. Tully also had a plan for extending the use of the "coordinated campaign"—plans under which Democrats in each state from the top of the ticket down would jointly do the things that it would be far more expensive to do separately, such as voter identification, registration and turnout programs. That kind of thing sounds so logical it should not have required a sales pitch, but candidates are often suspicious of even their party colleagues. So they had to be shown that the coordinated campaign could work in their states as it already had worked in many if not all of the thirty-three states that had adopted such an approach in 1990.

Tully developed a slide show he used to encourage groups of party workers, unions and potential contributors. When in the spring of 1991 Ron Brown convened a meeting of potential candidates and known fat cats at the Middleburg, Virginia, home of Pamela Harriman, widow of former Ambassador W. Averell Harriman and a very major Democratic contributor, Tully was there to make the case to the contributors that there was good use to be made of their money—and to the potential candidates that the 1992 campaign might not be as hopeless an exercise as they might think.

As Brown explained it later, "We were trying to get them to focus on the general election rather than the primaries"—and, not incidentally, to provide the funding for the plans. He told prospective candidates, he recalled, "We want you to designate us as your general election agents, so while you're fighting it out in the primaries, there's somebody focused on the general election period."

Mechanics aside, there also seemed to be a spreading awareness within the party that the ideological bickering of the past was a luxury Democrats could not afford when there were obvious issues of concern to voters. There was more talk about education and health care, less about the death penalty and who cast a vote for aid to the contras ten years earlier.

In June a speech by Governor Zell Miller of Georgia to a gathering of Southern Democrats in Raleigh, North Carolina, was given wide and generally approving circulation through the party—in large measure because Miller was a populist of impeccable liberal credentials who had carried one fifth or more of the black vote even against a black candidate, former Mayor Andrew Young of Atlanta, in winning the Democratic runoff for governor in 1990. In the key passage, Miller said:

"For too many presidential elections we have had things backward. We have chosen to fight on social issues rather than to run on the economic issues that shape the daily lives of American families. When the average American family stays up late into the night, they are not worrying about whether school prayer should be voluntary or mandatory, they are worrying about how to balance the checkbook and where they will find the money for junior's college tuition. Our party grew up around the economic issues that concern working Americans most deeply, and this is the common bond that unites us. But instead of rallying around those basic, unifying economic issues, we have allowed ourselves to be distracted by social issues that not only divide us but defeat us.''

Miller added this analysis of the 1988 fiasco: '' 'Dukakis liberal' became a code word for social values outside the mainstream of the middle class. Yet the basic error of the Dukakis campaign was not, as some suggested, its failure to answer the Bush assault on social issues. . . . Instead, the decisive, the devastating error of the Dukakis effort was its more profound failure to launch any assault of its own on economic issues, and because we failed to give people good reasons to vote for our nominee, the opposition was able to give them bad reasons to vote against him.''

The Georgia governor argued that each party had an ''elitist'' and a ''populist'' wing. Republican elitists, those most committed to protecting the wealth of the wealthy, were willing to campaign on the issues of the party's populists—social issues such as school prayer, the death penalty, abortion rights and gun control. In the Democratic Party, Miller argued, the elitists were the ones preoccupied with the social issues, while the populists centered on economic questions.

''The difference is that, unlike Republican elites, our elites demand that we run on their issues,'' he said. ''They are uncomfortable with economic populism and they historically tend to resist candidates who embody it. We also have a series of very active special interest groups, organized around liberal causes, that have imposed a filter through which only the purest of the politically correct can pass. To some, it is not enough to be pro-choice; it is demanded that the candidates favor taxpayer funding, even for abortion on demand. To others, it is not enough to endorse government support for the arts; it is demanded that candidates oppose any restrictions on the uses of arts funding, even if they are obscene. To still others, it is not enough to stand up for education; it is also demanded that candidates stand against every innovative idea that in any way infringes on the status quo—from teacher testing to merit pay.

"Don't get me wrong. I believe in a lot of the social issues which so many want our party to profess. But I also believe they cannot be the centerpiece of our presidential campaign. And to the extent that they are, we will not only continue to lose elections; ironically, we will also lose the very social goals that these Democratic elites regard as so important. . . . I did not become a Democrat to be a social liberal while ignoring fundamental economic choices. We must appeal to working families and the middle class. We have to again advance an economic agenda. We have to define it. We have to run on it. Because, my friends, that is the only way we will ever win."

One of those impressed by the speech was Bill Clinton, who spent the night in Atlanta with Miller and discussed it late into the evening. The speech, Miller told him, had been written with the help of three consultants—James Carville, Paul Begala and Bob Shrum. You should think about hiring them for your campaign, he told his colleague from Arkansas. As it turned out, however, those same consultants were very busy right then working for Harris Wofford in Pennsylvania and using the very same message Zell Miller had delivered at Raleigh.

Miller's line also was precisely the one being followed by the DLC—that the important thing was to focus on the middle class rather than wallow in the special concerns of Democratic constituencies. But by this point in 1991 it was a view not limited to the DLC. Attending the Democratic-dominated U.S. Conference of Mayors in San Diego that spring, Mayor Richard M. Daley of Chicago, for example, complained that the big-city executives were spending too much of their public attention on such high-visibility problems as AIDS and homelessness. "That's important," he said, "but we need to talk about the middle class. We need to focus more on education and things people are worried about."

Not all the tensions within the party had been resolved, of course. At the Cleveland meeting of the DLC in May, executive director Al From had deliberately excluded Jesse Jackson from the speakers' list with the full backing of Bill Clinton, thus assuring Jackson's appearance in the city for counterevents that week and his continued hostility toward the DLC. And the "delegates," many of them Washington lobbyists who had qualified by paying a registration fee, had passed a resolution that, among other things, objected to "quotas"—thus tacitly buying into President Bush's description of the Civil Rights Bill of 1991 then being debated in Washington as a "quota bill."

But by July there was at least the first stirring of an aggressive attitude toward Bush to replace the timidity that had been the rule since the 1988 election. Although the President's approval rating remained between 70 and 75 percent in public opinion polls, the most insightful professionals were pointing out that the "wrong track" number had crept up to 55 to 60 percent. And, based on studies of previous polls and election results, the evidence was that those who believe the country is off on the wrong track split two or three to one against incumbents. Such a split had occurred even in the Dukakis election, but the problem for the Democrats then was that a majority of the voters still thought the country was "heading in the right direction" rather than "off on the wrong track."

There was still, however, the problem of finding candidates. Bradley, Nunn and Mitchell were so adamant about not running that they were being written out of the equation. So was Lloyd Bentsen, although the Texas Democrat never shut the door entirely. In July, Gephardt announced that he would not be a candidate, and early the next month Gore followed suit. The stunner, however, was the August announcement by Rockefeller that he would not make the race because he did not feel prepared adequately for either a presidential campaign or the presidency.

Rockefeller's withdrawal was a particular jolt because it was clear that his candidacy was attracting enough interest across the party to have considerable potential for the nomination. And Democrats who knew him had relished the prospect of the patrician six-foot six-inch Rockefeller confronting a Republican president he held in such contempt. Moreover, Rockefeller had made it plain that he enjoyed the campaign and the prospect of running the country. "It's not just being president, not just the trophy," he said later. "You don't go there because it's there."

Rockefeller's explanation that he felt underprepared was a hard one for politicians to swallow; they are not often people afflicted with self-doubt and, on paper at least, the senator from West Virginia seemed as well equipped to make the race as anyone else in the field or even in the wings. The story that made the rounds was that his wife, Sharon Percy

Rockefeller, daughter of former Senator Charles H. Percy of Illinois, had opposed the campaign because it would force her to surrender the position she had just won as president of WETA, a leading public television station, in Washington, D.C. It was a job that would not permit her to campaign with her husband. Rockefeller himself called the conflict "another factor although not the major factor at all" in his decision. His wife, he pointed out, "had soldiered for me for twenty years" and he was reluctant to interfere with her career when she was enjoying particular success.

But the decisive element in the withdrawal, he said later, was his growing realization about how little he knew about national politics and what was involved in running for president. He recalled a trip to Texas where he had breakfast with Jack Martin, a street-smart operative in Austin who was Bentsen's principal political agent back home but whom Rockefeller had never met. Rockefeller was impressed by Martin, but when the breakfast was over, he said, "I didn't know if he was that smart or whether I just enjoyed the waffles."

When Lane Bailey, Rockefeller's closest adviser, presented him with a briefing book to study before he made his decision, he listed the names of nine professionals who might be considered for manager of the presidential campaign. "I had met three of them," Rockefeller said. The lesson he chose to draw was that if you are going to run for president, it takes some time to prepare.

Whatever the reason, Rockefeller's decision against running seemed to let some of the air out of the Democratic optimism. The inference again, inevitably, was that he had decided 1996 would be a better year—just as, incidentally, his Republican uncle Nelson had decided 1960 was not the right year to challenge Richard M. Nixon, a judgment he regretted for the balance of his political career.

With everyone running for cover, it now seemed that unless Mario Cuomo were to seek the nomination, the Democratic field would be a bunch of candidates who in other years would be on everyone's list—for vice president.

C H A P T E R   6

SECOND-STRING
SIX-PACK

The flight of the heavyweights from the 1992 Democratic field triggered the rush of second-line candidates. In the six weeks immediately after Labor Day, Doug Wilder, Tom Harkin, Bob Kerrey, Bill Clinton and, finally, Edmund G. (Jerry) Brown, Jr., the former governor of California, announced their candidacies. With Paul Tsongas already active for four months, the Democratic "six-pack" had been established as the successor to the "Seven Dwarfs" who had made up the party's field of candidates four years earlier—and was greeted with similar skepticism by the political community.

Although all six had impressive credentials in government service, at least on paper, none of them was then considered a truly national political leader. Wilder had gained some national prominence because of his precedent-setting success in Virginia; Brown had run for president twice before, but was distinctly in eclipse; Clinton was very highly regarded among his fellow governors, but not well known nationally.

The press and politicians quickly established a rough pecking order.

Kerrey, Harkin and Clinton were the candidates in "the first tier," if only because each held some statewide office. The others were consigned to "the second tier" for different reasons, with some conventional political logic. Tsongas's background was too unorthodox for him to be taken seriously. Few political professionals believed a black candidate could win, even if Wilder was serious about it. Jerry Brown was still viewed as "Governor Moonbeam" from his days in California and the two previous campaigns for Democratic presidential nominations in 1976 and 1980. He was the candidate best known to New Hampshire Democrats at the starting line but also the only one with negatives higher than his positives.

Only Ron Brown among prominent Democratic leaders seemed to find hidden virtues in the group. "I thought we had a lot better field than folks said," he recalled. "Part of it was just kind of getting some kind of perspective on the field." Some of the candidates whose absence was being bemoaned, such as Gore and Gephardt, were after all the same people derided as among the Seven Dwarfs four years earlier. Besides, Brown argued then and later, Bush's strength was being exaggerated. "There was no sense of direction," he said. "People were not enthusiastic about Bush, even those who said they would vote for him. There was a certain comfort level about him but . . . the country was sort of floating."

If any of the Washington-based candidates among the pack was particularly intriguing to Democratic professionals, it was probably Bob Kerrey. The political establishment in Washington and across the country always has some candidate it expects to do well because of how he looks on paper, without any real evidence that the voters are prepared to accept him. That was the case with then Senator Birch Bayh of Indiana in the crowded Democratic field in 1976, with then Senate Minority Leader Howard H. Baker, Jr., of Tennessee in the Republican competition in 1980 and with Senator John H. Glenn of Ohio in the Democratic campaign in 1984. Because they were formidable figures in Washington, it followed that they would be seen the same way elsewhere.

Kerrey raised similar expectations because in a single term as governor of Nebraska and three years in the Senate he had earned a reputation as an unorthodox but exciting political personality—the bachelor governor who had a relationship with Hollywood star Debra Winger while he lived in the governor's mansion in Lincoln—to the apparent delight of notoriously conservative Nebraskans. He was, in some particulars, a dream candidate for the Democratic Party at this particular juncture—a liberal largely immune from the usual Republican assaults on his patriotism because he had lost a leg and won the Congressional Medal of Honor as a Navy Seal during the war in Vietnam. When Kerrey opposed the attack on Iraq, no one dared accuse him of being faint of heart. And, beyond that, he was intelligent, articulate and engaging. He might have been the ideal candidate for vice president, to contrast with Dan Quayle and his credentials in the Indiana National Guard. If that would work, why not put him on the top of the ticket? It was a year in which Democrats were not being picky.

Kerrey himself had been thinking about making the race. "It had been on the radar screen in that I knew there were people asking me to run," he recalled. "Early in the year, I didn't seriously consider it. As the year wore on and there were fewer and fewer people in the race, I considered it more seriously." The prime factor, as it is with all candidates at one point or another, was simply deciding that he wanted to be president—"I had to cross a threshold," he said. But he also was clearly influenced, he said, by "the fact that Bradley didn't get in, that Rockefeller didn't get in, that Gore didn't get in, that Nunn didn't get in."

At the end of the war with Iraq, Kerrey felt more reason to run. "I thought it was desirable to beat Bush at the end of the Gulf War," he said. "I thought it was a mistake for Americans to get wildly enthusiastic over what was unquestionably a marvelous military effort but somehow struck to the heart of the citizenry in a frenetic way that I didn't like." Kerrey also had his own ideas of what he could do with the presidency. "I do have a vision," he said, "of what America could be like and what the world could be like if we did things differently today."

At the outset, it seemed clear that Kerrey had at least an identifiable market share available to him. In New Hampshire, many of the liberal activists who had been waiting for Rockefeller through the summer and had been left at the church or were now tiring of waiting for Cuomo rushed to support Kerrey. With Harkin in the field, it was clear that the Iowa precinct caucuses would be ceded to him and that the New Hampshire primary on February 18, eight days later than Iowa, would once again be the first testing ground.

This schedule was a reversion to the system that had dominated the presidential nominating process until a little-known one-term governor of Georgia, Jimmy Carter, won the Iowa caucuses in 1976 and made them what Howard Baker later called "the functional equivalent of a primary." Up to that point, the New Hampshire primary had been the first step in sorting out the candidates and establishing a pecking order for the rest of the contest for party nominations. But once Iowa began to get so much attention—as it did increasingly in 1980, 1984 and 1988—New Hampshire became the equivalent of a semifinal, the test that would narrow the field in either party to two or at the most three survivors with any realistic chance of being nominated.

Now once again the primary would be the focus of political attention through the rest of 1991 and those first weeks of 1992. Tsongas, Kerrey, Clinton, Wilder and Brown all hinted at one time or another that they might take the risk of campaigning in Iowa in the hope of embarrassing Harkin and winning an attention-getting second place. But in the end, none was willing to spend the kind of money and time away from New Hampshire that would be required for such a questionable prize.

In the precinct caucuses, party members gather at schools, libraries, firehouses and people's homes and vote openly for their choices. Although Tom Harkin had some detractors back home, it would have been foolhardy to imagine a liberal home-state senator being upset or even seriously challenged in a vote of activist, and generally liberal, Democrats.

The importance accorded New Hampshire was subject to the familiar complaints of editorialists, political scientists and many big-state politicians. The state was too white, too small, too homogeneous in its population, culture and industry, the argument went, to provide a fair test of national candidates. The entire Democratic electorate, it was noted, could be lost in a corner of the Bronx. But there were other arguments for the primary. The state was small enough to enable candidates without much money to compete on even terms with their more affluent rivals. The campaign lasted long enough for the candidates to have time to make themselves relatively well known to the voters and, not incidentally, to smooth out the rough edges in their candidacies. And the voters there, like the caucus participants in Iowa, enjoyed the national attention, and as a result took their responsibilities seriously.

The argument for the validity of the New Hampshire primary as a testing ground carried added weight this time because the state was suffering through the worst of the recession. The unemployment rate was slightly under the national figure, but more than twice what it had been in 1988 or what New Hampshire voters had come to expect. The state had lost 50,000 nonfarm jobs over the previous three years, 10 percent of the total. The five largest banks had been folded into larger ones or into new entities combining their resources. The rate of increase in those qualifying for welfare and food stamps was among the highest in the nation, and the bankruptcy rate was close.

The concern with the economy in the electorate was so pervasive, a poll made for *The Boston Globe* found only 17 percent of voters approved of President Bush's handling of economic matters compared to a staggering 74 percent who disapproved. This was the state that had propelled George Bush to the Republican nomination in 1988, but now his overall approval rating was only 42 percent, his disapproval 47. The bottom line was that, whatever people elsewhere thought of the primary, New Hampshire voters were clearly going to have much to say about the direction of the 1992 presidential election campaign.

So Kerrey followed his declaration of candidacy with a week of the intensely personal campaigning that characterizes New Hampshire primary politics, meeting a hundred Democrats in Katie Wheeler's home in Durham for two hours, then another fifty in Patty Blanchette's living room in Portsmouth an hour later, traveling from diner to bowling alley, from luncheon to coffee hour. This was how it was done, and those early audiences were attentive and receptive to the handsome young senator from Nebraska as he talked earnestly about the failures of the health care system and answered questions about whether he would be, in contrast to Michael Dukakis, tough enough to fight back against George Bush, a concern obviously in the forefront of those Democrats' minds.

Near the end of that first week, eating clam chowder at the Oar House in Portsmouth, Kerrey was asked what had surprised him. "It's a lot easier than I thought," he replied. It wasn't surprising that he felt that way. So far his contacts had been largely with the 3,000 or so New Hampshire Democrats most active in the party. The more important question of whether his appeal would translate to the 120,000 to 150,000 who might vote on primary day was still to be answered. And at this point all the candidates were so little known that opinion polls were essentially meaningless.

As November and December passed, the campaign in New Hampshire appeared to be taking shape. Tom Harkin had attracted a hard core of diehard liberals and labor leaders, many of the same people who had been behind Walter Mondale eight years earlier, and several figures from the political establishment, including former Senator John Durkin and a longtime legislative leader in Concord, Mary Chambers.

They liked it when Harkin argued that the Democrats had been "cheated out of our victory in 1988" by the failures of Michael Dukakis as a candidate rather than those of the Democratic Party. They liked it when he said, as he did repeatedly in the same words, "I think it's time for us to stand foursquare for the values of this party. It's time to say we weren't wrong, we were right." And they liked the way he tore into George Bush as he had when he declared his candidacy on an Iowa farm by saying, "I'm here to tell you that George Herbert Walker Bush has got feet of clay, and I intend to take a hammer to them." It was the old-time religion of the Democratic Party, the politics of absolution.

But as summer turned to fall and fall to winter, Harkin had not yet shown any sign that his support could be broadened beyond its liberal core. Kerrey had the "smart money"—the younger activists, many of whom had been with Gary Hart in 1984 and 1987 until the Donna Rice episode destroyed his candidacy.

Clinton's base lay with the few local Democrats who had formed a New Hampshire chapter of the DLC led by John Broderick, a Manchester lawyer, and a smattering of party activists including George Bruno, a former state party chairman who had been a friend of Hillary Clinton for almost twenty years. Tsongas was still being dismissed as a local phenomenon from across the border in Massachusetts with few supporters who were well known, although he did seem to have an interesting following of young people attracted to his economic message. If there was any significant support for either Wilder or Brown, it wasn't apparent to the naked eye.

But the tides of opinion in New Hampshire were not unaffected by what was happening elsewhere. On the contrary, it had become clear over the previous three or four primaries that a candidate needed some national credibility to score well in New Hampshire. That requirement was the reason that many candidates in both parties had been eliminated as serious factors in New Hampshire after flopping in Iowa.

In 1980, for instance, Howard Baker had given Iowa a secondary role in his campaign activity, planning to concentrate his time and money on New Hampshire. But after the Iowa caucus results came in with Baker a weak third behind George Bush and Ronald Reagan, Republicans in New Hampshire saw the contest as largely one between Bush and Reagan, and Baker never got off the ground. Similarly, in the Democratic campaign of 1984, John Glenn's campaign was fatally compromised by a fourth-place finish in Iowa while Gary Hart was given a strong push ahead by running a distant but still surprising second to Walter Mondale.

Even without Iowa as a factor in 1992, the New Hampshire primary was no longer an island. The voters followed the other preliminaries— the cattle shows and straw votes and debates—on their television screens. And, measured by the atmospherics that politicians use as a gauge when there is no hard data, Clinton was the candidate who seemed to be gaining the greatest momentum.

The governor of Arkansas had been a figure on the apron of the national stage for close to a decade. He was elected to the governorship in 1978, then defeated two years later when his constituents seemed to feel he had gone uptown on them too quickly, then resurrected with a comeback defeat of Republican Governor Frank White in 1982. He was prominent in the National Governors Conferences all through the 1980s and on everyone's list at one time or another for either national chairman of the party or vice president or—by 1988—even for the presidential nomination.

Clinton had a reputation as a strong personal campaigner, almost as effective as the recognized champion of Arkansas candidates, Senator Dale Bumpers. And he had enhanced his credentials as a national figure by becoming an active participant in the DLC, resigning his chairmanship of the group in 1991 only when he decided to make the presidential race. There were, however, rumors that he might have ''a little problem with the ladies,'' as an Arkansas Republican once put it to a visiting reporter in Little Rock, but none had ever been established as he won repeatedly by growing margins in his home state.

Another problem for Clinton was the fact he had pledged in his previous reelection campaign that if kept in office he would serve out the full term. He was known to have considered making a bid for the presidency in 1988, and in his 1990 race his opponent charged in a debate that

Clinton was using the Arkansas governorship merely as a stepping-stone to the White House. The pledge was the result. It was a tough race in which Frank Greer, Clinton's media adviser, said the governor at one point told him: "I'm in serious trouble. If I lose, I'll never run for dogcatcher, let alone president."

Clinton survived that challenge but he was left with the pledge, which stood as a public declaration of unavailability for the presidency. On one occasion when Ron Brown was feuding with the DLC, he twitted the rival group—and its chairman, Clinton—by saying it was too bad the DLC didn't have a candidate, what with Clinton having pledged to finish his gubernatorial term, which ran through 1994.

Still hung up on the question in the summer of 1991, although a small group of aides was already laying the early groundwork for a candidacy, Clinton spent the Fourth of July speaking at about a dozen public events, asking voters whether he should seek the presidency in spite of his pledge. He told them he had already fulfilled most of his term's planned agenda, and soon—by political osmosis or design—signs proclaiming RUN, BILL, RUN began to appear at his speeches. So, in the manner of all good politicians, he finally bowed to the will of the people.

In Clinton's announcement speech delivered in front of the Old Statehouse in Little Rock, he had impressed other politicians and reporters with the way he defined himself as a different kind of Democrat. He paid homage to the traditional Democratic concern for the disadvantaged but put emphasis on the concerns of middle-class taxpayers. And he demanded personal "responsibility" on the part of welfare recipients as well as corporate executives who milked their companies while workers lost their jobs.

"Middle-class people are spending more hours on the job, spending less time with their children, bringing home a smaller paycheck to pay more for health care and housing and education," he told the friendly audience in Little Rock. "Our streets are meaner, our families are broke, our health care is the costliest in the world and we get less for it. The country is headed in the wrong direction fast, slipping behind, losing our way, and all we have out of Washington is status quo paralysis. No vision, no action. Just neglect, selfishness and division.

"For twelve years, Republicans have tried to divide us—race against race—so we get mad at each other and not at them. They want us to look at each other across a racial divide so we don't turn and look to the White House and ask, Why are all of our incomes going down? Why are all of us losing jobs? Why are we losing our future?''

A few minutes later he defined what he offered this way: "The change we must make isn't liberal or conservative. It's both and it's different. The small towns and main streets of America aren't like the corridors and back rooms of Washington. People out here don't care about the idle rhetoric of 'left' and 'right' and 'liberal' and 'conservative' and all the other words that have made our politics a substitute for action. These families are crying out desperately for someone who believes the promise of America is to help them with their struggle to get ahead, to offer them a green light instead of a pink slip. This must be a campaign of ideas, not slogans. We don't need another president who doesn't know what he wants to do for America. I'm going to tell you in plain language what I intend to do as president. How we can meet the challenges we face—that's the test for all the Democratic candidates in this campaign. Americans know what we're up against. Let's show them what we're for.''

In the fall of 1991, Clinton made a series of shrewd moves to meet unspoken questions about his candidacy. He gave a series of three speeches on issues, including foreign policy, at his alma mater, Georgetown University in Washington, that were clearly intended to resolve doubts about whether this small-state governor understood the nature of the problems confronting the next president. And he attracted network television coverage simply because he made those speeches within a few miles of the Washington bureaus of the networks, which were obviously reluctant when money was tight to go to the expense of covering unproven candidates on the road. But they were quite willing to send a correspondent and camera crew on a ten-minute drive.

In September, Clinton turned up to speak at the Democratic National Committee's executive committee meeting in Los Angeles, encouraging obvious stories about the leader of the DLC in the lion's den. He came away with higher marks than any of the other candidates who showed up—Tsongas, Harkin and Brown. The speech was toughly partisan in attacking Bush but, most importantly, it offered a coherent view of the kind of approach Democrats needed to take against the incumbent president over the next year. A few weeks later he made a similar speech to the Association of Democratic State Chairs in Chicago and won even more enthusiastic reviews from party regulars who had viewed him with varying degrees of suspicion up to that point. Standing in the back of the room, Paul Tully, one of the doubters a few weeks earlier, was exuberant, turning to a reporter and delivering his ultimate accolade with a broad grin: "Now that was a general election message. That was big-time politics."

Clinton's performance was particularly strong when compared to those of his two supposedly most serious rivals, Kerrey and Harkin, before the same group. The senator from Nebraska concentrated on a lecture on the ills of the health care system in a speech that could not be faulted for substance. But it did little to reassure the Democratic leaders gathered at the Palmer House that this charisma they had been hearing about really existed.

Harkin, on the night before Clinton spoke, had delivered his usual speech extolling Democratic dogma, and describing the need for a "real Democrat"—by implication himself—rather than "a warmed-over Republican." Clinton rose to the bait forcefully. "I'm a Democrat by heritage, instinct and conviction," he told the applauding state chairs. "My granddaddy thought when he died he was going to Roosevelt. . . . These people call me a Republican because I want to change and push this party into the future, not pull it to the right or left."

Filing out of the room after the session, a prominent labor leader wearing a Harkin button stopped a reporter. "Clinton was terrific," he said, "I could see him doing very well in Michigan."

"What about Harkin?" the reporter asked, nodding at the button.

"I like Tom," the labor leader replied, "but let me ask you, was that speech last night the only one Tom can give?"

The Chicago meeting, coming on the heels of Clinton's success at the earlier DNC meeting in Los Angeles and the Georgetown speeches, seemed to crystallize opinion in the political community that he was now the front-runner in the Democratic field. Supporters of his rivals complained that the press was "anointing" the Arkansas governor for some devious reason of its own. But the press depiction of Clinton as the leading candidate accurately reflected the consensus that had developed among the party activists who were paying the most attention, in New Hampshire and nationally.

Reflecting later on his sudden designation as the front-runner, Clinton saw it as a mixed blessing. "First of all, I was very apprehensive about it," he recalled. "I was afraid that rising too fast, before the American people got to know me and had any kind of base on which to evaluate me, made me vulnerable, made me a target, and might tend to obscure my message. Although I think it happened basically because I seemed to be somebody who had really thought about these things and had a coherent view of what I wanted to do as president, and why I was running."

Clinton's stature was reflected most clearly in the new support he was getting from liberals who had become increasingly pragmatic as the evidence mounted that George Bush might be vulnerable after all. Clinton might not be their dream candidate—he supported capital punishment, for one thing—but he was certainly acceptable on most other issues and more than acceptable on the stump.

Looking back much later, Harkin was convinced the Chicago meeting had been the turning point in favor of Clinton and against his own candidacy. The Iowa Democrat believed that, contrary to the press consensus, he had won the oratorical competition at the Los Angeles DNC meeting and had been doing well otherwise. He had been given surprisingly high marks after a meeting with IMPAC, a group of relatively conservative Democratic big contributors. A survey of big-city mayors had shown they considered him the candidate who would be best for the cities. And when he gave his speech in Chicago that night, he had been received with warmth and enthusiasm.

The new consensus for Clinton, Harkin was convinced, was a product of some clever maneuvering by David Wilhelm, the young professional from Chicago managing the Clinton campaign, to orchestrate who said what to the reporters covering the meeting. "Sunday I got all the press reports about [how] Clinton had just blown them out of the water— *The New York Times*, the *Chicago Tribune*, AP, UPI," Harkin said. "There I was reading all these quotes from different state chairs. Well, every quote I saw was from a state chair who was a supporter of Clinton's—[Bob] Slagle of Texas, a couple of others. . . . This was Wilhelm at work, I know this guy. . . . Wilhelm got into my knickers big."

In fact, however, whatever the level of orchestration Wilhelm managed that day, the response to Clinton went well beyond what he had going in—and unquestionably came at a cost to Harkin and the other candidates. "From that moment on," Harkin said, "Clinton got a two-week bounce out of that thing, and I mean he was riding high. . . . To me, it was really a turning point because he was able to overtake me in the eyes of Democrats, the party structure . . . as the logical candidate, someone who could win, that type of thing."

Clinton, too, thought the Chicago speech was important in establishing himself with the party, as the first step in giving the campaign credibility to reach out to the electorate in what he called "ever-widening circles" of Americans paying attention to the campaign. "Those people thought I had something to say and they liked the way I said it, and there was a lot of passion," he said. "I think they thought I'd fight the fight; if they went with me that I'd hang in there."

In mid-December, the perception of Clinton as the leader of the six-pack was reinforced at a Florida state Democratic convention in Lake Buena Vista. In a straw vote, he beat Harkin, who had the backing of organized labor, by 54 percent to 31. Although the vote was intrinsically meaningless, Clinton's campaign had made a serious effort, spending some $50,000 on an elaborate effort to assure his success, and to demonstrate organizational as well as rhetorical ability. But the victory was most striking because it included many liberal Democrats from south Florida who in other times might have been more inclined to Harkin or Kerrey.

In fact, Clinton's strength was so obvious before the convention that Kerrey's state coordinator, a veteran of Florida campaigns going back to Jimmy Carter in 1976, state representative Mike Abrams, recommended against making any effort in the straw vote to avoid the embarrassment of defeat. By this point, the notion that Clinton was on a roll was so widespread that the Arkansas Democrat was raising about $700,000 a week. "Clinton was definitely the winner of the 'pundit primary,' " Paul Begala said later, referring to the preliminaries on which the political community established an early pecking order.

But Kerrey's campaign enjoyed at least a temporary lift that weekend as well, despite his decision against competing in the straw poll. His speech to the Florida convention was widely judged the most effective he had delivered in the campaign up to that point, both in terms of his diagnosis of national issues and his use of his own special résumé. Recalling his months of hospitalization after being so seriously wounded as a

Navy Seal in Vietnam, he made the case that he was living proof of the essentiality of good government services. It was an approach that allowed him to talk about service without seeming to be exploiting his Medal of Honor.

The next night Kerrey also was generally rated as the winner of the first nationally televised debate of the campaign, broadcast by NBC and moderated by Tom Brokaw. He came off as the hero in the sound bite that was shown repeatedly over the next two days. Kerrey's opportunity came as Jerry Brown was dominating the debate with a persistent assault on the corruption of everyone in politics except himself—now that he was no longer a state party chairman squeezing lobbyists for money. The other candidates and Brokaw appeared clearly annoyed as Brown insisted on playing his one note about corruption whatever the ostensible topic— to the point that the debate was being badly distorted. He and Brokaw also had a dustup when Brown insisted on repeating his 800 telephone number to appeal for campaign contributions, which Brokaw said violated the rules of the debate.

Finally Kerrey turned directly to Brown and said: "I've got to tell you, I resent all this . . . special interest stuff that you are putting out because you seem to be saying that I'm somehow bought and paid for. Is that what you're saying?"

"I'm saying you are part of a system that is bought and paid for," Brown replied, only slightly chastened.

"Well, I disagree with you," Kerrey countered, icily.

As dramatic moments in television go, this one wasn't in the league with Lloyd Bentsen's 1988 rejoinder to Dan Quayle that "you're no Jack Kennedy." But it was the one moment of that debate that anyone would remember, particularly since front-runner Clinton had taken a very deliberate above-the-fray attitude that made him appear almost a bystander in the ninety-minute broadcast. And for Kerrey supporters in New Hampshire, it was—finally—some of the evidence they had been seeking that he was capable of better things.

Indeed, up to that point, the Kerrey campaign had seemed to be one mistake or misjudgment after another. Part of the problem was that the Nebraska Democrat simply wasn't ready for a presidential campaign when he plunged into it in October. "There's lots of areas where I wasn't prepared," he said later. "I was conscious, very conscious that I was making the decision very late, the decision that I want to be president, that perhaps there should be four or five years between the moment that you decide you want to be president and the day when you first start to run.''

In fact, just as Kerrey was entering the campaign, one of his closest political allies and friends, former Representative John Cavanaugh of Omaha, was warning him that he wasn't prepared. ''John Cavanaugh can justifiably say, 'I told you so,' '' Kerrey conceded much later. But when Cavanaugh made the argument at the time, he recalled, ''I would ask back to him, 'John, okay, so what? Now that you've reached that conclusion, do you want me not to run?' ''

''No,'' he said Cavanaugh replied. ''I want you to run.''

''Well, okay, so I've got a weak hand, that's all. I've got to walk in and make them think I've got a full house.''

Kerrey's principal problem was simply the lack of a consistent and focused economic message, particularly in contrast to the prescription for economic revival being offered by Tsongas or the appeal to the middle class being made by Clinton. At the outset his Kennedyesque message— ''building for greatness''—was too much the rhetorical flourish for voters as preoccupied with the economy as those in New Hampshire. ''I still like the message that I had,'' Kerrey said later, ''but it didn't resonate with audiences concerned about losing their jobs. . . . We went into the teeth of an economic storm in New Hampshire.''

For a while Kerrey emphasized health care and his recommendation for a national health insurance program almost exclusively but, again, it was not direct enough. ''I failed to get it clearly inside a larger economic issue,'' he said. ''I didn't make it an economic issue.'' Speaking to a meeting of the unemployed in Concord one day, Kerrey wandered into discussing a proposal for cutting the number of cabinet departments from fourteen to seven—shades of Jimmy Carter—and describing health care reform as ''the most powerful economic engine,'' without ever getting to the obvious obsession of such an audience: jobs. Later in the campaign he began to talk about trade barriers and the Japanese, and their impact on the economy. One particularly striking commercial showed him on a hockey rink, an appropriate venue in New Hampshire, talking about how the United States left its net unprotected while the Japanese did not. But, again, it was one step removed from the immediate problem of those he was trying to reach. ''We had misread the audience with our television,'' he recalled. "It was a reflection of how I had misjudged the audience." As for that particular commercial? "It says nothing about their life. Their life isn't so much influenced by trade, though it is, [so] they're saying, 'We're out of work. So you run this fancy hockey ad, big deal. We're out of work.' "

Kerrey also had trouble dealing with his military record, trying to find a balance between being "naturally reticent" about talking about it and appearing to be exploiting his Medal of Honor. In that first debate on NBC, he made a conscious effort to deal with his personal history, mentioning his military service several times, only to find it backfired. "I'm aware that I've got to tell a story about who I am," he said later. "I know I've got to get that out. But after the first debate, I was gun-shy over referencing anything having to do with Vietnam, not just because there were negative editorials, but even my son said to me, 'My God, do you always [have to]? You mentioned it four or five times in the debate.' Even he noticed it."

Whatever his troubles, Kerrey clearly appeared to be at least in the ballgame in the final days of 1991. The same could not be said of Doug Wilder, who had found no fertile ground in New Hampshire, a state in which less than 1 percent of the population is black, and had made only a token effort to do so in any case. Nor was there any evidence that Jerry Brown's constant critique of the corruption of the political financing system was being taken seriously by New Hampshire Democrats worried about their jobs and businesses. Political reform was not high on their agenda.

Wilder's campaign had been something of a puzzle from its inception. Indeed, a few months before he decided to run, he had told a group of reporters over dinner in Washington that he probably wouldn't do it because he doubted a governor of less than two years' seniority could win the nomination. Nor was there any evidence to suggest either the Democratic primary voters or the electorate in general were prepared to accept a black nominee. He had defied that conventional wisdom in winning two statewide elections in Virginia, for lieutenant governor in 1985 and governor in 1989. But in each case he had won against flawed opponents by margins that should have been larger, and clearly would have been had he been a white candidate.

Wilder and his chief political adviser, Paul Goldman, were not deterred. Early in 1991 they were convinced that the Persian Gulf War would be politically irrelevant in a few months and that the condition of the economy would dominate the politics of 1992. And they were equally convinced that there would be a market in the new Democratic Party and the country for "the new mainstream"—their phrase for the moderately conservative approach the black governor had taken on fiscal and some social issues.

There was also the question of whether Wilder might not have been driven to some degree by his rivalry, real or imagined, with Jesse Jackson to become the dominant black political leader in the country. Although they both protested to the contrary, Wilder and Jackson always had a tense relationship. Jackson saw Wilder as too conservative on the issues he considered most important. Wilder had come up through the political system, sixteen years in the state legislature and then the lieutenant governorship, rather than the civil rights movement, and seemed at least mildly contemptuous of Jackson for not having played earlier in the political arena.

In his two statewide campaigns in Virginia, Wilder had adopted a policy of not accepting help from surrogates from outside the state, thus effectively closing the door to Jackson—in much the same way Lyndon B. Johnson had eliminated Robert F. Kennedy from consideration for vice president in 1964 by ruling that no one in his cabinet would be chosen. Now with Jackson apparently having put his presidential ambitions aside for the moment, there was room for another black leader— and one who had won a state governorship, while Jackson had refused to run even for mayor of the District of Columbia.

Wilder was a particularly prickly politician with a long history of continuing public spats with other Democrats as often as with Republicans. He had become involved in rhubarbs with his immediate predecessor in Richmond, Gerald Baliles, and with former governor and now Senator Charles Robb. He often ascribed these disputes to the feisty Goldman, but Wilder himself wasn't shy. When, for example, Democratic National Chairman Ronald Brown issued a routine statement in 1990 commending the tax deal between President Bush and Democratic congressional leaders, the Virginia governor quickly gave to the press and then fired off an angry letter asking Brown where he got the authority to put the party behind higher taxes.

In testing the presidential waters, he was equally contentious. In July of 1991, for example, he used a speech to a convention of Young Democrats to take a shot at Governor Mario Cuomo of New York, chiding "those who travel to Washington and deliver blistering speeches on fiscal responsibility but then return to their home states where they have blistered their own citizens with deficit spending and other fiscal torture." He seemed to be following a time-honored technique for getting attention— picking a fight with someone better known and thus, by implication, putting himself at the same level. But Cuomo refused to be drawn into the game.

With Bill Clinton as the acknowledged front-runner, Wilder attracted attention with a trip to Arkansas to enlist the public endorsements of several black state legislators who might otherwise have been considered Clintonites. A couple of weeks later he complained that Jesse Jackson "had asked people not to support me"—a charge the civil rights leader, who had taken himself out of the picture, denied. But none of this political gamesmanship could erase Wilder's principal problem. He was running in a primary in which virtually no blacks would cast ballots. And he faced the prospect that in the first eleven states that would hold primaries blacks made up 25 percent of the population in only one, Maryland, unless, as subsequently happened, Georgia moved its date forward. His only hope rested in a respectable showing in New Hampshire that would keep his candidacy alive for the Southern primaries in March, in which their large black constituencies could make themselves felt.

But there was no sign of any progress in New Hampshire and Wilder's situation was becoming increasingly awkward. On the one hand, he could not spend the kind of time the primary voters seemed to expect— "It was a little surprising to me, the one-on-one that was necessary," he said later. On the other, he was getting increasing heat from voters, the press and political rivals back home for neglecting the state. A compilation by *The Richmond Times-Dispatch* in October found the governor already had spent 111 days out of the state in 1991, much of the time campaigning. "People felt I should have had more gratitude for being elected, the first elected African-American in the country," he said, "and before I could even settle into the job, I'm talking about running for another job."

By contrast with Wilder's apparently unseemly haste, Jerry Brown had entered the campaign carrying the heavy baggage of almost twenty years as a most unorthodox player on the national political stage. His career in California grew out of his position as the son of a popular regular Democrat, former Governor Edmund G. (Pat) Brown. The younger Brown won a term as secretary of state, an office he used effectively toward his election as governor in 1974 as the successor to Ronald Reagan. Once in Sacramento, his "small is beautiful" style attracted wide attention from the media. He chose to sleep on a mattress on the floor of a modest apartment rather than live in the state-owned governor's mansion, and to ride around in a blue Plymouth rather than a properly gubernatorial limousine.

But Brown won high marks for his willingness to make unconventional appointments to state boards and commissions and to address the thorny problems of the energy shortage, the environment and farm labor law. Even some of his most severe critics credited Brown with having been far ahead of other political leaders in understanding the need for a more aggressive government role in protecting the environment.

Brown also was determinedly ambitious, entering the campaign for the 1976 Democratic presidential nomination and winning several late primaries after Jimmy Carter had effectively locked up the nomination. But Brown also was gaining a reputation as a politician who flitted from one fad idea to the next and for making abrupt changes in course. In 1978 he campaigned vigorously against California's Proposition 13, which sought to apply rigid limits to local taxation. But once the measure was approved in the state's June primary, the governor embraced it enthusiastically in the general election campaign—in effect, leading by running to the head of the parade—in which he won a second term.

When Brown set off on still another run for the presidency, this time challenging incumbent President Jimmy Carter in 1980, his credibility was seriously undermined by an erratic performance and he never won a primary. When he made a run for the Senate in 1982, he was buried by his own history and Republican Pete Wilson, who later moved to the governorship himself.

Brown was, however, a very different politician with an interest in ideas and a knack for recognizing emerging issues before they were obvious to everyone in politics. And he had the interest in examining ideas of a onetime Jesuit seminarian, which in fact he had been before going to Yale Law School. Dinner with him at El Adobe, a favorite restaurant of his in Los Angeles, could go on for three or four hours of exchanging ideas and arguments.

Once, on a visit to Washington in 1978, he spent a long evening with editors and reporters from *The Washington Star* testing his thesis that politicians should not present their decisions to their constituents as morally correct. To do so, he argued, would put those constituents who disagreed with him in the position of being not just substantively and politically but morally wrong. His dinner companions tested the thesis with one hypothetical situation after another and Brown seemed completely engrossed. It was not the kind of conversation that you would have with many politicians.

Brown also had the remarkable memory so common in successful politicians. One of us had dinner with him in San Diego one night in the fall of 1978 in which the conversation centered on the politics of the growing, although not yet fully visible, concern about the safety of nuclear power plants. When we encountered him next on a Los Angeles street corner in May of 1979, shortly after the accident at the Three Mile Island nuclear plant in Pennsylvania, he greeted us by asking: "Remember what I told you about those nuclear power plants?"

But Jerry Brown's uncanny ability to identify sore spots in the electorate was not matched by a talent for the laborious, painstaking work required to find solutions to those concerns. What he lacked in follow-through, however, he made up in chutzpah. He entered the 1992 campaign by somewhat grandly declaring his candidacy at Independence Hall in Philadelphia.

The inspiration for the setting and the lyrics came from veteran Democratic pollster and consultant Patrick Caddell, ostensibly out of politics and resettled in California. For several years, Caddell had been on the lookout for a candidate to test his theory of an electorate yearning for change, and to carry his message of political rebirth to it. He had tried with Gary Hart in 1984 and with Joe Biden in 1988, and now loaned that message to Brown, an old friend.

Brown said he was running against the "incumbent party of Republicans and Democrats alike" who had formed "an unholy alliance of private greed and corrupt politics" in Washington. It was a sentiment widely shared by the electorate of 1992 but exploiting this anger was one thing, finding a way to assuage it quite another.

Like George Corley Wallace of Alabama a generation earlier, Brown was demonstrating only that he could identify a significant vein of resentment against all politics as usual. There was no sign, however, that resentment alone would be enough to sustain Brown in New Hampshire or, for that matter, anywhere else.

Moreover, Brown was seriously compromised by the picture he had projected of himself over the years as a politician who kept reinventing himself. After his defeat for the Senate, he went into a de facto exile for several years, studying Buddhism in Japan and then working briefly for Mother Teresa at a refuge in India—before suddenly reappearing in California and running for, of all things, Democratic state chairman.

The notion of this man who had always disdained conventional political mechanics seeking such an office was mind-boggling, but now Brown insisted that he intended to do it and do it right. He got the job and at first that seemed to be the case. But his interest in nuts and bolts flagged after two years and he stepped down early in 1991 and began putting together a campaign for the U.S. Senate in 1992. The conventional wisdom held that he had a sufficient remaining core of support among California Democrats to be the favorite in the party primary for the nomination, but that he still carried too much baggage to win against a Republican in November.

At this point he heard from a former political adviser about how another Democrat, Lawton Chiles, had won a governorship in Florida by putting a $100 limit on campaign contributions. That gesture had proved to be an excellent metaphor for Chiles in presenting himself as a candidate free of the big-money special interests. But it also had produced about $5 million, enough to finance his campaign more than adequately.

Brown was fascinated by the idea. When one of us encountered him at a state party convention in Oakland early in 1991, Brown—still focused on a Senate campaign—inquired at length about how the Chiles strategy had played out. What he didn't seem to grasp was that Lawton Chiles had always limited contributions to his campaigns for the U.S. Senate and thus had built credibility as a reformist politician. Brown had just spent two years as a state chairman squeezing money out of big contributors. But the inconsistency didn't faze him. Who, he asked, knows the sin better than the sinner? He would use the $100 limit and an 800 telephone number to reach the broadest audience of voters who might be willing to risk that much in the name of clean politics. But as the New Hampshire primary campaign began in earnest, there was no sign this new reincarnation of Jerry Brown as a presidential rather than Senate candidate was proving persuasive.

Harkin's campaign also seemed stalled. As the candidates debated the differences among them on tax policy, the future of the economy and the complexity of the health care problem, the senator from Iowa still was being viewed largely in terms of his insistence on the old-time gospel of Democratic liberalism. His campaign manager, a veteran of New Hampshire campaigns named Kathi Rogers, continued to insist there was a market share there, and other longtime Democratic regulars agreed.

But there was also a growing suspicion that the electorate of 1992 was a different breed of cat. One reason was the growing evidence that Paul Tsongas, the most unlikely of candidates, was beginning to build a following among voters who agreed with his prescription of bitter medicine to revive the manufacturing sector of the economy.

As the year-end holidays approached, however, most voters in New Hampshire still had not begun to pay close attention. A poll for *The Boston Globe* found 40 percent of likely primary voters still undecided, a share large enough to put the entire poll into obvious question. But it did make clear that the contest was still to be shaped, let alone won or lost. And many of the political activists were still keeping their options open. They might be impressed by Bill Clinton or Bob Kerrey or even Paul Tsongas, but they still had not heard from the one Democrat many thought was the party's only possible savior—Mario Cuomo.

HAMLET ON
THE HUDSON

For more than seven years, ever since his keynote address to the 1984 Democratic national convention at San Francisco, Mario Cuomo had been a dominating figure in the party. In an era of bland politicians, he was vivid, complex, often vexing—always seeming to be larger than life, just as he appeared now to the six Democrats trying to be taken seriously in the early stages of the New Hampshire primary campaign.

In the preliminaries to the 1988 campaign, the widespread assumption in the political community was that the New York governor could win the nomination if he wanted it. Even as late as December of 1987, many Democrats believed he could have entered the competition and taken it away from Michael Dukakis or Richard Gephardt or any of the others of the Seven Dwarfs then in the field.

But Cuomo closed the door, or at least seemed to do so, with finality shortly before Christmas that year. Characteristically, he did so on a radio call-in show, thus delivering a small zinger to the reporters from Albany, New York City and Washington who had been pressing him for months

113

on his intentions. It was something he clearly enjoyed doing every once in a while.

In the runup to 1992, the situation had changed somewhat. Liberals were still intrigued at the possibility of a Cuomo candidacy. In California many prominent party figures were convinced he was the one candidate most likely to assure the Democrats the prize they had to have in the general election—California's fifty-four electoral votes, one fifth of the total needed to be elected. But the defeat of another Northeastern liberal, and an ethnic candidate to boot, in 1988 had emboldened the more conservative Democrats of the South and West to give more public voice to their view that a Mario Cuomo simply wouldn't sell with their constituents. He might win the nomination, the theory went, but he could not win the general election. How many times did the Democrats have to make the same mistake?

But Cuomo was not a politician who could be taken lightly, whatever the context in which he was operating. His force of personality, combative style and graceful use of the language all made him a candidate who could not be ignored or, more to the point, judged solely by such conventional measures as whether he was too liberal on the issues.

Some Republicans liked to talk smugly about how he would be the dream opponent—another leftist governor whose record in state government could be shredded. But others were less certain. He was no Michael Dukakis, that was for sure. This was a candidate who would get right in George Bush's face, and they were far from confident Bush would perform well under that kind of pressure.

Moreover, in a somewhat perverse way, the fact that his party was facing an uphill fight against an apparently unassailable Republican incumbent might make the campaign more attractive to Cuomo. The odds might be ten to one against him, but George Bush was the kind of opponent—a preppy, white-shoe Republican who had gone to Andover and Yale—that a candidate from New York City's borough of Queens might relish as an opponent. And the growing evidence of economic distress, which Cuomo was quick to recognize, was creating the kind of playing field that could favor a Democratic nominee who could identify himself convincingly with Americans suffering that distress.

Cuomo would have none of it. He already had been fending off questions about his intentions for most of the last two years. When one of us joined him in Albany one morning for a day of travel as he campaigned for reelection in 1990, he suggested we were planning "another dumb story" speculating on his ambitions for the presidency. And, drinking coffee as he flew toward Buffalo later that morning, he angrily rejected the suggestion there might be something about the elitist Bush he would particularly enjoy challenging.

"That would be self-aggrandizing," he said, banging the table for emphasis. "It would be the height of egoism and the height of selfishness." The only reason he wasn't ruling himself out entirely was the dark inferences that such a statement would encourage. "They'd say, 'He must have colon cancer, he must have a Mafia uncle.' "

Cuomo had always angrily resented the perpetual speculation that because he was an Italian-American he had something to hide in his background. This ethnic stereotyping had always been a sore spot with a man who came out of his St. John's Law School class with the highest honors, but could not even win an interview from the big Manhattan and Wall Street law firms to which he applied. In fact, his personal life had been investigated inside out—by the Republicans in his first race for governor, among others—and there was not a shred of evidence that he or his family had anything to hide.

Through the spring and summer of 1991, Cuomo continued to brush off the presidential talk. And this time he had finally found the formulation that he enjoyed using and seemed to believe defied the attempts of the Kremlinologist reporters with whom he liked to joust to find hidden meanings in his rhetoric. "I have no plans and no plans to make plans," he kept saying.

At the same time, however, Cuomo continued to take the occasional initiative that he had to know would feed the speculation, while arguing vehemently and forcefully that the fact he had strong views on, for example, the failures of the Bush administration didn't necessarily mean he was obliged to run for president, or was even thinking about it. He had a responsibility as governor of New York, he would say huffily; the inferences you draw are your own problem. If you want to write another dumb column, be my guest.

But he did nourish the speculation even while insisting it had no basis in fact. In May he criticized the Democratic Leadership Council for what he called its "implicit position that we have something we have to apologize for and now we have to move to the middle.'' He thus positioned himself as one liberal who was not prepared to wear a hairshirt because of the failures of Walter Mondale or Michael Dukakis.

In July, Cuomo unloaded another attack on Bush's record on the economy, and in August he went to Hyannis, Massachusetts, at the invitation of the United States Conference of Mayors, many of whose leaders were outspoken in their support for him as a potential presidential candidate. He delivered another stinging critique of Bush and laid out in a dazzling monologue his own prescription for beating him in 1992. Basically, he said, the Democratic leaders in Congress should pass their own economic recovery plan, let Bush veto it, and then have the party's nominee run against him on it. Then Cuomo tantalizingly told the mayors: ''I'll do anything you ask me to do—as governor.''

Cuomo insisted the situation never met the criterion he had set for himself in considering whether to run for president—simply that he would be the best alternative available. Long after the fact, he recalled describing his view to Michael Dukakis in 1987 this way: ''The way it works for me, I would have to conclude there isn't anybody as good as I am. Now there may be a different test that others apply, and I don't care much. That's the one I apply and I can't say that to myself. I can't say I'm better than you and I can't say I'd have a better chance than you.''

In the fall of 1991, nonetheless, it became increasingly difficult for Cuomo to argue he never even thought about it, even if only while shaving. The public pressure was becoming too obvious. And when Cuomo made a trip to California in September, he found many party leaders there—including an old friend, Representative Nancy Pelosi— who clearly wanted him to make the race in 1992. And some of those close to Cuomo thought they detected a quickening of interest.

In October, with the field stripped of the other acknowledged heavyweights, Cuomo began to send a somewhat different signal. The turning point was a breakfast at the Regency Hotel in Manhattan with a small group of longtime supporters and campaign contributors—a de facto committee planning the annual fund-raiser to finance his state campaigns. It was a group Cuomo said was ''like family . . . people who had been with me for fifteen years.''

Cuomo described it this way: ''One guy stood up, Vincent Albanese, who I have had tremendous respect for for a long time, a good friend.

He said, 'Mario, let me ask you a question. What about the presidency? We never ask you, out of respect,' he says, 'none of us have ever said anything to you. We get teased once in a while . . . they say that you could win.'

"I said, 'Well, you know, it's possible.' He said, 'What do you say about the presidency?' I said, 'Vincent, Matilda [Cuomo's wife] is sitting here, we've grown up together,' I said. 'I'm telling you I've never had a discussion with Matilda.' And Matilda said, 'That's right.' I said, 'I've never reached the point where I believe that I could say to myself, "This country needs me." ' I said, 'I know what I'm good at, Vincent, I'm very good at some things, I'm not so hot at other things. I just have never reached the point when I could say my country needs me.'

"He said, 'Well, that's very interesting and we believe that and we understand what you're saying, but what about us? What if we thought the country needed you?'

"Now, as simple as that sounds, you have to understand the setting," Cuomo related. "I hate asking for money. I took money from these people. I lost three elections in one year in 1977 to Ed Koch [the Democratic primary and runoff and, as the Liberal Party nominee, the general election for mayor of New York City]. . . . They have given me money. They never get anything because we just don't do business that way, and here this guy is saying, in effect, that you didn't think about us. And I said, 'I'll tell you what I'll do'—this is on the spot—I said, 'I will think about it for the first time and I'll be honest about it.' "

He would ask his son, Andrew, and some of his other political advisers, Cuomo told them, to take a look at the potential. The process, he suggested, would take less than six weeks. But there was, he reminded his old friends, the one problem of having to settle on a state budget.

"So I left," Cuomo recalled. "Before I got out of that room the press had been told about the conversation, which I'll never understand but obviously someone in that room . . . dropped a dime, because as soon as I walked out the door, somebody said AP has a story, and it couldn't have been forty minutes later."

Confronted when he reached Albany later the same day, Cuomo brushed off his talk at breakfast as a courteous but essentially perfunctory response to his supporters. "They said, 'Will you think about it?' " he related. "I said, 'Sure, I'll think about it. I'm always thinking about it.'

I said I'd have to be mindless not to think about it. I don't talk about it, but I think about it. Of course I do.''

Cuomo was adamant in insisting nothing had changed. ''I said absolutely nothing,'' he said. ''You can't honestly say you have a big story. If you're asking me did you say anything new, the answer is no.''

But there was indeed something new and different in Cuomo's position—a tacit acknowledgment that he was giving active consideration to running, that he could no longer say he had ''no plans to make plans.'' In Chicago ten days after his Manhattan breakfast, he said he was ''looking at'' the possibility of running and would make a decision soon. ''There's still time left until sometime in November,'' he said. ''By then you have to either be in or not be in. There's only a few weeks to go and we'll see.''

Over those ''few weeks'' the Hamlet on the Hudson continued to ruminate in public about a candidacy. Appearing on a cable television program on Long Island, he framed the internal debate this way: ''What does my heart tell me? Go out and tell them, Mario. Take your best shot, whether you win, lose or draw.'' At the same time, he said, ''Your head tells you: how do you do that and do the right thing as governor? I'm working on my head at the moment.''

In an interview with the editorial board of *The New York Daily News*, Cuomo conceded that the question was being treated more seriously this time around. ''The pressure has been greater,'' he said. ''The issues are different now than they were in '88, in '84. The economy is much worse. The recognition of the economy being worse is clearer than it ever has been. . . . I'm at a different stage of my career.''

Meanwhile, pressure to make a decision one way or the other increased, much of it applied—although indirectly—by Democratic chairman Ron Brown, who had once been a law student in a class taught by Cuomo at St. John's. Brown had made no particular secret of the fact he had hoped Cuomo would run, but publicly his priority at this point was getting an early decision so the party could move ahead in settling on a nominee.

In conversations with John Marino, the New York Democratic Party chairman, and Michael Del Giudice, another longtime political intimate of Cuomo, Brown urged that the New York Democrat make a decision as early as possible so that the field would be established. The threat of a Cuomo candidacy was freezing Democratic activists and contributors who by this point might have been choosing another candidate to support.

Brown was being burdened by the fact that his old professor Cuomo refused to accept his telephone calls, insisting their only communication be done through Marino or some other intermediary. "I was not talking to Ron Brown," Cuomo said. "Close as I was, I refused to talk to Ron Brown. I sent him one message . . . the governor's not going to talk to you and the reason the governor's not going to talk to you is he doesn't want to compromise you."

"It was almost like he thought I was going to trap him," Brown said later, "or I was going to encourage him to do something he didn't want to do, or put him on the spot, to push him toward a decision. . . . [His indecision] was not helpful, and that's why I tried to step up and exert some leadership. There was a major natural force hovering and it kept people from focusing. . . . It was very distracting."

Some of the candidates already in the field, and particularly those groping for a foothold among liberals, were predictably anxious to see the Cuomo question resolved. "A lot of my supporters in a lot of places were just hanging back, waiting to see what Cuomo was going to do," Tom Harkin recalled. "I heard it constantly." Bob Kerrey was having the same experience. "We were all standing in his shadow for the first ten or twelve weeks," he said later.

The way the active candidates viewed the prospect of a Cuomo candidacy reflected their different positions in the field. The conventional wisdom was that Cuomo would do the most direct harm to his fellow liberal Harkin because of his appeal to the same old-line regulars and labor, as well as his connection with black voters that the Iowa Democrat could not hope to match. Some Kerrey supporters were more sanguine about a Cuomo presence in the race, reasoning, somewhat simplistically perhaps, that Cuomo juxtaposed against the DLC candidate, Bill Clinton, might polarize the campaign and cast Kerrey as the centrist alternative who could draw from both ends of the spectrum. Kerrey, unlike Harkin, was seen as a candidate with potential in the South because of the special credential of his military record.

The most intriguing possibility, however, was that Cuomo would offer an opportunity for one of the other candidates—and Clinton in particular—to establish his political bona fides by defeating the New

Yorker in New Hampshire. The candidate who did that, the theory went, would be the giant-killer who would instantly take on mythic proportions for the rest of the contest for the nomination, and into the general election against George Bush. What better way to demonstrate that the Democratic Party had turned a corner than by defeating the quintessential symbol of old-fashioned liberalism, Mario Cuomo?

Paul Tsongas, never lacking for self-assurance, was convinced that his best chance to catapult himself to the head of the list of ostensibly "serious" candidates would be to defeat Cuomo in the New Hampshire primary. Someone who beat Cuomo, Tsongas was certain, could not be written off as no more than a regional favorite.

But the Clinton campaign was not so sure they should welcome such an opportunity. As Paul Begala, one of the key advisers to the Arkansas governor, put it later, "There was a lot of whistling past the graveyard. . . . A lot of that was us trying to pump ourselves up, get our juices flowing for the fight of a lifetime. Cuomo was not from Washington so it was not going to be very easy to make him the old politics. To do so would risk getting back on an ideological axis, where Clinton did not want to go. At the time, we were saying, 'Oh, yes, bring him on,' of course, because we have to. That's the kind of bravado, at least, that people in this business develop." But the truth, Begala conceded, was that "we were scared to death of him" because he was "such an 800-pound gorilla."

Meanwhile, the relationship between Cuomo and Clinton had become a touchy one. Cuomo was no admirer of the DLC and had been irked at the decision, which Clinton endorsed, to shut Jesse Jackson off the DLC speakers' program at the meeting in Cleveland earlier in the year. As the Democrats waited for Cuomo's decision, he gave an interview to *New York* magazine that made the relationship with Clinton even more tenuous. And, not incidentally, it raised some questions about whether Cuomo himself truly understood the special demands on the party to redefine itself for the 1992 electorate.

The magazine quoted Cuomo as disparaging Clinton's emphasis on welfare reform. "He says they shouldn't be on welfare forever," Cuomo said. "Maybe in his state they are. In my state, they're on for an average of two years." Questioned by *The Washington Post* about the remark, Cuomo explained it this way: "I don't want to make people on welfare a whipping boy—or lady, as is the case, since 80 percent of the people on welfare in my state and most states are women and children."

It was the conventional liberal argument on welfare. Cuomo surely knew, as did Clinton, that the two-year average was beside the point. The goal in welfare reform was to find a way out for the substantial number of families who had been trapped in the system for one generation after another. And Cuomo surely knew that one of the prime concerns of the conservative Reagan Democrats—the critical target group for the party in 1992—was their conviction that welfare costs were too high and too perpetual.

Cuomo also derided another Clinton idea—making college education universally available under a plan in which students would repay the costs through payroll deductions or with public service work. It was a notion, opinion studies indicated, with enormous appeal to the middle-class voters Clinton was targeting. But Cuomo wasn't buying. "Where do you get the money?" he asked. "Isn't this one of those big bureaucratic programs you're complaining about? Where are the details? . . . It's a lot of baloney." Asked about this comment, the New Yorker replied that he didn't want to get in a fight with Clinton, which was precisely what he had done.

For the Arkansas governor, the Cuomo attack was the ultimate political flattery, suggesting that he was the one, of all the party's dominant if still dormant potential presidential candidates, worth the attention. Indeed, at one point, some of Clinton's advisers urged him to go to Harlem and deliver a speech on crime that, implicitly at least, would be an attack on Cuomo. But Clinton himself scotched the idea. "I don't want to pick a fight with someone who's not running against me," he said. "If he's running, there's plenty of time for that."

Ron Brown continued to send his message through Marino and Del Giudice, adjusting the "deadline" as time passed and Cuomo continued to debate with himself. Mario could help things along by making a decision in early October or late October. Or how about by Election Day, November 5? Or what about Thanksgiving? But Election Day passed and Cuomo continued to ruminate.

"It was not helpful," Ron Brown recalled. "There was a major national force hovering when [political observers] were saying, 'This is a vice presidential field.' . . . I felt like we had to move the thing off dead [center]. We had to know what the field was and who the choices were. And as long as Mario and others were out there undecided, it kept people from focusing on what we had to do to get ready for a general election campaign. . . . People kept waiting for somebody else.''

On still another call-in program on public television the day after the election, Cuomo said: ''I'll complete the process as quickly as I can and let you know as soon as I can.'' Asked on November 14 if he would announce his decision by Thanksgiving Day or New Year's Day or Valentine's Day or St. Patrick's Day, he replied: ''All of those are possibilities.'' A few days later in Buffalo, he conceded feeling pressure to make up his mind. ''That means you have to rush your decision,'' he said. ''But if you have to rush your decision, and I don't have a [state] budget solution, then I would have to say no.''

By this point, Cuomo was presenting the issue in terms of the complex negotiations in which he was involved with Republican leaders of the legislature over a new state budget. But again the signals were mixed. At one point, he suggested he would have to resign as governor if he were to run, apparently holding this out as a possibility. But then he went on to say that would be ''a form of abandonment.'' In early December he told one interviewer that he ''never said'' he had to resolve all those state budget problems before reaching a decision to run. ''What I said is that I have to be sure that my running for president won't make it more difficult, won't make it worse for the state.''

Cuomo was also depicting himself, somewhat disingenuously, as lagging ''way behind'' the candidates already in the field. ''The people out there don't know who I am,'' he said at a press conference on December 5. ''Every time I meet somebody in Chicago, any group at all, maybe eighty percent of what the people say is, 'Gee, I didn't know you were that tall, I never heard you say that, Governor, I didn't know you had a sense of humor. Gee, I have this picture, I thought you were short, had baggy eyes and were very mean.' You've got to get to the people.''

Cuomo was also growing impatient with the press preoccupation with his future. ''You have all, every one of you without exception, commented on what a tiresome, repetitive process it is,'' he told reporters in Albany. ''So I will save you all the dilly-dallying, the shilly-shallying and the vacillations. Let's just put aside these tawdry meanderings and let's concentrate on the budget.''

A few days later, on December 16, Cuomo seemed to have developed a rationale for running even if the Republicans continued to thwart him on the budget. "If you made up your mind that they were doing this only to prevent you from running," he said, "then the solution would be to run. Then they would no longer have the motive to slow you up. And that would save the state, by running for president."

The issue of how a campaign would interfere with Cuomo's ability to perform as governor had always been one he cited to explain his recalcitrance. In the 1987–1988 cycle and again this time, he complained that a sitting governor couldn't take the time to run for national office. How could you spend weeks tramping through Iowa or New Hampshire when you were needed in Albany?

In fact, this was a straw man of impressive dimensions. Mario Cuomo was not some Bruce Babbitt forced to ride a bicycle across Iowa in 1987 trying to win a little press attention. He was not a Paul Tsongas required to stump day after day in New Hampshire trying to establish some credibility as a candidate. Cuomo was a national figure whose campaign from the start inevitably would draw heavy television network and newspaper coverage.

Perhaps most important, however, Cuomo seemed to have passed some invisible line, some indefinable point at which a politician becomes a celebrity and not just a political leader—a celebrity viewed with excitement and a certain amount of awe by ordinary people, essentially without regard to whether they agree with his politics. It is a rare status, bestowed in some mysterious way. Dwight D. Eisenhower had it when he returned from Europe to run for president in 1952. Nelson Rockefeller had it when he first ran for governor of New York in 1958. Robert Kennedy had it when he ran first for the Senate in 1964 and then for the Democratic presidential nomination in 1968. Ronald Reagan had it from the moment he announced his candidacy for governor of California in 1966. And now it was Mario Cuomo.

Whatever rationale he was using for staying out of the campaign, Cuomo was nonetheless positioning himself to make the race if he decided to do so. Marino gathered information on delegate rules and the primary and caucus process and drew up tentative lists of professionals for a campaign staff. Fund-raisers were alerted so that if he decided to enter the campaign he could raise the early money needed to qualify for federal matching funds. Cuomo himself met with Robert Shrum, a leading Washington consultant with campaign experience going back twenty years, to get his reading on how the campaign might be conducted. Cuomo agents scouted office space in Manhattan, Washington and New Hampshire.

The reports were encouraging. Money would not be a problem and, Marino reported, it would not be difficult to enlist the right people in the major states. "So all of it looked good except getting the [state] budget," Cuomo recalled. And by this time, the argument here centered on a gap of only about $200 million in a budget of $30 billion.

Cuomo blew hot and cold on whether there might be a deal, after all. At one point, he told the Republican leaders, he said, that he couldn't believe they would think it was in their interest to block his candidacy. "If I run for president and lose in the primaries, I'm dead meat," he said. "If I win, I'm gone and New York state has a president. How could that hurt any Democrat or any Republican? How can that hurt you?"

There was now a genuine deadline for his decision—December 20, the final day for filing to compete in the New Hampshire primary. Although it might have been possible for him to skip that test, he had already made it clear that he didn't intend to do it that way. If it was going to be a "go," it would start there.

Other Democrats and the press were growing impatient with the long public agonizing. At the Florida Democratic state convention, a write-in movement for Cuomo produced only 1 percent of the vote and there were choruses of booing and hooting every time his name was mentioned. Some professionals were suggesting that Cuomo already was playing "primary politics" by delaying his decision principally to rob his less-known rivals of time to compete.

On December 19, he told reporters in Albany that he wouldn't simply skip New Hampshire while leaving his options open for a final decision later, an option Ron Brown already had suggested would be damaging to the party. "The real deadline on New Hampshire is tomorrow," Cuomo said. "I wouldn't pocket veto the presidency."

On the contrary, those who talked to him early that evening were convinced he was up for the game. At one point, he asked Marino why, if he was going to run, "why wouldn't I go into Iowa?"—the Iowa precinct caucuses to be held eight days before New Hampshire. There were compelling reasons to focus for the moment on New Hampshire, but Marino liked what he was hearing.

Cuomo spent that night holed up in the executive mansion on Eagle Street in Albany, a sprawling Victorian house he had come to enjoy immensely once it had been improved with such refinements as a half-court basketball court. Talking at length with his son, Andrew, they speculated on the chances the Republicans would agree on a budget the next day, and Cuomo wrote two tentative statements—one a rationale for running without solving the budget stalemate, the other a statement explaining that he could not do it.

The morning of December 20, dozens of reporters and camera crews gathered outside his office on the second floor of the capitol, while others congregated at the gold-domed statehouse in Concord, where Cuomo's $1,000 filing fee and declaration of candidacy would have to be delivered by 5 P.M. Twenty-nine Democrats, nineteen Republicans and one Libertarian already had filed for places on the February 18 ballot, and during the day they would be joined by Harkin and Kerrey.

The declaration could not be filed with a fax or copy, but a signed original and check had been flown into Concord late Thursday and given to Joe Grandmaison, the New Hampshire political veteran who was acting as Cuomo's liaison, as a protection against the possibility of a snowstorm that would make it impossible for Cuomo to get from Albany to Concord in time.

Although it might have been legally acceptable for such a proxy filing to substitute for a personal appearance even without a blizzard, both Grandmaison and Marino recognized that would be seen as political arrogance in a state that likes to cut politicians down to size. "Joe desperately did not want that to happen," Marino said, "and I didn't want that to happen. I wouldn't do that in New York, let alone New Hampshire."

Grandmaison and Marino had become friends when Grandmaison also was serving as state party chairman a year or so earlier and, despite the differences in their bases and backgrounds, shared the most valuable asset for any political professional—street smarts. So it was not surprising that Marino had called Grandmaison in late October or early November to ask him if he might be willing to help if Cuomo decided to run.

Grandmaison had first come to national attention as the organizer of George McGovern's surprisingly strong showing in the 1972 New Hampshire primary, but he also had played key roles in several state and national campaigns thereafter—one of them as manager of Michael Dukakis's first campaign for governor of Massachusetts in 1974. So he replied that he was interested but only if he could be involved in more than New Hampshire. He wanted to be, he told Marino, "one of the five or six around the table" in a Cuomo campaign, to which Marino agreed.

On December 16, the Monday before the Friday deadline for filing, Marino called Grandmaison to ask, as the latter recalled, "what a schedule would look like" if Cuomo were flown into the state Friday to file the papers. The following day Grandmaison convened an instant committee to devise a schedule and then sent a fax to Marino's office in New York outlining a tentative plan and the steps that would have to be taken to prepare. By now the word was circulating through New Hampshire's small community of political activists and, Grandmaison said, "I started getting telephone calls from people who wanted to help."

Soon the list reached eighty or eighty-five people, including longtime liberal activists such as Sylvia Chaplain and prominent party figures such as former gubernatorial candidate Paul McEachern. The tentative schedule called for Cuomo to file his papers, hold a press conference in front of the statehouse, meet with sixty or seventy people who would make up the nucleus of his support and then meet with one of several networking groups of unemployed workers that had been formed in New Hampshire to talk about the economy. Grandmaison rented a bus and called Bob Molloy, another veteran state Democrat, and asked him to set up a sound system for the press conference. Marino dispatched a couple of advance men from New York to help with the mechanics.

At eight o'clock Friday morning Grandmaison positioned himself in the lobby of the Ramada Inn a block from the statehouse so he could keep in touch with Marino by using a pay telephone on the wall there. As the day wore on the crowd at the statehouse grew to 250 or so—the press, expectant supporters, the curious. People kept arriving and CNN kept showing a plane chartered for Cuomo poised on the tarmac at Albany. The candidate would be flown to Manchester and then driven the final eighteen miles to Concord. "Those of us from New Hampshire were getting somewhat giddy," Grandmaison said later.

But in New York, the optimistic enthusiasm Cuomo had displayed

Thursday night was missing. "Thursday night lifted my spirits immensely," Marino recalled. "By Friday morning I was talking to a different Mario Cuomo." The budget deal had not been made, after all.

Cuomo remained alone at the mansion on Eagle Street, making telephone calls and meditating. As the morning turned to noon to early afternoon, it was clear that time was running short. An alternative plan was developed to fly him directly to Concord if that were necessary. But it was also becoming clear that Cuomo wasn't going to do it. When Grandmaison placed his hourly call to Marino shortly after 3 P.M., the New Yorker told him: "Joe, he's going to announce at 3:30 that it's a no-go."

A few minutes later, just ninety minutes from the deadline, Cuomo broke the news to the reporters who had been spending hours guessing about his intentions. Citing the budget problem, Cuomo said: "It's my responsibility as governor to deal with this extraordinarily severe problem. Were it not, I would travel to New Hampshire today and file my name as a candidate in its presidential primary. That was my hope and I prepared for it. But it seems to me I cannot turn my attention to New Hampshire while this threat hangs over the head of the New Yorkers that I have sworn to put first."

Now that he had finally made the decision, Cuomo abandoned his coyness about whether he ever had wanted the prize. "I would be less than honest if I did not admit to you my regret at not having the opportunity to run for president," he said.

Cuomo conceded that it was possible to bypass New Hampshire and enter the race later but said he had no such intention. Instead, he said, he was meeting the "definitive deadline" set by Ron Brown. "You can't argue for that in logic or law," he said, "but I accept it and I understand the intelligence of it from his political point of view. Get Cuomo and everybody else out of the way and let's concentrate on the field we have."

At another point, he said: "I accept the judgment of the national chairman of our party that it would be in the best interest of the Democratic Party that I abandon any such effort now so as to avoid whatever inconvenience and disruption to the process is created by the uncertain possibility of another candidacy."

Whatever the reason, the Cuomo decision had cleared the air and defined the Democratic field. In the Clinton camp, it was obviously an important day. As Paul Begala recalled later, "We breathed a huge sigh of relief."

In Concord, Grandmaison walked from the Ramada to the statehouse and told the crowd Cuomo would not be coming after all. Before the sound system could be dismantled, however, Bob Kerrey arrived on the way to file his own papers with the secretary of state—and added a final bizarre touch to the day. "Kerrey walked up to the microphones," Grandmaison recalled, "and started, incredible though it may seem, started talking about the cost of energy"—at the moment the biggest political story in months had just broken.

With his television tuned to CNN in his office in Washington, Ron Brown was, as he said later, "incredulous watching his [Cuomo's] press conference." He had not spoken directly to Cuomo for months and had been forced to rely on messages sent through Marino, Del Giudice and the press. Now he felt he was being made the heavy who had forced poor Mario Cuomo to make this decision sooner than he might have liked. When Mike Royko of the *Chicago Tribune* wrote a column excoriating Brown for denying the Democrats their strongest candidate, Brown said, "I started getting the hate mail."

The notion that Cuomo had made the decision under pressure from Ron Brown was, on its face, laughable. Many of those close to the New York Democrat always had doubted that he would run, because he felt that obligation to his constituents and because he had always resisted the idea of having to go out and scramble for votes in unfamiliar territory.

Cuomo had always been extremely provincial, not just a New Yorker but a citizen of Queens who had never seemed at ease in Houston or Cleveland. Waiting for the decision that Friday in a television studio in Washington, Joe Klein, then a columnist for *New York* magazine and later with *Newsweek,* guessed an hour ahead of time that Cuomo wouldn't run. "He's probably saying to himself," Klein speculated, " 'St. John's is going to have a good [basketball] team this year and I won't be able to see the games.' "

Klein was being facetious, but in one sense he was not entirely off the mark. Although the budget deadlock was a serious problem for Cuomo, it didn't necessarily mean he couldn't run for the Democratic presidential nomination if—and this was the operative point—if he wanted the presidency badly enough. Most of those who run successfully for the White

House do indeed want the office with such a consuming passion that they will brush aside any obstacle, bend themselves into any configuration to get there.

Mario Cuomo was not one of them. Talking about it much later in his office in the World Trade Center in Manhattan, he put it this way: "I have difficulty with the notion of wanting it badly. I'm not sure what that means. I'm afraid some people want the office too much and I've always tried to guard against that. If you say, 'Did you have a great hunger for it?' I was always afraid of people who had too great a hunger for it. I thought they had the process backward. It shouldn't be that you desire the office and then you go out and get it. It should be that you are better than anybody else who's available. Otherwise, it's a very difficult thing to justify."

But if there were limits on Cuomo's ambition, there were others—in both parties—who were not so fettered.

C H A P T E R   8

CHALLENGE ON
THE RIGHT

Patrick J. Buchanan, the Republican right wing's angriest articulate voice on television and the nation's editorial pages, had always been dubious about George Bush. Sure, Bush supported supply-side economics—but only after Ronald Reagan put him on the national ticket in 1980; before then it was "voodoo economics." The same was true of his opposition to abortion; he was a politician whose views were a matter of convenience. Except on the Cold War, Bush seemed to lack the ideological moorings of a Ronald Reagan.

And now, after four years of Bush in the White House, the glories of Reaganism seemed increasingly distant. A few more years of this guy and old Dutch would be gone without a trace. Largely because of his doubts about Bush, Buchanan had thought seriously about running in 1987. But he feared his candidacy would serve only to dilute the potential base of support for another devout Reaganite, Jack Kemp. The idea never left Buchanan's mind, however, and he grew increasingly restive with

Bush's performance in the White House. If this was a committed conservative, the evidence was far from clear.

The notion of a television commentator and newspaper columnist running for president had been broached at other times. When Walter Cronkite was regarded by many as "the most trusted American," he was often touted as a potential presidential candidate. The same was true, to a lesser degree, of Bill Moyers, LBJ White House press secretary turned television sage. But Buchanan was different. Unlike Cronkite, he had a long identification with the Republican Party and had served in the White House under two Republican presidents, Nixon and Reagan. And, unlike both Cronkite and Moyers, he had a sharp ideological identification that had built him something of a cult following among like-minded conservatives who watched him regularly on such political talk shows as *The McLaughlin Group, Crossfire* and *The Capital Gang*—all with substantial audiences of political junkies.

In the fall of 1991, shortly after Buchanan had hinted he might run, a television colleague covering a David Duke rally at Evangeline Downs race track just outside Lafayette, Louisiana, found himself beset by white men in jeans and work caps all with the same message—as one put it: "When you go back home, tell old Pat to run."

In fact, Buchanan more than a year earlier had begun thinking actively about challenging the incumbent president, when Bush reneged on his promise not to raise taxes and joined the Democrats in the budget agreement. "Like a lot of conservatives," Buchanan said later, "I felt he'd broken the main commitment he'd made for us."

By January of 1991, Buchanan was putting his toe in the water, accepting an invitation from Governor Judd Gregg of New Hampshire to speak at a party dinner in Manchester. Buchanan realized that Gregg was trying to use him to send a message to President Bush that he had better give the state more of his attention. But symbiosis is what politics is all about, and the appearance also served Buchanan's purpose. It gave him a chance to test his message and cement an already close relationship with Nacky Loeb and Joseph McQuaid, the publisher and editor, respectively, of *The Union Leader*, the unfettered voice of conservative extremism in Manchester that still was a major influence in the state's politics.

But the context changed abruptly that night. "I got up to speak,"

Buchanan recalled, "and when I got down, this guy put a camera in my face and said, 'There's explosions in Baghdad.' So I said we've all got to get behind our president."

With Bush presiding over a popular war in the Persian Gulf, Buchanan told McQuaid, "it would be ridiculous to have any kind of conservative challenge." As the war was playing out even more successfully than Bush might have dared to hope, such a challenge seemed even more ridiculous.

The war had caused a political problem for Buchanan in other ways because he had been one of the few conservatives to take a firm and characteristically outspoken position against military action, arguing vehemently that there was no national interest in the Gulf worth the risk of American lives. For his trouble, he noted later, the conservative *Washington Times*, which regularly ran his column, made him the first inductee in its Wall of Shame. His opposition to Bush on Gulf policy was a stance that put him in the company of, among others, George McGovern, and dismayed other rightists less devoted to what they called "the new isolationism."

Meanwhile, George Bush was enjoying the political fruits of vindication. Buchanan, a native Washingtonian, recalled being particularly impressed by the June 10 parade to celebrate the victory in the Persian Gulf—troops and tanks passing on Pennsylvania Avenue while Stealth bombers flew by overhead. "You just said, 'This guy's invincible,' " Buchanan remembered thinking. "There hadn't been a parade like that in my hometown since Eisenhower. The whole country loved it."

As Bush's postwar approval ratings began to fade, however, Buchanan's interest in running against him was revived. The "triggering event" for Buchanan was Bush's decision—"that cave-in," Buchanan called it—to accept the 1991 Civil Rights Act, which had become an issue of intense symbolic importance to liberals and conservatives alike. Bush had vetoed a similar measure in 1990 and fought the new version for months, insisting in the face of heavy conflicting evidence that it was a "quota bill"—one that would require American employers to establish quotas for minority employees, or risk extended and expensive litigation.

The decision was more stunning to Buchanan because it came on the heels of what he saw as a great triumph for conservatives in general and

George Bush in particular, the Senate confirmation of Clarence Thomas for the Supreme Court. "Then he turned around and said, 'I'm going to sign the quota bill'—the quota civil rights bill—after he'd said, 'I'm not going to sign it, I'm not going to sign it, I'm not going to sign it.' " Buchanan wrote an angry newspaper column calling the Bush decision a betrayal following a long series of betrayals.

When his sister, Angela—known as Bay—read the column in California, she called and told him he should stop just writing angry columns and run for president.

The off-year election returns also began to suggest there was something different in the political water right now. Buchanan was impressed by Harris Wofford overturning a deficit of more than forty points in the opinion polls and winning that Senate election in Pennsylvania. And he noted that David Duke, although losing his race for governor of Louisiana to Edwin W. Edwards by a three-to-two margin, had captured a majority of the white vote and more than 60 percent of the non-Catholic white vote.

"What the elections told me," he said later, "was . . . there's really a movement out there, that if you could ignite it against the establishment of both parties, it might really go somewhere." Trying to measure his potential, sister Bay, who was to become his campaign manager, telephoned Nacky Loeb at the *Union Leader*, a call that produced a front-page editorial under the headline: RUN, PAT, RUN. For Buchanan, this was critical. "So then you knew," he recalled, "that if you went in there [the New Hampshire primary], you could pretty much count on strong support from the *Union Leader*, without which there's no sense going in there for a conservative against a sitting president."

From the outset, Buchanan's campaign was predicated on the notion that the New Hampshire primary offered his only real opportunity. His strategy would have to be, he said later, "score big in New Hampshire or come home." He knew economic conditions in the state were disastrous and thought he might be the vehicle for sending a message to the White House—that Bush had been too cavalier in his treatment of the state whose Republican primary had been so important to him four years earlier. He believed that Bush lacked the kind of hold on Republicans that Ronald Reagan had enjoyed; there were no Bushites as there were

Reaganites, no Bush Democrats as there were Reagan Democrats. And there was the history of the New Hampshire primary electorate defying the conventional wisdom and the establishment.

This was, after all, the state in which Eugene McCarthy had captured 42 percent of the Democratic vote in 1968 against President Johnson, a showing that ultimately forced Johnson out of the campaign. Buchanan remembered that phenomenon well. He was in New Hampshire at the time as a campaign aide to Richard Nixon, running in the state's Republican primary against Governor George Romney of Michigan. Nixon's one-sided victory there put him on the comeback trail to the White House—and Buchanan with him. New Hampshire was also the state in which Reagan came within a point of upsetting another incumbent president, Republican Gerald R. Ford, in 1976. "It wasn't a total lark up there," Buchanan said later. "You knew you could do something."

Buchanan also counted on the novelty of someone like him in the field. "What I knew I had going up there was a damned good story," he said. "Somebody coming off a talk show and challenging the president of the United States is good copy in a boring political season." His only concern, he said later, "was somebody else would get in there, [William] Bennett, [Pete] du Pont or even Duke," depriving him of "the clarity of coming off the talk show."

And with Bush still giving New Hampshire a cold shoulder, Buchanan figured he could use to good effect what he called "the old he-cared-enough-to-come" pitch to frustrated voters, a reference to the slogan Nelson Rockefeller used to upset the absent Barry Goldwater in the Oregon Republican primary of 1964.

So, on December 10, just ten weeks before the primary, Buchanan went to Concord and declared his candidacy. In his announcement speech at the state capitol, he urged "a new nationalism" and policies to "put America first." He touched the sore spots of resentment, particularly of foreign aid, and stressed generational change. "This race is not about personalities and it will not get into personalities," he told his supporters. "George Bush served bravely in America's great war. George Bush is a man of graciousness, honor and integrity who has given half a lifetime to his country's service. But the differences between us now are too deep. He is yesterday and we are tomorrow."

At another point, he defined it this way: "He is a globalist and we are nationalists. He believes in some pax universalis; we believe in the old republic. He would put America's wealth and power at the service of some vague new world order. We put America first.''

Despite his insistence that he would not "get into personalities,'' Buchanan made a point of defining the ideological differences within his party in terms of Bush's actions. "We Republicans can no longer say it is all the liberals' fault,'' he said. "It was not some liberal Democrat who declared, 'Read my lips: no new taxes,' then broke his word to cut a seedy back-room deal with the big spenders on Capitol Hill. It was not Teddy Kennedy who railed against a quota bill, then embraced its twin. It was not Congress alone who set off the greatest spending spree in sixty years, running up the largest deficits in modern history. . . . No, that was done by the men in whom we placed our confidence and our trust and who turned their backs and walked away from us.''

Buchanan also was talking with increasing frequency about immigration, having deduced from what he heard that this, too, was a hot button with American workers worried about competition for their jobs. And, characteristically, he did it with the kind of extravagant and often inflammatory language that persuaded liberals he was racist and anti-Semitic. The latter was a particular problem for Buchanan, guaranteeing him clutches of Jewish demonstrators at many of his campaign appearances.

The question of whether Buchanan was an anti-Semite came to the fore when, during the debate over the wisdom of military action against Iraq, Buchanan buttressed his argument against it on a television program by pointing out, correctly, that Israel had a direct national interest in destroying the Iraqi military capacity. But, as usual, he voiced it in terms that invited a hot response: "There are only two groups beating the drums for war in the Middle East—the Israeli defense ministry and its amen corner in the United States.''

The comment drew a wrathful column from A. M. Rosenthal of *The New York Times* accusing Buchanan of anti-Semitism. That column, in turn, set off a debate over Buchanan's history of controversial pronouncements and columns on issues having to do with Israel, including his long-running argument that the case against John Demjanjuk, accused of being a Nazi war criminal known as "Ivan the Terrible,'' was flawed. Fellow conservative William F. Buckley wrote a long article in his magazine, *National Review*, in which he concluded that many of the things Buchanan had written or said about Jews "could not reasonably be interpreted as other than anti-semitic in tone and substance."

For those like ourselves who had known Buchanan for twenty-five years or more—back to the time Richard Nixon was running in New Hampshire in 1968—the question was vexing and complex. On the one hand, there was no question that Buchanan's prose and rhetoric was never run through a filter of sensitivity toward any group and, in cases involving Israel, could be seen as a reflection of anti-Semitism. On the other, if the definition of anti-Semitism requires an automatically hostile reaction to Jews and their interests, we believed from long personal exposure that Buchanan did not qualify. But whatever the truth of the matter, it was a label that had been firmly affixed to the conservative commentator and one that would stick to him in this campaign.

Although his declaration of candidacy centered more on foreign policy than domestic issues, Buchanan also touched some nerves when he included this passage: "When we say we will put America first, we mean also that our Judeo-Christian values are going to be preserved and our Western heritage is going to be handed down to future generations and not dumped into some landfill called multiculturism." When the statement caused a stir, Buchanan "explained" it this way on the David Brinkley program on ABC television: "I think God made all people good, but if we were to take a million immigrants in, say Zulus, next year, or Englishmen and put them in Virginia, what group would be easier to assimilate and would cause less problems for the people of Virginia?"

Interviewed on *The MacNeil/Lehrer Newshour*, Buchanan conceded that God created all men equal "in their basic natural rights" but added: "He did not create them all equally assimilable in an English-speaking society which . . . [has] British institutions and has basically a Euro-American culture. . . . I think when you decide on legal immigration, that matters of culture, of language or religion, of ethnicity have got to be taken into consideration. . . ."

This was the essential Buchanan. On the face of it, it might be impossible to deny that some groups are more easily assimilated into American society than others. That reality has played a part in immigration policy and law at times. But Pat Buchanan never used restrained language when it was possible to be colorful and provocative. And what could be more provocative than suggesting that some groups should be regarded as garbage being cast into that "landfill." It was the kind of language that made his columns and commentary so striking. But it was also the kind of language that seemed to appeal to the least noble attitudes of his followers. Although Buchanan looked down his nose at David Duke, his tactics sometimes were identical, and he made no bones of the fact he was appealing for the support of the Duke admirers.

In practical political terms, this perception of Buchanan imposed limits on his ability to reach beyond the most angry and reactionary of the extremists of the right, to enlist conservatives toward the center. He wasn't respectable enough for them. Thus, when one of us attended a Buchanan speech in a small New Hampshire town one snowy Sunday night, at least four or five couples who had been in the audience made it a point to say that although they were disappointed in George Bush and had attended this meeting, they would never—never—vote for Pat Buchanan. Maybe, one elderly woman said, she could bring herself to vote for a Democrat just this once, someone like that Paul Tsongas. "George Bush is a fool," she said, "but Mr. Buchanan is too scary."

Buchanan entered the primary campaign with few illusions about his potential. He acknowledged that it was "almost impossible" to take a nomination away from an incumbent president and that New Hampshire had many Republican loyalists who would stick with Bush in a primary even with their reservations about him. So Buchanan's hope was to expose the weakness of the president and force him to the sidelines as Gene McCarthy had done to Lyndon Johnson.

"If I get 45 percent," he told reporters in Concord that day, "they'll be writing their résumés in the Roosevelt Room the next morning." But there was also always that tantalizing possibility of defeating Bush and winning the nomination himself. "You might be ranked twenty-seventh but you got a title fight right up there in New Hampshire," he said later.

The reaction within the Bush campaign was more annoyance than concern. "We weren't entirely blindsided but we were a little surprised when Pat decided to get in," Charlie Black recalled. The conservative community in Washington is tightly knit and relatively small, and news passes rapidly through the grapevine. Ten days before his announcement, Black heard about a meeting at which Buchanan told his fellow right-wingers: "All right, I'm going to run, so now's the time, those of you who want to, now's the time to go call up Black and cut the best deal you can."

Bush himself was "offended" by Buchanan's decision, Black said. "Bush looks at things on the basis of personal relationships and he thought that he and Buchanan had always had a good personal relationship when they were around the White House together," Black recalled. "He didn't look at it in ideological terms like Pat does. 'Why would this guy want to run against me? We get along.' . . . He considered it another irritant but not an insurmountable problem."

The initial problem for the Bush campaign was that it still lacked either much structure or staff. The time set aside earlier for basic organizational work for the national campaign had to be used as well for preparing for an immediate test in New Hampshire. And the word that came back from Republicans there was consistently disturbing. Tom Rath, the Concord lawyer and Republican activist who had seen the threatening implications of Harris Wofford's success in Pennsylvania, was warning that Buchanan could get 30 to 35 percent of the vote against George Bush simply on the basis of the economic distress in the state.

Bob Teeter, the Bush campaign chairman, ordered a poll and the news wasn't good. "It showed," Black said later, "a great deal of Republican disaffection over the economy and a potential for a big protest vote against Bush." Few believed the threat of the Buchanan challenge had much to do with ideological divisions within the party. "I never heard anybody think it was ideology," Jim Lake said. "They all thought it was the economy."

But George Bush still resisted accepting that judgment, perhaps misled by economic statistics that understated the extent of the economic problem, particularly in New Hampshire. At one point, Teeter told his colleagues: "Boys, the president just doesn't get it. He sees the numbers and the numbers belie some of the suffering and personal experience out there." Even if he had accepted the idea that the economy was driving the electorate so completely, Bush appeared unable to do anything about it. When the White House finally realized in November that public concern about the economy had crystallized into a significant problem for the president, he stalled. Word went out that his plan for economic recovery would come in his next the State of the Union address to Congress—a full two months in the future.

This was the quintessential example of the Washington establishment response that baffles ordinary Americans elsewhere. In the capital, the State of the Union speech is one of the revered annual rituals: a joint session of Congress, members of the cabinet and the Supreme Court filing in to listen on the House floor, the galleries packed with the president's family and other Very Important People; the bright lights of national television, the president being led through the clutching senators and congressmen to the podium, the copy of the address being handed up to the Speaker of the House.

But to millions beyond the Beltway it is just another of those Washington ceremonies that interrupt the television schedule. The connection between the State of the Union address and whether you are going to have a job next week or meet your mortgage payment next month is tenuous. Bush may have thought he was reassuring his constituents with his promise to deal with the economy in late January, but it was hardly the kind of gesture likely to inspire their confidence. And, more than anything else, that reassurance was the political imperative of the moment, nationally and, more to the point, in New Hampshire.

"His credibility . . . on economic issues was so low that a lot of people wanted to vote against him to send a message," Black recalled. "Everybody who went up there [to New Hampshire] . . . [was] impressed with the fact that people were hurting and scared. They were just scared. It was different than anything I'd ever seen."

The result, Bob Teeter said later, was that the Bush advisers now knew that Buchanan could not be overlooked. "Obviously, it didn't take a great deal of genius to know that we had a hell of a problem," he said. The campaign's immediate goals at first, not expecting a primary challenge, were to establish Bush's credentials on the economy—that is, to impress on the electorate that he was concerned and had a plan to do something about it. And Teeter had thought there would be three months or more, while the Democrats were fighting with one another in the early primaries, to get that job done without distractions.

"In retrospect," Teeter said, "the Buchanan candidacy turned out to be incredibly damaging. . . . We thought we had one more window where we could get those things done . . . [but] we spent all that time fighting Pat Buchanan.''

Black noted that Buchanan had declared his candidacy at precisely the point the Bush campaign was just getting organized. ''All this time,'' he said, ''we should be gearing up, assembling a staff, building infrastructure, organizing the states, picking state leaders—we've got a big campaign on our hands in New Hampshire . . . we had to do it all at once and we never got ahead of the curve.''

Like the Democratic candidates who had been on the ground for weeks and in some cases even months, Buchanan now discovered just how preoccupied with—perhaps even obsessed by—the economy New Hampshire voters had become. After the initial flurry of major media attention, Buchanan enjoyed the new experience of campaigning, principally traveling with a small entourage—press secretary Greg Mueller and a handful of reporters—to drop in at diners, walk through stores along the main streets, visit the unemployment lines. ''It was great, I loved it,'' he said later. ''The most vivid impression you got was that they were really down. I was very moved by the whole thing.''

Retail campaigning in New Hampshire was hardly a new experience for Buchanan. But when he traipsed around the state with Dick Nixon in 1968, Nixon was the Republican establishment candidate, and here was Buchanan challenging the party establishment. Also, working New Hampshire as a candidate was quite different from tagging along behind somebody else, doing his errands.

Back then, Buchanan was the ever-uptight Nixon's buttress against an ever-inquisitive press, keeping us at bay as best he could. He played a key role in one of Nixon's most famous con jobs on reporters, on the first morning of his 1968 campaign in the state. The night before, Nixon had held a party for reporters at the old New Hampshire Highway Hotel in Concord at which he promised that relations would be different between him and his longtime tormentors. Then, as we slept, assured by Buchanan that nothing was scheduled early the next morning, he and Nixon slipped off to shoot television commercials with a stacked audience at a local town hall. Buchanan then and later managed to share Nixon's contempt for much of the news media (but not Nixon's paranoic fear) while getting rich as a member of it, and maintaining friendships in its ranks.

Now, twenty-four years later as a candidate himself, every day there seemed to be a new and striking case history from which to learn. An old woman breaking into tears while talking about her financial problems. A worker lined up outside a paper mill in Berlin waiting for his Christmas turkey and suddenly looking up at the Republican visitor and telling him: "Save our jobs." The owner of a submarine sandwich shop in Laconia relating how he ran a help-wanted advertisement for a part-time delivery-man offering pay just above the minimum wage and no health insurance, and received 250 applications from as far away as Nashua, more than an hour down the road.

Buchanan began to understand that Bush's perfidy on the tax bill was less important than these immediate concerns, and his own rhetoric began to change as he learned more. This phenomenon was common in the strange politics of 1992. Politicians usually set their own agenda, but this year the voters were determining what the topics would be.

Buchanan described it this way: "You go up there obviously with your own speech and your ideas and the more you talk to these people and the more you listen to them, the more what they say and what they think and what they're concerned about, the more that is worked through what you say, until what you say, you're speaking their language, their hurt and you're talking to their concerns, and I think it comes through."

Bush, meanwhile, was trapped in a political dilemma. On the one hand, it was risky for him to pay too much attention to New Hampshire and the challenge from some right-winger from a television talk show. That would suggest he was taking Buchanan too seriously and inflate the importance of the challenge. On the other hand, Tom Rath and Judd Gregg in New Hampshire and his advisers in Washington were telling him it was essential for the president to demonstrate that he remembered how important New Hampshirites had been to him four years earlier, that he recognized the dimensions of their problem, and that he was going to do something about it.

By December, while still delaying his official candidacy, Bush was beginning to show himself as a candidate by taking part in carefully staged media events elsewhere. In Chicago on the day Buchanan announced his candidacy, the president dropped in for a hamburger at the Billy Goat Tavern, a blue-collar lunchtime and after-work hangout for many workers from the Chicago newspapers nearby—but hardly a natural venue for the preppy president from Andover and Yale. Another day it was chicken-fried steak at Cafe 121 in Coppell, Texas. Still another was a visit to a Head Start center in Maryland. But like a celebrated earlier trip to a J.C. Penney's outside Washington to buy socks, none of these gestures rang true. And more to the point, none of them impressed the skeptical electorate of 1992. The time for media events had passed; it was time for some evidence George Bush understood these voters and their fears and was capable of doing something about it.

In New Hampshire, meanwhile, there were some small signs that Buchanan was hitting a nerve. By late December an opinion poll published by the *Concord Monitor* showed the president leading Buchanan among Republican primary voters, 58 percent to 30 percent. Those were the dimensions of a comfortable victory for anyone in most circumstances, but the figures also could be read as a warning signal to an incumbent president. If Buchanan was truly at 30 percent, the potential for serious embarrassment obviously was there. The White House began to react, dispatching more surrogates into the state, approving additional money for Medicaid costs, opening a passport office at the closed-down Pease Air Force Base near Portsmouth. "You got the sense," Buchanan said, "that something was happening or he [Bush] wouldn't be paying it all that much attention."

The expectations game was important, as it always is in presidential primaries. George Bush needed not only to win the February 18 primary but to do so with a vote impressive enough to put this upstart challenger in his place, to make Buchanan be seen as just some nut taking a flyer. Just what kind of showing would achieve that goal was far from clear, however. The conventional wisdom seemed to be that a 30 percent showing for Buchanan would not be entirely surprising; even the most popular politicians usually have a third of the electorate against them. But what if Buchanan got 35 percent? How would the press and political community interpret that? The goal in the Bush campaign, Charlie Black said, was to hold Buchanan under 40 percent and win by at least twenty points.

The campaign was never joined in the conventional sense—indeed, could not be. An incumbent president cannot spend weeks in New Hampshire attending coffees and visiting diners and bowling alleys or taking part in candidate forums sponsored by interest groups. Especially not against some television commentator. Bush already was universally known, and inevitably so was his record. His campaign would have to be his performance in the Oval Office and elsewhere. But once Buchanan declared himself, it was clear that the president's attention was focused on New Hampshire.

It was obvious, for example, why the rescheduled trip to the Far East had suddenly been converted from one designed to reassure the United States' allies into an economic pilgrimage. Leaving Andrews Air Force Base for Australia, Bush told reporters: "Let me make very clear the focus of this trip. My highest priority is jobs. . . . One way to get this economy growing again is to open up markets abroad for American jobs and services." Nor did many mistake the targets when Bush told the Farm Bureau Federation at Kansas City: "Do not listen to those prophets of doom, those frantic politicians who say we are a second-class power."

The Bush campaign operation, finally rid of the heavy hand of John Sununu running the show from the White House, began doing the mechanical things—sending in surrogates, organizing committees of supporters, setting up telephone banks, sending out mailings, planning and buying time for advertising—that these same Republicans had done so well in so many campaigns. At this point the Bush strategists also were insisting that the campaign would be about "family values" and the "stature gap" between Bush and his less-experienced rivals. Besides, they kept saying, when all is said and done, people "really like" George Bush. Once "the message gets out there" the problems will be solved. And Samuel K. Skinner, the new White House chief of staff, already was planning to shake up the communications office. In short, Bush's advisers were using the classic rationalization of the incumbent in trouble: it's not a failure of the candidate or policy, it's just a failure of communication.

In New Hampshire, Buchanan was finding his footing as a candidate and clearly feeling his oats as well after the first three weeks in his new career. "Mr. Bush, you recall, promised to create 30 million jobs," he delighted in telling one audience after another. "He didn't tell us he would be creating them in Guandong Province, Yokohama or Mexico." When Bush was scheduled to arrive in Tokyo, his challenger plastered a map of New Hampshire on a factory wall in Manchester and turned a giant searchlight into the heavens in an ostensible attempt to help the wandering president find the state. He told crowds that the voters of New Hampshire should "put a Denver boot on Air Force One" and maybe Bush would have time to come and see them then.

The next day Vice President Dan Quayle arrived to make Bush's case. "I understand you want to send a message," he said. "We've got the message. The president understands the problem and is going to do something about it. But please don't send us a message of protectionism. Please don't send us a message of isolationism." But the attempts to reassure New Hampshire Republicans that Bush was on top of their situation obviously were undermined by pictures on every television news broadcast of the president in Tokyo passing out and vomiting into the lap of Prime Minister Kiichi Miyazawa.

Finally, on January 15, just more than a month before the primary, the president himself arrived to campaign in person. But the day, built around a carefully choreographed meeting in the camera-friendly Exeter Town Hall, didn't quite work out as the Bush managers had hoped. Local Republican leaders were calling the visit a "mea culpa tour" designed to allow his followers to vent their anger at him, then get on with the business of reelecting a Republican president.

Unsurprisingly, it was the unevenness of Bush's own performance that thwarted the best-laid plans. He clearly had some trouble convincing himself this was the right approach. At the Exeter meeting, he seemed to hit the right note, telling the Republicans who had been given tickets: "I've known this economy is in a free-fall. Maybe I haven't conveyed it as well as I should have, but I do understand it." But he also continued to insist things might not be as bad as everyone imagined. "There are some fundamentals that are pretty darn good," he said at one point.

Nor could he resist a familiar complaint about his political opponents, saying: "I'm sick and tired of every night hearing one of these carping little liberal Democrats jumping over my you-know-what." He wasn't going to buy some "fancy quick-fix," by God. And, anyway, his political rivals are just "these people who just discovered New Hampshire on the road map." When someone tried to press Pat Buchanan's no-tax pledge on him, Bush reacted by turning away angrily. But—as was the case with that Democratic T-shirt—he could not leave it alone, telling his audience there was "talk about pledges and all that" when what was needed was a pledge to elect more Republicans.

The president also displayed his penchant for goofy non sequiturs, explaining to listeners in Dover that, whatever his burdens, he felt blessed: "Don't cry for me, Argentina." When he tried to refer to the Nitty Gritty

Dirt Band, it came out: "Nitty Ditty Nitty Gritty Great Bird." The most memorable moment, however, may have been when he appeared to read a stage direction from a card: "Message: I care." The president was supposed to summarize his message to the state by saying, "I'm here, I'm listening and I care" but, as Charlie Black observed later, "It got Bushized . . . he has this method of shorthanding everything." Or, as Jim Lake put it, "He was reading the words that had been put down there, because he didn't get it."

The bottom line was that the single day of campaigning was a mixed blessing, at best. Bush attracted substantial audiences and was received warmly on a bitter cold day. As the day progressed, the president seemed more at ease and his listeners more receptive. Rhona Charbonneau, the Republican state chairman, told traveling reporters at Portsmouth that Bush should win "at least 70 percent of the vote" against Buchanan, thus setting a standard that sent chills through his campaign operation. It was another case in which the cheering of the moment obscured the political realities.

By the end of the day, George Bush still had nothing to say that was persuasive about how he could help these frightened New Hampshire voters. And his advice to "stay tuned" for the State of the Union address still two weeks away was less than reassuring. A small-businessman and longtime Republican who had attended one event, a meeting in a hangar at Pease, told a visitor: "It was just some slogans and stuff. He's going to have to do better than that." In an editorial, *The Nashua Telegraph*, which had supported candidate Bush four years earlier, put it this way: "Bush did his best to appear his aggressive best, but unless he can match this attitude with specifics, his campaign forays will lack realism."

Bush didn't seem to grasp the seriousness of his situation. By now, polls were showing his approval rating consistently below 50 percent, and the "wrong track" number was running 75 percent or higher, a red-alert for an incumbent. But the president was making awkward little jokes about how he had soiled the prime minister's suit and trying to get by principally on a smile and a friendly wave from the steps of Air Force One. Even when, a week after his visit to New Hampshire, Bush dropped his opposition to an extension of unemployment benefits, he earned little political credit. Why in the world had he been fighting for weeks against an action that presidents of both parties routinely took in tough times?

By the time the State of the Union day arrived, expectations for the president's speech had been built to a level that he could not possibly fulfill. He tried determinedly, with a combination of bluster and blue smoke and mirrors. He evoked those fading memories of the triumph in the Persian Gulf, saying of the recession as he had of Saddam Hussein's invasion of Kuwait: "This will not stand. . . . We can bring the same courage and sense of common purpose to the economy that we brought to Desert Storm and we can defeat hard times together."

He challenged the Democrats in Congress to pass his economic plan by March 20 and threatened them with political retaliation if they did not do so. "From the day after that, if it must be, the battle is joined," he said. "And you know, when principle is at stake, I relish a good fair fight."

It was obviously an empty threat. Bush was in no position—and both sides knew it—to talk about joining any battle on the economy. Moreover, the specifics of the economic program on which he was staking so much were less than revolutionary—a reflection of the fact this was a president dealing with the prospect of another $400 billion deficit in the next fiscal year. Bush ordered a change in income tax withholding so that most taxpayers would enjoy an immediate increase in take-home pay— about a dollar a day—that would be made up in lower tax refunds in April 1993. He also recommended a temporary tax credit for first-time home buyers, a $500-a-year increase in the personal tax exemption for children, a reduction in the capital gains tax rate, an investment tax allowance, and more flexibility in the use of proceeds of Individual Retirement Accounts for home buyers and to pay medical and education expenses.

There was nothing intrinsically wrong with any of these proposals, and some of them—most notably the capital gains tax reduction—were things the president had been pushing all along. But, again, after all the weeks of building attention for the address, Bush had done nothing to suggest he understood the urgency of the concern in New Hampshire and elsewhere about economic distress.

The perception of his proposals as marginal was reinforced when Jack Kemp, his secretary of housing and urban development, described as "gimmicks" such things as the reduction of withholding to put more money into circulation. "I cannot sit here," Kemp said in a television interview, "and retain my credibility and say that allowing people another thirty dollars a month is going to spur economic recovery"—a judgment Kemp ruefully conceded was not "artful" when scolded by the White House a day later. But voters also had caught wise. A *Washington Post* poll quickly showed that 70 percent of the voters felt the plan did "not go far enough" on the economy and that half the voters were still saying the president does not "understand the economic problems people in this country are having."

Bush's managers were, nonetheless, encouraged. At least Bush now had something that could be called "the plan" on the table. And by setting that March 20 deadline for action, he appeared to have put the ball into the Democrats' court. This was conventional politics—control the agenda, force the other side to react to your initiative. But in the politics of 1992 there was already a growing body of evidence that playing the political game well by the old rules might not be relevant. And with his State of the Union address, the president had played his only real high card in the contest against Pat Buchanan in New Hampshire.

The president's campaign stepped up the attack on the conservative challenger, arguing that "a vote for Pat Buchanan is a vote for Ted Kennedy" and running a heavy concentration of television commercials trying once again to make the point that Bush "cared" about voters in the upcoming primary. "This state has gone through hell," the president said in one thirty-second spot. "It's gone through an extraordinarily difficult time and I am determined to turn this state around." With his official declaration of candidacy just a few days away, Bush granted "exclusive interviews" in the Oval Office with virtually every news outlet of any size in the state—urging voters, as he put it to *The Nashua Telegraph,* to "vote for me and send a message to the United States Congress."

After making his announcement of candidacy in Washington on February 12, six days before the primary, Bush flew to Concord and told the Republicans there: "I believe government is too big and it costs too much." Who could argue with that? But polls continued to show the rebellious attitude of those Republicans. One survey found, for example, that 93 percent of Bush supporters were backing him because they thought he would be the best president, while fully 53 percent of Buchanan supporters were intent on sending a message of their discontent with the president.

The president flew back into the state for a day and a half of campaigning over the final weekend before the vote, but he had little new to say about the central issue of the primary that Pat Buchanan and the five remaining Democratic candidates had been talking about now for several months. At Nashua, Bush told a rally of supporters, "I really honestly believe the people of New Hampshire are a little bit tired of the negative advertising and attack-dog tactics coming from the left and the right." It was a curious and unpersuasive statement coming from a man who just four years earlier had won the New Hampshire primary with a blast of negative advertising against Senate Minority Leader Bob Dole.

The president also was trying to remind Republicans of what was at stake. The central question, he told a pancake breakfast Sunday morning, was: "Who do you want to be president of the United States?" A late television commercial made the same argument, showing Bush as a towering success in foreign affairs and citing the special role of the primary. "In New Hampshire," the announcer's voice said, "we have a special responsibility. We don't just vote, we choose presidents."

Meanwhile, Buchanan had found another weak spot in Bush—his failure to follow up his State of the Union call for an added $500 a child tax exemption by omitting that specific item from legislation sent to Congress. A Buchanan television commercial showed Bush making the promise, with the voice-over saying: "Today he's abandoned your tax cut. Even his advisers admit it was just a speech for New Hampshire." Buchanan also was running, for the first time, commercials centered on his own plans and policy proposals, an obvious attempt to lift himself beyond the send-a-message rhetoric. And the challenger himself was as extravagant as ever, telling his volunteers that they would "cut through the hollow army of King George like a knife through butter."

Perhaps the most revealing thing about Bush's final campaign swing into the primary state was the fact that he brought movie star Arnold Schwarzenegger with him as what he told voters in Goffstown was a "special treat" for them. The audience loved it; reporters at the event thought the reaction was clearly more enthusiastic to "The Terminator" than to the Leader of the Free World. But whatever the reaction, this was the oldest of the old politics, the quintessential media event in a state whose citizens had been signaling frantically for six months now that they needed bread rather than circuses. The final opinion polls showed Bush with a comfortable lead—60 percent to 33 percent according to CNN, 54 to 26 according to *The Boston Globe*—but hardly a ringing testimonial to George Bush as either a president or candidate.

When primary day finally arrived, Buchanan profited politically by an anomaly, an error in the exit polls—the survey of voters leaving their polling places after they had cast their ballots. These polls generally have been quite reliable indicators of the actual returns. They cover a large sample of voters and because they are made outside the polling place, the poll-takers are assured they are dealing with actual voters, not just "likely" or "registered" voters. By the time of the 1992 election, there was only one exit poll of any moment, a survey conducted by an operation called Voter Research and Surveys. It was financed jointly by the television networks and leading news organizations that once sponsored their own separate surveys at great expense, usually producing basically identical results.

In theory, the polls are intended primarily to provide an understanding of how the vote broke down—which candidate won by how much among voters of different races, ages, economic circumstances, ethnic backgrounds and ideological identification. But on election days they become a running account of who's ahead and by how much, as the data accumulate in the computer systems of the sponsoring news organizations. Although the information is supposed to be closely held, the findings race through the political grapevine all day.

On February 18 the first exit polls had Buchanan running far behind with only 26 to 28 percent of the vote. But by early afternoon, they were finding a tight race in the Republican contest, each candidate with 49 percent of the projected vote. In midafternoon Buchanan went running and when he returned, he recalled, "Somebody said you and Bush are only about four points apart." The challenger and some of his friends drove over to a steakhouse in Nashua and on the way back began to hear the first actual returns, showing him ahead of the president in the raw vote in Manchester. "We were really sky-high," he said. More to the point, the final exit poll figures showing Bush with 48 percent of the vote and Buchanan with 42 created a mind-set in the press that the president was about to suffer a serious political embarrassment, a de facto defeat even as he was winning.

"I got an enormous benefit out of the fact that the exit polls were showing the race incredibly tight," Buchanan said later. "It looked like Bush was going to get the shock of his life. It looked like he was in real danger in New Hampshire and I think a lot of reporters started writing their leads and the talk around town . . . was that [there was] crisis management at the White House. All that crisis management and early returns [that] showed it closer than it was, was a tremendous benefit to me."

Buchanan had been hoping "to do what McCarthy did"—that is, run so far ahead of expectations—to be the "winner" even while losing. But he also had been nourishing "way in the back of your mind" the thought that there might be a political miracle in the making. And now the figures from the exit poll were suggesting that might be possible.

The same thoughts were running through the Bush campaign, particularly after Charlie Black and Jim Lake flew into Manchester and heard about the final exit poll numbers—and reports from Republican leaders that the turnout had been extraordinarily high. Black and Lake were supposed to be the spin doctors for the president on this occasion, charged with putting the best possible face on the results, as the hard returns continued to show Buchanan with more than 40 percent of the vote and Bush under 50. "That was scary there for a couple of hours," Black said, "because I never had it in mind that, hell, we could lose this, but I had it in mind if it was fifty-two to forty-eight we were in for a long primary season."

Mary Matalin, recalling that first primary night, said "you can't underestimate the shock value of that exit poll." The campaign staff, she said, was "in panic," so much so that a conference call was made from Washington to about 300 campaign operatives around the country to try to combat the impact. Teeter got on the line, she said, saying, "Don't worry; it's our low-water mark," but the damage to staff morale was done. "We'd won and everyone said we lost," Matalin recalled. "We were demoralized." And analysts on the air, she said, were asking "why we weren't doing better." By the time the official figures came in, she said, "the press couldn't pull back," continuing to report Buchanan's big surprise, "and that attitude was absorbed by field [the field staff]. . . . We never should have had that conference call."

Black and Lake met with Judd Gregg and Tom Rath at the Center of New Hampshire Holiday Inn in Manchester, then telephoned Teeter back in Washington. They recommended that the president quickly make a statement claiming victory but expressing generosity toward the Republicans who supported Buchanan, and repeating his understanding of their concern with the condition of the economy. But Bush was angry and refused to go to his victory celebration and make a statement. "The mood he's in right now," Teeter reported to his colleagues, "you wouldn't want him to do it anyway."

Finally, the president issued a statement that conceded the results were not all that he would have wanted. "This election was far closer than many had predicted," he said. "I understand the message of dissatisfaction." At the White House, press secretary Marlin Fitzwater underscored the recognition that Buchanan had become more than a minor annoyance, announcing that Bush would be campaigning virtually full-time from February 25 through March 10, the date of the Super Tuesday primaries, when voters in eleven states, seven of them in the South or border states, would go to the polls.

Back in Manchester, Black and Lake told television interviewers and reporters gathered at the Tara Sheraton Wayfarer that "a win is a win" and that they should remember poor George Bush had been under constant assault not only from Buchanan but also from all the Democratic candidates, while Buchanan had been enjoying a free ride.

Meanwhile, armed with what appeared to be more than 40 percent of the vote, Buchanan was exuberantly claiming victory. "Tonight we began as a little rebellion that has emerged into a full-fledged middle-American revolution," he told his cheering supporters. "We are going to take our party back from those who have walked away from us and forgotten about us." At another point he shouted: "Buchanan's brigades met King George's army . . . and I'm here to report they're retreating back into Massachusetts!"

The final official figures, however, were not as devastating to the president as either the exit poll that preconditioned the press and political community or the earlier returns that seemed to validate the exit poll.

Bush ended with 53 percent to 37 for Buchanan, with the other 10 percent representing votes for minor candidates and, more often, write-ins for Democrat Paul Tsongas. Just what skewed the exit poll was never entirely clear, but one theory was that more Bush supporters refused to respond to the poll-takers than did voters who had just cast their ballots for Buchanan.

But even given the inaccuracy of the head-to-head figures, the exit poll was full of warning signs for the president. Only 7 percent of the Republican primary voters, for example, listed the war in the Persian Gulf among the three issues they considered most important in making their decision. By contrast, half said it was the economy, one fourth cited taxes and one fifth the problems of the health care system. Almost 90 percent said the economy was ''not very good'' or ''poor.''

The question now was what Buchanan could do for an encore. ''I knew damned well that George Bush was not going to step down from the presidency of the United States and give Pat Buchanan the Republican nomination by virtual default,'' he said later. And if Buchanan had been harboring such notions, they were quickly dispelled. Black found him having a celebratory drink with his friends at the Wayfarer election night, and told him: ''Congratulations, Pat, get some sleep, because you've got thirteen primaries in the next three weeks.''

Buchanan understood that moral victories, even those exaggerated by a faulty exit poll, were not going to do it. ''You're going to have to beat him in a state and break it open,'' he recalled telling himself, ''and Georgia was the one we picked.''

C H A P T E R   9

SWIMMING AGAINST THE TIDE

One night in early November of 1991, Paul Tsongas was having dinner with two reporters at the Country Place in Merrimack, New Hampshire. Casually, he mentioned that he supported term limitations on officeholders. When the reporters seemed surprised, he said he didn't talk about it in the campaign because he feared it might be a distraction. "I've got to be a Johnny-one-note on the economy," he said. "I want people to say, 'This son of a bitch knows what he's talking about.' "

In his six months as a candidate for the Democratic presidential nomination, Tsongas had probably accomplished that purpose. Starting with his eighty-six-page tract, *A Call to Economic Arms*, the fifty-year-old former senator from Massachusetts had established himself as a political scold on what the Democratic Party needed to do to save itself, and the country as well. The party had to abandon its long tradition of bashing business and instead make common cause with it. There could be no true economic revival without a strong manufacturing base, and until there was a healthy economy, all the social goals of the Democrats would remain beyond their reach. It was a thesis that was antithetical to traditional liberalism but not dissimilar to what was being heard from the more moderate voices in the party, and particularly the Democratic Leadership Council.

At that stage, Tsongas's views seemed essentially irrelevant. Although he had been out there as a declared candidate since April 30, he was still being lumped into the "second tier" of candidates, with Doug Wilder and Jerry Brown, a step below the supposedly more serious challengers, Bill Clinton, Bob Kerrey and Tom Harkin. There was no mystery about why. Tsongas had left the Senate in 1985 after a single term because of cancer, a non-Hodgkin's lymphoma, and had none of the conventional credentials for a candidate. Nor was he a compelling campaigner capable of electrifying an audience.

Tsongas himself was philosophical about all this, comforted by his certainty that he had the answers on the economy. "Nobody ever says to me, 'You're wrong on the issues,' " he said. "They say, 'You don't give a good speech,' or 'You're a Greek.' "

Tsongas was accustomed to being a lightly regarded underdog. He had come up through the political ranks in his native Lowell, Massachusetts, a mill town of 100,000 people forty miles from Boston that had been struggling for two generations, first to save and then to replace its old manufacturing base. Tsongas had served on the city council, then as a Middlesex County commissioner before being elected to the House of Representatives in 1974. After two terms he won a Democratic Senate primary in 1978 against two better-known rivals and then defeated an incumbent Republican, Senator Edward W. Brooke, who had been weakened by ethics charges.

Tsongas had won that Senate seat the same way he was now trying to win a presidential nomination—by relentlessly pressing his views on the electorate without benefit of either flashy advertising or a vivid public personality. When he entered the Senate primary, he ran some attention-getting commercials showing Massachusetts voters trying to pronounce his name—and failing spectacularly. The novel approach essentially solved that problem. From that point forward, however, the Paul Tsongas campaign was Paul Tsongas droning on the issues.

Before his cancer was diagnosed, Tsongas had been thinking about running for president in 1988—a piece of personal history that, in retrospect, he found ironic. If he had been well enough to run that year, the context would have been all wrong. "If I had been in New Hampshire in 1988," he said, "the discussion would have been about how much your condo appreciated the month before because those were boom times, and someone like me would have been irrelevant."

In any case, Tsongas put his ambitions on ice while he was undergoing treatment, until sometime in 1990. He was serving in those days on the boards of directors of several corporations, largely for high-technology firms, and was struck by his fellow directors' concern, he said later, about "the decline of the United States" and the frustration they felt "about our refusal to acknowledge the problem."

He was seeing evidence everywhere. "I remember driving down Route 93 from Lowell to Boston and passing people or being passed by people driving very expensive cars," he said, "and saying to myself, 'Don't they realize that there's a real capital problem in the United States, and if you spend $40,000 on a Japanese car . . . ?''

So Tsongas decided to write a book, and over a Thanksgiving vacation on Cape Cod began working on it. By the end of the year, he saw several options for himself—simply push the book, find some like-minded candidate to support—Senators Bob Kerrey of Nebraska and Bill Bradley of New Jersey were the two he had in mind—or run himself, either in a full-scale campaign or a symbolic candidacy in New Hampshire.

It soon became clear to him that running was the only alternative if he hoped to get any attention for his ideas about the economy and Democratic Party. He tried to arrange to speak about his ideas at a National Press Club luncheon in Washington, for example, but the press club turned him down. "It was obvious I had no forum to speak from," he said. So, with a clearance from his doctors, his wife and his three daughters, he and his longtime political intimate, Dennis Kanin, began to plan a campaign early in 1991.

Tsongas was not a naïf. He understood from the outset that he would be the object of ridicule, although he may not have fully appreciated the news media's fixation on the preposterous notion of "another Greek from Massachusetts." He enjoyed telling campaign audiences about breaking the news to an old friend that he was "thinking of running for president," to which the old friend replied: "President of what?"

"That was the basic reaction," Tsongas said later. "Everybody was very skeptical." And he had his own doubts as well. "You lie in bed at 2 A.M. in Lowell, Massachusetts, and you think, 'You gotta be kidding, that you'd actually run for president.' " But the tipping point came— "the moment where I guess I decided in my own heart that something had to be done"—when he listened to President Bush deliver his State of the Union speech to the Congress after the Persian Gulf War, and be received with wild demonstrations of pride in the military success that had just been achieved.

"When he got to the domestic side," Tsongas recalled, "he said we were the most productive nation on earth, and it was obvious he would not use his enormous political capital to deal with the realities that all of us saw out in the private sector. That was the moment where I was comfortable that even though there would be ridicule about running . . . there was a purpose to be served." It was something he could do, he decided, to meet "the obligation of my survival" of his cancer.

Over the next few months, Tsongas's sense of purpose was sorely tested. Money was hard to raise; the prosperous Greek-Americans who had contributed so heavily to Michael Dukakis in 1988 now felt betrayed and in no humor to help another candidate with superficially similar credentials. Where Dukakis had raised some $10 million in the year before his campaign, Tsongas raised less than one tenth as much. His operation was thin—his old friend Kanin as campaign manager once again; Andy Paven, an experienced advance man as his traveling companion; Ed Jesser, a street-smart Boston operative, as a consultant; a small handful of other pros; and his corps of volunteers in New Hampshire. Tubby Harrison, a Boston-based poll-taker who worked for both Dukakis and Tsongas, called it "two or three people doing it on rubber bands."

Said Tsongas: "It was like a death march. No money. It was just slogging it out."

The low point, Kanin said later, was the second half of 1991, when the campaign was being ignored and bringing in hardly any money. "Nineteen thousand dollars a week for a presidential campaign—that's laughable," he said. When Kanin learned that a poll was to be taken by *The Boston Globe*, he borrowed against federal matching funds due to the campaign in January to finance a television commercial that might— and did—give Tsongas enough recognition to make a respectable showing.

The bad news was consistent. During the summer, Tsongas took his wife, Niki, and their daughters on a "vacation trip" to Iowa, where the first Democratic precinct caucuses would be extremely important if home-state Senator Tom Harkin didn't run. "It was like slogging through this sort of marsh of indifference," Tsongas said later.

Nearing the end of the year, Tsongas was desperate enough to con-sider folding his starving campaign. Instead, he violated a promise he had made to himself, exercised some stock options and sold $50,000 worth of stock he had always thought of as a college fund for his daugh-ters. The news continued to be discouraging.

"In early January [of 1992] in Florida," he said, "there was a *New York Times* poll that showed I had two percent of the vote, a seven percent favorable, eleven unfavorable national rating. I remember I was sitting in the back seat of a car being interviewed when this reporter showed me that poll and said, 'What do you think about this?' I wanted to slit my wrists [but] I said, 'Oh, that doesn't mean very much.' "

In fact, the polls aside, the Tsongas campaign had begun to show some visibility in New Hampshire that some of the most astute political players recognized. With the Iowa precinct caucuses written off as a legitimate test of strength because of home boy Harkin, New Hampshire would be the first measuring stick of 1992. And Tsongas was approaching it as other long shots had done in the past—some successfully, some not—by grinding away at the consciousness of the electorate.

With the primary still more than three months ahead, he already had spent thirty days in the state and Niki was making less-heralded appear-ances two or three days a week. Tsongas had more than 150 volunteers in place, many of them young people who kept showing up outside other candidates' events, holding up signs proclaiming themselves: ANOTHER ECONOMIC PATRIOT FOR TSONGAS. If money was lacking, commitment was not.

There were indications that ubiquitousness might be paying divi-dends. An opinion poll in late fall showed most prospective primary voters didn't know much about any of the candidates but still placed Tsongas first, with 24 percent, with Harkin, the candidate who had spent the second-most time in the state, next with 12. Whatever progress Tson-gas had made, however, was being dismissed by his rivals as a predictable reflection of support for a senator from a neighboring state. But Tsongas had not run for office in Massachusetts for thirteen years and had been out of office for seven, and a benchmark poll during the summer had shown him with only 7 percent of the vote, hardly a testament to a local favorite.

On the national political stage, Tsongas was essentially invisible, as *The New York Times* poll he had been shown in Florida demonstrated. But he had gone through many of the obligatory rituals of presidential year politics, speaking at state party dinners and meetings whenever possible, showing up at the relatively few cattle shows the Democrats were staging for their candidates this year and growing increasingly sophisticated about the way the game was played.

He had a lot to learn. Shortly after he had announced his candidacy, he attended a state party candidate forum with Harkin in Wisconsin and was stunned to hear the Iowa Democrat call for an end to the "bullshit" in politics. Eating dinner with a reporter in San Diego a few days later, Tsongas recounted the incident. "He was so emotional," he said of Harkin, "he actually said 'bullshit.' "

Most everyone else in the political community already knew that this was a Harkin shtick—borrowed from another liberal candidate, then Senator Fred Harris of Oklahoma, who had tested the same shock technique in 1976. But Tsongas, at this stage of his campaign, was not much for gimmicks. The furthest he had gone—and he delighted in repeating the line over and over—was in accusing his rivals of offering "Twinkie economics—tastes good but no nutritional value."

But New Hampshire offered a different kind of opportunity for a grit-it-out, straight-ahead candidate with the self-assurance of a Paul Tsongas. Because it was such a small state, it was manageable even for a candidate having a far harder time raising money than his fellow Greek-American had found it four years earlier.

More to the point, because the economic conditions in New Hampshire were among the worst in the nation, there was a more receptive audience for a candidate so single-minded about creating jobs. And that receptive audience included a high proportion of white, middle-class, suburban and small-town voters who were not accustomed to living with direct threats to their livelihood. Furthermore, many of them were independents who could cast ballots in either party's primary if they had a reason to do so.

Many also were voters willing to read that eighty-six-page book. "The book was in demand," Tsongas said later. "Here we were with no money having to print more books because of the demand"—ultimately some 250,000 copies. There were, it appeared, serious voters abroad in 1992 who were determined to get answers. "People would say, 'On page forty-three, you said so and so,' and they would challenge me," he recalled. "What we gave them was something they could digest."

Tsongas was a more effective candidate with relatively small groups of people willing to listen to what he said rather than focusing on how he said it. His slight frame, sad-eyed, dour expression and the faint suggestion of a lisp seemed the antithesis of conventional charisma expected of presidential candidates grasping for attention. He was widely derided. When doctors put President Bush on a "bland diet" after his illness in Japan, David Letterman defined it as "dining with Paul Tsongas."

But he had a deadpan self-deprecating humor that often surprised his listeners and captured their attention. Handing out the lengthy booklet explaining his economic views, he would say with a slight smile, "Hang on to this, it's going to be valuable someday."

He enjoyed turning his political baggage against himself, telling audiences, as he told a group of self-important students at St. Paul's School: "When I got into this race, I went to the Swiss consul. I asked what would it take. We talked about falsifying of birth records. That wouldn't work. So I decided I'm Greek and I'm proud of it." Complaining about the reluctance of Greek-Americans to contribute to his campaign after their experience with Dukakis, he promised, "Next time I'm going to be Swedish." When the arrival of Sam Donaldson of ABC News diverted the attention of an audience in Nashua, Tsongas said: "Remember, I came here to see you. He came here to see me."

But he had an edge that surfaced at times. When one of those St. Paul's students kept pressing him to give the answer he wanted to hear to a question, Tsongas replied: "I'm not running a massage parlor. I'm not here to make you feel better. My job is to give you a better country." When a student at Dartmouth, Tsongas's alma mater, who opposed nuclear power plants chided him for serving on the board of a power company operating such facilities, and began explaining the health hazards from radiation, Tsongas fired back: "Don't ever lecture me about cancer. When you've had it and dealt with it, then we can have a discussion."

In the first debate among the Democratic candidates, he came through the television camera as diffident and preachy and perhaps a trifle smug— "Saint Paul," as he became known within the campaign. "It was just awful," he said. "It was an embarrassment to everybody in the campaign." Determined to do what needed to be done, Tsongas found a debate coach to advise him on how to dress and how to handle himself when the cameras were on him. His performances in subsequent debates were consistently improved, and he was able to add to his repertoire little jokes about his politically correct suits and ties.

Meanwhile, Tsongas's determined insistence on talking about the strengths and weaknesses of various economic proposals helped keep those issues at the center of the debate—and gave New Hampshire voters more insight into who the serious figures were in that debate. Clinton, it was obvious, was also a policy maven who could hold his own with Tsongas or anyone else in arguments about whether there should or should not be a tax cut for the middle class, investment tax credits or reductions in capital gains taxes. Although his views on health care were more fully developed, Kerrey also could talk with some apparent authority on economic issues, and Harkin finally produced a little booklet of his own about jobs, sketchy though it may have been. That left Jerry Brown, who was still framing every issue in terms of the way campaign money corrupted the political process.

The economic debate among the Democrats also served, inadvertently, to underline the failure of President Bush to confront the situation with a credible program of his own. Bush often complained about being "bashed" so much by the Democrats, but he gave them repeated openings with his own faltering campaign.

By the end of 1991, a rough pecking order had developed among the Democratic candidates in New Hampshire that did not necessarily reflect national opinion with precision, or the judgments of the political cognoscenti. With Mario Cuomo finally out of the way—for this cycle at least—Bill Clinton had become the leader of the pack in the primary campaign. He had become the acknowledged front-runner nationally with his series of attention-getting speeches and his success in the Florida straw vote.

Meanwhile, although not in the national picture, Tsongas had used quite a different route—through the back roads of the state—to establish himself as the principal rival to Clinton in terms of poll figures on the primary.

Neither Kerrey nor Harkin had found a significant footing in the state, and Brown and Wilder were not even in the picture. The conventional wisdom had it that either Kerrey or Harkin was likely to be the "real" competition for Clinton once they started spending money on television commercials—to which Tsongas replied, "They said that in September." Many professionals were convinced Tsongas would plunge like a stone once the voters realized they were nominating a president rather than applauding a local boy.

Tsongas was too different in too many ways. His description of himself as a "pro-business Democrat" was only the beginning of his apostasy. He was the only Democrat in the field who opposed the "strike-breaker replacement" legislation that was a first priority of organized labor. He supported nuclear power. He called the middle-class tax cut, which only Harkin joined him in opposing, "generationally irresponsible" because it would add to the federal deficit. He was the most outspoken free-trader in the field, joined only by Clinton in supporting the North American Free Trade Agreement that labor also opposed on grounds that American jobs would be lost to Mexico. Sure, he was liberal on social issues, including abortion and gay rights, but he was always harping on "old Democrats who are into giveaway, giveaway, giveaway, antibusiness corporate-bashing." If more of the liberals had known of his support for term limitations, they wouldn't have been surprised.

Then there was the question of Tsongas's health. He claimed the cancer had been cured and he had the statements of his physicians to support him. He competed with nationally ranked senior swimmers in national meets. And he had run an early commercial in which he appeared vigorously swimming the butterfly stroke in his Speedo suit. But, still, a man who had suffered from cancer? Paul Tsongas as the Democratic Party nominee for president of the United States was simply unthinkable.

None of this early handicapping of the candidates could be taken too seriously, however. At the same point in the 1984 campaign, the two leading candidates in New Hampshire were supposed to be former Vice President Walter Mondale and Senator John Glenn; the eventual winner, Senator Gary Hart, was no better known than either Kerrey or Harkin. The problem with the early judgments was that the only voters paying close attention were probably the 3,000 or 4,000 Democratic activists across the state, the ones whose names were on the state party's mailing lists. Their support was important to the candidates as a credential but, as Mondale had discovered eight years earlier, guaranteed nothing with the primary electorate at large.

Thus, the opinion polls being taken as the campaign year began in earnest and well into January were not being regarded too seriously by political professionals. They understood the polls were principally reporting unformed or only partially formed opinions based on the national press exposure of some of the candidates, especially Clinton, and the most assiduous personal campaigning within the state, especially that done by Tsongas.

But even if the polls were suspect, the perception of the New Hampshire campaign as an odd contest between Mr. Inside Tsongas and Mr. Outside Clinton was having an effect of its own, making it far more difficult for either Kerrey or Harkin to make himself a major element in the equation. Some of the liberals who might have been expected to sign on with one or the other of them—former gubernatorial candidate Paul McEachern, former state party chairman Larry Radway, former state party executive director Ricia McMahon—had chosen Clinton instead. By early January, it already was apparent that Jerry Brown, the best known of the candidates at the outset because of his previous campaigns in New Hampshire, was going nowhere. And Doug Wilder's campaign had hit such a dry hole that there was not even a ripple when he announced early in January that he was giving up the race to concentrate on affairs in Richmond.

There were also the usual also-rans trying to catch a political lightning bolt. Larry Agran, whose only credential was his brief service as mayor of Irvine, California, kept showing up at party functions and debates, demanding to be heard. To avoid embarrassing him in his home state, Democratic National Chairman Ron Brown had allowed Agran to speak at that Democratic National Committee meeting in Los Angeles in September, a gesture that Agran took as a certification of his bona fides. Lenora Fulani, candidate of the New Alliance Party, also kept protesting her exclusion from party events, sometimes backed by busloads of supporters from New York.

Eugene McCarthy, too, was campaigning in New Hampshire again, revisiting the scene of his glory twenty-four years earlier. But his campaign now seemed to consist largely of swapping old war stories with older reporters in the bar at the Wayfarer. Ralph Nader was running a write-in campaign as the symbol of "none of the above."

Two Chicago political consultants, Phil Krone and Don Rose, were conducting a write-in campaign for Mario Cuomo out of a second-floor office in Concord—and, to no one's surprise, Cuomo was being just ambivalent enough to make the possibility intriguing. Asked by *The Boston Globe* if he intended to repudiate the write-in campaign, he replied: "How can I not approve of people saying, 'You're so good, you should be president'?"

Just six days before the primary, Cuomo kept a long-standing date to speak at the Kennedy School of Government at Harvard and threw another log on the fire of speculation with a rollicking attack on Bush. Asked again why he wouldn't repudiate the draft, he countered: "In my own state, they're saying lousy things about me. If they're saying nice things about me in New Hampshire, I'm going to encourage them."

The Cuomo write-in campaign was being taken more seriously than others on the fringe because there was a long history of such campaigns succeeding in New Hampshire. In 1964, Ambassador Henry Cabot Lodge won the Republican primary entirely on write-in votes, defeating two candidates whose names were on the ballot, Barry Goldwater and Nelson Rockefeller. President Johnson also won the Democratic primary in 1968 on write-in votes; he had been unwilling to take the possibility of challenge seriously enough to qualify for a place on the ballot. (Johnson's victory, however, was widely interpreted as a setback when McCarthy won an embarrassing 42 percent of the vote against him, and it was shortly afterward that LBJ announced he would not seek another term.)

Krone and Rose were mailing postcards to 75,000 Democratic households, tailored for each locality, explaining how they could write in the New York governor's name. The question was simply whether the field of active Democrats was so unsatisfactory that a substantial number of voters would try to write a new "Mario scenario" before it was too late. Or was it more likely that the seriousness of the concern with the economy would make voters less likely to play around with might-have-beens and concentrate on the choices they were being offered?

By February, it was no longer possible for Tsongas's rivals or the press or anyone else to simply write him off as some local aberration. He was running even or ahead of Clinton in opinion polls whose validity increased with each passing day as more voters took an interest in the campaign. He was attracting large audiences of voters who, more to the point, now hung on every word. His lack of charisma had become a kind of charisma in itself, and he could depend on appreciative laughter when he greeted audiences with small jokes about the new and fashionable red ties he was wearing these days for the television cameras.

In short, the political atmospherics had changed through some mystical process hard to understand. "I think there is a smell to candidates," Tsongas said later, "and if the smell is he's going to lose, there's no interest . . . when I began to move in the polls, what seemed like a ludicrous campaign then began to smell like something that was possible."

Suddenly, Paul Tsongas had become the flavor of the month in the Democratic competition in New Hampshire. The candidate who could go unrecognized in a restaurant two months earlier now found a dozen cameras fighting for position to film him—swimming laps for exercise in an indoor pool. The case against him had been that he had no chance to win, and now that argument, Tsongas recalled, "began to break down."

On February 9, nine days before the primary, he arrived at a Sunday afternoon meeting at Daniel Webster College in Nashua and found more than 500 voters, nine television crews and perhaps fifty reporters from all over the world waiting for him. "What are you all doing here?" he asked in mock surprise and obvious delight as he walked onto the platform.

What they were doing there, they demonstrated, was trying to find out if this man had answers to their economic concerns. Tsongas talked for more than forty minutes, then remained on the podium for another two hours answering questions on every aspect of economic and domestic policy. No more than a dozen or two of his listeners drifted out as Tsongas mixed his earnest exposition with small dashes of the kind of humor that seemed appropriate for a Sunday afternoon meeting like this one.

It was a meeting strikingly similar to one Gary Hart had held in Nashua two days before he upset Fritz Mondale eight years earlier—an audience driven by interest in the candidate, people who arrived two or three at a time in their own cars, not a crowd bused in by an advance team. The message was plain: this was a year when slogans and sound bite politics weren't enough. Even a candidate prescribing bitter medicine could get a hearing if he was serious about what he was saying.

By the time the campaign reached its final weekend, Tsongas was clearly on a roll—a stature reflected in the final Democratic debate at St. Anselm's College in Goffstown. Led by Jerry Brown, the other candidates sniped at Tsongas on his support for nuclear power. The issue had once been a volatile one in New Hampshire although that was no longer true. But it gave Tsongas's rivals an avenue for attack. "Paul," said Bob Kerrey, "we're not trying to gang up on you. We're not saying you're wrong all the time, but this time you are."

In fact, they were trying to gang up on him, just as candidates always do on any front-runner. Unlikely as it might have seemed only six weeks earlier, Paul Tsongas had arrived. But as he did, attention had already been drawn away from the economic issues he was riding, toward something entirely different—the matter of Bill Clinton's personal life.

TABLOIDMANIA

In early August of 1991, about two months before Bill Clinton's decision to seek the presidency, it was Hillary Clinton who raised within the Clinton political circle the specter of her husband's reputation as a womanizer. The rumors had hovered over him through his gubernatorial years, but the sources of them had such little credibility that not even *The Arkansas Gazette*, which editorially was a severe Clinton critic, had seen fit to publish them. Still, with speculation growing that Clinton would seek the White House in 1992 after all, his wife's antenna for political trouble was fine-tuned, and it was picking up plenty of signals.

Just weeks before, the conservative *Washington Times*, which did not take undue pains to be objective, had reported unverified rumors that Clinton had "extramarital affairs, illegitimate children and (had) used drugs," and *The New Republic* and right-wing columnist George Will had made references to similar rumors in pontificating about the proper role of the news media in dealing with them.

"These rumors are just flying around," Frank Greer, Clinton's media adviser, recalled the governor's wife saying at a meeting of political insiders at the mansion in Little Rock. "This is getting out of control. You may not have made a decision," she told her husband, "but if we want to move toward making a decision to run for president, we've got to deal with this." According to Chicago political sources, when Richard M. Daley, mayor of the city, was approached early to back Clinton, he expressed reservations because of the womanizing rumors. The prospective candidate's wife offered to talk to Daley about them, but the proper and staunch Irish Catholic Daley cringed from the notion of discussing such a subject with the man's wife.

Greer himself had been tracking down the rumors, going back to Clinton with each one. One that was getting particular currency was that Clinton had fathered a black child with a television newscaster from an Eastern city, which he flatly and heatedly denied. In fact, at one closed-door meeting with Democrats in Chicago at which he was running a gauntlet of questions about alleged philandering, he snapped: "Listen, I don't have a black baby!" The notion that Clinton would have a hidden child out of wedlock somewhere was certainly not in keeping with his strong policy position in favor of firm government action against deadbeat fathers—men who abandoned children and ducked out on paying child support.

Another old turkey that nobody in the inner circle was particularly worried about was a lawsuit against Clinton by a disgruntled former state employee named Larry Nichols. In it, he protested his firing and alleged that Clinton as governor had used state funds in the romantic pursuit of five separate women, one of whom Nichols identified as a Little Rock former television reporter and later nightclub singer named Gennifer Flowers. Nichols, who Greer said later "wanted to be a little Ollie North," had lost his job for using state phones to make more than 400 calls in behalf of the contras in Nicaragua.

During Clinton's 1990 reelection campaign, Nichols had held a press conference on the steps of the capitol in Little Rock to announce his lawsuit and the names of the women. But not one word was written in Arkansas at the time, Greer said, "because the press in Arkansas knew Larry Nichols, they knew it was off-the-wall, unsubstantiated, and it was completely untrue," as the local reporters concluded after further investigation.

The continuing rumors of other Clinton dalliances, however, led to a discussion within the Clinton inner circle about the matter, and whether they held the same potential for trouble of the sort that had driven Democrat Gary Hart from the 1988 presidential race. Clinton, Greer recalled, "agonized about this a lot—whether or not, since Gary Hart, the rules had changed; whether or not, in a hopeful sense . . . the press did feel they had to have substantiation from two sources or whatever, or whether or not somebody could just make something up, and say it and get it in print, and all of a sudden it's taken a life of its own. My naive sense was no, I had a lot of faith in the journalistic community."

Greer said he told his candidate: "Bill, it's not that bad. You know, people just can't make things up." To which Clinton would reply: "Frank, given these new rules, somebody *can* just make it up." Nor did Clinton and his advisers know, Greer said later, "that the tabloids would be paying them several thousand dollars to make it up."

Greer and other insiders advised the Clintons to seek some opportunity to reassure the voters about their marriage and commitment, as a means of coping with the rumors. Much earlier, after the Hart debacle, Clinton had told Arkansas reporters that he didn't think public officials had to answer what he called "have you ever" questions and he didn't intend to. The insiders argued that without doing so he could deflect the rumors by acknowledging that his marriage like many others had had its difficulties but was in good shape now.

The whole business grated on Clinton, Greer recalled. He would argue that the news media's attitude toward marital problems involving individuals in public life was itself potentially destructive. "What we're really doing with the standards that journalism and politics have set today," Greer recalled Clinton saying, "we're encouraging people to split up and divorce. If you're divorced, then nobody will ask any questions about you. But if you have some difficult times and work things out, you make a real effort to keep your marriage together, then you have to pay a price."

Also discussed at some of these meetings in August, Greer recalled, was the matter of Clinton's military record, or lack of it. "He always said, 'You know, I didn't serve in the military. I basically got a high lottery number. But Frank, I opposed the war in Vietnam. I didn't want to serve, and I was really thankful when I got a high lottery number. But it's never been an issue here because every time it's come up, the people involved, they all said that I did nothing wrong and that they'd back me up.' ''

Greer replied, he remembered later, that a lot of other people at the time opposed the Vietnam War and didn't serve, "and if you didn't do anything wrong in terms of avoiding the draft, it isn't going to be a problem." That judgment, Greer said later, "I felt in my core."

In any event, it was decided that the proper forum for flushing out the rumors of womanizing and other problems of Clinton's personal background was a popular breakfast meeting of Washington reporters organized by Godfrey Sperling of *The Christian Science Monitor*. Greer arranged for both of the Clintons to be guests in late September.

On the weekend before, many of Clinton's closest supporters from around the country were called into Washington to assess the political landscape and evaluate the pros and cons of a Clinton presidential candidacy. Attending at the Washington Court Hotel on Capitol Hill were representatives across the spectrum of Democratic political thought, and several openly expressed concern about the womanizing rumors. Clinton in effect rehearsed the "nobody's perfect" defense he was preparing for the Sperling breakfast.

The day before the breakfast, Greer had a conversation about Clinton with Gloria Borger of *U.S. News and World Report*, and he suggested that she ought to show up the next morning. About half an hour into the breakfast, the have-you-ever question hadn't come up yet so she popped it the most benign way she could. She reminded Clinton that he had talked about "a zone of privacy" regarding his personal life, and wondered whether he would talk about it.

Clinton, smiling, said: "I thought you would never ask." He then went on to say that his stated refusal to get into that area of questioning in the past stemmed from "all those rumors about me during my race for governor that were sparked by a disgruntled state employee [Nichols] who was working for my opponent. Those were false, and I said so at the time."

Clinton duly recited the preplanned response: "What you need to know about Hillary and me is that we've been together nearly twenty years. It has not been perfect or free from problems, but we're committed to our marriage and its obligations—to our child and to each other. We love each other very much.''

And that, Clinton and his political advisers hoped, would be that. That statement, Clinton said, ''ought to be enough'' to satisfy the have-you-ever question. Acknowledging that his marriage had ''problems'' was as far or farther than any previous presidential aspirant had gone publicly in alluding to marital infidelity.

What Clinton was counting on was an adherence by the news media to the time-honored journalistic code of reporting verifiable facts, not rumors of unproved allegations. At least the mainstream press, that is, as opposed to such embarrassments to the mainstream press as the supermarket gossip tabloids, to which nothing was sacrosanct. What he didn't figure on was that after the Gary Hart experience of the previous presidential election, important elements of the presumably more responsible news media had developed an itchier trigger finger on reports of personal misconduct by celebrated individuals in public life.

The standard of a generation earlier for deciding what and what not to report about a politician had been whether the alleged misconduct affected the performance of the duties to which he or she had been elected. That standard explained why it was possible for candidates for the highest public offices to entertain mistresses on the side or continue to be chronic drinkers without disclosure. If a senator showed up falling-down drunk on the Senate floor, that would be hard not to write about, but short of that, the code was to say or write nothing.

The subsequent disclosures, however, of President John F. Kennedy's dalliances, and then the Hart episode in which the Colorado senator seemed to be flaunting his extramarital escapades, made the news media collectively defensive about looking the other way when such activities were known about. Still, there remained within the mainstream news media generally a contemptuous attitude toward the sensationalist supermarket tabloids, which forever were reporting on such things as clandestine relationships between extraterrestrial beings and beautiful movie stars, and the like.

At first, it seemed that this contempt would continue to isolate the gossip and sex magazines and newspapers from the arena of responsible journalism, simply because mainstream practitioners would continue as they always had to treat them with disdain, in the manner of straight cops at the precinct station toward one bad apple on the take. When *Penthouse* shortly after Clinton's announcement of candidacy ran a raunchy, paid interview with a self-described rock star groupie from Arkansas named Connie Hamzy, in which she alleged merely that she had a near-encounter with Clinton in a North Little Rock hotel back in 1984, only CNN's *Headline News* of any national media mentioned it—and only once after swift damage control by the Clinton campaign of the sort for which it would soon became celebrated.

Prior to the CNN mention, a young and alert campaign press aide, Steve Cohen, had heard a local radio talk show host discussing the *Penthouse* article. He informed young, boyish-looking George Stephanopoulos, then Clinton's deputy campaign manager, who rounded up affidavits from several Clinton associates who saw the encounter. All swore that it was "Sweet Connie," as she called herself in the interview, who approached Clinton and that he had summarily rebuffed her. As soon as CNN mentioned the interview, Stephanopoulos showed the affidavits to the cable network and the story was dropped. Thereafter Cohen was known in the campaign as "Scoop," and the hopeful assumption was that the worst was over on the womanizing problem.

Clinton's very impressive performances in the early Democratic cattle shows, early fund-raising strength and notable endorsements by now had propelled him into the New Hampshire primary as the news media's consensus front-runner for the Democratic nomination. And with Mario Cuomo finally taking himself out of contention, he set his sights on victory there although Clinton pollster Stan Greenberg's internal polling had him in second place behind New Englander Tsongas, at about 20 percent.

Winning New Hampshire could in one swoop dispose of any charge that Clinton was a regional candidate, and at the same time set the stage for a decisive blow in the Super Tuesday tests, predominantly in his region of the South, shortly afterward. The campaign ran a sixty-second television spot in which Clinton simply faced the camera and talked about his plan for economic recovery. Almost at once he shot into the lead, with 37 percent in Greenberg's polling to only 25 for Tsongas.

"It's very interesting what people took away from that ad," Clinton recalled later. "What they really liked about it was its general emphasis on health care and jobs, and the fact that it seemed specific, and that there was a plan they could write for. . . . What gripped them was that I seemed to have a plan . . . and that it seemed to be a long-term plan, that I wasn't just promising to be in thirty or forty days and turn the world over.'' Like Tsongas's eighty-six-page booklet, he said, it was "counterintuitive . . . to what normally works in politics, which is the emotional thirty-second ad and all that.''

"New Hampshire was the place,'' Clinton said, "but '92 was the year in which people really wanted to believe that they could be brought into the system [again]. They were properly skeptical of all the claims, and they thought at least if you were specific, even if you had to change or modify your position over time . . . that at least you had thought about the problems and you were moving beyond traditional politics.''

New Hampshire was also proving to be an ideal place for the Clinton message. "People used to talk about how New Hampshire wasn't a good place to start [the presidential election process],'' Clinton said later, "that it was not a good microcosm, it was more antigovernment. . . . This year it was a very good place to start, because while the economy objectively in some ways was no worse than several other states, the unemployment, food stamp and welfare rolls had tripled in three years. The average welfare recipient in New Hampshire was a middle-class person.'' A lot of them, he said, had their property taxes "folded in with their mortgage payments, so a lot of the welfare checks were coming in to unemployed white-collar people to keep their families in their homes. . . . So what you had was a state that was just riveted in its focus [on the state of the economy]. . . .

"It turned out in '92 that in all these town meetings people were really concerned with . . . mostly mainstream economic bread and butter issues. I think you couldn't get through there if you hadn't thought about and focused on what you believed and why, and what you would do. And nearly everybody who came out of there and went on to the other states was much improved [as a candidate] by the process.

"Because the state is so small, you couldn't leave New Hampshire without a human face on the problems of America. You couldn't campaign in New Hampshire without being able to call the name of somebody who had lost his job, or call the name of some child whose family had problems. You just couldn't do it. They were just there, staring you in the face all the time. It was an incredibly emotional experience.''

Tsongas, however, was proving to be a formidable candidate in his own backyard. Like the tortoise in the fable, he had been assaulting the New Hampshire electorate inch by inch, tirelessly, and voters had a familiarity and a comfort level with him that neither Clinton nor any of the other three remaining Democratic contestants—Kerrey, Harkin or Brown—brought into the nation's kickoff primary. As Clinton's fortunes rose and fell over the next eventful weeks, Tsongas kept persevering like the determined swimmer he was, and his widely acclaimed aquatic television commercial showed him to be.

On January 16, all the trouble started for Clinton. It was a Thursday, which Clinton campaign strategists came to call "garbage day," because that was when the supermarket tabloids released the first copies of their new issues. The *Star*, a leading such tabloid, sent out an advance of its next issue that picked up on the dog-eared 1990 Larry Nichols lawsuit and ran with it.

Actually, the story had appeared a few days earlier in the *Daily Mail* of London but had drawn no attention in the United States. In any event, the Clinton campaign already had denials from the five women involved, including Gennifer Flowers, but that fact did not stop one so-called mainstream newspaper, the sensationalist tabloid *New York Post*, and then the rival *New York Daily News*, from latching on to the story in a big way. The *Post* headlined its story "Wild Bill" and the *Daily News* announced it as "I'm No Gary Hart." Another tabloid, the *Boston Herald*, and the Fox television network, also given to tabloid journalism, jumped aboard as well.

Clinton now got his first real taste of the news media of 1992 in full pursuit. As he entered the Sheraton-Tara Hotel in Nashua for a conference on health care issues, reporters, photographers, television cameramen, light and sound technicians flocked around him. Forewarned by his staff about the tabloid story, Clinton benignly dismissed it as "old news" already "thoroughly investigated, and it's not true." He noted that it "comes up as I start to do a little better" in the campaign, resurrected by a gossip sheet "that says Martians walk on earth and cows have human heads."

The candidate called the old lawsuit "totally bogus," brought by a man "fired for making illegal phone calls [who] tried to bribe me into giving him money, and I just wouldn't do it." Clinton moved along on the sea of shouting interrogators through the hotel lobby and onto an elevator, seemingly unruffled.

Frank Greer's "faith in the journalistic community" was being put to the test. *New York Post* editor Jerry Nachman defended picking up the supermarket tabloid story on the grounds that "there are filed court papers" and hence "absolutely public information," although the case had lain dormant for about two years, brushed aside by the Arkansas press as garbage. The managing editor of *The Arkansas Democrat-Gazette*, John Robert Starr, was reported by *The Washington Post*, in fact, as saying there was "no substance whatsoever to the charges," that Nichols was "not a credible fellow" and that "he had no evidence, nothing, except he heard the same rumors the rest of us have heard." Nachman, though, insisted that "it's become part of what we do in campaigns, going over the character thing."

That was true enough, especially since the Gary Hart self-destruction, helped along by an accommodating *Miami Herald* and others in 1987. There was a very major difference this time, though. These supposed members of the mainstream press, albeit with one foot firmly in the tabloid gossip business, did not go out, investigate and find the story themselves, establishing its truth prior to publication, as the *Herald* had done on the Hart liaison with Donna Rice five years earlier, at a considerable expenditure of time, effort and money. They simply picked up the *Star* yarn and ran with it on the technically valid but ethically questionable argument that it was in the public domain in the form of a lawsuit (soon dropped with abject apologies from Nichols, who disavowed his charges).

The managing editor of the *Daily News* at the time, Matthew Storin, made the case for his newspaper, in a tough circulation battle with the rival *Post*, that "a lot of people aren't going to run this story and they're going to end up running it a day later. So why not run it now?" He argued that Clinton "is running for president. Let's put it out there and have him react to it. If no one comes forward and backs him [Nichols] up, we'll all know it was a pig in a poke and go on to the question of capital gains."

That approach might have been valid had the Nichols lawsuit just been filed. But it had already been scrutinized by the Arkansas press, well aware of the womanizing rumors about Clinton, and judged not to be credible. The fact that it was picked up by a supermarket tabloid should have hung a handle-with-care label on the story in the eyes of mainstream editors, and indeed most of them either ignored the story altogether or gave it inside-page placement. *The Washington Post* had its media reporter, Howard Kurtz, write a story that featured the role of the news media as much as the stale allegations themselves—an approach that soon would be adopted by other news organizations as the story developed and they became ethically defensive about their own decisions on dealing with it.

The CNN shouting match, *Crossfire*, pitted Nachman against a Democratic television advertising consultant, Mandy Grunwald, who argued forcefully against devoting valuable television time to this kind of warmed-over rumor veneered by an old lawsuit and published in a supermarket tabloid. Grunwald was a business partner of Frank Greer but not then a part of the Clinton campaign, busy with other clients running for the Senate.

Had the whole matter died there, Clinton might have been out of the woods on the womanizing rap. But near the end of the next televised debate among the Democratic candidates, moderator Cokie Roberts of ABC News and National Public Radio, in what Greenberg later called "a fairly scurrilous form of journalism," injected the matter into the news media mainstream beyond argument. She asked Clinton to comment on "concern on the part of members of your party that these allegations of womanizing, that the Republicans will find somebody and that she will come forward late, and that you would lose the all-important Democrat women's vote."

Clinton replied that the allegations were "an example of what the Republicans have been trying to do to me for years," and he branded them as "a pack of lies" that his repeated elections in Arkansas proved were not a deterrent to his electability. He concluded by saying the Republicans should not be rewarded for "the kind of rumor-mongering negative and totally irrelevant stuff that they won on four years ago. I don't think the American people are going to fall for it again. And I know people who are bleeding and hurting in New Hampshire are not about to be sucker-punched by it." The reminder to voters of the Bush negative campaign of 1988 was one that would be heard repeatedly from Clinton, and with good effect, as the campaign progressed.

But it didn't stem the allegations. On the following Thursday, the next "garbage day," the *Star* outdid itself. Clinton had just returned to New Hampshire from Washington with his newly hired political consultant—James Carville, the more flamboyant member of the Carville and Begala team that had helped steer Harris Wofford to his upset Senate victory over Republican Dick Thornburgh in Pennsylvania in November. The team was a hot property after that surprise success and several presidential candidates had competed for its services, but Clinton had won out.

Carville hadn't planned to go to New Hampshire that day but he got a call from George Stephanopoulos at Washington National Airport. "I think you ought to come up to New Hampshire with us," Stephanopoulos told him. "You just had the sense, I don't know why," Carville recalled later, "you knew something was going to happen that day."

The governor was slated for another busy campaign day in the state, but he seemed his usual laid-back self as he came into the lobby of the Inn of New Hampshire, a top-grade Holiday Inn in downtown Manchester. He chatted amiably with several reporters and was pulled to the side by Mark Halperin, the ABC News producer in his traveling party. Halperin asked him a number of questions and Clinton responded, then went up to his room. Clinton was routinely late in starting his campaign day, so we thought nothing of it on this occasion.

In his private suite, however, Clinton discussed with aides what Halperin had questioned him about: the *Star* was prepared to unload on Clinton again. Stephanopoulos got hold of an advance copy sent by telephone facsimile to the hotel. It was an eye-popper, bearing the headline: "They Made Love All Over Her Apartment." Gennifer Flowers provided a first-person account of how, by her testimony, Clinton over a period from 1977 to 1989 had often jogged from the state capitol to her apartment and turned it into a veritable playground of sexual athletics.

The tabloid also reported that Flowers had turned over some fifteen taped telephone calls with Clinton from December 1990 until recent days, and it quoted from one it said had taken place between Clinton and Flowers on the previous September 23, about a week before his formal declaration of presidential candidacy. Flowers had been expressing concern about the pressures she was encountering from the news media, and the tape had the voice identified by Flowers as Clinton's saying: "If they ever hit you with it, just say no and go on. There's nothing they can do. I expected them to look into it and come interview you. But if everybody is on record denying it, no problem."

The story did not come totally out of the blue to Clinton. He had indeed talked recently to Flowers, whom he acknowledged he knew and whom he had helped get a $16,000-a-year state job with an agency that handled appeals on rejected unemployment benefit claims. She had told him of the tabloid press pursuing her and offering her as much as $50,000 to say that she had had an affair with Clinton.

It was this pursuit, Clinton said later, to which he was referring in conversation with her—while declining to verify that it was his voice on any particular tape. This development, clearly, was much more serious than the first, but maybe—just maybe, some of the Clinton advisers hoped—most of the mainstream press would again lay off it, considering the very suspect source. In case that didn't happen, though, it was time to gear up for damage control, "to get out there as fast as we could with our side of the story," Carville said later.

When Clinton finally headed for Claremont, Carville stayed behind in Manchester and contacted Hillary Clinton, who knew all about the Nichols lawsuit and the Flowers rumors and indeed about the woman's phone calls to the governor. She was in Atlanta, and when she heard the news she said she was ready to fly wherever the strategists decided, to be with her husband to help throw water on the fire. It was tentatively decided that she should go to Washington, where Clinton would meet her to do some television show that night, possibly ABC News's *Nightline* if it could be arranged.

After that, Carville proceeded to confer by phone with campaign operatives in Little Rock and Washington on how best to cope. The Little Rock headquarters was put to work tracking down a year-old letter from Flowers's lawyer, Robert M. McHenry, to Little Rock radio station KBTS threatening to sue because a talk show host had "wrongfully and untruthfully alleged an affair between my client, Gennifer Flowers, and Bill Clinton."

Surely that letter would convince the mainstream press that a hard-pressed Flowers had made up the story for money—and indeed the *Star* subsequently acknowledged it had paid her an unspecified sum for the interview and tapes. As soon as the letter was located, copies were reproduced for inquiring reporters.

Without a sign that the day was in any fashion out of the ordinary from the routine on the campaign trail, Clinton, accompanied by Stephanopoulos and Begala, set off by van for a plant tour and talk in Claremont, on the western side of the state. The weather was miserable, wet and foggy, making it impossible to fly. But it was decided that the candidate had to maintain the appearance of normality in the face of this latest threat.

On top of that, Clinton knew he had to return to Little Rock that night to deal with eleventh-hour appeals for a stay in the scheduled execution of a man named Rickey Ray Rector, sentenced to death for the killing of a police officer. Holding the life of any person in one's hands is a huge responsibility under any circumstances, but this particular case presented Clinton with a dilemma quite beyond his immediate political travail.

The convicted forty-year-old man had, eleven years earlier, turned the gun on himself after having shot the policeman, destroying part of his own brain and turning himself into, in the word of his lawyer later, a "zombie" with severely impaired mental faculties. As a man unable to understand now what he had done or even to comprehend death, the lawyer argued, "his execution would be remembered as a disgrace to the state."

Clinton, however, was firmly on record as a presidential candidate in support of the death penalty, and his position on that issue drew a major distinction with the opposition of the old liberal Democratic leadership from which Clinton was so determined to separate himself in voters' eyes. The odds were strong that he would let the execution take place, but both decency and prudent politics required that he spend the day of the execution in his Little Rock office giving the matter of the requested executive clemency thorough consideration and reflection.

First, though, was the matter of getting through the campaign day in New Hampshire. As his van rolled through the bleak winter storm and across hazardous icy roads, Clinton kept his mind occupied by reading *Lincoln on Leadership*, a gift from Mario Cuomo. By the time he arrived at the American Brush Company in Claremont, a successful small business that made paint brushes, word of the *Star* story had reached the press corps traveling in other campaign vans—one of which bore Halperin, toting a copy.

He and ABC News correspondent Jim Wooten circulated it among the host of reporters whose vans had arrived in advance of Clinton's small motorcade. They read the Flowers account with a mixture of professional interest and titillation, and when Clinton came into the small foyer of the plant in a crush of television and still cameras, and tape recorders held over the crush to pick up his words, they bombarded him with questions.

Clinton was physically trapped in the small foyer. "The story is not accurate, the story is just not true," he said, obviously chagrined. "She's obviously taking money to change her story." Putting aside his precampaign vow not to discuss reports of marital infidelity, Clinton knew he had to respond. He acknowledged that he had received calls of distress from Flowers, but he said he had told Hillary about each one and that she had advised him to return the calls.

"I did call her back every time she called me," Clinton said. "She said she was frightened, she felt beleaguered, she felt pressure, she felt that her life was being ruined by people harassing her" and later "offering her bribes to change her story." He also said he had told Flowers "to just tell the truth," and when advised that the *Star* story had made no reference to that, Clinton responded: "Well, I'm sure they didn't put that in there. I told her that several times." He also noted that "the lady had a lawyer that threatened to sue people who were saying the very thing that she's saying, just a year ago."

Clinton went onto the work floor of the paint brush plant, mingling easily with the employees and finally standing up on a high platform and delivering his standard stump speech as if nothing untoward had happened to upset his campaign. When he was through, however, he disappeared up the front stairway to the plant's offices, where he was closeted with Stephanopoulos and Begala, conferring by phone with Carville in Manchester and his other political advisers in Washington and Little Rock.

"We were trying to figure out how deep the wound was," Stephanopoulos said later, "and whether we had to go for radical surgery right away, or if we had time to stabilize the patient and keep moving."

The weather outside was getting progressively worse, and it became clear that Clinton wasn't likely to make his next scheduled event at Plymouth State College to the northeast.

While we reporters pondered what to do with this developing story growing out of a questionable account of marital infidelity first aired by a supermarket tabloid of general disrepute in mainstream journalism, copies of the letter from Flowers's lawyer to the Little Rock radio station had been faxed to the Claremont factory and were distributed by Clinton aides. The letter made it easier for most of us to decide that the whole business had to be reported. Here, after all, was a presidential candidate who, by responding to reporters' questions and then going behind closed doors for a couple of hours to confer with his campaign strategists in what clearly was a crisis atmosphere, had altered his campaign day and advanced a story that had the potential of destroying his candidacy. Had those of us bird-dogging Clinton that day simply ignored what was going on, we would have left ourselves open by that point to allegations of cover-up and favoritism toward Clinton.

The question had become not whether to report what had been published and its aftermath, but how—in what context. It was, to be sure, the tail of American journalism wagging the dog, but reporting the consequences now seemed to most of us there unavoidable. So a line of reporters formed at the single pay phone in the American Brush Company cafeteria to dispatch the news of the latest womanizing scandal that had rocked the presidential hopes of Bill Clinton.

Some major newspapers, like *The New York Times*, handled the story gingerly the next day, the *Times* relegating it to eight inches over the headline, "Clinton Denounces New Report of Affair," on an inside page. But on its evening news show on the night of the Claremont scene, WMUR-TV in Manchester carried a vivid report showing Clinton bombarded with press questions, and shortly afterward the Associated Press moved a story from Claremont as well. The major television networks, however, did not report what was going on in this critical day in the Clinton campaign, except for a brief reference in a Clinton profile on NBC.

It was after 7:30 that night, after the network evening shows, when Clinton finally came down to the front office area of the plant amid much confusion about whether he was going on to Plymouth or back to Manchester. Several of us in the press entourage piled into a van that we thought would be following Clinton, but in short order realized that we had lost sight of the Clinton van. What we didn't know at the time was that Clinton had abandoned all notions of going on network television that night and instead had gone on to Manchester, where he boarded a plane back to Little Rock, flying much of the night in order to be at his desk to give full attention to the unhappy matter of the scheduled Rector execution. More than two hours after our press van left Claremont, with a Clinton volunteer from Florida at the wheel driving for the first time on icy New England roads, we returned to Manchester only fifty miles away, still in the dark about his whereabouts.

In the meantime, ABC News, which in its wisdom had decided after all its spadework not to report the *Star* story or Clinton's very public responses on its network evening news show, did decide to devote *Nightline* to an analysis of the ethics of running the story. Whether by intent or not, this approach amounted to bringing the supermarket tabloid report into so-called responsible journalism by the back door.

When the possibility of getting the Clintons on the show fell through, its producers began casting about for other guests. They settled on Larry Sabato, a University of Virginia political science professor who had recently written a book called *Feeding Frenzy* on the handling by the news media of campaign rumors and scandals, and Jonathan Alter, a young media critic for *Newsweek*, and were looking for a third participant. Someone had seen Mandy Grunwald on *Crossfire* a week earlier and decided she would fit the bill. As things turned out, *Nightline* and its host, the self-assured Ted Koppel, got more in her than they had bargained for.

Grunwald strolled into her firm's office at about eight o'clock that night, after it was clear the Clintons wouldn't be making the *Nightline* appearance and she had been confirmed for the show. Greer and Greenberg were still on the phone, as they had been all afternoon, talking to Carville in Manchester and campaign manager David Wilhelm and other Clinton strategists in Little Rock in what had turned out to be a floating conference call.

She told them she was going to do the show. "What do you want me to say?" she remembered later asking them. "Oh, don't worry about it. You'll be fine," was the reply, and they went back to their conference call. Here was what was potentially a critical moment in the campaign, and as the brainstormers were agonizing over how best to defuse the bomb, along came the perfect vehicle in which to do it, handed to them with a big bow around it—and they told Grunwald in effect, she said, to wing it!

Wing it, she did, with a vengeance. "I'm enough of a student of television, and I watch Koppel enough," she recalled later, "that I knew that he hadn't done anything on the primaries, and he hadn't done anything about the election in fact, and it was three weeks to go [until the New Hampshire primary].'' Grunwald went home and planned what she was going to say ''as I was washing my hair,'' she said, ''and I was actually a nervous wreck. I know enough about politics to know it was kind of a big moment. I didn't have such a sense of self-importance that I thought it was going to make or break the campaign, but I knew the heat of the day was intense.''

After years of prepping clients for television appearances, she was faced with having to prep herself, and she found being the one going before the cameras intimidating. Once she got there, however, she performed like a veteran defense lawyer. Koppel, after comments from the other guests, turned to Grunwald, asking whether it was possible to put that sort of story in proper ''perspective, or does it develop a sort of momentum of its own?''

GRUNWALD: Well, programs like this are not a help, Ted. This is the first program that *Nightline* has done on any topic relating to the Democratic presidential candidates. You haven't been talking about the middle class. You haven't talked about why Bill Clinton has captured people's imagination. Here you are—

KOPPEL: Oh, now, now wait a second. Wait a second. You're making a charge that's not accurate. We've done a number of programs on the middle class. We've done a number of programs on—

GRUNWALD: You have not.

KOPPEL: —the issues, unemployment. You're quite right. We haven't done a program on Bill Clinton.

GRUNWALD: But here we are just a couple of weeks before the New Hampshire primary. People are about to go out there and vote. . . . They have real concerns. And you're choosing with your editorial comment, by making this program about some unsubstantiated charges that . . . started with a trashy supermarket tabloid. You're telling people that something you think is important. That's not context. You're setting the agenda and you're letting the *Star* set it for you.

KOPPEL: All right, let me—

GRUNWALD: And I find that troubling.

Grunwald aggressively accused *Nightline* and Koppel of sleazy journalism—introducing the womanizing allegations in the guise of a serious discussion of journalistic ethics. The usually composed Koppel seemed taken aback and defensive. Grunwald's very public scolding of Koppel on his own show dominated it, shaking its pretense of being a responsible forum for discussion of the ethics of handling an attack on a public figure paid for by a sensationalist supermarket gossip and scandal sheet. For many viewers long irritated by Koppel's rather know-it-all treatment of guests, Grunwald became an overnight heroine, and not only in the Clinton campaign.

Her feisty performance did not, however, end the crisis atmosphere, or a debate within the Clinton camp about what to do about it. The Washington contingent, according to Greenberg later, did not want Clinton to go on the air at once, fearing he was not properly prepared, but "we hadn't quite realized how much he had already responded" to direct questions in Claremont.

"The idea was to get out front of the thing as soon as we could," Carville said later, "and get out our explanation. At that point, we knew the thing was going to be what we call in the campaign a cluster fuck—I mean, you know when you're gettin' it."

Once it was clear that Clinton could not do *Nightline* that night, the staff had begun casting about for another early opportunity. ABC's *Good Morning America* the next morning was one possibility, but the producers were unwilling to give Clinton what his aides felt was a sufficient amount of time to tell his side of the story. Instead, another ABC program on prime time Friday night, *20/20*, was offered, but Clinton declined, saying he did not wish to make what would clearly be a political appearance on the night Rector faced death. The situation gave Clinton and his aides time to gather their wits and decide what to do.

Clinton spent the next day as scheduled in seclusion in Little Rock, as he always did when pondering whether to grant a reprieve to someone on death row or let the execution go forward. Begala, to bolster his candidate's spirits, at one point sent the governor an adage favored by Georgia secretary of state Max Cleland, who had suffered the loss of three limbs in Vietnam: "Life breaks us all, but some of us emerge stronger in the broken places."

While Clinton reflected on this, on Rector's fate and on the events of the last days, his staff nailed down two weekend national television appearances for him, the first on the next day, Saturday, on the CNN *Newsmaker Saturday* show and the following morning, Sunday, on ABC's *This Week with David Brinkley*.

With those two appearances settled, however, another offer came from Steve Kroft, a correspondent on CBS's *60 Minutes*, the nation's most-watched news show. Kroft pointed out to Stephanopoulos that the show would go on Sunday night immediately after the Super Bowl. The offer was too good to refuse, considering the Clinton campaign strategy to get the Clintons before the largest possible audience.

On the condition that there would be no sensational promotion of the appearance, the Clinton strategists agreed to give CBS an exclusive interview, to be taped Sunday morning. The other appearances were canceled, with apologies. CNN was particularly rankled because its Saturday show had bumped Mario Cuomo to make room for Clinton.

"We broke the commitment, thereby starting a very rocky relationship with CNN for the rest of the campaign," Begala said. "We did the right thing strategically. I feel bad that we gave a commitment and had to break it, but when *60 Minutes* offers you a special edition after the Super Bowl with an audience of a hundred million viewers, you say yes. And when they say the condition is you cancel CNN, you say okay."

Clinton declined to stay Rector's execution, and it took place on schedule. The next day, Saturday, the Clintons returned to New Hampshire for an upbeat, morale-boosting rally in a Manchester high school gym, after which they headed for Boston, where their segment of *60 Minutes* was to be taped late the next morning. They were checked into the Ritz-Carlton hotel off Boston Common and tried to relax with some friends and key political advisers. Among them for the first time was Mandy Grunwald, who, after her performance on *Nightline* and her recognized expertise in television, had been asked to come to Boston to help prepare the Clintons for the taping.

It turned out, she said later, that they didn't need much prepping. It already was their instinct, she said, to do what she had done—"not to just sit there and be defensive, but to lash back at the press" and to express their "personal outrage at the process." Beyond that, Grunwald recalled, "nobody told them what to say about their marriage. They knew what they wanted to say. It was actually very emotional, both in the prep meetings and watching *60 Minutes*, to hear them talk about their marriage." According to others, when Hillary Clinton was asked at one point in the prep session how she felt about her family, she started weeping, expressing concern about how the show would affect their daughter, Chelsea, then eleven years old.

There was more prepping the next morning but the Clintons were ready. The taping took place in a private room with fireplace in the hotel, with the Clintons sitting side by side. According to a key Clinton adviser in the room, just as the interview was to start, *60 Minutes* senior producer Don Hewitt, who had been a producer of the famed first 1960 debate between John Kennedy and Richard Nixon, knelt down at Clinton's left elbow and said: "When he asks you if you committed adultery, say yes. It will be great television. I know. I know television. The last time I did something like this, Bill, it was the Kennedy-Nixon debates and it produced a president. This will produce a president, too."

The Clinton adviser said later: "I was dumbfounded. This guy was coaching my candidate to confess adultery on his show! Clinton listened impassively."

Kroft indeed tried repeatedly to get at the issue of infidelity in more than an hour of questioning. Each time Clinton would recite his standard reply—that he had not had an affair with Gennifer Flowers, but that he had been responsible in unspecified ways for "wrongdoing" and for "causing pain in my marriage."

While contending that he had "said things to you tonight and to the American people from the beginning that no American politician ever has," he balked at Kroft's specific question about committing adultery, saying that he was "not prepared tonight to say that any married couple should ever discuss that with anyone but themselves."

The closest he came to implying infidelity was when he said near the end of the interview: "I think most Americans who are watching this tonight, they'll know what we're saying, they'll get it, and they'll feel that we have been more candid. And I think what the press has to decide is, are we going to engage in a game of 'gotcha'?" Clinton recalled a time "when a divorced person couldn't run for president, and that time, thank goodness, has passed." Then he asked: "Are we going to take the reverse position now that if people have problems in their marriage and there are things in their past which they don't want to discuss which are painful to them, that they can't run?" And his wife weighed in: "I don't think being any more specific about what's happened in the privacy of our life together is relevant to anybody besides us.''

Perhaps Clinton's most effective moment came when Kroft, trying to characterize the Clintons' relationship, said he thought "most Americans would agree that it's very admirable that you've stayed together—that you've worked your problems out and that you've seemed to reach some sort of understanding and arrangement—'' Clinton broke in: "Wait a minute, wait a minute, wait a minute. You're looking at two people who love each other. This is not an arrangement or an understanding. This is a marriage. That's a very different thing.''

Hillary Clinton added: "You know, I'm not sitting here, some little woman standing by my man like Tammy Wynette. I'm sitting here because I love him, and I respect him, and I honor what he's been through and what we've been through together. And you know, if that's not enough for people, then heck, don't vote for him.''

The sense of the campaign strategists watching the interview on closed-circuit monitors in a control room was that Clinton had taken some hits but had survived. Afterward, he had lunch with members of *The Boston Globe* editorial board and spoke of his dilemma on being less than explicit about the have-you-ever question. "If I say no, you all will just go out and try to prove me wrong,'' he said at one point. "And if I say yes, that will mean there is no end to it. I'm not complaining, though. I signed on for the whole ride. If I made any mistake, it was talking about all this at all.''

While Clinton was at the editorial board lunch, his wife was in another room in the hotel having sandwiches and beer with some old Boston friends, including Rick Stearns, a fellow Rhodes Scholar and McGovern campaign alumnus with Clinton. The candidate walked in while Begala was on the phone with his wife, like Begala a transplanted Texan, telling her how the taping had gone. Clinton took the phone. "Well, Diane,'' he said, "I think it went pretty well until they showed me that picture of the sheep. I told them it was Begala. I hope you don't mind. I gave him up for a good cause.''

When the show came on after the Super Bowl that night, to an estimated audience of 34 million viewers, the interview had been cut to about fifteen minutes, but it was packed with drama and unprecedentedly personal revelation by a presidential candidate and his wife about their marriage. Nevertheless, Begala said later, "we were very angry with the editing," and realized the campaign had made a mistake in not insisting that the interview be done "live to tape"—doing one run-through for the allotted air time and no more. If so, it might have caught another dramatic moment, when a television lamp tipped over and Clinton grabbed his wife off the sofa to safety.

But the one thing that the Clinton strategists regretted most about the cuts, one of them said later, was one observation by the candidate. "No one wants to be judged," he had said at one point, "on the worst moment of his life."

That moment, for Clinton, was not over. The next day at the Waldorf-Astoria in New York, the *Star* produced Flowers at a press conference. Dressed in a bright red jacket with her brassy blond hair flowing from conspicuously dark roots, she did not make the most compelling witness as she insisted Clinton was "absolutely lying" in saying they had never had an affair.

"I was Bill Clinton's lover for twelve years and for the past two years I have lied to the press to protect him," she said. "The truth is, I loved him. Now he wants me to deny it. Well, I am sick of all the deceit and I'm sick of all the lies."

Prior to the playing of selected portions of the tapes she said she had made of Clinton phone calls, Flowers insisted that "when people hear my tapes, I think they will realize that I am not a woman that he saw and spoke to infrequently. My tapes go far beyond what Bill described." But when excerpts were played, only twelve minutes out of an hour or more she said she had made available to the *Star,* nothing definitive was heard to establish an affair between them.

Much later, Carville argued that the very fact that the tapes were presented with segments omitted was the best evidence that if presented whole they would have vindicated Clinton. "Why would someone present the tape and take something out of it?" he asked. "The only reason they'd take something out of it is because there's something in there that they don't want you to hear." Carville noted that there were twelve separate edits in the tape, and he pointed out that in a court of law, "there's a good reason for the rule that unless something is whole, it's not evidence."

CNN, which Clinton had given short shrift in canceling its Saturday news show and preferring *60 Minutes,* carried the event live and all the other network news shows picked it up that night. Democratic National Chairman Ron Brown immediately condemned CNN for practicing "trash journalism and titillation television" but Tom Hannon, CNN's political director, defended the live coverage. "We think our viewers are entitled to a direct opportunity," he said of Flowers, "to evaluate her credibility in an adversarial context with reporters."

The whole womanizing story, which up to now had been treated as if it had fenders by *The New York Times* and with all the affection usually afforded a dead fish by other news organizations in the mainstream, had finally made the jump from the supermarket counters of America into the nation's living rooms. In the past, such stories had been enough to bury political candidates. But here was one who took this one head-on, and was surviving.

Although a *Boston Globe* poll in New Hampshire reported a sharp drop in Clinton's support, internal opinion samplings by Greenberg for the campaign found that Clinton's backing in the state, which had been going up rapidly, was stalled by the Flowers story but leveled off rather than plunging. "There was some shifting around in who was supporting us, as a result of the story," he said later. Clinton, he said, "lost ground with older women but gained ground with younger men, which is what you'd probably expect, given the issue."

But subsequent focus groups, Greenberg said, found that voters "hated Gennifer Flowers—men too, but women particularly. They knew she was paid. They didn't know whether she had an affair or not, but what they did know was the source of the story was Gennifer Flowers, which undermined her story. . . . They knew it was tabloid, they knew it was money. . . . The most important thing we learned was their comfort with the way Clinton was addressing the question."

At the same time, the Clinton campaign did its share to paint Flowers as the wicked witch in the piece, and in the process to make the mainstream news media feel uncomfortable about the way they were taking their lead from a gossip tabloid. In fact, Carville said later, "I think Gennifer Flowers [the story] had a positive impact on the coverage, because I think after everybody went through it, no one felt very good about it. It was my job, I was out there trying to make people feel bad about it."

Nationally, other polls were indicating public annoyance with the focus on Clinton's personal life. In an ABC News survey, 80 percent of those asked said they didn't think the issue of whether Clinton had had an extramarital affair should be an issue in the campaign.

The most politically embarrassing aspect of the whole business was turning out to be a remark the voice identified as Clinton's on one of Flowers's tapes had made about Mario Cuomo. The voice referred to Cuomo as a "mean son of a bitch," and when Flowers suggested that the New York governor might have "Mafioso" connections, the voice replied, "Well, he acts like one."

While still challenging the veracity of the tapes, Clinton told reporters he was trying to reach Cuomo to apologize. Cuomo in turn told reporters that Clinton "ought to save himself his quarter," deploring the taped remarks as "part of an ugly syndrome that strikes Italian-Americans, Jewish people, blacks, women, all the different ethnic groups." Clinton publicly apologized, saying that "if the remarks on the tape left anyone with the impression that I was disrespectful to either Governor Cuomo or Italian-Americans, then I deeply regret it. At the time that conversation was held, there had been some political give-and-take between myself and the governor, and I meant simply to imply that Governor Cuomo is a tough and worthy opponent." Cuomo was not pleased, but he eventually cooled down, although he told us later that Clinton never did reach him then to apologize personally.

If the Flowers affair did not severely damage Clinton in New Hampshire, it did generate concerns among Washington politicos about "electability" and speculation that other Democrats might enter the race, particularly an irate Cuomo. *The New York Post* did its bit to push that development along with this headline regarding Cuomo's response to the alleged Clinton remarks: "Cuomo Says Clinton Talks like Bigot."

Cuomo reiterated that he was not a candidate, but when self-starters from Chicago moved into New Hampshire and set up shop for a Cuomo write-in effort without his blessing, he ran true to form. "I wouldn't presume to interfere with the good people of New Hampshire," he said. "Who am I to tell the people of New Hampshire, 'You shouldn't do that'?"

Beyond the customary Cuomo tease, there were few other prospective new starters in view. House Majority Leader Richard Gephardt seemed to some to leave the door open a crack to a late presidential bid, but nothing came of it. The polls in New Hampshire, where righting the dismal economy held the voters' concentration, continued to indicate that Clinton had weathered the storm, for all the doubts about his "electability" flourishing among assorted reporters, columnists and political wise men in Washington.

The other Democratic candidates in the field began to complain, in fact, that the Flowers story had so dominated the news and kept the focus on Clinton that they were dropping off the political radar screen. A *USA Today*/CNN poll nationally found 42 percent of Democrats surveyed favoring him to only 16 percent for the runner-up, Jerry Brown. And although Paul Tsongas continued to be Clinton's strongest rival in New Hampshire in local polls, the fact that he trailed Brown nationally reflected how lightly regarded he remained as other than a regional candidate.

For Clinton, the fact that the Flowers story had originated in a supermarket tabloid, that she had been paid for it, and that she herself was therefore seen as less than credible, had enabled him to dodge the bullet. But just as he did, another was winging his way—also out of his past.

C H A P T E R   1 1

DODGING THE DRAFT

After a few days out of New Hampshire, Clinton returned on Wednesday, February 5, feeling terrible physically. He struggled through a speech at a school in Concord and then took to his bed with a fever at Days Hotel, where the Clinton campaign was headquartered. On top of his physical condition, Clinton was worried about a story he knew was about to break regarding his draft record—and not in some sleazy super-market tabloid this time, but in *The Wall Street Journal*—a fortress of mainstream journalistic respectability.

Sure enough, the next morning—another Thursday, another "garbage day" in the Clinton campaign lexicon—the newspaper quoted a retired army recruiter in Arkansas, Colonel Eugene Holmes, as saying that Clinton in 1969, during the Vietnam War, had signed up for the Reserve Officers Training Corps (ROTC) program at the University of Arkansas Law School to avoid the draft, and then "was able to manipulate things so that he didn't have to go in."

Clinton was stunned, especially because Holmes was the source of the story—a man who repeatedly over the years had told inquiring reporters that Clinton had behaved correctly in the matter.

Clinton had been studying at Oxford on a Rhodes Scholarship at the time and as an ROTC enrollee he was given a further deferment and permitted to return to England to finish that program. He said then that he intended to enter the law school, and the ROTC program, in the fall of 1970 but in the fall of 1969 he decided not to go into ROTC upon finishing at Oxford and asked to be put back in the draft. He was reclassified 1-A on October 30 but in the first draft lottery on December 1 he drew a number too high for induction. In the fall of 1970, with no draft worries, he enrolled at the Yale Law School, not Arkansas.

Those at least were the facts known and acknowledged by Clinton at the time the story broke. Holmes had now told the *Journal*, however, that he was led to believe in 1969 that Clinton had planned to return to Arkansas and enter the law school there later that year, and would not have received the deferment otherwise.

Like the womanizing stories, this one also was an old turkey that had been chased around the political barnyard in Arkansas by reporters during Clinton's earliest gubernatorial campaigns and, after inquiries with Holmes and other military and draft officials, abandoned as unworthy of continued pursuit. But now the *Journal* also quoted Opal Ellis, the Republican executive secretary of the draft board in Clinton's hometown of Hot Springs, as saying the town was "proud to have a Hot Springs boy with a Rhodes Scholarship" and that Clinton pressured the draft board to defer him and accordingly the board "was very lenient with him" and "gave him more than he was entitled to."

The Clinton campaign was caught unprepared. For all these years, Clinton had relied on Holmes to verify that he had done no wrong regarding the draft, and his aides continued to do so. It was, Begala acknowledged later, "a mistake. What if Holmes got hit by a beer truck?" He and other aides immediately sat down with Clinton to review the whole story once again, prodding his memory.

Carville was on the shuttle en route from Washington to New York to make a speech when he picked up a copy of the *Journal* and glanced at the story. "I can remember just having a pit in my stomach all morning, giving the speech," he recalled. He phoned Stephanopoulos in New

Hampshire, telling him, "Man, this thing don't have the right kind of feel to it." The other political advisers in New Hampshire had already reached the same conclusion—that if they thought they had been through fire over Gennifer Flowers, the real inferno was just flaring.

Again it was damage-control time. All pertinent papers from Clinton's draft file were faxed from Little Rock to Manchester, digested and used as a base to subject the candidate, fever and all, to a dry-run press conference on his draft history.

The next morning, as Clinton walked into the lobby of the Sheraton-Tara in Nashua—the same place he was first confronted by a host of reporters and cameramen on the Larry Nichols lawsuit allegations barely three weeks earlier—he was mobbed again and bombarded with questions about the *Journal*'s draft story. "I was not seeking to avoid military service by this [signing up for the Arkansas ROTC]," he insisted. "I could not have known that this [high] lottery number would come about or that all the lottery people wouldn't be called."

As for suddenly deciding to decline the ROTC deferment and subject himself to the draft, Clinton insisted that because several of his friends from Arkansas had been killed in Vietnam, "I just didn't feel right about having a four-year deferment" through Oxford and then law school. "I put myself into the draft when I thought it was a one hundred percent certainty that I would be called." And regarding Opal Ellis's remarks that he had put pressure on the draft board, Clinton said he "had absolutely no conversations with her to that effect, ever," adding that "she's had twenty-three years to tell this story and has never done it before." He called the whole business "an unbelievable rewriting of history."

The Clinton press office in Little Rock, meanwhile, released a brief chronology of Clinton's draft record and called the allegations "recycled Republican charges . . . first raised when Clinton ran for governor in 1978 by a retired air force lieutenant colonel, who then was working for Clinton's Republican opponent. They were false then, and they are false now." And Stephanopoulos in New Hampshire handed out copies of an *Arkansas Democrat-Gazette* story of the previous October in which Holmes was quoted as saying he had dealt with Clinton on his draft status "just like I would have treated any other kid."

But what media critic Sabato had dubbed the "feeding frenzy" was on. At a town meeting in Exeter that night, Clinton was hit with the question again, and he insisted that "I did not do anything wrong, and I certainly didn't do anything illegal."

The new charges nevertheless dominated the political coverage the next day, but at another question-and-answer session at New Hampshire Technical College in Stratham, no voter raised the issue and the staff began to hope that the worst was over. Greenberg meantime had conducted a focus group—a roundtable discussion with selected voters to gauge public attitudes—and found little concern or ill-will toward Clinton over the latest development in the news.

At that point, however, came what Carville later called "one of the biggest mistakes I think I made. He [Clinton] was really sick and he wanted to come home, and I said, 'No, goddamn, what we found is, if you stay out of the news cycle you get clobbered up there.' " That, indeed, was what had happened to Ronald Reagan in the 1976 Republican primary in New Hampshire, when he left the state brimming with confidence on the final weekend, leaving the field to President Gerald Ford, and lost narrowly. And in 1980, George Bush spent the final weekend of the primary basking in sunny Texas while voters shivered in New Hampshire—and wound up voting for Reagan.

Now Carville argued: "What you need to do is get Hillary and Chelsea, bring them up to the Ritz-Carlton in Boston. Let's get room service there, let's just take him out one time a day and just go into New Hampshire, and get our side of the story." But he lost the argument. "I guess I just didn't hold my ground," he said later in discussing his "mistake." "We all went down to Arkansas that weekend and the whole thing just went to hell in a handbasket. You could see, Tsongas was coming up before that, there were some little signs for concern but nothing [concrete]. But that Sunday night poll was just awful, and you knew it was real."

At the governor's mansion that night, the key political strategists and Clinton held a stock-taking meeting. David Wilhelm recalled that "we did not feel the necessary urgency during that meeting because we had some evidence from focus groups that when people were presented with an explanation of the draft [story], they seemed to be satisfied. I guess what we forgot," he said, "was that you have to get that message out, you have to explain it. The fact that a focus group knew the explanation was not sufficient for the rest of the people who were not part of that focus group, who had not been given that explanation."

Shortly before midnight, Greenberg called in with his latest polling numbers from New Hampshire, and the news was worse than anyone had thought. "Meltdown," he told Carville, giving the rough numbers showing Clinton to be in a free-fall, from a high-water mark of 37 percent to 17 in only a few days, with Tsongas surging into the lead and campaigning now, remarkably to many, with the aura of a winner. "This was not shades of gray," Greenberg said later. "We had a whole new race."

A new *Boston Globe* poll had Tsongas pulling essentially even with Clinton. "We started ripping up the schedule," Wilhelm said, "trying to see what we could do to get this back on schedule." A conference call involving Clinton, Carville, Begala, Wilhelm, Greer and Greenberg was patched together. One idea floated was to buy television time for Clinton to field questions from callers. Another was to have Clinton go on the attack, blaming the Republicans for slandering him. Still another, advocated by Greer, was to prepare television ads with Clinton attacking the tabloids and appealing to the voters for fair play.

"We decided we had to do everything possible to change the dynamic," Greer recalled. "We had to get past the feeding frenzy [of the news media]."

The team, with the Clintons overseeing it all, set to work then and there. Begala and Stephanopoulos started on a short speech text for Clinton, a departure from his customary extemporaneous style. Hershel Gober, the Arkansas state director of veterans' affairs, was awakened and called on to tape a testimonial for his boss they had written and that Greer then rushed to New Hampshire radio stations. A still sick and weary Clinton finally turned in, understanding full well that the fate of his presidential bid was now hanging in the balance, and would likely depend on what happened over the remaining eight days before the New Hampshire primary.

Early the next morning, Monday, Bill and Hillary Clinton and aides flew back to New Hampshire, with the candidate working over Begala's speech text hitting hard at the notion that the latest questions about Clinton's veracity—about "Slick Willie" as his critics increasingly referred to him—was the work of a "Republican attack machine" honed in the

1988 presidential campaign. Clinton was slated to deliver the fighting speech at the Nashua airport but the authorities refused to grant clearance for a political use of the premises.

Another, much more significant factor, however, was about to alter the day's plans drastically. Mark Halperin, the same ABC News producer who had figured in the confrontation of the candidate regarding the Gennifer Flowers story earlier, met the plane and handed Stephanopoulos a copy of a letter that was to throw the campaign into a tailspin again.

The letter, long and anguished, had been written from Oxford in December 1969 by the twenty-three-year-old Clinton to Colonel Holmes, explaining, after thanking Holmes "for saving me from the draft," why he had decided to withdraw from the Arkansas ROTC program and submit himself to the draft after all. The letter was written only days after the lottery had given him such a high draft number—311—that he was safe from induction.

The young Clinton confessed his thorough opposition to the Vietnam War, saying he had earlier taken a minor job with the Senate Foreign Relations Committee so that in some small way he could work daily "against a war I opposed and despised with a depth of feeling I had reserved solely for racism in America before Vietnam." He wrote of having "written and spoken and marched against the war," going "to Washington to work in the national headquarters of the [anti–Vietnam War] Moratorium, then to England to organize the Americans here for demonstrations here. . . ."

Clinton went on that he had studied the legality of the draft when he was an undergraduate at Georgetown and "came to believe that the draft system itself is illegitimate." No government "really rooted in limited, parliamentary democracy should have the power," he argued, "to make its citizens fight and kill and die in a war they may oppose, a war which even possibly may be wrong, a war which, in any case, does not involve immediately the peace and freedom of the nation."

There was a basic difference, he wrote, between World War II and the wars in Korea and Vietnam on this latter score. He praised two Oxford friends who were conscientious objectors and said he himself had considered that option but "decided to accept the draft in spite of my beliefs for one reason: to maintain my political viability within the system." He had prepared himself for "a political life" and was determined to pursue it. In other words, he was saying, he understood that his political future risked being jeopardized by draft resistance and he wasn't willing to run the risk.

At the same time, Clinton wrote, after signing the ROTC letter of intent "I began to wonder whether the compromise I had made with myself was not more objectionable than the draft would have been" because he had no interest in ROTC "and all I seemed to have done was protect myself from physical harm," as well as deceiving Holmes "by failing to tell you all the things I'm writing now."

After Holmes had cleared his draft deferment, Clinton wrote, "the anguish and loss of my self-regard and self-confidence really set in." Before leaving for the fall term in Oxford, he said, he sat down and wrote a letter to the chairman of his draft board in Arkansas saying "I couldn't do the ROTC after all and would he please draft me as soon as possible." But he never mailed the letter, young Clinton went on, "because I didn't see, in the end, how my going in the army and maybe going to Vietnam would achieve anything except a feeling that I had punished myself and gotten what I deserved." So he went back to England.

Clinton closed the letter by saying he hoped that "my telling this one story will help you to understand more clearly how so many fine people have come to find themselves still loving their country but loathing the military, to which you and other good men have devoted years, lifetimes, of the best service you could give."

After Stephanopoulos read the letter, Begala recalled, "for the ten thousandth time in the campaign, he says, 'We're through.' He hands me the letter, and just like George, the first thing my eye sees is, 'thank you for saving me from the draft.' I gotta tell you, my knees buckled." It had the ring of a death knell to Clinton's presidential hopes. And the line about "political viability"—that he had acted to save his own political future—wouldn't help either, nor would the closing reference to "loathing the military." All in all, the letter had disaster written all over it, or so it seemed.

When Stephanopoulos handed the letter to his candidate as the Clintons along with Carville and Begala crowded into a small room in the airport, Clinton scanned it and seemed unperturbed. He turned to his wife and said: "This is mine. I remember writing this letter." Her response, Begala recalled, was, "This is terrific. This is exactly what you were thinking at the time. This proves everything that you were saying, Bill''— that he had indeed, as he had said all along, voluntarily made himself available for the draft.

The youngest of those present, Stephanopoulos and Begala, did not see it that way, but the man with the best political antenna on the staff, Carville, agreed. "When the letter hit," he recalled later, "they said, 'Oh God, this is the end of whatever.' And I said, 'Get that sumbitch and put it in the paper, man. Make this thing as public as we can get anything.' ''

Begala recalled his partner declaring to Clinton, "This letter is your best friend.'' Here, Begala said, "was the generation gap, because George and I were looking at each other and saying, 'Are they reading the same letter we are?' The younger set argued, Begala recalled, that "what the press is gonna do, they're not going to [read] it in its entirety," but instead would pull out the most damaging phrases. "Hillary and James said, 'We've got to make them read it in its entirety. That's why we've got to take it to voters. . . . This letter will free us. It won't sink us.' ''

His reasoning, Carville said, was that "this was a story people felt. It showed that he was sort of tortured by the whole thing. People were tortured by the war. If you were Bush's age (at sixty-seven a World War II veteran) or George or Paul's age (both in their early thirties and post-Vietnam), it looked like a bad deal. If you were my age (forty-five and a Vietnam-era veteran), there was a real sort of anguish. The people I served with, I can't tell you the people who said, 'Look, he just didn't want to get his ass shot off. That's fine with me.' Who did?''

Carville said he recognized the political risks in Clinton's reference to Holmes "saving me from the draft'' and salvaging his own "political viability,'' but believed that the letter "taken in its whole'' would be a plus for Clinton. "If we go out and get in front of it and make it public, then people think you've got less to hide. There's very little doubt he joined the ROTC not to be drafted.''

The question now was how to handle the letter to turn what at first blush appeared to be a political suicide note into an affirmation of Clinton's credibility on the draft issue. At Halperin's request, Clinton agreed to an interview with the ABC reporter on the story, Jim Wooten. First he delivered his planned speech vowing to "fight like hell'' against the same

"Republican attack machine" that had done in Michael Dukakis in 1988, attempting at the same time to get the campaign focus back on his economic agenda. "For too much of the past couple of weeks," he said, "this election has been about me, or rather some false and twisted tabloid version of me, when it should have been about the people of this state."

The references to the 1988 Bush campaign against Dukakis were more, however, than simply a smokescreen behind which a candidate under attack could hide. Well aware of the growing mood in the country against negative campaigning, generated in considerable part by revulsion to those 1988 tactics and best remembered in the Willie Horton prison furlough story, the Clinton campaign deftly hung Horton around the necks of the Republicans generally, and Bush in particular, especially later. "The divide-and-conquer strategy helped George Bush and Roger Ailes convince people," Clinton told his Nashua audience, "that the greatest threat to their jobs, schools, children and future in 1988 was a convict named Willie Horton and a governor named Michael Dukakis."

After the speech, Clinton toured a yogurt factory in nearby Londonderry and then went into a small room there for his interview with Wooten, arguing that the letter supported what he had said all along about his draft record. Then the candidate returned to Manchester and waited for the evening television news, and Wooten's public disclosure of the letter. But Wooten before the show informed Clinton that there were some aspects about its surfacing that he wanted to check out.

Wooten didn't know it at the time, but the source of the letter to ABC News was retired Lieutenant Colonel Clinton Jones, deputy to Holmes at the Arkansas ROTC in 1969. Jones, saying later that he was merely "trying to get some facts on the table," denied that he was involved in any "Republican plot" or that he had been paid by anybody to release the old letter.

It turned out that Jones was in Myrtle Beach, South Carolina, at this time and had asked a hotel clerk there to make some copies of the letter for him. The clerk spirited away a copy for himself and faxed it to a friend in Washington, who in turn sent one copy to Clinton's Washington office and another to, of all people, former Air Force Major General Richard Secord, a convicted player in the celebrated Iran-contra affair, who then sent it to ABC's *Nightline*. This string of events once again brought the show's host, Ted Koppel, into the Clinton campaign saga when he received the letter quite independent of Wooten, who didn't have any idea, either, that Koppel by now also had it.

Carville, as already noted, wanted Clinton to make the letter public post-haste, and to the widest audience possible. But Clinton, aides insisted later, felt honor-bound to Wooten to let him break the news in what would have been a major journalistic scoop. Campaign aides did, however, go about the mechanics of arranging for advertising space in the main New Hampshire newspapers. The sooner the better was the attitude, Greenberg said. The strategists didn't want the story to break in the final days of the primary, he said, or for that matter smack in the middle of Super Tuesday.

The Clintons flew off for a major fund-raising dinner in New York at which the candidate managed to mangle the famous Mark Twain quote about reports of his death being "greatly exaggerated," saying instead that reports of his own demise were "premature."

On the flight back to New Hampshire, the Clintons were in an unusually good mood. He was still physically in great distress from the cold or flu he could not seem to shake, and he astonished the few reporters flying with him by popping prescription pills with seeming abandon. He and his wife played pinochle with a couple of reporters and reminisced about their days in the Vietnam antiwar movement and Southern politics, including the bizarre case of another governor, Bill Allain of Mississippi, whose problems made Clinton's pale by comparison. It was Allain who in the last days of his 1983 campaign was confronted by accusations of liaisons from a group of alleged homosexual transvestites—and was elected anyway.

The plane landed in Keene after midnight, and Clinton insisted on searching out an open Dunkin' Donuts shop, where he devoured a bowl of soup and a couple of bagels with tuna salad. Then, as the others in the party watched, weary but bemused, the candidate settled into a long discussion on health care with a surprised late-night customer. If Clinton was worried about the latest bombshell that was about to fall on his campaign, he gave no indication of it.

All but lost in the intense focus on the approaching New Hampshire primary were the Iowa precinct caucuses held that night. With native son Tom Harkin in the presidential race, all the other candidates had prudently decided to save their time and money and leave the state to him. But not wanting to be embarrassed in his own backyard, Harkin had spent an inordinate amount of resources there in winning 76.5 percent of the vote. It was like kissing your sister, and at the price of a chance to make a stronger showing in New Hampshire, where he was going nowhere. Tsongas, sending a stealth representative into the state late, finished third with 4.1 percent behind "uncommitted," which had 11.9 percent.

The Iowa caucuses, critical in other presidential years, had been reduced to a footnote in the story of the 1992 campaign. Business was so slack in the bar at the Hotel Savery, the traditional wall-to-wall hangout of assorted political operatives, reporters and junkies, and in Guido's restaurant that Guido himself, who reveled every four years in greeting the Peter Jenningses, the Tom Brokaws and the John Chancellors of the television news firmament, went abroad during caucus week.

The action remained in New Hampshire, and on the next afternoon, Koppel got into the picture again. He called David Wilhelm, the campaign manager in Little Rock, telling him it was "important that the governor and I talk." The subject, naturally, was the Clinton letter. Here was ABC News once more bringing bad news to the campaign, making some in Little Rock wonder whether the network had become the channel for Republican antics. But Koppel, knowing Secord's history, was himself wary of the circumstances by which the letter had come to him, and the motivation of its sender. He told Wilhelm only that he was "under the impression that my source might have gotten it from someone in the Pentagon." Only when Wilhelm told him did Koppel find out that his own ABC colleague Wooten had a copy of the letter and had already interviewed Clinton about it.

Koppel knew that a critical aspect of the campaign had fallen into his lap and he invited Clinton onto *Nightline*. Stephanopoulos handled the negotiations, and when he asked Koppel where the letter had come from, Koppel pleaded ignorance again, once more saying it was his "impression" that it had come from the Pentagon.

"We went bananas [at Koppel's answer]," Begala said. "We decided we'd call a press conference, release the letter, and announce that the Pentagon had put this out, and that we were going to go on *Nightline* and talk about it." If it was true, here was a grand opportunity to really nail the Republicans not only for going negative against Clinton on the sneak but also possibly for breaking the law by circulating material protected by privacy laws.

The next day, Clinton himself called Koppel, telling him he wanted to release the letter but wanted to confirm that the source had been the Pentagon, as Koppel had indicated. "It was clear in our minds," said Mickey Kantor, the campaign chairman, who was listening in on the call, "that from Ted Koppel's perspective [the letter] came from the Pentagon," or Clinton never would have made such a public charge. So Clinton went out and held a news conference in a Manchester Airport hangar while aides handed out copies of the letter.

Clinton reported that Koppel had "confirmed to me that it is his understanding that ABC received a letter from two different sources, both of whom got it from the Pentagon. If this is true, the leak violates the Federal Privacy Act." He disclosed that he would be appearing on *Nightline* that night to discuss the whole matter.

Koppel later in the day called back, Kantor said, saying "he had talked to his lawyers" and backed off, saying he had learned that the letter had not, in fact, come from the Pentagon. That left Clinton with a bit of egg on his face—and without a very strong counterattack issue with which to divert attention from his own problems.

Later, on a flight to Claremont, Clinton seemed depressed to reporters aboard his small plane. As he walked up to his seat he said hello to Tom Edsall of *The Washington Post*, who with his wife, Mary, had just written an insightful book about how the Democratic Party, in the public perception that it pushed policies benefiting blacks, had contributed to the flight of conservative whites to the GOP in the Reagan-Bush era.

Another reporter, Curtis Wilkie of *The Boston Globe*, told Clinton he had recently written that he was the best-positioned Democratic candidate to address the problems of race raised by the Edsalls, to which Clinton lamely replied: "I was." Wilkie asked: "What do you mean, 'I was'?" Clinton caught himself. "Oh, hell, I am," he said. "It's just that I'm so busy fighting wars that are twenty-three years old. . . ."

Much later, Clinton told us that even in these most trying moments, he never thought about quitting the race. Had his wife asked him to, he might have, he said, "but she never did. I was glad [the allegations against him] happened in New Hampshire because I trusted those people

. . . I thought I got in the race for certain reasons, and nothing anybody said or did affected those reasons, or what I thought was my ability to do the job. I just figured I'd hired out for the whole race, and if the people wanted to take me out, they were free to do it at any point along the way, and I was going to stay until they made that judgment.

"It never occurred to me to quit, not a single time. To me, quitting would have been the worst thing. Getting beat in an election is not a dishonorable thing to have happen, and I certainly could have understood it if at any time along the way the voters had decided they just didn't want to take a chance. They didn't know me, they knew all this bad stuff about me. Why should they risk this thing? I figured the best thing for me was to plow ahead every day and demonstrate a commitment to the things and people who had gotten me into the race."

That same night in Dover, Clinton gave one of his most memorable speeches of the campaign before the local Elks Club, a deft mixture of emotion, defiance and counterattack. Playing off the popular ridicule of Bush's reference to "the vision thing" that critics said Bush lacked, Clinton said that public service in politics was "the work of my life" and that his dreams for the country were his "vision thing." He said he hoped parents in the audience "never raise a child without the vision thing. . . . Life would be bleak and empty without the vision thing."

Then Clinton began talking about gratitude in public life. He noted that Bush had been resurrected politically in 1988 by the voters in the New Hampshire primary after having run third in the Iowa caucuses, yet in the next three years as president had spent only three hours in the state, "mostly on his way to and from Kennebunkport, while you tripled your unemployment, welfare and food stamp rates."

He went on: "They say I'm on the ropes because other people have questioned my life, after years of public service. I'll tell you something— I'm going to give you this election back, and if you'll give it to me, I won't be like George Bush. I'll never forget who gave me a second chance, and I'll be there for you till the last dog dies."

After the speech, Clinton seemed emotionally drained, but still ahead was his appearance on *Nightline* to address the Holmes letter. Before airtime, Koppel asked Clinton to read the letter on the air, but Clinton declined. So Koppel by his own choice and with Clinton's assent, read the whole thing, consuming a major portion of the half-hour show, as

Clinton sat listening attentively and merely confirming by nods the sentiments expressed therein.

When Koppel was finished reading, Clinton told him that "the important thing is that the letter is consistent with everything I've been saying for the last eighteen years, since I was first asked about this in late 1978 [when he was running in Arkansas]. I was in the draft before the lottery came in. I gave up the deferment. I got a high lottery number and I wasn't called. That's what the records reflect. A Republican member of my draft board has given an affidavit in the last couple of days saying that I got no special treatment and nothing in the letter changes that, although it is a true reflection of the deep and conflicted feelings of a just-turned-twenty-three-year-old young man. I felt that at the time."

Koppel then asked Clinton for his views on the draft generally, and how he thought the issue would "play in your neck of the woods, down South, where indeed support of the army is a stronger issue than perhaps most other parts of the country." Clinton replied: "I was reelected five times to run things, in tough times, with no help, by good people who heard all this stuff. If you're looking for somebody that's already been tested, you ought to go with me."

The judgment of the campaign staff afterward was that once again the candidate had survived a major test. "I know that show got us out of the woods with the press," Begala said. Koppel, he said, treated the interview "the way it ought to be treated. It wasn't just a sort of ambush, gotcha, chickenshit journalism." Reporters, just as Begala and Stephanopoulos had done, had seized on the damaging phrases for their morning stories, but after they saw *Nightline*, began to see it as Carville and Hillary Clinton had. The polls did not show any immediate upturn, however, and the jury that counted would not be in until primary night, now six days away.

The draft story seemed to hang on in New Hampshire, more than had the womanizing rap against Clinton. "When people don't know you," he reflected in an interview much later, "even if they don't want to believe something bad about you, in the early going at least an election can be a process of elimination. So that if they hear two bad things about you instead of one, I think the question then is, should you be eliminated?"

The draft allegations, he said, "came to have legs partly because the press thought that there was still more to come out. The story just stayed alive, and there was this whole question whether everybody knew everything they needed to know and I had told them everything they needed to know, and if there was something they didn't understand. . . . It lingered in the news longer, and frankly, my opponents felt more comfortable raising questions about it [than about the womanizing allegations]."

This final stretch came in retrospect to be the finest hour of the Clinton campaign to many of its campaign warriors. After Cuomo had taken himself out of the picture in December and Clinton had moved ahead in the New Hampshire polls and had become the recognized front-runner, the hope had been to win the state and then roll south into the Super Tuesday primaries to sew up the nomination then and there. "If we had won New Hampshire," Carville said later, "that would have shut the whole thing down." But the Flowers story had further fueled the issue of the trustworthiness of "Slick Willie" and softened him up somewhat, and the draft story had put him on the ropes.

Now the struggle was to get him back up to a respectable showing in the state, feeding the spin that Tsongas as a New Englander should have been the favorite there all along. "We came to believe," Greenberg said later, "that getting 25 percent and having as much space between Kerrey, Harkin and us as between Tsongas and us was the threshold we needed to pass" to come out of New Hampshire in credible shape.

To achieve that goal, Carville said, it was necessary to get Clinton maximum exposure in the final days, and he was more than willing to go all out. "We were answering everything, we were taking it as it came," Carville said of every opportunity offered to get the candidate on television and radio, and before large crowds.

At the same time, the Clinton campaign, part of which was in Little Rock, part in Washington, part in New Hampshire and part wherever the candidate happened to be, became centralized in New Hampshire for the do-or-die push. "The sense," Mandy Grunwald recalled later, "was all hands on deck. . . . My sense was it was the first of the war rooms" that subsequently were set up in each primary state along the road toward the nomination.

Mickey Kantor came to Manchester and functioned, in Carville's words, "like a trainmaster," presiding over early-morning meetings at which everyone got his two cents in on what the candidate needed to say and do to survive down to the wire. "Mickey was very impressive," Grunwald said. "There were a lot of disparate voices and he really got everybody organized. That was an incredible week in terms of each day there was a major television test that Clinton put himself through, any one of which, given how fragile the campaign was, could have blown up the campaign."

After the *Nightline* show, there were two paid television appearances in which Clinton fielded questions from voters, one in a small town-meeting format and one a call-in, plus a debate on the final Saturday night and a spot on one of the network Sunday morning interview shows. Instead of opting for the most controlled environments in which risks of off-the-wall questions could be avoided, Grunwald said, "his reaction was, 'Let me out there.' He was working twenty hours a day and he wanted as many forums as possible to connect with people."

In advance of the two paid appearances, the campaign ran a statewide promotion ad for them with Clinton personally urging voters to watch, observing that he knew they had heard a lot *about* him and now he wanted them to hear *from* him. Greer set up a "roadblock" for the promotion— buying all available television for a specific time slot in the Boston area and New Hampshire—so that anyone watching television on any channel would see it. Successful fund-raising, in the midst of all the travail, brought in $1 million in February, enabling the Clinton campaign to take such aggressive actions.

A research firm was hired to round up a small group of undecided voters for the first paid Q-and-A session, and in neither that one nor the telephone call-in show did anyone ask about Gennifer Flowers. There was one question touching on Clinton's draft problems, but it was indirect and easily answered—would he, if elected, be able to perform the functions of commander in chief. The campaign strategists breathed a modest sigh of relief.

Tsongas, meanwhile, was enjoying his own rising fortunes, but not gloating, and declining to be drawn into the controversy over Clinton's draft record. "This too will pass," he said at one point. "I didn't get depressed over the hard times and I'm not going to get euphoric over the good times."

As *The Boston Globe* poll finally showed Clinton making a modest recovery but still about eight percentage points behind Tsongas, he began to address directly the question of whether his scandal-ridden campaign could win. "I'm electable," he told a voters' panel in Concord. He had always been able to overcome negative attacks in the past, he said, "and

I will, if there is enough time. . . . If you say I'm electable, by definition I'm electable.''

Tsongas, holding to the high road, said that the draft issue was "worthy of discussion but should not be the total focus of this campaign," adding that he considered Clinton a friend and that the frenzy over his record during Vietnam was "irrational." Vietnam war hero Kerrey, while saying he was "tremendously sympathetic to Governor Clinton's dilemma" and that "the Vietnam War is not an issue in 1992 and should not be," continued to run radio ads raising the question of Clinton's electability. In the final debate of the primary, however, none of the other candidates raised his personal problems—a critical factor for his man, Kantor said later, because "they allowed Bill Clinton to get back on message."

In the final days, the Clinton campaign bore down. In addition to the early-morning mass meetings, Kantor held smaller sessions with smaller circles of advisers at which specific problems or television events were thrashed out, after which he would assign one or two of the principals to boil down the conclusions and present them to Clinton, so that he would get the most important points of view without an accompanying Babel. In advance of that week's debate and later ones, the advisers would come up with questions, Grunwald recalled, much tougher than any that ever were asked. Carville especially, she said, reveled in "scaring the hell out of his candidate for no reason at all."

From all this, Greenberg said later, "the solidarity of the campaign was first forged in New Hampshire," rather than descending to bickering in a crisis period as often happened in high-stakes campaigns. "Everybody was in the same hotel, it was like a college dorm," Carville recalled. "In some ways, it was the most fun part of the whole campaign. In the culture of the Clinton campaign, New Hampshire was not that much of a nightmare because it was fun. There was real camaraderie up there."

Clinton and Tsongas campaigned energetically and effectively down to the wire. Clinton beat a steady path to the television stations in Manchester, riding next to the driver in a van with aides and occasional reporters. On one such trip as the primary approached, he told us he was certain there was nothing else in his past that could be thrown up at him, and that all he could do now was reach as many voters as he could and answer all questions tossed his way. He seemed neither optimistic nor pessimistic, just determined to pack as much voter contact as he could into the remaining hours. At the same time, aides distributed 20,000 videos of Clinton making his pitch, enabling voters to watch him in their own living rooms, at a time of their own choosing.

For all this effort, the Clinton campaign on primary eve was apprehensive. "The whole landscape had changed in a period of two weeks in New Hampshire," Greer said. "The day before the primary, the polls still had Clinton going down, and if you looked just at the numbers, we were on the precipice of coming in third, which would have been disastrous." But Clinton that night had a more optimistic feeling, born of his intensive exposure to the voters in the final, frenetic week.

Tsongas had benefited from Clinton's absence from the state on the weekend the draft story broke, and he too was driving to the finish before large and enthusiastic crowds that would not have seemed possible to any impartial observer who had seen him retailing rather forlornly across the state months and months earlier.

In the end, both men reached the goals they had sought down the homestretch—Tsongas an impressive winner with 33 percent of the Democratic vote and Clinton just managing the 25 percent that his strategists believed he needed to survive the state on an upbeat note and head toward presumably more favorable circumstances and political climate in the South.

For the other Democrats, New Hampshire seemed the beginning of the end: Kerrey 11 percent, Harkin 10 percent, Brown 8 percent, Cuomo 4 percent on write-ins, and consumer advocate Ralph Nader 2 percent, also on write-ins.

Tsongas had won but Clinton's survival forced him to share the spotlight on his big night, and doubts about his appeal outside New England remained strong. As for Clinton, he was prepared to make the most of the situation, to declare his second-place finish as a glass half full rather than half empty. As the exit polls came in that afternoon, Begala was the first to make the point within the campaign that Clinton had to cast the result not as a near-miss but as a comeback. There was some dispute later whether Begala or Grunwald actually came up with the expression "The Comeback Kid," but Clinton used it that night to describe himself—in a primary election he had been on the way to winning handily until two stories out of his past had risen up and nearly knocked him out of presidential contention.

At the suggestion of Joe Grandmaison, the former New Hampshire state party chairman who had been in Cuomo's corner until he finally folded his cards, Clinton went down early to his supporters, to accentuate the positive before his finish was cast by others as a defeat. He had taken a lot of hits, he told the voters of New Hampshire that night, but no more than the people of the Granite State had taken through the Reagan-Bush years. And if nothing else, he concluded, "at least I've proved one thing: I can take a punch."

In getting through the trial by fire in New Hampshire, the Clinton insiders believed they had learned important lessons about their candidate, about the news media and about the mind-set of the voters in the 1992 election year, and what they had to concentrate on as the Democratic nomination moved on to the next tests.

"It was clear just in the tracking of numbers," television consultant Grunwald said later, reflecting on the experience of New Hampshire, "that there had been no meltdown after Gennifer Flowers; there had been after a weekend of the draft story. We did not understand [at first] what the alchemy between the two issues was, what long-lasting question it raised about Clinton. . . .

"We also didn't realize how lucky we were to have an election [then]. If we had had that three-week period in December instead of in January, if there hadn't been a vote, so that you all knew and we all knew how people, real people, feel about all this, both those issues could have festered. And they certainly did from one point of view, but they could have festered in a different way, and maybe been lethal, I don't know. But it was very fortunate in retrospect that you had a moment when people could say, 'No, this doesn't matter. We're real people, We reject the notion that this is what's going to determine our president.' And I think that was crucial to the timing of it . . . the ability to have people ratify your point of view, and we obviously took advantage of that in terms of what he [Clinton] said on election night."

The long-lasting question to which Grunwald referred was the credibility, the trustworthiness of Bill Clinton, at the core of the womanizing and draft issues and inherent in the nickname "Slick Willie" first laid on him in Arkansas and emerging increasingly now. It was true, as Grunwald suggested, that New Hampshire curtailed the festering of those two issues with voters. But it was also true as she indicated that they continued to fester among a news media that had not yet picked up on what the voters were saying about those issues.

In permitting Clinton to survive with a respectable second place, they were saying that in themselves the allegations of womanizing and draft-dodging didn't matter, except as they might reflect on Bill Clinton's credibility to do what he was saying he would do to deal with the faltering economy being neglected, in their eyes, by the man who had been in the White House for the previous three years.

With the New Hampshire primaries for both parties concluded, the spotlight that had focused so relentlessly on that small state would now, in the next weeks, swing wildly from one state and region of the country to another. On the next Sunday, February 23, Democratic voters would caucus in Maine, and two days later both parties would conduct primaries in South Dakota. Then, in a rush, primaries or caucuses would be held by one or both parties on the following Tuesday, March 3, in seven states: Georgia, Maryland, Minnesota, Colorado, Idaho, Utah and Washington state; on March 7 in South Carolina, Wyoming and Arizona; and on March 8 in Nevada.

Then, on March 10—Super Tuesday—would come the preconvention season's single busiest day at the polls, with primaries in Texas, Florida, Louisiana, Mississippi, Tennessee, Oklahoma, Massachusetts and Rhode Island and caucuses in Missouri, Delaware and Hawaii. The candidates obviously could not compete with equal intensity in all of these state contests after New Hampshire, so targets had to be chosen. On the Republican side, as already noted, Buchanan chose to make his major stand against Bush in Georgia; among the Democrats, each candidate had his own priorities based on local support and hopes as the campaign plunged into this most frenetic travel period of the year.

In all these states, for Bill Clinton the same question remained a haunting roadblock to the Democratic nomination. Could, and would, the voters believe and trust this relative stranger from Arkansas who was asking to lead the country for the next four years?

Many who had soured on President Bush, or hadn't made up their minds about him and were uncertain about Clinton and Tsongas, yearned for another choice. Two nights after the New Hampshire primary, they suddenly had one.

BILLION-DOLLAR
MESSIAH

At 4:16 P.M. on Saturday, June 1, 1991, at the Hilton Plaza Inn in Kansas City, a man named Jack Gargan stood before a regional meeting of an organization called the Coalition to End the Permanent Congress and announced that he was setting out to elect H. Ross Perot president of the United States. He knew the exact time, Gargan said later, because he checked his watch. "I knew I was making history so I wanted to get it right," he said.

"You heard it here first," he told the applauding audience of fellow critics of a Congress that had built up a huge federal deficit. Perot, the famed Texas self-made billionaire businessman, "is too modest to seek the office," said Gargan, "but I think he's too patriotic to refuse."

Afterward Gargan, who had been urging Perot to run, phoned his quarry in Dallas and told him: "Well, the fat's in the fire." But Perot, as he had repeatedly told Gargan, said it was out of the question. "Well," Gargan replied, "that's what a draft is." Recalling that conversation later, Gargan added: ''He never gave me any encouragement, but he never gave me any discouragement, either.''

Gargan's idea of Perot running for national office did not hit the hard-charging Texan out of the blue. According to retiring Chrysler Corporation chairman Lee Iacocca in an interview on *Larry King Live* after the 1992 election, ''Ross and I almost did it two years ago, but we decided a third party wouldn't cut it.'' He and Perot, Iacocca said, had done an ''Alfonse and Gaston'' act on which of them would be the presidential candidate and which his running mate, before abandoning the idea.

Gargan, a sixty-two-year-old semiretired financial planner from Tampa driven to political action by his outrage against the congressional pay raise and the savings-and-loan scandal, was the head of an organization known as THRO, for Throw the Hypocritical Rascals Out. He had met Perot for the first time only days before the Kansas City meeting, when he called on the Texas business tycoon in his office in Dallas. Gargan told Perot, he said later, that ''you are the only person who can turn this country around, and my job is to see that you run for president.''

Most men who had never run for even the lowliest public office might have been bowled over by the proposition. But according to Gargan Perot ''was intrigued,'' and even engaged in Gargan's speculation about ''possible vice presidential candidates [to run with him]. I left the meeting, with him saying that he was a businessman, not a politician, and that he was not interested. But I remember when I left, he said, 'You know, Jack, I'm a man of action. If I see a poisonous snake, I don't call a committee to kill it.' And I said, 'Well, Mr. Perot, I'm a man of action, too, and when I see a man who ought to be president, I go out to get him.' '' It seemed a serendipitous meeting, and Gargan took it from there.

A few days later at a THRO town meeting in Seattle, he asked those in attendance: ''What do you think of Ross Perot for president?'' Again he got an enthusiastic response, as indeed he continued to get as he traveled the circuit of anti-Congress, anti-establishment citizens like himself.

Although Gargan had not met Perot before he visited him at his Dallas office, the two men had talked on the telephone. In 1990, when THRO began to get some national publicity, Perot had called its founder and offered his help. Gargan told him he didn't need any right then but wouldn't forget his offer. In April 1991, Gargan invited Perot to address a meeting of about sixty better-government groups in Tampa, but Perot begged off, pleading another engagement. Soon after, THRO's steering committee met and unanimously voted to ask Perot again. Gargan did so, promising him a big audience by throwing the meeting open to the public. Perot said he'd be there.

That was enough for Gargan, and after his first in-person meeting with Perot on May 30 he flew to Kansas City and made what he now calls his "historic" announcement of the Draft Perot movement. Then he began making plans for the Perot speech that he saw as the spark that would ignite the drive to put him in the White House.

On November 2, about 3,000 residents of the Tampa area packed into the Thomas Jefferson High School to hear the rags-to-riches Texas celebrity. Gargan had run a newspaper ad in *USA Today* announcing the meeting and forty-two state representatives of THRO showed up. When Perot arrived, he was greeted with signs held aloft throughout the audience, paid for by Gargan, that said: PEROT FOR PRESIDENT and ROSS FOR BOSS.

On hand to introduce him was 1980 independent candidate John B. Anderson, recruited by a friend to do so although Anderson had never met Perot. Anderson in his 1980 campaign had built on the work of former Governor George Wallace of Alabama in 1964 in opening state ballots to independent presidential candidates, becoming the first such candidate to qualify for ballot position in all fifty states. Anderson said later he was "mildly taken" with Perot at the time "because of his plainspoken ways," although he recalled that Perot was not overly enthused about being introduced to the crowd by him. "Ross wanted the band to play "the Star-Spangled Banner" rather than my introduction," Anderson remembered.

Perot's theme was "It's Your Country"—a slogan that voters all over America came to recognize as synonymous with the super-patriotic, feisty computer services magnate. As he spoke, eight or ten THRO members planted by Gargan in the front row began to chant: "Run, Ross, Run!"

When the speech was over, to ringing cheers and applause from the audience, Gargan got up and made the pitch again. "I don't know about you folks," he said, "but I think this is the man who ought to run for president." The place erupted in cheers again, as a smiling, noncommital

Perot stood there waving. At the airport, Gargan pushed him again. Perot told him: "I'm a businessman, not a politician." But when Gargan would not let up, Perot said, "We'll see," and boarded the plane.

"I just kept on his case," Gargan said later. In phone calls and letters over the next three months, he continued to urge Perot to run. "You have no idea what support you have out there," he would tell his target, but the answer was always the same: "Jack, I'm not a politician."

In THRO's newsletter to more than 100,000 members around the country in late January 1992, Gargan ran a box that said: "If you think Ross Perot should be a candidate for President of the United States, here's his address. Here's his phone number." In short order, Gargan said, "his secretary told me he was absolutely inundated with letters and phone calls."

Ross Perot was hardly the first nonpolitician to come down the pike and find himself the quarry of others who wanted him to run for president. But most of those who got anywhere at all were recruited by politicians, not a host of private citizens. That was so with Generals Dwight Eisenhower and Douglas MacArthur, and in both cases they made their entry into presidential politics through the Republican Party, not as independents. Members of THRO and others who wrote or phoned Perot were Republicans, Democrats, Libertarians and independents of several stripes, and they were motivated not simply by the inspirational Perot story and his no-nonsense, it's-that-simple approach to problem-solving.

An essential ingredient of their interest in him was their increasing disgust with politics-as-usual, with the whole political process and with the men and women who practiced it professionally. That was the reason most members of THRO were involved in that organization, and many, many others who were not members shared their frustration with the way things were in the politics of the country. Ever since the election of John F. Kennedy in 1960, voter turnout had dropped every four years, until by 1988 only about half of all eligible voters bothered to cast votes for president.

Anti-incumbency seemed to be sweeping the country and veteran members of Congress by the scores began announcing their intention to retire, either out of concern that they would be rejected at the polls or because they too were frustrated with the inability to get things done. Perot over the years had built a reputation in business—and in derring-do, as in the rescue by a Perot-hired team of his employees held hostage in Iran—as, he would put it, a can-do kind of guy. When he talked about "cleaning out the barn" or "looking under the hood," listeners understood what he was saying. Coming from a politician, it all might sound like hokum, but Ross Perot not only wasn't a politician but he clearly shared the contempt for them felt by millions of average Americans as another presidential election approached.

Gargan kept calling and writing Perot, urging him to become a candidate, to no avail—until Gargan got a phone call from Perot in late February telling him that he was going to be on the CNN's *Larry King Live* interview show. Unbeknownst to Gargan, another private citizen, lawyer-businessman John Jay Hooker of Nashville, had also been on Perot's trail, trying to persuade him to become a presidential candidate. The previous October, before Perot made his speech to THRO in Tampa, Hooker, a former Democratic gubernatorial and senatorial candidate in Tennessee, had telephoned him and made the same pitch as Gargan had, coming at Perot from a somewhat different angle.

"Let me ask you a question," Hooker began. "Do you think the country is governable, with the deficit we have, and the racism and the rest of it? What would you do?" The questions started Perot's motor, and he began to talk. "Twenty minutes later he stopped," Hooker recalled. "I never had heard a stronger voice. He rang a bell with me. All the talk, he said, was about dividing the pie, when the answer was you had to make the pie bigger." Perot made the argument that was to become familiar to television viewers and listeners in the next months, that the answer to economic recovery was rebuilding the nation's manufacturing base and then expanding American exports. It was exactly what Hooker wanted to hear.

Through November and December, Hooker had been calling Perot three or four times a week, he remembered, with Perot always saying he wasn't interested in becoming a candidate but nevertheless continuing the conversations. "On December 18 I bet him a dollar he would run. He bet he wouldn't," Hooker said.

In early February, Perot was in Nashville to do a radio interview. The night before, he met with Hooker and they talked for four hours in Perot's room at the Stouffer Hotel, during which time Hooker told him at one point he could be "another Eisenhower." Perot replied: "I'm no

Eisenhower," to which Hooker responded: "You could be. Give people a chance to make you one."

In advance of the meeting, Hooker had been doing research on how an independent candidate for president gets on the ballot in the various states. He had talked to Richard Winger, a California expert in the field, and Winger had sent him several memos, which Hooker had dispatched to Perot, writing across the top of the first one: "Ross: We've got plenty of time. Let's go!"

The next morning, after the radio show, station WLAC had a small reception for Perot to which about fifty prominent citizens of Nashville were invited. Perot spoke and answered questions. To Nancy Sanders Peterson, a local businesswoman, Perot came off as another politician getting ready to be a candidate, although he hadn't said so, limiting himself to critical comments about President Bush and Congress. Finally, she raised her hand and, as she recalled later, said: "You sound a lot like a Monday morning quarterback. . . . Are you going to run? If not, why? And if you won't be head coach, who would you recommend?"

Perot dodged, saying he would be a square peg in a round hole in the White House. But she pressed him: "Well, under what conditions would it take for you to run?" Perot pondered for a moment, then blurted: "I really am not interested in being in public life, but if you feel so strongly about it, register me in fifty states. If it's forty-nine, forget it. If you want to do fifty states, you care that much, fine, then I don't belong to anybody but you. I would not want to run in any of the existing parties because you'd have to sell out."

A reporter for *The Nashville Tennessean* wrote a short story about the reception under the headline "President Perot?" and so did *The Nashville Scene,* a local alternative weekly, but neither got much attention outside Nashville. Hooker, though, saw an opening and seized it, functioning in the next months as a sort of midwife to the birth of a Perot candidacy.

First he called an old friend, Bert Lance, the former budget director in the Jimmy Carter administration and later Democratic Party chairman in Georgia, for advice. Lance told him he had to get nationwide publicity for what he was doing, and he suggested interviews with prominent Washington correspondents or with Larry King.

Hooker was a frequent viewer of the Larry King show and liked that idea. He didn't know King but one of his good friends, John Seigenthaler, retired editor of *The Nashville Tennessean*, did. Hooker got him to call King and ask him to accept a phone call from Hooker. "Tell the guy to call me," King said. Hooker did, filling King in on his conversations with Perot, although he did not mention the business about running if voters put him on the ballot in all fifty states.

It so happened that Perot was already scheduled to be on King's show, but Hooker sparked King's interest in Perot's presidential musings. (Later, at a chance meeting with Seigenthaler, King told him: "If you hadn't called, I never would have taken that call. Now I'm making history.")

When Perot phoned Gargan and told him he was going to be on the show on February 20, that was the first Gargan knew about it, because he and Hooker were unaware of the Draft Perot activities of the other. "All this time," Gargan said later, "Ross never once told me about John J. Hooker and he never told John J. Hooker about me"—behavior that later became more understandable as Perot insisted that the whole draft business had developed strictly from spontaneous combustion among his "volunteers."

Subsequently, a producer for the Larry King show called Gargan to ask whether it would be a good time to ask Perot about a presidential candidacy. He wasn't in his office but his secretary, who was privy to the conversations her boss was having with Perot, said she was sure it was.

Hooker had also been urging Patrick Caddell, the longtime Democratic pollster now living in California and informally advising Jerry Brown in his own insurgent presidential campaign, to talk to Perot. Caddell had long believed that the country had grown so disillusioned with politics-as-usual that voters were ready to rebel through the ballot box, if only they could be persuaded they could make a difference, and if only there was someone on the scene who could so persuade them.

Caddell had done polling for Hooker in his unsuccessful runs for statewide office in Tennessee but had not heard from him in some time when Hooker called out of the blue and asked him what he thought about Perot as a presidential candidate. Caddell told him it was an intriguing idea and in fact, although he had never met Perot, had been thinking about calling him. Hooker, who had mentioned Caddell to Perot as someone with ideas about insurgent politics, encouraged him to do so.

Caddell called, telling Perot he knew he didn't want to run for president but wanted to talk to him about building a political movement. Caddell flew to Dallas, where Perot met him at the airport for a long lunch and talk, in which Perot continued to express no interest in running but listened intently as Caddell laid out his thoughts about the possibilities of an anti-establishment movement.

Caddell at that time was involved in a project dealing with interactive television that dovetailed with Perot's own interest in creating "electronic town-hall" meetings through which to cull public sentiment on major issues. The two hit it off. Among other things, Caddell told Perot that as a result of John Anderson's legal steps in winning ballot access in Ohio in 1988, he could not be kept off the ballot anywhere if he did decide to run. Later, back in California, Caddell sat down and wrote Perot a long personal letter laying out why he should do so.

On the day of the Larry King show, Perot and his wife, Margot, checked into the Hay-Adams Hotel just across Lafayette Park from the White House, had dinner, and Perot departed for the CNN studio while she returned to their room to watch the show on television. King, noting the mood of voters who "wished somebody else were running, and some undoubtedly have this guy in mind," began with the obvious question: "Are you going to run?"

Perot's response was unequivocal: "No."

"Flat no?" King asked. The answer wasn't what he had been led to believe it would be from his conversation with Hooker.

"Getting all caught up in a political process that doesn't work," Perot said, ". . . I wouldn't be temperamentally fit for it." King reminded him that Hooker "is strongly urging you to do it." Perot acknowledged that he was getting "a tremendous number of calls and letters," but he then changed the subject, giving King's audience a taste of prime Ross Perot as a national Mr. Fix-it.

The host began a long discussion of what was wrong with America by asking him to "give me something Ross Perot would do if he were king." Perot replied that if he had one wish "it would be to have a strong family unit in every home. It's the most efficient unit of government the world will ever know." Then he launched into a sermon that would soon be familiar to millions of Americans:

"The first thing I'd like for you to do, all of you, is look in the mirror. We're the owners of this country. We don't act like owners. We act like white rabbits that get programmed by messages coming out of Washington. We own this place. The guys in Washington work for us. They are our servants. . . . The second wish is that everybody in this country would start acting like an owner. . . . The third thing I'd ask for is the electronic town hall. . . . With interactive television every other week, say, we could take one major issue, go to the American people, cover it in great detail, have them respond and show by congressional district what the people want. Now don't you think that would kind of clear Congress's heads about whether or not to listen to folks back home or listen to their foreign lobbyists on an issue? Sure it would."

Perot was just getting warmed up. Soon the Rossisms were flowing out like a swollen river:

On shaping up American business: "If we have a losing football coach, we know what to do—get a new coach, get a new quarterback, start with basics, clean it up. . . . Our primary problem in this country now is to create taxpayers. You create taxpayers by building strong growing companies. . . ."

On special interests in Washington: "Let's clean up the system first. . . . We pass a simple law. We, the owners of this country, tell the guys: pass a law that if you were elected or appointed or worked in Washington, you cannot be a lobbyist for a foreign government, foreign individual for ten years. You go to Washington to serve, not to get rich. . . ."

On trade with the Japanese: "When they do a negotiation for an industry the most experienced people in their industry put together a plan. We've got a bunch of young people that blew up balloons in the election. . . . My favorite story is when they brought trucks into the United States and got them declared cars, and cut the import tariffs from twenty-five percent to two and a half percent. That's like getting an elephant declared a horse at the dock."

On dealing with the federal deficit: "We can't waste a year on stupid jump-starts. Novocain-in-the-knee shots, that sort of thing."

King interrupted to get the conversation onto the crop of candidates who at this point were challenging President Bush. Perot said he respected them for running but added "there's some wonderful people in the country who ought to be running who are not. I wish they would run." It wouldn't, however, "be appropriate for me to name any," he said. But he did have kind words for Democrat Paul Tsongas when King asked about his eighty-six-page agenda for economic revival.

"He is thinking," Perot said. "It is orderly. It is logical. It involves pain. It involves sacrifice. That's another thing—not to aim it at any one candidate—look for a candidate that has the guts to look you in the eye and tell you, 'This won't be pretty.' [Just as Ross Perot was now doing.] You know, going to the dentist to get your teeth fixed has a little pain attached to it, but it has a long-term benefit. We cannot go from where we are to where we need to be on a pain-free trip."

As for President Bush, Perot said that "in all candor" he didn't believe he understood business; that in his overriding interest in international affairs he just "doesn't like to work on domestic issues [but] I think he realizes now he's got to get into it. My unsolicited advice, and I hope it doesn't offend him, is to get a bunch of people around him that understand this and go to work on it night and day." When King asked whether he would volunteer, Perot replied: "Only if they're serious. And I will not be used as a Hollywood prop . . . because they've used me before. . . ." He didn't elaborate—not right then.

It was not until a caller from Plattsburgh, New York, asked Perot what voters "as the owners of this country" could do to tell "the people in Washington and all the other bureaucrats to do what we want them to do" that he gave the listeners and viewers a hint of what specifically he had in mind.

"Well, it's this simple," he began. "You know, I go back to when people are always asking me to run and I explain to them that one of the reasons I don't want to run is I don't think any one person can do this job. . . . For example, whoever you decide to back, you're going to have to stay in the ring after Election Day. . . . Just that one person . . . has got to have your organized visible support to make this system work. . . . We can have a revolution in this country. I urge you to pick a leader that you're willing to climb in the ring with, stay with, stay the course."

For the moment, Perot let it go at that. After a few more callers, none of whom picked up on what Perot was suggesting, and with time running out for the show, King very casually made one more try at the obvious question:

KING: By the way, is there any scenario in which you would run for president? Can you give me a scenario in which you'd say, "Okay, I'm in"?

PEROT: Number one, I don't want to.

KING: I know, but is there a scenario?

PEROT: Number two, you know, nobody's been luckier than I have. And number three, I've got all these everyday folks that make the world go round writing me in longhand—

KING: Is there a scenario?

PEROT (riding right over King's question): —now that touches me. But I don't want to fail them. That would be the only thing that would interest me. And so I would simply say to them and to all these folks who are constantly calling and writing: if you feel so strongly about this, number one, I will not run as either a Democrat or a Republican, because I will not sell out to anybody but the American people—and I will sell out to them.

KING: So you'd run as an independent?

PEROT (as if King weren't there): Number two, if you're that serious—you, the people, are that serious—you register me in fifty states, and if you're not willing to organize and do that—

KING: Wait a minute. Are you saying—wait a minute.

PEROT: —then this is all just talk.

KING: Hold it, hold it, hold it, hold it—

PEROT: Now stay with me, Larry—

KING: Wait, wait, wait. Are you saying—

PEROT: I'm saying to the ordinary folks—now I don't want any machine—

KING: —this is a "Draft Ross Perot on an independent—"

PEROT: No, no, no. I'm not asking to be drafted.

KING: Okay.

PEROT: I'm saying to all these nice people that have written me—and the letters, you know, fill cases—if you're dead-serious—

KING: —start committees—

PEROT: —then I want to see some sweat—

KING: —in Florida, Georgia—

PEROT: —I want to see some sweat. Why do I want to see some sweat? I said it earlier. I want you in the ring. Why do I want you in the ring? Because I can't do the job, and nobody can do the job, unless you will go in the ring.

In the course of a few minutes, Perot had gone from unwilling citizen to reluctant candidate to the Man in the White House telling his supporters that he won't be able to get the job done unless they stick with him after the election. King seemed bowled over by the news scoop that appeared to have dropped smack in his lap.

"Well, wait a minute," he said to Perot, finally able to get a full sentence in. "Are you saying groups all across America, all across America, can now, in New York, Illinois, California, start forming independent groups to get you on the ballot as an independent, and you would then, if this occurred in fifty states with enough people, you'd throw the hat?"

PEROT: I'm not encouraging people to do this—

KING: If they did?

PEROT: —but the push has to come from them. So, as Lech Walesa said, "Words are plentiful, but deeds are precious." And this is my way of saying, "Will you get in the ring? Will you put the gloves on? And do you care enough about this country to stay the course?" Now I want your promise, also, that, if we [Perot laughs], you know, got lucky and climbed the cliff, you wouldn't climb out of the ring the day after election. You're going to have to stay there for the fight. Then all of these changes could be made.

Now he was wound up and ready to close the sale. "Now recognize," he said, "you're listening to a guy that doesn't want to do this. But if you, the people, will on your own—now I don't want some apparatus built. I don't want two or three guys with big money around trying to do this. Between now and the convention we'll get both parties' heads straight. Number two, I think I can promise you're going to see a world-class candidate on each side. And number three, by the convention, you might say, 'Cripes, you know, it's all taken care of.' "

In other words, Perot was suggesting, such a grass-roots effort would so scare the Democrats and Republicans that they would start listening to the average voter. "But on the other hand," he said, "we're set, and if you're not happy with what you see and you want me to do it, then I don't want any money from anybody but you, and I don't want anything but five bucks from you because I can certainly pay for my own campaign—no ifs, ands and buts—but I want you to have skin in the game. I want you to be in the ring. Now then, God bless you all who have written me and called me. The shoe is on the other foot.''

Having made his pitch, including the suggestion that volunteers kick in five dollars apiece just so they would feel they had a stake in the effort, Perot turned to King. "I expect everybody to go very silent at this point, Larry," he said, like a kid saying to the American people, "Put up or shut up," with the expectation that they would shut up. "That puts it to bed," he concluded.

Or so Ross Perot thought, or said he thought. The moment the show was over, the CNN switchboard in Washington lit up and stayed lit up. And when Perot got back to his hotel room, his wife met him incredulously with "I can't believe you did that!" Perot assured her that "it'll never happen," but moments later an envelope was shoved under the door. When Perot opened it he found a five-dollar bill—the first "skin in the game" from an anonymous supporter.

In Dallas, Perot's longtime lawyer and friend, Tom Luce, a 1990 Republican gubernatorial candidate importantly bankrolled by Perot in that losing effort, was working out on his treadmill at home and watching, unaware in advance of Perot's appearance. "I almost fell off," he remembered. And in Los Angeles, Hooker was sitting in a hotel room watching the show with Caddell when Perot made his offer to "the owners" of the country. Hooker and Caddell were elated that he had taken that step, and Caddell thought the fifty-state ballot challenge a particularly brilliant if risky move.

King meanwhile had gone from the CNN studio to his radio studio in suburban Arlington, Virginia, for his late-night call-in show. On the air, he started getting calls from listeners who wanted to know how they could reach Perot. "I told them I had no idea," King recalled. Perot had left no phone number to call, or address to write, at the end of the television show.

Early the next morning at Perot's office in Dallas, the switchboard was engulfed with calls. The volume was so great that Perot authorized the leasing of an 800 toll-free number, and in the next two weeks, more than a million individuals phoned asking what they could do in their own cities and towns to get Perot on the ballot. Employees of Perot Systems manned the phones, taking names, addresses and skills, without much idea of where to go from there.

Perot persuaded Luce, an unsuccessful Republican gubernatorial candidate in 1990 whose campaign debt of nearly a million dollars had been picked up by Perot, to organize the effort. He also asked Luce to call Caddell and solicit his advice on ballot access. Caddell flew to Dallas again and conferred with Luce, assuring him that Perot could not be blocked from any state ballot. (Much later, however, Luce pointedly told us that while Caddell had sent many memos to Perot, he had played no larger role than Hooker, Gargan ''and thousands of other people who were calling Ross . . . and throwing their two cents in.'')

Perot also told Luce, the lawyer remembers, that Gargan had researched the ballot access question thoroughly, and he asked Luce to meet with him and other informed Gargan associates. Perot was concerned, Luce said, that he not put people around the country to great effort if legal prohibitions would render their activities fruitless.

Gargan meanwhile, acting on his own, set up a coordinating committee in Washington, assuming his embryo efforts and experience in insurgent politics would be his ticket to a key role in the campaign. Gargan recruited Lionel Kunst, another veteran congressional critic and political maverick, ballot access expert Winger and others, telling Perot he was putting together a team that could be trusted and knew what to do to organize a successful petition drive.

Soon after, Luce called Gargan and asked him and his associates to come to Dallas. On March 7, they met with Luce at the Hyatt at the Dallas–Fort Worth Airport. Luce brought with him a platoon of lawyers from his own firm who, according to Winger, were ''totally ignorant about ballot access,'' and apparently none too happy to be dealing with ''outsiders.'' Luce said later the meeting was informative and ''got us way down the road,'' but he still hadn't satisfied himself it was doable.

When Gargan reported on the coordinating committee he had set up in Washington, he recalled later, ''they didn't like that at all. The shit really hit the fan. There was a very conscious effort of some of Luce's subordinates to dump me quick. They felt I was a threat to them. They branded me an opportunist. I told them all off.''

Luce acknowledged later that ''there was some friction early on'' about the opening of the Washington office and "resistance to that in the sense that I didn't think that ought to be done with respect to people that Ross really didn't know, and they ought not to be out using his name in raising money under his name when Ross had said he didn't want people contributing money." (Perot had, however, talked on the Larry King show about people putting "skin in the game.")

In any event, shortly afterward, Gargan was ordered to shut down the Washington office. Perot was upset, he was told, because when the office phone was called, "somebody's answering it saying, 'Perot for President.' " Gargan was aghast. "That's what grass roots is all about," he replied. But the office was shut down. "My theory is that Ross wanted to maintain top-down control," Gargan said later. "That's his style." The incident was another signal of things to come.

At the Dallas airport meeting, Gargan and his group cautioned Luce and his associates to avoid problems with the Federal Election Commission, before which Perot had already filed as a candidate under the agency's strict watchdog stipulations on any presidential campaign activity. They also immediately raised questions about Perot financing his own campaign, as he had said he would do in giving his supporters "a world-class campaign."

"I thought it was a mistake for him to use his own money," Gargan said later. Another of the "outsiders," a Washington public relations man named Mike Foudy, agreed. "I felt that if he just financed it out of his hip pocket," he said, "he would run the risk of being tagged a dilettante." He and others thought it was a much better idea to accept the limit of $100 from any one person, as Jerry Brown was doing. But Perot had made up his mind.

Gargan and his associates wrote to Perot, telling him he was making a mistake, to no avail. As they feared, cartoonists began drawing Perot with bags of money as his ticket of admission to the presidential race. "Tom, this is just the beginning," Foudy recalls telling Luce at the time. "Perot wanted to be drafted," he said later, "but he wanted it to be a controlled draft."

The immediate question that had Luce and the lawyers anxious, Winger said later, was getting on the ballot in Texas, which had an early deadline for the filing of petitions. The law stipulated that no one could sign who had voted in that year's primaries, which were in March, so that left only two months to collect the 55,000 signatures required. Consideration was given to hiring a firm to get them but the "outsiders" argued that it would be bad public relations for a campaign that was supposed to be driven by volunteers—the folks Perot had dubbed "the owners" of the country—to buy "hired guns" of the sort Perot spoke so vehemently against to do the job. Luce's lawyers were skeptical that volunteers could pull off this relatively sophisticated distilling of prospective petitioners, but finally agreed that the task should be left to the grass roots, which were already stirring in Texas and around the country.

Quietly, there was one prominent former political professional traveling to Dallas during this early period giving advice to Luce and Perot's chief business associate, Mort Meyerson, without any compensation. Hamilton Jordan, the prime architect of Jimmy Carter's winning presidential bid in 1976 and later his White House chief of staff, shared Perot's view that the country was in decline and needed basic reform, and he volunteered his help.

Jordan had been out of active politics, except for a brief unsuccessful bid of his own for a Senate seat from Georgia, since Carter left the White House, and at the time was a key executive at Whittle Communications in Knoxville, Tennessee, in its ambitious program to improve classroom education. He had been supporting the candidacy of Paul Tsongas as, he said later, "the only person in either party telling the American people the truth" about what needed to be done. But intrigued by Perot, Jordan began spending his weekends in Dallas, counseling Luce and Meyerson in whatever ways he could, but never expecting to get involved any deeper.

Perot during this period started working the television news and talk shows with a vengeance. He did CBS's *60 Minutes* and the Phil Donahue show, after which MCI, which by now had installed 100 new lines into the mushrooming Perot operation, reported a jam of 18,000 calls in one thirty-second period—unprecedented in telephone history. The response was so immense that a computerized call-routing system was installed from Tampa.

In mid-March, Perot addressed the National Press Club in Washington. He went through his litany of what was wrong with the administration and Congress, including the lack of business sense in coping with the recession. Of the $4 billion deficit, he mused that "maybe it was voodoo economics. Whatever it was, we are now in deep voodoo, I'll tell you that.''

Although Perot repeatedly disdained sound bites, nobody was better at spinning them out than he was. In this one he managed in a few words to remind voters what George Bush originally had called Ronald Reagan's economic agenda, which Bush then embraced, and then to ridicule his famous characterization of trouble as "deep doo-doo." But he never mentioned his own political musings until the first questioner asked: "Will you run for president?" Only then did he repeat the fifty-state challenge that had triggered the avalanche of phone calls around the country. He said he had told Larry King that "it's too complicated," but "to my amazement, and I guess everybody's amazement, there are people at work in fifty states on their own initiative. Now, will it happen? I don't know. The ball is in the owners' court.''

Later the same day, Perot did a long interview on C-SPAN, the public affairs cable outlet, repeating that if the people who had been writing to him "on their own, as the owners of this country, want to go out in fifty states with nobody programming them, nobody telling them what to do, and put me on the ballot as an independent, I will run as their servant.'' In all that followed, Perot continued to insist "the owners" were doing all the petition-gathering and other organizational efforts on their own with "nobody programming them, nobody telling them what to do.'' But his own very strong insistence on maintaining tight control of everything said and done in his name or concerning him ran directly counter to that contention.

Perot also said in the C-SPAN interview that if the fifty-state stipulation was met he would be obliged to name a running mate to qualify for ballot access in certain states. "I will have to have a vice president who I feel is a more qualified person than I am,'' he said. "I will not just reach for an empty suit to play golf and go to funerals. This person will have to be totally qualified to replace me if anything should happen to me.'' He said that "the acid test is could that person be chief of staff''—a unique notion of how a vice president would serve, reminiscent of Reagan's toying with the idea of putting former President Ford on the ticket with him in 1980 in what came to be referred to as a "co-presidency.''

Shortly afterward, citing the pressures of time, Perot selected a "provisional" running mate as a stand-in for his eventual choice, for the purposes of ballot qualification. He chose an old friend, former navy combat pilot and decorated Vietnam War hero, retired Vice Admiral James B. Stockdale, who had spent seven years as a prisoner of war in North Vietnam. From the start, it was clear that Stockdale did not meet Perot's own qualifications to serve as vice president, but he was, after all, only to be a seat-warmer for Perot's eventual choice.

All was not smooth sailing for Perot in these early public exposures, for all his talent in dominating an interview with his filibuster answers and it's-that-simple dismissals of tough questions. Appearing before a meeting of the American Society of Newspaper Editors, he bristled in the face of direct inquiries about his intentions and record, asking at one point: "Do we have to be rude and adversarial? Can't we just talk?" Once again, under pressure, Perot signaled things to come.

He was also learning the perils of speaking his mind, as when he threw out the idea on the NBC *Today* show that a fortune could be saved by eliminating Social Security benefits for wealthy individuals like himself. Attempts to get him to spell out in further detail how he planned to reduce and eventually eliminate the huge federal deficit were brushed aside with a promise to provide a comprehensive plan later.

Early on, also, came another warning signal—that Ross Perot was a man with light regard for the privacy of others and a penchant for sleuthing. In mid-April, *The Wall Street Journal* reported that two months earlier Perot had sent a lawyer and two airplane pilots in his employ to interrogate a prison inmate in Missouri about his claim that he had piloted an American Blackbird spy plane bringing George Bush from Madrid in 1980. The flight was alleged to have taken place after secret meetings with Iranian officials as part of the "October Surprise" to delay release of American hostages until after the Carter-Reagan election campaign, in which Bush was running for vice president.

The man, Gunther Russbacher, known as a veteran con artist with a record of falsely claiming associations with well-known people, was declared a fraud by the Perot aides after he was unable to answer questions about the Blackbird's operation. Perot acknowledged that he had sent his men to investigate after an appeal from Russbacher that he had been railroaded, but he dismissed the inquiry as "a simple surgical check on his credibility" and insisted he had no intention at all of trying to implicate

Bush in an October Surprise that could have rocked his hopes for reelection.

As Perot continued to work the television news and talk show circuit, Perot-for-president petition campaigns were springing up all over the country in a self-starting political operation unprecedented in its scope. The "owners" were picking up the ball that Perot had put "in their court" and running pell-mell with it. But their efforts were not entirely self-starting in many places. Perot's first financial filing with the Federal Election Commission showed he had spent more than $400,000 of his own money—still a far cry from his boast that he was ready to spend whatever it took—$100 million or more—to give the voters that "world-class campaign," but hardly peanuts either. And for all his expressed disdain for "hired guns" in politics, he started conferring with some of the best of them in Washington, a city he had derided in his National Press Club speech as one of "sound bites, shell games, handlers and media stuntmen who posture, create images and talk—shoot off Roman candles but don't ever accomplish anything."

As the Perot phenomenon grew, Perot also instructed a number of his key employees at Perot Systems, many of them former military officers, to oversee the development of the Perot petition efforts in the various states, dispatching them to give local volunteers guidance on how to qualify for the ballot in each state. In some states, more than one group sprang up, creating tensions and sometimes clashes. The Perot emissaries—later dubbed "the whiteshirts" by some of the "outsiders" because of their immaculate appearance and austere manner—reported the disorder back to Dallas, and Perot was not pleased.

But the petition drives were having such astonishing success all over, and the fledgling Dallas operation was having such trouble keeping up, that the grass-roots effort—the "prairie fire," some called it—just kept spreading of its own momentum, for all of Perot's penchant for control. Perot, with his talent for the pithy, told British interviewer David Frost that his volunteers were "moving like locusts across a wheat field."

The polls told the story: A *New York Times*/CBS News survey in late April had Bush ahead with 38 percent of those surveyed, to 28 for Clinton and 23 for the upstart Perot. A *Washington Post*/ABC News poll a couple of days later had it even tighter: Bush 36 percent, Clinton 31, Perot 30. Veteran political consultants began to sit up and take notice.

David Garth of New York, who had managed John Anderson's independent campaign in 1980 that got only 7 percent of the vote, drew this comparison: "We had no money. If Perot is in the twenties [in the polls] and can spend $100 million, and if he runs the right kind of campaign, he can get one third of the vote and win [in a three-way race]."

In Texas, where the petition drive was going gangbusters in spite of the stringent stipulations of the law, a poll by Texas A&M among 674 likely voters had native-born Texan Perot running first, with 35 percent, to 30 percent for Texas transplant Bush and 20 percent for Texas neighbor Clinton. "Put Perot against Bush and ask who is more the Texan," said veteran Republican pollster Richard Wirthlin, "and it won't take two seconds to answer that one."

The political implications were obvious: at a minimum, in a close race between Bush and Clinton, if Bush could be denied his "home" state and its thirty-two electoral votes, Perot could be the Bush spoiler. But although it was clear from the start that Perot had a special dislike for the president, he insisted that if he got into the race, it would be to win.

After what his volunteers had already achieved, Perot told David Frost, "Now it's my turn. I owe them a world-class campaign and they want a victory, not a 30 percent effort. . . . Let's go back into my life. I don't ever compete to be second or third. That is a characteristic, and I will admit it openly, and anybody that's ever been around me will say once you hunker down for the competition, whatever it is, you compete to win."

In the short span of two months—from Perot's appearance on *Larry King Live* to the end of April—the feisty Texas billionaire had moved from the status of oddity to potential political monkey wrench—or more. As the primary competition played out within the Democratic and Republican parties, the little big man with the crew cut and salesman's palaver was casting an increasingly long shadow over the presidential politics of 1992.

CHAPTER 13

NOT LISTENING

Two days after the votes were counted in the New Hampshire primary, President Bush—or, more precisely, White House chief of staff Sam Skinner—made a decision that on its face seemed to have nothing to do with the president's aspirations for reelection. A man named John E. Frohnmayer was fired as chairman of the National Endowment for the Arts. For those who knew who he was, however, the message was clear: Pat Buchanan had torn a gaping hole in the Bush campaign's right flank that required immediate repair.

In informed conservative Republican circles, the firing of Frohnmayer meant a recognition at the White House that Buchanan now constituted a serious political threat, not so much for the Republican nomination, but to the party unity essential to Bush's reelection chances in the fall. Bush simply could not afford defections among the right-wingers, so red meat had to be tossed their way, and quickly. John Frohnmayer was that red meat.

As chairman of the NEA, Frohnmayer for several months had borne the brunt of conservative rage for allowing federal funding of graphic and in some cases sexually explicit art. In October, Bush himself had suggested Frohnmayer should think about stepping aside. But like many presidents, this one found it difficult to do the face-to-face dirty work, and Frohnmayer hung on through weeks of continuing controversy and not-very-subtle hints that he had overstayed his welcome. "It was," one campaign insider said, "a comedy of errors."

It was no coincidence, however, that Frohnmayer, a lawyer from Oregon, was thrown overboard the same day Pat Buchanan attacked the NEA for "subsidizing both filthy and blasphemous art" and made it clear that he intended to make that record part of the debate in the March 3 Republican primary in Georgia. As Jim Lake put it later, "There was a real concern about the right, not just in Georgia. . . . [The firing of] Frohnmayer was a symbolic gesture to the right that needed to be done."

In a sense, Georgia was an ideal place for Buchanan to use the Frohnmayer issue in his campaign to force the president into retirement. Originally the conservative commentator-columnist had hoped to go from New Hampshire to the South Dakota primary on February 25, but he had been shut off the ballot there on a technicality. And when he appealed to Clayton Yeutter, the former secretary of agriculture who had taken over as chairman of the Republican National Committee, he was—to no one's surprise—brushed off.

But the Georgia primary a week later offered special opportunities. It had always been fertile ground for the most conservative Republicans. In 1976 Ronald Reagan defeated President Ford there by more than two to one, and in 1980 Reagan trashed George Bush, with 73 percent of the vote to 13. The hard-core Republicans in Georgia were white, suburban and conservative, but anyone could vote in either party's primary so there was also the possibility of a heavy turnout among "born-again" or evangelical Christians, who the poll-takers said had made up 60 percent of the Republican primary vote in 1988. It was not an electorate that would be happy with the federal government paying for dirty pictures.

Buchanan was well aware that he could not sustain his candidacy indefinitely simply by beating expectations as he had done with 37 percent of the vote in New Hampshire. "Somewhere you've got to beat the president in a primary," he said, "and then this firestorm we've talked about has got to ignite. There's no question that the daunting number of primaries in the next three weeks is an enormous hurdle to overcome, which is much higher than the first one.''

Just what Buchanan expected this ''firestorm'' to accomplish was never entirely clear. By the time the votes were counted in New Hampshire, the deadline for qualifying had already passed for more than thirty primaries. But Buchanan also suspected that if he could actually defeat the incumbent president, the doubts about Bush might force him to the sidelines and open the situation for someone, if not necessarily for Buchanan himself. On the other hand, he also recognized that Bush was a tenacious politician who unquestionably could amass the needed delegates if he simply slogged through the rest of the primaries, whatever his winning margins. In many states the Republicans, unlike the Democrats, awarded their delegates on a winner-take-all basis, which meant that victories in the expectations game—such as Buchanan's in New Hampshire—were worth nothing at the cashier's window, however gratifying they might be otherwise.

The one thing that was clearest to Buchanan was that the Georgia primary would be a great deal different from the test in New Hampshire. Although there was some obvious economic distress in parts of the state, the unemployment rate was only about 4 percent, well below the national average, and there was no single-minded preoccupation with economic issues as there had been in the earlier primary. The answer obviously was a strategy that relied most heavily on the social issues that would touch the nerves of those culturally conservative evangelicals who had become such an important element of the Republican Party.

Thus, it was no surprise when Buchanan unveiled a thirty-second television commercial playing on the NEA funding. It included a clip from a film called *Tongues Untied* that showed slow-motion pictures of gay black men in leather harness and chains dancing while the legend on the screen read: ''This so-called art has glorified homosexuality. Bush used your tax $$$ for This.'' And the audio said: ''In the last three years, the Bush administration has wasted our tax dollars on pornographic and blasphemous art too shocking to show. This so-called art has glorified homosexuality, exploited children and perverted the image of Jesus Christ. Even after good people protested, Bush continued to fund this kind of art. Send Bush a message. We need a leader who will fight for what we believe in.''

The accusation against Bush was obviously a bit of a stretch. The film-maker had received a $5,000 grant from the Rocky Mountain Film Institute, which had received the money from the American Film Institute, which in turn had received it from the NEA. And Bush supporters in Georgia howled that the ad was so tasteless it would backfire. "It just caused a firestorm down there," Buchanan recalled later, "and the Bush people went berserk." But the ad obviously struck a nerve with some voters.

And although Buchanan had been uneasy enough about the ad to have it test-viewed by his mother, the attack on the gays was a natural for a candidate who sometimes referred to them as "the pederast proletariat" and argued that AIDS was a divine retribution being visited on gays because of their sexual orientation. So Buchanan refused to back away from a commercial he insisted made a valid point. "The president has spoken about obscene and blasphemous art," he told reporters, "but he hasn't done anything about it. It's a pattern. He says one thing and does another."

The White House and Bush campaign strategists also understood the new realities of campaigning in Georgia rather than New Hampshire. The firing of Frohnmayer was not the only gesture made to the conservatives in the aftermath of New Hampshire and the recognition that Buchanan's showing there meant he was going to be a continuing problem. "It put him in good enough shape so we had to campaign at least through Super Tuesday," Lake said. So the White House also chose this time to put a hold on a proposed regulation that would have required churches to report any gifts over $500 to the Internal Revenue Service. The regulation was intended to give the tax collectors a cross-check on charitable deductions, but the churches feared it would have a chilling effect on their contributors, who would resist having their names included on government lists.

The Bush campaign also reacted sensitively to complaints from some evangelical leaders because its general chairman, former Secretary of Commerce Robert Mosbacher, had held a meeting with a gay rights organization—explaining that it had been held for the purely "personal reasons" of Mosbacher, who had a daughter who was openly gay. The White House also moved to stifle a plan by the Department of Veterans Affairs to open some veterans' hospitals to nonveterans as an experiment, an initiative that had evoked a hot response from the veterans' organizations that are so important as social centers in many smaller Southern communities.

The Bush campaign believed that the less intense focus on the economic issues in Georgia might allow the president to take approaches that might have been seen as irrelevant and even counterproductive when used on voters preoccupied with their jobs. One of those was Buchanan's vigorous opposition to the use of military force in the Persian Gulf a year earlier, a position that presumably would not sit well with Southern voters, who polling data indicated were more patriotic and supportive of the armed services than other Americans.

The campaign quickly produced a thirty-second television commercial featuring retired General P. X. Kelley, the former commandant of the Marine Corps. The spot described Buchanan as "Wrong on Desert Storm, Wrong for America" and depicted Kelley saying: "When Pat Buchanan opposed Desert Storm, it was a disappointment to all military people . . . and I took it personally. I served with many of the marines who fought in Desert Storm. The last thing we need in the White House is an isolationist like Pat Buchanan. If he doesn't think America should lead the world, how can we trust him to lead America?"

The commercial was noteworthy because it was such a direct attack on the challenger coming at a time when President Bush still was refusing to mention his name, thus observing a long outdated political myth that simply mentioning your opponent exalts his status. Bush was still talking about "those who didn't support us then and . . . those who second-guess us now" on the war, as if the voters didn't know about Pat Buchanan. In a speech to South Carolina Republicans in Charleston three days after New Hampshire, Bush said, "Let's not listen to the gloom and doom from all those intense talking heads"—his favorite phrase for those like Buchanan who appear on television talk shows—"who are happy only when they say something negative."

Although Buchanan may have been on the defensive on the Persian Gulf, he had issues of his own that seemed likely to have sting in the South. One of them was that Civil Rights Act of 1991 that was the last straw drawing him into the campaign in the first place. Speaking to the annual Conservative Political Action Conference in Washington, Buchanan made his case against the "quota bill" in terms of class warfare. "Now if you belong to the Exeter-Yale GOP club," he said, "that's not going to bother you greatly because, as we know, it is not their children who get bused out of South Boston into Roxbury, it is not their brothers who lose contracts because of minority set-asides, it is not the scions of Yale and Harvard who apply to become FBI agents and construction workers and civil servants and cops, who bear the onus of this reverse discrimination. It is the sons of middle America who pay the price of reverse discrimination advanced by the Walker's Point [Bush's Kennebunkport home] GOP to salve their social consciences at other people's expense. If I am elected, my friends, I will go through this administration, department by department and agency by agency, and root out the whole rotten infrastructure of reverse discrimination, root and branch.''

It was rhetoric worthy of George Wallace in his heyday twenty years earlier when the Alabama governor used to talk about the "the average citizen—your steelworker and your beautician" being wronged by the social manipulation of the liberals and "pointy-headed bureaucrats who couldn't park a bicycle straight." More to the point in 1992, it was rhetoric aimed directly at the supporters of David Duke, the rabble-rouser from Louisiana who had failed to qualify for the Georgia ballot. Although the former Ku Klux Klan leader was still officially a challenger to Bush and Buchanan, his campaign had never lifted off the ground even enough for him to qualify for federal matching funds. And, although Buchanan had once considered Duke a potential rival—he threatened mockingly in December of 1991 to "sue that dude for intellectual property theft"—he now knew that potential Duke voters could be reached with the right rhetoric.

Campaigning in small towns in the South, Buchanan was a master of innuendo and riposte in playing on their resentments. When he told an audience, for example, that his hometown of Washington had been a fine place "before all that crowd came rolling into town and took it," no one imagined he was talking about the liberal bureaucrats. The same was true when he complained in an interview about walking down Connecticut Avenue and finding "these guys playing bongo drums . . . in the town I grew up in.''

He was a master of derision, describing the vice president as "Little Danny Quayle" and establishment Republicans as "kennel-fed conservatives" and "Exeter and Yale Skull and Bones Republicans." He drew hoots of appreciative laughter when, borrowing a line from a television comedian, he said, "You know, I have a lot of respect for Teddy Kennedy. What other fifty-nine-year-old do you know who still goes to Florida for spring break?"

Buchanan's campaign in the Georgia primary was not, however, a well-crafted exercise. Indeed, he spent the entire weekend after the New Hampshire primary stumping in Florida, a state in which he knew he had no chance of winning and one that awarded its delegates on a winner-take-all basis. And after a two-day bus trip through small Georgia communities like La Grange, Perry, Fitzgerald, Griffin and Fayetteville, he detoured off for two days in South Carolina, in whose primary four days after Georgia's he was no factor, before finally returning to the Atlanta suburbs where the votes were.

On another day he ducked over to Tupelo, Mississippi, to put flowers on the graves of two Buchanan ancestors who had served in the Confederate army. When asked about the rationale behind his scheduling, he shrugged and laughed.

Bush, meanwhile, was focusing narrowly on what he saw as his challenger's vulnerabilities as well as his own. But he was still a snakebit candidate. With the primary just a week away, the president flew to California for a campaign fund-raiser and, with Barbara Bush at his side, paid a call on Ronald and Nancy Reagan that was designed to produce a public embrace for the network news. Instead it was an embarrassment. Reporters and camera crews who accompanied the Bushes to the Reagan home in Bel Air were left behind a gate wrapped in plain brown paper. There was no photo opportunity, no comment—only an official White House still photo showing the two couples smiling awkwardly into the camera.

Nor did Reagan attend the fund-raiser at the Century Plaza, a short block from his office. There was, the press was told, a previous commitment. The incident was all the more embarrassing because it came on the heels of a story in *The Washington Post* about the problems Bush was facing in winning California's fifty-four electoral votes. The story said Reagan had told friends that one of Bush's troubles was that "he doesn't seem to stand for anything"—which was just what Pat Buchanan was telling other Republicans every day. In Washington the whole episode was written off as "Nancy's revenge." It was no secret that Nancy Reagan had never been a Bush enthusiast from the time he was chosen for the ticket in 1980 over her friend Paul Laxalt.

Bush's campaign in Georgia was largely a return to the so-called values issues and media events that he had employed with such success in the 1988 campaign. Speaking to a party rally in Atlanta, he drew cheers when he played off Buchanan's slogan, declaring "We put America first so long as we put family first" and repeated such bromides as "parents know better than some bureaucrat in Washington, D.C." and "yes, we believe there's a place for voluntary prayer in our children's classrooms."

There was nothing subtle about the Bush strategy. On the final Sunday before the primary, Episcopalian Bush had been scheduled to attend services at the Peachtree Presbyterian Church, one of whose parishioners was an old friend. But early that week the campaign, in a message to the born-agains, announced he would attend services, instead, at the First Baptist Church of Atlanta, a congregation of some 15,000 Southern Baptists whose services were regularly televised to a wide audience throughout the state.

The economic issues that had dominated the Republican campaign were largely overlooked in Georgia. But in an election eve interview published by *The Atlanta Journal* on primary day, the president took a further step to clean up his image, confessing that the 1990 budget agreement with Democratic leaders of Congress that raised taxes had been a "mistake" he would not repeat. "Listen," he said, "if I had it to do over, I wouldn't do what I did then for a lot of reasons, including political reasons." Bush said he thought the deal would result "in total control of domestic spending and now we see Congress talking about raising taxes again."

In a separate interview the same day with conservative columnist Cal Thomas, Bush also pointed to the tax increases Ronald Reagan had felt obliged to approve in 1982 but later was sorry he had accepted. "But he had to do it and he regretted it," the president said, "and I had to do it and I regret it." The strategy was obvious. Bush and his campaign advisers had recognized that reneging on "read my lips" had become such a continuing vulnerability that there was no choice but to try to put it behind him once and for all.

When the votes were counted election night, it was clear that Bush had not yet solved his political problems. He won Georgia with a respect-able 64 percent of the vote, an improvement of eleven points over his New Hampshire total, to 36 for Buchanan, almost identical to his vote in the earlier primary. "We've done it again," the ebullient Buchanan told his followers without explaining how losing almost two to one qualified as a success. Bush confined himself to another written statement designed to placate the rebellious within his party. "To those who have been with me in the past but did not vote for me today, I hear your concerns and understand your frustration with Washington," he said, implying that these were protest votes against some amorphous "they" rather than George Bush personally.

The figures from exit polling and returns from other primaries on March 3 sent warnings to both candidates. Bush won Maryland by 70 to 30 percent and Colorado by 68 to 30—with Buchanan achieving his 30 percent in each state without doing any significant campaigning in either. That performance suggested that the conservative commentator's candi-dacy was almost irrelevant, because there were 30 percent of Republican voters opposed to Bush anywhere. That point had already been demon-strated in South Dakota, where 31 percent of Republicans cast their votes for "uncommitted" after Buchanan failed to win a place on the ballot. Viewed in that light, Buchanan's strenuous campaigning in New Hamp-shire and Georgia was worth about 6 or 7 percent.

On the other hand, the evidence that this hard core was consistently testing out at 30 percent was a menacing reality for the president. These were, after all, Republican primaries, and defections of that scale from an incumbent Republican president were more than he could accommodate in the general election.

The exit polls in Georgia and Maryland also uncovered some bad news for George Bush. In each state one Republican in seven said they intended to vote for a Democrat against Bush in November and more than one third said they disapproved of Bush's performance in office. And despite the Bush campaign's attempts to exploit the Persian Gulf War issue in Georgia, only 12 percent of voters there said it influenced their votes. In short, although the president seemed to have a clear field toward the nomination for a second term, he had done little or nothing in these first primaries to alter the perceptions that made him a vulnerable incum-bent. And his campaign was still being compromised by tensions and poor communications between the White House staff under Sam Skinner and the political operation being run by Bob Teeter.

Criticized on the outside as being ruthlessly political, the Bush operation on the inside in 1992 was at times laughably scrupulous. According to Mary Matalin, who was chief of staff at the Republican National Committee before becoming the Bush-Quayle campaign's deputy manager, White House counsel C. Boyden Gray imposed a rule requiring strict separation of political and policy discussions, presumably to avoid running afoul of Federal Election Commission regulations. Yeutter and other party officials, Matalin recalled, "could not meet with any cabinet member unless there was a lawyer present and no policy discussions took place. One time Boyden found out that we were having a meeting with Lou Sullivan [secretary of health and human services] to talk about black turnout, black registration, and Boyden canceled the meeting." Matalin sighed: "See what I mean about the White House?"

When Skinner took over from the dictatorial Sununu, she said, the White House and the campaign committee moved on their own tracks. "There was no synergy," she said, "and if you don't have it, you're certainly not going to get it in the middle of the campaign." If she had to talk to somebody on the White House staff about a political matter, Matalin said, she had to notify Teeter, who would call Skinner, who would call Gray to get approval. "People at the White House were freaked out," she said. If she called someone there to convey or ask for information, she said, she was likely to be told: "I can't talk to you."

As a result, Matalin said, "an immediate impediment was put up between the two structures." In addition, she said, "we soon discovered that the English language was heard in two different ways. We heard it politically and they heard it governmentally." In other words, when the campaign was addressing a matter in terms of the reelection effort, the White House continued to look at it in policy terms. Something that might be considered helpful to advance the president's reelection would not be timed for optimum political impact because the White House did not think in those terms, and did not look to the campaign for political guidance.

Such problems, however, mattered more in the long term than in the short. Buchanan was effectively all through as a challenger, although he obviously threatened to be a continuing irritant to the president. The conservative commentator had used an appearance on the David Brinkley show on ABC to send what he called "a signal . . . that I was ready for a cease-fire in place" if he lost in Georgia. If Bush were the nominee, he said, he intended to support him in the general election.

But when Newt Gingrich, the Georgia congressman who served as Republican whip in the House, and longtime Bush political lieutenant Rich Bond, now chairman of the Republican National Committee, both lashed out at Buchanan because of the NEA commercial, and Gingrich on television compared him with David Duke, Buchanan got his back up. He said he would fight it out all the way to the end. "I said, 'California, here I come.' . . . and so you were sort of locked in to going to California"—to competing through the final primaries in early June. "Tell Little Richard [Bond] we'll see him in Orange County," Buchanan said, for emphasis. Bond had replaced Yeutter as party chairman in a move to bring more partisan political experience to the post. But in this instance Bond's aggressive style only seemed to exacerbate the situation.

In the days immediately after the Georgia vote, the president plunged into full-scale campaigning across the South while his advisers in the White House and campaign operation conducted a semipublic debate over whether he should be behaving politically or presidentially. Bush himself, off for appearances in Florida, South Carolina, Tennessee, Louisiana and Oklahoma, said he wanted to make it clear "we're not taking anybody for granted." But Mosbacher told an interviewer that the president had "a million things to do" in Washington and should be back there.

The testiness and tension in the Bush campaign was apparent when even the usually good-humored White House press secretary, Marlin Fitzwater, lost his cool at the persistent questioning of the president and what he was doing. When Bush was about to make a speech at Oklahoma Christian University, most of the White House reporters were gathered in a press center in a building nearby to listen to the speech piped in on closed-circuit television and to write their stories, a customary procedure on White House trips. But Fitzwater suddenly walked in, ordered the sound turned off and told the reporters if they wanted to hear the speech, they would have to go to the auditorium. "I'm sick of all you lazy bastards," he said. The incident was trivial and Fitzwater later apologized, but it added more fuel to the perception of a campaign under great stress.

Buchanan, meanwhile, was continuing to display what was clearly overweening self-confidence, given his record to this point. Visiting the Alamo in San Antonio, he declared: "They said he's beat me seven to nothing. He's going to have to beat us fifty nothing. We're going to find some state where we take the king down and after that we're going to win and win and win."

As a practical matter, however, Buchanan had little left in his arsenal. He was shut out in the Super Tuesday contests on March 10, losing all eight Republican primaries by huge margins. He had hoped to attract a heavy vote in Michigan from blue-collar culturally conservative voters who had rallied behind George Wallace a generation earlier. But when the votes were counted on March 17, he came away with only 25 percent of the vote in Michigan, 23 in Illinois. The Michigan result, he said later, "was a great disappointment." He still had federal matching money available, nonetheless, so he tried several other states because "we needed a place to go before we went to California." But even in North Carolina, the home ground of arch-conservative Republican Senator Jesse Helms, he was able to get only 22 percent of the vote. It was clear by now that Buchanan's grand dreams of scuttling the president somewhere on the road to California had gone up in smoke.

One old political and personal friend, however, counseled him against carrying the fight to the Golden State. He called Nixon, now an expatriate in New Jersey but still the self-styled world's greatest political expert, after his Michigan loss to report his progress. "Nineteen [defeats] for nineteen. Not bad, eh?" Buchanan informed him. Nixon replied: "Buchanan, you're the only extremist I know that has a sense of humor." But Nixon warned him about California: "Bush is going to lose [the state] and they'll blame you."

If George Bush had a problem, however, it was not Pat Buchanan; it was his own weaknesses as a candidate and national leader, and particularly the poverty of his understanding of, and interest in, domestic issues. His flaws were never more evident than they were in the wake of a jury verdict freeing four policemen who had been shown on a videotape beating a black man named Rodney King a year earlier. The riots that exploded in South Central Los Angeles were the most destructive in the history of the United States—fifty-three deaths, more than 2,000 injured, 5,000 fires that destroyed hundreds of small businesses, damage estimated to exceed $1 billion. Millions upon millions of Americans watched them unfold on their television screens as the first hours of racial rage evolved into days of epidemic and systematic looting and burning.

Nothing in Bush's public career, his service as president for more than three years or his own intellectual interests, had prepared him for this crisis. Rather than flying to Los Angeles to confront the situation, the president remained in the White House for nearly a week, groping for a way to deal with a challenge in which the politics was far more complex than in attacking Saddam Hussein.

His first response, at a state dinner, was as insensitive as it was baffling: "The court system has worked. What's needed now is calm respect for the law. Let the appeals process take place." The president of the United States apparently was unaware that an unsuccessful prosecution has no right of appeal—that the Fifth Amendment in the Bill of Rights stipulates: ". . . nor shall any person be subject for the same offence to be twice put in jeopardy of life or limb. . . ."

Two days later Bush made a televised speech telling Americans that the turmoil in Los Angeles was "the brutality of a mob, pure and simple" rather than an emotional protest against either the verdict in the Rodney King case or conditions in the inner city. He also dispatched agents of the Justice Department and, later, a special team headed by David T. Kearns, the former Xerox executive serving as deputy secretary of education, to report on what the federal response should be.

Conspicuously out of the loop in those first days was the man who should have been most logically at the center of things, Jack Kemp, the former congressman from New York serving as secretary of housing and urban development. Kemp had won high marks for his aggressive promotion of a Republican urban agenda that included, among other things, a plan to allow public housing tenants to purchase their apartments, and the creation of urban enterprise zones in which tax incentives would encourage creation of jobs in the inner cities.

Because of that history, Kemp probably had more acceptability in the black community than any other Republican since Nelson Rockefeller twenty years earlier. But Bush had always considered Kemp a bore because he was so focused on issues and had such complicated ideas for confronting problems. When Kemp was on the list of potential vice presidential nominees in 1988, a friend of Bush cautioned us that there was no chance Kemp would be chosen. "George has visions of Jack arriving for lunch carrying a bunch of manila folders under each arm,'' he said. Moreover, despite Kemp's credentials as a devout advocate of supply-side economics throughout the Reagan years in the White House, he was viewed with suspicion by some of the most extreme conservatives within the Republican Party because of his determined advocacy of efforts to broaden the party by attracting more black voters.

As criticism of Bush's languor increased, the White House—as well as campaign operatives—began to recognize the president was suffering new political damage. The first reaction predictably was blame-placing. Press secretary Fitzwater was trotted out to say: "We believe that many of the root problems that have resulted in inner-city difficulties were started in the sixties and seventies''—when the Democrats were promulgating all those social welfare programs that didn't work. The line was so preposterous it offered an easy target for the leading Democratic candidate, and Bill Clinton quickly seized it, saying: "It's just amazing. Republicans have had the White House for twenty of the last twenty-four years and they have to go all the way back to the sixties to find somebody to blame. I don't care who's to blame. I want to do something about the problems.''

Bush, who had been scheduled to travel to Los Angeles long before the rioting, finally arrived on the scene six days after it had erupted— with Jack Kemp now conspicuously at his side for window-dressing. Bush made the obligatory rounds and was photographed talking with schoolchildren, inspecting a burned-out shopping center, meeting with merchants in Koreatown and black church leaders. "We are embarrassed by interracial violence and prejudice," he said. "We're ashamed. We should take nothing but sorrow out of all that and do our level best to see that it's eliminated from the American dream. We will do what we can.''

The television film showed an empathetic president but, as was the case with the economy, Bush had built no credibility on the question of what to do about the condition of American cities. He was confronted repeatedly by pickets and hostile questioners. When one suggested he was spending too much of his time with the wealthy, Bush replied: "I don't want to sound defensive, but why do you assume I am only concerned about Beverly Hills?'' The answer, of course, was that he had never demonstrated any concern for South Central Los Angeles until it went up in flames.

By the end of the visit, Bush was touting what he called an "action agenda" that he intended to press back in Washington. Unsurprisingly, it was made up largely of proposals from Kemp that the president had shown little or no interest in pushing for three years. But, with the polls showing Bush having lost five percentage points in a week, presumably because of the riots and his failure to respond more forcefully, Kemp was now back on the first team in the photo ops and the policy discussions alike—George Bush's new best friend.

The president himself was suddenly very visible in demonstrating his concern for the disadvantaged, popping up one day at a prenatal care clinic in Baltimore, another day with some black children at a playground in the Anacostia section of the District of Columbia. As always, however, there were little misfires to remind everyone that George Bush had a tin ear. On the second day of his trip to Los Angeles, he visited Scott Miller, a firefighter hospitalized in critical condition after being shot during the riots. The president commended Miller on his courage but, apparently at a loss for small talk, added: "I'm sorry Barbara's not here. She's out repairing what's left of our house [at Kennebunkport]. Damned storm knocked down four or five walls. She says it's coming along." Bush obviously was not equating the storm damage at his fancy Walker's Point vacation retreat with the riot damage in Los Angeles. But it was characteristic of him to say something that would allow that inference to be drawn. Miller, flat on his back, no doubt felt real sorry for poor George.

As a practical matter, there may have been nothing Bush could do immediately about the politics of the riots in Los Angeles. "By definition," Charlie Black said later, "Republicans are on defense when you've got inner-city riots and problems at the top of the news. . . . It was very unfortunate timing politically because it came at a time when you already had economic unrest and a lot of people had this insecure feeling about where the country was and where it was going. To have the worst urban riots in our history and people killed and all that, and huge problems for rebuilding and everything in a major city, it just reinforced the bad feelings about the country and about the government."

But it was also true that the riots had presented an opportunity for the president to display on a critical domestic issue the kind of national leadership he had shown in the war in the Persian Gulf only fifteen months earlier. The hard truth, however, was that this president was as unable to present himself as credible on urban problems as he had been on the economy. The riots, like the primaries earlier, had exposed political weakness rather than uncovering political strength.

George Bush's problems by this time were transcending the storm damage at Kennebunkport and the riot aftermath in South Central Los Angeles. It was true that by early June the focus on the riots had blurred and Pat Buchanan was out of the campaign, at least temporarily, for heart valve surgery after losing to Bush in every primary along the way. But the time and resources it took to deal with him made the Buchanan challenge, Teeter acknowledged later, "incredibly damaging."

Original plans to spend the first three or so months of the year getting the president's economic message in shape and sold to the voters, he said, had to be postponed. "I thought we had one more window where we could get those things done," he said, "but the window closed. . . . We spent all that time fighting Buchanan. . . . We knew he was a threat on the right. You just had to look at New Hampshire." There never was, Teeter said, "a big pro-Buchanan vote, but he became a vehicle for everybody who was mad at Bush on the economy."

And now, in addition to the Democrats harping on the president's failure to cope with the stagnant economy, there was this fellow Ross Perot stirring the bushes with his increasingly disturbing petition drive to put his name on the presidential ballot in all fifty states. It was impossible to predict how that phenomenon would play out, but it was abundantly clear already that Perot had no love for George Bush and was daily poisoning the political well against him with his wisecracks about the country being in "deep voodoo."

And then there was the trouble within Bush's own political family. Sam Skinner at the White House was infinitely more likeable than the departed Sununu but the reelection campaign was finding that the White House operation under him simply was not politically attuned to the opportunities of incumbency, or geared to exploit them. And proposals submitted from the campaign seemed to be going down a black hole.

It wasn't like that at all in 1984, when Jim Baker was the White House chief of staff masterminding the Reagan reelection campaign, or in 1988, when he oversaw the early Bush campaign while serving as Reagan's secretary of treasury and finally took over as campaign manager.

Baker was a man who knew how to make decisions quickly and firmly and get them implemented effectively and without delay. But Jim Baker was now Secretary of State James Addison Baker III, perched loftily over at Foggy Bottom and trotting the globe in a huge government jet on missions of war and peace. The last thing he wanted was to descend once again into the trenches of unseemly campaign politics. But something had to be done.

Two key White House figures who had often been at odds on economic matters, budget director Dick Darman and Bill Kristol, Vice President Quayle's chief of staff, encountered each other one day in this spring of uneasiness in a corridor of the Executive Office Building adjacent to the White House where each had his office. They agreed that genuine efforts had been made to make the political operation in place work under Skinner, and that they would continue to try. But maybe, they agreed, the only alternative was to get Baker back, and sooner rather than later.

That sentiment was widely shared at the reelection committee as well. Jim Lake was telling Teeter around the same time: "If we don't make a change over there [at the White House], we can't win." And there was probably only one individual who could persuade Baker to return—the man who had made him secretary of state, the president of the United States. Some internal lobbying clearly was in order.

On the Democratic side, meanwhile, Bill Clinton also had survived his party's primary in New Hampshire and had headed south, leaving behind the wintry weather and, he hoped, the pesky allegations of personal misbehavior that had nearly derailed him there. He knew he could count on a warmer climate in his native region. But how warm the voters would be, in this mecca of true-blue patriotism, to a candidate with a shady draft record was a question that still needed answering.

C H A P T E R   1 4

SALVATION

On primary day in New Hampshire, hours before Bill Clinton proclaimed himself the Comeback Kid on the strength of his second-place finish, chief Clinton strategist Carville was on a plane headed for Atlanta and the Georgia primary two weeks later, on March 3.

An old hand in Southern politics who had run the successful gubernatorial campaign of Democrat Zell Miller, now strongly in Clinton's corner, Carville figured that the Georgia primary, standing by itself on the Southern political calendar a week before the Super Tuesday collection of presidential primaries and caucuses dominated by Texas, Florida and other Southern states, could be the early breakthrough for his candidate. Miller conveniently had persuaded his legislature to move the Georgia primary date forward, out of the clutter of Super Tuesday, a move that offered Clinton a golden opportunity. With luck—and hard campaigning—Georgia could restore Clinton's image as a winner after the scars inflicted on him in New Hampshire, and set him up to emerge as the clear front-runner after Super Tuesday.

In focusing on Georgia, the Clinton campaign was assigning a low priority to the next two state contests on the calendar—the Maine caucuses and the South Dakota primary—without quite conceding them to the other candidates; neither of them would mean much if Clinton could win Georgia and then do well on Super Tuesday.

Tsongas, counting on at least a regional boost from his New Hampshire victory, set his immediate sights on Maine but also staked claims in the Maryland and Colorado primaries and in caucuses in Washington state, all on the same day as the Georgia primary, in the hope of offsetting an expected Clinton victory there. A Tsongas sweep from coast to coast would go a long way toward demolishing his image as a regional candidate. Concerned about such a sweep and deciding that Tsongas would be too strong in Maryland, especially in the Washington, D.C., liberal suburbs, the Clinton campaign assigned a higher resource priority to Colorado than to Maryland, while still focusing mainly on Georgia.

Tsongas also made a flying trip to South Dakota where, at a cattle auction, he stood out like a fully clothed man in a nudist colony. Kerrey and Harkin also headed for South Dakota and its primary a week away in a fight for identity as the Midwest candidate and modest salvation from their weak showings in New Hampshire. That left Jerry Brown, who elected to concentrate on Maine, on the basis that his guerrilla-style campaigning might be more effective in the low-turnout caucus process.

Brown, playing on Tsongas's support for nuclear energy, mobilized Maine's environmental activists and embarrassed Tsongas by holding him to a virtual tie. The first official tally was Tsongas 30 percent, Brown 29, Clinton 15, Harkin 5 and Kerrey 3. Although Brown claimed an edge on the basis of the final results later, in the perceptions game that dominated the news media coverage at this stage of the race, Tsongas's appearance of victory, however close, was what mattered.

Just as Clinton had done in New Hampshire, Tsongas chose to emphasize the positive—his margin over Clinton, not Brown, saying of the Maine result, "I feel fine about it. My fight is with Bill Clinton at this point."

Tsongas's view that the race had already become a two-man affair between himself and Clinton escaped most observers that early, but not Clinton. "The whole sense of how to deal with Tsongas came from Clinton," Grunwald remembered. "Right after New Hampshire, the campaign lost its equilibrium because you went from being in a multi-candidate field where it wasn't clear who would emerge from the pack to being in a virtually two-person race. And instead of being in this intimate setting where you could drive to everything and all you focused on was WMUR [the Manchester television station], then you were all over the map. It was a very different kind of campaign, and it took everybody a while to both focus on the message point of view and a logistical point of view, how to make that transition.''

"There was a period of time,'' Greer agreed, ''probably for about five days to a week, where through polls and focus groups in Georgia, Maryland and Colorado we were trying to assess how we should adjust the message of the campaign. More so than at any other point in the campaign, it was a point at which we were a bit adrift for a short period of time, probably because we had thrown everything into figuring how to come out of New Hampshire as the Comeback Kid. . . . And we were going into a territory like Georgia where we didn't know how the draft story was going to play.''

Grunwald remembered that ''Clinton was the one who really pushed everyone and said, 'Look, we are not doing this right. This is a two-person race. We have got to compare my plan to his [Tsongas's] plan and focus people on the economy, and which economic approach is going to work.' He dragged the campaign into the right message.''

Kerrey and Harkin, however, were not ready to concede that the race had already shaken down to Clinton against Tsongas. Each reasoned that if he could post a victory over the other in South Dakota, he could gain a toehold in the campaign as the prime challenger to Clinton, on the assumption still widely shared that Tsongas would fade outside New England and the East. And so the senators from neighboring Nebraska and Iowa worked the cold and barren prairie state as if it were a main event.

The other three major candidates, plus the super-longshot former mayor of Irvine, California, Larry Agran, joined them for a debate on farm and rural issues in Sioux Falls the Sunday night before the primary, but the real contest in the state remained between Kerrey and Harkin for practical survival.

Kerrey, who had started earlier than Harkin in South Dakota and had campaigned in a notably lower key, scored an impressive victory over him on primary night, winning 40 percent of the vote to Harkin's 25. Clinton, who had made little effort in the state, managed 19 percent, ahead of Tsongas's 10 and Brown's 4. Kerrey told cheering supporters: "Tonight we struck gold in the Black Hills of South Dakota . . . and tonight we begin a rush for gold, a rush for delegates in the South, the West and throughout this country."

As already noted, the next week's voting schedule, dubbed "Junior Super Tuesday" by the phrase-makers, included in addition to Georgia, Maryland, Colorado and Washington state, a primary in Utah and caucuses in Minnesota and Idaho.

What Kerrey did, however, was go south first, with the idea of ambushing Clinton there, only to shift gears and head west—too late to claim that region for his own. "The whole calculus," he told us after the election, "was that having finished third in New Hampshire, it was essentially over." Had the 1992 process begun in South Dakota, where he had a base, Kerrey said, the whole year might have been different. But, he said, after his New Hampshire showing out of his home region "in order for me to get back in the race, I had to get up on the board in the Western caucus states, and failed to do it. . . . Tactically it was probably a mistake to go into the South right after [the South Dakota primary]. If I had been smart, right after South Dakota I would have driven all the way to the West."

But south Kerrey went—and immediately made, in his own view, another mistake. Speaking at Spelman College in Atlanta, he did what he had said he would not do. Clearly in the context of the furor over Clinton's draft record, Kerrey stated flatly that "Bill Clinton should not be the nominee of our party because he will not win in November." If Clinton was nominated, he said, he was "going to be opened up like a soft peanut" in November. Shortly afterward, in a news conference, Kerrey said it wasn't Clinton's draft history that bothered him, but rather his insistence on blaming others for his current political problems concerning that record.

"I don't object if anybody who in conscience said, 'The [Vietnam] war is wrong and I will not serve,' " Kerrey said. "But that is not what we have. There is an effort to say, 'Once again my draft board did this,' or 'This was an honest mistake,' or 'Republicans were trying to do this to me.' There is an evasion of responsibility. And that is the problem and difficulty I have." He also lamented the fact that "it was the men and women who went to Vietnam who suffered when they came home, and all of a sudden all the sympathy in this campaign is flowing to somebody who didn't go."

The remarks, in light of Kerrey's earlier reluctance to criticize Clinton's draft history, were immediately taken by the assembled reporters as political hardball from a candidate scrambling to elbow his way back into contention, and Clinton deftly treated them as such. In a written statement from Denver, where Clinton was doing spadework in advance of the Colorado primary, he said: "I don't know which Bob Kerrey to respond to—the Bob Kerrey who repeatedly told the people of New Hampshire that he did not want this issue discussed, or the Bob Kerrey who's trying to tell the people of Georgia this is an issue today. . . . I hope that tomorrow he'll wake up as his old self, remind himself he came home as an opponent of the Vietnam War, remind himself of the facts of my case, that I did nothing dishonorable or wrong."

Demonstrating his own instinct for the political jugular, Clinton went on: "It appears that Bob Kerrey, like George Bush, would rather play politics with patriotism than address problems here at home. That's what George Bush will do in November when he points out that Bob Kerrey opposed Operation Desert Storm even after the conflict began." Working in a reference to Kerrey's opposition to the very popular Persian Gulf War effort was an old trick of Tricky Dick Nixon, and completely worthy of him.

"In retrospect," Kerrey told us after the election, "I made a mistake going after Clinton on the draft. It was an unusual moment at Spelman College." He had just given a speech, he said, "during which I ad-libbed a reflection about being in airborne school in Georgia." There, he said, he had been "stunned" that the enlisted men in his battalion "were mostly black, mostly from poor families and they did not seem to be qualified to be in airborne. And I said at the time to this black audience, mostly black kids, 'I bet a lot of these kids died.' I remembered that, I remembered the nature of the privilege that I felt, to have been able to go to college and get into officer candidate school, and how college mattered. And that was the message."

After the speech, Kerrey said, someone came up and told him he was one of Kerrey's drill instructors at the time and agreed. He told

Kerrey about a program that "lowered the standards of eligibility for the draft in 1968 and went out and got 100,000 poor kids who otherwise wouldn't have qualified, drafted them and sent them to Vietnam. So then I go into a press conference and I was asked about Bill Clinton's draft, and I just went high-order explosion.

"It was viewed as a calculated move. It was an emotional response to the moment, and a mistake. You don't get into a campaign and get all emotional, particularly on an issue like that, and drive something like that out. Because when I got to Colorado, that's all I heard about. So instead of going into Colorado as somebody who had won a Western state [South Dakota] in a primary, I went into Colorado as a guy who had just gone after Clinton on the draft in Georgia, which didn't help me much."

That one foray was the only one Kerrey made into the South in the week before the Georgia primary—a fact that fed the impression that he had gone down there directly from his South Dakota victory to hit Clinton between the eyes on the draft, to his own political benefit. In any event, he said later, his relations with Clinton, with whom he had served as a fellow governor, were "strained" thereafter.

With or without comments from Kerrey on Clinton's draft record, the issue was supposed to face its acid test in the South. The region's reputation as the most pro-military, patriotism-on-your-sleeve region in the country was well deserved. Dixie supplied an inordinate share of the nation's men and women in uniform and housed an overabundance of its military installations, thanks to the seniority of many of its members of Congress sitting on, and often chairing, strategic committees. But after the solitary Kerrey assault, little of a substantial nature was heard about Clinton and the draft thereafter. And in Zell Miller in Georgia, Clinton had one of his most outspoken and aggressive supporters and surrogates anywhere in the country. Miller, a decorated veteran, cast Clinton as a much-put-upon victim of scurrilous attack.

When Clinton came to Atlanta after his runner-up finish in New Hampshire, Miller told the cheering crowd that "maybe they'll stop treating him like the only fire hydrant at a dog show." He painted Tsongas as a pro-business Republican in Democrat's clothing and warned that he would lead the party "back down that well-worn path of defeat" that the Democrats knew so well, by being "on the side of the big CEOs and against the rights of shareholders."

Clinton himself, acting quickly on his view that he was now in a two-man race against Tsongas, took up the same theme in Colorado, where he hoped to prevent that feared Tsongas coast-to-coast sweep and at the same time establish himself as more than a Southern candidate. In a slashing, provocative press conference in Denver, he took after Tsongas as a "soulless economic mechanic" whose proposals to benefit business first at a time workers were in dire straits "smack of trickle-down economics." He ridiculed praise of Tsongas as having the courage to oppose middle-class tax cuts of the sort Clinton proposed, saying he was "tired of what is cold-blooded being passed off as courageous. . . . I fail to see," he went on, "what is courageous about telling people who have already been plundered in the 1980s" by the Reagan-Bush tax policies that benefited rich Americans "at the top of the totem pole who made a killing in the eighties" that there will be no tax cuts for them.

An indignant Tsongas replied: "Is Bill Clinton now our resident expert on courage? To suggest that saying yes to middle-class tax cuts is an example of profiles in courage is a phenomenally interesting definition of the term." Tsongas charged that Clinton's concern for the middle class was being driven by polling data indicating proposing tax cuts was good politics rather than good economics, and that if enacted they would drive up the federal deficit. This latter charge particularly angered Clinton, who had said repeatedly in talking of the tax cut for the middle class that he would make up for it by imposing higher taxes on the wealthy—the "fairness" theme that key Democrats in Congress also were pushing as a way of continuing to picture the Republicans as the party of the well-to-do.

In launching this attack on Tsongas, Clinton was revealing a developing resentment toward what he saw as a carping righteousness in the former senator. But Clinton was motivated in his verbal assault by more than passion. He was determined to focus the campaign now on his differences with the New Englander, and to underscore Tsongas's most glaring vulnerability—that he sounded like a Republican trying to win Democratic primary votes.

"I believe that the chief factor in the decline of America and our productivity is our failure to develop the capacity of our people and to organize our economy to compete and win," Clinton said in Denver. "Paul Tsongas believes the main factor is our failure to provide tax incentives to American business. . . . If you want somebody who talks tough but acts easy on the people at the top of the totem pole, you should vote for Senator Tsongas. If you thought the policies of the eighties were basically sound but need some good fine-tuning, you should vote for Senator Tsongas. . . . Franklin Roosevelt didn't get this country off its back by saying the only thing we have to fear is lack of venture capital.''

Clinton continued the attacks on Tsongas in television ads using a 1991 quote from *The Boston Globe* that had him saying if elected he would be ''the best friend Wall Street ever had''—a quote Tsongas said was taken out of context. Tsongas called party chairman Ron Brown urging him to get all the candidates to desist in negative campaigning, warning at the same time that ''if we continue like this for another three or four months, then we will have a very battered and bloody party'' going against Bush in the fall. He accused the Clintonites of having ''this kamikaze attitude that if they don't get [the nomination] they're going to take everybody else down with them.'' In the same breath, however, Tsongas said he had approved television ads of his own ''that demonstrate that we know how to fight back. We're now in a counterpunch mode.''

The next night in a debate in Denver, there was no smoking of any peace pipes. The battle was joined by Clinton in discussing energy policy in a state known for antinuclear environmental activists: ''We do not need to do what Senator Tsongas wants to do—to build hundreds of more nuclear plants to become energy independent.''

Tsongas broke in angrily: ''That is a lie. That is a lie. That is a lie.''

Clinton shot back: ''You don't want to build more nuclear power plants? Say you don't, then. Let's get you on record for the first time. Say it. Just say no. Just say no.''

Tsongas sidestepped the challenge, countercharging that Clinton had been running a ''misleading'' ad against him, and trying to pass the peace pipe. ''Take a pledge, let's all agree,'' he said. ''No ads. No attacking each other. No ads against each other.''

''What about your ad, Senator?'' Clinton asked, referring to Tsongas's latest ''counterpunch.''

''I started yesterday because you've been on my back for a long time,'' Tsongas said. He renewed his call for Clinton and the others to take a no-attacks pledge: ''Put your hand up. Put your hand up, Bill. No negative ad. Put your hand up.'' Clinton and the others ignored him.

Clinton, in going after Tsongas on the nuclear issue, was aware that it could benefit Jerry Brown, but his objective, again, was to keep Tsongas from winning both Maryland and Colorado and slaying his regional albatross. And he wasn't the only one to attack Tsongas. Kerrey and Harkin, both wanting to replace him as the alternative to Clinton, tried to undercut him with a Western audience to whom he was a stranger.

"I hate to keep reminding my friend Paul Tsongas that manufacturing is not the engine that drives our economy," Harkin said. "The engine is people." And Kerrey hit him as a Yankee out of his element. "Paul, you're from Lowell, Massachusetts, there's no question about that. You understand manufacturing in New Hampshire," he said. "What gives me pause is whether or not you understand agriculture and Western issues."

Tsongas shot back, reminding Kerrey he had run what was widely seen as a protectionist—and ineffective—ad in New Hampshire, and challenged him to air it in Colorado. "It was a lousy ad," Kerrey acknowledged. "Why would I want to put something on the air that didn't work?"

"The issue," Tsongas replied loftily, "is not whether it worked, but what you believe in." Saint Paul was in his pulpit again. At one point, Clinton remarked: "No one can argue with you, Paul, you're always perfect." Tsongas snapped back: "I'm not perfect, but I'm honest."

The Tsongas bashing continued, less heatedly, in two more debates over the weekend, one in Atlanta and the other at the University of Maryland. In the latter, Harkin charged that Tsongas had started the negative attacks against him as far back as the summer, and called for "no more of this self-righteousness." And Clinton defended his own ads on Tsongas's pro-business economic agenda, arguing that "the American people are entitled to know what the differences between our positions are, and if you won't tell them, somebody needs to."

Even as Tsongas was again pleading for his rivals to lay off negative ads, he was airing a new one on radio criticizing Clinton for an embarrassing gaffe relating to Jesse Jackson, in an obvious attempt to capitalize in Georgia, where blacks were expected to constitute as much as 40 percent of the primary vote.

Four days earlier, as Clinton was sitting in a television studio in Little Rock doing a series of interviews via satellite with out-of-state stations, an aide told him—erroneously—that Jackson had just endorsed Harkin in Jackson's native state of South Carolina. Unaware that there was a microphone open to a station in Phoenix, Clinton blurted out: "It's an outrage! It's a dirty, double-crossing, back-stabbing thing to do!" He then instructed an aide to call Jackson, according to a tape supplied by the Phoenix station, KTSP, and "say, 'Listen, I came to his house at midnight, I have called him, I have done everything I could for him.' . . . To hear this on a television program is an act of absolute dishonor. Everything he has bragged about, he has gushed to me about trust and trust and trust. It's a back-stabbing thing to do. . . . We'll see if I embrace him in public. . . . If he wants to talk to me about it, fine, but this is a terrible way to find out about it. . . ." (Media adviser Frank Greer observed later, laughing: "I warned him a thousand times about microphones.")

Now, in advance of the South Carolina March 7 primary, Tsongas's ad said of Clinton: "He didn't wait for the facts. No, Bill Clinton didn't wait to find out if it was true. He just attacked. The man he attacked, Jesse Jackson, the Reverend Jesse Jackson—Paul Tsongas doesn't go around attacking respected national leaders like Jesse Jackson."

Jackson, ever cool, had played down the incident, saying "the press would like to make this into an issue of controversy between the two of us, but we should not allow the campaign to be diverted onto these side issues." But the episode—and the fact that Jackson, while not formally endorsing Harkin, had campaigned with him in South Carolina—added one more page to the book of uneasy relations between Clinton and Jackson. It didn't help Clinton's image as the surefooted, controlled political robot, either.

Among black voters in Georgia, however, Clinton had more than enough other leadership support to weather the minor squall. Beyond Governor Miller, he also had an array of prestigious black leaders behind him, including Mayor Maynard Jackson of Atlanta and Congressman John Lewis, one of the authentic heroes of the civil rights movement of the 1960s. Such backing, along with Clinton's own established rapport with Southern blacks in an exceedingly low general turnout of only 9.2 percent, brought Clinton a sweeping victory in the state on March 3—despite last-minute jitters by Carville.

The success with the black vote in Georgia, Greenberg said, was "a learning experience" on how well a Southern white candidate with his own ties to other elements of the black political leadership and a connection of his own with black voters could do without Jackson prominently in his corner. It was a lesson that sustained Clinton in future dealings with him.

A severe case of nervousness nevertheless had gripped the Clinton strategists on the morning of Georgia and the other March 3 primaries. If their candidate didn't do extremely well in Georgia, beating expectations of his strength in a Southern state, and Tsongas ran a close second while winning Maryland, Colorado and Washington state, Clinton would be in trouble.

Clinton won a whopping 57 percent of the Georgia vote in the field of five against only 24 percent for Tsongas, with the other three candidates in single digits. Most significant, in polls taken as voters left their voting places, four of five Georgians interviewed said that Clinton's draft history had no effect on how they voted. If the draft issue was not buried, it certainly seemed to be in a comatose state now.

Tsongas, however, was not finished, nor was Jerry Brown. The former Massachusetts senator, showing strength outside of his home region, beat Clinton in Maryland, 40 percent to 34, won the Utah primary with 33 percent to 28 for Brown and only 18 for Clinton, and also Washington state's caucuses. Brown, a recipient of the fallout from Clinton's attacks on Tsongas on the nuclear issue, surprised again in Colorado by edging Clinton 29 percent to 27, with Tsongas at 26. Harkin salvaged the Idaho caucuses, with 30 percent to 28 for Tsongas and 11 for Clinton, and the straw poll at the Minnesota caucuses, with 27 percent to 19 for Tsongas and 10 for Clinton, but these latter two tests were insignificant and Harkin was on the ropes.

More so was Kerrey, who ran no better than fourth in any of these states and abandoned the race two days later, retracting his earlier observation that Clinton was unelectable. "With each passing day," he said, "it is clear that the only unelectable candidate is George Bush."

Clinton had won only one of the six tests on Junior Super Tuesday but it clearly had been the most important one, as a preview to the Southern-dominated Super Tuesday collection of primaries and caucuses a week later. Also significant, Stephanopoulos said later, was Brown's victory in Colorado, denying Tsongas grounds to claim he was a truly national candidate. "I think I could make the argument," he said, "that

Brown won Clinton the presidency when he won Colorado. I think if Tsongas wins Colorado, you're in a different ballgame.''

After the fact, Tsongas agreed that the Colorado defeat was the one that finally doomed his campaign. To try to counter the nuclear power issues, he and Dennis Kanin had decided to run a rebuttal commercial over the final weekend but they could not come up with the money to produce and air it in time. "So we went from an eight-point spread to third place," Tsongas said. "That was the moment the brass ring was lost."

Greenberg's polls found a 10 percent "bounce" for Clinton out of the Georgia victory—an increase in his standing in the polls—and it helped convince other Southerners, Greenberg said, that a Clinton vote was okay even after all his publicized troubles, especially concerning his draft record. Also, he said, no polls were taken in Florida after the Georgia result, so the message of Clinton's acceptability flowed in there from Georgia unfiltered.

On the next Saturday, Clinton topped his Georgia showing in the South Carolina primary, winning 63 percent of the vote, in spite of the flap over his outburst against Jackson, to only 19 for Tsongas.

Eight states were holding primaries on Super Tuesday, March 10— Florida, Louisiana, Mississippi, Oklahoma, Tennessee and Texas in the South and Southwest, plus Massachusetts and Rhode Island—and three were holding caucuses—Delaware, Hawaii and Missouri. Clinton concentrated on his home region, but Tsongas made a substantial effort in Florida to add another state to Maryland as evidence that he could win outside New England, and once again the sparks flew between Tsongas and Clinton.

Clinton homed in on Tsongas as an advocate of old-fashioned Republican trickle-down economics and an increased gas tax, and his campaign ran a television ad in Florida, which it had first used in Georgia, that took dead aim on the Sunshine State's high elderly population. It quoted Tsongas's campaign pamphlet as proposing "a cut in cost-of-living adjustments for older Americans," leaving the distinct impression that Tsongas was talking about all Social Security benefits, when in fact he was referring to Medicare only. "This made Tsongas go ballistic," Greer recalled, while straight-facedly defending the ad. Tsongas accused Clinton of lying about him.

Meanwhile, in a debate in Dallas, a relentless Jerry Brown, determined to elbow his way into the limelight, took after the front-running Clinton. He seized on a photograph taken with Senator Sam Nunn, a strong Clinton supporter, at a Georgia "boot camp" for predominantly black first-time offenders. Clinton and Nunn, he said, looked like "colonial masters" in what he said was "almost a Willie Horton" in attempting to play the race card—an allegation resented by Clinton. When Brown also noted that Arkansas had no state civil rights law—Clinton's state legislature had rebuffed his attempt to get one—Clinton snapped: "Jerry, chill out. . . . Nobody has a better civil rights record than I do."

In all this, Tsongas said very little, but later in a Dallas news conference Clinton inadvertently re-ignited his feud with Saint Paul when he said of Tsongas's favoring tax incentives for business rather than a middle-class tax cut: "We cannot put off fairness under the guise of promoting growth. It won't work. It's not America."

Tsongas, apparently under the impression Clinton had said "it's not American" and hence had questioned his patriotism, erupted the next night in Florida, charging that Clinton was using "code words" to foster division. Reporters checking tape recordings of the Clinton news conference confirmed that Tsongas had erred, but it was clear his onetime friendly attitude toward Clinton had turned to ashes. He insisted that Clinton was slurring his Greek ancestry and declared that "this is one Greek who fights back"—an allusion to fellow Massachusetts Democrat Michael Dukakis, widely criticized in 1988 for failing to respond to attacks by the Bush campaign.

Tsongas escalated the war of words in Fort Lauderdale by holding up a teddy bear and saying: "This is my opponent—pander bear." Clinton, he charged, "will say anything to get elected," referring to Clinton's call in Connecticut to save the Seawolf nuclear submarine that was to have been built at Groton but was now slated to be scrubbed. Clinton shot back: "You want to talk about pandering. It wasn't me that went to New York and said I'd be the best friend Wall Street ever had. That was Senator Tsongas."

And so it went over the final weekend before Super Tuesday as the candidates campaigned frenetically to cash in on the campaign's single richest day of delegate gathering yet. Tsongas's talk of Clinton pandering to older voters on Social Security and tax cuts, Kantor argued afterward, helped rather than hurt Clinton. And by now, Greenberg said, Clinton had found "clarity in our contrast with Tsongas—Bill Clinton for people, Tsongas for more trickle-down—and we decided that was all we'd talk about." On Saturday, Clinton won lightly contested caucuses in Wyoming and Tsongas did the same in Arizona, and on Sunday Brown ran first in Nevada, but all eyes were on the bigger prize on Tuesday.

All eyes, that is, except Harkin's. As voters went to the primary polls and caucuses in eleven states, he faced the reality of his shortage of funds and diminished appeal of his aggressively, even defiantly, old liberal message and quit the race. His withdrawal in advance of the Michigan primary a week later was somewhat surprising, inasmuch as Harkin's strong labor support might have been expected to make him a contender there. As it was, by pulling out, Harkin—who subsequently endorsed and campaigned for Clinton—gave Clinton the opportunity to play up his basic differences with Tsongas on key labor issues in the state.

Super Tuesday was a bonanza for Clinton. He won eight of the eleven contests decisively, including delegate-rich Texas and Florida, the latter one state in the South that Tsongas had hoped to salvage. Instead, it was not even close: Clinton 51 percent, Tsongas 35, Brown 12. Tsongas managed to win only his own state of Massachusetts, neighboring Rhode Island and the Delaware caucuses.

"The people of the South heard the worst about me," Clinton said, "but they saw the best." As for Tsongas, he remained defiant—and bitter. "Super Tuesday was meant to eliminate somebody like me," he said. "Well, I'm still here." And he added: "I'm going to tell you something, Bill Clinton. You're not going to pander your way into the White House as long as I'm around."

With a widening lead in delegates—728 by one count to 343 for Tsongas—Clinton now set about seeing that Tsongas would not be around much longer. From the beginning, the Clinton strategists had looked upon Illinois, which along with Michigan would hold its primary the next Tuesday, as the place where their candidate could nail down the Democratic nomination. Mayor Richard Daley of Chicago, eldest son of the legend, and his politically savvy brother Bill, a Chicago banker with strong union ties, did not publicly endorse Clinton but gave the nod for many of their supporters to help him.

In addition, Clinton's campaign manager in Little Rock, David Wilhelm, was a young but veteran political strategist from Chicago who had played a critical role in Rich Daley's mayoral campaign. His knowledge of the Illinois political terrain, coupled with the opening in Michigan afforded by Harkin's withdrawal, poised Clinton for a knockout blow against Tsongas, now seen as the remaining but severely weakened obstacle to the nomination. Brown, as from the beginning, was regarded more as an irritant than a threat. The day before Super Tuesday, the Clinton campaign started running negative ads against Tsongas in Illinois, charging that his economic plan was pro-business and antiworker.

In targeting Illinois as the key, Kantor said later, "we played off what happened, frankly, to Al Gore in 1988, when Gore should have been in fairly good shape after Super Tuesday but didn't have either the resources or the plan for Illinois or Michigan." The Clinton campaign had both, and as in New Hampshire the main campaign operation was shifted from Little Rock to Chicago to facilitate decision-making and implementing.

While Kerrey and Harkin remained in the race, Clinton had sought to claim the mantle as the Washington outsider in a year when Washington was taking its lumps. Their departure made it harder for Clinton to make the case, but the incentive continued to be great. Two days after Super Tuesday, the House of Representatives voted, 426–0, for full disclosure of all the bad checks written on the House's internal bank by 296 present and fifty-nine former members. The development was only the latest contributor to the antipolitics mood gripping the country, and Clinton was not hesitant to try to capitalize on it.

The notion, however, that Clinton could ever be regarded as an outsider anywhere politics was being played was laughable. He was the consummate politician, as comfortable in the back rooms as in voters' living rooms—a fact that served him well, especially in places of high-powered urban politics like Illinois and Michigan.

In Illinois, Carville said later, "the fact that Tsongas couldn't deal with the Chicago politicos hurt him. Because even non-Chicago people [would say], 'These guys are a fact of life, and the fact that you can't deal with these people is a sign of weakness.' In Michigan, I think the fact that he couldn't deal with labor problems was damaging, even among some nonunion voters, [who said,] 'Those are the facts of life in Michigan. Good politicians have to be able to deal with unions in Michigan.

Good politicians have to be able to deal with ward leaders in Chicago.'
. . . The most effective Republican politicians in those states don't beat
up on ward leaders and labor because voters see that as a sort of measure
of leadership. . . . Bethesda [an upscale Washington, D.C., suburb] was
the perfect place for Tsongas.''

Both states, however, provided good laboratories for measuring the
public appeal of contesting economic proposals, with unemployment at
8.5 percent in Illinois and 9 percent in Michigan, highest in the Midwest,
and both well above the national average. In Michigan particularly, Clinton made much of Tsongas's opposition to a key litmus-test issue for
organized labor—federal legislation that would bar hiring strikebreakers
as permanent replacements for striking employees.

Visiting an auto parts plant in Detroit, Tsongas patiently explained
his reasons to workers brought together to ask him questions, and they
clearly were not mollified. Tsongas, in a blue satin United Auto Workers
jacket, looked as out of place with these blue-collar workers as he had at
the cattle auction in South Dakota weeks before. Tubby Harrison, Tsongas's pollster, said later: ''The problem with our candidacy is that there
was no political message at all.'' That is, when Tsongas asked voters to
sacrifice, such as paying a higher tax on gasoline, they ''were never told
how they would get something back,'' he said.

Jerry Brown, seeking to fill the vacuum with labor after Harkin's
withdrawal, worked the union halls diligently, also always in one or
another UAW jacket presented to him along the way. He embraced organized labor's opposition to the North American Free Trade Act (NAFTA)
being pursued by Bush and given conditional approval by both Clinton
and Tsongas. Brown by now was establishing himself as the Zelig of the
1992 campaign, as in the Woody Allen movie character who, chame-
leonlike, took on the characteristics and appearance of whichever group
was at hand.

In a debate in Chicago on the weekend before the two primaries,
Brown said he would not ''give George Bush a blank check to go down
there and send his business buddies who will abandon workers in Illinois,
Michigan and this country to get two-dollar-an-hour cheap labor.'' It was
a message that played well with blue-collar workers in both states, and
Brown won the endorsement of the Michigan teamsters and a number of
other local unions.

Perhaps the most significant pair of campaign events during the hectic week, however, concerned the issue of racial harmony. Clinton first went to Macomb County, the nearly lily-white middle-class suburban enclave just north of heavily black Detroit famed as the "home of the Reagan Democrats," and made an emotional plea for an end to racial divisions and suspicions.

"I do not believe we have any hope of doing what we have to do in America unless we can come together across racial lines again," he said at Macomb County Community College before a sedate audience that was hardly the redneck stereotype of the Reagan Democrat. "This is a crisis of economics, of values," he said. "It has nothing to do with race. . . . The one thing that it's going to take to bring this country together is somebody's got to come back to the so-called Reagan Democratic area and say, 'Look, I'll give you your values back, I'll restore the economic leadership, I'll help you build the middle class back.' But you've got to say, 'Okay, let's do it with everybody in this country.' "

The next morning, Clinton went before a black congregation at the Pleasant Grove Baptist Church in Detroit and repeated essentially the same message. Telling his audience about his words to the Macomb audience the previous day, Clinton said: "I come here to challenge you to reach out your hand to them, for we have been divided for too long. . . . On Tuesday, tell the people of Macomb County, 'If you'll give up your race feelings, we'll say we want empowerment, not entitlement, we want opportunity, but we accept responsibility, we're going to help be a part of the change.' "

The two visits were an intentional effort to present Clinton as an unorthodox politician, a "different kind of Democrat." "We wanted to show," Wilhelm said later, "that Bill Clinton's message of linking economic opportunity to individual responsibility was a message that would sell among Reagan Democrats as well as African-American voters. . . . The critique of the Democratic Party in recent years has been that it is impossible to do that. If you are going to succeed in regaining the support of Reagan Democrats, or white ethnic middle-class voters, you have to do things that push off the base vote of the party.

"That twenty-four-hour period, maybe better than any other, demonstrated how Bill Clinton's message mattered," Wilhelm said, "and elicited support from wings of the party that people thought simply could not work together. . . . The message of individual responsibility, which so many felt was a message that was oriented toward those who had left the party because of the perceived permissiveness of the party, elicited just as much enthusiastic support from African-American voters as it did from any other group.''

All this was reminiscent of the posture of Robert Kennedy in his 1968 presidential primary campaign in Indiana, when he successfully ran as a tough law-and-order candidate while holding the overwhelming support of black voters. ''We talked about it,'' Wilhelm recalled. ''I wouldn't say that it was a model that we were trying to emulate, but we certainly knew enough about that race and understood he had a populist appeal on economic issues but also emphasized law and order and responsibility to one's community and family. And maybe somewhere in our subconscious, that race, and that month of his, was something that helped us.'' But rather than a positive model that drove the Clinton campaign, he said, ''if anything, it was more a desire to learn from the mistakes of the most recent Democratic campaigns—an unmodel, if you will.''

Carville said later that the Clinton strategists ''always wanted to have this kind of going-against-the-grain element in the campaign.'' Ironically, he said, there was discussion within the campaign earlier of having Clinton demonstrate his willingness to go against the grain by opposing the reelection of Congressman Gus Savage, a prominent, entrenched black Chicago Democrat accused of sexual harassment and other misconduct. But a good opportunity did not present itself at the time, and the gambit of showing Clinton bucking up against a traditional Democratic special interest group was held for another occasion—with considerably more political impact when it occurred. The idea, Carville said, was ''if you took it on in one arena, you sort of had to take it on somewhere else. You couldn't just attack racism. You couldn't just go lecture [one side].''

Clinton himself called it ''counter-scheduling.'' Later, he told us: ''I thought the only way for a Democrat to build a coalition for change, that is, for me to get a mandate in the election to do something instead of just be against somebody else, [was] to try to show that I would say the same things to everybody everywhere. And you had to go into territory that wasn't particularly friendly to your message and say things that people didn't necessarily want to hear, because I think we've all got to do some things to change. And I thought that on race and on economics, that was very important to say. There were other issues too, on education, on crime. I thought those things had to be said, and I did. Really, as a deliberate strategy, no Democrat had tried to do it since Bob Kennedy, and I felt then . . . and I still feel that there is a kind of hunger for that out there.''

One other, inadvertent case of going against the grain during this week caused the Clinton campaign considerable heartburn when Hillary Clinton, chatting with voters and reporters at the Busy Bee coffee shop in Chicago, defended her role as a professional woman pursuing her career at the same time she was the wife of a state governor.

In a debate the night before, Brown had charged, going beyond what had been reported in a newspaper story, that candidate Clinton was "funneling money to his wife's law firm . . . the kind of conflict of interest that is incompatible with the kind of public servant that we expect as president.'' Clinton denied it and strenuously defended Hillary. "I don't care what you say about me,'' he told Brown, "but you ought to be ashamed of yourself for jumping on my wife. You're not worth being on the same platform with my wife.''

Now, when she was asked at the coffee shop whether there may have been an appearance of impropriety in her law firm's dealings with her husband's administration, she said: "I suppose I could have stayed home, baked cookies and had teas. But what I decided was to fulfill my profession, which I entered before my husband was in public life.''

Professional women found no fault with that answer, particularly in this "Year of the Woman'' when the nation's majority gender was reaching conspicuously for a greater share of political power. But from other quarters, chiefly among conservatives and religious fundamentalists, came the suggestion that she was denigrating women who played the homemaker role. Perhaps more than anything else Hillary Clinton said in the campaign, that offhand remark caused her grief down the road.

It did not, however, alter the outcome in the Illinois and Michigan primaries the next day, in which her husband won in each state with 51 percent of the vote. Tsongas was second in Illinois with 26 percent, but Brown, by virtue of his hard campaigning and pro-labor rhetoric, beat him out for second in Michigan, where Tsongas's pro-business views seriously hurt him with labor.

The nomination now appeared to be in hand for Clinton. Party chairman Ron Brown began to put the word out that he considered the nomination settled, and that the party ought to close down the competition and get on with planning for the fall campaign. But Jerry Brown insisted that the Arkansas governor would not "be given a coronation" and that he himself intended to challenge him all the way.

Tsongas, running a more conventional campaign than Brown and more dependent on contributions for television advertising, staff and travel, announced two days later that he was "suspending" his campaign because "we simply did not have the resources" to continue.

"The obligation of my survival has been met," he said, alluding to his recovery from cancer, which he said had been a factor in his decision to run. "It's been a helluva ride." One thing he would not be, he said, was a spoiler by staying in the race and attacking Clinton when it was clear he himself could not be nominated. "That is not what I'm about," he said. "I did not survive my ordeal [against cancer] to be the agent of George Bush's reelection."

Jerry Brown, though, had no such qualms. It was clear that he, like Jesse Jackson in 1984 and 1988, was shifting from a serious pursuit of the nomination to leadership of a cause on which he could build a longer-range movement of the politically disenchanted—and sustain this latest phase of an erratic personal career. Bill Clinton would have to press on, to another phase—and another hurdle—on the path to his lofty objective, this time back east to Connecticut and then New York, land of tabloids, talk shows and one of the most demanding electorates anywhere.

WINNING, BUT LOSING

Paul Tsongas's sudden "suspension" of his campaign caught the Clinton strategists by surprise. They thought the man from Lowell, Massachusetts, would be looking to his neighboring state of Connecticut, next on the primary calendar, to regroup for a final showdown in New York two weeks thereafter, but they were wrong. Tsongas said later that he thought he could win Connecticut but "you looked at New York and all you could see was [Clinton advertising] in Buffalo and Schenectady and no chance to respond."

Confident of winning both Illinois and Michigan, Carville and Greenberg on the eve of those primaries had pressed for Clinton to go into Connecticut to knock Tsongas out. Greenberg said later his polling showed Clinton to be within a couple of points of Tsongas and that victories in Illinois and Michigan would push him ahead. It was seen by them as a no-lose situation; if Tsongas were to win Connecticut it could be written off as a regional victory only, and the showdown would be in New York anyway.

Consequently, the Clinton campaign started running television ads against Tsongas in the Hartford area while low-balling Clinton's prospects in his backyard. But when Tsongas took himself out, the Clinton campaign—prodded by Hillary Clinton's friend and adviser, Susan Thomases—intensified its focus on New York, leaving an opening for Jerry Brown. As in Maine earlier, he worked Connecticut diligently. At the same time, many in the Tsongas operation refused to fold up shop, hoping a strong showing for their man would persuade him to stay in the race after all.

From Illinois, Clinton had returned to Little Rock and by the time he reacted to the Tsongas withdrawal and got to Connecticut he had missed the Thursday news cycle and was not into the campaign dialogue with Brown until the Friday before the primary.

The combination of Brown's guerrilla campaigning and the resurrection effort in Tsongas's behalf caught the high-riding Clinton in a squeeze. Brown hammered him as an establishment politician riding a corrupt process to the nomination who would lead the Democratic Party to another defeat in November. When it was disclosed that Clinton had just played a round of golf at the all-white Little Rock Country Club, Brown accused him of "an arrogance, a complacency, a smugness," and Clinton, acknowledging that playing there was "a mistake," vowed not to do so again until the club was integrated. Tsongas earlier had accused Clinton of pandering to Connecticut voters by endorsing continued work on the Seawolf nuclear submarine program at Groton slated for termination by Bush, and the allegation appeared to hurt him.

Clinton painted Brown as a spoiler who would say or do anything to win votes and "wouldn't mind reelecting George Bush" by so doing. To which Brown replied: "What is this, the Politburo? There is only the candidate picked by the power structure? I'm not the spoiler. Slick Willie is the spoiler. If he gets the nomination, he is going to ruin the whole Democratic Party."

Brown promised to give Clinton "a wake-up call" on primary day and he did just that, eking out a 37 to 36 percent upset over him in Connecticut, with Tsongas drawing 20 percent as a withdrawn candidate. Exit polls indicated that Brown had been the clear beneficiary of that withdrawal, with 35 percent of his voters saying they would have cast ballots for Tsongas had he remained in the race, to 23 percent who said they would have voted for Clinton. With Tsongas still running, these polls suggested, he would have won about 40 percent of the vote and Brown would have dropped to third. That result would have been less embarrassing to Clinton than losing, however narrowly, to Brown. Clinton consoled himself, aides said later, by attributing the setback to "buyer's remorse"—having just about made the purchase, having second thoughts before leaving the store.

A more serious cause for concern to Clinton came out of the same exit polls. When the voters were asked whether they thought he had "the honesty and integrity to serve effectively as president," 48 percent said no, to 46 who said yes. The result was ominous after all Clinton had been through, and as he headed into the New York primary with a revived Brown on his neck. It was one thing to win a string of primary victories and quite another to do so with the voters still believing you couldn't be trusted in the White House—a troublesome cloud looking toward the fall campaign against Bush.

Going into Connecticut, Greer said later, "everybody thought he was preordained. All of a sudden, people were saying, 'We don't think we want this guy,' and then we're going into the meat grinder of New York." Greenberg said his own polling immediately after the Connecticut loss showed the race even in New York. "We sat on it," he said of his poll, because the press perception was that Clinton remained comfortably ahead there, "but we knew we were potentially in trouble."

The problem was not simply in New York, Kantor said later, but nationally, and particularly in the political community in Washington, where Clinton already had been pronounced dead and buried a few times and had to be dug up each time. There was, he said, a "Bill Clinton Is Flawed Club" in Washington, so "we couldn't afford to lose a primary, because people were not ready to join the cause" and in fact some Democrats were poised "to look for somebody else to walk into this race." And with loose cannon Jerry Brown as the sole active opponent, the course of the next two weeks was not predictable.

The Clinton strategists approached New York—the city, not so much the state—as if it were a hornets' nest, and with good reason. Its television, radio and tabloid newspaper corps had a deserved reputation for sensationalism to the point of political cannibalism. They took pride in their image as the bully boys in the toughest neighborhood anywhere.

Jerry Nachman, editor of *The New York Post*, who seized the first *Star* story on the Larry Nichols lawsuit and bled it into the journalistic mainstream, was quoted in *The Washington Post* as observing: "This is New York. Everything else is an out-of-town tryout."

Local columnists, licking their chops to get their shots in at the front-runner from Arkansas, charged the rest of the press corps with rolling over for him and vowed to make up for the kid-gloves handling. It seemed as if the New York news media felt they had to live up to their bad reputation—and many did.

For Clinton, there was also the question of the volatile Mario Cuomo. Prior to the Connecticut vote, Cuomo had observed that Clinton, with whom he had had some celebrated run-ins, was close to having their party's nomination "locked up." Now, however, when Brown made a pilgrimage to Albany as a resuscitated contender, Cuomo proclaimed that "the presumption of ascendancy for Clinton is now rebuttable." Brown rejoiced that "we've gone from a conclusive presumption to a rebuttable presumption." In a left-handed compliment, Cuomo said either Clinton or Brown would be better than Bush but that he wasn't going to endorse either one. "I don't think it would help them much," he said. "I'm not so popular myself right now."

Recognizing that he could no longer afford to ignore Brown and concentrate on the fall election against Bush, Clinton in New York stepped up his criticisms of a Brown proposal for a federal 13 percent flat tax across the board for all Americans. Clinton bashed the idea as regressive and a "war-on-New-York tax" because it would eliminate the income tax deduction for payment of state and local taxes that in high-tax New York would mean "a $4 billion bill" for taxpayers in the state.

Brown meanwhile turned up the heat on Clinton, describing him as the "scandal-of-the-week" candidate who was "taking the Democratic Party for a ride" to defeat. As Brown got more and more personal, party chairman Ron Brown stepped in, reprimanding him as having "crossed the line in terms of inappropriate attacks" against Clinton in a "scorched earth policy." Brown, campaigning in Wisconsin, which also had a primary on April 7, brushed the chairman's admonitions aside. "The trouble is, there's such a trail here that the media has to keep bringing stuff out. Our party chairman does a disservice to somehow cover it up and be quiet about it." To Ron Brown, he demanded: "If you can't be neutral, then step aside, because this insurgency doesn't stop.''

Jerry Brown's tactics, and tenacity, were particularly disturbing to the party chairman because his prime objective all year had been for the party to have a brief, decisive and bloodless primary season in order to focus on the general election challenge to Bush as early as possible.

In the white-hot political atmosphere of New York, Clinton found himself fending off blows daily. At a fund-raiser in Manhattan, an AIDS activist accused him of "dying of ambition," producing one of the rare occasions on which Clinton lost his temper in public. "If I were dying of ambition," he said rather incongruously, "I wouldn't have stood up here and put up with all this crap I've put up with over the past six months. I understand you're hurting," he went on, but "you can't stop hurting by trying to hurt other people." And when the heckler continued to berate him, Clinton blurted: "I've had about enough of this. I have listened to all these attacks, attacks on me [for not caring about the victims of AIDS]. That's just a bunch of bull. Don't you understand that one of the problems in this country is we all devalue each other? We've got to go back to putting some value on the integrity of people's lives."

At a Harlem hospital center, New Alliance Party candidate Lenora Fulani interrupted a Clinton speech and demanded "democracy" in the form of opening debates to herself and long-shot Democratic candidate Larry Agran. After she had gone on for about fifteen minutes of heckling, Clinton finally walked out, shouting: "I want to thank those of you here who really want democracy. I think Harlem should fight for free speech. Free speech in Harlem! Fight for the First Amendment!"

The Clinton campaign decided that the best way to cope with Brown, and to get Clinton's message out amid the in-your-face news media frenzy that was New York, was to debate Brown directly and repeatedly. In one such debate, Clinton ran into another buzz saw when a local reporter asked him a question in a way that required a straight answer. He gave it, but his penchant for fudging and evasion won out in the end—to his further political discomfort. The question was about past drug use, and his standard answer when asked on all previous occasions had been the one that he had given only four days earlier before the editorial board of *The New York Daily News*, according to the Associated Press: "I have never broken the laws of my country."

That response, like all the previous ones, should have tipped off the press corps, especially in light of Clinton's history of dissembling on tough questions, of the cute evasion. For years, according to veteran Arkansas reporter John Brummett, he had been saying in his home state in response to questions on drug use that he had never broken any of its laws. Yet for some reason no reporter had gotten the picture, and had asked the obvious follow-on question—until now. One of the panelists at a candidates' forum over WABC-TV was Marcia Kramer, a WCBS-TV reporter who had been traveling with the Clinton entourage and was familiar with his talent for dodging verbal bullets. When she read the answer he had given to the newspaper, she said later, "it was like this alarm bell went off in my head."

So she pressed him. Reminding him that he often bristled when referred to as "Slick Willie," she observed that his answer on drug use seemed to have been carefully crafted. Okay, he hadn't broken the laws of his country. What about any state law or one of another country when, for instance, he was a student at Oxford?

"I've never broken any state laws," he answered, "and when I was in England, I experimented with marijuana a time or two." Then he added: "And I didn't like it, and I didn't inhale, and I didn't try it again."

The answer was vintage Clinton, and perhaps as revealing about him as any answer he had given all year concerning his political thought process. He had known perfectly well each time the general drug-use question had been asked over the years what the inquirer really wanted to know, but each time he had given a lawyer's response—answer only the specific question asked and don't volunteer anything beyond. Even now he threw up that defense for all his past dissembling. He told reporters after the debate: "I said I've never broken the laws of my country, and that is the absolute truth." Had the *Daily News* editors "asked me the same question," he said, "I would have given the same answer."

The next day, Clinton again defended his previous dissembling. In 1987, he said, when he was first asked in Arkansas about drug use, "I said what I believe in. I think there is a limit to what people ought to have to say. But I am running for president now. People finally asked me a direct question. I gave them a direct answer."

The afterthought—"and I didn't inhale"—was also revealing of Clinton's habit of trying to minimize something that might hurt him politically, as well as opening him to a ridicule that lasted throughout the campaign. It was always a mystery how someone with such sensitive political antennae about most things could fail to anticipate the political fallout of such a ludicrous and self-serving alibi.

The admission of brief marijuana experimentation twenty-three years earlier, in what was a typical act of his generation, was in itself no big deal. As Clinton himself observed, 1988 presidential candidates Bruce Babbitt and Al Gore had similarly acknowledged marijuana use during the Vietnam War era without apparent harm to their candidacies. But the incident fueled the sense among many voters that Clinton was a man who was someone other than he presented himself as being; there always was something that had to be pried out of him, and then he would always have some tortured explanation or alibi. He had ridiculed Paul Tsongas earlier as being ''perfect'' and had admitted that he himself wasn't, yet his imperfections seemed to surface only when someone else dug them out or when he was backed to a wall to acknowledge them. And even then, he seemed more often than not to dodge and weave.

The episode was equally embarrassing, or should have been, to the great army of reporters—ourselves included—who had followed Clinton's political career for a decade or more, were familiar with his standard response of not having ''broken the laws of my country'' on drug use, and had never followed up with the obvious question. But such lapses in the press corps were hardly new.

In 1959, for example, when President Dwight D. Eisenhower, asked at a White House news conference to provide a major decision in which then Vice President Richard M. Nixon, expected to seek the presidency in 1960, had been involved, Eisenhower replied that ''if you give me a week, maybe I can think of one.'' The answer was read as a blow to Nixon's claim of high-level experience, yet at the next news conference a week later, nobody asked Eisenhower whether he had been able to ''think of one.'' So perhaps Clinton knew what he was doing when he continued his dodge on past drug use well into the 1992 campaign.

On the other hand, two polls of nationwide sentiment, released at this time, one by a New York television station of New York voters and the other by *The New York Times* and CBS News, underscored the scope of continuing voter doubts about Clinton's trustworthiness. Asked again whether he had the ''honesty and integrity'' to be president, 57 percent of those in the New York poll said no, to only 29 who said yes, and in the national survey the responses were 54 percent no, 26 yes.

These figures understandably shook the Clinton camp. The New York tabloids were now having a field day with "I didn't inhale" as Clinton's advisers brainstormed on how they could get the dialogue back on their candidate's economic proposals and differences with Jerry Brown. Although the New York airwaves were now being choked with political news and candidate appearances and interviews, the Clinton campaign suddenly proposed a series of six more debates, a rate of one a day, until primary day. The gambit by Clinton's admission was an effort to get past the clutter of renewed reportage about his personal past in the press and go directly to the voters.

All that voters "have heard is bad stuff dumped on them about me," he said, and what with distortions in the news media about his positions, "at least the people who watch the debates will hear them." At a black church in Queens, Clinton lamented: "I have seen myself turned into a cartoon character of an old-time Southern deal-maker by tabloids and television ads—a total denial of all my life's work." Hank Morris, a New York Democratic consultant, translated for *The New York Times:* "They decided they'd rather debate Jerry Brown than the New York press."

The strategy in one sense worked, because Brown and the questions asked in the debates stuck essentially to substantive issues like taxes and welfare. But in Clinton's eagerness to go directly to the voters, he fell prey to yet another peril of the television era—the scandalmonger masquerading as journalist, in the presence of talk show host Phil Donahue. Donahue, whose bread and butter was sensationalism but who sought to lacquer it with a veneer of serious demeanor, single-handedly sought to bring the campaign dialogue back to where it was in New Hampshire by resurrecting the Gennifer Flowers story.

Donahue subjected Clinton to a rehash of all the old questions, starting with: "Now, Governor, may I just characterize what I think may be some of the suspicions or the concerns of some Americans?" He then launched into a general recitation of "suspicions fueled by allegations," to which Clinton responded with his standard comment that his marriage had had problems but was solid now. He and his wife had never separated, Clinton said, but "it was none of your business if we did."

Donahue went on: "Part of the 'Slick Willie' problem is caused by what some analysts see as your ability to deflect questions and to give answers which really don't speak—" Clinton broke in: "We need the ability in politics to deflect some questions," he said. "You folks would kill us if we didn't." The studio audience applauded in agreement.

Still, Donahue perservered, asking about marijuana smoking and inhaling. Clinton was exasperated: "What difference is it if I said I inhaled or not?" Donahue replied: "The difference is the appearance of dancing around these issues . . . the pattern of tap-dancing around direct answers to potentially embarrassing questions."

At one point Clinton told him: "I don't believe I or any other decent human being should have to put up with the kind of questioning you're putting me through." And when Donahue still pressed on, Clinton told him that if he kept up the same line of inquiry, "we're going to sit here a long time in silence, Phil." Again the audience applauded.

Clinton operatives later sought to make the best of the situation by saying the exchange had demonstrated once again their candidate's ability to stand up to hostile questioning, and had evoked sympathy for him in the face of Donahue's opportunistic sprint on the low road. That no doubt was so, as evidenced in the comment of one young woman when Donahue raced into the audience, microphone in hand, for reaction: "I think, really, given the pathetic state of most of the United States at this point— Medicare, education, everything else—I can't believe you spent half an hour of airtime attacking this man's character. I'm not even a Bill Clinton supporter, but I think this is ridiculous." The studio audience cheered and applauded.

Several days later, Clinton appeared again on the Donahue show, this time with Jerry Brown, and the host astonished both candidates by informing them minutes before airtime that he intended merely to introduce them and then step aside, letting them debate without interruption. Donahue's surprising abstinence—perhaps the product of the audience disfavor with his behavior in the first Clinton appearance—resulted in one of the best, most serious, issue-oriented exchanges of the whole campaign. Clinton, Frank Greer said later, had come to the studio with a tough game plan to deal with another expected verbal wrestling match with Donahue. Instead, he said, "we had about four minutes to game-plan'' how to deal with Brown without the specter of Donahue hanging over the debate.

Getting in the ring with the electronic media bully boys had one other positive moment for Clinton. In an interview with one of New York's most obnoxious but popular drive-time radio hosts, Don Imus, who had regularly been referring to Clinton as "Bubba," the candidate informed him that where he came from, Bubba was a synonym for "mensch," Yiddish for somebody who was the salt of the earth. Thereafter, the Clinton operatives always referred to the Imus interview as one of the brightest spots of the days in "the meat grinder."

Clinton was also helped by a decision by Jerry Brown to proclaim, first in Connecticut but then more conspicuously in New York, that he wanted Jesse Jackson as his running mate. Jackson had remained anathema to many Jewish voters in New York City, where they often constituted as much as 40 percent of the Democratic primary vote, ever since his slur in the 1984 campaign about New York being "Hymietown." But in an apparent effort to cut into the black vote, Brown showed up at a Jackson voter registration rally in downtown Manhattan and latched on.

Jackson made clear he was not endorsing Brown, praising him faintly only as "a man who brought substance to the campaign," but Brown threw his arm on Jackson's shoulder and proclaimed: "Reverend Jackson has made himself available, and we're going to make him available as the next vice president of the United States." Jackson replied that he was "honored by his request" but said his objective was "to empower the people. If by chance the party's nominee [pointedly not specifying Brown] were to make such a request and the convention were to ratify it," Jackson said, "I would be honored to accept it."

The reaction in the Jewish community was not long in coming. As Brown was telling the Jewish Community Relations Council the next day that "the number one goal for survival of a free society is healing the division between black and white," Dov Hikind, a state assemblyman from Brooklyn, broke in. "You insult the Jewish community by picking Jesse Jackson," he shouted. Anyone who had accepted the support of Louis Farrakhan, the Nation of Islam leader who once called Judaism a "gutter religion," Hikind said, was unacceptable as a vice presidential nominee. Others in the room tried to quiet the heckler, and he was finally hustled out of the room.

When Brown tried to defend his decision, saying that as a longtime defender of Israel he would be making the decisions as president, someone else called out: "What happens if you die, Governor?" Others in the audience made a point of collaring reporters and telling us they had no problem with a black as vice president—but not Jackson. If Clinton had any worry about winning the Jewish vote in New York, it vanished with Brown's gesture to Jackson and black voters. "A vote for Jerry Brown is also a vote for Jesse Jackson," warned *The Jewish Press*, an influential weekly.

That night, Greenberg polled Jewish voters regarding the Jackson matter and found, he said, that Brown "had dropped into single digits. It was a massive and immediate collapse." When we asked Brown much later why he had indicated he would choose Jackson as his running mate if nominated, he said he was well aware "that Jackson had problems in New York [among the Jewish community] but he had strengths elsewhere. And I thought it was important to say something real in all the talk about change. I was trying to basically lay out a really different alternative."

A new peril for Clinton surfaced on the final weekend before the New York vote. Paul Begala was walking through the lobby of the Clinton headquarters hotel when John King of the Associated Press strolled over. "I'm going to ruin your night," he said. "Clinton got a draft notice."

Begala thought nothing of it, because he recalled that Clinton had mentioned earlier that he thought he had gotten something like that but it had never turned up. But now an old political opponent in Little Rock revealed a 1969 letter indicating that Clinton had indeed received a draft induction notice in April of that year, which did not square with the impression he had left when the first stories about his draft record had broken during the New Hampshire primary. Then he had said he signed up for the ROTC program at the University of Arkansas in anticipation of being drafted in the fall of 1969, making no mention that he had actually received an induction notice before applying for the ROTC slot.

Clinton insisted now that he had simply forgotten about the notice, that it had arrived in England after the induction date indicated had passed, that he had contacted his draft board in Hot Springs and was told to ignore it. "They said, 'Look, this is a routine deal. We will extend this. Don't worry about it. You will have to come home this summer and make some decision,' '' he recalled. Grilled about the latest development by reporters outside his midtown Manhattan hotel, Clinton sought to brush the matter off. ''I'm sorry if twenty-three years later it looks unusual,'' he said. ''But I can tell you at the time it never occurred to me as being anything unusual.''

The tabloids leaped on the latest wrinkle in Clinton's draft story, but *The New York Times* barely gave it a yawn. The campaign had long since moved on to other issues, although campaign strategists for President Bush, tracking the story diligently, were tucking it away for future use. It got barely more mention than an interview with Hillary Clinton in the new issue of *Vanity Fair* magazine in which she said it was ''apparently well known in Washington'' that President Bush had had an extramarital affair. The tabloids jumped all over that one, with such headlines as ''Hillary Goes Tabloid'' and ''Hillary's Revenge.'' The candidate's wife promptly said it was a ''mistake'' for her to respond to a question that way, ''but nobody knows better than I the pain that can be caused by ever discussing rumors in private conversation.''

More of a cloud hanging over Clinton on the eve of the New York primary was the ''suspended'' candidacy of Paul Tsongas, who had won 20 percent of the vote from the sidelines in Connecticut and in whose behalf a stealth campaign was being waged in New York. Tsongas sparked the hopes of supporters by saying on one of the Sunday network interview shows that he was considering reentering the race, based on his and Clinton's showings in the New York primary. Tsongas's vote in Connecticut had been a key factor in Clinton's loss to Brown there, and aides feared recent history could repeat itself in New York, with much more dire results.

Those concerns, however, were unwarranted. Clinton won New York decisively with 41 percent of the vote, and the vote for Tsongas— 29 percent, good enough for second place—proved to be a windfall for the Arkansas governor by pushing Brown, with 26 percent, into third place and out of serious contention once and for all. The Tsongas vote of about 279,000 without an active candidate was, however, notable as an indication that many Democrats nervous about Clinton and his past were still looking for some other option to him. In Wisconsin, where Brown had hoped to spring another upset, Clinton won over him, 38 percent to

35, with 22 for Tsongas, who said later that he would have reentered the race only if Clinton had lost to Brown in both New York and Wisconsin. When that didn't happen, he said, "the idea had no legitimacy."

Clinton also won lesser victories over Brown in Kansas and Minnesota that helped produce headlines the next day that he had scored a "sweep"—a psychologically important pronouncement, Kantor said later. "For all practical purposes," he said, "it ended the nomination process and quieted down all the naysayers and doomsayers in Washington."

Relieved, Clinton at a victory party in New York called the experience of the primary there "like a ride on the Coney Island Cyclone, with ups and downs and twists and turns. And now that I'm through it all, I admit, I've had a ball." He even had kind words for Jerry Brown, who graciously conceded defeat but still gave no sign of bowing out of the race—and the diminishing national spotlight on him. Tsongas, however, faced reality for a second time and announced he would not be reentering the contest for the nomination.

Clinton appeared home free for the nomination at last, although he vowed to press on, not wanting to leave the impression in Pennsylvania, the next major state on the primary calendar, or any of the others where Democrats had not yet voted that he was taking them for granted. It should have been a time of rejoicing and relaxing within the Clinton inner circle, but it was not—again because of the exit polls. As after the Connecticut primary, they showed that nearly half of all Democratic voters in the New York primary surveyed believed Clinton lacked the "honesty and integrity" to be president. Many Brown and Tsongas voters told the exit pollsters they preferred independent candidate Ross Perot, who was climbing rapidly in the polls, to the Democratic front-runner.

Another poll by *The Washington Post* taken a few days after the New York primary produced the same ominous result. To the "honesty and integrity" question, 55 percent expressed no confidence in Clinton, to only 34 percent who did, and when asked for their presidential preference, voters surveyed put Perot in a virtual tie with Clinton—Clinton 24 percent, Perot 23—behind Bush's 37 percent. Clinton was faring no better in this poll despite the fact 55 percent said they disapproved of the way the president was handling his job.

Reflecting later on the intensive, bare-knuckles scrutiny he underwent leading up to and through the New York primary, and on the clinging doubts about him, Clinton told us: "The only thing that bothered me about it was, I felt there for several months there was such a discord, a disconnect, between how the people I met and talked to and communicated with, the people who watched the town meetings on television, felt and how everybody else in the world felt. The cumulative impact of these repeated stories was that I couldn't be defined in any other way.

"But I finally realized that the only way I could ever change that was by hanging in there and doing what I was doing; that the voters would make a decision ultimately. . . . It was extremely frustrating, but what we finally did was to try to settle on a long-term strategy to try to deal with it. It was a very deliberate decision by me that I had to find a way to get people to define me in terms of the whole person I was."

"I kept saying, 'We're winning, but we're losing,' " Greer recalled. "The serious problem was winning the nomination and then being so wounded that you can't win the general. And we always ran the campaign [in a way] so that we could win in November. We had to stand back and figure how we win the war as opposed to fighting each battle tactically" in the primaries.

The key to doing so was finding out what it was exactly that was causing Clinton to "lose while winning"—to fail to overcome voters' doubts about his trustworthiness to sit in the Oval Office, even as they were expressing their preference for him over the available alternatives. It was, although the Clinton insiders did not put it quite this way, like the old Henny Youngman joke: "How's your wife?" "Compared to what?" As long as the "what" was Brown or Tsongas, Clinton was going to win among the growing number of Americans who were fed up with George Bush. But another "what" was coming along in Perot, and the jury was out on him.

One reason for Clinton's problem was obvious: he always seemed to be sliding off questions, giving evasive answers unless nailed down with specific questions, as in the go-around on smoking pot. Donahue, for all his deplorable excesses, was right about that. But beyond that, why weren't voters really buying into what was a genuine American success story: poor boy, broken home, hard worker, rising to be governor of his state at a remarkably early age, commended by his peers as the nation's best?

The Clinton strategists decided to find out the answer, and thus was born what came to be called inside the campaign "The Manhattan Project"—an intensive research undertaking to gauge voter attitudes and concerns about Bill Clinton to learn what they knew and didn't know about him. The name was used inside the campaign to connote an all-out research effort but not advertised because of the nature of the real Manhattan Project—the search for the unlocking of the atom and development of the atom bomb. What the researchers discovered was not going to assure victory, but the information culled from the project, they hoped, would help them get Clinton through the wall that was blocking him from becoming a competitive general election candidate.

The day of the New York primary, Kantor called in Carville, Greenberg, Grunwald and the other top strategists and told them, with New York apparently won, to break off and make the study, with an eye to the long-term problems of perception facing Clinton looking to the general election. Greenberg and his partner, Celinda Lake, Carville and Greer set out in a series of discussions with academics and politicians, polls and focus groups to crack the enigma of candidate Clinton.

What they learned over the next several weeks was that the Bill Clinton the voters were seeing bore little resemblance in most important ways to the Bill Clinton they knew. The details of his womanizing and draft problems were not the problem, Grunwald said later. Voters knew all they wanted to know about each, and in fact the focus on them, she said, "blocked out other information about him." They liked the toughness of him, she said, and were intrigued by his ability to survive, "but they had this sort of shorthand—Gennifer Flowers, draft, I didn't inhale—and they didn't know anything more."

One of the first focus groups, in Allentown, Pennsylvania, according to Greer, uncovered that the voters gathered together "had no idea where this guy had come from and what he stood for. They thought he had been born with a silver spoon in his mouth. They thought that he was a child of privilege, that he had gone to all these Ivy League schools, and wasn't that much different than George Bush. It was phenomenal, shocking to us, but it shouldn't have been because we hadn't done any biographical work since one spot in New Hampshire."

Voters, Grunwald said, figured, " 'How could a kid from Arkansas, which they of course thought chauvinistically was some two-bit state, wind up at Oxford and Yale and governor? Well, his daddy must have helped him.'. . . When they learned that not only did his daddy not do anything, but there was no daddy, and he had worked for everything he had in his life, and he had worked very hard against some pretty decent odds, it totally changed their view of who he was, what he had been through, what he was proposing for the country.''

At the same time, however, Greer recalled, the voters tested ''thought he was always political, he was always cutting the corners, rounding the edges, not shooting straight.'' One voter bowled over the focus group operatives by observing that if Clinton was asked what his favorite color was, ''he'd say, 'plaid.' ''

With Pennsylvania the next primary and Brown trying desperately to shoehorn himself back into the picture by working the labor vote, the Clinton strategists decided to address Clinton's revealed problem immediately. They rejected one idea for Clinton to give a kind of tell-all Richard Nixon ''Checkers'' speech and instead started running a lengthy biographical television spot that started: ''His father died just before he was born, and his mother and her family struggled to give him better opportunities, to preach that with hard work, faith and a good education, anything was possible.''

At the same time Clinton returned more forcefully and consistently to his economic message, and to the case that he understood out of his own humble middle-class experience in Hope and Hot Springs, Arkansas, what working people were going through in the clinging recession. A second television ad was aired showing a mother who had lost her health care and a man whose lifelong job had been snuffed out in a plant closing, with Clinton talking about his agenda for change and concluding with a line from his Comeback Kid speech in New Hampshire: ''Some people say I've taken some hits lately, but nothing like the hits the American people have taken.''

Clinton also did statewide television town meetings from Philadelphia and Pittsburgh with advance promotions in which Clinton himself urged voters to tune in, as was done in New Hampshire at the time the womanizing and draft stories had the campaign on the ropes. And he gave another of his ''against the grain'' speeches at the University of Pennsylvania's Wharton School. He told the students that their celebrated business school was ''a powerful symbol of where our country went wrong in the 1980s . . . where Michael Milken got the idea to use junk bonds to leverage corporate buyouts" and where Donald Trump, "who glorified the art of the deal," learned his moves. Photographs of both hung on the school's "Wall of Fame," he noted, "until Trump went bankrupt and Milken was on his way to jail." He urged them to put morality back into business, and the students cheered and applauded the challenge.

In one sense, Clinton's running "against the grain" was curious. It seemed to defy another characteristic of him as a politician—an inordinate desire to please everyone all the time. That inclination was never clearer than in another speech during the Pennsylvania primary—on Earth Day at Drexel University. Clinton dealt with virtually every environmental issue on the table, comparing his positions with Bush's. But what made it memorable was a single digression. He suddenly began talking about how as a small boy he had been surprised to discover after he moved "into town"—Hot Springs—that there were just as many snakes, spiders and tarantulas on the ground as there had been in Hope. Then he added: "We had to figure out how to make them our friends rather than our enemies."

On the stump, Clinton's primary victories by now had given him the aura of a winner, if only in terms of the Democratic nomination. When he toured Philadelphia's famed Italian Market one morning, vendors and customers alike crowded around him reaching to shake his hand as he examined the wares with Mayor Ed Rendell at his side. But he was never completely out of the woods. From across the street at one point, a man called out to him, and when Clinton looked up, he heard this shouted question: "If you cheated on your wife, what would you do to the country?" Clinton forced a weak smile, waved the man off and turned back to surveying the unmenacing carts of broccoli, corn and other less toxic subjects.

The presumptive Democratic nominee was hearing discordant notes from another quarter in Pennsylvania as well. Democratic Governor Robert Casey, skeptical of Clinton's ability to win in the fall and noting the low primary turnouts, said in an interview: "We've got a tiny minority of Democrats voting for Bill Clinton, and he is winning every race without generating any sparks, any enthusiasm, any momentum. . . . People have a tremendous unease about him." Clinton's strategists recognized the same thing, but were not happy to have the Democratic governor of the state saying so publicly. Casey, an outspoken foe of abortion, had long been arguing that the party was on the losing side of the abortion issue, and Clinton was pointedly for abortion rights.

None of this criticism made any difference when Pennsylvania Democrats went to the polls on April 28. Turnout again was low, with the outcome a foregone conclusion, and Clinton beat Brown by more than two to one, 57 percent to 25, with 13 for Tsongas. Much more significant for the Clinton inner circle was the fact that when the network exit pollsters again asked the "honesty and integrity" question, 62 percent answered that they thought Clinton had those qualifications, to 34 percent who said no. "Bill really felt we had turned the corner," Greer said.

Some minor headaches remained, including pressures from Jesse Jackson. After a meeting with Clinton in Kansas City three days before the Pennsylvania vote, Jackson left without endorsing him and was quoted in a New York tabloid interview as saying: "I see myself as a running mate for the Democratic Party. . . . If I am rejected this time, I am prepared to react." It seemed like the same old stuff Jackson had tried with Michael Dukakis in 1988, but he quickly backed off, saying "at no time did I threaten the candidate or the party over the vice presidency or anything else." In any event, Clinton was not ready to undertake the selection of a running mate yet and he wasn't about to let Jackson under the tent, as would soon become abundantly clear.

On May 12, however, Clinton did announce a three-person task force headed by Warren Christopher, deputy secretary of state under Jimmy Carter, and aided by Vernon Jordan, a prominent Washington lawyer and former head of the National Urban League, and former Governor Madeleine M. Kunin of Vermont. They began extensive conversations with party leaders about the choice and eventually started interviewing possible selections.

Clinton was sweeping through the remaining primaries routinely now and focusing his campaigning increasingly on President Bush. When America's worst race riots broke out in Los Angeles, Clinton was quick to criticize Bush's initial comment that "the jury system has worked." He expressed hope that the president "would at least acknowledge that the facts of the case as evidenced by the film lead a lot of Americans, and not just black Americans, to wonder about the accuracy of the verdict." Later he chastised Bush for waiting so long to embrace the proposals of his own housing secretary, Jack Kemp, for urban enterprise zones and other initiatives to address inner-city problems.

The final primary day, June 2, in California and five other states, which earlier had been expected to be decisive, was an anticlimax, with Clinton again winning everything in sight including Jerry Brown's home state, which the Arkansan won by 47 percent to 40. By now, most of the "buyer's remorse" appeared to have subsided, at least among Democratic primary voters.

Still, however, Clinton continued to trail Bush in the national polls and was in danger of falling into third place behind Perot, who was climbing fast and grabbing all the headlines. "There was nothing we could do to break through," Stephanopoulos recalled. "Even when we won we were judged by the exit polls." Large numbers of voters told the pollsters that they really preferred Perot—to the point, Stephanopoulos said, that the exit polls "became more important than the actual results."

To Begala, it was "the worst time in the campaign" because "we were doing everything right, honing our message, and Clinton was hitting his stride, but we were being totally eclipsed by Ross Perot." Greer agreed. "The low point emotionally was the night of the California primary," he said. "We had won the nomination, and we turned around and coming down the track was this train, and written on the headlights was 'Ross Perot.' "

Clinton also hit bottom emotionally on the night of his California victory because of the exit polls indicating voters would have voted for Perot had he been on the ballot. "Nobody was laying a glove on him," Clinton told us later. That night, he said, "was much more of a low point than what had happened in New Hampshire. Because when I was in New Hampshire, I felt I had really connected with those people. They had been coming in big numbers even when I was dropping in the polls, and I knew that if we could find a way to appeal to their innate sense of fairness, that they would in some sense decide that my campaign should go on."

But after that, through the California primary, he said, "every primary was a struggle. I thought if I could just get through and win the nomination and there were three people who wanted to be president, that in a way the whole primary trial would be a plus, and there would then have to be some balanced scrutiny of the record and positions, the complete character of each contestant, and that I would have an opportunity from June to July to carry out our strategy. . . . But a lot of people just shut it down. They weren't listening.''

Through this period, Clinton displayed a frustration with the news media's continued focus on what he called ''process questions.'' After having survived all the personal allegations and the challenges of all comers, the appearance of a page-one story in *The New York Times* on the prospects for a brokered convention was illustrative of his complaint. Although he himself was a political animal to the core, he felt there was too much political clutter going on for his policy message to get through. He wanted to talk about his economic and other proposals, not about polls, the ''horse race'' and such things as whether Perot helped or hurt him or Bush more. In a long interview with him as his car was stalled in a San Francisco traffic jam around this time, Clinton conveyed his coolness to such questions on sheer politics and process.

Much later, campaign press secretary Dee Dee Myers observed: ''Bill Clinton is part policy wonk and part political strategist, and he's very good at both. He really enjoys the give-and-take of politics, he really enjoys the day-to-day demands of governing. What he found out was that every time he uttered a word about politics, he got tremendous coverage. When he talked about policy, nobody listened. And so as the campaign went on he learned to say less about politics, because when he did, that was what ended up being the lead of everybody's story.'' For this reason, Greer said later, ''we counseled him not to talk process.''

On the advice of Hollywood television situation comedy producers Harry Thomason and his wife, Linda Bloodworth-Thomason, and others on the staff, Clinton found that one way to get beyond the news media's focus on process questions was to work the television talk show circuit. Since the Manhattan Project had established clearly that voters still did not have a clear idea of who Bill Clinton was, the best and most cost-effective way to deal with the problem was television exposure, and then more television exposure, offbeat or otherwise, and hope voters would start paying attention. What's more, he couldn't seem to get enough of talking to them. During a break in one appearance on the Larry King show, King asked him whether he wasn't worn down by the pace. Clinton seemed surprised at the question. ''I love this,'' he said.

The whole focus on the talk shows, especially of the pop culture variety in the period after the California primary, Grunwald said, was known inside the campaign as "the Arsenio strategy," after Clinton's appearance on the Arsenio Hall late-night show. There, he played "Heartbreak Hotel" on his saxophone, wearing dark shades and looking and sounding cool to that special audience not likely to be reached with a heavy speech on his economic agenda.

Grunwald said she had become particularly interested in the approach when a chambermaid at a hotel in Wisconsin during that state's primary told Clinton, "I saw you on Donahue. You were great!" The woman, Grunwald said, did not seem to be the type who read the newspaper every day or followed the campaign, but her reaction "was very much a personal one—'I know you. I have a sense of who you are.' " There was a whole audience of prospective voters out there that was not being reached on a personal level by traditional means, but could be reached. And, an important consideration to a campaign running low on money at the end of the primary trail, the talk show circuit was free.

Shortly after the Arsenio show, Clinton did a national town meeting on television and then another with young voters on the MTV cable outlet. To the surprise of many, the questions from the young audience revealed mostly the same concerns among the music video set that were on the minds of their square elders—jobs, the economy and fears about the future.

The Clinton campaign, in addition to being on the lookout for ways to reach untapped audiences, also continued to seek means to show the candidate "going against the grain," to demonstrate that he was indeed a different kind of candidate. An opportunity was about to present itself in this regard, handed unwittingly to Clinton by an irreverent member of the MTV generation—a young rap entertainer who called herself Sister Souljah.

CHAPTER 1 6

JETTISONING JESSE

With Bill Clinton now on an apparently unimpeded course to the Democratic nomination, one question lingered within the party: what to do about Jesse Jackson. Ever since he had decided to get into elective politics as a candidate for the 1984 nomination, the civil rights leader had been a mixed blessing for the Democratic Party and its candidates.

Jackson's unprecedented candidacy had an enormous significance to black voters, who took great pride in his ability to compete effectively at the highest level of American politics. His most obvious appeal was to the young blacks he urged to stay in school, stay away from drugs and take part in the process. But beyond them, particularly in that first campaign in 1984, he reached effectively into all segments of black society. A few leaders such as Andrew Young, a close adviser to the Reverend Martin Luther King, Jr., and later a congressman and mayor of Atlanta, viewed him with a jaundiced eye because of their experience with his showboating style during the civil rights movement. But most blacks of all levels of educational and economic achievement admired his audacity and determination. Jackson held his own, or more than his own, in televised debates with white candidates, and "Run, Jesse, Run," was not just a chant from the young.

But it was equally true that Jackson was a red flag to more conservative white voters, in the South and the industrial Northeast and Midwest. They were intimidated by his in-your-face style and saw him as a political radical demanding special treatment for blacks at their expense. Jackson himself was not inclined to mute his demands in the interest of keeping these whites within the Democratic Party.

On the contrary, his position was that he represented the party's single most loyal voter bloc and the one whose fealty was absolutely essential to the success of any Democratic presidential candidate. As a result, in both 1984 and 1988 he had brought about public confrontations with the party's presidential nominees that had given many voters the impression—largely unjustified—that they had caved in to the civil rights leader to buy his endorsement and support.

In 1984, Jackson had finished third far behind Walter Mondale and Gary Hart in the contest for the Democratic nomination. Yet rather than throw in behind the ticket of Mondale and Geraldine A. Ferraro, he stood aside as the leader of a separate force, reconfiguring his candidacy as a movement and sailing through the convention in San Francisco, and the entire summer, without delivering an endorsement. Finally, he agreed to attend a meeting of prominent black Democrats in St. Paul on Labor Day weekend, although also insisting on a separate meeting of his own with Mondale at the nominee's home just outside the city.

After that session, Jackson and Mondale were driven to the parking lot of a school nearby for a press conference—where, with Mondale standing uncomfortably at his side, Jackson pointedly refused to use the word "endorse" to express his support for the ticket. Later that night, under pressure from other prominent blacks at a meeting in the St. Paul Hotel, Jackson finally delivered his endorsement. But the whole episode sent a picture through the television networks of the civil rights leader jerking around the Democratic nominee for president. It was an image that persisted throughout that campaign—and was clearly a contributing factor to Mondale's inability to win even 30 percent of the white vote in the Deep South states such as Alabama, Georgia, Louisiana and North Carolina with large black populations.

Four years later, Jackson finished second—but a distant second—to Michael Dukakis and, again, made the most of his opportunity, withholding his endorsement until a convention-eve session in an Atlanta hotel after another media circus of several days' duration. This one was set off by Jackson's learning from the press, rather than directly from Dukakis himself, that Senator Lloyd Bentsen of Texas had been chosen for the vice presidential nomination. The mistake had been purely mechanical, a case of a misplaced telephone call. But Jackson wasn't willing to let it go by, when a display of indignation and bruised feelings obviously could give him added leverage at the convention.

Once again the electorate was being given apparent reason to believe another Democratic nominee was caving in to Jesse Jackson. And, once again, a Democratic presidential nominee was beaten by embarrassing margins among white voters in the South and some working-class areas of the Northeast and Midwest. Although few would argue that Jackson was the prime factor in those defeats, there was little doubt, considering the role of race in American politics of the 1980s, that among many white voters he was a heavy piece of political baggage.

The pattern had become clear in presidential and, alarmingly for Southern Democratic leaders, many statewide contests, as well. In states with large black populations, white candidates with any identification as liberals needed only 30 to 35 percent of the white vote because they could count on winning 90 percent of the black vote. But, paradoxically, the states in which these candidates needed the fewest white votes were the ones where it was most difficult to enlist them. Their best opportunity lay in states such as Tennessee, Kentucky or Arkansas, where they needed 40 percent or more of the white vote because there were relatively fewer blacks—and the Democrats were not identified as ''the black party'' with which some white voters were so reluctant to identify themselves.

A racial pattern sending a similar message emerged in the Democatic primaries when Jackson was an active candidate, particularly in 1988. His share of the white vote was consistently largest in those states in which the black share of the population was smallest. It was easier for white liberals in Oregon, for example, to identify with Jackson and his boast of a ''rainbow'' than it was for white working-class voters in New Jersey or Michigan.

This time the situation was different. Jackson had not competed in the primaries, and his refusal to run for mayor of the District of Columbia in 1990 had diminished his validity as a serious political figure. But he was still an influential voice with black Americans, and his relationship with Bill Clinton and the Democratic Leadership Council had not been a comfortable one. He had not forgotten that Clinton was chairman of the DLC at the time he was barred from speaking at its Cleveland meeting in May of 1991. The situation had been further exacerbated, moreover, by the incident during the primary season when Clinton, mistakenly thinking he was sitting at a dead microphone, blew up angrily when misinformed that Jackson had endorsed Tom Harkin in South Carolina.

Jackson originally responded with an unusually mild statement, but on second thought decided to take offense. "I'm disappointed with his overreaction without verification," he said in an interview on CNN, which repeatedly ran the clip of the outraged Clinton. "I'm disturbed by the tone of the blast at my integrity, my character. I felt blindsided by what I finally saw and heard him say." As was the case with the Lloyd Bentsen episode four years earlier, Jackson wasn't going to miss an opportunity to react to any perceived slight.

Clinton had followed a policy of maintaining a distance from Jackson throughout the primary period, and his advisers were telling reporters privately that this was the way it was going to be. Jackson had no delegates, they argued, so he had no special claim on a place at the convention in New York or in the general election campaign. More to the point, by this stage of the campaign Clinton had enlisted valuable support from black officeholders such as Representatives John Lewis of Georgia and Mike Espy of Mississippi and Mayors Maynard Jackson of Atlanta and Kurt Schmoke of Baltimore. If the goal was to increase black turnout, which declined precipitously from Mondale to Dukakis, these officeholders could deliver just as well as Jesse Jackson. Or, at least, so the theory went.

Clinton's campaign through the primaries had appeared carefully staged to avoid the kind of identification with black leaders and causes that could thwart his more obvious appeal to the Southern whites and Reagan Democrats elsewhere, who were essential to his prospects of building a winning coalition in the general election. Clinton's appearances at black events often seemed timed so that they would be too late for the television network news that night or so that they would be overshadowed in newsworthiness by other events.

And, happily for Clinton, although there was muttering from a few black leaders, most of them were pragmatic enough to understand that the first imperative was to elect a Democratic president after twelve years of Ronald Reagan and George Bush. So they let his neglect slide in a way they might not otherwise have done. The prickly Jackson might be grumbling there in the background, the Clinton managers said, but he was no longer the only game in town.

There were, however, some prominent Clinton supporters, particularly in the South, who thought the Arkansas governor needed to do more to separate himself from Jackson and had advised him to find a way to emphasize that distance so it would be clear to white voters. None of Jackson's white competitors in 1984 and 1988 ever had confronted him in any seriously forceful way, even when, in 1984, there were the allegations of anti-Semitism after his reference to New York as "Hymietown."

The one candidate who ventured into open criticism of Jackson was Senator Joseph Biden of Delaware at an early stage of the preliminaries to the 1988 contest. And Jackson had come back at him so harshly that the lesson for other campaigns was to tread very softly. But this time Jackson seemed less insulated from criticism, and Bill Clinton was told on more than one occasion that he could help himself immensely by, as one longtime party activist and fund-raiser in Alabama put it, "telling old Jesse where to stuff it."

There was never any evidence that Clinton approved such a strategy explicitly, but late in the spring—whether inadvertently or not—he followed it.

En route to a June 13 appearance before a meeting of Jackson's Rainbow Coalition in Washington, Clinton learned that the previous night the group had heard from Lisa Williamson, a rap singer known as Sister Souljah who had caused a stir with some angry rhetoric in the aftermath of the Los Angeles riots. On May 13, *The Washington Post* had published a story about an interview in which Sister Souljah was asked if she thought the violence had been "wise."

She replied: "Yeah, it was wise. I mean if black people kill black people every day, why not have a week and kill white people? . . . In other words, white people, this government and the mayor were well aware of the fact that black people were dying every day in Los Angeles under gang violence. So if you're a gang member and you normally would be killing somebody, why not kill a white person?''

Clinton had decided he should address the Sister Souljah rhetoric before a black audience, just as he had been telling home truths to other audiences such as those in Detroit and Macomb County during the Michigan primary campaign and in his blast at business greed at the Wharton School during the primary in Pennsylvania.

So, with Jackson sitting at his left in a conference room of the Sheraton Washington Hotel, Clinton chastised the Rainbow Coalition for giving the rap singer their conference as a forum. Her remarks to the *Post*, he said, had been ''filled with a kind of hatred that you do not honor today and tonight.'' He added: ''If you took the words 'white' and 'black' and reversed them, you might think David Duke was giving that speech.''

Jackson, who had listened in silence while staring stonily ahead, was clearly nonplussed. ''I don't know what his intention was,'' he told reporters who quickly crowded around him afterward while a gospel singer sang in the background. ''I was totally surprised.''

Later, after meetings with Clinton and his own advisers, Jackson held a press conference at which he defended Sister Souljah, arguing that she had been ''misunderstood'' and suggesting she had been misquoted when, in fact, the interview had been tape-recorded by the *Post*'s reporter. Jackson's willingness to defend the rap singer quickly recalled his silence eight years earlier when one of his most militant supporters was Louis Farrakhan.

But now Jackson's focus was on the critic rather than the object of the criticism. Clinton, he said, had shown ''very bad judgment'' in assailing her at the Rainbow meeting. ''It was unnecessary, it was a diversion,'' Jackson said. ''I don't know why he used this platform to address those issues.''

Clinton had tried to couch his criticism by depicting the rap singer's rhetoric as foreign to the purposes of the Rainbow Coalition and by making a point of citing his own ''mistake'' earlier in the spring when he played golf at an all-white country club in Little Rock. ''We have an obligation, all of us, to call attention to prejudice wherever we see it,'' he said. But there was no question that he had confronted Jackson on his home turf in a way that was certain to attract heavy attention from the news media, a situation almost certain to evoke a response.

Jackson said later that he "really was stunned and amazed" by Clinton's remarks. The two men had met for about thirty minutes in a suite in the hotel before the conference session, and Clinton had given no hint of his intention to raise the question of Sister Souljah's remarks. Moreover, Jackson recalled, he thought he himself had shown restraint repeatedly in the months before the meeting, passing up more than one chance to take what he called "a clear shot" at the Arkansas governor.

During the height of the Gennifer Flowers controversy, Jackson said, he had telephoned Clinton "to express my sensitivity and concern" about the preoccupation of the press with the issue, at the expense of attention to more important concerns—just as he had done, he said, with Gary Hart during the Donna Rice episode in 1987.

A week or so later, Jackson said, he had called Clinton again to urge him to consider a reprieve for Rickey Ray Rector, the brain-damaged convicted killer scheduled to be executed in Arkansas. Clinton told him, Jackson said, that he was "praying about it" but that all legal options apparently had been exhausted. The day after the execution, Clinton flew to Washington to appear before a meeting sponsored by the Rainbow Coalition, whose members were not happy about Clinton's permitting it to go forward. But, Jackson said, they "chose to be restrained in their displeasure about what had happened the very night before.

"We did not make it a point by which to define him, which we could have done because our people were in that mood," Jackson said. "They were very angry about it. . . . We could have reacted to our displeasure by disinviting him." Instead, he said, Clinton was given "a fair hearing" and "left unscarred. . . . It was not a showdown moment because we chose not to make it a showdown moment."

The next dustup came when Clinton erupted in that television studio about Jackson campaigning with Harkin in South Carolina. This time, Jackson said, he thought they had reached an agreement to avoid such problems in the future. Clinton had called him at about two o'clock in the morning to apologize for the outburst, Jackson recalled, and the two agreed that henceforth they would communicate with each other privately when either had a complaint, before going public. The policy, said Jackson, would be "open lines before we have open mikes. . . . This was another time that we could have shot at him if that were our interest."

What Jackson called the "accumulation of signals" of ill will continued to build, he said, while he himself continued to show restraint. Next there was the visit of Clinton and Senator Sam Nunn to a Georgia prison camp the day before the March 3 Georgia primary—a ploy Jackson figured was designed to produce pictures and stories "calculated to be on the front page" that would depict Clinton as tough on crime. Jackson called the visit "a version of the Willie Horton situation," but again one on which he showed restraint. And then there was Clinton's "mistake" two weeks later in playing golf at an all-white country club in Little Rock, a breach that Jackson again allowed to pass with what he considered great restraint.

In Jackson's view, there was a pattern of consistent behavior on Clinton's part from the time he shut Jackson out of the DLC convention in Cleveland in 1991 clear through to his attack on the rap singer at the Rainbow conference. "There was a straight line from that meeting to Souljah," he said.

After Clinton had made his remarks and the conference session ended, Jackson and Clinton returned to the hotel suite. By this time, Jackson was seething. "I said, 'You violated us. Why did you do this?' " he said he told Clinton. The governor replied, Jackson said, that he was "offended" at the allegation, pointing out that he had praised the Rainbow Coalition highly and that his remarks on Sister Souljah had been just a fraction of what he had said. But Clinton, Jackson noted later, produced from his pocket a piece of paper containing the text of Sister Souljah's controversial observations—proof that Clinton had come primed to make an issue of them.

The meeting between the two men was sufficiently civil, however, that, as both said later, Jackson invited Clinton to come back to the meeting later and play his saxophone. "Even then," Jackson said, "we didn't realize the political ramifications and calculation of what had happened."

Clinton's remarks, nonetheless, had struck a nerve with the press and attendees at the conference, to which Sister Souljah had been invited as a participant to a youth workshop. "Afterwards," Jackson recalled, "people were enraged. They were prepared to go [outside the hotel] and confront him [Clinton] at his car, go to his hotel and other kinds of things,'' until dissuaded by Jackson.

Jackson's anger built when Frank Watkins, a longtime close adviser, informed him that he had been warned in advance that Clinton was going to say something newsworthy. ''I got word from one of the reporters that this was going down,'' Watkins said later. ''I didn't know exactly what it was, but that he was going to do or say something that would be offensive to the Rainbow, and this was part of their 'counter-scheduling' strategy.''

Much later, Clinton while acknowledging his campaign's use of a ''counter-scheduling'' strategy on other occasions, as in his Macomb County, Michigan, speech, insisted that it didn't apply to the Sister Souljah incident. ''There were some people, some folks in our group, who really thought I should go there as counter-scheduling and just take her on,'' he said, ''which was the way it got played, what I said. I made a deliberate decision that I didn't want to do that because I didn't know her, I had never had any contact with her, and also because even though Jesse and I had had differences, I was immensely impressed with his Rebuild America, his economic plan, and I was there in effect trying to compliment him for emphasizing some things that had not been empha-sized before on his part. . . .

''So I read what she said and I decided that I should make a very different point, which I honestly tried to make . . . although because I was there on Jesse's doorstep and because I had done so much counter-scheduling before, it's not the way it came out. The point I was trying to make when I read about what she had said . . . was here was this obvi-ously really articulate, really intelligent, really passionate young woman, clearly a role model, who was saying things that I strongly disapprove of. . . . But the importance of her to me was how urgent it was for us to take on these tasks and to take them on together, because we were in danger of losing a whole generation. You had all these kids that were out there in trouble and then you had young people like her who were doing well but were so alienated that they couldn't be reached.

''So the point I was trying to make was a very different one than the one that came out, which was that we didn't have a lot of time and here's somebody saying something that I strongly disapprove of who's obviously representative of a certain point of view, and we'd better move and move now to try to bring these folks back in the fold. That's the point I was trying to make. As it turned out, because I was there with Jesse and because of the past habits of counter-scheduling and maybe [because] there were some people in my crowd who wanted me to deliver a different message that I deliberately decided not to deliver because I didn't think it was the right thing. I wanted to reach out an olive branch to someone I strongly disagreed with as a way of symbolizing what I thought we had to do. So I kind of regretted the way it came out, actually.''

There was still another complicating element in the situation. Well before the meeting, Clinton and his strategists had decided they would ''shut down'' any speculation about Jackson as a possible vice presidential nominee by telling him early that he wouldn't be selected. To temporize as Dukakis had done in 1988, they feared, would set off another round of controversy and raise unrealistic expectations in the black community that would have to be disappointed.

Thus, during one of their private meetings that day—Jackson thought it was the first, others the second—Clinton told Jackson that he wouldn't be his running mate. As Jackson recalled it, Clinton said: ''I've made a choice about my ticket, and given our calculations, I don't think that would work.''

Jackson said he replied that his advisers also had done some calculations on how his presence on the ticket could change the election arithmetic in a positive way. He said he offered to give Clinton an analysis that was ''at least worth assessing and calculating.'' Clinton said he would read it. But after the blowup over Clinton's remarks about Sister Souljah, Jackson said, he decided not to provide the material to him.

Long after the fact, Clinton described to us in positive terms his decision to inform Jackson directly that he wasn't going to be on the Democratic ticket. ''I told him that I was not going to select him,'' Clinton said. ''I did it basically out of personal respect. I did it because . . . I thought he was a very important part of the Democratic coalition and a very important leader in America, because I wanted to have a good, honest, open relationship with him, and I just wanted to do it personally. It's not something I wanted to delegate, something I wanted to do on the phone, and it was coming on time for me to make a decision. I was getting close to a decision and I wanted to look him in the eye and tell him myself. I think it was something I should personally do.''

Asked what the reason was for not selecting Jackson, Clinton diplomatically observed that he was already moving toward another choice that would be an "utterly different, unconventional decision." He added, however, that "I just didn't think it was the right thing to do at this time . . . either substantively or politically." His uneasy history with Jackson went unmentioned, but certainly was a factor, along with the obvious question of whether any black candidate, and this one especially, would hurt rather than help the ticket "at this time."

Jackson said later that he knew the Clinton campaign would suggest—as it did—that he reacted heatedly to Clinton's remarks on Sister Souljah "because we were disappointed" about being shut off the ticket, "but that was not the case at all." If he was going to react angrily to that circumstance, Jackson argued, he would have been much more likely to do so four years earlier after he had received several million votes in the primaries. (He had, however, complained at length in 1988 about hearing the news from someone else that Dukakis had picked Lloyd Bentsen.)

"This had strictly to do with insulting our audience," Jackson said, a view he came to hold with greater force the more he thought about it. "He [Clinton] actually was talking to the TV audience," he said. "He was not talking to the people who were there. He was using the people who were there as a platform to spread his message."

This perceived slight was the issue on which Jackson's anger finally focused as his friends and advisers drove home the point to him. As Watkins told him the day after the conference: "The guy came into your house, kicked you in the balls, and turned around and walked out." Jackson, Watkins said, "still didn't want to believe it," but finally did.

If there was any doubt about Jackson's anger, he resolved it over the next few days. He complained bitterly and repeatedly that Clinton had abused his hospitality in an attempt to reach the white working-class voters who had deserted the Democratic Party in large numbers in the previous three campaigns. Jackson said the presumptive nominee had "again exposed a character flaw" by conducting what amounted to "a very well-planned sneak attack without the courage to confront but with a calculation to embarrass" Jackson himself. The Clinton strategy was designed, the civil rights leader told *The New York Times*, "purely to appeal to conservative whites by containing Jackson and isolating Jackson." It was an excellent piece of political analysis but not one designed to improve the relationship between the civil rights leader and the Arkansas governor.

Clinton and his advisers professed to be surprised by the intensity of Jackson's anger, but Clinton refused to back down. Talking to reporters at Little Rock, he said: "I bragged on the Rainbow Coalition and its programs. I criticized divisive language by Sister Souljah. If Jesse Jackson wants to align himself with that now and claim that's the way he felt, then that's his business."

Reached by *The New York Times*, Jackson replied with one of his typical formulations: "The attempt to align me with her is an attempt to malign me with her." Appearing on the CBS program *Face the Nation* a couple of days later, Jackson added: "As we reached out, Bill Clinton pushed off and so we don't want to interfere with the campaign, nor do we want to be a foil for any tricks."

Ten days after the original incident, Jackson was still beating the same horse. The night before he was to speak at the annual meeting of the U.S. Conference of Mayors in Houston, Jackson received a call from an old ally who had been one of the chairmen of his 1984 campaign, Mayor Maynard Jackson of Atlanta. Maynard Jackson's message was direct: it is time, he told Jesse Jackson, to cool down this feud with Clinton. When the press asks you about it in Houston, give them a "no comment." Otherwise, they won't pay any attention to your own proposal for an urban investment bank.

For his part, Maynard Jackson was fully behind Clinton. He had followed his own advice and turned aside questions about the Sister Souljah incident. And in a closed meeting of Democratic mayors, Maynard Jackson had taken the lead in making the case for what proved to be a strong declaration of support for the economic program Clinton had announced only two days earlier, and now was bringing before the conference. Nor was Maynard Jackson alone; other black mayors such as Sharpe James of Newark and Norman Rice of Seattle also were quick to praise the Clinton initiative.

But when Jesse Jackson arrived, it was clear he wasn't ready to take Maynard Jackson's advice and put the whole thing behind him. Although he used his speech to the mayors to call Clinton's economic program "a step in the right direction [that] shows an authentic concern for the urban crisis and the need to reinvest,'' he pointedly refused at a press conference to endorse Clinton.

And he was obviously unready to forget Sister Souljah. Clinton, he told reporters, was trying to "distance" himself from Jackson to seek white votes. The civil rights leader was derisive about Clinton's argument that he had been speaking out of anger at Sister Souljah's rhetoric. "When Bill Clinton said he's left the all-white country club," he reminded reporters, "he didn't say he left because of moral outrage. He just said he'd left."

Clinton could have made his point about Sister Souljah, Jackson suggested, by simply not attending that Rainbow Coalition meeting. "If the issue was distancing," he said, "there was distance before he came." When a reporter pointed out to him that he had nice things to say about Clinton's economic program, he looked up with a thin smile and replied: "I have been consistently nice. I have good manners."

When the press conference ended, Jackson took a reporter aside outside the conference room and explained he had no choice but to respond to Clinton's "distancing" strategy. "He used our meeting to do it," he said. The notion of Jackson complaining about a politician using someone else's forum was laughable on its face; he had made a career of transforming other leaders' events into forums for himself.

But the message was obvious that Jackson was in no hurry to heal the breach. On the contrary, he may have had visions of another "summit" meeting such as those Mondale and Dukakis had granted—the kind of media event that would be catnip for the press and television cameras soon to be gathered in huge numbers for the nominating convention at New York.

Press attention was meat and drink for Jesse Jackson. When he was campaigning for the party ticket in the general election campaign of 1988, he used to telephone the national editor of *The Washington Post* and others to brief them on his schedule for the day. But as a player on the fringe, that kind of attention wasn't being paid until the controversy over Sister Souljah. Now, as one longtime Jackson friend put it, "You'll notice he was back on the front page of *The New York Times* last week. It's been a long time since that happened."

But Clinton and his managers were just as determined that there would be no such attempt at rapprochement. Jackson didn't have any delegates this time, they said, and he was not going to be given special treatment. "Why in hell do we have to deal with him at all?" a Clinton confidant asked in tones that answered the question.

After the fact, Clinton and his advisers insisted there had been no deliberate, carefully contrived plan to affront Jackson, that the whole episode had been a natural next step in the policy Clinton was following of "going against the grain"—telling audiences things they didn't necessarily prefer to hear. As Mickey Kantor, chairman of the Clinton campaign, described it, "We had a whole campaign . . . of going to Macomb County and going to a black church [in Detroit], going to Floyd Flake's church [in New York] and then going to an Orthodox Jewish dinner, to try to show symbolically, as well as in terms of what Clinton wanted to do programmatically, that he wanted to bring disparate communities together in this country. His immediate gut reaction was that [what] Sister Souljah had been saying, in effect, in her music was the antithesis of what Bill Clinton was trying to do."

Within the campaign, Kantor said, the discussion centered not on "Bill Clinton standing up to Jesse Jackson" but instead on the candidate being consistent in his approach. "We were so focused on what he had been doing, and what we had tried to project for months at that point became the issue—that if you go before the Rainbow Coalition, you don't just back off of that issue and tell them what they want to hear."

"Had we gone to Rainbow and not said something about it," George Stephanopoulos said later, "you think that every Republican . . . wouldn't have been on us for that? They'd have beaten the crap out of us."

So Clinton and his advisers discussed how Jackson might react, how angry he might be—but not whether to take the risk. "He couldn't go in front of this audience and not say something," Kantor said. "It would be impossible for Bill Clinton. . . . Not saying anything was a continuation of the same kind of politics which had led us to get our clocks cleaned in every election."

According to Paul Begala, Clinton originally intended to make public his criticism of Sister Souljah shortly after the riots in Los Angeles in a speech before the Show Coalition, a group of Hollywood celebrities that was active in raising money for the Democratic campaign. The plan was to make the point that people in the entertainment business had a moral responsibility to speak out when one of their own was advocating racism. But the event in Los Angeles, he said, proved to be "a philanthropic thing" at which such a scolding speech would have been out of place.

"So he put the speech on the shelf," Begala recalled. "It was not going to be a central thrust of the campaign but he just felt that he was going to be Bill Clinton and put appeals for racial unity in all of his speeches. . . . Then he felt something of a moral obligation if you see something like this, to speak out against it, to be against racism wherever you see it. Then time passes, two or three weeks, and Clinton's going to be at the Rainbow Coalition and Mandy Grunwald notices on the program the day before is Sister Souljah, so what do you do? It's pretty easy for Clinton. You have to be true to yourself. You have to be true to your views. So we dusted off the appropriate parts of the Sister Souljah speech and gave it there."

But, Begala insisted, "it was not, as some think, an overt attempt to find something to stick in Jesse Jackson's eye for the sake of doing it. . . . The purpose of the speech wasn't just to piss off Jesse."

All this sounded reasonable long after the fact. But it was also true at the time that some Clinton strategists were encouraging the idea that this was a candidate who would not be kowtowing to Jesse Jackson and just might find a way to prove it. Nor was it any secret that Clinton was getting advice from allies, particularly in the South, that he needed to make his independence from Jackson as clear as possible. And that, in turn, would involve a deliberate strategy that the timing in this case seemed to suggest. If Sister Souljah's rhetoric was so offensive, why did Clinton have to wait an entire month? Was there no other way to make his message heard? Was it necessary to drop the bomb on Jackson at a Rainbow Coalition conference without giving him any advance notice?

Longtime Jackson-watchers have come to realize, however, that Jackson's anger is sometimes more tactical than emotional, a display turned on and off as another way to achieve some specific purpose. In this case, the continuing attacks by Jackson right through the mayors' conference in Houston already had served to put him back in the Democratic equation as a force with whom Clinton apparently would have to reckon before the Democratic convention opened in New York in three weeks.

Within the Clinton campaign, however, there was no inclination to accord Jackson anything that looked like special treatment. The candidate and his advisers all were fully aware of the experiences of Mondale and Dukakis—and with the political price each had paid. Dealing with Jackson was notoriously difficult, as the Clinton managers were also aware.

"Somebody said [Mondale campaign manager] Bob Beckel met with him seventy-two times," Carville said. "I couldn't meet anybody on the face of this earth seventy-two times." The bottom line was a decision simply to ride out Jackson's rage and avoid any appearance of being too conciliatory. "Nobody ever said there'd be one of those big summit meetings," one Clinton adviser said.

This approach rested heavily on the confidence that Clinton could rely on those other black leaders. "Bill Clinton did not need an envoy to the African-American community," Mickey Kantor said later. "He did not need a visa." When John Lewis earlier said of Clinton, "He can walk the walk and he can talk the talk," Kantor said, "in the African-American community that was remembered." And Clinton, said his press secretary, Dee Dee Myers, "just wouldn't cede the turf to him [Jackson]."

In political terms, however, the issue was less whether Clinton could enlist heavy black support without Jesse Jackson than whether he could win more support from Southern whites and Reagan Democrats in the north by taking on Jackson so directly and visibly. As the campaign wore on, it became apparent that, premeditated or not, the Clinton posture toward Jackson resonated throughout the electorate. As Stephanopoulos put it later, "It stood for something larger than what it was"—dramatic evidence this was a "different kind of Democrat."

We heard about it repeatedly from Democrats in the South all through the general election campaign. As Al LaPierre, executive director of the party in Alabama, recalled: "People would come up to me and say, 'Dammit, we've finally done something right. . . . It was really amazing that one instance worked so well." And we heard it from blue-collar workers in the industrial states outside the South. Kevin Mullaney, an electrician in North Philadelphia, later told one of us, "The day he told off that fucking Jackson is the day he got my vote."

Just how much of a price Clinton might pay in terms of black support for affronting Jackson was impossible to determine. Clinton was winning heavily among blacks during the primaries. But, unsurprisingly, black turnout in the primaries was far lower than it had been when Jesse Jackson was a candidate.

The task in political arithmetic was simple enough—whether whatever losses in the black vote Clinton might suffer from a lower turnout in November would be offset by the message he had sent to white Democrats. At the moment, however, another problem was looming ever larger in Clinton's aspirations to collar white Democratic votes. His name was Ross Perot.

SEARCHLIGHT ON
INSPECTOR PEROT

While President Bush was methodically if uninspiringly disposing of the challenge of Pat Buchanan, and Bill Clinton was surviving the pitfalls of the Democratic primaries and his own past, the phenomenon of Ross Perot and his bandwagon of volunteer "owners" of the country had continued to roll on. It was fueled up to now essentially by the high-octane energy of the glib, fast-talking Texas billionaire as he worked the television talk show circuit, assuring his admiring millions of supporters that if only they would "stay in the ring" with him, together they would crack the gridlock in Washington and change America.

He was, as he had promised, putting some of his own money into the drive to place his name on the ballot in all fifty states, but the $400,000 in his first filing with the Federal Election Commission was only small change by his reckoning. From Maine to California, voters were opening petition offices and manning petition tables in shopping malls at their own expense to advance the cause.

As the weeks flashed by, however, Perot found himself increasingly pressed on the talk show circuit to get beyond the clever one-liners and sound bites of the sort he continued to decry from "the politicians," and spell out exactly what he had in mind to end the recession and eliminate the nation's staggering deficit. When he did use hard figures and they were questioned, he would duck, or promise an explanation later.

One claim was that he could cut $180 billion by eliminating government waste, fraud and abuse; another was that he would save $100 billion a year by asking well-off older people like himself to decline monthly Social Security and Medicare checks to which they were entitled. When his figures were challenged on the NBC News show *Meet the Press*, he grew testy and insisted the numbers had been given to him by a government expert "whose name is a household word," but he declined to supply it.

In a speech before the American Newspaper Publishers Association in New York in early May, Perot announced that he was going to cut back on his whirlwind schedule of television appearances and interviews to focus on getting ready for a full-blown candidacy. He said he would "spend all my time building an organization, finalizing a strategy and developing carefully thought out positions on each of the major issues." These were all undertakings his effort badly needed, as he confessed to the publishers.

"Night and day," he said, "there is saturation bombing. There are Patriot missiles going down air shafts in my office from all your good reporters wanting to know my position on everything from mosquitoes to ants."

Lack of specificity was not Perot's only problem at this point. As the phenomenon continued to exceed expectations, threatening to make him a very serious factor in the fall outcome of the presidential campaign, news media scrutiny was intensifying proportionately. Even before Perot burst on the political scene, he had a reputation as a man with a short fuse and a suspicious nature. Now individuals who had been subjected to either, or said they had been, began to tell the world. And reporters began to probe for whatever they could find that would reveal who this man who would be president really was, and what made him tick.

The publisher of *The Fort Worth Star-Telegram*, Richard L. Connor, came forward with a story that Perot three years earlier had threatened to release compromising photographs of one of the newspaper's employees in retaliation for the publication of an unfavorable story about his son, Ross Jr. "I was just stunned by it," Connor said. "It was sort of seamy, extremely mean-spirited. . . . I remember how shocked I was that this guy would stoop to that level." Perot's response was that he had called to "complain about the accuracy of a story" but that he had made "no comments of a personal nature about anyone."

This and similar stories soon gave rise to the characterization "Inspector Perot"—a man with a fixation for investigating others, allegedly with the intent of digging up dirt that could be used as threats, or out of a suspicion or fear that someone else was acting out of suspect motives.

An Associated Press reporter in Washington, John Solomon, routinely checking on Perot's finances as he became a more formidable prospective candidate, dug out Nixon White House logs from the National Archives indicating that Perot, far from being the Washington outsider he claimed, with nothing but contempt for establishment politics, had been—as Solomon wrote—"the ultimate insider." Solomon quoted former Richard Nixon White House aide Peter Flanagan to that effect, and another Nixon White House hand, convicted Watergate figure Charles Colson, called Perot "an amazing operator," unmatched in his ability "to muscle himself in quicker [than others] into the president's own confidence."

The AP reporter found White House memos indicating that Perot in private meetings with Nixon had offered to spend $50 million in public relations efforts to boost Nixon's image, including purchase of the ABC television network and a major newspaper, and another $10 million to establish a pro-Nixon think tank. Colson said Perot "never put up a nickel" but "parlayed that offer" into Oval Office access. Perot denied it all, saying Nixon aides would try to get money from him for various "beautiful and strange ideas," but that he always turned them down.

The AP story also reported that the Nixon White House had intervened with the Internal Revenue Service after it had questioned Perot's deduction of a political contribution to the 1968 Nixon campaign on his corporate tax return and had interceded with other agencies to assist Perot in various financial disputes, indicating he knew the levers of Washington power to push, and pushed them.

Such stories only fed Perot's deep conviction that the Republican Party and the Bush White House were out to get him. At the time this story first appeared, one of us had an hour's interview with Perot in his Dallas office. When he was asked whether he believed the Bush campaign had planted the story with the AP reporter, Perot replied without hesitation: "Sure I do. Do you really think anybody could dig through all the files of the Nixon Library, with everything scattered all over the place? I think if you talk to that reporter, he'll tell you he found it all piled in one place. That's what he told me."

But Solomon, who found the papers in the National Archives, not the Nixon Library, told us it was Perot himself, when the reporter talked to him on another matter, who said some things that gave him the idea to check the Archives, and that he had never talked to anybody in the Bush administration or the Republican Party in advance of finding the Nixon logs and memos relating to Perot.

At first, the critical stories about Perot did not make a dent in the spread of his movement or the success of his volunteers around the country in collecting the petitions in the various states necessary to place his name on the November ballot. The first state where volunteers qualified him, without any appreciable effort by Perot or his Dallas associates, was Tennessee. But the first major test came in Texas, where state law required 53,000 signatures of Texans who had not voted in the state's March 10 primary to be collected in five weeks' time. The Texas volunteers produced more than 200,000 names, delivering them to Secretary of State John Hannum in an elaborate ceremony on the steps of the state capitol on deadline day.

Without the enlistment of professional politicians—Perot made a point of emphasizing that fact in our interview—the Texans for Perot staged a cheering, foot-stomping parade up Austin's broad Congress Avenue. It was complete with cowgirls on horseback and a banner stretched from one curb to the other reading AMERICA IS READY FOR YOU, ROSS PEROT, toted by about twenty supporters chanting, "Goodbye Bush, Hello Perot!"

At the capitol, volunteers carted nearly a hundred boxes of signed petitions and piled them before a platform where Perot addressed the crowd of several thousand under a wilting sun, giving them his standard speech about giving the country back to its "owners." Commending their efforts, he said that all the political experts had said "ordinary people couldn't get this done," but "you showed 'em." Still, he played it coy, saying only that he would announce whether he would be a candidate "whenever we're ready."

The stories about Perot's past were coming faster now, tarnishing his shining armor. *The Dallas Morning News* reported that Perot's father in 1955 wrote a letter to then Senator Lyndon B. Johnson of Texas asking his help in getting his son released from active duty in the navy after only two years of the four-year hitch required upon his graduation from the Naval Academy. Perot said he had no recollection of the matter.

Several days later, the Associated Press reported the existence of another letter, this from Perot himself to Representative Wright Patman of Texas, again asking help in winning early release from the navy because, Perot wrote, he found it to be "a fairly godless organization" marked by "drunken tales of moral emptiness" and promiscuity on the part of his fellow sailors.

There were also stories of a Wall Street fiasco in which he lost a fortune, of a broken pledge of $2.5 million to the Ronald Reagan presidential library, and of a complaint from Republican Senator Warren Rudman of New Hampshire, mentioned as a possible Perot running mate, that a private investigator claiming to be working for Perot was nosing around about him.

The Republicans, just as Perot had been saying, started what appeared to be an orchestrated assault on him. The day after the Rudman complaint, House Minority Leader Bob Michel called Perot "frightening" and a "demagogue" with a dangerous streak of "authoritarianism." The next day, White House press secretary Marlin Fitzwater labeled Perot "a pig in a poke and a dangerous and destructive personality," adding: "Being afraid of the unknown may soon make people ask, 'What kind of monster are we buying here?' "

These observations came on the heels of a most impressive showing for Perot in the Oregon primaries of both major parties. The networks' exit polls found that an astounding 45 percent of Democratic voters and 41 percent of Republicans said they were going to vote for Perot in November. In addition, he received 13 percent of the Democratic primary vote and 15 percent of the Republican on write-in ballots. Also, the *Los Angeles Times* poll had him surging ahead in California, with 39 percent of those surveyed to 26 percent for Clinton and 25 for Bush. The attacks on "Inspector Perot" didn't seem to be hurting him much as he continued to work the television and radio talk show circuit—in spite of his announcement that he would be laying off to concentrate on his much-awaited plan for cutting the deficit.

What was hurting, however, was the ability of the close Perot associates who were trying to run the quasi-campaign, lawyer Tom Luce and business lieutenant Mort Meyerson, to cope with the organizational challenges growing with every passing day. More and more states were undertaking and completing petition drives and calling on Dallas to produce Perot for celebrations just like the one in Austin that marked the filing of petitions for Texas ballot access.

A televised rally linking supporters in six states by satellite from Orlando, Florida, developed glitches and attendance at some sites was disappointing, indicating a lack of the sort of professional planning Perot had said he didn't want, but that Luce and Meyerson were coming to believe was essential.

The trick was finding the right political pros who could solve the organizational problems while accepting Perot's insistence that the campaign be an unconventional one, to match his unconventional style. His image as the anti-establishment nonpolitician was a central element in his appeal and could be tarnished by the arrival at the Dallas headquarters of a team of "hired guns" so recently and thoroughly criticized by Perot.

For several weeks now, as already noted, Luce had been conferring with Hamilton Jordan, who had volunteered his services on a part-time basis without pay. Jordan was a thoughtful and not entirely conventional political strategist who understood and appreciated Perot's unconventional approach to politics. "I read everything I could get my hands on about Perot," he said later, and was impressed with him.

On his own, Jordan began to work up charts laying out his ideas for a Perot campaign beyond the petition phase, presenting them to Luce and Meyerson for their consideration and, if they chose, for Perot's, whom he had never met. He made the basic case that voters were so hungering for reform that they would take some risks with a newcomer, but that, as he put it later, Perot could not be "scary or worrisome" and hope to keep their support. He noted that Perot in starting out as a newcomer had "the advantage of writing largely on a clean slate," but if the campaign "didn't define Perot, other people would define him."

Compared to other recent third-party or independent candidates,

Jordan noted, Perot had the advantages of financial resources, broad appeal and intensity of support without the limits of any narrow ideology. But in the end, he warned, Perot would have to answer satisfactorily one question: "Can he govern?"

Jordan argued that Perot as a newcomer to politics could not be expected to know everything and that he could finesse that shortcoming by sticking to the central problem of righting the economy, and a few other issues such as education and political reform about which he had definite ideas, and saying about other issues raised: "We'll argue about these after we fix the economy. Your government is broke and doesn't have the resources to fix these problems. . . . All these things are important, but we can't do anything about them until we deal with the core issues. All these emotional issues, if all you care about is how to settle these issues, go somewhere else. Don't vote for me."

He was trying, Jordan said later, "to come up with an honest way to deal with the fact that Perot wasn't well versed on a hundred issues, and that wasn't what people wanted from him anyway. They wanted to know where he stood on these kinds of gut issues." This approach would underscore his concentration on the issue most on voters' minds and would validate another concept of Jordan's—that Perot would be well served by campaigning unconventionally in what he called "a learning posture"—conspicuously on his own, without press coverage.

One week, he suggested, Perot would hold a town meeting somewhere off the beaten path, meet with workers, do a couple of interviews. The next week he would spend his time talking to people calling in on the Perot 800 number phone bank; the next, he would go for a briefing by AIDS researchers; then go to his home town of Texarkana and make a speech on who Ross Perot was. The next week, he would call on Sam Nunn, a Clinton backer, for a talk on defense issues and on Warren Rudman, a Bush backer, to discuss the budget deficit.

"My point was," Jordan said later, "without sacrificing your unconventional style, this was a way to go out and put yourself in a learning posture, show people you're concerned about all these things and, in fact, develop useful kinds of information." Perot, he said, was "a quick study. I thought he would in fact learn, and I thought it would look good to the American people."

Jordan also had ideas for putting the volunteers to work once the petition drives were completed, arguing that they constituted the campaign's ''muscle'' that would atrophy if not exercised. He suggested holding 20,000 ''Perot parties'' in private homes around the country to recruit more volunteers, and a ''Project Greyhound'' in which volunteers in Texas would be trained in political organization and sent out by bus through twenty or twenty-five smaller states, mostly in the West, to give direction to local Perot supporters.

Luce and Meyerson liked these ideas because they did seem to be within the framework of the unconventional campaign on which Perot was insisting. But the campaign nevertheless continued essentially on the petition-gathering track, along with Perot's seemingly tireless appearances on television news and talk shows. In late May, the two Perot lieutenants, overwhelmed by the mushrooming growth of the Perot phenomenon, broached the subject of Jordan coming aboard full-time, after first softening up Perot on the need for professional help—again within the framework of Perot's insistence on an unconventional campaign without ''handlers.'' Jordan was reluctant, but intrigued.

Around the same time, Luce called Ed Rollins, the manager of Ronald Reagan's 1984 reelection landslide, who, after his somewhat stormy tenure as head of the Republican congressional campaign committee in which Bush had tried to force him out, was back in private consulting practice in Washington. Rollins recalled later that he had been watching the Perot grass-roots operation in his home state of California and was fascinated by it.

''The volunteer movement was really something unbelievable,'' he said. ''I kept saying to Teeter and others in the Bush campaign, 'Don't underestimate this thing. This thing is very, very powerful.' There was discontent in the country, which obviously was something I had watched closely through the congressional committee, and I saw real dangers in Bush's reelection.'' Bush's broken tax pledge, Rollins recognized, had resulted in ''an underbelly that was very soft'' and a ''wrong track'' reading on the direction of the country that spelled real trouble.

At this time, Governor Pete Wilson of California, an old Rollins friend, asked him to go out to California and help him run the state for the whole Republican ticket, but when Bush got wind of it he blew the whistle on the idea. There was a minor furor in political circles as a result and Luce, hearing about it, phoned Rollins and invited him to talk in

Dallas. Patrick Caddell previously had also discussed the Perot campaign with Rollins, but he told both of them he couldn't get involved. One reason was that Rollins's wife, Sherrie, had just taken a high-profile political job in the White House, as head of the Office of Public Liaison, dealing with various public interest groups.

About a week later, Luce and Meyerson were in Washington and had dinner with Rollins. The best he could do, he said, was provide advice "from afar" and assist them in finding others who could help, but it had "to be totally stealth" in fairness to his wife.

Luce and Meyerson called again from Dallas a week later. "We've gone to Ross," Rollins was told. "This won't work, doing it behind the scenes. We want you out front, we want you public, and we want to get a Democrat." Rollins suggested Caddell, and when he was vetoed came up with Jordan. "Hamilton's out of politics, he understands the outsider campaign," he said.

The two Perot lieutenants, already working for weeks with Jordan, called him, he remembered, "and said, 'We've got a crazy idea and want to try it on you' "—pairing him with Rollins. "I told them that I was flattered, that I was interested, that I was surprised," Jordan said, "but that I didn't think they had thought it through, because I thought there would be a potential firestorm among their own supporters when they did this, because it seemed at variation with what Perot had been saying— no handlers, and all that."

But the two Perot aides wanted to pursue the idea, and the result was a meeting over Memorial Day weekend in Jordan's office in Knoxville among Luce, Meyerson, Jordan and Rollins. "We both were very reluctant and had significant reservations," Rollins recalled. Luce and Meyerson pressed them, asking what it would take to get them aboard. Rollins said Perot offered only to match what they were making in their current jobs and would require that they have no other clients—no problem for Jordan, who was out of politics. (Much later, Jordan showed one of us an uncanceled check from Perot for a month's pay—$75,000—that he hadn't decided to cash, sensitive to the "hired gun" label.)

Shortly afterward, Jordan and Rollins went to Dallas to meet Perot. Beforehand, they discussed the campaign again with Luce and Meyerson, and Rollins said later he made a point of warning what it would be like. "What Perot has to understand if you hire people like us, we're very visible," he told them. "Part of the campaign will be, I'll be on television talking about strategy and tactics, and if he's going to go batshit every time that occurs, how are we really going to be able to do the job?"

Jordan, however, was less inclined to see his role as a public spokesman, and more than Rollins he bought in to the Perot idea of an unconventional campaign that would be compatible with the notion that Perot was a different breed of cat. They agreed between themselves, however, Rollins said, "that there could be only one campaign manager," and that Rollins would have that day-to-day role and Jordan would focus on broader strategy and message.

Luce and Meyerson had reservations about whether Perot would buy the arrangement, but they said they would take it to him—the first of many missions of shuttle diplomacy required by the nature of Perot's modus operandi. "Hamilton and I walked out of there that night saying, 'Shit, he's not going to buy off on this,' Rollins recalled. 'He's got reservations. He hasn't a clue what's involved here.' We had bad vibrations."

The next day, however, when they met with Perot for about five hours, he appeared to buy in to everything that had been proposed. "He couldn't have been more charming," Rollins said. "He thought this was great, just what we needed, no reservations about anything."

Jordan came armed with more charts, having read Perot correctly as someone who liked to deal with visual aids rather than reading long-winded papers. He presented them, making such points as the importance of Perot staying on the message of his campaign regardless of the flak thrown up at him. Perot seemed to grasp readily the need for that kind of discipline. "I found him smart, shrewd, charming, quick on the uptake— and in some ways naive," Jordan recalled.

After the meeting sealing the deal, Jordan went off to a summer camp he runs for cancer-stricken children but in the next several days made trips to Perot petition operations in Tennessee, North and South Carolina and Georgia to appraise them for himself. "I was very impressed with what I saw," he said later, not only with how effectively they were being run but with the sincerity and commitment of the people attracted to the movement.

Rollins remembered later, "I walked out of there that night saying, 'I may have just met the next president of the United States.' " He called

Sherrie from the airport and said the same thing. "She was terribly upset, so I flew back and went to my cabin to think about it." By now the word was getting out—from Rollins himself, the Perot aides were convinced—and he was besieged with phone calls from fellow Republicans trying to talk him out of it. Jim Lake of the Bush campaign was dispatched to Rollins's hideaway in the Shenandoah Mountains to dissuade him, in vain. In the end, Rollins joined the Perot army as field general—to the continued chagrin of Sherrie Rollins, who decided she would have to resign her White House job, despite Bush's sympathetic understanding of her situation. She remained very publicly committed to his reelection.

"I had argued with her," Rollins said later, "that if they were smart, the president would say, 'Listen, this is what marriages are all about today. I've got the best Rollins, and if her idiot husband wants to go off and work for this nutcase, so be it.' He would have been a hero to every working woman in America."

The arrangement, announced at a press conference in Dallas but dribbled out first in the press and confirmed by Sherrie Rollins's resignation, was big political news. Here was Ross Perot, vehement foe of professional politicians as corrupters of the political process, hiring two of the biggest names in the business. Luce put the most positive spin on it he could. "It is very comforting to me," he said, "and I know it is very comforting to the volunteers, to know they'll have people who will be with us who have been through this before and can help us in terms of expertise."

Jordan, who had been skeptical about how it would go down with the volunteers, was pleasantly surprised. "It showed Perot had a sort of Reaganesque ability sometimes to have it both ways," he said after the campaign. "He said he was going to do it his own way, and he brings in two hacks, two hired guns, and everybody says, 'Boy, that was smart.' "

Indeed, the move brought new and instant credibility to the Perot campaign. Here were two high rollers taking a flyer with Perot, and Perot was being a realist in recognizing that his grass-roots movement had graduated to another level, requiring the help of professionals who had been down the road before. Rollins, it was true, had overseen the fairly easy reelection of an extremely popular president in a conventional campaign, but Jordan had ridden a little-known long shot into the White House, although he hadn't been able to keep him there for a second term.

The fact that Jordan was a Democrat and Rollins a Republican made the case, intentionally, that the Perot movement was a haven for the disaffected in both major parties.

At the same time, said Sal Russo, a California consultant and Rollins associate who also joined the operation in Dallas, the hiring of Jordan and Rollins brought closer press scrutiny to the campaign. "When Ed was hired and Hamilton was hired," he said, "I think the press thought, 'Well, shoot, amateur night in Dixie is getting pretty serious.' "

Bush made no immediate comment on the development, and in a subsequent news conference dodged questions on Perot. Clinton, however, said the hirings showed that Perot was "a politician like the others seeking the presidency," adding, "I'd like to know how much they were both paid to do it." Ron Brown, the Democratic party chairman, chimed in: "I think it makes a travesty of Ross Perot's claim that he's not seeking handlers and doesn't need handlers."

Perot put his new team in place one day after the publication of yet another major poll chronicling the remarkable climb of his political fortunes. The latest *Washington Post*/ABC News survey had him leading the field with 34 percent to 31 for Bush and 29 for Clinton. And the network exit polls in three major states on the final primary day of the season brought more good news for Perot: 46 percent of the Republicans surveyed in California and 33 percent of the Democrats said they would have voted for him had his name been on the primary ballots; in Ohio, 46 percent of the Democrats and 32 percent of the Republicans; in New Jersey, 35 percent of the Republicans and 29 percent of the Democrats. Jordan and Rollins appeared to be taking the reins of a runaway political horse.

Around the Perot headquarters, the atmosphere was heady and homey. Russo was taken with the innocently warm mood that prevailed. He first met Perot at a birthday party for him at the headquarters, where middle-aged "Perot girls" in patriotic costume sang a homemade Perot song and, Russo remembered, "did a dance routine right out of twenty-five years ago. It was hokey but kind of fun—Americana personified, and it controverted the idea that the era of the volunteer was over."

A story was told at the party of how a telephone worker was up in the ceiling installing a line when this little guy in a close-cropped haircut came along. "Hey, bud, would you mind passing up that wire?" the worker asked him, whereupon Ross Perot stood there and fed the line up to the worker, never identifying himself. "After the birthday party," Russo said, "I never saw that Ross Perot again."

The negative stories continued to roll off the nation's presses against the wealthy Texan. A comment on an ABC News talk show that he would not appoint homosexuals or adulterers to his cabinet got the gays upset, if not the adulterers. "I don't want anybody there that will be a point of controversy with the American people," he said, nor would it be "realistic" to lift the ban on homosexuals in the armed forces.

The Dallas Morning News reported that lawyers for Perot had gotten a Dallas judge to permit Perot security guards to search a Perot tenant's house without a warrant after the man was nine days late in paying his monthly rent of $7,500. *The Washington Post* reported Vietnamese officials claiming that Perot, a vehement critic of North Vietnam for allegedly holding American prisoners long after the Vietnam War, had later discussed the possibility of Perot investments there—a charge that particularly outraged Perot. There were stories recounting his onetime proposal for a police sweep on Dallas neighborhoods for illegal drugs, brushing aside constitutional guarantees of privacy and due process; about questionable business dealings; about hiring private eyes to sleuth on the extramarital and other activities of employees and business competitors, and even investigating his own children.

Vice President Quayle also got into the act, digging out a statement Perot had made on ABC News's *Good Morning America* about eight months earlier in which he said "Germany and Japan are winning" in world competition because "they got new constitutions" after their defeats in World War II. Addressing the conservative Federalist Society in Washington, Quayle in boosting Bush said "it would be a very bad idea to replace a genuine statesman with a temperamental tycoon who has contempt for the Constitution of the United States." And so it went.

The worst of it all came in a *Washington Post* story reporting that Perot had investigated George Bush and his sons in 1986 and informed Bush, "in what Perot portrayed as a friendly warning, that two of Bush's four sons were said to be involved in improper activities." Perot, the story said, informed Bush that "a Florida investigator told him that one son had visited a known gun smuggler." On Christmas Eve that year, it went on, "Bush sent Perot a short handwritten note defending his sons. 'They are all straight arrows,' he wrote, 'uninvolved in intrigue.' "

Bush, who up to now had restrained himself about Perot, finally lashed out. In an interview on ABC News's *20/20* show, yet another of the free airtime programs being worked by all the candidates to an unprecedented degree in this campaign, the president said of the *Post* story: "If he was having my children investigated, that is beyond the pale. . . . Leave my kids alone. . . . I am sick about it if it's true, and I think the American people will reject that kind of tactic." Quayle added: "Imagine Ross Perot having the IRS, the FBI and the CIA under his control."

Perot spokesman James Squires accused the White House of mounting "a series of hysterical attacks designed to mischaracterize Ross Perot in the public's mind," in a tactic that was "the staple of Republican presidential politics for more than a decade." Perot himself called the story "part of an election year fantasy carefully crafted by the Republicans . . . to destory my credibility." He added: "Do I run around the world hiring investigators? No . . . I'm not an investigative personality."

In any event, Jordan and Rollins were finding out that they had a candidate on their hands who may have walked the straight and narrow personally but carried a lot of baggage in his business past and in his present notions, and also was a loose cannon who went wherever he wanted whenever he wanted and said whatever he pleased to whomever he pleased. That was fine for an average citizen, but potentially disastrous for a presidential candidate whose every movement and utterance were held up for scrutiny and criticism. Perot's assurances when Jordan and Rollins signed on that he was going to listen to them and accept certain imperatives of major league campaigning were beginning to ring hollow in their ears.

"In fairness to Perot," Jordan said, contrasting his early campaigning with Jimmy Carter in advance of 1976, "we made our mistakes when nobody was watching. Carter had two years to learn the game, to be in Iowa. This guy was like he was just dropped out in a parachute in the middle of the Super Bowl and was supposed to know exactly what to say and do."

Perot would spend whole days calling reporters and editors complaining about stories that he said were unfair or untrue, frustrating Jordan and Rollins in their efforts to get decisions from him on broad operational and strategy questions vital to the effective development of the campaign. Jordan at one point told him, "Ross, you've got a powerful message. You're on a message track and you've launched it, and at the end of the campaign, if you've stayed on that message track, you'll be elected president. Every day when you get out you should think about nothing but staying on your message. Every day, when everybody else gets out, they're gonna try to drag you off of the message. The Republicans are going to do it, the press is going to. If you stay on it, you win. If you don't stay on it, you lose." Perot, Jordan said, "understood that in the abstract, but he was just incapable of doing it."

One problem was that Perot was enthralled with television. He would make his own appointments, then fly off without telling Jordan or Rollins where he was going or what he was doing. Sometimes they would flick on a television set and see him there in midinterview, generously sprinkling pithy one-liners on a variety of subjects over the airwaves, all the while insisting that he could not sound-bite an answer to this or that question of substance.

On one occasion, he showed up for the NBC News *Today* program for an interview with Katie Couric and stayed for the full two hours, getting himself twisted in knots over his notion of having affluent older Americans like himself give up their Social Security and Medicare benefits. He finally insisted he was only talking about asking them to do so voluntarily. He said he'd gladly do so himself, and also work without pay if elected president, to which a caller replied: "Well, you can afford to." This was hardly staying on the message that could win for him.

Through all this, Perot insisted that only he could speak for himself. He bristled whenever Rollins, a political games-player, would go on television and talk strategy. Perot would call Rollins, Russo said, and ask him: "How do you know what I think unless you ask me? How can you answer any questions?"

Perot got particularly exercised, Russo recalled, when Rollins went on television and effectively disinvited Jesse Jackson from any involvement in the Perot effort. Jackson at the time was talking to Perot on the phone in what Rollins saw as an effort to use a relationship with Perot as leverage on Clinton, who was largely cold-shouldering him. Rollins,

Russo said, "drove a stake in Jesse Jackson's heart, when he believed, I think correctly, Jackson was just using Perot as a stick to beat up Clinton, to get things." Rollins told Jackson, Russo said, that the Perot campaign "was not seeking his support. It completely chopped Jesse's legs off and completely wiped out his leverage with Clinton." All this, however, went over Perot's head and he blamed Rollins for driving away a helpful source of support.

Perot's idea of press relations, Rollins said, was to do all the talking himself and to have a bunch of what Perot called "sweet young things" dealing with reporters because reporters "wouldn't be mean to them."

Through all this, the public focus continued to remain on the petition drives, which were gaining ballot access for Perot in state after state. The progress provided a ready catalyst for moving Perot around the country, but always before wildly partisan crowds of volunteers emulating the Austin rally by personally presenting the requisite thousands of signatures, followed by an inspirational thank-you speech from the man himself. Over the course of a week in mid-June, he flew from Sacramento and Irvine, California, to Denver, then Boston and Annapolis, where a flotilla of private boats accompanied him to the site of a dockside speech. Reporters wanting to cover this odyssey were obliged to scramble on their own for commercial aircraft because the unconventional campaign of Ross Perot did not have provision for the conventional press plane.

Perot was greeted like a savior by his adoring followers, but behind all the cheering Jordan and Rollins began to note that the negative stories and other allegations against their candidate were beginning to take their toll. A *New York Times*/CBS News poll had ominous portents. While Perot remained in a virtual tie with Bush, 32 percent for the president, 30 for Perot and 24 for Clinton, the percentage of voters who had a negative opinion of the Texas billionaire had more than doubled in the last six weeks. The survey found specifically that Perot's suggestion that well-off older Americans give up Social Security and Medicare benefits to help cut the federal deficit had only 10 percent support, even among Perot backers.

"The numbers on top still looked pretty good but the internal numbers started to look terrible," Jordan said later. "Perot just looked at the top, but you'd look under it and you'd see that the negatives had tripled in three or four weeks. Underneath we were cruising toward a big drop."

One of Jordan's charts spelled it out. "Perot has dominated the political press for the last thirty days," it said. "The pressure to define Perot has increased proportionately." While "Perot has worn well," the chart said, "there will be a day of reckoning" if the campaign failed to shift gears.

"There was just an enormous question mark [about Perot] all through May and June," Jordan said later. "This guy had come like a comet out of the sky. We were in that bubble for about thirty or forty days and people were asking, 'Who in hell is this guy?' "

As the end of June approached, Jordan and Rollins understood that unless some steps were taken to stem Perot's slippage and particularly to define him in more definite and favorable terms, the criticism of him, which he and his loyalists were convinced was motivated by the Bush campaign, could destroy his chances to be elected. They worked up elaborate remedies for the decline. All they had to do was sell them to Perot. They would soon learn, however, that it would take a salesman of Perot's own talent to close the deal.

PICKING THE
SOUTHERN LOCK

When President Bush in May 1991 was discovered to have an irregular heartbeat after a day of considerable physical exertion, and the public spotlight inevitably swung onto Vice President Quayle, Bill Clinton was among the first Democratic leaders to sound the alarm. "As the weeks and months go by," Clinton said, "he [Bush] will have to answer to the American people about this issue: does he believe, and does he believe again in 1992, that the vice president is the best person in America to succeed him if he's unable to continue?"

At the time, Clinton, as governor of Arkansas, had not yet disclosed that he would seek the presidency in 1992, but the issue of presidential succession was on his mind—unlike most Americans. Although lip service often was paid to the importance of having the person "a heartbeat away" from the presidency who was best qualified to assume that awesome responsibility, and presidential nominees always said it was a prime, or *the* prime consideration in their selection of a running mate, history suggested it was too often otherwise.

Voters certainly did not seem to take the matter seriously into their thinking on how they would vote in a presidential election, the best illustration being their support of Bush after his surprise choice of Dan Quayle. If they had, they would have punished Bush for selecting a running mate they told pollsters repeatedly and emphatically they did not believe was qualified to sit behind the great desk in the Oval Office.

When the time came for Clinton to choose the 1992 Democratic vice presidential nominee, he obviously had all the customary political factors in mind—characteristics that would help him get elected. But according to all those who dealt with him in his preparations and deliberations for making the choice, the matter of possible succession to the presidency was critical from the start. His campaign chairman, Mickey Kantor, said later that when Clinton in his presence privately charged Warren Christopher with the principal role in the search for a running mate, he instructed him to use "one criterion only—'If something happened to me, who would make the best president of the United States?' "

Clinton, Kantor recalled, told Christopher, " 'You pick the best person. Give me the best people.' He was going to pick the person, [but] we started out with a fairly lengthy list and went through an extremely detailed process." Aware that five of the previous nine vice presidents— Truman, Johnson, Nixon, Ford and Bush—had gone on to become president, Kantor said, Clinton recognized that he could be selecting a future president and took that responsibility seriously.

One reason, Begala suggested later, was that Clinton was particularly mindful of the matter of mortality, his father having died at such a relatively young age—only twenty-nine when he perished in a car accident just months before the birth of his son Bill. "It sounds too much like psychobabble," another insider said later, "but when you lose your father like that, I would suspect that as a dimension to your approach to this kind of question, you think of your own mortality."

Clinton's press secretary, Dee Dee Myers, said the candidate also wanted someone "who had experience where he was weak," such as in foreign affairs and Washington, and who "shared his world view" as a new Democrat. But his "overriding concern," she said, "was, he was not going to be a nominee who picked Dan Quayle. He thought that that was just a crass political decision. He blamed Bush totally. Most people sort of thought, 'Oh, Quayle, what an idiot,' but Clinton looked at it and thought, 'Oh, Bush, what a dumb choice,' because he sees everything in the context of history—everything—about the presidency, and for him it was an irresponsible decision on Bush's part to choose this man who [in Clinton's mind] was clearly incapable of being president.''

Clinton himself, in an interview later, was more diplomatic in discussing Bush's choice of Quayle, but it all came down to the same thing. ''I thought he [Bush] seemed to have acted rather quickly and to have been motivated by political concerns—more about categories than substance, the kind of thing they always accuse the Democrats of,'' Clinton said. ''Quayle was from the Midwest, he [Bush] was from someplace else, and Quayle was from the conservative wing of the party, Quayle was part of the new generation. It was something that looked good but wasn't. . . . The president picked him because the categories seemed right, even if the first question [was he qualified to be president?] didn't get asked or answered.

''My determination was, let's ask the first question first. And I looked over dozens of names of people, dozens. When Christopher was managing this process for me, I always said, 'I've got to have somebody that if I drop dead, would be a good president. That is the first criterion.' Then I wanted somebody who really understood this time, and I wanted someone who was generally in harmony with the direction that I had staked out, not somebody who would agree with me on everything, but generally in harmony with the direction. And finally, if I could find him, I wanted someone who had some strengths or experience that was different from my own.''

Clinton's observation at the time of Bush's irregular heartbeat reflected that view and, according to Kantor, he also believed that the process used in selecting Quayle and too many other recent running mates, Democratic as well as Republican, had not been ''dignified'' in terms of the treatment of prospective choices. It was not that the choices themselves were not good ones—Carter's selection of Mondale and Dukakis's choice of Senator Lloyd Bentsen of Texas were considered particularly distinguished—but Clinton was not enthusiastic about the manner in which they were picked.

Early in the process, Kantor said, he, Clinton and Christopher all read up on the history of vice presidential selection and Clinton concluded that the process itself had to be ''done correctly,'' that it should be "dignified and should be confidential. . . . The whole experience of [picking] vice presidents affected him, and obviously Quayle was part of that process."

Ironically, the view that the procedure for selecting a running mate should be carried out in utmost privacy was also held by Bush in 1988 when he picked Quayle. Aides said he thought the very public selection processes used by such recent Democratic presidential nominees as Jimmy Carter in 1976, Walter Mondale in 1984 and even Michael Dukakis in 1988, wherein they summoned or met the persons under consideration in the glare of television lights, had been "demeaning." Consequently, Bush was determined not to put the Republicans he was considering as his running mate through anything like that. So he never personally interviewed any of them about the job, and the result was Dan Quayle.

Clinton by contrast always planned to interview personally the individuals whom he would most seriously consider, but insisted that the process of drawing up an initial long list and winnowing it down would be done in the greatest privacy, in deference to all those whose names were thrown into the pot. And when that list had been winnowed, he instructed that those on the short list be afforded special privacy and dignity in how they were treated.

About the only presidential nominee since World War II who openly acknowledged that he didn't apply the "best qualified" yardstick in making his choice of a running mate was Republican Barry Goldwater in 1964, who told reporters he had chosen a feisty, extremely partisan but pedestrian upstate New York congressman, William E. Miller, because "he drives Lyndon Johnson nuts." In the end, however, most nominees select the person calculated to provide the most help in winning the election, or risk the least harm.

The operative axiom, in fact, is that a running mate does not necessarily have to help the ticket, but he or she should not hurt it. In 1968, when Richard Nixon was casting about for a ticket mate, his pollsters found that all prominent Republicans tested would be a drag, and that Nixon ran strongest alone. The result was his choice of a relative nobody, Governor Spiro T. Agnew of Maryland (who didn't remain a nobody for long).

Clinton was not, obviously, blind to all the conventional factors of geography, age, ideology and the rest that traditionally went into the choice of a running mate. But a measure of how subordinate they were in his thinking was the fact that his political advisers, who ate, drank and slept such calculations, were given a minor role in the selection process. In fact, according to Greenberg, one of their specific recommendations was ignored—that Clinton not choose a fellow Southerner to run with him.

"The political team," Greenberg said later, "was asked for a general memorandum on the criteria that they would recommend on selection. Mandy had conversations around with the consultants on our thinking on it, and drafted a memo." But that memo, according to Greenberg, included "a specific provision that [the choice] not be a Southern candidate." He remembered, he said, "specifically putting [in] a footnote, because I dissented from [that provision] because I thought that Gore was the right choice."

Greenberg said he and his fellow consultants "never had a unified view of who the choice ought to be, nor were they an integral part of the decision-making process. There was a general memorandum that went to Clinton and went to Christopher, and Clinton individually conferred with us on our thinking about it." As a political junkie himself, Clinton would "sometimes run names by" the political types, Greenberg said, "but the campaign team was not part of the ongoing process of selecting the VP."

Assisting selection task force members Christopher, Kunin and Jordan was Mark Gearan, a 1988 Dukakis campaign aide who later became director of the National Governors Association, and who in that capacity had become a close aide to Clinton, then chairman of that association.

Although, Gearan said, "there certainly was a school of thought that you needed to broaden the age, geographic, ideological, religious element of the ticket," Clinton in his instructions "took those subjects off the table." As a result, the long list of about forty names that was put together by the task force was not limited to prominent elected officials. Some business leaders and academics were also on it, Gearan said.

When the process began in early June, Christopher personally solicited the views of about ten to fifteen senators and some House leaders, and Clinton talked to many of them and a number of governors by phone, Gearan said, always keeping his own counsel. "I think he asked everybody in sight, from pollsters to chambermaids, what they thought," Grunwald said, "but never saying, 'Well, here's what I'm thinking.' "

At the same time, another team of legal experts headed by Washington lawyers Richard Moe and Victoria Radd set about compiling research on every phase of the public records of the individuals on the long list, on a strictly confidential basis. Moe, who had been chief of staff to Walter Mondale when he was vice president and had become an expert in the vice presidential selection process, had written papers for the Democratic National Committee on the subject and was one of the first people with whom Christopher conferred. Summaries of the public records of those on the long list were written and given to Christopher, who reported on them to Clinton. This process had become standard practice in both parties at least since 1972, when Senator Thomas Eagleton of Missouri failed to inform party nominee George McGovern that he had undergone shock treatments for depression, and was dropped from the Democratic ticket.

By mid-June, the list had been reduced basically to five names— Senators Al Gore of Tennessee, Bob Graham of Florida, Bob Kerrey of Nebraska and Harris Wofford of Pennsylvania and Representative Lee Hamilton of Indiana, who had won national prominence as an even-handed chairman during the televised Iran-contra hearings.

Another set of lawyer teams was assigned to the vetting process, also an outgrowth of the Eagleton affair. One team was formed for each of those on the short list, who submitted answers to a questionnaire, after which the lawyers checked for anything in that prospective candidate's background that might be a disqualifying factor. Reports again went to Clinton by way of Christopher. No political operatives were involved in the vetting, one of the lead lawyers said later, and "the process was not driven by political considerations."

According to Greenberg, a sixth name was also in the mix for a time—Governor Cuomo—but he was never vetted by the lawyers. "I know a message was delivered to Clinton that Cuomo was interested," he said later. Traditional considerations were fed into the assessment, he said, such as "whether New York and New England would come across [for Clinton] in any case and what the cost would be elsewhere, particularly in the South, if he were on the ticket." Also, the pollster said, there was sentiment for a "nonpolitical" choice, and Cuomo's selection would have been seen widely as one of political ticket balancing—an Easterner, a liberal, a Catholic with a Southerner, a moderate, a Baptist.

Cuomo said in an interview later that although he had "a couple of conversations" with Christopher, he "never" indicated any interest in being on the ticket. He brushed aside reports at the time that he had hung up abruptly when Christopher began describing the thorough vetting process in terms Cuomo saw as reflecting on his ethnicity. "There never was any objection to any investigation," Cuomo said. "If that had been the question, my answer would have been, 'I'm certain you have done negative research [on potential rivals for the nomination]' because they did, 'and I'm certain you included me.' So, in my case, it would be easier, because you wouldn't have to go through that [vetting] process."

Gore was the first to be interviewed by Clinton, under circumstances worthy, Gearan said, of "a bad detective movie." In keeping with Clinton's insistence on total secrecy, Gearan engineered an elaborate scenario to avoid the news media and it worked. Clinton was in Washington for the National Education Association convention in mid-June and was staying at the Capitol Hilton downtown. Gearan rented a room two floors below Clinton's where no reporters or staff people were staying, under his wife's maiden name, Mary Herlihy.

Late that night, with Clinton in his suite and reporters and cameramen keeping watch in the hotel lobby, Gearan in a rented car with driver picked Gore up at the Senate. They drove to the hotel's service entrance, where a door was quickly opened and closed as Gore was whisked out of the car and taken by freight elevator to "the Herlihy Room." It was now about eleven o'clock, and Gore, a morning person, was getting weary while Clinton, a night person, was just getting warmed up. He walked down the vacant stairwell two flights for the meeting.

Gore had been told it would probably last about an hour, but it went on for two and a half hours in the living room, while Gearan and Bruce Lindsey, Clinton's longtime personal aide and friend from Arkansas, waited in an adjoining bedroom, watched television and periodically glanced at their watches. Clinton, Gearan said he learned later, was very impressed by a man he had not known well before. Gearan and the driver took the exhausted senator from Tennessee back to Capitol Hill.

About a week later, Clinton interviewed three more finalists, one at a time, in "the Herlihy Room" at the same hotel—Graham, Hamilton and Wofford, each for about an hour, with the same cloak-and-dagger scenario engineered by Gearan. The press stakeout had grown in size and frenzy and Hamilton compared the stealth entry to an underground meeting he once had with Libyan strongman Muammar Qaddafi.

At one point John King, the Associated Press reporter, checked Gearan's shoes, because he had spied a pair of shoes getting out of the car as the service entrance door was closing and hoped to make an identification of the mystery arrival. On another occasion, a camera crew in a van chased Gearan's car, tried to film the occupants through the closed window and reported later that it wasn't clear whether the person in the front seat was Christopher or a woman. Which caused Gearan, the occupant, to wonder: "Do I look like a woman, or Warren Christopher? I'm not sure."

The fifth finalist, Kerrey, went to Little Rock from Nebraska for a late-night interview with Clinton that lasted about an hour and a half. Contrary to some reports, Clinton aides said later, the presidential nominee gave serious consideration to Kerrey, and the defeated presidential candidate said he was satisfied that was so. He wasn't lusting after the job, he said after the election, but "I thought I could help him win. I still believe I could have, much in the way that Al did, and in the end, I don't think as much as Al did. He asked me in Little Rock who I'd recommend and I recommended Gore."

While he could have projected the same generational appeal on the ticket with Clinton, Kerrey, who is single, said, "it would have been Bill, Hillary and Bob, instead of Bill and Hillary and Bob and his wife." Clinton never told him that was a factor, he said, "but I'd be surprised if it wasn't," though not a major one.

It was now July and the nominee was close to making his decision. In the final week before he reached it, Greenberg said, he along with Carville and Stephanopoulos were called in by the nominee, but by that time the short list had been settled on without much influence from the political arm of the campaign. The virtue of an all-Southern ticket in Texas, where Perot was now threatening Bush in a state critical to the president's reelection chances, was obvious, although the campaign strategists insisted to the end that that consideration was not prominent in the selection.

Several days before the announcement, Clinton summoned Gearan from Washington to Little Rock to start preparations for it. Continuing to carry out Clinton's insistence that the whole matter of vice presidential selection be handled with dignity and style, Gearan pulled together a group of Democratic operatives who had been involved in it in the past— Eli Segal from the McGovern campaign, Dick Moe and Mike Berman from the Mondale campaign and John Sasso from the Dukakis campaign—to work out the details. Then Christopher at Clinton's direction flew to Gore's home in Carthage, Tennessee, for a final review.

It so happened that Graham, planning to seek reelection to the Senate in November if he wasn't picked by Clinton, had to file the next day, July 9, or forget it. So Clinton had to make up his mind that night. Christopher, Lindsey and Gearan had dinner at the Capitol Hotel in Little Rock and then drove to the executive mansion in Lindsey's red convertible, with the top down, causing another press frenzy as reporters and cameramen besieged the task force chief for some inkling as to the choice. Gearan said later he still didn't know who it was going to be, but he had a fair idea.

In a living room, Christopher again reviewed the bidding on the finalists before Bill and Hillary Clinton, Gearan and Lindsey. The conversation soon settled on Gore, and after some more talk, Clinton simply said, "Okay, that's it, let's give him a call." He got up and went over to a phone, whereupon Lindsey suggested that the historic moment ought to be captured on film. So Clinton waited while Lindsey got Chelsea's Instamatic or some other family camera and snapped the scene. Then Gearan took another picture as Clinton got through to Carthage, where he heard the senator's wife, Tipper, on the other end of the line. He said he hoped he hadn't awakened her, but he had to. Gore was on the phone in a flash in another room, where staff aides were taking another picture.

Clinton told him he had thought about it and, as Gearan remembered, said, "I think you'd be an excellent choice and I'd like you to run with me." There was a brief pause and then Clinton flashed a thumbs-up sign to the others in the room. Clinton told his new running mate that Gearan would be flying to Tennessee early the next morning to bring the Gores to Little Rock for a press conference the next day.

In the end, Greenberg said, one strong point in Gore's favor in his view was that because Clinton "did not come out of the primaries well defined, the Gore choice had the advantage of reinforcing the image as young, moderate, smart, Southern, and an antipolitical choice—a choice that would seem to be nonpolitical in its motivation, because it wasn't the typical balancing."

Hamilton, for example, would have seemed "too conventional a choice," Greenberg said, "and we felt we had to do something unconventional. Given our relative inexperience, we couldn't do something that would make us look like we were jeopardizing national security, but we did need to do something that said, 'This ticket is different.' Hamilton would have been a good choice, but it would not have created excitement around the ticket. It wouldn't have sent the message that these were a new kind of leaders." Begala agreed. He called the selection of Gore "the defining decision of the campaign."

Grunwald argued later against the notion that Clinton was motivated by a "Southern strategy" to cut into Bush's base in Dixie, especially with Perot still in the picture at the time. "My sense is he did it because they [Clinton and Gore] share an attitude about public service that he felt comfortable with," she said. "And Gore is as serious about the issues he cares about [as Clinton is]." Dee Dee Myers said Clinton mused to her the day before the announcement that Gore would be a "risky" choice, and she gleaned from that comment that "he liked the risk factor about it, that it wasn't a political decision, that this was the person who met his criteria, and that people couldn't say this was the obvious, politically correct choice."

Clinton to the end, indeed, clung to his insistence that his overriding consideration was that the person chosen be the one best qualified to assume the presidency if anything were to cut short his own tenure, and that he was committed to meet his responsibility for assuring qualified presidential succession.

By all his stated criteria, Clinton said later, "I thought Gore was the best. Even though there was not the age difference that a lot of people thought I needed, or the regional difference that a lot of people thought I needed, or the ideological difference a lot of people thought I needed . . . it turned out to be a great choice."

Among the chores still to be completed was notification of the finalists who had not been selected. Clinton called each of them personally the next morning, avoiding the fiasco that Dukakis had suffered four years earlier when Jesse Jackson learned from a reporter in an airport that Bentsen, not himself, had been picked as the Democratic vice presidential nominee. "There are some things," Dukakis campaign alumnus Gearan said with a grin, "you learn from history."

The introduction of the youthful, joyous Bill and Hillary and Al and Tipper team the next day outside the governor's mansion in Little Rock was a smash hit. Clinton said of his choice: "The man standing beside me today has what it takes to lead this nation from the day we take office." That was something George Bush would be hard-pressed to say about his selection, if indeed he decided to keep Dan Quayle on the Republican ticket at the approaching Republican convention.

Clinton said later that his selection of Gore "had a lot to do with my election. I think in a funny way it was one of those decisions that was bigger than you might have thought. . . . I didn't sense it was going to be as electric as it was until we walked out the back of the governor's mansion at the announcement, and I looked at him and Tipper and their kids, and Hillary and Chelsea, and for the first time it just hit me like a bolt; this is going to be an awesomely popular thing. I didn't really know it until then, but somehow it made a statement to the American people about me. I took them seriously because I took the job [of vice president] seriously, and I really picked someone that was smart and accomplished and strong and even younger than I was.

"It worked and I don't know why it worked, but it was another one of those things. Maybe '92 was a year where all these counterintuitive decisions worked. Maybe it will never be that way again, but my gut feeling is that it always will work for a nominee for president to pick a person that he believes would be a superb president and in whom he has confidence, because the relationship becomes apparent to the American people. It sort of resonates, it has a harmony, it has a feeling. People get it."

From start to finish, the process of selecting the 1992 Democratic vice presidential nominee had been precisely what Clinton had ordered—orderly, dignified and confidential. The serendipity of the choice itself was not fully appreciated at the time, but that would come before long.

CHAPTER 19

NEW YORK:
SETTING A TONE

Although the choice of Al Gore had been politically invigorating, the thousands of Democrats who began to gather in New York for the party's national convention had valid reasons to be uneasy.

For a generation, conventions had not served their original purpose—making a decision on a nominee for president. That decision now was foreordained by the results of primaries, precinct caucuses and state conventions in all fifty states. But a convention was still a valuable ritual to the party, quite beyond the exposure the ticket would be given by four days of press coverage. It was an opportunity for Democrats from different regions and different backgrounds to find the political commonalities that bound them together and to agree to tolerate their differences.

A Democrat from Montana could learn from a delegate from New Jersey, for example, why it was important for their party to put itself on record for more jobs in the inner cities—and the Montanan could explain to his fellow Democrat why a gasoline tax is political poison in the Far West.

Quite beyond that, the conventions were revealing exercises in defining the differences between the two political parties. Anyone who watched both conventions inevitably would be struck by the contrast between the white middle-class homogeneity of the Republican delegates and the extraordinary diversity of those who called themselves Democrats. And anyone who listened would be similarly struck by the differences between the parties in the issues they chose to emphasize and the positions they adopted as part of their dogma.

Most important politically, the conventions were supposed to send the nominees for president and vice president into the general election campaign with the cheers of the delegates ringing in their ears, and the attention of the voters focused positively on what they had to say. The three major television networks—ABC, CBS and NBC—had decided against gavel-to-gavel coverage in favor of an hour or so of prime time each night, arguing that the news value of the conventions merited only that much attention, but raising the obvious suspicion they knew where the money was. The full conventions still would be available through CNN, PBS and C-SPAN, nonetheless, and the number of households with cable television now exceeded those that did not have that option. Most major newspapers also provided saturation coverage of even the most banal and predictable events.

For the Democrats, however, conventions seemed too often to be minefields—occasions on which the party compromised its nominees rather than helped them. The most chaotic had been the 1968 Democratic convention in Chicago that nominated Hubert Horatio Humphrey of Minnesota—but only after four days of fiercely angry protests in the streets by demonstrators against the war in Vietnam, tumult within the convention hall itself and ultimately a crackdown on the protesters that an investigating commission later described, accurately, as a "police riot."

Humphrey and his running mate, then Senator Edmund S. Muskie of Maine, eventually recovered to the point that Humphrey lost to Republican Richard Nixon by only a whisker. But it was impossible to believe that the ugly images from that convention had not made Humphrey's campaign far more difficult than it otherwise would have been. Indeed, that conventional wisdom had become so deeply ingrained in the Democratic Party that it had not held another national convention in Chicago despite all of the city's attractions as a site for any political celebration.

Four years later, in Miami Beach in 1972, the Democrats indulged their new fervor for small "d" democracy to the point that they projected a picture of a party totally lacking in discipline. The most convincing proof was the fact that the nominee, George McGovern, was not introduced to make his acceptance speech until well after 2 A.M. EDT, late enough to be past bedtime for most voters in all the mainland time zones. McGovern then compounded the political felony of the disorderly convention by choosing a vice presidential nominee, then Senator Thomas Eagleton of Missouri, whose electric shock therapy fell so far short of political correctness that Eagleton eventually had to be replaced on the ticket.

In 1980 the convention voted to nominate President Jimmy Carter for a second term over the challenge of Senator Edward Kennedy of Massachusetts, once again ratifying the results of the primaries. But the most memorable television images of the convention were those of the hapless Carter pursuing Kennedy around the podium on the final night trying to arrange the traditional tableau of victor and vanquished, hands clasped and held aloft in a show of political unity—what politicians call "the armpit shot."

Four years later the convention in San Francisco that ratified the nomination of Walter Mondale was electrified by his choice of then Representative Geraldine Ferraro of New York to be the first woman nominated for a place on a major party ticket. But the convention was marred repeatedly by internal bickering—one of the memorable images this time was of black delegates booing Andrew Young, one of the certifiably genuine heroes of the civil rights movement. And Mondale used his acceptance speech to indulge in some of the most politically destructive candor in the annals of American politics by telling the nation that, yes, if he was elected he would raise taxes.

This time the man responsible, Democratic National Chairman Ron Brown, was determined that this was going to be a different kind of convention. He had spent three years bringing the party apparatus from the depths of the defeat in 1988, plotting and cajoling to get an early de facto decision on a nominee for 1992 and preparing a campaign plan to give the nominee a quick start. And along the way he had built his own reputation to the point that no one thought of him as "Kennedy's man" or "Jesse's man" but as a political leader of rare skill and sophistication.

He wasn't going to fritter all that away with some disaster in Madison Square Garden.

What Brown understood from the party's twelve years out of power and from the way the 1992 primaries and caucuses had played out was that his fellow Democrats were energized by the possibility of recapturing the White House. And, given the condition of the economy, they were not in a humor to argue endlessly over how many ideological nuances could be stuffed on the head of a pin. Brown was prepared to tolerate dissent but he was not willing to allow it to spoil his convention.

Many of Brown's fellow Democrats—the activists and professionals and hangers-on as well as the delegates—were more tempered in their optimism. They had watched the opinion polls showing Bill Clinton running third behind George Bush and Ross Perot, with his support threatening to drop below 20 percent and his negatives still at a dangerous level. They were aware that the turnout in the primaries after New Hampshire had been consistently and conspicuously low, a potential warning signal for the general election, when any Democrat profits from a high level of voter participation. And, most of all, they were still wondering if there were not some "other shoe" about Clinton's personal life that might drop during the general election campaign and cost them the opportunity that seemed to be there. The young governor of Arkansas had shown himself to be a remarkably tenacious candidate, but he clearly had not resolved all the doubts about himself.

There was, however, another current running through the Democrats who gathered in New York that weekend—pragmatism. They, too, had understood, if perhaps dimly at first, the message of the primaries. They recognized that this was not a time to argue about ideological purity. They were, after all, about to nominate a candidate who favored the death penalty, had a mixed record at best on the environment and talked about the "responsibility" that welfare recipients must demonstrate. The weakness of George Bush, they understood, was his failure to come to grips with the serious concerns of the electorate on domestic problems. If they could get through this convention without making a hash of things, perhaps Clinton could prove he had the ability to provide a convincing alternative.

One clear measure of the difference in this Democratic convention was the fact there were so few sticky problems to be resolved. Even the protests in the streets were minor league. Militant blacks like Al Sharpton and Gus Savage marching outside might be worth a few paragraphs or a few seconds on the local news in New York and Chicago, but not on the networks.

The most pressing problem was what to do about Jesse Jackson, who may have lacked the delegates to be a factor on the convention floor but remained an important party leader whom Ron Brown was determined to enlist—under his own terms. And the basic rule was that no one who had not endorsed the ticket would be allowed to speak at the convention. "At that point, believe it or not, I thought I was in charge," Brown said later.

In the days leading up to the convention, Brown held several conversations with Jackson. They had been friends for years and often political allies. Four years earlier Brown had served as Jackson's convention manager, so he had the credentials to make the case. The message was plain: You've got to be inside and the only way to be inside is to endorse the candidate. It's the best thing for you and for the party. "He knew that I was real clear on how to be inside rather than outside," Brown recalled.

But the civil rights leader also knew that he held few high cards. "He didn't have 1,200 delegates [as in 1988]. . . . There were no options there. It wasn't that hard a sell," Brown said.

Hard sell or not, Brown was credited with defusing a potentially serious problem. As George Stephanopoulos put it later, "The single best decision we made, one of them was, 'you only speak if you endorse.' It was the best rule we ever had. . . . It was easy, it was a one-liner. . . . [Brown] was able to do that piece of business and it was a masterful job. It made sure it wasn't a traditional Democratic convention."

Jackson said later there never was any specific demand from Brown that he endorse Clinton as a price for a place on the convention schedule. "That was not the truth," Jackson said. "The opposite of that took place. There were no preconditions." He said Brown called on him at his Rainbow Coalition office in downtown Washington twice in the days leading up to the convention, on each occasion discussing possible times for his speech. Jackson said he "remained noncommittal" on whether he would endorse Clinton but that Brown understood that he, Jackson, had no intention of giving a convention speech that would damage the party. Whatever the details of those conversations, however, it was clear from

Brown's repeated public statements that Jackson was aware of the prime requirement for qualifying for the speaking program and chose to meet it.

Jackson made a point of endorsing the "ticket" rather than Clinton specifically, and of doing it on his own television show on the Saturday night before the convention opened. And appearing on NBC's *Meet the Press* the following morning, he was still complaining that Clinton was trying to distance himself from some elements of the Democratic coalition, obviously meaning blacks and himself. "I think at this stage that pushoff has insulted and infuriated a lot of people," he said. But whether Jackson acknowledged it or not, the critical requirement had been met. Jackson was more or less on board, and it had been accomplished without Clinton paying public obeisance to him.

Then there was the matter of handling Governor Robert Casey of Pennsylvania, an adamant opponent of abortion rights who had been preaching all year that the Democratic Party's commitment to choice was offensive to those Democrats who disagreed, and destructive politics as well. But Casey had irked Ron Brown during the platform hearings when he insisted on characterizing the party position as "abortion on demand"—thus adopting the inflammatory language of the most extreme conservative opponents of abortion rights. Now Casey was having daily press conferences pressing his demand that he be given a place on the speaking program to present his dissent.

But the Pennsylvania governor, although the head of his state's delegation, had not endorsed Bill Clinton so Brown simply shut him out on that basis. The Republicans quickly complained that Brown's "gag rule" was stifling dissent in his own party, but if many delegates were upset, it was never apparent. Even within the Pennsylvania delegation, there were leading Democrats impatient with Casey and anxious to get on with the business at hand.

At one point Brown tried to reach Casey over the telephone in his delegation on the floor, hoping to find some formula to end the impasse. But when that attempt failed, Brown never followed through, a lapse he said later was a "mistake." But the party chairman had a sense of proportion about Casey's complaint. "It was getting old, really," he said.

The controversy that received the most attention from the press was probably the most artificial—the demand from Jerry Brown and his rabid followers that the defeated candidate be allowed to address the convention. In fact, Brown was always entitled to speak because his name was going to be put into nomination, and the rules allowed him to use that time to be heard. What Ron Brown would not give him, however, was a formal place on the program with the other defeated competitors for the nomination—Paul Tsongas, Tom Harkin and Bob Kerrey. They had endorsed Clinton so they were entitled. So was Governor L. Douglas Wilder of Virginia, who had gone along after appearing to be flirting with a defection to Ross Perot. But Jerry Brown had not, so he would not be given the same opportunity. It was that simple.

The former California governor characteristically milked the situation for all it was worth, holding media events such as a brief visit to a soup kitchen in Spanish Harlem the day before the convention opened. He sneered at the demand for an endorsement as "enforced uniformity" and insisted it would be no more than a "verbal fig leaf." On the floor at the opening Monday night session, his supporters chanted "Let Jerry Speak!" and at one point rushed toward the podium as if to take it over. The disruption was so noisy that at one point the following night, Ron Brown turned over one of his functions, as presiding officer, to Representative Nancy Pelosi of California so that he would not be there to evoke more chants.

Jerry Brown also had produced what he modestly called a "humility agenda"—the idea of "Jerry Brown" and "humility" together was mind-boggling. He wanted the party to adopt, as part of the convention rules, calling on members of Congress to return their pay raises, surrender many of their perks and, presumably, solve the basic problem of money corrupting American politics. But Brown didn't have the votes to change either the platform or the rules, and Ron Brown had devised the floor schedule in a way that would minimize the exposure given to this lonely dissenter.

But the press abhors a news vacuum and, lacking any real story, reporters and camera crews pursued the Jerry Brown protest, forcing Ron Brown and some agents of the Clinton campaign to try to reach an agreement that would elicit the California Democrat's endorsement and give him a formal place on the program. In retrospect, some of them thought Jerry Brown would have liked to make such an agreement but was unable to control his own supporters enough to make a commitment that could stick.

Ron Brown, once again taking the lead in dealing with an imposing ego, held several conversations with Jerry Brown and some of the ostensible leaders of his campaign, but without success. "There was no decision-making process in that campaign," he said later. Others had a similar experience. "His supporters were so riled up, I think it was hard for him to pull back," James Carville recalled. At the same time, he said, Brown "didn't want the dance to end."

Moreover, the would-be negotiators were having a difficult time even determining just what Jerry Brown was seeking.

"We were a little bit like the press," Carville said. "We never knew exactly what they were thinking there because it was like the Oklahoma weather. Every fifteen minutes you talk to them it was somebody else and something different. But clearly the thing was that we weren't going to make any deals." Or, as Stephanopoulos put it, "Jerry couldn't figure out how to do it . . . he couldn't figure out the politics of his own people."

Brown told us later, however, that he had made specific requests directly to Clinton in a telephone conversation of what it would take to win his endorsement. He wanted the $100 limit on contributions and the prohibition of political action committee money included in the party platform, he said, which would have then given him "a rationale" for the endorsement. He said he understood as a practical matter that Congress probably would not enact such legislation, but Clinton "didn't even offer a carrot. They didn't want to give my candidacy any credibility."

When Brown did finally speak, as he was nominated early Wednesday evening, he offered his by now familiar attack on "the influence of power and money" without any endorsement of his party's ticket, although he did promise to "fight for this party." But now that the "controversy" was over and there was no "story" left, the speech was given the scant press attention the entire episode had deserved.

Jerry Brown had brought something new and entirely different to the 1992 campaign with his $100 limit on campaign contributions and his 800 telephone number. And he had attracted some support among those most alienated from the system, many of them young people who didn't know about his history of reinventing himself for every new situation.

But he had also left such a bad taste in so many Democratic mouths as to raise doubts that he would ever have substantial influence in his party again.

Meanwhile, the convention offered a program designed to send the clear message that the Democratic Party of 1992 was a different party from what it had been, and its nominee truly "a different kind of Democrat," independent of the constituency groups—the "special interests," according to the Republicans—and committed to middle-class Americans worried about their jobs and health care. There were all the usual Democratic touches of political correctness; one night the benediction was offered in English and then in Navajo. But the first priority clearly was projecting an image that would not repel independents and Reagan Democrats watching in their homes across the nation.

Of the three keynote speeches, only one seemed to rouse the audience. Former Representative Barbara Jordan was as impressive as always in terms of her rhetoric but she never mentioned Bill Clinton. And Senator Bill Bradley, back in the arena in which he had played ten years as a star of the New York Knicks, never managed to capture the full attention of the delegates.

The most compelling and intriguing keynote came from Governor Zell Miller of Georgia, written in concert with Clinton campaign advisers, including his old friend Paul Begala. Miller used conventionally partisan tough language about George Bush and the Republican Party: "For twelve years the Republicans have dealt in cynicism and skepticism. They have mastered the art of division and diversion. And they have robbed us of our hope." And he took the convention's first open shot at Ross Perot's claim to be an outsider: "If he's an outsider, folks, I'm from Brooklyn. Mr. Perot's giving us salesmanship, not leadership."

But the key passages were those designed to tell the vast television audience that Bill Clinton was not just a friend of the working class but a product of it:

"I'm for Bill Clinton because he is a Democrat who does not have to read a book or be briefed about the struggles of single-parent families, or what it means to work hard for everything he's received in life. There was no silver spoon in sight when he was born three months after his father died. No one ever gave Bill Clinton a free ride as he worked his way through college and law school."

The Miller speech also was designed to underline the positioning of Clinton as someone different from the liberals of the past. "Bill Clinton," said Miller, "is a Democrat who has the courage to tell some of those liberals who think welfare should continue forever and some of those conservatives who think there should be no welfare at all that they are both wrong. He's a Democrat who will move people off the welfare rolls and onto the job rolls."

The platform adopted the following night was similarly tailored to reflect the putative transformation of the party, on the off chance that voters might read it. Although the platform made the customary genuflection to liberal dogma on most social issues, it also included some planks that never would have survived the editing process in other recent conventions. One said: "We offer a new social contract based neither on callous, do-nothing Republican neglect nor on an outdated faith in programs as the solution to every problem."

Clinton and the convention program did not ignore the liberals, of course. On the same day the platform passed, Clinton's only public appearance was before the National Women's Political Caucus, where he made a point of reaffirming his support for abortion rights. And on the podium that night, the party's commitment on the issue was underlined even more clearly by the appearance of six Republican women who had decided to vote Democratic in 1992 because they supported choice on abortion.

The speakers that night also included two victims of AIDS who spoke movingly about the need for a more concentrated federal effort to deal with that scourge—Bob Hattoy, an environmentalist working in the Clinton campaign, and Elizabeth Glaser, who had contracted AIDS through a blood transfusion and unknowingly passed it on to two of her children, one of whom had died.

By Wednesday, the third day of the convention and the night on which Clinton was to be nominated, all of the potential problems seemed to have been resolved and the Democrats were reveling in their satisfaction. They were holding a convention without self-immolation, even sending positive messages. The notion that they might actually win the election began to seep into their thinking. The reservations about Clinton that had seemed so disturbing only a few weeks earlier had receded.

There was even some good news from other quarters. A new *Wash-*

ington Post/ABC News poll had Clinton leading Bush, 42 percent to 30, and the faltering Perot down to 20. A week earlier it had been Bush 35, Clinton and Perot 30 each. The electorate clearly was reacting to the choice of Gore and the early display of enthusiasm in Madison Square Garden.

Mario Cuomo was to deliver the speech nominating Clinton, although it had taken some persuading by Ron Brown in the weeks before the convention. On the face of it, the question of who delivered the nominating speech shouldn't have mattered much. But Cuomo held a special place as an icon of the liberals and his relationship with Clinton had been testy. Brown wanted to tie up still another political loose end, to send his nominee into the general election campaign under the most auspicious circumstances. And, predictably, the Cuomo speech couldn't be arranged without some contortions.

"Mario wasn't returning Clinton's calls [then], so I called Mario," Brown recalled, "and we had a terrific conversation, talked for maybe fifty-five minutes about everything, fifty-five minutes of him telling all the reasons he couldn't speak at the convention. He'd done that."

Finally Brown played his trump card, telling Cuomo: "This is my convention. I brought it to New York, you're my law school professor, you're the governor of the state. I'd look silly if you don't come and do something and make an appearance at the convention."

The next day, Brown said, Cuomo called back and, as Brown remembered it later, the conversation went about like this:

CUOMO: How long is that speech supposed to be?

BROWN: As long as you want it to be, Mario.

CUOMO: You really want me to do this, don't you?

BROWN: Yes, I really want you to do it.

CUOMO: Clinton really wants me?

BROWN: Yeah, Clinton really wants you to do this.

CUOMO: I think I have been much more persuasive on this issue, but I'm going to defer to your judgment.

So Cuomo wrote the speech over the following week and went to the Garden Wednesday afternoon to rehearse it for the Clinton advisers assigned to help him. "They hated it and I didn't like it either," Cuomo said. The speech didn't do enough, they decided, to "equate" Cuomo and Clinton, so the New York governor went back to his office, rewrote some of it, and this time everyone was satisfied once a few minor changes were made.

The result was a rhetorical tour de force—the Democratic Party's premier orator singing the praises of its presidential nominee, excoriating the opposition Republicans and—most importantly—making common cause with a governor of Arkansas in their definition of their party and their mission:

"Bill Clinton believes, as we all here do, in the first principle of our Democratic commitment: the politics of inclusion, the solemn obligation to create opportunity for all of our people, not just the fit and the fortunate—for the aging factory worker in Pittsburgh and the schoolchild in Atlanta, for the family farmer in Des Moines and the eager immigrants sweating to make their place alongside of us here in New York City and in San Francisco.

"For all the people . . . from wherever, no matter how recently, of whatever color, of whatever creed, of whatever sex, of whatever sexual orientation, all of them equal members of the American family, and the neediest of them, the neediest of them, deserving the most help from the rest of us. That is the fundamental Democratic predicate."

An hour later, the ritual of the roll call completed, Clinton was nominated on the first ballot with 3,372 votes to 596 for Jerry Brown, 209 for Paul Tsongas and 74 scattered among other candidates. When the vote from Ohio put Clinton over the top, the television networks showed him celebrating with Hillary at an Arkansas party at Macy's a long block from the Garden—a block he walked to claim his prize. Tradition dictated that the nominee would not go to the convention hall until he was ready to deliver his acceptance speech, but Bill Clinton was not a politician inclined to allow tradition to interfere with an opportunity for more positive television exposure. The walk was a carefully crafted bit of show business supervised by Clinton's Hollywood friends, Harry Thomason and Linda Bloodworth-Thomason, with television bringing the triumphant Clintons—Bill, Hillary and Chelsea—along the sidewalks of New York amid cheering crowds.

All that remained was the acceptance speech. Unsurprisingly, the nominee talked longer than might have been prudent, some fifty-four minutes, long enough for one network to cut away to show a child in the audience who had fallen asleep. But Clinton used the speech to spell out his basic message to the largest television audience he had ever enjoyed to that point.

There was nothing subtle about his appeal to the political center. "One sentence in the platform we built says it all," he said. "The most important family policy, urban policy, labor policy, minority policy and foreign policy America can have is an expanding entrepreneurial economy of high-wage, high-skilled jobs. And so, in the name of all those who do the work and pay the taxes, raise the kids and play by the rules, in the name of the hardworking Americans who make up our forgotten middle class, I proudly accept your nomination for president of the United States."

When the applause and cheering died down, Clinton added even more pointedly: "I am a product of the middle class and when I am president, you will be forgotten no more."

Like most acceptance speeches, Clinton's was largely a codification and compilation of all the things he had been saying during his long march toward the nomination. He defined the "New Covenant" he had been describing for months—with the obvious hope of persuading the press to seize on the phrase as a latter-day "New Deal" or "New Frontier"— this way: "The New Covenant is a solemn agreement between the people and their government based not simply on what each of us can take but what all of us must give to our nation. We offer opportunity. We demand responsibility. We will build an American community again."

The speech touched off the final demonstration of the convention— thousands of Democrats cheering and singing on the convention floor while their new champion, his family and his political allies danced to "Don't Stop Thinking About Tomorrow" and sang "Circle of Friends" on the podium. It was a moment of glory Bill Clinton clearly had been imagining for at least a decade now. But even at the height of his political success, he found himself sharing top billing with another story, and another severe critic of the status quo—Ross Perot.

TEXAS HARA-KIRI

In the six weeks or so leading up to the Democratic National Convention, the volunteers for Ross Perot had continued to make impressive progress in their petition drives around the country. But behind the scenes in Dallas, where political professionals Jordan and Rollins were digging below the surface "horse race" numbers in the polls—who's ahead and who's behind—the campaign was going around in circles.

As state after state was falling in line toward the objective of ballot position in all fifty jurisdictions, Jordan and Rollins, and Luce and Meyerson, too, were aware that it was imperative to shift from the petition-gathering mode, which in large measure was self-generating at the local level, to a real campaign mode. One difficulty was that from the Dallas end, the field operation of about thirty-five people had been placed—by Perot himself—in the hands of the head of his personal security force, a former military officer named Mark Blahnik who had absolutely no political experience.

Blahnik by the professionals' judgment was a nice enough fellow, but hardly the man to take a civilian army of volunteers and whip it into an effective campaign organization. Asked later whether Blahnik was a problem, Jordan threw his head back, laughed, and said: "He was Perot's security guy running the field for us. Does that sound like a problem? That was the Perot way."

It was not just Blahnik, but the fact that most of the field operatives— individuals sent from Dallas out to the states to help on ballot access and, eventually, to sort out internal disputes among the volunteers—were also political neophytes recruited from the ranks of Perot Systems. "Perot took great pride in his field staff," Sal Russo remembered. "He talked to them at all levels." They were regarded by the professionals as "Perot's ears and eyes of what was going on in the fifty states," Russo said, and were dubbed "the whiteshirts"—a spit-and-polish bunch, mostly military veterans, with close-cropped hair and conservative suits and ties, right out of the Perot dress manual that he always insisted did not exist.

"As this thing started, Perot made Mark political director," Rollins said, "and Mark was scrambling, one of these guys working twenty hours a day trying to do all things for Perot. These were nice young guys, never been in a campaign, didn't have a clue, and they're out there with this grass-roots mob, spending money like wild with no concept about anything relating to politics. Once they got the petition drives done, they didn't know what to do next. But from day one, Perot made very clear we were not to have anything to do with his volunteers or his field staff. That was the first warning signal," Rollins said. "After the first day, if I'd had a gun I'd have blown my brains out." Instead, he stayed on and hoped for the best.

So did his old business partner, Russo, who had the same misgivings. "Perot was definitely a control freak," he said. "Nobody ever knew everything that was going on [but him]. He departmentalized things for security reasons," and that was one reason the security staff was so important to him.

Many of the volunteers in the various states, however, were very suspicious of the whiteshirts, coming in to what the volunteers had been led by Perot to believe would be their own show. Part of the problem, Russo said, was that the whiteshirts dispatched from Dallas "were used to the military command structure, [which was] 'good luck' with volunteers. And part of it was, because this was a self-starting volunteer army around the country, thousands of dedicated, loyal Americans who saw an opportunity to take their country back were well motivated. But you had in the mix a couple of charlatans, crooks, thieves and assorted bad people who saw this as some sort of gravy train. . . . I think 99.9 percent were the dedicated, hard workers, but there were rotten apples in the mix— embezzlers, I think there was a child molester. So there was a shakedown period where they tried to weed out the bad apples, or there were people who were just mentally unbalanced.''

One of Perot's earliest supporters, a man named Pat Clancy in Oklahoma, said he asked the whiteshirts who dropped in on him: ''What have you got to do with the Oklahoma grass-roots effort?'' He told them, he said later, ''to butt out and go back to Texas.'' But in the end, he said, he was forced aside.

There were also cases, Russo said, of competing Perot volunteer groups in one town, and the whiteshirts were sent in to referee and make a choice on the local leadership, leading the individual or faction who lost out to charge strong-arm methods from Dallas. Soon a string of negative stories of this nature filled local newspapers around the country, tarnishing the image of the movement as a bottom-up crusade. Finally, another veteran of the Jimmy Carter campaigns with outstanding credentials as a field organizer, Tim Kraft, was brought in to ''work with'' the Perot-anointed chief of the whiteshirts.

Kraft, a cool-headed operative who largely orchestrated Carter's 1976 breakthrough in the Iowa precinct caucuses, set himself to welding the Dallas operatives and the volunteers in the field and held a training session in Dallas. There were, he acknowledged later, ''the usual turf battles and resentments toward politicians'' among many volunteers, particularly within states, ''but it wasn't anything we hadn't seen before'' in other campaigns.

''We weren't going to change the fundamental fact that this was a volunteer-driven campaign,'' Russo said later. ''We wanted to utilize the volunteers in a way that could have caused Perot to win. We never lost sight of the volunteers' role, because it was the one unique advantage he had. We weren't organized to do that, but we could have been. We could have put on the most awesome grass-roots campaign ever assembled in America.''

Beyond the headache of revamping the volunteer effort from a petition-collecting to a campaign mode, the most important task for the professionals now was to define Ross Perot in terms that would make him the most formidable vote-getter possible, before the opposition was able to define him in ways that would cast doubts about him among undecided voters and strip away the considerable support he already had.

That effort to undermine Perot's image and reputation was already well under way. Shortly after the California primary in which the network exit polls found a remarkable groundswell for Perot among both Republican and Democratic voters, the Bush campaign held four sets of focus groups in Fresno and Riverside, California, Columbus, Ohio, and Paramus, New Jersey—the town where the celebrated Willie Horton story first was identified as a decisive issue for Bush in the 1988 campaign.

It was at the earlier Paramus focus group that the story of the black convicted murderer furloughed from prison in Massachusetts who committed rape and mayhem in Maryland caused Michael Dukakis's credibility to plummet, especially when paired with his vetoing of a state bill requiring public school teachers to lead their classes in daily recitation of the pledge of allegiance.

This time around, the focus groups produced nothing quite so dramatic as ammunition for a Bush campaign on the attack. But according to Fred Steeper, the Bush pollster, comments from the voters did confirm marked uneasiness about the modus operandi of Ross Perot—the stories about spying on employees and competitors and so on. The participants expressed a sense that there was something weird about the little man from Texas with the huge bankroll. The Bush campaign concluded that playing on that perception could cool off the red-hot Perot, as the Willie Horton and flag-pledge stories had started the front-running Dukakis on his downward slide in 1988.

The focus group reactions to Perot, Charlie Black said later, were "pretty damned favorable to Perot," but there were some negative observations, "like, 'He sounds like a dictator, has to have his own way, a one-man band.' And the stuff on spying was coming out, the beginnings of Inspector Perot—all that was surfacing, so it was clear that that was the way to pin him down."

One major problem for the Bush campaign created by Perot, Bob Teeter said later, was the fact that "he was forcing the country almost exclusively onto a message that was our worst"—dealing with the economy. And no matter what Perot said, it was perceived as anti-Bush, as well as being basically conservative, thus drawing conservative Republicans from Bush's base. At the same time, Teeter said, Perot was bringing Democrats into the process, "at least a significant number of whom would not have voted" at all had he not been in the picture.

That Perot was, indeed, anti-Bush, was beyond question. In our interview with him in May, he had talked again and again in critical terms about the Bush administration, never once commenting on Clinton until asked, and then he had little to say about him. Bush himself professed to be in the dark about why Perot was so hostile to him. During a break in an interview with Larry King later in the year, Bush asked King: "What's Ross Perot got against me? You know him better than I do."

Charlie Black had two theories. "Bush was always the kind of guy Perot looked down on because he never made real money," Black said. But more likely, he said, the hostility came from the fact that in 1986, Perot had asked Reagan to send him to Southeast Asia to look for Americans missing in action from the Vietnam War. "Guess who got to call Perot back," Black asked, "and say he couldn't go over there?"

The challenge of driving up Perot's negatives, Black said he realized from the positive comments, would be much harder than nailing Dukakis had been four years earlier. But in this case, he noted, the American news media was already engaged. "It was more like 80 percent the press, with us stoking the fire as we could," he said.

Bush himself, according to Mary Matalin later, never shared the view that his campaign should go after Perot. He thought that Perot would "implode" and that Clinton was always the primary foe, she said, but "there was not a major dispute [within the campaign] because the people who were arguing to attack him [Perot] were vehement about it and were making good sense. The president's attitude was, he was not enthusiastic about it because he had his own feelings about where the Perot candidacy was going. But he literally said, 'You guys get paid to worry about this, so do what you have to do'—something like that. It was not a concern to him." In other words, it was the same old George Bush, holding his nose while others did something he said was distasteful to him—but not distasteful enough for him to call off the dogs.

Later, Matalin said, some in the campaign "tried to take credit" for shooting Perot down with the attack strategy, "but the truth is, we were supposed to take a few surgical strikes [at Perot]. It was not even like an affirmative, signed-in-blood decision. But the discussion led toward the feeling that we couldn't get back to getting Bush's positives up'' as long as Perot was riding high. "All summer our goal was to get Bush's positives up. Darman and some of the others were of the persuasion that you couldn't get near to getting Bush's positives up until you got Ross's negatives up. You would continue to be an uncredible messenger on the positive side if there was some other guy who was credible trashing him every day. Then it snowballed.''

As first one administration source and then another, each on his own, she insisted, weighed in against Perot—Quayle, Fitzwater, party chairman Rich Bond, drug czar Bob Martinez, others—it became, she said, a "spontaneous eruption.'' With Bush resisting going into "the campaign mode'' and everybody in his camp anxiously and nervously "waiting for the campaign to start,'' Matalin said, ". . . the Republican community inside the Beltway takes it as a signal and they start shooting away, and it just got out of control.''

She and David Carney, the White House political director, "sat back there and laughed, and said, 'We love to see our campaign collapse into place.' We were not supposed to nuclear bomb the guy. It was supposed to be a little bit of Death by a Thousand Cuts.''

Matalin and Carney, she said later, tried to make the argument that it was not wise to alienate the Perot supporters with overt attacks on their hero. "Just common sense will tell you,'' she argued, "we're gonna need these guys. He is not going to make it all the way through. People are not going to waste their vote. . . . We thought in the end these guys were going to largely come our way, and why make them crazy?''

In Dallas, though, Perot's closest associates like Luce and his son-in-law and campaign counsel, Clay Mulford, were convinced that they were witnessing Son of Willie Horton—the full-blown rebirth of the intentional, carefully orchestrated negativism of the 1988 Bush campaign hatched out of those original Paramus focus group soundings. They cited a column by Thomas Oliphant in *The Boston Globe* at the time laying out what had been culled by the Bush campaign from those focus groups as evidence of the Bush "dirty tricks'' team at work again. In doing so, they were stretching the definition of dirty tricks quite a bit, but what they read was enough to convince them that it was 1988 all over again, but with independent Ross Perot, not Democrat Bill Clinton, cast by the Bush campaign as Michael Dukakis.

Luce later noted a sequence of events that followed swiftly after the focus group sessions. First Bush said of Perot to reporters that "it's too much of a gamble to put the country in his hands." Then Fitzwater said "it's shocking and frightening to see that kind of bizarre behavior on the part of a presidential candidate." Then Black said the next day that "the thing that gives people some hesitancy is Perot's MO. He's authoritarian, his use of investigators." Then Quayle raised the question of "having the IRS, the FBI and the CIA under his control. Who would be investigated next?" From June 21, the day Oliphant's column appeared, Luce said later, "starting for about the next ten days, almost on a daily basis, a new surrogate [was] trotted out to use words like 'bizarre,' 'frightening,' 'shocking,' 'investigator.' There was a concentrated attack, and polls showed it was causing his numbers to go down."

Clearly, Luce was never going to be convinced that all this occurred without careful orchestration, especially after the experience of 1988. Even press criticism, he insisted, had Republican origins, and he knew that was so because reporters would bring him fax copies bearing derogatory information about Perot on Republican Party letterheads. "All that stuff was being fed by the Republicans," said Luce, himself a former GOP gubernatorial candidate.

He was not suggesting, Luce said later, that there was some kind of conspiracy between the press and the Bush campaign to get Perot. Rather, he said, the press was by now investigating Perot independently and the Bush campaign contributed to a developing feeding frenzy, making "a conscious decision to take their guns off Bill Clinton, and let him get off the ground." That, he said, "was their fatal mistake. He was winded, he was down for a nine count and they let him go to a neutral corner and get well, because they turned all these guns off of Clinton onto Perot, and concentrated on Perot for three weeks. In doing so, they let Bill Clinton completely withdraw from the front pages of the papers, get out of the vortex of the negative press that Bill Clinton was in. In that time he redid his economic plan, people quit talking about Gennifer Flowers, and he came back with the Democratic convention and his economic plan. . . . It enabled him to sound substantive while Bush was throwing rocks at Perot."

The Clinton strategists agreed completely. The Manhattan Project had established that it no longer was the substance of the womanizing and draft issues that bothered voters, but what came off as his excessively "political" answers, summed up in "Slick Willie." In this period, Wilhelm said later, "we began, and he began, filling in the answers to some of those questions, first by introducing him biographically and [as] a human being" on the talk shows.

At the same time, Clinton was reworking his economic plan, which he felt needed updating in light of what had gone on in the campaign, and in the country's economic outlook. Although he continued to rail against such pet peeves as "deadbeat dads" who ducked out to avoid paying for their child care responsibilities, and to trumpet his "domestic peace corps" whereby America's youth would get college educations in return for community service, he knew the election would not turn on either issue. They were what Grunwald called "mirage issues," just as, the Clinton campaign was now convinced, were the issues the Bush campaign was pushing regarding Clinton's "character." So Clinton zeroed in on the economy, and as he did, as Greer said later, "fate shined on us."

It was just then, Wilhelm noted, that "Ross Perot and George Bush got into a shoving match, and at the time they were being political, we put out our [new] economic agenda. I think that was one of the key periods of the campaign," he said, "because we were teetering after the California primary, and I actually think that if George Bush had gone on the attack [against Clinton] during that period, we might have suffered nicks and cuts that we could never have recovered from.

"But instead, he and Perot tussled, giving us almost a free opportunity for people to give us a second look. They took that second look, so that by the time the Democratic convention rolled around, I think people were already starting to look at Bill Clinton differently. . . . The Bush people's failure to really hit us when we were down, providing us an opportunity to introduce Bill Clinton, and for Bill Clinton to introduce himself, was very, very critical."

"The Republicans made a fatal mistake turning their howitzers on Ross Perot," Stephanopouios said. "It gave us an opportunity to come up the middle."

Clinton told us later that the Bush-Perot squabbling helped him because "by then the whole country was where New Hampshire was. They were very worried about their economic circumstances. They were really worried about a government that didn't function; they were sick and tired about the politics of blame; they just wanted something done." The bad blood between Bush and Perot, for whatever reason, "was palpable," Clinton said, "and the American people basically wanted the president to worry about them and not about some other politician."

Perot, always suspicious about the involvement in his campaign of "hired guns," as he still called them, didn't quite blame Jordan and Rollins for the assault on his reputation in the news media that was going on all this time. But, according to Russo, Perot would observe that "there had never been an unfavorable newspaper story written about me until you guys came along"—a testimony, if nothing else, to Perot's limited reading habits. He also stepped up his charges that Bush was using dirty tricks against him, to the point that GOP chairman Bond called in to Perot on the Larry King show one night and challenged him to produce "one shred of evidence" to back up his bombast. The campaign, it began to seem, was becoming one big television talk show.

In the face of the attacks on Perot, and with the conviction of his associates that it was now open season for the Bush forces on Ross Perot as some kind of weirdo, the matter of defining him in positive terms, and without wasting any more time, became imperative. That was where the professionals, Jordan, Rollins and the troops brought in largely from GOP ranks by Rollins, came in. They knew how to do it and had proved so in the major leagues of politics. But there was always the question of whether what they knew how to do would square with Perot's own views of how to campaign, and whether they could convince him that they did know.

"The hiring of people doesn't have anything to do with whether you have an unconventional campaign or not," Luce said later. "I wanted to run a professional unconventional campaign, and I don't think that's an oxymoron. We went to great lengths to make sure that both Hamilton and Ed were signed on to running an unconventional campaign." They agreed, Luce said, but "there was disagreement with Ed subsequently as to how we defined, 'unconventional'. . . . I knew Hamilton had a good understanding and wanted to run the campaign in a very different way."

Perot was strong in emphasizing, Luce said, "that the way campaigns were run was part of what we were running against, part of what we were trying to change. And we were always trying to define as we went along how we could do it better. . . . In that early phase, we were clearly doing things differently and in an unconventional way. The rallies were planned by the volunteers; they were not planned by advance men.''

This approach, in what Luce called ''the petition phase,'' was continued after the arrival of Jordan and Rollins, ''and neither one proposed changing that phase of what we were doing. We couldn't ever reach agreement on what we were going to do going forward.'' Disagreements over novel ideas and the timing of carrying them out mounted, even as the arrows of criticism kept raining down on Perot. ''It frustrated Hamilton and Ed,'' Luce said, ''but you have to understand that what Ross thought was important was to talk about issues and communicate about issues. Ross was continuing to do that every time he appeared on television. As far as he was concerned, the campaign was doing just fine. Ross always felt that when he was appearing on television, talking directly to the American people, that was the way to campaign.''

As for professional politics and its way of doing business, Luce said with a wan smile, ''he looked at it as if it were a virus, and he was afraid to let the antibodies get into his bloodstream.''

As Jordan sought to strike a responsive chord with Perot with his charts on long-range thinking and planning, Rollins and others began peppering Luce and/or Perot with memos pressing for decisions on specific key matters that needed resolving at once. One of them was picking a real running mate to replace the stand-in, Admiral Stockdale. The first deadline for filing an official slate for the fall election was August 11 in South Dakota, and after that, one memo dated June 22 warned, ''the deadlines begin to cascade.'' The memo added that ''we should take at least one month to do a minimal background review of the potential candidate—unless we want to 'surprise' the nation as Bush did with Quayle. This means we need a name by the second week of July.'' The memo also suggested that the selection of the running mate might be made at the time of Perot's declaration of candidacy, the date of which also had not been nailed down.

A longer campaign plan dated July 1 said the choice of a vice presidential candidate ''may be the single most important decision Mr. Perot makes. Vice presidential candidates rarely add a great many votes to a ticket, but they can often do great damage. A careful strategy to orchestrate the buildup, announcement and aftermath must be devised. We cannot allow a 'Quayle unpreparedness' incident to strike the campaign.''

Perot, according to John Jay Hooker, the Nashville businessman/ politician who was one of the earliest Perot enthusiasts, had already discussed some names with him, some conventional like Paul Tsongas, Warren Rudman and General Colin Powell, and some quite unconventional. These included Bernadine Healy, director of the National Institutes of Health, Sharon Rockefeller, president of public television station WETA in Washington, D.C., and wife of Senator Jay Rockefeller of West Virginia, and Anne Armstrong of Texas, former Republican Party co-chair and ambassador to England under Reagan. James Squires, the former *Chicago Tribune* editor who was a Perot spokesman and adviser, said a New York federal circuit judge, Amalya Kearse, a black woman, was high in Perot's considerations.

Hooker also heard from other sources inside the campaign that radio and television reporter Cokie Roberts was on the list. Roberts, who heard the report and was as astonished as others who heard it, said the only explanation she could think of was that she had written an opposite-editorial-page piece in *The New York Times* that Perot may have seen as favorable to him although she certainly had not endorsed his candidacy. She said she asked Luce and he denied it. Also denied by the Perot campaign was another name floating about—former Reagan Attorney General William French Smith. Smith, however, was already automatically disqualified by virtue of the fact he was dead. In any event, at this point Perot kept dodging on a vice presidential choice.

The June 22 memo also pleaded for ''a tight schedule of focus groups and polls,'' both of which Perot was dead-set against. ''Why should I pay good money when I can pick up a newspaper,'' he would thunder, ''and read the polls there for free?'' The memo pleaded for data to help determine what was and wasn't working: ''This campaign is swinging at a fast pitch in a darkened stadium. We may be hitting, because we can hear the screams of the fans. But we have no idea where the ball is going.'' But Perot thought polls and focus groups were simply to find out what people wanted, and then to pander to them. ''I'm not a parrot,'' he would say, according to Russo. The professionals would tell him that he might be spending millions on a message people didn't understand, and it was prudent to find out. But he still wasn't buying. Money for polling, Russo said, finally was hidden in another budget item.

Still another memo pressed Perot on another key matter: "We have to make a final decision on the convention by next week or our options will be very limited. This could be another defining event in the campaign and must be carefully done. If we are doing fifty, five or one convention, we have to start now." Jordan was proposing state conventions in each of the fifty states together with one grand national affair over two days, held in some huge arena or park.

Also under consideration, Russo said, were five regional conventions at such sites as the Rose Bowl in Pasadena and Shea Stadium in New York, or even what he called "a Woodstock in someplace in Missouri or someplace in the middle of the country, have parades from all over the country assembling and have a million people. Actually we called Guinness [Book of Records] to find out what the record was for the most people ever assembled in America." The biggest free event, he was told, was a New York Philharmonic concert in Central Park, which drew nearly 900,000, and the largest paid event was a rock concert in San Bernardino, California, attracting more than a million.

"The idea would be to try to break that record," Russo said. "We had all that Hollywood entertainment support, and it would be just a week-long celebration of America." Joe Canzeri, one of the Republican Party's premier advance men who helped "handle" Quayle in the 1988 campaign, was aboard for Perot now and he was convinced it could be done. But again the planners couldn't get a decision from Perot.

A one-page, single-spaced memo dated June 30—with the narrowest of margins to satisfy Perot's limited patience with written presentations— repeated the same points about a running mate and his announcement of candidacy and told him pointedly: "We are starting to see erosion in our support because voters do not believe you are addressing issues. We need a comprehensive plan to release our issues papers in a way to put this issue to rest." But that to Perot was conventional politics and he wanted no part of it. Wasn't he out there on television telling voters where he stood?

Finally, there was the urgency to counter the attacks. "We must convince voters that Perot is not a jump into an unknown void," one internal paper said. "Attacks on Perot will continue centering on converting the driven, can-do, patriotic, successful businessman into a quirky, sick, obsessive, paranoid billionaire. The best thing we can do is recognize that there can be doubt sown in the mind of the electorate. That doubt can kill us because it will stop momentum and slowly erode our base vote.''

Another memo warned: ''Given the pummeling the campaign has taken in the past two weeks, it is more important than ever to have our media and advertising in place. The two lines of attack which seem to be taking hold are Perot's suspected 'authoritarian' tendencies and his lack of specificity. Paid advertising will go a long way to deflect both attacks.''

But Perot was cool to paid television as well. When Jordan proposed that a biographical film be produced to show on television or have Perot go on live in conjunction with the 20,000 ''Perot home parties'' he had recommended, to give the state volunteer organizations something tangible to do and expand the Perot base, he balked at the cost. ''Why don't we just do it on Larry King?'' he asked. ''I'll just get Larry to give me an hour. All you guys know how to do is come up with ideas on how to spend my money.'' What Perot could not or would not grasp was that it was essential for his campaign to control the message that went out, to convey specific information to counter reports and impressions that were hurting him.

Perot seemed to see no urgency in the matter, but the professional staff was now near desperation. Another memo dated July 3 pressed for a ''generic defense—a commercial designed to be put on the air quickly to defend against any number of attacks while a specific defense spot is being prepared.''

But money was always an issue with Perot—and whether he could trust those who were asking for large chunks of it for what he saw as conventional campaigning. When Rollins was unable to find a firm budget for the campaign, he went to Perot, he recalled later, and asked him: ''Are you for real on the $150 million figure? You've got to understand, I've been around a lot of rich people who keep saying 'Whatever it costs to get elected,' but I haven't seen many of them actually dip into their pocket. You've got to understand, it's gonna cost at least $150 million just to stay even with the two national committees in the presidential campaign, and you've got the added burden that you've got to be on television all summer defining yourself.''

Also, he said he told Perot, he couldn't pay the professional consultants who had broken ranks with their own parties "what you pay your security guys." But Perot, Rollins said, denigrated all of them as "hired guns," when "in his particular case we were there because we believed in change, or in him. It was sort of like the volunteers were honorable and we a bunch of whores because we took money."

On another occasion, Rollins said, he got the idea of putting up 5 million Perot yard signs all over the country on the Fourth of July. "There never had been 5 million yard signs," he said, "and my strategy was to make people think. 'Gee, I'm joining something, I'm not such a kook to be out here thinking I'd be, being for Perot.' You look out into the neighborhood and all of a sudden you see twenty or thirty signs, and they're on prominent Republicans' or Democrats' front yards.

"So I went in to Perot, and Perot goes, 'So what is this gonna cost?' And I said, 'Well, a buck or two apiece.' He goes, 'Ten million dollars for yard signs? Can't they make their own yard signs?' I said, 'Ross, they're not going to make their own yard signs. That's not the idea behind this. This is tremendous advertising.' But he wasn't having any of it."

Nor did Perot want to send a mail piece to the millions of individuals who had called the Perot phone bank in Dallas volunteering to help. Jordan said Perot's "computer nerds" had compiled lists of millions of names apparently just because they were there, with no plan or intention to do anything with them, other than sending some names out to state petition drives early in the game. The neglect was frustrating to the professionals, who saw, as Jordan put it, "an enormous army out there waiting to get orders." But Perot's attitude about direct mail, Rollins said, was "this is junk I get on my desk every day that I throw out. I'm not going to spend any money on junk mail."

Rollins despaired. "All the tools which you normally use in a political campaign weren't there." When Rollins worked up a campaign budget for submission to Perot, it came to $152 million. "I prepared it with all of his people," Rollins recalled. "What I tried to do was surround him with all of his people because I knew he wasn't comfortable with us— quote—political whores. I thought if I surrounded him with his own people, they get to realize we know what we're doing, we're professionals, we're not trying to rip him off and spend his money. Ironically, he was being ripped off," Rollins said. "Tom Luce didn't know from shit.

Every vendor would walk in the door, and say, 'Gee, I want to sell you this list of 7 million names of hot political activists.' What they'd sell to the [major party] national committees for one tenth of a penny per name, they'd sell to the Perot thing for a buck. Contracts that Luce had already entered into were absurd, because they just didn't know. It was every vendor's dream. The vault was open."

Luce and Meyerson said they would submit the Rollins budget to Perot for him, because, they told him, "when you're dealing with money Perot is very, very sensitive and we don't want you to take the brunt of it." When Perot saw it, Rollins said, "he blew up, and cut the budget in half, arbitrarily. He eliminated the whole issues division," where budget expert John White was working up the plan for deficit reduction and economic recovery that Perot had promised to deliver to the voters. When White submitted the plan, Rollins said, Perot hardly looked at it.

"These guys keep sending me big thick books," Perot told Rollins. "I don't want big thick books." Perot set the base budget at about $72 million with the understanding separate big-ticket items like the expansive convention ideas, if agreed on, would be up for negotiation with him.

Luce and Meyerson told Rollins, he said later, "just please bear with us. He will spend whatever you need in the end. He just doesn't trust you or your guys. He thinks you're trying to rip him off." Rollins replied: "Well, that's a hell of a nice environment to be working in." Every time he came over to the campaign headquarters, where Rollins was moving new staff in, he'd erupt. "He'd say," Rollins recalled, 'What the hell's going on here? We're building a Pentagon here.' "

Rollins argued that the Perot operation "was very bare bones" compared to the Clinton and Bush campaigns. "He kept saying, 'You don't understand the way I do things. I want a little guerrilla squad. I want to get the job done, I don't want this big army, this big bureaucracy. That's why I've always been better than my competitors.' I said, 'Ross, you don't even understand what the mission is. You can't get by with guerrilla operations. Your candidacy has got to be different from any other candidacy, but I assume you want to win.' " ("Maybe it was a false assumption," Rollins said much later.)

But the most serious problem about money was Perot's reluctance to spend it on the production of the television commercials the professionals insisted were absolutely essential, immediately, to define him in a positive light and "stop the hemorrhaging" caused by the negative stories and attacks on him. At one point, David Wolper, regarded by many as the best maker of documentary films in Hollywood, and Gerald Rafshoon, Jimmy Carter's media man in 1976 and 1980, were brought in to talk to Perot, but he found them too glitzy for his tastes.

Rollins, undeterred by Perot's unexpected penny-pinching, sought the services of Hal Riney, one of the most successful—and expensive— television advertising men in Los Angeles. Riney had produced the famous "Morning in America" ads for Ronald Reagan's 1984 reelection campaign, managed by Rollins, and he was known for his effective "feel-good" style demonstrated in those Reagan ads. His work tended to the emotional, and the thought was that he would be the ideal man to capture the high spirit of the Perot movement.

While Rollins was talking to Riney, Jordan, knowing Perot's attitude about "big-league guys who charge high prices," tried a parallel track. Luce told him about a young Dallas television ad man named Andrew Wilson and Jordan hired him to do a quick biographical commercial on Perot to hold the fort. With Perot's obstinacy in mind, Jordan told Luce: "I can sell this kid, because he's not costing a lot, and he's local."

In a mere thirty-six hours, young Wilson produced a superb if a bit ragged five-minute commercial, mostly from stock footage, that was cut into sixty-second spots. It captured the essence of Ross the Good and presented other people in the context of their own personal experience with him in a straightforward way, devoid of slickness. One sixty-second segment shown to Perot started with a woman talking about her husband, who had been taken prisoner in Vietnam in 1965. She told about receiving a phone call out of the blue in 1969 from Perot, whom she had never met, saying, "I'd like to know what I can do to help your family." He did help, she said, until her husband was released. The spot then showed him saying, "Ross Perot is a very unusual person. He looks for things that ought to be done because it's the right thing to do, and then he tries to figure a way to do them."

The spot then showed Perot's sister talking about him growing up in Texarkana and worshipping his father, then presented a Perot shipmate in the navy, then Mort Meyerson on Perot as a businessman, and finally Perot's wife, Margot, simply talking about how they had met and how he had always told their children, "It's not what you have, but what you are, that's important."

It was a terrific ad produced for only $12,000 under severe time pressure—and Perot hated it. When Jordan showed it to him, he went ballistic, berating Jordan in the most offensive language and calling it the worst he had ever seen. He complained that the spot—a first, rough cut—didn't have the POW story straight, that he didn't like something his sister had said, and that the lighting on his wife was terrible. Taken aback at the ferocity of Perot's assault on him, Jordan left shaken—and recognizing that this could be the beginning of the end for him in the Perot campaign.

"This young guy produced that in thirty-six hours, and if he had five more days, no telling what he would have come up with," Jordan said. "But I was trying to get something on the air. We were starting to fall apart. . . . When we showed this to people who knew Perot, they cried." And when he showed it to a meeting of Perot state coordinators gathered in Dallas, the reaction was immediate and positive. "They all said, 'Put it on right now,' " Jordan recalled.

Jordan was at the end of his rope, particularly in light of his treatment at Perot's hands and what seemed the futility of it all, given Perot's attitude. When Perot called him shortly afterward in what Jordan saw as the closest Perot could bring himself to an apology, he told him: "You know, Ross, I'm not accustomed to people talking to me like that. You talk about high-paid help and all of this. Why the hell did you bring us in, if you weren't ever going to listen to us?"

A couple of days later, in the first days of July, Jordan went over to Perot's office and told him he was leaving. "It was probably a mistake to hire us," he said. Perot answered, according to Jordan: "It probably *was* a mistake to hire you guys. The difference between you and Rollins is, I like you. I don't like Rollins and I don't trust him. He's got Washington disease. He talks to the media too much. This is just another business deal for him. These leaks have got to stop."

Rollins had been accused of leaking from the start, with stories about himself and Jordan going to work for the Perot campaign. He flatly denied that he leaked but at the same time said later that Perot and his unpolitical associates did not understand that "public people" like himself talked to the press as part of the job of communicating the views of the campaign. For that reason, he went on headline television interview shows, which drove Perot crazy. At the same time, however, Rollins said later that Perot would be critical of Jordan in conversations with him.

In any event, Jordan told Perot he was getting out as soon as he could find a gracious way to do so. "Where I got stuck was, I couldn't figure a way to get out. I didn't want to be seen jumping ship. I wanted to get out, but I really didn't want to harm him. I still believed in what he was trying to accomplish." But he told Luce, Meyerson and Rollins he intended to leave.

Meanwhile, Rollins had convinced Riney to try his hand. "He does great Americana-type stuff," Rollins recalled, "so I thought, 'Boy, this would be a natural—Perot with his stories of his famous charitable givings and all that stuff, his Norman Rockwell office and Remingtons. These two are a match made in heaven.' " They had one good meeting, Rollins said, with the soft-spoken Riney, who uses his own voice on many of his commercials, apparently making a good impression. But afterward Perot balked. "Someone had told Perot that Riney had once spent a hundred thousand dollars putting a goat on the top of a mountain," Rollins said, and he wasn't going to spend his money on any such stunt.

Rollins assured Perot that if it had happened—and Riney later told Rollins he couldn't recall any such incident—there would have been a sound advertising reason. The original plan was for Riney to do a television documentary on Perot, but Perot insisted on writing the script himself, Rollins said, and when Riney looked at it, he said it would take three and a half hours of airtime to do it.

Riney proposed instead, Rollins said, "that we talk conceptually about what we're gonna do," and tried to explain to Perot what the process was—first the approach, a script and storyboards before shooting anything. "Perot was, like, 'I want it tomorrow,' " Rollins said. "Riney would say, 'If you want something tomorrow I can do something tomorrow, but it's not going to be what I would be proud of, and what you would be proud of.' "

Perot's response, Rollins said, was "You don't understand, I get can-do people. When I wanted to move food to Vietnam, I got these can-do people. We had the planes loaded and there." Rollins told him he could do that, too, but moving food on a plane to Vietnam was "not what it takes creative talent to do.'' The real problem, Rollins said, was that a friend of Perot's in Dallas with a local background in radio and television, Murphy Martin, kept telling him ''he didn't need to hire Hollywood crews at fancy prices'' and he could get a couple of local cameramen and do the job for a song. ''That was sort of going in Ross's ear,'' Rollins said.

Rollins, however, pressed for using Riney, although Luce and Meyerson, knowing Perot, told him he was pushing his luck. ''I thought it was that important,'' Rollins said. ''If Hal Riney walked on us, it would be so hard to get somebody good, to get up and functioning, you'd lose another three or four weeks. So I pushed hard to get Riney.''

Riney went ahead and made a quick commercial in New York, using the man-in-the-street technique of testimonials for Perot interspersed with street scenes of voters being petitioned for their signatures on corners and in malls—heavily in the emotional, touchy-feely mode for which he was celebrated. Perot hated that one too and Riney was sent back to the drawing board.

Rollins had Russo get hold of Riney's ''Morning in America'' spots for Reagan in 1984 to show Perot, but he never said what he thought. ''There was a feel to Riney's stuff,'' Russo said later. ''That was the feel we wanted, but if Perot didn't like it, that was a clue we had a big problem. . . . Unfortunately, the first Riney spots didn't have a lot of facts in them, but that wasn't their purpose.'' It may have been, Russo said later, ''that Perot is an engineer, and engineers by their training are always looking for the facts, they have a slide rule, they're calculating, and they're always doing things in a sequential order. Suddenly you come in with a television spot that's supposed to connect with people's emotions. An engineer is not going to like that.''

Another conversation with Perot centered on money. ''Tell me what one of these things costs,'' he asked Riney. Riney replied, according to Rollins, ''Well, Ross, I can't give you a specific cost. It depends on how much it costs to shoot.'' Perot shot back: ''Hal, I've never dealt with anybody who couldn't tell me the price of what they're selling.''

Rollins told Perot that when he headed the Republican congressional committee and ''we absolutely were going to lose with twenty percent of the vote, we'd send out two guys with a video camera. It would cost $3,000 just to do that. It was just garbage, knowing they were going to lose. If you're going to spend $120,000 a minute to put an ad on the air—He goes, 'What?' And I said, 'Well, that's what a minute of prime time costs.' And he goes, 'No way. You guys are nuts if you think I'm going to spend that kind of money when I can get an hour free on Larry King.' "

Riney told him he could make a cheaper commercial, for $50,000 or $75,000, but he had to think about the quality and the fact that the commercial would be seen over and over again and had to have staying power. Perot told them to go back and talk to Luce, and as they left the office, Rollins said later, "Perot walks me down the hall, Riney goes ahead, he puts his arm around me and says, 'Everything's going to be okay, don't worry about this. We'll get this thing worked out.' Meanwhile, he calls Tom [Luce] over to his office and tells him, 'Tom, get rid of this guy [Riney]. How outrageous. His prices are absurd.' "

"The next day there was a story in *The Wall Street Journal*," Rollins said, and he was asked for a comment. "I said, 'It's unfortunate it didn't work out. Hal Riney's the best in the business. It just didn't work out.' Perot just went batshit. He thought I had taken Riney's side against him, and how could I do that?" I walked back and said to Riney, 'Hal, you just saw the end of this campaign. This guy obviously doesn't want to be president.' "

On Friday night, July 10, according to Rollins, he had dinner at the home of Tom Luce and his wife. "In the course of the dinner, Tom must have gotten up ten times to take a call from Perot," he said. "He was really worked up over [a report that] ABC was going to go with a story about one of his daughters [involving] a college professor. As Tom explained the story to me, it had been a serious relationship and Perot had had them under surveillance. The college professor had claimed Perot had confronted him and said, 'My daughter's never going to marry a Jew.' He was really worked up over the story."

Jim Squires said later that the story, which had been kicking around for months and had repeatedly been raised by reporters interviewing Perot, drove him crazy, not only because it painted him—erroneously, he said—as prejudiced but because it was an embarrassment to his daughter, now married and a mother.

On the next day, Perot, who had avoided set-piece political appearances before special interest groups, preferring to address friendly audiences of his volunteer supporters, agreed with grave reservations to speak to the National Association for the Advancement of Colored People in Nashville. Rollins and Squires had been telling Perot there were certain major forums in the summer he had to address. "These people aren't for me," Rollins said Perot told him, but he finally relented, but barred the usual advance work that was routine in a conventional campaign.

It was a disaster. Insisting on preparing his own remarks, Perot got himself into a rambling recollection of his childhood in Texarkana and how his parents had brought him up free of racial prejudice. Even in the hardest times, he said, his father always made sure to pay his black employees because, he would say, "they are people, too, and they have to live." During the Great Depression, he said, his mother would always feed hoboes who came to the door hungry, "many of them black."

In the course of discussing the sick economy, Perot observed that "it's going to be a long, hot summer. . . . Now I don't have to tell you who gets hurt first when this sort of thing happens, do I? You people do. Your people do. I know that. You know that."

A young listener called out: "Your people? Our people!" And somebody else demanded: "Correct it!" Perot didn't seem to hear what had been said, and he plunged ahead, seemingly unaware that his words had offended some in the audience as patronizing. Later, talking about crime in the cities, he said: "Now good, decent people all over this country, and particularly your folks, have got bars on the windows and bars on the doors, and they're sitting up at night with a shotgun across their knees. And we have abandoned their neighborhoods to crime."

As Perot spoke, his words drew frowns from NAACP leader Benjamin Hooks and other officials on the platform behind him. Flying back to Dallas, an aide tried to explain to Perot why his words had offended many in the audience. It happened that CNN had broadcast the speech live, and that night Perot telephoned the CNN bureau in New York, where the Democratic National Convention was about to open. In conversations with anchorman Bernard Shaw, CNN president Tom Johnson and Tamara Haddad, a producer for Larry King, Perot kept complaining about how the news media was out to destroy him, saying over and over, "This is the last straw!" He was offered airtime to defend himself but declined.

Later, Perot offered an apology—sort of. "It never occurred to me that they would be offended and if I offended anybody in any way I certainly apologize," he said. But the wolves were on him. What Perot said, observed Ron Brown, the Democratic national chairman, "shows a man who is out of touch with real people out there." And Brown's Republican counterpart, Rich Bond, said Perot's performance "underscores the fundamental tin ear that Ross Perot does have when it comes to national politics."

Rollins, learning what had happened, remembers thinking, "This thing is over. I'm getting out of here. . . . I was getting up every day, spending fifteen hours with my people, trying to win. And he clearly had decided that he didn't want to win."

Luce and Meyerson were talking to Perot all weekend, and on Monday, Rollins said, "they said, 'This thing is not working. He doesn't want to run the kind of campaign you want to run.' I said, 'Well, that's obvious. What he doesn't understand is that if he doesn't run a campaign, he can't win. I'm not trying to run Ronald Reagan's campaign all over again. But you've got to go on television, you've got to define yourself. There's certain elements in the campaign to get your message out. You're not willing to do any of them. If we continue to do what we're doing now, we've dropped nine points in a week. By the time the Democrats are finished with their convention we'll be down another five points and then the Republicans will batter the shit out of us for a week.' I said, 'We'll be sitting here at ten points at the end of the summer and we'll never be able to get back in this race again.'

"Meyerson said, 'Isn't there some in-between?' I said, 'There's no in-between. You either run a campaign or you don't run a campaign. We are not running a campaign. . . . We don't have a press operation, a field operation, we don't have any commercials, we don't have any goddamn thing. We have a candidate who on his whim gets on television and says whatever the hell he wants to say. He won't study the issues. I promise you, we're going to lose it all.' "

Luce and Meyerson went over to see Perot again and came back asking, Rollins said, "Okay, what will it take?" Rollins, exasperated because he had sent numerous plans on what decisions were needed with no response from Perot, agreed to give him one last plan.

On Tuesday, Rollins, Jordan and the other professionals sat around waiting to hear from the candidate. By this time, the word was circulating that Jordan was unhappy and wanted out. All fingers pointed at Rollins again, but he denied again he had leaked the story, arguing that reporters were calling from the Democratic convention. Jordan, trying to pick his own time and manner of leaving, denied the report.

On Wednesday morning, at a staff meeting, an irritable Luce began complaining again about leaks and blaming Rollins, telling him, Rollins remembered, "You're the only one who has a stake in getting rid of Hamilton." Rollins told him he would be the last one to want to see Jordan, another proven professional, leave. But Rollins's reputation for talking to reporters made it a hard sell.

That morning, Jordan remembered, the top staff people "had a great meeting" of two or three hours with Perot in which he indicated acceptance of all the recommendations made to him and "how to roll them out" in an orderly and effective way. Jordan was encouraged.

A few hours later, Luce, Meyerson and Rollins went to lunch where, depending on who tells the story, Rollins resigned or was fired. Perot, Luce told Rollins, "wants all of the professionals out of here." Rollins told him that if he and his people went, there would be nobody left "but the Perot Systems people," but Luce was adamant. Rollins later characterized his departure diplomatically as "a mutual decision" but added, "if I had said, 'No, I don't want to leave,' I'm sure they would have fired me." Luce said it was more direct than that.

That afternoon, in Luce's office, Jordan said, Perot "told me two things. He told me he was going to get rid of Ed because he said he didn't trust Ed, and that he hoped that I would stay. He said, 'If you're not going to stay, though, I'd rather that you leave now with Ed, and not have two big stories instead of one big story.'

"And I said, 'Well, Ross, will things continue as they have been?' And he said, 'Well, I don't know. Am I going to turn everything over to you and other people to make all my decisions? No. You also should know that I may just decide to pull the plug on this whole thing.' That was the first time I'd heard him say that, and I didn't believe him when he said it.

"He said, 'This thing is unbelievable. My family's privacy has been invaded.' He had asked me several times, 'What is it like if you make it to the White House?' I said, it just gets worse. It doesn't get any better. He said, 'I just can't stand for my kids to be public figures. . . . What was it like for Amy Carter?' I said, 'It was different. Amy Carter was a little girl. Your kids are, comparably speaking, grown-up.' It really weighed on him that what he did was going to have consequences for his children. He was very sincere about that.''

In fact, Jordan said, at one point he told Squires, the press spokesman, ''he was willing to give the press the number of his kids, but he wasn't going to give them their names!''

Shortly afterward, Rollins went into Jordan's office, told him he was leaving and asked whether he would be leaving with him. He was about to have a press conference to break the news. Jordan told him Perot had asked him to stay, and he felt after denying he was leaving earlier he could not do so now. Jordan said later, laughing: ''I damn sure didn't want to go out with Ed Rollins. I didn't want to go out under that same cloud.''

That night, Perot called Luce and Meyerson and asked them to come to his house. There, Luce said later, ''he told us he decided he was not going to run. He told us all the reasons that have now become known. He told us everything he said the next day plus what he later revealed about his daughter. He just said he saw no need to put his family through this.'' But he did not explicitly say, Luce said, what it was concerning his daughter that had driven him to his decision.

''He told me he wasn't going to get back into the race,'' Luce said. ''I've known Ross for over twenty years. I've been probably as close a friend as he had, and I don't think he would have lied to me about it. . . . I think if he intended to come back, he would have asked me to stick around.'' Instead, Luce went back to his law firm in Dallas, which still represents Perot.

Squires, who also talked with Perot the same night, said there actually were four stories concerning young people close to Perot—two of his daughters, Ross Jr. and David Meyerson, son of Mort Meyerson, who Perot thought of as another son—that drove him to abandon his candidacy. In addition to the one alleging surveillance of an old flame of one of his daughters and one concerning the second daughter's wedding, only later revealed, Perot was upset about public statements regarding the campaign that the two young men had made, convincing him that all four of his loved ones were being damaged by the campaign.

The next morning, Perot's announcement hit the country like a bombshell, and nowhere more so than at the Democratic National Convention in New York, where the delegates were looking forward to presidential nominee Clinton's acceptance speech that night. If Perot was aware that he was stepping on Clinton's big night, he showed no signs of it as he told assembled reporters and the live television cameras why he was not going to run after all.

His reasons were so farfetched that we were moved in our newspaper column to write from New York: "If Ross Perot were Pinocchio, his nose would be growing all the way from Dallas to here after the whopper he unleashed on the country to explain why he was leaving millions of dedicated volunteers in the lurch."

"Now that the Democratic Party has revitalized itself," he said, taking note for the first time of that alleged phenomenon, "I have concluded that we cannot win in November and that the election will be decided in the House of Representatives [if he remained a candidate and no one received the required majority in the electoral college]. Since the House of Representatives does not pick a president until January, the new president will be unable to use the months of November and December to assemble the new government." Continuing the campaign, he said, "would obviously put [the election] in the House of Representatives and be disruptive to the country . . . so therefore I will not become a candidate."

He did, however, urge Perot volunteers in New York state to complete their petition drive "so that everybody running for president will know the names and addresses of all the people who are unhappy with the way things are today." That request started speculation almost at once that Perot was playing some sort of game—speculation that began to grow in intensity not too much later in the year.

The immediate reaction was one of shock and, among Perot's millions of volunteer supporters, a mixture of deep disappointment and anger. Asked at the news conference how he would respond to the charge that he was a quitter, Perot said: "People can say anything they want to say. I'm trying to do what's right for my country. Now, that probably makes me odd in your eyes, but that's what I'm trying to do." After parrying some more questions, Perot turned and strode out of the room and the campaign headquarters, without so much as a thank-you to his staff and phone bank volunteers now faced with a new deluge of calls from bewildered and heartsick Perot loyalists.

It was left for Meyerson to say that Perot "knew he would hurt the volunteers and that he feels deep regret about that.'' Nothing probably hurt the volunteers more than the fact that he had not told them that personally.

In the end, Rollins said later, ''I think he realized the job of being president was a lot tougher than he thought. My sense was when he got into this thing he saw it as a little volunteerism in Washington—'I'll go there for a couple of years and straighten the mess out.' And then he realized it wasn't gonna be fun, but a very tough political environment. I said to him one time, 'You know, this thing is like war, Ross.' He said, 'No, this is not like war. People don't lose limbs. Those are people who are tough.' I said, 'I promise you, Ross, you may not lose limbs, but it's as close to war as you'll ever find. You're trying basically to dismantle the political system of America. There are so many people with vested interests in you failing. They're going to do everything possible [to beat you].' '' Perot apparently came to agree that Rollins was right.

Suddenly, the 1992 race for the presidency was turned upside down. The remaining contenders swooped down quickly on the remains. Speaking to the Perot volunteers from Wyoming, where he was vacationing, Bush said he shared ''many of their same principles . . . and we welcome them warmly into our campaign.'' And in New York, Clinton, who watched the Perot press conference on television with aides who didn't know what to make of it all, walked into another room to place a call to Perot. He also took time from preparations for his acceptance speech to invite the shocked Perot army ''to join us in our efforts to change our country and give our government back to the people.''

Some in their disappointment switched at once, including a Democratic delegate who had been prepared to cast her vote for Perot and came out for Clinton. But many others, refusing to believe that their dream of taking back their country from the politics-as-usual crowd behind the leadership of the feisty independent from Texas who had called on them repeatedly to ''stay in the ring'' with him, hoped against hope that they had not seen the last of Ross Perot.

TWO FOR
THE ROAD

Ever since Michael Dukakis came out of the 1988 Democratic con-vention with a seventeen-point lead in the polls and quickly lost it, it had been remembered how, in the period before the Republican convention, he had gone back to Massachusetts and tended to state business—while the Bush campaign methodically chewed him up. The Clinton strategists were determined that there would be no repetition. Clinton and new running mate Al Gore were going to hit the ground running out of New York, and keep running until November 3. The question was how and where.

Well before the convention, the Clinton planners had settled on a cold electoral college strategy—in which states they were going to work hardest and deploy the most resources, in which states they would make some effort in hopes of winning or forcing Bush to spend his resources, and which states they would largely ignore either because they appeared to be safe for Bush or could be reasonably counted on as safe for Clinton.

In the four years leading up to the election year, party National

Chairman Ron Brown and his able and intense political director at the Democratic National Committee, Paul Tully, had already done the spade-work on a specific 1992 electoral college strategy. After a meeting in a Washington suburb in 1991 at which all the prospective Democratic presidential candidates were briefed, newspaper stories reported that the plan was so specific that certain states already were being written off, obliging Brown to say, with fingers crossed, that a fifty-state strategy was being planned. That was true enough, but tentative plans were for some of the fifty to get little more than a nod.

The plan also included tighter linkage than in recent years between the Democratic national ticket and state tickets in what was called a "coordinated campaign" strategy. In previous years, and particularly in 1988 with Michael Dukakis at the head of the ticket, many local and statewide candidates had run away from the national standard-bearer, especially in the South where the nominated liberal jeopardized their own chances of election. This time, the hope was that they would embrace the ticket enthusiastically.

Tully was a bear on making the coordinated-campaign idea a func-tioning reality in the Democratic Party as it had been for years in the Republican, and on electoral vote targeting. And in assigning priorities in allocation of campaign resources to the various states, he was a walk-ing, fast-talking encyclopedia of political facts and figures. He conveyed his treasury of information and analyses in a trademark patois of word abbreviations of Ds [for Democrats] and Rs [Republicans], generously seasoned with grunts and punctuated by raised eyebrows, wide grins and flailing arms. Understanding Tullyspeak was an essential prerequisite for fellow campaign workers and reporters alike who wanted to grasp what really was going on. Once Clinton had the nomination secured, Tully was dispatched to Little Rock to lend his general and specific political savvy to the campaign headquarters.

The party's electoral college strategy had as a central precept that the string of industrial states from New York and New Jersey, through Pennsylvania and Ohio, into Michigan and Illinois would be the key to victory. David Wilhelm, the Clinton campaign manager, who was overseeing the electoral vote strategy from Little Rock, emphatically shared this view. As a native of small-town Ohio who had cut his political eyeteeth in Illinois, running winning campaigns for Senator Paul Simon and Mayor Richard Daley in Chicago, Wilhelm knew the territory.

In mid-April, two memos blossomed from the Democratic camp that, taken together, were to have far-reaching ramifications for the Clinton campaign. On April 15, Steve Rosenthal of the Democratic National Committee political staff wrote one to his bosses, Ron Brown and Tully. Five days later, Carter Wilkie, a young campaign aide then working in Indianapolis in advance of the Indiana primary and unaware of Rosenthal's memo, wrote another and sent it to "Clinton strategists and staff" in Little Rock.

Rosenthal specifically proposed a pair of "nationwide voter-registration bus caravans" to set out immediately after the Democratic National Convention, one from New York bearing presidential nominee Clinton and the other from Los Angeles with the yet unselected vice presidential nominee in the lead bus. The scheme, Rosenthal wrote, would be "a way to keep the media focused on our 'momentum' and also as another way to avoid any lag (à la Dukakis) following the '88 convention."

Rosenthal proposed that the nominees ride the buses for a full three weeks, or at least drop in on them from time to time with celebrities and well-known elected officials filling in as surrogates. All "would take part in a series of rallies in large and small cities, suburban and rural areas— based on our targeting," the memo said, and the two bus caravans would meet in Houston for one final rally two weeks before the Republican National Convention there.

"The message that would come out of this," Rosenthal wrote, "is that the Democratic campaign has hit the ground running, is organized and is taking its message directly to the American people . . . as a takeoff on the old 'whistlestop' campaigns." The memo made clear that the caravans would be focused on voter registration that could "utilize the skills of the union organizers" available to the campaign and would work through "each state's coordinated campaign plan" to benefit all candidates on the Democratic ticket.

Wilkie's April 20 memo, which did not specify travel by bus although that was the logical means of transportation for the region he wanted covered, was pegged originally for three approaching primaries along the Ohio River. "The Indiana, Kentucky and Ohio contests," he wrote, "come at a time when Clinton must tell his life story, connect with ordinary Americans and begin to define himself as a Democrat in touch with traditional, middle American values. Both banks of the Ohio River are populated by Democrats who are mainly economic populists and social traditionalists. Rather than visit southern Ohio, Indiana and Kentucky at separate stages, the campaign should take advantage of the regional culture and local TV markets that transcend state boundaries and schedule an old-fashioned, three-state swing. . . ."

Wilkie suggested that such a tour "place a premium on visits in small settings in small towns, i.e., a speech to local Democrats from the front porch of a supporter's home, the steps of a county courthouse, or the pulpit of a Methodist church." This approach, he wrote, would "remind people of the forgotten Democratic Party roots in small-town, traditional middle-class American communities and the aspirations of the forgotten middle class."

Wilkie was intrigued by the cultural roots that had buried themselves into the soil of Appalachia through West Virginia, Ohio, Kentucky and Indiana—economic populism and social traditionalism—and thought he saw a kinship with Clinton's own roots and agenda. To take a sounding on his scheme, before writing the memo, he had phoned his friend Mort Engelberg, a Hollywood producer and political junkie who amused himself advancing campaign trips for Clinton and previous Democratic candidates. He asked Engelberg whether such a trip through this region, with stops at settings reflecting the culture of the region mentioned in his memo, was feasible. Engelberg said why not?

Wilkie bounced his idea off local reporters, and they reacted very positively toward it. Most of them, Wilkie said later, did not work for news organizations that could afford to send them on the very expensive jet plane trips the candidates made, and this was their shot "to be the boys on the bus" in their own bailiwicks.

So Wilkie put his thoughts on a single sheet of paper, made photocopies and sent the memo to Wilhelm and other members of the Clinton senior staff. That same day or the next, Wilkie said, Bob Boorstin of the Clinton staff called back and told him: "Great! We're going to do it— after the convention." No mention was made of Rosenthal's memo of five days earlier, which specifically called for his proposed bus caravans to set out at that time.

Wilkie remembered the letdown. "I was so depressed," he recalled. "I said, 'You guys don't understand. We've got these primaries.' " If the trip was done after the convention, he said, "nobody will be around. You'll be wasting your time." But that was the decision.

Several weeks before the Democratic convention, Engelberg was on the phone with Bev Lindsey, then Clinton's campaign scheduler. They talked about what was going to be done after the convention and Engelberg expressed weariness with the old, conventional routine of the nominees flying from one media-market airport to another and another, holding tarmac rallies with, as Engelberg put it later, "a bunch of white politicians in suits." What about, he suggested, a bus trip?

Around this time Rosenthal had sent another version of his original memo to Wilhelm, an indication that no action had been taken on the basis of that first one. Wilhelm as the Clinton electoral vote specialist felt strongly that in order to win the two states with which he was most familiar, Illinois and Ohio, it would be important to muster downstate support for Clinton—outside Chicago and Cook County in Illinois and outside Cleveland in Ohio. A good way to do so, he became convinced, was by sending Clinton through the southern parts of these battleground states—and others in the Rust Belt of the East and Midwest, an idea that coincided with Wilkie's scheme.

"We had Bush in the White House, we had Perot not leaving television studios, we had Bill Clinton—who was not very well known yet by the American people but was really extraordinary at person-to-person campaigning," Wilhelm said. "We knew we would be attacked as liberals who don't understand the values of middle-income America, and we had to leave New York, and had to go somewhere, and we'd already figured out what the showdown states were. Why not take a trip through [them], showcase Bill Clinton at his best, which is in a very grass-roots style of campaigning, which would put the lie to what certainly would be attacks on him as some sort of tax-and-spend liberal?"

Wilhelm saw the states bordering on the Ohio and Mississippi rivers as the key to the election, and what better way to reach them? Trains were out; they were too expensive and the atrophied rail system limited too severely the routes that could be taken.

Traveling by bus in the jet age seemed at first comical. After all, hadn't jet travel and television communications revolutionized presidential campaigning? Nearly a third of a century earlier, Richard Nixon, the victim of a foolish pledge to campaign in all fifty states before Election Day, had stretched himself so thin in 1960 going to places with insignificant numbers of voters and electoral votes that he crossed the finish line bedraggled, exhausted—and defeated. Over the next eight years, as he plotted his comeback in presidential politics, Nixon had learned his lesson. When he ran again in 1968, and won, he adopted the tarmac strategy that had become standard ever since—focus on major media markets, make quick hits in and out of them by jet for maximum television coverage, and leave the boondocks largely to the vice presidential nominee.

But Engelberg, who had produced the *Smokey and the Bandit* movies and understood the romance of the open road, saw the possibilities of taking the Clinton persona and message to the highways and byways. "Having been on the road with this guy in one way or another for the past year," he said later, "I found that the times I was with Clinton and he was in unstructured kinds of situations [were] real good, because he was good in one-on-one informal stuff. It also elevated him, because he seemed to respond to that kind of environment."

At the outset, Engelberg said, he found "no great enthusiasm" for the idea of a bus trip among the top campaign strategists in Little Rock—although many later claimed at least a portion of its paternity. Engelberg phoned fellow Californian Mickey Kantor, now chairing the campaign from Little Rock. Focused as nearly everyone in Little Rock was at the time in discussions on the vice presidential selection and convention plans, Engelberg said, Kantor seemed to him not to have heard about the idea. "Literally, Mort had to fight for it," Kantor said later. "A lot of people at first [said], 'Oh, God, you put two Southerners on a bus—what would it look like?' " But then a consensus started to build for it, he said.

Engelberg, Kantor said after the election, "was insistent and incessant, and so was Bev, in our doing it, and other people picked it up, and now, today, you will find many mothers and fathers to that idea". . . . In any event, he said, "it doesn't matter whose idea it was. It worked."

The one major figure in the campaign who admitted that he didn't think much of the idea at the time was Carville. He said later it started out "a sort of mediocre idea" but caught on and became "symbolic" of the Clinton style and campaign.

Engelberg recalled pitching Kantor that "if we did this, it should be issue-driven—every stop we made should not be a rally but a message kind of event, and we should stay out of the big cities, but hit the big-city media markets" along the way. Also, he made the case that having the presidential and vice presidential nominees together coming directly out of the convention would be an irresistible magnet for press coverage, on both the national and local levels. "I kept saying that if you keep these guys together we'll have a great hunk of the national press corps with us, plus the fact that a bus as opposed to a plane means we'll have a lot of local people, which if nothing else I guarantee you we'll own [for example] the Columbus media for the day before and the day we're there. I always felt we would dominate the media."

For one thing, Engelberg said, echoing Wilkie's view, a lot of local newspapers "cannot afford the twelve or fifteen hundred bucks that a seat on the plane costs today, but a hundred and fifty bucks for a seat on the bus meant, for example, we could get a lot of Philadelphia media on board in New York to make the trip with us and stay on an extra day [through Pennsylvania]."

After the idea had been weighed in Little Rock for several days, Engelberg recalled, Kantor called back and gave him the go-ahead. The first step was laying out a route. Engelberg knew the bus trip would be leaving from the convention in New York, and the original thought was to have it end in Little Rock. Considering where the major battlegrounds were, most of it as Wilhelm also noted easily fell in place—across New Jersey, into Pennsylvania, Ohio and on west. At this time, Clinton had not selected his running mate, but Engelberg deduced—without any inside information, he said later—that Gore and Hamilton were the finalists. So he planned two preliminary routes, one dipping down from Ohio into Tennessee in the event Gore was the choice and the other going up into Indiana if it was going to be Hamilton.

Next, Engelberg in conjunction with Bev Lindsey and then Susan Thomases, who had taken over scheduling, set out to find specific places to go within the framework of Wilhelm's battleground states strategy. Still well in advance of the convention, Engelberg flew to Philadelphia, the obvious first media market to exploit after leaving New York, rented a car and started driving west. Accompanying him was Bruce Garamella, a veteran advance man. First, though, they decided on Camden, New

Jersey, across the Delaware River from Philadelphia, as the initial stop outside New York, at a General Electric aerospace plant that had suffered sharp cutbacks but had a strong worker retraining program of the sort Clinton was advocating.

Engelberg and Garamella then worked their way across Pennsylvania, with guidance from Carville, who knew the state well after having run the Wofford campaign, and Celia Fischer, the Clinton state coordinator working out of Philadelphia. They drove up to Valley Forge and other likely places in eastern Pennsylvania looking for picturesque sites that also had activities that dovetailed with the Clinton message, finally settling on York for the first overnight. They also chose what was billed as "the world's largest truck stop" at Carlisle, "a good place to do infrastructure—talk about bridges and highways," Engelberg said. "And it just so happened that it was a very interesting kind of picture, because as far as the eye could see you've got these giant semi-trailer trucks, a very picturesque café there. . . . We knew it would be a good picture there, [the candidates] walking around with a bunch of truck drivers and hopefully sitting down and talking infrastructure."

As Engelberg and Garamella meandered their way through Pennsylvania and Ohio, it became clear that the tour was not likely to make it all the way to Little Rock in the time allotted, so it was decided to terminate it after a thousand miles in St. Louis, in another targeted state. The selection of Gore as Clinton's running mate turned out not to be a factor in the scheduling, and the first trip was routed through Indiana, not Tennessee, after all.

Some ranking members of the staff remained cool to the whole idea. One of them, encountering Engelberg at the convention, asked him what he was up to. When he told him, the reply was, "Oh, yes, you got your way. We're doing the bus trip." Engelberg said later, "I felt like Lee Harvey Oswald, like I was being set up as the single assassin; everything short of Fair Play for Cuba leaflets in my hotel room." And he told *The Boston Globe*'s Curtis Wilkie: "If you find some bones on the side of the road along the way, they'll be mine."

Engelberg as busmeister leased only eight buses for the trip, one assigned to each of the candidates and the rest for staff and about 150 newspeople of various descriptions, and a couple of vans for television and still cameramen. He had a small team of assistants led by twenty-year-old Jason Goldberg, who loaded twenty-five pounds of ice, sandwiches and a case of soft drinks on each bus for the first day—totally inadequate since there was no stop for lunch or dinner before arriving in York late that first night. The second day the order was increased to 800 pounds of ice and sixty cases of soft drinks.

There were other opening-day snafus. Planning in advance, Engelberg sent the vans on ahead, figuring "they could get this wonderful shot of the bus after we come out of the [Lincoln] Tunnel [to New Jersey], with the New York skyline in the background." But on the way to the tunnel, the motorcade passed the vans, stuck in traffic. And before the motorcade reached the toll booth for the New Jersey Turnpike that would take the entourage south to Camden, Secret Service agents reported the presence of a stowaway, a homeless woman, on one of the staff buses. The motorcade had to be halted at the toll booth to disembark the unwelcome interloper on the campaign that bragged it was "Putting People First." So much, Engelberg laughed later, for "the well-oiled machine."

Otherwise, the scheme of conveying the Clinton message along the route worked out well. At a turnpike rest stop about eight miles north of Camden, the motorcade stopped and took aboard six workers from the GE job retraining program who visited with Clinton and Gore and briefed them on what they would see at the plant. This approach was followed throughout this and subsequent bus trips.

But it was not logistics, good or bad, that became the trademark of what some signs along the way were soon calling "Bill and Al's Excellent Adventure." It was the men and their message of generational change, delivered in words and in their strikingly youthful and vigorous appearance, together with their young, blond and stylish wives.

"Change is the key to your security," Clinton told the workers at the Camden plant. "The other side is saying we've been in charge for twelve years and if you want change, vote for more of the same. That approach doesn't make sense. Their approach has failed."

Along the way, Clinton and Gore made a special pitch to the supporters of Ross Perot, now that he had withdrawn. At a New York rally kicking off the bus trip, two Perot organizers in New York state had announced their conversion to Clinton, and the Democratic nominee and his running mate pounded away at their message of change at every stop. The Perot pullout had helped give Clinton, *The New York Times* reported, the largest bounce recorded after a party convention in fifty years, putting him 24 percentage points ahead of Bush, 55 to 31, in the *Times*/CBS News poll.

The Republican opposition seemed stunned by the aftermath of the Perot decision, catapulting the Democratic ticket into such a lead. Appearing with Bush in Provo, Utah, on the second day of the Clinton-Gore bus trip, Republican Senator Jake Garn ridiculed the Democratic pair as "a team of pretty boys," but that flip dismissal failed to grasp a political phenomenon that was now being revealed on the open highways through Pennsylvania.

When the bus tour arrived in York near midnight, two hours behind schedule, for the first overnight stay, a crowd of several thousand people were waiting outside the candidates' hotel. "This happened for the next five days," Engelberg recalled. "It was what you would like to do if you're a good advance man, but it just happened. That was the first time I felt, 'Something's going on here.' " Mark Gearan, who was now assigned as Gore's chief aide, said: "We weren't competent enough to advance that kind of trip. Every advance kid we had was in New York. We just rolled out of there hoping for the best. Something else was happening."

The stop the next day at "the world's largest truck stop" in Carlisle was all that Engelberg had hoped for. Bill and Al, dressed casually in sport shirts and slacks, climbed into the cab of a semi—Bill behind the wheel, naturally. Both went into the diner and sat at the counter discussing things like speed limits and other trucker concerns with the customers, while Hillary and Tipper played some miniature golf outside.

At a rest stop along the Pennsylvania Turnpike, Bill and Al tossed a football around in the best Kennedy tradition, and the next day, at Weirton, West Virginia, they had an opportunity, not to be passed up, to tap the Kennedy legend again. Speaking beside a bust of Kennedy, who had visited the troubled steel town during his 1960 campaign as FDR had done in 1932, Clinton reminded the crowd of Kennedy's visit and his message then and his own message now, that "it's time for a change."

On into Ohio the bus tour rolled. After a stop for a discussion with farmers at the farm of Democratic state chairman Gene Branstool outside of Utica, a small town northwest of Columbus, the buses went on past a crossroads where Branstool had informed Engelberg he could produce a few hundred people. When they got there late that night, more than 3,000 were waiting. Clinton and Gore got out and spoke, as they were increasingly obliged to do as the bus trip itself began to take on the reputation of a happening.

But it was the appearance and the style of Clinton, Gore and their wives as much as the campaign rhetoric that seemed to capture the small-town crowds and the hundreds who gathered at crossroads and other truck stops along the way. Gore particularly, so stiff and earnest in his failed 1988 presidential bid that he became the brunt of robot jokes, became more relaxed and even playful in the role of second fiddle.

Running mates as a rule seldom campaign with the standard-bearer, and when they do it is almost always in a subordinate, even subservient role, but Clinton saw to it that Gore got nearly equal billing. He invited Gore to answer voters' questions addressed to himself, especially when the subject was one on which Gore had superior background, such as the environment. And Gore developed into a first-class crowd warm-up speaker, with a laugh-getting ritual that became standard on the tour.

After reciting a long list of Bush-Quayle failures, he would intone: "Bush and Quayle have run out of ideas. They've run out of energy. They've run out of gas, and with your help come November, they're going to be run out of office!" He would wind up his pitch by shouting: "It's time for Bush and Quayle to go!" Then he would ask the crowd: "What time is it?" And on cue the roar would come back: "It's time for them to go!"

Clinton, his head thrown back in boisterous laughter as if he were hearing the routine for the first time, would then step up to the micro-phones. Gesturing to Gore, he would say, as he did at one stop in Wilmington, Ohio: "I made a pretty good decision, didn't I? It would suit me for this election to be based on the first decision George Bush made [as a presidential nominee in 1988] and the first decision I made."

In a more serious vein, Clinton often would tell crowds that the one reason he had selected Gore was that he believed him to be the best person to assume the presidency if anything were to happen to him. And compared to the way Bush was keeping his stand-in, Dan Quayle, at arm's length, the embrace emphatically conveyed the sense that here was a genuine relationship of mutual respect and confidence.

By this time Al Gore was like a kid who couldn't be dragged off the roller coaster at an amusement park. The Gores had been scheduled to drop off the tour when it reached Louisville and go home to Tennessee, but as the departure point approached, Gore turned to Gearan and asked: "Why are we leaving?" When Gearan told him briefing sessions were planned for him home in Carthage, he said they could be done on the bus, that he wanted to stay to the end.

The Clintons and the Gores took to riding for hours in the same van, visiting and, in the case of the two men, experiencing a bonding that became obvious to their fellow bus travelers. After the longest of days, they would sit on the bus talking, talking, talking, while the rest of the entourage groaned for them to get off and go to bed. Soon, when Gore would go into his warm-up and end with, "What time is it?" weary reporters would shout back: "It's time for us to go!" On one occasion later, when the two ticket mates sat in Clinton's bus, locked in a post-midnight gabfest at the end of the day's schedule, aides took to rocking the huge bus back and forth to get them out.

As the buses moved on, dipping into Kentucky and Indiana and on into Illinois, the crowds grew larger and more enthusiastic. Often there were protesters present, usually toting anti-abortion signs, but except for them the mood was cheerful and even celebratory. As the buses sped by more crossroads in the middle of nowhere, signs began to crop up saying: GIVE US EIGHT MINUTES AND WE'LL GIVE YOU EIGHT YEARS. The appeal proved irresistible to the two candidates, who would stop the motorcade, hop off, shake hands and say a few words, thus assuring further late arrivals down the road.

Gene Randall of CNN ribbed Engelberg, suggesting he had hired extras to move from crossroads to crossroads to give the illusion of Clinton's crowd appeal. (It would not have been the first time. During the 1988 Iowa caucuses, most of the cars in a motorcade across the state by televangelist Pat Robertson were packed with supporters, who piled out at each stop and quickly assembled to hear their man make the same speech he had made at all the stops before.)

On the final night of the trip, a crowd more than doubling the local population waited two hours beyond the scheduled arrival time in Vandalia, Illinois, site of the state's first capitol where Abraham Lincoln served in the legislature. It was just the kind of setting that Carter Wilkie had in mind when he wrote his memo back in April. Clinton told his listeners that Lincoln "is turned over in his grave tonight to think of what George Bush and Dan Quayle have done to the Republican Party and the United States of America." And the next day for the trip's windup, another crowd estimated at 30,000 jammed downtown St. Louis streets in a scene more typical of late October in a presidential election year. The bus trip had succeeded far beyond expectations, and the team of Bill and Al was cemented in a way that George and Dan never could, or would, be.

After the election, Charlie Black of the Bush-Quayle campaign credited his opponents with a master stroke in the bus trip coming directly out of the Democratic convention. The practical effect, he said, was "they turned a four-day story into a twelve-day story" by extending that very successful convention beyond its adjournment and maintaining the bounce derived from the convention itself against attempts even then by the Republicans to cut the Clinton-Gore team down to size.

Beyond that, Jim Lake said, the timely withdrawal of Ross Perot at the end of a successful convention, followed by the bus trip, was golden for Clinton. "The minute he [Perot] bails out in the middle of this halo [the convention], all these people who were anti-Bush become pro-Clinton," Lake said. "Clinton and Perot couldn't have sat down and planned it better. We didn't know it at once, but we soon saw it."

Before the final rally in St. Louis, Bruce Lindsey asked Engelberg to send him a memo with his thoughts on how another bus trip in some future time should be done, based on what he had learned from this one. On the plane back to Los Angeles, Engelberg wrote it out in longhand, advising at the outset, "Let's not kill the goose that laid the golden egg," but wait a month before trying it again. When he got home, he typed it out, intending to send it by fax to Little Rock the next morning. But when he got up, he found a message to him on his fax machine, informing him that there would be another bus trip in ten days.

The second trip picked up basically where the first had left off, in East St. Louis just across the Mississippi River in Illinois. This time, Engelberg recalled, "everybody wanted a piece of it"—staff and press alike. Fourteen buses were required to handle the increase, and special props were built, including what Engelberg called "a rally in a box." It was a small stage equipped with a sound system that could be folded up into the undercarriage of Clinton's bus. Before leaving, Engelberg's crew practiced setting it up until they could do it in seven minutes, while the candidates were working the ropeline, shaking hands with voters. (The aforementioned Pat Robertson motorcade across Iowa four years earlier also had such a contraption.)

The Secret Service also stepped in, armor-plating the front of Clinton's bus and installing bulletproof glass, with the idea that he would be able to stand up and wave to crossroads crowds as the bus went by—a notion that did not calculate Clinton's seeming inability to resist stopping. "They came to see me," he would tell aides, "I'm going to get out and talk to them." Television lights were installed inside the bus so that crews could come in and do their job without first having to set up all their cumbersome equipment.

The second bus trip was a much shorter affair, up the Mississippi for less than three days with stops in small riverfront towns in Missouri, Iowa and Wisconsin, then ending in Minneapolis. Many stops along the way were called "impromptu," but often local Democratic officials, notified of the bus route, would advise the campaign that they intended to have a crowd at this or that crossroads or truck stop. If the crowd materialized, the motorcade would then stop, and most times it did. As a result, the motorcade would roll up hours late to the entrance to the hotel or motel where the candidates would be staying overnight. As late as 2:30 A.M. in small towns on the route, hundreds or even thousands would be waiting to greet them. And of course Gore would have to ask them "What time is it?" and Clinton would have to give his own answer: "Time for a change."

The highlight of the first day was a visit to Hannibal, Missouri, Mark Twain's boyhood hometown, where Clinton quoted his observation that "petrified opinion and old ideas never did anything to break a chain or free a human soul." While Bill and Al weren't quite Tom Sawyer and Huck Finn, they did do a fair imitation of small-town boys who hadn't forgotten their roots. The notably articulate Clinton started talking about his "momma" and beginning his remarks with phrases like, "Well shoot, folks."

At Burlington, Iowa, before a massive crowd with the muddy Mississippi flowing slowly by, he talked about how "I've grown up loving the land that borders this river," and "all the troubles this river has seen." He would also make a point of telling the crowds that "Al still lives on a farm'' in Carthage, Tennessee, although Gore had spent much of his time as a youth in Washington as the son of a United States senator and still put in most of his time there.

By now they were behaving like a couple of brothers, if not twins, with Clinton frequently telling crowds that ''Al and I'' would do this or that for them when they were elected, and with Gore referring to ''the Clinton-Gore team.'' Clinton didn't seem to mind a bit, and continued laughing at Gore's introduction, which he was now laying on with voice rising and arms flailing.

At a forum in Davenport, Iowa, when Clinton was asked a foreign policy question and gave a short, unimpressive response, Gore took the microphone and recalled that President Bush in a recent speech had emphasized how important it was to have an experienced voice on the end of the line when a crisis call came into the White House in the middle of the night. When Bush's wealthy friends called, Gore said, he always answers at once, but ''when the average American family calls up'' to tell him how bad things are, ''they're getting a disconnect.'' Clinton stood there wearing a slight grin that suggested he was wishing he'd have said that.

Pat Deluhery, an Iowa Democratic state senator watching the team at work at the Davenport forum, told us afterward concerning Clinton: ''He's made two fabulous choices. First he's picked this guy [Gore] and then this bus thing. People love it. They have to come out and see these two young guys who look and act like they're ready to go.''

At the final stop of the second trip, another large crowd waited in the rain for hours in downtown Minneapolis for Clinton's arrival. From his bus, he called the crowd over a cellular phone, with his words hooked up to a microphone, apologized for being so late and asked them not to leave. They stayed, and when he got there, Clinton stood before a statue of the venerated Hubert Humphrey, with another former vice president from Minnesota, Walter Mondale, standing by. As he started to brag on Gore, about to call him the best vice presidential selection ever, he stopped, grinned, and added: ''who was not from Minnesota!''

The Republican convention was now only days away, so Bill and Al put their buses away for a while, but afterward resumed their Excellent Adventure. In all, they made seven full-fledged bus trips and two others for parts of a day before election day. The trips, Engelberg mused later, "became sort of a metaphor—symbolic of this campaign: this is for everybody. The difference in the bus as opposed to Harry Truman's train trips, if you wanted to see Harry Truman, you had to go down to the train station. The beauty of these bus trips was that we took the bus to a Head Start center, or we took the bus to a factory, and in a sense we were bringing the campaign to the electorate."

As Clinton and Gore thus rolled merrily along toward the fall campaign, the team of Bush and Quayle was stumbling toward the Republican convention in Houston. Bush was continuing to insist that he had no thought of discarding the man he had said in 1988 was qualified to be president. But others in their party, after four years of Dan Quayle remaining that celebrated heartbeat away from the presidency, still had their doubts. They wondered how firm George Bush really was on the point—and whether anything could be said or done to change his mind.

STILL NO
JACK KENNEDY

While the Bill and Al traveling road show was playing to smash audiences across small-town America, the Republican team of George and Dan—Bush and Quayle—was doing solo acts, as the two had all through the previous four years, intentionally keeping their distance. With Pat Buchanan disposed of as a threat to Bush's renomination, the president preferred to get back to governing and leave the campaign stumping to the vice president, who in spite of endless ridicule from the Democrats and in the news media had proved to be an effective drawing card and record-breaking fund-raiser for his party.

Ever since Bush had shocked and dismayed many fellow Republicans at the party's national convention in New Orleans four years earlier by selecting the young and gaffe-prone Hoosier senator as his running mate, political duets by the two were few and far between. The reason was understood by all who had witnessed or read about Quayle's disastrous run as the Republican vice presidential nominee in 1988 and his erratic performance as Bush's understudy in office thereafter.

Two episodes haunted him from the 1988 campaign. The first and best remembered by voters was his ambush at the hands of Democratic vice presidential nominee Lloyd Bentsen in their debate in Omaha. Much of that debate was focused on Quayle's youth—he was forty-one at the time but much younger-looking and immature—and hence on his qualifications to take over the presidency if fate were to so dictate.

Quayle was defensive. "It's not just age, it's accomplishments, it's experience," he said at one point. "I have far more experience than many others that sought the office of vice president of this country. I have as much experience in the Congress as Jack Kennedy did when he sought the presidency. . . ."

Bentsen stiffened, then glared at Quayle. "Senator," he said in a rejoinder from which Quayle would never recover, "I served with Jack Kennedy. I knew Jack Kennedy. Jack Kennedy was a friend of mine. Senator, you are no Jack Kennedy."

Quayle was stunned, as the audience erupted in applause and laughter. That one exchange became a political albatross around his neck thereafter, to the point that, once elected, the young vice president chose to turn it into a joke. At a book party on the occasion of our account of the 1988 campaign in which the debate exchange was reexamined, Quayle graciously came, stood up and said: "I knew Teddy White. Teddy White was a friend of mine. And believe me, you guys are no Teddy White."

But politically, Dan Quayle's reputation as an inexperienced naïf could not be laughed off. Neither could the second experience that left scars on him from the 1988 campaign. That was the Bush campaign's assigning of handlers to hold a tight rein on him as he stumped through the smaller towns and states, the customary fate of vice presidential nominees. They saved him from some but not all the political pitfalls he encountered, but he chafed at their close supervision and at news stories about it.

He began to blame the handlers, longtime professional consultants Stuart Spencer and Joe Canzeri, for not permitting him to be himself—which, when he was, sometimes had embarrassing results. Losing his temper at one point, he told reporters: "There is not going to be any more handler stories, because I'm the handler." He dubbed himself "Doctor Spin" and told reporters that if they had any questions to come to him, not to one of the handlers. But Spencer and Canzeri continued to watch over him, and he survived the campaign.

As vice president, Quayle insisted on having his own people around him, and he functioned politically on a much freer rein than during the campaign, but still under the general direction of the Bush administration's political operation, as was expected of any vice president. Bush continued to insist that he had made a good choice but did not go out of his way particularly to showcase that choice.

Quayle was given a few special assignments and met with the president weekly for a private lunch, in the pattern of Bush himself when he was Ronald Reagan's vice president. And like Bush under Reagan, Quayle was a fawning man-in-waiting, ever loyal and outspokenly supportive of Bush in every way. In inner counsels, however, he spoke up much more often than Bush ever did at political and policy staff meetings with Reagan. He was regarded as a strong voice for conservative viewpoints within the Bush administration, bolstered by his astute and politically attuned chief of staff, Bill Kristol, and others.

Outside the administration, however, Quayle continued to be regarded as the pratfall-plagued political mistake. Although he went for months at a time without saying or doing anything to reinforce that reputation, he slipped occasionally enough to keep it alive and the brunt of public ridicule. That fact governed his usefulness for the president. On the one hand there was a desire to put him in situations where he could combat the impression of being a dim bulb. On the other, there was always the realization that he could misstep, and an understanding that his role as emissary for the president did not always carry the force desired. Still, Dan Quayle was vice president of the United States, and that fact alone counted for a great deal, especially in the international diplomatic community.

After less than two weeks in office, Bush sent the new vice president to South and Central America to perform largely ceremonial duties, as a way of getting his feet wet. He performed adequately, except for an observation in El Salvador that the United States was committed to "work toward the elimination of human rights" in the region.

Shortly afterward, back home, when the Republican National Committee's executive committee censured former Ku Klux Klansman David

Duke upon his election to the Louisiana state legislature as a Republican, Quayle commended the party for its "censorship" of Duke.

On a trip to the Pacific, he treated the locals at a military base in Honolulu to a little geography lesson: "Hawaii has always been a very pivotal role in the Pacific. It is in the Pacific. It is a part of the United States that is an island that is right here." And in Pago Pago, American Samoa, pronounced "Pango Pango" but which Quayle called "Pogo Pogo" as in the old comic strip, he referred to the local children as "happy campers," which was taken as condescending. These slips were trivial, to be sure, but they got much press attention and froze the image of Dan Quayle as an empty suit.

His interest in golf, which he had played with considerable skill and dedication ever since college, also became a prominent trademark, and not always in a constructive manner. On the same Pacific trip, after a round on the local links in Singapore, he showed up late for dinner at the home of the fuming prime minister, who greeted him with "I hear you had some golf."

Back home again, Quayle rewarded what came to be known in the press corps as "the gaffe watch" with his twist on the slogan of the United Negro College Fund, that "A mind is a terrible thing to waste." Run through the Quayle language mangler, it came out "What a waste it is to lose one's mind, or not to have a mind, is being very wasteful. How true that is."

Dan Quayle, as vice president just as vice presidential candidate, was always good for a laugh. But for Republican politicians, especially those already looking ahead to the prospects for a second Bush term, "the Quayle problem" was no laughing matter. A *Washington Post*/ABC News poll in early August of 1989 found that 52 percent of 1,022 persons interviewed didn't think Quayle was fit for the presidency and 38 percent said Bush should get himself another running mate in 1992.

On and on it went. Visiting the site of the latest San Francisco earthquake, Quayle called it "a heart-rendering sight" and judged that "the loss of life will be irreplaceable." Voters continued to laugh and shake their heads. But a vice president has a constituency of one, and that one remained firm in his support. Bush in November told *The Dallas Morning News* that Quayle "absolutely" would be on the ticket with him in 1992 if he wanted to be.

Quayle's reputation, however, was inhibiting his ability to perform the traditional job of presidential emissary abroad. After the Bush administration's invasion of Panama in early 1990, he was sent to Latin America to smooth sensitivities and explain the American decision, but Venezuela and Mexico declined to receive him. It was on this same trip that he bought the infamous "anatomically correct" doll in Valparaiso, Chile, that added to his image as a sophomoric clown. A March 1990 Gallup poll found 54 percent said he wasn't qualified to be president and 49 percent thought Bush should dump him in 1992.

But Dan Quayle had his strengths, too. For the 1990 congressional campaign, he raised a record of more than $15 million for party candidates. And when Bush decided to go to war in the Persian Gulf to turn back the Iraqi invasion of Kuwait, Quayle was a visible, outspoken defender. Even then, though, Quayle seemed to do himself no good politically. Speculation began that one of the stars of the American military effort, General Colin Powell, chairman of the Joint Chiefs of Staff, might and ought to replace Quayle on the Bush ticket in 1992. A *New York Times*/CBS News poll of 1,252 adults found 56 percent viewed Powell favorably to a dismal 19 percent for Quayle.

In May, the hospitalization of Bush for an irregular heartbeat after a day of jogging and other strenuous physical exercise gave higher visibility than ever to "the Quayle problem." A *Time* headline asked: "Is He Really that Bad?" with a poll showing 52 percent of those surveyed thought Bush should bounce Quayle and 24 percent saying they would be less likely to vote for Bush if he didn't. The *Newsweek* cover, showing Quayle swinging a golf club, was no better: "The Quayle Handicap . . . Is He a Lightweight—Or Smarter than You Think?"

When Bush was asked whether he might reconsider keeping Quayle on the ticket, he shot back: "Do you want that by hand or do you want it by word?" He said he would prefer not emulating a former vice president, Nelson Rockefeller, who once conspicuously replied to a heckler's taunts by extending his middle finger into the air. Quayle, the president said, was getting "a bum rap in the press, pounding on him when he's doing a first-rate job. And I don't know how many times I have to say it, but I'm not about to change my mind when I see his performance and know what he does."

In the next weeks, Quayle traveled to Japan and India and shortly afterward to Eastern Europe on what were essentially gaffe-free trips, but few reporters went along and it didn't seem to matter anyway. A mindset had taken hold with the American people that Dan Quayle was in over his head. Fortunately for him, it was a view that George Bush either didn't share or hoped wouldn't make any difference to voters in 1992 just as, apparently, it hadn't in 1988.

At home, Quayle took on his own legal profession, complaining there was entirely too much litigation going on, charging it was undercutting American competitiveness in the global market. It was a view that came out of the President's Council on Competitiveness headed by Quayle, which critics attacked as a pro-business vehicle for end-running government regulations.

Quayle had no shortage of critics, even in the funny papers. Garry Trudeau, author of the "Doonesbury" strip, resurrected the story of an Oklahoma prison inmate who was put into solitary confinement in the final days of the 1988 campaign when he was about to hold a news conference charging he had sold drugs to Quayle when Quayle was in law school. A strip character was portrayed as having been told the Drug Enforcement Administration had a file on Quayle. It turned out there was such a file but the DEA had found the accusations to be groundless. But it was a fact that the inmate, Brett Kimberlin, serving a fifty-one-year term for drug smuggling and a bombing, had been put in solitary on orders from the Bureau of Prisons days before the 1988 election.

Through all this, there continued much speculation about Quayle's political fate and much wishful thinking among his critics that Bush, out of his own political travail, would finally ditch his hapless vice president. But from the start of the planning for 1992, it was always identified as the Bush-Quayle campaign, with the president continuing to give Quayle his unqualified endorsement.

In the fall, as economic conditions failed to improve, Quayle was among those inside the administration who pressed for the president to speak out. At one point, according to Bob Teeter, the vice president called him in and said, "We've got to do something." Much more than Bush, Quayle had been out around the country, and he knew that the sense of drift was eroding the president's support. But the argument from Darman and others that recovery was around the corner was the one Bush wanted to hear, and it prevailed.

Early in January of the election year, Quayle was the beneficiary of a largely favorable series about his vice presidency in *The Washington Post* by two of its top reporters, David Broder and Bob Woodward, but even in that series his problem was identified, by Republican Senator Warren Rudman of New Hampshire. "Dan Quayle has a long way to go to be really qualified to be president in terms of leadership qualities," Rudman said, "for a very unfortunate reason not of his doing—and that is the perception with which he is held by the American people."

When the Pat Buchanan challenge emerged in New Hampshire and began to look serious, Quayle was dispatched there to bring the message that Bush cared, but it was the sort of message that could not be delivered effectively by a surrogate. Quayle's words could not counter the feeling of resentment, fed by Buchanan, among New Hampshire Republicans, who, after all, had bailed Bush out in their 1988 presidential primary after he had finished an embarrassing third to Bob Dole and Pat Robertson in the Iowa caucuses. Buchanan poked fun at Bush's decision to send "little Danny, the pit puppy," to do political battle for him.

Quayle's trip to the first primary state came only hours after word from Tokyo that Bush had gotten sick and collapsed at a state dinner, and that fact focused as much or more on the same old question of presidential succession as on Quayle's political mission. As soon as Air Force Two landed in Nashua and Quayle stepped off to field the press's questions, he was asked about his qualifications to take over if necessary. "I'm ready," he said, and ended the press conference.

But Bush's unhappy experience in Japan put Quayle and the possibility of succession in the limelight once more. *The Manchester Union Leader,* supporting Buchanan, ran a cartoon showing a beaming Quayle on a map of the United States, surrounded by the horrified faces of five citizens. The caption was "Home Alone," after the popular movie then playing about a wild youngster left at home by his parents.

Later, walking along a ropeline at a shopping mall outside Manchester, a woman stopped him as he shook her hand. Reporters were kept too far away by Quayle's Secret Service agents to hear the conversation, but the woman, a lawyer named Karen Heller, later recounted it to us.

"I don't have it in for Vice President Quayle," she said. "In the past I've been a Bush supporter. Right now I'm undecided and I told him that. I said I like him as a vice president and I like him as a man, but I like him as a vice president only if I know that he would never be president, which of course no one can guarantee. I said to him, if the polls showed that his being the vice president was a hindrance to President Bush's campaign, what would he advise President Bush to do?'' Quayle, she went on, ''sort of avoided the question'' and told her ''the polls were nothing . . . but manipulated by the media.'' Later, she said the conversation hadn't changed her mind, and she thought Bush should drop him from the ticket.

Quayle tried to put the best face on the Buchanan challenge. He said it was helpful because ''it's already energized the president's campaign. . . . We're starting the campaign earlier than we had anticipated.'' His enthusiasm was genuine, because in private he had been pressing for getting the campaign into high gear. He told voters: ''I understand you want to send a message. We've got the message.''

Nevertheless, New Hampshire voters gave Buchanan a surprising 37 percent of their votes against an incumbent president. Three days after the primary, Quayle took his case for Bush to the Conservative Political Action Conference in Washington. Without mentioning Buchanan by name, he lectured the audience that ''the only real question facing us today is whether our president will enter the general election campaign from a position of strength or from a position of weakness. Anyone has the right to wage a symbolic campaign,'' he said, ''but it would be irresponsible to endanger all that we have achieved.'' And he told his fellow conservatives that opposing Bush would ''risk being out of power for a generation.''

Quayle did not mention what a defeat in November would do to his own ambitions, but that went without saying. As Buchanan faded, Quayle was able to breathe easier, but there was always something to bring him unfavorable publicity. In April, a report of the General Accounting Office, Congress's investigative arm, disclosed that he had been using military planes to go on golfing junkets. He said in some cases political events were involved and he had partly reimbursed the government, but again tongues wagged from coast to coast.

On May 19, at the Commonwealth Club of California in San Francisco, Quayle finally carved out his own voice in the campaign as the defender of ''family values.'' He blamed the riots in Los Angeles on ''lawless social anarchy'' that was the result of a ''breakdown of family structure, personal responsibility and social order.'' And he called for "social sanctions'' against women ''irresponsibly'' bearing children out of wedlock. He chose as his target one of the most popular television situation comedies in which the central character, unmarried, gave birth.

"It doesn't help matters,'' Quayle said, ''when prime-time TV has Murphy Brown—a character who supposedly epitomizes today's intelligent, highly paid, professional woman—mocking the importance of fathers, by bearing a child alone, and calling it just another 'lifestyle choice.' ''

If Quayle wanted to set off a firestorm, and there were indications he intended to do just that, he could not have picked a better, higher-visibility target. Many viewers ridiculed the spectacle of Quayle taking on a fictitious television character, but others saw his remarks as a fusillade in the continuing battle over abortion. His right-wing constituents, who had come to look upon him as their chief advocate and protector within the Bush administration, applauded his initiative, while abortion rights activists condemned him.

The creator and executive producer of the television show, Diane English, one of the latter, said: "If the vice president thinks it's disgraceful for an unmarried woman to bear a child, and if he believes that a woman cannot raise a child without a father, then he'd better make sure abortion remains safe and legal.''

The White House at first backed up Quayle, though without much visible enthusiasm, and then Bush retreated by saying he was "not going to get into the details of a very popular television show.'' But Quayle had struck a sharp chord and was playing it for all it was worth. "It's a speech that had to be given, an important speech,'' he told reporters. "I know it's risky territory when someone like myself begins to talk about values. It can come across, perhaps, as preachy, as moralistic.'' But, he said, "the discussion will get beyond Murphy Brown and it will give me an opportunity to talk about values.''

The day after the Murphy Brown speech, Quayle took that opportunity outside a predominantly black school in South Central Los Angeles. "Hollywood thinks it's cute to glamorize illegitimacy,'' he said. "Hollywood doesn't get it.'' Before Quayle was through, he found himself in an exchange with actress Candice Bergen, the real-life Murphy Brown. And in the process he moved into the forefront of the whole focus on "family values" that the Bush-Quayle strategists hoped not only would reinforce their ticket's support among the party's right wing but also would provide a vehicle for getting at the "character" issue against Clinton.

From all indications, Quayle and his staff hit on the idea themselves and rode with it before the top campaign people realized he had done so. It never would have happened in the 1988 campaign, but Dan Quayle's days as putty in the hands of handlers were over, especially with the campaign working overtime this late in the year to shore up its conservative base and Quayle its most popular active figure on the party's right.

Soon after the Murphy Brown assault, Quayle followed up with an attack on the nation's "cultural elites," who, he told a Southern Baptists convention in Indianapolis, "respect neither tradition nor standards. They believe that moral truths are relative and all 'lifestyles' are equal. They seem to think . . . that fathers are dispensable and that parents need not be married or even of the opposite sexes. They are wrong." And as for the "scorn of the media elite" that he said had been rained down on him since his Murphy Brown speech, he said, "I wear their scorn as a badge of honor."

Clinton did not let this one go by without comment. "How dare Dan Quayle talk that way about anybody?" he said. "I'm tired of people with trust funds telling people on food stamps how to live." But Quayle was on a roll now. "Now that we have your attention," he told reporters in North Carolina, "tune in, stay tuned, because we're going to talk about values." And in New York, he castigated the distribution of condoms in the city's schools and blamed its many problems on "the entrenched government establishment and its liberal ideology."

Quayle began to sound like vice presidential predecessor Spiro Agnew, who in the Nixon administration had gone to war against what he called "radical liberals" and the "nattering nabobs of negativism" in the news media. And it was at this juncture too that Quayle joined the Republican onslaught against Ross Perot with his description of the Texas billionaire as a "temperamental tycoon."

But just when Quayle was hitting his stride, he put his foot in his mouth again. At a children's spelling bee being supervised by Quayle at the Luis Muñoz Rivera Elementary School in Trenton, New Jersey, twelve-year-old William Figueroa correctly spelled the word "potato" on a blackboard. Quayle, trying to be helpful, told him: "That's fine phonetically, but you're missing just a little bit." With coaxing from Quayle, the boy added an "e." Quayle had been given a yellow flash card with the word misspelled and simply passed on the misspelling.

In the local newspaper, *The Trentonian*, the boy was quoted as saying the incident "showed that the rumors about the vice president are true—that he's an idiot." Later, he told an Associated Press reporter that Quayle "is an okay guy, but he needs to study." So much for Dan Quayle being taken seriously. Signs began to appear in his speech crowds reading MR. POTATOE HEAD and other variations.

All these happenings stirred the concern that already existed within the Bush campaign about what Quayle on the ticket might do to what now appeared to be the president's very uncertain reelection chances. One Republican senator, James Jeffords of Vermont, was openly suggesting that dumping Quayle would help Bush in the fall. Quietly, campaign chairman Bob Teeter had a poll taken testing how Quayle and other possible running mates would affect the strength of the Republican ticket. Experienced pollsters like Teeter knew that the identity of the vice presidential nominee seldom had any appreciable impact on the outcome of an election, but bad numbers in the right hands could help make the case for deep-sixing the erratic young man from Indiana.

Teeter's poll, Kristol said later, "didn't make much difference. It didn't show as much as he hoped it would show. If it had showed a more dramatic result, it could have been used to bolster the dump-Quayle scenario." Still, according to others close to the campaign, some key figures did press for the vice president's removal, but rather halfheartedly in light of Bush's stated intentions and the lack of strong supportive polling data.

Those said to be interested to one degree or another in replacing Quayle included, in addition to Teeter, campaign director Fred Malek, Charlie Black, Rich Bond and Jim Baker, although in Baker's case and standard practice for him, he stayed in the background. The basic argument, one insider said later, was that Quayle was "baggage we don't need" in what already was becoming an uphill fight.

Among those being mentioned by the dump-Quayle insiders to replace him were Dick Cheney, first, and then Bob Dole because both had been under public scrutiny, Cheney in his confirmation hearings when he went to the Pentagon, and Dole as a former presidential and vice presidential candidate, and either one could stand a frisk.

Fortunately for Quayle, Kristol said later, "the people involved never had the nerve to really move beyond talk to conspiring. There were a couple of weeks there where I was worried, where we took a couple of acts to try to make sure to flush out the possible conspirers."

When a *Wall Street Journal* story appeared indicating some conservatives thought Quayle ought to step aside for his own sake, and other stories in the same vein followed, it was taken in the Quayle camp as a tipoff that the wolves were out. So were rumors about Bush's health, immediately squashed by Bush's doctor. The president called it "a crazy time on rumors" in which it was being suggested that not only he but his wife and Marilyn Quayle were ill. "I don't know what's going on," he said—perhaps forgetting how rumors about Dukakis's health had been spread by his own campaign in the summer of 1988 as part of the effort to reduce his lead in the polls.

Kristol, according to conservative stalwart Paul Weyrich, began calling "movement conservatives" like himself, warning that talk of dumping Quayle was "fairly serious." Kristol, Weyrich said, "urged those of us who had been favorable toward Quayle to make our views known, which we tried to do. The trial balloon was such that Bush understood that he would have a problem if he selected another nominee."

The argument he put forward, Weyrich said, "was not that this would be a betrayal of conservatives, because he could have picked somebody just as conservative." But the Democrats, he warned, would "make you reargue your initial judgment [on Quayle], and I don't see how that helps you. Even if you get somebody else, you're already stuck with that decision. If it was wrong, it was wrong four years ago. If you get somebody else, it's going to suggest that you didn't know what you were doing and you made a terrible mistake. Unless you want to say that, which presumably you don't, I think you'd be very hard-pressed to come up with somebody else."

Weyrich said he told this to Malek, Jim Pinkerton, one of the most conservative White House aides, and—importantly—to the president's son George W., known as "Junior" to the insiders, who he understood conveyed it to his father. "I continued to believe," Weyrich added, "that very few people vote on the basis of the vice presidential candidate. While

Quayle didn't help him any, I don't think he hurt him that much. If Quayle were the problem, then George Bush never would have been at ninety percent approval rating during the Gulf War, because Quayle was such a liability. That didn't affect anything. . . . He would have been fodder for nightclub jokes but he would not have been an issue.''

When a reporter asked Bush, "Is the vice president's chair a little uncertain these days?'' he replied, "No, it's very certain.'' But that didn't stop what he called a media feeding frenzy.

Two days later, Quayle went on the Larry King show and again got into the headlines when King asked him, following on the Murphy Brown flap, what he would do if his own young daughter became pregnant when she grew up. Quayle said he would "counsel her and talk to her and support her on whatever decision she made" but that he would "hope that she wouldn't make that decision [to have an abortion].''

Somewhat lost in the resulting furor over a seeming contradiction with his firm anti-abortion position was another exchange on the show. Asked whether he might take himself off the ticket, Quayle said he had had "a number of discussions" with Bush, "and believe me, if I thought that I was hurting the ticket, I'd be gone. I want George Bush reelected.''

That, one insider said later, "opened the door a little to the pressure. But having opened the door, it was important to close the door.'' So Quayle went to see Bush, got from him firsthand that he did indeed want him to stay on, and "then we put that word out,'' this insider said, "and closed the door we had opened. It was surprising how well it worked.'' When a reporter asked Quayle flat out on July 24, after he had met with Bush, whether he would be staying on the ticket, Quayle replied: "Yes,'' declining to provide details of his talks with the president. A couple of days later in Birmingham, Alabama, Quayle said the question of his seeking reelection as vice president was "a closed issue,'' and that "the president has never wavered on this issue, in public or in private. The only people who are bringing this up are my opponents and the media.''

Concerning the halfhearted dump-Quayle effort, Kristol said later: "What was striking was their lack of resolution and boldness. I'm not sure that a strong and bold attempt to depose Quayle wouldn't have worked. I'm amazed that we were able to bluff them back as easily as we could. . . . They just didn't have the guts to force the issue.''

Of more concern inside the Bush campaign as the Republican National Convention approached was the chaos within the campaign itself, and the war that continued to go on between the campaign and the White House. More and more, talk was heard of the return of Jim Baker, ensconced in the prestigious and demanding position of secretary of state and resisting being pulled back into what he saw as the demeaning game of politics.

When Ross Perot bailed out on the final day of the Democratic National Convention, sending Clinton surging in the polls and Bush falling back, the president's appeal to Perot supporters came from Baker's ranch in Wyoming, where the two old friends were enjoying their annual fishing vacation. A few days later, the word was out: Baker would be back to take over the troubled campaign. Nothing was said about when and in what capacity, but Republican political workers everywhere were saying the sooner the better, and it didn't matter what the title. Wherever Jim Baker was, he was always in charge, and things got done.

It was with that expectation, or at least hope, that the ragged forces of the Bush-Quayle campaign and White House headed for Houston and the coronation of the same ticket that had brought the Republican Party victory four years before.

HOUSTON: CAVING IN
TO THE RIGHT

The week before the Republican National Convention opened, its tone was set by the party's platform committee, gathered in Houston to write the document on which President Bush ostensibly would run for a second term. The Republicans routinely held their platform sessions in the days immediately before their conventions to assure the party another week of press and television attention. And the plan this time was to highlight a different topic each day—domestic policy, foreign policy, national defense, family values—and force the press to focus on them one by one.

As a practical matter, however, there was only one issue that was likely to get any attention. It was whether the platform would include the same tough provision against abortion rights that had been written into the documents of 1984 and 1988, calling for a constitutional amendment forbidding abortion even in cases of rape and incest. In fact, there was never any doubt about the intentions of the Bush campaign. When the platform committee held preliminary hearings in Salt Lake City in May,

Bob Teeter had passed the word to abortion rights supporters that the campaign would give "not one inch."

But the way the issue played out was important, nonetheless, because it would be a measure of the relative strength of moderate Republicans and the hard-line social issue conservatives, including the Christian Coalition led by evangelist Marion G. (Pat) Robertson and the followers of the redoubtable Phyllis Schlafly, leader of the Eagle Forum. If there was one issue likely to define their concepts of "family values," it was abortion.

Beyond that, the issue was intriguing because it was one on which George Bush had pushed himself into an extremist corner with a position potentially damaging in a close election.

The president's stance on abortion had changed radically over the years. As a candidate for the Republican presidential nomination in 1980, he had described himself in New Hampshire as opposing abortion and federal funding of abortions, but also opposed to a constitutional amendment that would overturn *Roe* v. *Wade*, the 1973 Supreme Court decision that legalized abortion. In an interview with *Rolling Stone* magazine early in 1980, Bush had conceded that his principal rival at the moment, Ronald Reagan, "opposes me for not wanting to amend the Supreme Court decision on abortion," and added: "I happen to think it was right." In short, he held what became known as the pro-choice position.

But once Bush joined Reagan's ticket, he became an echo on his opposition to abortion rights. His position had undergone some "evolution," he said in 1984. He now favored a "human life amendment" although he would add exceptions for rape and incest as well as for circumstances in which the life of the mother was threatened. By 1988, Bush was going a step further. "My position has evolved, and it's continuing to evolve in favor of life," he said in a debate with Democratic nominee Michael Dukakis at Winston-Salem. "I'm for the sanctity of life and once that illegality is established, then we can come to grips with the penalty side. And, of course, there's got to be some penalties . . . to enforce the law, whatever that may be."

When the press quickly raised the question of whether he now intended to prosecute women who had abortions as well as the physicians who performed them, campaign manager Jim Baker held a quick press conference to explain the candidate didn't mean that at all. And Dukakis was so inept a candidate he never fully exploited the opening he had been given. Shortly after taking office, Bush cleared up how far he would go: "After years of serious and sober reflection on the issue, this is what I think: I think the Supreme Court's decision in *Roe* v. *Wade* was wrong and should be overturned. I think America needs a human life amendment.''

As president, moreover, Bush continued to harden his position. He vetoed District of Columbia appropriation bills that would permit local tax funds to be used for clinics that performed abortions. He opposed the use of fetal tissue in medical research. And, finally, he approved the so-called gag rule that prohibited personnel in federally funded abortion clinics from even discussing abortion with pregnant women.

But because Bush had made that "evolution"—essentially a total turnaround—on the issue, he continued to be pressed on whether he might evolve even further. But five days before the platform committee was to meet, he made it clear that wouldn't happen. "No matter the political price—and they tell me in this year that it's enormous—I am going to do what I think is right,'' he said. "I will stand on my conscience and let my conscience be my guide when it comes to matters of life.''

The politics of the abortion issue were not as clear as Bush suggested. Opinion polls found few voters who would claim they planned to base their vote primarily on the abortion issue, and they were divided about evenly in most surveys. But Supreme Court decisions permitting states to impose restrictions on the right to an abortion had energized the pro-choice groups and given the issue new pertinence with voters not preoccupied with other questions. Studies of some election returns had found that a small percentage of Republican women, most often in the suburbs, would cross party lines to vote Democratic on the choice issue if the differences between the candidates were clear. The one thing all the political experience had shown, as Bush well knew, was that the politician who tried to straddle the issue got the worst of both worlds.

As the platform committee assembled in Houston, it was obvious that there would be no significant change in the abortion language, although there might also be included some other wording, perhaps in a preamble, that would recognize that other views could be acceptable within the party. This was the so-called big-tent approach advocated by the late Lee Atwater when he was the party's national chairman. Charles Black, the campaign adviser assigned to oversee the platform deliberations, said, "We won't change the substantive language" of previous planks, but added, "there might be some additional recognition of diversity."

But as far back as the May hearing in Salt Lake City, Schlafly had made it plain she would consider any softening language "a cave-in" on the part of George Bush, and it was soon apparent the religious right committee members were equally unyielding.

Nor were there any formidable voices urging change. One group, Republicans for Choice, was led by Ann Stone, a political consultant in Washington, and another, the National Republican Coalition for Choice, by Mary Dent Crisp, a moderate who had once been vice chairman of the party. But neither was made up of Republican heavyweights with any influence. The only other dissenters from the hard line were some office-holders facing campaigns for reelection, including then Senator John Seymour of California and Senator Arlen Specter of Pennsylvania, who were arguing for leaving the abortion issue out of the platform entirely.

There were also some Republican governors from states with heavy concentrations of Republican moderates who were pro-choice, including Pete Wilson of California, William Weld of Massachusetts and John McKernan of Maine. But whether they would be willing to challenge the president on the issue at the convention was unclear. Wilson, the most potentially influential, was heading the Bush campaign in his state and not inclined to defy his candidate in Houston.

The subcommittee voted seventeen to three to retain the language of previous platforms after a parliamentary ploy was used to prevent any substitute being brought directly to a vote. The debate was emotional and sometimes bizarre. One committee member, Virginia Phillips of Alaska, described how she had been obliged by a medical condition to have an abortion as a young woman. She reported that "it wasn't a Sunday afternoon stroll" but instead a traumatic experience. The subcommittee chairman, a lawyer from North Carolina named Mary Potter Summa, confided that she was four and a half months pregnant and very aware of "what is in me. It's not a rock. It's not a Coke bottle. It's a human life"—and, she added, one that was kicking her and pressing on her bladder at that very moment.

The following day the full committee ratified the subcommittee action, rejecting by eighty-four to sixteen an attempt to remove the plank entirely and shouting down by voice votes other attempts to amend it or add some softening language to the platform. The pro-choice Republicans never came close to enlisting the twenty-seven votes they needed on the 107-member committee to bring a minority report to the convention floor, or the majority of six state delegations that also would have allowed that procedure.

The issue would have been effectively throttled if, on the same day the platform committee voted, Bush himself had not taken what was essentially a pro-choice position in an interview on NBC. Asked what he would do if one of his granddaughters wanted to have an abortion, he replied, "Would I support my child? I'd put my arm around her and say, if she were trying to make that decision, encourage her not to do that. But of course I'd stand by my child, I'd love her and help her, lift her up, wipe the tears away and we'd get back in the game."

"So in the end the decision would be hers?" the interviewer asked.

"Well," Bush replied, "who else's could it be?"

That, of course, was precisely the point of the pro-choice movement—that the decision should rest with the woman involved—"who else?" But neither Bush nor Dan Quayle, who had given a similar answer to a similar question about his daughter a couple of days earlier, seemed to see any conflict between their private feelings of protectiveness toward their own families and their extreme positions on abortion as a public policy question.

The platform plank, like those in 1984 and 1988, finally read: "We believe the unborn child has a fundamental individual right to life which cannot be infringed. We therefore reaffirm our support for a human life amendment to the Constitution, and we endorse legislation to make clear that the Fourteenth Amendment's protections apply to unborn children. We oppose using public revenues for abortion and will not fund organizations which advocate abortion. We commend those who provide alternatives to abortions by meeting the needs of mothers and offering adoption services. We reaffirm our support for appointment of judges who respect traditional family values and the sanctity of innocent human life."

The abortion plank was not the only one on which the religious right showed its political muscle in the preliminaries to the Republican convention. The platform also specifically opposed "any legislation or law that recognizes same-sex marriages," supported "home-based schools," celebrated "our country's Judeo-Christian heritage and rich religious pluralism" and said "elements within the media, the entertainment industry, academics and the Democratic Party are waging a guerrilla war against American values."

The attention given to these questions was striking in the face of the whole year's experience with the electorate's concentrated focus on quite a different question—the condition of the economy. But here, too, there was a development that Bush didn't need. At the subcommittee level, a group of supply-side Republicans led by then Representative Vin Weber of Minnesota managed to insert language calling the 1990 tax increase Bush had approved "a mistake." Bush himself had used the term, but it was still jarring enough in the party's official platform that the White House ordered the word "recessionary" substituted in the final version.

The harsh and defiant Republican tone also was evident in a bitter attack by the party's national chairman, Rich Bond, on Hillary Clinton. In a speech to the Republican National Committee, he drew a picture of Clinton as president being advised by "that champion of the family, Hillary Clinton, who believes kids should be able to sue their parents rather than helping with the chores as they are asked to do. She has likened marriage and the family to slavery." The description was an outlandish interpretation of an essay Hillary Clinton had written for the *Harvard Education Review* in 1974 entitled "Children Under the Law."

The Bond attack was an indication that Republican strategists were now convinced—mistakenly, polls soon showed—that Hillary Clinton was so unpopular with the voting public that she was vulnerable to direct attack. It was a strategy no one could recall being employed against a candidate's wife so directly even in the days when Eleanor Roosevelt was a controversial figure. Clinton clearly didn't share that assessment. "That's pitiful, they're getting pitiful," he told reporters traveling with him in Pittsburgh. "This comment by Bond is pathetic. . . . It's going to be very difficult for the American people to take them seriously if they can't do any better than that."

Bond also joined with Dan Quayle in an attack on the news media that was fuel for the same social conservatives most caught up in the abortion question. Bond's complaints were the predictable ones about the press favoring Clinton over Bush. But they conveniently ignored the press coverage of the Gennifer Flowers episode and Clinton's draft history, which had made the Democratic nominee, at least in Republican eyes at that moment, most vulnerable.

But Quayle had a better ground for his charge of "sleaze" in the news media. *The New York Post* had just front-paged a story about a book that quoted a deceased ambassador as having said he had arranged a place for an assignation between then Vice President Bush and his longtime assistant, Jennifer Fitzgerald, in Switzerland in 1984. The gossip about Bush and Fitzgerald had been making the rounds in Washington for years and had been investigated thoroughly by several news organizations without a shred of evidence uncovered to support it. The result was that most newspapers ignored the "story" until the New York tabloid put it into the public arena—and gave Quayle a legitimate beef.

The Bush campaign, however, had a bigger problem even before the convention formally opened. The political dialogue was depicting a party that was angry, defensive and—most important politically—preoccupied with issues such as abortion and homosexual rights that were not the ones of prime concern to the voters. Many of the mainstream Republicans and longtime Bush supporters already assembled in Houston were clearly upset about how the abortion issue and harsh rhetoric would play with like-minded Republicans and independents back home.

After listening to Bond, for example, Elsie Hillman, a national committee member from Pennsylvania and chairman of the Bush campaign there, told one of us: "Not all of us agree with all of that, you know." She added that it was necessary for the president to provide some positive reinforcement for regular Republicans with positions on issues important to them. "He's not there yet," she said. "He has to give them a reason, just a glimmer of a reason."

Instead, coming into the convention, the Republicans and their president continued to send conflicting signals about what their message would be. In interviews over the weekend before he was to go to Houston, Bush said he would be making some new proposals on the economy. He thus invited speculation that his acceptance speech would be still another attempt to seize control of that issue before it was too late—and none too soon, as polls showed the "wrong track" number approaching 75 percent.

In another interview over PBS after the convention opened, Bush inadvertently fanned that speculation by saying in response to a question about his second term that "you'll see plenty of new faces, plenty of changes.'' With demands from the party's right wing that Secretary of Treasury Nicholas Brady and budget director Richard Darman be dumped right then to demonstrate basic economic change, CNN took Bush's remark and ran with it. CNN reporters on the convention floor and elsewhere were assigned to seek out cabinet members and ask them whether they expected their heads to roll. Soon the convention was awash with rumor as one after the other the cabinet heads ducked and weaved—but none fell.

The rhetoric in Houston, however, was centered far more on ''family values'' and on the characters of Bill and Hillary Clinton than on cabinet changes, or on how to produce more jobs for the nine million Americans who were unemployed. And no speech was more stunning than the one Pat Buchanan, Bush's onetime rival for the nomination, delivered on the convention's opening night:

''The agenda Clinton and Clinton would impose on America—abortion on demand, a litmus test for the Supreme Court, homosexual rights, discrimination against religious schools, women in combat units—that's change, all right. That's not the kind of change America needs, it's not the kind of change America wants, and it is not the kind of change we can abide in a nation that we still call God's country.''

Buchanan contrasted Bush as a young fighter pilot with Clinton: ''I'll tell you where he was. When Bill Clinton's time came in Vietnam, he sat up in a dormitory in Oxford, England, and figured out how to dodge the draft. Let me ask the question of this convention: Which of these two men has won the moral authority to send young Americans into battle?''

But of all the passages in Buchanan's take-no-prisoners assault, none hit with as much force as this one: ''My friends, this election is about more than who gets what. It is about who we are. It is about what we believe and what we stand for as Americans. There is a religious war going on in this country for the soul of America. It is a cultural war as critical to the kind of nation we shall be as the Cold War itself. And in that struggle for the soul of America, Clinton and Clinton are on the other side and George Bush is on our side.''

Buchanan's prime-time appearance had been the product of extensive negotiations with the conservative commentator who had made such a harsh case against Bush during the early primaries. Bob Teeter originally believed there was too great a risk involved in letting Buchanan speak in prime time. He feared that Buchanan might use the occasion to endorse Bush with such faint praise that his tepid support would set off a new round of damaging stories about the president's problems with conservatives.

But the Bush campaign's polling numbers were telling them there was still work to be done to solidify the conservative base. So Jim Lake was dispatched to New York during the Democratic convention in July to negotiate with Bay Buchanan, Pat Buchanan's sister and campaign manager. At a meeting at the Star Delicatessen, Lake told her that Pat would have to agree to endorse Bush. She replied that he fully intended to do so. The key questions were when—Buchanan insisted on a prime-time appearance because "we had three million votes" in the primaries—and whether Buchanan would make the endorsement in the speech or beforehand.

In subsequent negotiations over the next three weeks, it became clear that Buchanan wanted to do it during the speech itself. He had consulted Richard Nixon, his old boss, who advised him that was the right time to get the maximum effect. But Teeter continued to be suspicious, fearing that the campaign was being set up for a damaging embarrassment. He agreed to go ahead only after Lake reported that Buchanan would show the speech to the Bush campaign managers forty-eight hours before it was to be delivered. Lake told Teeter he was confident the endorsement would be unstinting. "I trusted them [the Buchanans] to do what they promised. . . . [I told them], 'If you screw me, I'll be dead forever.' "

The result was a meeting in convention director Craig Fuller's trailer at the Astrodome on the Saturday night before the convention's opening on Monday, when Buchanan would speak. Bay Buchanan brought the text and while Fuller read it, Lake faxed a copy to Teeter, who was at the White House talking to Bush about Buchanan's convention appearance. The language was sufficiently enthusiastic for Teeter to reassure his candidate. None of the Bush insiders, however, saw the pitfalls in the harsh language Buchanan was planning to use to attack Bill and Hillary Clinton and make his case that a religious war was under way.

"I read the speech and it had a great endorsement," Lake recalled later. "I really paid no attention to anything else. I was totally concerned with, Is this going to be a strong endorsement of George Bush? Is it going to make our conservative base happy?"

Thus, the eventual backlash came as a surprise to the Bush strategists.

"Even that night at the convention," Lake said, "I didn't sense any of that . . . the offending stuff didn't really become an issue for forty-eight hours."

Buchanan himself insisted that he delivered the three things that the Bush campaign asked him to do in the speech: praise Reagan, who would follow him on the platform, endorse Bush and "take apart" Clinton. "I came home and wrote the speech in that order, to those specifications," he said later. And he insisted that his speech did no harm to Bush's chances. As he was delivering it, he said, "the Bush people were cheering their heads off." It was the "subsequent demonizing and trashing of the speech" by the news media that did the damage, he said.

Buchanan's speech was the distillation of the case the delegates of the religious right felt driven to make at Houston—that there was a moral high ground they occupied. Their political adversaries were not just wrong on the substance, they were morally wrong. As Pat Robertson put it to the cheering delegates, "When Bill and Hillary Clinton talk about family values, they are not talking about either families or values. They are talking about a radical plan to destroy the traditional family and transfer its functions to the federal government."

On the convention floor, the mood of the religious right delegates was heady at their influence—and hostile to those they saw as their enemies. A middle-aged man brimming with barely suppressed rage accosted one of us on the convention floor and said: "I watch you on television all the time and I hate everything you say." When it was suggested that was why television sets have off buttons, he was not mollified. He insisted he had "one thing I'm going to say to you whether you like it or not." The one thing: "You can't be a Christian and be a Democrat."

This moral element was something new at this level of American politics. In the past, extremists on both ends of the ideological spectrum had demonstrated hard edges of hostility and anger; no one who was there could forget the Barry Goldwater delegates shouting their rage at the press at the 1964 Republican convention in San Francisco. But the argument had always centered on who was "right" and "wrong" in their approach to government. It had usually been possible for conservatives and liberals to behave with civility and even good humor toward those with whom they totally disagreed; indeed that was still the case where they came together regularly—in Congress, for example. But the delegates of the religious right were a different breed of activists who believed those who disagreed with them were not just wrong, but evil.

The Bush campaign strategists later tried to dismiss the reaction to the tone of the convention as little or no factor in the general election campaign. "We went in at thirty percent and we had a hell of a base problem," Teeter said, "and we came out with about forty percent and we did get a lot of that base back." The argument that the images of the convention had cost Bush "a big chunk of votes," Teeter said, was never supported in the campaign's polling figures.

Teeter said Buchanan's speech was "not helpful" and conceded there were things the campaign might have done differently at Houston, that "in those famous words, mistakes were made. . . . But it was not as big a thing at the time and it was not a giant negative."

Charlie Black contended that "the convention itself wasn't bad" but that the campaign had not been effective in managing how it was interpreted. "The mistake we made in the convention, in my opinion, is we lost control of the spin," he said, particularly in the first few days. The imperative, he said, was always to get the conservative base energized, and the Houston meeting accomplished that.

Lake also was puzzled by the criticism the convention's tone evoked. "I had no idea it would cause as much backlash as it did," he said. "We still felt we had to, we still did have to, tie down the base. We hadn't done that yet and that was why we wanted Buchanan there."

But reporters at the convention were finding many mainstream conservatives alarmed and dismayed by the tone and religious content of the rhetoric, the pictures of Pat Robertson and Jerry Falwell perched in the VIP section of the Astrodome, the repeated attacks on abortion rights and homosexuals.

The morning after Buchanan's speech, one longtime Bush supporter from the Farm Belt, a middle-aged woman who worked as a vice president of a major corporation, telephoned one of us to talk about it. "It wasn't just the speech," she said, "it was the people all around me cheering while Buchanan was saying those things. What's happened to my party?" Then she burst into tears, sobbing and saying over and over, "I can't believe what's happening here."

But George Bush himself had given his supporters license by his own predilection for casting politics in moral terms. Speaking to the Knights of Columbus a few days before the convention, Bush said: "I stake my claim to a simple belief: the president should try to set a moral tone for this nation. I believe that a central issue of this election year should be: who do you trust to renew America's moral purpose, who do you trust to fight for the ideas that will help rebuild our families and restore our fundamental values?"

In one sense, that approach might have been chalked off to Bush recognizing that Clinton might be vulnerable on the trust question because of Gennifer Flowers and his waffling on the draft. But Bush had employed a very similar approach in 1988 when he used the controversy over the pledge of allegiance to the flag to suggest that Michael Dukakis might be less patriotic than a president should be. The fact was that Bush would do whatever it took, and if that involved firing up the religious right's sense of moral outrage, so be it.

The offensive on family values continued to dominate the convention through its third night and the official nomination of the president for another term. Bush himself appeared on the podium with his wife, Barbara, five children and twelve grandchildren to produce what were designed to be the ultimate family pictures for the television cameras. But the rhetoric that night was not equally benign. Marilyn Quayle, wife of the vice president, presented herself as a member of the baby boom generation quite different from Bill Clinton.

"We are all shaped by the times in which we live," she said. "I came of age in a time of turbulent social change. Some of it was good, such as civil rights. Much of it was questionable. But, remember, not everyone demonstrated, dropped out, took drugs, joined in the sexual revolution or dodged the draft," she said to wild cheers from fellow moralists in the hall. "Not everyone believed that the family was so oppressive that women could only thrive apart from it."

In his acceptance speech, Dan Quayle sounded the themes that were the message of the whole convention. "Like so many Americans, for me, family comes first," he said. "When family values are undermined, our country suffers. All too often, parents struggle to instill character in their sons and daughters only to see their values belittled and their beliefs mocked by those who look down on America. Americans try to raise their children to understand right and wrong, only to be told that every so-called lifestyle alternative is morally equivalent. That is wrong.

"The gap between us and our opponents is a cultural divide. It is not just a difference between conservative and liberal. It is a difference between fighting for what is right and refusing to see what is wrong."

Not all of the Houston rhetoric was red-hot. Ronald Reagan delivered what may have been the best speech of the convention using his usual mix of the partisan and the inspirational. Barbara Bush's speech following Marilyn Quayle's was a conspicuously low-key encomium to her husband. And, in the face of the convention's drumfire of criticism of homosexuals and homosexual rights, there was a striking emotional reaction to the speech of a forty-four-year-old woman who was HIV-positive, Mary Fisher, daughter of industrialist and Republican fund-raiser Max Fisher.

By the time Bush arrived to deliver his acceptance speech, expectations for the occasion had reached towering proportions. The conventional wisdom among politicians and press was that this was his single last best opportunity to regain control of the campaign agenda and present himself as a convincing voice on the economy. But the speech fell far short. Bush did advance some obvious attention-getting proposals—for an across-the-board tax cut, increases in the personal tax exemption, reductions in capital gains tax rates. But there were no specifics about how much and just when.

The one new proposal on the fiscal situation was a plan to allow taxpayers to specify that 10 percent of their taxes would have to be used for deficit reduction—an idea his own administration had pooh-poohed as unworkable in congressional testimony earlier. Indeed, the hollowness of the Bush economic program was clear the following morning when campaign chairman Teeter announced that the plan would be sent to Congress after the November election. The implication was that the voters would have to take it on trust—from a candidate whose lack of credibility on economic issues had put him on the defensive for the entire campaign.

Carville, the Clinton strategist, said later that Bush's failure to make himself credible on the economy was the real convention failure, not the extremist excesses. "I thought they were hurt more by what they didn't say than what they said," he observed. "They had a chance to draw some economic distinctions and talk about some things that were just left out on the table. If you use your convention to get your base back, that's not a very good way to use a convention. You've just got to take your base for granted.

"They just couldn't show enough, as far as I was concerned, of Falwell and Pat Robertson, who are much more visible to people than Buchanan is, or Marilyn Quayle. . . . People out there know who Falwell and Pat Robertson are. That hurt more. They could have been out there talking about the football scores. It isn't so much what you say but what you don't say. . . . The idea that some Republican strategists were saying they couldn't win by talking about the economy [was ridiculous]. They couldn't win without talking about it. Or health care, or something. Most people don't wake up in the morning thinking they're in a religious war. Most people don't wake up in the morning worrying about gays."

The week in the Astrodome nevertheless had given Bush a bounce in the numbers. *The Washington Post*/ABC News survey immediately after the convention showed Clinton leading, 49 percent to 40, compared to 60 percent to 34 before the convention. Other surveys found similar figures—leads for Clinton ranging up to 14 percent where they had been running consistently above 20 percent before Houston.

But the convention also had exposed significant fault lines in the Republican Party. There were clear gulfs between the Christian Coalition social conservatives, who made up perhaps one third to one fourth of the delegates, and the mainstream Republicans who had been the heart of George Bush's original base. But even if Bush suffered no serious defections from either group against Bill Clinton in November, they would not be enough together to elect him.

And the convention had offered essentially nothing to the independents and Reagan Democrats the Republican president needed to win a second term, or to those who had supported Ross Perot earlier in the year. The central issue was the economy and the central question whether George Bush could offer a coherent program to come to grips with that problem. But the answer from Houston had been that "family values" were the issue and "Can you trust Clinton?" was the question.

The stage was now set for the general election campaign, and the Republican Party still didn't have a handle on how to salvage the presidency of an incumbent who had yet to make an effective case for a second term. So, as in 1988, some other way would have to do.

GHOST OF
WILLIE HORTON

Well before the bashing of Bill Clinton at the Republican convention, the Bush campaign—which its candidate had vowed would leave the negative tactics of 1988 behind and take the high road in 1992—had been back on the attack again. The prime target had been Ross Perot until his withdrawal in mid-July, but once he seemed safely out of the way, the Bush strategy turned to the task of cutting Clinton down.

Four years earlier, the situation for Bush had been markedly the same. Then as now, he was running as much as seventeen percentage points behind the Democratic presidential nominee after the rival party's convention. And then as now, with his own support stagnant, his strategists decided that the route to victory would be not to make voters feel better about him, but worse about his opponent.

In 1988, the vehicles had been the Willie Horton prison furlough story, Dukakis's veto of a state bill mandating recital of the pledge of allegiance in Massachusetts schools, his membership in the American Civil Liberties Union, pollution in the Boston Harbor and other issues equally critical to the state of the nation. Their use had been widely credited with Dukakis's fall and defeat—and widely criticized as demeaning to the political process. Bush had vowed this time around that he would not tolerate such doings, but as with other categorical pledges, he didn't keep this one either when political necessity seemed to dictate the imperative of "going negative" against Clinton.

Just as in 1988, when focus groups by the Bush campaign had identified the Willie Horton and other stories as exploitable vulnerabilities of Dukakis, similar sessions, as already noted, found the soft spots in public attitudes about Perot that were then put to practical use. They also found that Clinton, in spite of his string of primary victories, remained the subject of considerable public doubt and mistrust. Other focus groups by the Clinton camp itself uncovered the same doubts, and the campaign labored diligently in the later primaries and thereafter to dispel them, by giving voters more information about Clinton's humble beginnings, storybook struggle and climb to political prominence.

The focus groups run by Stan Greenberg and associates found that while such matters as the allegations of womanizing and draft-dodging against Clinton remained in voters' minds, he was able to overcome them by focusing the campaign on the voters' economic worries and offering a plan to deal with them—while Bush spent his time taking shots at Perot. By the time the fall campaign came around, Grunwald said, "people had already factored in" the personal issues in making their judgments about Clinton.

But the Bush campaign continued to believe, on the basis of their own focus-group findings in April and June, that Clinton could be damaged with voters by raising such issues of "character and trust." Once Perot had stepped aside, pummeled by negative stories about him that the Perot campaign was convinced came directly from the Bush operatives, they were free to turn their fire on Clinton.

Only two days after Perot's pullout, during a Bush visit to Utah, Senator Garn reopened the issue of Clinton's draft record. Noting that Clinton had written that he chose not to go to Canada to avoid the draft because "at twenty-three he was thinking of his future political career," Garn told 15,000 listeners at Brigham Young University: "We don't need those kinds of politicians in either party, so let's vote for those candidates who have the courage of their convictions."

Two days after that, Quayle joined in, suggesting during a television satellite hookup to Ohio stations that Gore "was probably put on that [ticket] because he went to Vietnam. I am sure Bill Clinton does not want to talk about character and some of the other things, so I think Al Gore was put on the ticket to shore up Bill Clinton's inadequacies."

At the same time Bush, while claiming to be staying out of "the campaign mode" until the Republican convention, began criticizing Clinton's revamped economic plan, trotting out the standard Republican tax-and-spend indictment against Democratic liberals and charging that Clinton could not be trusted to guard the nation's security. Bush told some defense workers that the military budget, which Clinton was targeting for cuts modestly below Bush's own, was "more than a piggy bank for folks who want to get busy beating swords into pork barrels." These were, however, criticisms on policy positions and as such perfectly legitimate, if exaggerated.

Meanwhile, though, Bush's agents were at work, with a vengeance. Among the president's most loyal—and outspoken—defenders was the Bush-Quayle deputy campaign manager and political director, Mary Matalin, a savvy and saucy tough-talking operative with blue-collar, suburban Chicago roots. A veteran foot soldier in the Bush political ranks who was instrumental in his survival against Bob Dole and Pat Robertson in a drawn-out fight for delegates in Michigan in 1988, Matalin had carried much of the load as political director at the Republican National Committee during the illness of her close friend Lee Atwater. Having moved over to the reelection committee, she had spent much of the summer seething over the indecision and chaos between a politically rudderless White House and the campaign, and yearned for Bush to get into the fray with both feet.

Beyond all that, Matalin was particularly frustrated at what she saw as a pattern of distortion on issues by Clinton, and the failure of the news media to call him on it. In a speech in Houston, Clinton had charged that Bush if reelected was going to cut funds for local law enforcement, which, she said, "was a total lie." The campaign's opposition researcher, David Tell, by this time had compiled a substantial file of what Matalin called Clinton's "evasions and slickness," and it was decided to put out a "lie of the day" press release, subsequently toned down to "distortion of the day."

Up to this time, the communications division of the campaign was putting out erudite daily "talking points" in newsletter form for the campaign field offices and the press. But, Matalin recalled, "they were so boring we stopped reading them ourselves. I said we've got to do something different." The result, she confessed later, "was high wisenheimer." In the most slashing, bitter—and often sophomoric—language, Matalin, press aide Torie Clarke and the White House political operative Dave Carney began collaborating on a new, livelier version designed to grab attention. They succeeded, beyond their expectations and, eventually, their desires.

The press releases started going out in late July and caused no ripples at first. Matalin, however, in defending the offensive against Clinton, denied to a *New York Times* reporter that the campaign was repeating personal charges against him. "The larger issue is that he's evasive and slick," she said. "We've never said to the press that he's a philandering, pot-smoking draft dodger."

"The way you just did?" the reporter asked.

"The way I just did," Matalin replied. "But that's the first time I've done that. There is nothing nefarious or subliminal going on."

Putting negative remarks in circulation by denying having said them was an old Dick Nixon trick. Ron Brown immediately jumped on the exchange, and using another old political trick, "absolved" the perpetrator and blamed a higher-up. "Anyone who knows Mary Matalin," he said, "knows she is a true political professional. She would never have used such a vicious smear unless she was instructed to do so." He noted a news conference back in April at which Bush said he had "made specific instructions in writing to our people to stay out of the sleaze business." Brown asked: "Is this insubordination or obedience? Is his political director getting a public reprimand and a private pat on the back?"

That was just the start of it. On Sunday, August 3, Matalin issued the fourth of her "distortion of the day" press releases headlined: "Sniveling Hypocritical Democrats: Stand Up and Be Counted—On Second Thought, Shut Up and Sit Down!" Some twenty statements by or about Clinton were printed, together with sources, usually newspaper articles. One of them quoted Clinton aide Betsey Wright as saying she was in charge of dealing with "bimbo eruptions," an accurate quote and description of what Wright was doing in Little Rock—coping with new allegations or reported allegations of other womanizing episodes by Clinton floating around or being investigated by various news organizations.

The Clinton campaign immediately demanded that Matalin be fired for violating Bush's no-sleaze policy. It was an uneasy moment for James Carville, who was romantically involved with Matalin but still politically at war with her. He empathized with her, while recognizing that she had blundered, to the benefit of his own candidate. Clarke, traveling with the president, defended the press release, but shortly afterward White House deputy press secretary Judy Smith released a statement on Air Force One saying "the president is determined to keep this campaign out of the sleaze business."

White House chief of staff Skinner phoned Matalin and told her the president wanted her to apologize. Matalin, ever the political animal, thought that was a bad mistake. Her immediate attitude, she said, was " 'Do you really want me to apologize?' I thought that was a bad political thing. 'Fire me, don't make me apologize.' The pure, dispassionate political analysis was, 'Fire me or defend me,' but don't do like, 'She's sorry.' I knew we'd get crucified if we tried to have it both ways." Skinner backed off and Matalin put out a statement that only by a stretch of the imagination could be called an apology.

"With respect to our project to expose daily the negative campaign against the president and the hypocrisy of our opponents," she wrote, "it would appear to some that I might have violated, at least in spirit, the president's dictate to the campaign that we avoid references to Governor Clinton's personal life. I regret if the tone of my statement left the wrong impression in that regard." Then she added: "I stand by my criticism of the Clinton campaign and the Democratic Party for their unprecedented hypocrisy and for daily disparaging, in the most egregious and personal terms, the President of the United States."

Matalin said later her chief concern was that the incident had "stepped on the story" of a good campaign day for her boss. When he finally called her from the plane, she said, "I started crying. 'I'm sorry, I've ruined your day.' " Bush told her, she said, not to worry about it, that it was about time somebody hit back at all the attacks against him. "He understood the overarching objective of that memo," she said, and told her to keep it up, but not get carried away. And because it was a time when everybody else was standing back and letting the Clinton campaign hit at him, she said, he appeared to appreciate what she had tried to do.

In an interview in *The Washington Times* about a week later, Bush said of the incident that he "got cross-threaded with Mary Matalin, who I support strongly in her taking the attack to the enemy, but only because one characterization out of twenty [the "bimbo eruptions" reference] seemed to me to be doing that which I said I wouldn't do."

Matalin insisted later "it was never the campaign's strategy to personally attack Clinton. Even the woman's stuff. As the resident woman," she said, "I was the sounding board for this stuff. And I knew from the Sperling breakfast [the Washington reporters' group at which the Clintons had openly discussed their marital situation] that that was off the table, not because he was so good [in defending his marriage], which he was, but because she [Hillary Clinton] was so good. I remain convinced that one of the things that sealed Gary Hart's fate was the pitiful, painful pictures of Lee Hart standing behind him, looking like just what she was—the cheated-on wife. And I thought that the voter reaction was going to be, 'If Hillary can take it, we can take it, and it's nobody's business.'

"So that part of the character issue was never on the table," she said. "What was on the table and became perceived as a negative attack against him [Clinton] was the nature of his character . . . that you really gotta think about—do you want this man in the White House? This is what I was trying to tell that *New York Times* reporter. . . . You've got to know who your president is, somewhere and sometime. You've got to have some sense of who this guy is, and if he won't tell you the truth about his past, why should you believe what he's saying about your future?"

Beyond the personal reference to Clinton's earlier womanizing troubles, the Matalin press releases, which she continued daily after her "apology" but without a focus on his past personal problems, were embarrassingly amateurish in their wild swings at him. She took to referring to him as "Boy Clinton" and to his campaign bus as "the pandermobile," peppering her comments with pathetic efforts to be cutting and cute at the same time. She wrote, for example, that Clinton's bus had just "brie-zed through Wisconsin's Dairyland yesterday, trying to peddle a tax policy with more holes in it than a pound of Swiss cheese.'' Or this one: ''Slick Willie's tax-and-spend chickens come home to roost—with a few surprises still hiding in the henhouse.''

Matalin said afterward that for all the handouts' shortcomings, they were a tonic to Bush field workers as frustrated as she was at their candidate's and campaign's lack of sharp counterpunching. ''For as sophomoric as you all thought it was,'' she said, ''it was the first positive reaction [the campaign headquarters] got from the field. My two biggest phone days [with approving calls from the field] were Murphy Brown and 'bimbo eruptions.' . . . The field force—the county chairmen, the thousands of little workers, they loved them. They went crazy. They thought they were funny, they remembered the points because they were couched in these metaphors. . . . We had to give them something, so I gave them something. They loved it. It inspired them to fight.'' And in the process, she insisted, a lot of information on Clinton damaging to him got out to the public.

The trouble, though, was that also in the process, the whole exercise, which came off as exceedingly mean-spirited to those not among the Bush faithful, played directly into the hands of a prime Clinton strategy—to paint the 1992 Bush campaign as a carbon copy of 1988, as Son of Willie Horton. In the environment of an electorate up in arms against politics as usual, fanned by the complaints of Ross Perot, this strategy proved to be a critical ingredient in the election's outcome.

From the very start of the campaign, the Clinton strategists had made a point of reminding voters of the Willie Horton and other 1988 negative attacks on Dukakis. Every time Bush or a Bush surrogate said the slightest thing that could be taken as a disparaging word about Clinton, his operatives would immediately cry their version of the old Ronald Reagan line against Jimmy Carter in 1980: ''There he goes again.''

The fact was that there was very little in the 1992 Bush attacks on Clinton that came close to the 1988 allegation that Dukakis's irresponsibility had turned loose a convicted murderer who was black who then went out and raped a white woman. That blatant appeal to racial prejudice, wrapped up in the charge that Dukakis was soft on crime, hit a low in negative campaigning that even the 1992 Bush operatives—while publicly defending it as factual—recognized had to be avoided this time around.

Well before her ''distortions of the day'' backfired, Matalin noted, "they had been bashing us all year and calling us negative campaigners. That was irritating the president and was a very frustrating environment." Ron Brown as Democratic party chairman in fact had been calling Bush a dirty campaigner ever since 1988, "and had largely sucked you guys [the press] in," she said, and it was then conveyed to the public, conditioning voters to believe it. "But that notion that we were negative campaigners," she acknowledged, "did back us off of doing negative ads. Many discussions about advertising of the negative variety included how hard you guys were going to come down on us."

(In the October 1992 issue of *Harper's* magazine, *Harper's Index* reported that the name Willie Horton was mentioned sixty-nine times in *New York Times* articles from January through August of 1992, compared to only thirty-three times during the 1988 presidential campaign in which Horton was made a live issue by the Bush campaign.)

Matalin recalled that she and Teeter wanted to consider doing ads on Clinton's Arkansas record between the two conventions but "were dissuaded because of how you all would respond." There was, notably, nothing wrong with pointing up an opponent's record in office, provided it was not distorted. But so spooked had the Bush campaign become by the ghost of the Willie Horton that its 1988 predecessor had unleashed on the voting public that it pulled its punches—and still got hammered for "going negative."

The Bush strategists, Matalin said, thought if the voters didn't have a memory of Willie Horton, the press would remind them. "If it was branded negative campaigning, whether or not it was," she said, "people had this knee-jerk reaction to it. We did not think we could withstand the press assault, given this sort of article of faith that we were negative campaigners."

Teeter said later he thought more significant than the Clinton camp intimidating the Bush strategists directly against going negative was how the press was already conditioned to expect negative campaigning from the Bush campaign. "There was a disproportionate interest [among the press] in what was a negative commercial and what was a negative speech and when we were going to do it and if we were going to do it," Teeter said. "I think that probably in the broader sense the conditioning of the press and to some degree the public from '88 limited how you could attack and what you would do negative. . . .

"I don't think anybody ever had any views that you weren't going to attack Clinton or run any negative commercials because they said, 'There they go again.' " At the same time, he said, "you almost went into the campaign knowing that your degrees of freedom on negative spots because of '88 were less than they were in '88." At the same time, the public mind-set on Bush as a negative campaigner gave Clinton a freer hand to hit at him. "There was nothing we could do to make people think we were more negative than Bush," Stephanopoulos said. "There was just no way."

Within those limitations, though, Bush and his campaign did their best to undercut Clinton in the voters' eyes. Addressing the annual convention of the Catholic lay organization the Knights of Columbus in New York, the president immodestly asked: "If you're looking to restore America's moral fiber, why buy a synthetic when you can get real cotton?" He reiterated his unflinching opposition to abortion—unflinching, that is, since joining the Reagan Revolution—and took some glancing shots at Clinton without mentioning his name.

"Some think it's okay to hand out condoms in schools," he said, "but oppose amending our Constitution to allow our kids to put their hands together in prayer." And later: "I believe that a central issue of this election year should be, 'Who do you trust to renew America's moral purpose? Who do you trust to fight for the ideas that will help rebuild our families and restore our moral values?' " The words "trust" and "family" and "values" were becoming staples in his speeches, all obviously for comparison purposes with the scandal-scarred Clinton.

Others, meanwhile, were being much more direct. After Bush had said in an interview in *Time* that he would fire anyone henceforth who dealt in private innuendo, including "the issue of marital infidelity," he remained silent when his campaign general chairman, Robert Mosbacher, told reporters marital fidelity "should be one of the yardsticks" for measuring the candidates. A CNN reporter at a Kennebunkport news conference had asked Bush directly about recurring reports of infidelity involving himself and he had angrily denied them and castigated the reporter for raising the issue on nationwide television. Mosbacher said those reports were "totally uncorroborated" whereas Clinton lacked credibility "based on what he has denied and what he hasn't denied."

Bush took no action when U.S. Treasurer Catalina V. Villalpando, before the New Jersey delegation at the Republican convention in Houston, offered a more direct slur against Clinton. She linked him to former San Antonio Mayor Henry Cisneros, a Clinton supporter who three years earlier had withdrawn from public office after acknowledging an extramarital affair, by asking: "Can you imagine two skirt-chasers campaigning together?" Bush's response was, "Nobody is going to be able to control everything that everybody says." And he didn't seem to try as other Republicans used the Houston convention to attack his Democratic opponent, directly or by inference, on everything from draft-dodging to womanizing and drug use.

Immediately after the convention, Bush took up the call. The election, he told a large crowd in Woodstock, Georgia, standing in a driving rain, "is a choice about the character of the man you want to lead this nation for another four years," and "about families and leaving the world a better and more prosperous place." And with his customary tough-guy words that belied his easygoing, preppy manner, he told the crowd: "So you tell Governor Clinton and that Congress, 'If you can't run with the big dogs, stay under the porch.' "

Bush spoke after one of the GOP's meanest pit bulls had warmed up the crowd with a stinging attack on Democratic "weird values," referring to the hot story of the hour, a nasty child custody fight between movie actors Woody Allen and his former lover, Mia Farrow, in which Allen had declared his love for one of her adopted daughters. "I call this the Woody Allen plank," Gingrich oozed. "It's a weird situation, and it fits the Democratic Party platform perfectly. If a Democrat used the word 'family' to raise children in Madison Square Garden, half their party would have rebelled and the other half would not vote. . . . Woody Allen had nonincest with his nondaughter because they were a nonfamily." A Bush spokesman afterward said only that "the president does not want to make Woody Allen an issue."

On other occasions in other places, Bush hewed to legitimate criticisms of Clinton on issues ranging from auto fuel efficiency, in Michigan, to free trade agreements with Mexico, in Missouri, but always with an emphasis on "trust." Compared to 1988, to Willie Horton and flag pledges and Boston Harbor, he was on the high road, but that didn't stop the Clinton campaign from saying "there he goes again," especially when surrogates did the mud-slinging for him and he remained mute.

Wilhelm said later that while the Clinton campaign "certainly reminded people" of the Bush record on negative campaigning, "the best teacher of that was 1988."

After Labor Day, when the president appeared in ultraconservative Orange County, California, with former President Reagan and another of his party's hand grenade specialists, Representative Robert Dornan, he held his tongue as Reagan needled Clinton as a draft evader and Dornan called him "Chicken Little of Little Rock." Clinton, Dornan said, spent his time during the Vietnam War "eating compulsively to the point of exhaustion . . . throwing darts [and] drinking ale" in an Oxford pub while other Americans his age fought and died. To that, a Bush spokeswoman said Dornan was "entitled to his opinion—free speech."

Bush himself was careful, with the ghost of Willie Horton always hovering, to leave the personal shots at Clinton to such surrogates. Aides continued to press him to make the case for himself, for what he would do in a second term to right the economy and address the other demanding problems on the domestic front. Finally, in a carefully constructed speech before the friendly Economic Club of Detroit, among the nation's most prestigious forums for discussing the state of the economy, Bush on September 10 laid out an "Agenda for American Renewal" that essentially was a repackaging of his old conservative remedies, with a few new concepts.

The first was a proposal to downsize, or as he put it to "right-size," the federal government. He said he would cut the White House operating budget by one third if Congress would do the same with its own. Another was a broad pledge to extend to European and Pacific Rim countries the free trade approach proposed for Mexico. The rest was a retread of such ideas as the line-item veto, congressional term limits, capital gains tax rate cuts, urban enterprise zones, tuition vouchers for school choice, voluntary earmarking of income taxes for deficit reduction, a cap on product liability damage suits and a ban on political action committee contributions.

Although the speech was largely a rehash of Bush proposals rejected or ignored by the Democratic Congress, it was at last a coherent recitation of what Bush intended to do in his second term. Insiders credited Jim Baker and his team for pulling it together and orchestrating its airing and distribution to the electorate—a cohesion and decisiveness sadly lacking all year, until Baker's move from the State Department to the White House.

Bush repeated the highlights that night in a five-minute paid television appearance and the campaign prepared a slick twenty-nine-page brochure of the plan. "We had satellite links to everyplace," Jim Lake recalled, "and we spent a lot of money sending out those 'Agenda for American Renewal' magazines with the plan in it—and it lasted one day. We should have carried on with that for two weeks, a long period of time, driving that home. But something came up that caused us to get off of that."

That weekend, Lake said, as the campaign's communications director he tried to get Baker or his chief lieutenant, Bob Zoellick, to go on the major network interview shows to tout the plan, "but Baker wouldn't do it. It was a way in my opinion to send a signal that this is important, this is real, and to send a signal to the press corps that Baker had really put his reputation on the line here; this must be something good. But we weren't able to get that done." The signal that many in the press corps expecting a strong follow-up got, instead, was that once again Jim Baker, who never wanted to be pulled back into the dirty business of politics in the first place, was keeping his distance.

One thing that "came up" at this time was the potential for reopening the whole draft issue against Clinton. Quayle was scheduled to address the annual convention of the National Guard Association in Salt Lake City in mid-September, and the campaign decided that Bush should replace him. Learning of the switch and anticipating a broadside attack, the Clinton campaign got its candidate invited to speak right after the president and prepared a strong rebuttal. Reporters from around the country rushed to the convention to witness the bloodletting firsthand. Surely Bush would seize the opportunity to raise the issue of Clinton's failure, under still suspicious circumstances involving a flirtation with the Arkansas ROTC program, to serve in the military during the Vietnam War. The fact that Bush had decided to take over from Quayle, and that Clinton had changed his own schedule to appear on the same day, added to the anticipation of fireworks.

Instead, the guardsmen, the news media and the national audience watching on television were treated to an episode that well illustrated the manner in which the Bush camp's concern about being painted once again as an agent of negativism in politics affected the 1992 campaign dialogue. Bush, leading off, took pains to discount what he said was "a great deal of speculation . . . that I was going to come out here and use this forum to attack Governor Clinton." He went on: "I want to tell you, I do feel very strongly about certain aspects of the controversy swirling around Governor Clinton. But I didn't come here to attack him."

Bush then launched into a defense of Quayle and his service in the Guard, an issue in the 1988 campaign, praising him for his "candor," lack of which Clinton had been accused regarding his own draft record. He worked his way around to raising the issue of "using influence to avoid the military," without pinning it explicitly to Clinton. And he argued that such questions "matter because, despite all our problems at home, we can never forget that we ask our presidents to lead the military, to bear the awful authority of deciding to send your sons and daughters in harm's way."

Bush, telling of a letter sent to him by the mother of a helicopter pilot who had died in the Gulf War, stammered as his voice choked, noting that this was a responsibility that faced all presidents. "And does that mean that if you've never seen the awful horror of battle that you can never be commander in chief?" asked this World War II combat pilot. "Of course not, not at all," he answered himself. "But it does mean that we must hold our presidents to the highest standard, because they might have to decide if our sons and daughters should knock early on death's door."

The softness of the president's allusions to Clinton surprised the governor and his entourage. A strong defense of his draft record had been prepared but was scrapped when Clinton learned on his way to the convention that Bush had not attacked him directly. The Democratic nominee then spoke without notes about his support for a better-equipped National Guard and a better-educated work force to restore economic well-being at home.

Afterward both sides declared "victory," the Bush camp for keeping the Clinton draft record in the news without attacking him on it, the Clinton side for what its strategists said showed the draft issue was behind them. More notable was the fact that Bush had the ideal forum for taking the gloves off against Clinton on what his strategists said they believed was still a killer issue against him, and he fired what essentially was a blank cartridge. Once again the concern about being painted as too negative had intruded.

With less than seven weeks to go to the election, Bush still trailed Clinton badly, by 15 percentage points in the latest *Washington Post*/ABC News poll. The time had come for Bush to stop playing Mr. Nice Guy. Six days after the gentle encounter in Salt Lake City, he finally went bareknuckles on the draft issue. In a radio interview with ultra-right-wing talk show host Rush Limbaugh in New York, he attacked what he called Clinton's "total failure to come clean with the American people" on the matter. His opponent's "fundamental difficulty," he said, "is that he has not told the full truth, the whole truth, nothing but the truth."

Bush told his host that he wasn't "trying to make it a big issue" but that "it's not going to go away." Inaccurately charging that Clinton in his famous letter to Colonel Holmes had called the military "immoral," Bush said: "I have a very different concept of military service. I'm sure I would never call the military immoral." Clinton had said in the letter he considered drafting Americans for the Vietnam War "illegitimate" and wrote of the dilemma for young men like himself who loved their country but "loathed the military." But Bush went on: "I believe that the commander in chief should not have a mind-set to say the military is immoral. Now, maybe he's changed his view on that. . . . Let's find out. Let's let him level with the American people."

Clinton was asked about Bush's remarks as he campaigned in Chicago with Admiral William C. Crowe, the former chairman of the Joint Chiefs of Staff under Bush and Reagan who had recently endorsed him. He pointed to Crowe and said he "has more credibility on truth-telling than George Bush" and wouldn't have endorsed him had he shared Bush's views on the subject.

The specter of Willie Horton continued to intrude. Floyd Brown, a filmmaker who in 1988 under "independent expenditure" provisions guiding the Federal Election Commission had on his own produced and aired a television ad showing Horton, was at it again. This time he prepared ads providing a telephone number viewers could call to hear what he said were the taped conversations between Clinton and Gennifer Flowers. Bush campaign lawyers complained to the FEC demanding that Brown be required to inform contributors that his Presidential Victory Committee had nothing to do with the Bush-Quayle campaign. At the same time, White House press secretary Fitzwater called Brown's activities "despicable" and said they "have no place in the American political system."

Four years earlier, Bush professed to be equally appalled at Brown's Willie Horton ad, while conveying basically the same message from the stump. This time, with good reason to believe that the womanizing issue against Clinton had long since flamed out, he told reporters "we will do everything we can within the law to see that this man does not use my name in raising funds for these nefarious purposes."

Late in September, the Bush strategists decided that their best shot at Clinton might, after all, be his Arkansas record, which could reasonably be attacked without unleashing a torrent of criticism about going personally negative. They sent the president and Air Force One on a dizzying 2,500-mile encirclement of Arkansas, putting down in all six states bordering Clinton's home base—from Missouri to Oklahoma, Texas, Louisiana, Mississippi and Tennessee—and hitting at his stewardship as a five-term governor. Up to this point, he said, "I have resisted the urge to focus on Governor Clinton's record. But I must tell you, I am very tired of the distortions, tired of the half truths. And the stakes are too high to let America be deceived by a negative campaign. So today I have chosen to lay it on the line, talk about my opponent's record . . . in Arkansas. . . . And that means explaining the Grand Canyon that separates his rhetoric from the reality of his record."

Bush said Clinton's environmental record was so bad and "the rivers are so polluted, the fish glow in the dark." On crime, he said, his opponent was a "Doberman pinscher" as a candidate but a "Chihuahua" as governor. And in an allusion to the old draft issue he offered an observation of which Tricky Dick Nixon himself would have been proud. Asked about it at a rally of supporters at the airport in Shreveport, Louisiana, Bush said: "No, I am not going to talk about the draft today. I'll let the American people make up their own minds about that. All I will say is that I am proud I put on the uniform of my country."

In the end, it always seemed to come back to the draft issue, and by implication the question not only of Clinton's honesty in dealing with it but also his patriotism—another throwback to the Bush campaign of 1988. Then it was Dukakis's veto of the state bill requiring school teachers to lead their students in recitation of the pledge of allegiance to the flag, recommended to him by his legal advisers on grounds the bill was an abridgment of the First Amendment.

Clinton learned of Bush's attacks on his Arkansas record on the same day the governor was campaigning at Michigan State University, site of what would have been the first of a series of presidential debates had Bush not balked at participating. He challenged the president to make his charges face-to-face, but Bush preferred long-range firing at this point.

The Clinton team in Little Rock was now cautiously confident, but driving hard. All hands took to heart the blunt reminder of the campaign's overriding focus that Carville after the Democratic convention had posted in the "war room," where daily strategy and "rapid response" to Bush's attacks and revealed vulnerabilities were determined:

> Change vs. more of the same.
> The economy, stupid.
> Don't forget health care.

Campaign manager Wilhelm remembered later that on the next night, September 24, Paul Tully, whose state-by-state targeting was now the heart of the campaign's strategy, said: "We still have work to do, but we're ninety percent of the way there." It was a goal toward which Tully had worked heroically despite many disappointments through all his adult years, and he was relishing the prospect. After another of the prodigious dinners of good food and good talk for which he was known, Tully retired for the night a happy man, and died in his sleep.

The loss hit the campaign hard, personally and politically. Clinton broke off campaigning and attended a memorial service at the Washington Cathedral at which he was only one of hundreds of Democrats, famous and unknown, who paid homage to a man who had brought zest and wisdom to the party's quests for the presidency over the years. Many young men and women who had learned campaign organizing—and the joy of playing hard, dedicated politics for causes beyond themselves—under Tully's guiding hand, came from around the country to say goodbye to him.

The campaign moved on, and in spite of the Bush campaign's awareness of the perils of being seen as more negative, Clinton's patriotism, like Dukakis's in 1988, was coming to the fore as a late-campaign issue. Congressman Dornan on the House floor began to raise questions about a trip Clinton had made to Moscow as a tourist while he was a student at Oxford in 1969, during a school break (one of as many as 60,000 Americans to visit the Soviet Union that year). Clinton had said he didn't remember much about it other than walking around looking at the sights, or who he may have seen there. He did remember, he had said, meeting a Georgetown professor and peace activist at a train station in Norway.

The question of Clinton's activities while he was a student abroad took on a sinister wrinkle when *Newsweek* reported that several pages appeared to be missing from the State Department's passport file on him. The discovery came, the newsmagazine said, as the department was attempting to respond to requests from several news organizations under the Freedom of Information Act investigating a rumor that Clinton had considered applying for foreign citizenship as a means of escaping the draft. But the FBI, which was ordered to investigate the allegation of the missing pages, reported a few days later that the file appeared to be intact. The very disclosure that the State Department had been searching through Clinton's passport files, however, triggered suspicions of Republican dirty tricks that soon would surface, and be exploited by the Clinton campaign.

Dornan kept pressing the case, even winning an audience with Bush and Jim Baker in the Oval Office to urge that the Moscow trip be made a major issue in the final, critical month of the campaign. The blatantly pro-Bush *Washington Times* ran a banner headline on the trip, but the story seemed to be going nowhere until Bush appeared on CNN's *Larry King Live* on the night of October 7, from San Antonio.

When King asked Bush about the Clinton trip, he replied: "I don't want to tell you what I really think because I don't have the facts. But to go to Moscow, one year after Russia crushed Czechoslovakia, not remember who you saw there. . . . You can remember who you saw in an airport in Oslo but you can't remember who you saw in Moscow?" He criticized Clinton's previously disclosed participation in demonstrations against the Vietnam War in England and demanded that Clinton tell the American people "how many demonstrations he led against his own country from a foreign soil. . . . I cannot for the life of me," he said, "understand mobilizing demonstrations and demonstrating against your own country, no matter how strongly you feel, when you're in a foreign land."

Once again, the Bush strategy was tied to events of the past, in a country and at a time voters were hurting economically and fed up with harping on personal questions about the candidates. Clinton's spokesman, George Stephanopoulos, called Bush's performance a "sad and pathetic ploy by a desperate politician. If he worried as much about what most Americans are going through in 1992 as he does about what Bill Clinton did in 1969," he said, "we'd all be in much better shape. He sees the handwriting on the wall."

Once more the Clinton operatives were saying "there he goes again" on negative personal attacks. Two days later, Bush appeared to be backing off, responding to a question about Clinton's trip on ABC News's *Good Morning America*. "Clearly, if he's told all there is to tell on Moscow, fine," he said. "I'm not suggesting there is anything unpatriotic about that. A lot of people went to Moscow. And so that's the end of that as far as I'm concerned." One reason may have been that mention of Moscow, according to Greenberg, sent Clinton's poll numbers climbing.

Later that very same day in Cincinnati, however, Bush said he would continue to criticize Clinton for "demonstrating against your country in a foreign land when soldiers . . . are dying in Vietnam. . . . It is wrong to demonstrate against your country when your country's at war," he repeated, "and I'm not going to back away from that one single bit."

The more Bush went on the personal attack, the more he was inflicting wounds on himself. *The Washington Post* reported a survey by Brown University that found 52 percent of those polled in Boston—admittedly a heavily Democratic city—believed the president was responsible for keeping the campaign on the low road, to only 15 percent who blamed Clinton. A Brown professor, Darrell West, was quoted as saying: "Bush is losing the blame game. In 1988, Bush was much more negative than Michael Dukakis but wasn't blamed for it. . . . A lot of the press coverage has accentuated the idea of Bush attacking."

The ghost of Willie Horton had indeed come back to haunt the man who had made him famous four years earlier. Bush had other specters chasing him now as well. They were face masks and head masks of chickens that were appearing at campaign rallies for both Bush and Clinton around the country, together with signs that read CHICKEN GEORGE—manifestations of voter dissatisfaction with Bush's foot-dragging on long-proposed televised debates with his Democratic opponent. Time was getting short, and the odds were still long against him. George Bush could not afford to be called "chicken" much longer.

SMART BOMBS
VS. BUCKSHOT

Even before Labor Day, the conventional opening date for presidential general election campaigns, the Clinton strategists had already fired the first shots in what had come to be called "the air war"—the competition for votes through paid television and radio commercials.

The Clinton ads began running in August, a week after the Republican National Convention, and where they were run was just as significant as when. Eschewing the traditional general election practice of advertising nationwide on incredibly expensive network television, the Clinton planners targeted specific battleground states and began assaulting them with unprecedentedly heavy buys in cheaper local markets. In the process, they left many states uncovered by paid commercials and abdicated the broad national television audience to the Bush campaign—at least in the realm of purchased time.

The Clinton strategists' unconventional timing and targeting sent a distinct message: they were determined not only to define their candidate in their own terms before the Bush campaign did it for them, but to do so intensively in the key states that could win the election for them. From the outset, it was clear that their first priority was controlling the agenda, and delineating the critical zones of combat, for the air war of 1992.

"We wanted to define Clinton in those battleground states before they defined us," Mandy Grunwald, the campaign's advertising expert, said later. From August through the election, she said, the Clinton campaign ran about twice as much paid television in the selected battleground states as the Bush campaign, which hewed largely to the traditional approach of buying mostly network time. "We had two weeks on the air when they didn't have a single spot on the air, which was unbelievable," she said. "It was just stupid of them, and for another three or four weeks we were outspending them at higher point levels [intensity of airtime] in those states."

The goal, Grunwald said, was to have two tracks running simultaneously in the target states—one defining Clinton in the most positive terms, one criticizing Bush and keeping him on the defensive. There was a desirable third track as well, she said, which was responding to Bush's attacks. "You can live in a world where you have to pick two out of three," she said. "You can't live in a world where you have to pick one out of three. . . . We didn't want to be in a situation in a battleground state where we could only run one track, and a lot of this walking away from the network[s] was born of the desire [to run two tracks]."

The targeting strategy grew out of the experience of a Clinton team whose strength was running statewide rather than presidential campaigns. "We all come from running Senate and gubernatorial campaigns," Grunwald said, "and knowing what it takes in a . . . [particular] state to win a campaign. And a lot of our focus was, we were going to treat Michigan and Colorado and Georgia as we would treat [them in state races]."

The conventional wisdom among politicians holds that paid advertising is less important in presidential elections than in campaigns for lesser offices, because candidates for president get so much news coverage—"free media," in the lexicon of political operatives—that the commercials have less impact.

There is obvious validity in that view, at least to the extent that in presidential campaigns it is far more difficult to build or alter a perception of a candidate with advertising alone. For example, in Jimmy Carter's 1980 campaign against challenger Ronald Reagan, the president's strategists made television commercials designed to depict him as a strong leader. But when run they were juxtaposed against news stories on the television networks showing him being jerked around by the Ayatollah Khomeini in the Iran hostage situation.

Television and, to a lesser degree, radio commercials can have an effect on voters, however, when by endless repetition they are a prime source of the "information" the voters receive about a candidate. And, more importantly, they can have an effect when used to reinforce perceptions of a candidate already in the voters' minds.

In the 1992 contest, the Bill Clinton strategists scheduled their television spots onto the tracks Grunwald talked about. First, they pressed their own case with saturation coverage in the key states—"smart bombs" zeroing in on specific targets with pinpoint precision. Second, they underlined reservations about President Bush that already had been identified by the opinion polls all through the primary season and summer. And when necessary and when they had the resources, they responded to Bush's attacks. But more often Clinton did so himself, and quickly, through the ample free media that the heavy general election coverage brought him.

The first sixty-second spot, run in ten states targeted by the campaign as critical to Clinton's election prospects, used footage of the candidate reaching into crowds to shake hands on the post-convention bus tour, at his desk as governor and delivering his acceptance speech in Madison Square Garden. The accompanying text emphasized his promise to raise taxes on those who earned more than $200,000 a year and invited voters to write for a copy of his economic plan.

As read by the announcer, it was a distillation of the message Clinton had been sending all year and would continue to send—that Clinton was the candidate of change and economic progress. At the same time, the commercial was an attempt to inoculate him against the attacks on his record as governor of Arkansas that the campaign expected from President Bush:

"Something's happening. People are ready, because they've had enough. Enough of seeing their incomes fall behind and their jobs on the line, enough of a government that just doesn't work. They're ready for change. And changing people's lives—that's the work of his life. Twelve years of battling the odds in one of our nation's poorest states. Arkansas now leads the nation in job growth. Incomes are rising at twice the national rate. Seventeen thousand people moved from welfare to work. That's progress, and that's what we need now. Change, real solutions. Bill Clinton has an economic plan to rebuild America that invests in our own people. Education. Training. Eight million jobs in the next four years. Those making over $200,000 have to pay more. The rest of us get a break. It's a plan to put people first again. And six Nobel Prize economists say it will work. For people, for a change, Bill Clinton for President.''

In targeting more than 80 percent of the $35 million to $37 million available for advertising in battleground states, and even in particular markets within those states, the Democrats enjoyed a luxury resulting from the fact that they entered the general election campaign with such huge leads in so many states. They could safely count the electoral votes in these states as assured, or at least as assured as anything ever is in a presidential election campaign. ''We never bought network television time until the last two weeks,'' Grunwald said. ''That's never been done.''

Using the targeting profile that had been developed early in the year by Paul Tully, the campaign held weekly meetings in Little Rock to make the decisions about where to spend how much in the days ahead. Such flexibility was permitted by the fact that as many as fifty media buyers were standing by to put in the orders when those decisions were made. The decision-makers, in addition to Tully himself before his death, regularly included David Wilhelm, Stan Greenberg, field director Craig Smith and Grunwald. Also, the others in the campaign with extensive political experience in statewide races in the battleground states knew the media markets and what it took to win in them.

The strategists decided to ignore two groups of states in placing their commercials. One was made up of those clearly beyond reach because they were so congenitally Republican—such hopeless cases as Virginia, Kansas and Nebraska. These states were, in effect, written off even though at the time there were polls showing Clinton running even or ahead of Bush in most of them. Indeed, at the outset, the earliest polls showed Clinton clearly trailing only in one of the fifty states—Utah.

Some of these were difficult calls. Early in the campaign, polls were showing Clinton leading by eight to ten points in Alabama, and Democrats there had been in Clinton's corner early. But the Clinton strategists realized it was likely to be difficult ground in the long run—possible but not likely. In some cases, the key consideration was simply figuring the cost-benefit ratio. Florida, for instance, looked susceptible to Clinton throughout the campaign but a full-scale media assault on the state would have cost several million dollars—too much to pay for the potential benefit. As Wilhelm put it one day during the campaign: ''We don't need to win them all. We don't need 450 electoral votes.''

The toughest decision may have been one against an intense effort in Texas. Here again early polls were encouraging, and the Clinton managers were intrigued by the possibility of defeating George Bush in his home state or, at the least, forcing him into spending much of his treasure to protect his base there. Moreover, the campaign in Texas was headed by Gary Mauro, the state land commissioner and one of its two or three most skilled political operatives, and he was arguing, perhaps predictably, that Texas was within range for Clinton.

In this case, the brain trust in Little Rock temporized, spending a small amount of the ''soft money'' available through the Democratic National Committee to buy some test commercials while postponing a final decision into October, when Texas finally was effectively written off. As Grunwald put it later, ''We walked away from a lot of states where we held leads . . . there were a lot of temptations out there.''

The most politically significant, and risky, decisions were those to withhold advertising in states in which Clinton seemed to be in an unassailable position, including not just such traditionally Democratic bastions as Massachusetts, West Virginia and Rhode Island, but some of the major states whose electoral votes were crucial—California, New York and Illinois. ''Our gamble was,'' said Grunwald, ''that [we] would not need advertising to win these states.''

This strategy required a certain amount of nerve on Wilhelm's part. When what had been a lead of close to thirty points in California narrowed to under fifteen late in the campaign, he and his California campaign director, Los Angeles lawyer John Emerson, had to decide whether the state's fifty-four electoral votes were still safe or needed to be reinforced with advertising, financed from an emergency contingent fund. They decided the Clinton margin would hold in this case, but there were several such questions raised in other states during the course of the campaign.

The key factor in all these decisions was Greenberg's polling data. Some of the runaway states might be getting tighter but, the polling expert kept saying, there was no reason to panic. This approach, Grunwald said later, "meant that California watched seven weeks of negative ads about Bill Clinton and never heard an answer." But by not buying advertising in the nation's most populous state, Grunwald estimated, the campaign saved between $5 million and $7 million of a total advertising budget of $35 million, or enough to allow saturation commercial coverage in the most closely contested major states.

In Ohio, for instance, the Clinton campaign was spending more on television than the candidates in the leading statewide races, buying as much as a thousand rating points a week—meaning the average viewer would see the Clinton spots ten times during that period. "Our premise was," Grunwald said, "if we're going to contest, we're going to run a full campaign. . . . If we're there, we're going to own the airwaves. And if we can't do that, let's not be there."

By contrast, the Bush campaign never enjoyed that same luxury. As Bob Teeter said later, the first priority for the Republican operation was to lift Bush's numbers in the national opinion polls, so that he would appear competitive and voters would begin to focus on the choice between the two men. In short, the incumbent president still had to establish his credibility. Until that happened, there was no point in spending money to try to pick off the electoral votes of particular states. The only course available was to spend most of the Bush money on network television— spraying buckshot everywhere—and that was what was done through most of the campaign, at least until the final two weeks.

(Through September, the air war was waged between the Clinton and Bush camps. But in the end, the Ross Perot campaign spent more than either of the major party campaigns on television advertising—about $45 million. As in the Bush campaign, most of it went for network television, with a large proportion on longer programs rather than spots. But Perot was never a direct combatant in the air war because he never became fully engaged in the charges and countercharges that the Republican and Democratic candidates directed at each other. Instead, the Perot spots late in the campaign were aimed largely at undercutting the press, to counter its contention that the independent candidate had no realistic chance of winning the White House. In one commercial, Perot was shown saying: "You got to stop letting these people tell you who to vote for.

You got to stop letting these folks in the press tell you you're throwing your vote away. You got to start using your own head.")

The reliance on the networks obviously meant that the Bush campaign was spending relatively as much money in states the president already was assured of winning as in those where he needed a breakthrough. But given the goal of improving his national position, it didn't matter much whether whatever new support could be elicited came from states that were closely contested or not.

The Bush strategy, even if dictated by circumstances, did mean that in many states seven weeks or more passed in which Bush campaign attacks on Clinton did indeed go unchallenged by Clinton commercials. But Clinton was able to answer personally on the free media, or through his surrogates and state campaign operations. That was one of the reasons for the weekly meetings in Little Rock—to keep the campaign "always vigilant," as one adviser put it, against the possibility of any nasty surprises.

If there was a clear difference in the advertising strategy of the two campaigns in deciding when and where to run their commercials, there was an equally stark contrast between the content of their commercials. And that contrast spoke volumes about the shape of the campaign.

Once Clinton strategists had managed a certain amount of inoculation against attacks from the Bush campaign, they followed the first two tracks mentioned by Grunwald more or less simultaneously. One was intended to define the governor of Arkansas as a "different kind of Democrat"— not another traditional liberal in the mold of Walter Mondale or Michael Dukakis—who represented change and, for the electorate, hope of a serious attack on the fundamental problems of the economy. The other was a strategy of keeping the voters' attention focused on George Bush and on the economic issues that, all the polling data continued to tell the Clinton campaign, were still the prime concern, even preoccupation, of most of the voters of 1992.

In this regard, Grunwald said, the model for her was the 1980 Reagan television strategy against Carter—another "incumbent president in a weak situation and people very worried about the economy." Although Reagan campaigned on the stump to "get the government off the backs of the American people" and "stand tall in the world," she said, "neither of those phrases ever appeared in his advertising . . . ninety percent of his spots were about the economy. . . . It amazed me how single-minded and focused the advertising was.''

One of the early positive Clinton commercials announced ''The Clinton Plan'' and showed the Democratic nominee leaning on his desk talking into the camera: ''Government just isn't working for the hardworking families of America. We need fundamental change, not more of the same. That's why I've offered a comprehensive plan, a real plan to rebuild America, create 8 million new jobs, invest in education and job training, insure quality, affordable health care for all. We're going to ask the rich to pay their fair share so the rest of America can finally get a break. A plan to put government back on your side. Read it yourself. Together we can make America work again.''

Another thirty-second commercial also focused on the economy and economic fear in particular. It bore the legend ''The Republican Record,'' and under those words showed a kind of political odometer tracking the number of unemployed as the figure moved up past 9.5 million Americans out of work. As the figure grew, the announcer said: ''You're looking at the results of years of Republican neglect. The highest unemployment in eight years. The Republicans actually stalled the extension of unemployment benefits, blocked a middle-class tax cut that would help the economy, cut Medicare for senior citizens and tried to reduce college loans. . . . The worst economic record since the Great Depression. Aren't you ready to say enough is enough?''

The commercials designed to depict Clinton as a ''different kind of Democrat'' showed the presidential nominee and his running mate, with this voice-over description: ''They're a new generation of Democrats, Bill Clinton and Al Gore. And they don't think the way the old Democratic Party did. They've called for an end to welfare as we know it, so welfare can be a second chance, not a way of life. They've sent a strong signal to criminals by supporting the death penalty. And they've rejected the old tax-and-spend politics. Clinton's balanced twelve budgets and they've proposed a new plan investing in people, detailing $140 billion in spending cuts they'd make right now. Clinton-Gore. For people, for a change.''

Clinton had used the welfare issue to help define himself as different throughout the campaign, particularly in the South and, perhaps to a lesser extent, with audiences of blue-collar Reagan Democrats in the Northeast and Midwest. One thirty-second spot showed Clinton speaking from the governor's mansion in Little Rock and saying: "For so long government has failed us, and one of its worst failures has been welfare. I have a plan to end welfare as we know it—to break the cycle of welfare dependency. We'll provide education, job training and child care, but then those who are able must go to work, either in the private sector or in public service. I know it can work. In my state we've moved 17,000 people from welfare rolls to payrolls. It's time to make welfare what it should be—a second chance, not a way of life."

The Bush campaign also ran positive spots that attempted to combine, at least by implication, his stature as a world leader and military hero. But what was missing was any coherent message to answer the central question of the campaign—whether he now could be relied upon to confront and deal with the economic distress. His first sixty-second commercial attempted to create a dramatic atmosphere with film of war planes taking off, a computer printing out his message and music building in the background while he was shown, in an excerpt from his acceptance speech, saying: "The world is in transition. The defining challenge of the nineties is to win the economic competition. To win the peace, we must be a military superpower, an economic superpower and an expert superpower. In this election, you'll hear two versions of how to do this. Theirs is to look inward, ours is to look forward, prepare our people to compete, to save and invest so we can win. Here's what I'm fighting for: open markets for American products, lower government spending, tax-relief opportunities for small business, legal and health reform, job training and new schools built on competition ready for the twenty-first century."

Another Bush commercial run later attempted to use his role in the Persian Gulf War and on the world stage. It showed pictures of Scud missiles and fighter planes, hostages and President Boris Yeltsin of Russia interspersed with labels such as "Persian Gulf Crisis—1991" and "The Coup against Gorbachev—1991" and, more to the point, "Today's Unknown Threat." At the end the camera zoomed in on the leather chair behind the president's desk in the Oval Office and the legend that appeared on the screen read: "President Bush. Commander in Chief."

The sound track had President Bush announcing: "Just two hours ago allied air forces began the attack on military targets" and simulated the voices of news broadcasters saying such things as "if revolutionaries and terrorists are armed with nuclear and chemical weapons, it may pose new challenges to the President.'' Finally an announcer was heard saying: ''In a world where we're just one unknown dictator away from the next major crisis, who do you trust to be sitting in this chair?''

This approach was the heart of the Bush campaign's case—that Bill Clinton lacked the experience and character to be trusted in the White House, while George Bush already had demonstrated his ability to function in a crisis. But the problem for the Republicans was that this pitch was simply irrelevant in terms of the 1992 electorate. The voters already knew what Bush had done in the Persian Gulf and had factored it into their tentative decisions.

They also knew the Cold War was a thing of the past. The Bush campaign appeared to have forgotten, perhaps out of necessity, that the first question of politics is, ''What have you done for me lately?'' And what it lacked in its arsenal of commercials was even one that could make a convincing case for Bush on domestic issues. The Republican strategists tried once, with a five-minute commercial derived from his speech to the Economic Club of Detroit, but it fell so flat they dropped it within days.

Lacking a positive case that voters would see as pertinent, the Bush strategists relied heavily on negative commercials—again aimed at raising questions about Clinton they hoped would lead voters into making comparisons. Clinton's record as governor of Arkansas was a target off and on as the campaign progressed. One early—and funny—spot showed fast-forward film of state legislators applauding while Clinton signed bills in Little Rock, a clip of Clinton himself playing the saxophone, with bluegrass music in the background. Said the announcer:

''To pay for his increased spending in Arkansas, Bill Clinton raised state taxes. And not just on the rich. He increased the sales tax by thirty-three percent, imposed a mobile-home tax, increased the beer tax. He assessed a tourism tax, created a cable TV tax, supported a tax on groceries. And now, if elected president, Bill Clinton has promised to increase government spending 220 billion dollars. Guess where he'll get the money.''

Such ads were mild stuff compared to what the Bush campaign of 1988 had run against Dukakis. But two others, perhaps the most vivid and memorable commercials of the campaign, struck at Clinton in the same sinister way that marked the Bush ads of four years earlier.

The most controversial was a thirty-second spot that used a *Time* magazine cover from the heart of the primary season in April showing a photo-negative image of Clinton with the headline: "Why Voters Don't Trust Clinton." The ad seemed to imply that the magazine was currently raising the question. The voice-over announcer said: "He said he was never drafted. Then he said he forgot being drafted. He said he was never deferred from the draft. Then he said he was. He said he never received special treatment. But he did receive special treatment. The question then was avoiding the draft. Now, for Bill Clinton, it's a question of avoiding the truth."

The commercial backfired, however, when legal action by protesting *Time* officials persuaded the Bush campaign to take it off the air—thus reinforcing the constant needling from the Clinton campaign that the Bush campaign was playing old-fashioned "dirty-trick" politics. As a practical matter, the spot probably fell short in another way by, once again, stressing an issue voters already had taken into account. Those who were going to vote against Clinton on the draft didn't need to be reminded; those who were not were not likely to be persuaded at this point. Grunwald later called the ad "a colossal mistake . . . we found it made people angry . . . to keep harping on the draft issue."

The single most evocative commercial of the year was a thirty-second spot showing black-and-white images of storm clouds gathering, with thunder in the background, and dissolving to a barren landscape on which a single buzzard was perched on a leafless branch of a dead tree. The legend across the screen read: "America Can't Take That Risk."

Although the pictures seemed to suggest the aftermath of nuclear war, the message dealt with Clinton's record in Arkansas: "In his twelve years as governor Bill Clinton has doubled his state's debt, doubled government spending and signed the largest tax increase in his state's history. Yet his state remains the forty-fifth worst in which to work, the forty-fifth worst for children. It has the worst environmental policy, and the FBI says Arkansas has the biggest increase in the rate of serious crime. And now Bill Clinton wants to do for America what he has done for Arkansas. America can't take that risk."

The repeated attacks on Clinton's record as, to use one Bush phrase, "the failed governor of a small Southern state" was a throwback to the attacks on Michael Dukakis's service as governor of Massachusetts that were so successful for Bush in 1988. But the differences in the situation were too clear to have the same effect. Dukakis had never controlled the 1988 agenda so was kept on the defensive; Clinton had been on the offensive since July. More to the point, Bush was no longer a candidate with a clean slate; he was now a president with a record to defend.

The Clinton campaign had recognized from the outset, nonetheless, that many voters would feel they didn't know much about the challenger and that many others might have erroneous ideas about him. One, as noted earlier, was that Clinton had come from a privileged background because he had attended Georgetown University and Yale Law School. So, in addition to spots trying to put his Arkansas record in a more positive light, the Clinton campaign ran one early sixty-second commercial confronting the trust issue with excerpts from a biographical film used at the Democratic National Convention.

It included black-and-white still pictures from Clinton's youth, including his meeting with President Kennedy, mixed with color film of the candidate reminiscing about his life. "I was born in a little town called Hope, Arkansas, three months after my father died," Clinton said on the film. "I remember that old two-story house where I lived with my grandparents. They had very limited incomes. It was in 1963 that I went to Washington and met President Kennedy at the Boys Nation program. And I remember just, uh, thinking what an incredible country this was, that someone like me, you know, had no money or anything, would be given the opportunity to meet the president. That's when I decided that I really could do public service because I cared so much about people. I worked my way through law school with part-time jobs, anything I could find. After I graduated, I really didn't care about making a lot of money. I just wanted to go home and see if I could make a difference. We've worked in education and health care, to create jobs, and we've made real progress. Now it's exhilarating to me to think that as president, I can help change all our people's lives for the better and bring hope back to the American dream."

The Clinton campaign also was quick to respond—using the third track—to that most graphic ad showing the barren landscape. Less than twenty-four hours after it aired, the Clinton strategists countered with a thirty-second commercial in battleground states carrying such legends as "Bush ads are misleading and wrong" and "Arkansas leads the nation in job growth." The ad cited such sources as CBS and the Bureau of Labor Statistics and had an announcer say: "No wonder *The Washington Post* says George Bush is lying about Bill Clinton's record, and why *The Oregonian* concluded, 'Frankly, we no longer trust George Bush.' "

But if there was a critical moment in the air war, it had far less to do with what voters thought about Bill Clinton than what they thought about George Bush. Despite all the efforts of the Republican strategists to prevent the campaign from becoming a referendum on Bush, both sides discovered that it was just that.

Beginning with the first negative commercial against the president, the Clinton managers found that their single most effective way to undermine him was to show Bush himself on the screen. That spot and several others depicted Bush making a statement, then flashed on the screen a legend refuting his claims—thus reminding the electorate of his failures.

The spots were often tricky. In the first one, the president was shown saying, "The economy is strengthening," while the legend cited unemployment at a six-year high. Not mentioned was that Bush had made the statement in October of 1991, and the jobless rate peaked in March of 1992. In another, Bush was shown in 1988 saying, "We will be able to produce 30 million jobs in the next eight years," followed immediately by the voice of an announcer saying, "Under George Bush, more private sector jobs have been lost than have been created."

Bush was also shown saying, "And I am an environmentalist," to which the announcer retorted: "The Sierra Club says Bush allowed this administration to, quote, 'gut clean air rules.' " Then Bush: "I want a kinder and gentler—" and the announcer: "Uh, uh. We can't afford four more years."

Some of the claims in the Clinton and Bush negative ads were subject to dispute on the facts and the sometimes misleading juxtaposition of information. And both campaigns were aware that in 1992 every news organization of any seriousness had "ad police" on the job—reporters examining the factual claims in the spots and refuting them when they didn't hold up, thus offering ammunition to the opposition that a revival of Willie Horton was taking place.

Mandy Grunwald said the Clinton campaign tried to reinforce the credibility of spots by citing official or quasi-official sources—the Bureau of Labor Statistics, the census bureau or perhaps some newspaper or magazine. "Almost every major charge we used came through a third-party citation," she said. But the key was using Bush himself.

"With Bush we, as often as possible, had him use his own words and what we found in our research was . . . it was more credible [and] people thought it was more fair: 'It's true. He said it himself. It's his own words. I remember when he said that.' " In short, it was "more devastating" to be fair—or at least to appear to be fair.

In key battleground states like Ohio and New Jersey, the Clinton strategists found, Bush's approval ratings that began at 32 or 33 percent when the general election campaign opened could be driven down to 26 to 27 percent with heavy use of commercials in which he appeared speaking for himself.

"The ads kept it focused and kept his job performance [ratings] down," Grunwald said. Indeed, every time the president's approval rating would creep up to 29 or 30 percent, she recalled, "we would pump up the focus on Bush."

The Bush managers would not concede that using their candidate out front was a negative. But two opinion surveys made at midcampaign indicated that voters found Clinton commercials more believable and they blamed Bush more than Clinton for the negative aspects of the campaign.

As the campaign went on, it became clear from the design of the Bush commercials that the president's strategists were getting a similar message from their own research. That was why they were using commercials like the barren landscape with the buzzard in the tree, instead of showing Bush himself. And it was clearly the reason they began running spots showing not Bush but supposedly ordinary citizens talking about him or Clinton, taped in a shaky, amateurish fashion that was supposed to suggest sincerity or, at least, an absence of slickness.

One showed eight people sitting in booths eating breakfast at an International House of Pancakes restaurant in St. Louis. The "conversation" included these remarks: "I still have a lot of confidence in my president." . . . "I feel we need Bush to keep us from a big-spending Congress." . . . "I don't trust Clinton." . . . "The man says one thing and does another." . . . "First he denies it and then he says, well maybe it happened. You can't trust him." . . . "Clinton gets in, what we're going to see are more taxes." . . . "One thing that's got me definitely for Bush is I remember what happened the last time we did things the way Bill Clinton wants to do them."

A similar commercial shot at a union rally in New Jersey was clearly aimed at stopping the erosion from the Republican president on the part of blue-collar Democrats who had voted for Reagan and Bush in the past.

It had voters saying about Clinton: "I don't believe him. I don't believe him one bit." . . . "I don't know much about Clinton except promises." . . . "He tells everybody what they want to hear." . . . "Well, he wants to spend more money, and the only place he can get it is from the taxpayers." . . . "Higher taxes." . . . "Less food on the table." . . . "Broken promises." . . . "Less clothes on the kids' back." . . . "I don't know how we can take any more taxes." . . . "Less money to go to the doctor." . . . "He's raised taxes in Arkansas. He'll raise taxes here." . . . "Just less of everything."

The commercials sought in capsule form to make the case Bush had to make for a second term—that Clinton could not be trusted and that Bush was the safe choice. And because voters always feel there is some risk in voting for a challenger, the spots had some effect, at times raising Clinton's negatives a few points.

But as was the case with the entire Bush campaign, the spots were missing the point. The voters were looking for evidence that the president had a plan for dealing with the economic situation, and there was no such evidence in the commercials. On the contrary, they reinforced the suspicion that Bush was playing the old-fashioned negative politics-as-usual that the voters had shown repeatedly all year they would not accept.

(At the very end of the campaign, the Bush strategists tried one final negative ploy. They ran a heavy schedule of radio commercials that were tailored for specific states with claims that, for example, a Clinton administration would shut down off-shore drilling and take away hundreds of thousands of jobs in Louisiana, or that he would impose energy taxes that would raise utility bills "over $350" in Maine, Michigan and Maryland. The radio spots ran too late to get much press attention, but the Clinton campaign quickly responded with radio rebuttal ads of its own, with an announcer saying: "It's the same old story. George Bush will say anything to get elected. He said so himself. . . . So the next time you hear a George Bush ad, ask yourself, isn't it time for a President who will fight for American jobs?")

Through all this, Bill Clinton stayed "on message" about the economy. He knew the key to winning was pounding Bush relentlessly on the issue, and in that effort he was soon to have considerable help, from a familiar source.

CHAPTER 26

HE'S BACK!

Almost from the moment old sailor Ross Perot threw himself over the side in a Dallas news conference on the final day of the Democratic National Convention, he had regretted the political drowning attempt. He had not gauged the depth of anger and sense of abandonment that the act would create among the millions of volunteers who had put themselves on the line for him and his "movement." And his departure without a special word of explanation or apology to them was particularly grating. Meyerson conveyed those sentiments to him as Perot contemplated in seclusion what he had done and how he had done it.

At 4:45 A.M. Hawaii time on July 16, the ringing of a telephone had broken the predawn hush in the home of a former Vietnam prisoner of war and Perot friend named Orson Swindle. Sleepy-eyed, Swindle roused himself and heard the voice of Darcy Anderson from the Perot headquarters in Dallas.

"I've got some bad news," Anderson told him. "Ross is pulling out."

"What?"

Swindle, appointed the Hawaii coordinator and manager for the campaign by Dallas only two weeks earlier, was dumbfounded. Anderson told him to turn on his television set because Perot would be going on live shortly. Swindle slipped into his clothes and drove at once to the Perot petition drive headquarters in downtown Honolulu. By this time, CNN was reporting that Perot was about to quit, and volunteers began streaming into the office—a scene being repeated in cities and towns across the mainland as word leaked out.

The mood was a mixture of bewilderment and disbelief. "These were just average people," Swindle said later, recalling the scene. "They had no particular sophistication about politics. That's the last thing they had. They came from diverse backgrounds. Some were out of work, some were housewives, some were hardworking people fortunate enough to have a job. We sat around and started talking, and they said, 'Orson, you know him. You've got to go back and talk him into staying in this damn thing.' So everybody just immediately committed to [the idea that] we're going to get him back into the race. We started laughing, and the mood shifted from one of sadness to one of challenge."

Swindle and Bob Hayden, the campaign's self-starting state coordinator in California, were of the same mind. They talked and Hayden initiated a "fax network" to other state coordinators urging them to meet in Dallas that weekend at their own expense to take stock and "talk to Ross." Perot was alerted and he passed the word for them to come ahead. It was, after all, their movement and their country, and they were "the owners."

On Friday night, one day after his pullout, Perot appeared again on *Larry King Live*, from New York, and in the course of the interview talked about mobilizing his shocked troops into an army of patriots to keep the heat on Bush, Clinton and congressional candidates. At one point he described his own chance of election as a "very, very, very long shot," but that thinnest of reeds was seized by some Perot stalwarts to hope that he could be made to change his mind about an active candidacy. "I have not gone away," he said. "I will stay with them right through the end. I will help and support them any way I can, and play any role they want me to."

On Saturday, July 18, about forty people gathered at the campaign headquarters in north Dallas to press their case on Perot. Swindle was not among them, his plane to the mainland having been repeatedly delayed. In advance, they had met and worked out with Hayden the questions they wanted to ask Perot and who would ask them. Then they were taken by bus to the headquarters, presumably to keep the press at bay. Reporters were barred as the man himself walked into the old campaign press room, his old jauntiness having never left him.

According to Cliff Arnebeck of Columbus, Ohio, one of those present, Hayden had prepared a statement on behalf of the others to read to Perot, but Perot brushed it aside and launched into a monologue of his own. "I know you wouldn't be here if you didn't want me to be your candidate," Arnebeck remembered Perot saying. But there might be a better way, he went on, to accomplish the goals that the movement had set to reform the politics of the country. That was to put out a platform for change and maintain an organization behind it, which he would support financially.

Then, as Arnebeck remembered, Perot told the volunteers that "if neither party steps up to the plate and addresses our issues, we can get back into this," adding, "If anybody thinks I've quit, they may be in for an October surprise. The ads are in the can." He had referred to them the night before on the Larry King show, calling them "killas from Manila."

In the course of his remarks, Perot spotted someone operating a video camera, and he ordered it turned off. His paranoia about the press had not been diminished by his withdrawal, although reporters had been kept outside.

Perot, according to Arnebeck, went on to discuss conversations he had had with Mikhail Gorbachev and Boris Yeltsin about helping their country's terrible economic state, in return for information about American POWs and MIAs. Then the state coordinators were invited to ask Perot questions. One by one, Arnebeck said, "they were all saying there was one thing he could do to keep the movement alive, and that was to come back into the race."

Perot heard them out but gave them no reply. Afterward, Arnebeck remembered, some Perot staff people—the whiteshirts—circulated among the volunteer leaders telling them that Perot had not been happy about the meeting, and that the visitors had not been forceful enough in pressing him to become a candidate again.

The next morning, on Sunday, the state coordinators met again, this time at the Sheraton Park Central hotel not far from the campaign headquarters, and again Perot staffers, according to Arnebeck, were telling them that they hadn't leaned on Perot hard enough to get back in. It so happened that attending another meeting at a nearby hotel was John Anderson, the 1980 independent presidential candidate. A delegation including Arnebeck was sent to talk to him about the wisdom of forming a third party.

When Anderson was told of the previous day's discussions and Perot's allusions about returning to the fray, he expressed the opinion, Arnebeck recalled, that Perot was just having second thoughts and regrets about his precipitous retreat. He had created a major credibility gap for himself, Anderson said, and if he entertained any thoughts about coming back he ought to do so at once. He could justify his action by saying the volunteers would not buy his plan of reform without him at the head of it, and therefore he was obliged to bow to their wishes and stay in the race. The longer he waited, Arnebeck recalled Anderson saying, the wider his credibility gap.

Arnebeck and the others returned to the Sheraton Park Central where the second day's meeting was under way and conveyed to others the advice Anderson had given. Together with the urgings from the whiteshirts, the idea of pressing Perot to come back into the race had a rebirth. Among those in the forefront in addition to Arnebeck were the Texas coordinator, Jim Surer, and Donna Gilbert of Alaska.

Swindle had arrived by now and he walked into the meeting "not knowing a single person in the room," he said. "I looked around and I was exposed to my first example of some rather bizarre people who had tagged along to this movement. I sat there in utter amazement, picking out the personalities—that one's got a political agenda of his own, this is a real freako that wants to find a big train he can jump on to ride. Everybody there was emotional. There was movement on the part of several of these people—'We're just going to draft Perot.'

"When they started talking about how they were going to force Perot, I got up and said, 'Hey, guys, I'm Orson Swindle. I don't know any of you and I certainly respect your enthusiasm for what you want Mr. Perot to do. But I do know him and have known him for some time, and the one thing you are not going to do is force him to do anything. The man will go in the other direction.' ''

Swindle in effect took over the meeting for what he later called ''a grieving session'' about Perot's withdrawal and what to do next, and he was not happy about the efforts of Arnebeck, Gilbert and the others to lean on Perot. But they persevered anyway, urging the group to agree to a statement calling on him to stay in the race, ''not to force him to do something he didn't want to do,'' Arnebeck said later, but in line with Anderson's counsel ''to give him a credible basis on which to reenter the campaign after saying he had dropped out.''

Swindle was presiding when Arnebeck suddenly got up, went to a blackboard behind him, Swindle said, and started writing something to the effect of ''We hereby reaffirm our support of Ross Perot for president of the United States.'' Swindle tried to intervene. ''I said, 'What in the hell are you doing?' He said, 'We're gonna draft Perot.' I said, 'Go sit down, please. We've got a lot of things to talk about.' ''

One by one, however, the state coordinators walked up and signed their names to the draft resolution on the blackboard. That afternoon, the blackboard was moved to another location, where Donna Gilbert asked for a vote on it. Swindle, informed that Perot was on his way over, balked but ''they finally pressed on with this so-called draft statement,'' he recalled. ''Everybody was on it but me.'' When Perot walked in and saw the blackboard, Swindle said, ''he just bristled.'' Hayden, according to Arneback, said to Perot: ''Ross, this isn't a setup. I didn't know about it.''

Perot sat in a chair and invited the others to sit around him in a semicircle so they could talk. Some pulled up chairs and others sat on the floor. They started to give vent to their feelings of disappointment. A woman from Colorado, Arnebeck said, told Perot she had sacrificed a great deal to join him and he had let her down. Another coordinator read a letter from a Vietnam veteran, Arnebeck recalled, that said: ''I didn't want to go to Vietnam but I had to. I was drafted. Now you're being drafted.'' Perot, according to Swindle, replied, ''You just don't understand.'' In addition to the reasons he had given publicly for withdrawing, he said, ''I have some personal reasons.''

When somebody asked him whether he had failed to anticipate the flak he was going to get from the press, Arnebeck said, Perot said that as far as he was concerned, it was nothing compared to what prisoners of war had to go through, but he didn't realize what an ordeal it would be for his family. "If this goes out of the room, I'm out," he quickly added, implying that if his enemies knew they could reach him through his loved ones they would subject his family to even more abuse. But he was no more specific than that.

Some of the coordinators told Perot what Anderson had said about the need for him to move quickly, to close his new credibility gap, if he were to get back in the race. He seemed to some to be wavering. At one point he observed that if the other candidates didn't shape up to their satisfaction "I suppose we could be the 800-pound gorilla and come back in." At another point he suggested that the coordinators go back to their states and find out how their volunteers felt, but they told him it wasn't necessary—they all wanted him back in the race. (They meant, to be sure, those who hadn't already left the Perot movement in scorn at his betrayal.)

"I think I should talk to my family," Perot told the coordinators. He went out of the room with some of the whiteshirts. Some of the coordinators began to feel they were pressing him too hard and if crowded too much he would indeed balk. So they sent a representative in to tell him they weren't demanding an immediate answer. But shortly afterward, as Swindle recalls it, Perot came out and told the coordinators: "My decision is, if you want to know right away, I'm not going to do it." He told them to go home, think about it, and come back in a couple of weeks, when they would then talk about the future of the movement.

At the end of July, the coordinators gathered in Dallas again, but this time without the "troublemakers" who had tried to force a draft on Perot, who were not invited. By this time, Arnebeck and others in the draft effort had concluded that Perot had not wanted to be drafted then for the simple reason that he had already decided on a grand strategy: he would lie low for the next two months and, as he had said at the first meeting, come back and spring an "October surprise." If he had returned as an active candidate right then, obviously, he would have opened himself to a resumption of the investigations of his business practices, his penchant for investigating others, and all the rest of what was summed up under the label Inspector Perot.

Much earlier, Perot had argued to his political advisers that the smartest—and most frugal—thing for him to do was to stretch out the petition drives until September. "Perot used to say," Hamilton Jordan recalled, " 'y'all always want to spend my money. We need to keep our powder dry.' " With the Democratic and Republican nominees not shifting into high gear until after Labor Day, he thought, he could easily wait until then himself. Perot's campaign counsel and son-in-law, Clay Mulford, also said Perot often talked of waiting until September, before going all out.

Jordan produced charts that showed that it was a myth that voters waited until after the World Series to make up their minds on how they would vote. In fact, Jordan told Perot, 90 percent had pretty much decided by Labor Day. Therefore, he argued, mindful of Perot's constant interest in getting the most for his buck, resources spent early would be directed at a much larger universe of undecided voters than money spent late in the campaign. But Perot clung to the idea that he could hold off—an idea that dovetailed with the scenario of withdrawing in July to avoid the intense press scrutiny and getting back in late in the game, when he could bring his immense wealth to bear in television advertising.

Those who came to the late July meeting, however, did not harbor thoughts that Perot was anything but sincere in his statements that he did not intend to get back into the race unless the failure of the two major parties to straighten up forced his hand. Without the folks who wanted to draft Perot, Swindle said, "it was a far more calm meeting. The emotion was there, but it was far more controlled emotion. Some people had fallen by the wayside. We obviously saw in that first meeting that some of those people did not have his best interests at heart, did not have the movement's best interests at heart. So some changes were made. We relied greatly on Perot's field staff [the whiteshirts] to select who would come down there."

Having weeded out Rollins, Jordan and the other professionals, the purge of undesirable elements among the volunteer forces was now under way, leading to numerous stories of heavy-handed incursions by the whiteshirts at the grass-roots level and reinforcing the image of Perot as a control freak. Swindle later chalked up most of the complaints to local leadership squabbles among factions, but there was no doubt that Dallas had made its authority felt.

"The charlatans came out of the woodwork for this thing," Swindle said. "All the fringe elements, people who wanted to make a fast buck on T-shirts, it was just everywhere." There were also problems of meeting Federal Election Commission requirements, and all of this taken together "got to Perot," Swindle said, because "Perot is a man who likes to be in control." And the trouble with grass-roots politics, Swindle said, was it resisted control. "The minute you'd try to invoke any control, they'd say, 'This is grass roots, we don't want any top-down.' Then they'd say, 'By the way, will you send us some money?' "

In any event, the second phase of the Perot operation was not going to tolerate such goings-on. "We came back decidedly more orderly, more focused," Swindle said. "The group consensus was we definitely wanted to get Ross back in, but we knew we had to get him on the ballot in all fifty states so we decided we would form an organization." Thus was born United We Stand America.

On August 6, Swindle sent out a memo to the state Perot offices justifying the choice of people invited to the latest Dallas meeting: "They were essentially those with whom the field coordinators and Ross Perot were most knowledgeable and with whose leadership and organizational skills they were most comfortable." Swindle concluded: "Please, folks, let's cut out the internal positioning and get on with the really important issues at hand—insuring the election of Ross Perot as the next president. ACCEPT THE APPOINTED LEADERSHIP! We have work to do."

Decisions were made to reduce the operations in California and other states that had already placed Perot on the ballot—about twenty-five at this stage, and Perot agreed to continue to fund the petition drives in the other states. That willingness fed the theory that Perot was intending all along to get back into the campaign later. "It was open," Swindle conceded. "Why else would we want to put him on the ballot if it wasn't open?" It was Swindle's notion, in wanting to see Perot back in eventually, that if he could be qualified for ballot position in all fifty states, it would then be hard for him to refuse to run, especially when his own credibility was at stake.

The one place where a major financial burden was involved in achieving ballot position was New York state. Perot committed to bankroll that effort and also to give each of the fifty states a minimum of $7,500 a month for operating expenses, with more for the larger states. The rationale, Swindle said, was to keep the volunteers together until United We

Stand America could be put on its feet after the election. But outside the Perot operation, the suspicion remained among some that he was holding his troops in readiness for that threatened "October surprise." Swindle discounted that as too farfetched. "If it was a scheme," he said later, "my God, surely we could have come up with something better than this. We never recovered from the July 16 withdrawal."

So the petition drives continued, with Perot pumping about $6 million into his movement in July, bringing his total to $12 million with more to come. Meanwhile, he stayed in the news with the publication of his long-awaited plan to deal with the federal deficit, a bit of bad-tasting medicine that called for cutting spending by about $416 billion and increasing taxes by $302 billion, including a high-profile boost in gasoline taxes reaching fifty cents a gallon in five years. He brought out his overall plan in a paperback book called *United We Stand: How We Can Take Back Our Country* that with the help of self-purchases hit the best-seller lists and climbed rapidly.

At the Republican National Convention in Houston in mid-August, departed campaign manager Ed Rollins predicted that Perot would be back in the race before November, a notion fed by a Perot response on NBC's *Today* show when asked whether he'd consider doing so if either of the two parties failed to come up with a satisfactory agenda. "I wouldn't have a choice," he said, if that's what his volunteers said they wanted—which after all was what they had said explicitly to him only a month earlier in Dallas. "I do belong to them," he said, "and it would be their decision, whatever they feel is appropriate."

By this time, Perot had been qualified for ballot position in thirty-six states, with another six on the verge, with petitions filed but not yet verified. Swindle's notion of forcing Perot's hand by reaching the fifty-state goal seemed well within reach now.

Perot himself, however, continued to play guessing games. On September 11 he paid an undetected call on White House chief of staff and de facto Bush-Quayle campaign chief Jim Baker at his home, for an undisclosed reason. In a C-SPAN program the next day, asked again about running, he said: "If the volunteers said, 'It's a dirty job but you've got to do it,' I belong to them. . . . Let's try to get the two parties to step up to the plate. If they don't we'll do what we have to do." But then he added: "But there's no plan for an October surprise or a September surprise. There is nothing planned."

By September 15, Perot was on the ballot in forty-seven states and the District of Columbia, and a *Washington Post*/ABC News poll found that 16 percent of likely voters were saying they intended to cast their ballots for him whether he was running or not. On September 18, Perot said on the *Today* show that he might be "trapped" into running because he wanted to buy television time to talk about his economic plan but the networks "won't sell it to me unless I declare as a candidate. So I may be the first guy in history that had to declare he was a candidate so he could buy TV time." Jim Squires later vouched for the accuracy of this rationale for Perot getting back in.

On September 19, the target of fifty states was reached with qualification in Arizona, which was overseen by Swindle himself. From Phoenix, he flew to Dallas and applied the heat on Perot directly. By this time, Swindle said, Perot "was now thinking, 'We're gonna do this thing.' I said, 'Ross, you've got to do it now. You don't have a choice. They're not doing what you said they had to do. They're not changing. . . . Bush cannot win this election. It looks like Clinton is going to win it and damn it, let's go beat Clinton. You've got to keep your word now.' We started talking about how to do it."

Swindle wasn't the only one over the summer who had been nagging Perot about getting back in the race. John Jay Hooker from Nashville, who in a sense assisted at the birth of the Perot presidential adventure from near the very start, had continued his telephone courtship of the Texan. In frequent conversations, Hooker appealed to Perot's sense of personal pride and integrity, telling him repeatedly that his reputation— his place in history—would always be tarnished if he didn't make up for the July withdrawal that had shattered his credibility. In his melodramatic but persuasive fashion, Hooker told Perot he owed it to his country, to his family, even to his mother in heaven to put things right by getting back into the race.

On September 22, Perot threw out another tantalizer. He said on CBS's *This Morning* show that he had "made a mistake" in dropping out and giving the two parties a chance to address the important issues on their own. On the way out of the studio, he ran into Democratic

National Chairman Ron Brown, who was just going in for an appearance. Perot at Brown's request waited until Brown was off the air and the two went into a makeup room to talk.

"Neither you nor I want to see George Bush reelected," Brown told him. "We should spend all our waking hours to see that that doesn't happen." Perot replied, according to Brown: "You don't understand. I have to talk to my volunteers."

BROWN: Come on.

PEROT: No, you don't understand. My volunteers decide.

Brown tried to persuade Perot that Clinton shared a lot of his positions on the issues and said he'd like to talk to him further about it. Whereupon Perot invited him, and other Clinton campaign leaders, or even Clinton himself, to go down to Dallas to talk to the volunteer leaders themselves.

The two parted, and when Brown got down to the lobby he spied Perot on a pay phone. He learned that Perot was calling Baker to extend the same invitation to the Bush campaign. Perot got on a plane and flew to Washington to meet Baker that afternoon, and that was how it came to pass that the Clinton and Bush campaigns found themselves, in effect, paying homage to Perot in the vain hope of keeping him out of springing an October surprise after all.

Squires said later that all this time Perot really was pressing to get Clinton to accept three principles regarding the budget deficit that would have persuaded him not to get back into the race: acknowledging publicly that the price to voters would be painful, that new revenues would have to be raised and that entitlement programs would have to be cut. Talks were held with Clinton campaign chairman Kantor, Squires said, to no avail.

On September 28, high-level teams from the Bush and Clinton campaigns dutifully trooped to Dallas to genuflect before the Texas billionaire and assembled state coordinators and make pitches designed, with little hope by now, to deter him from reentering the race. The Bush team included campaign chairman Teeter, White House National Security Adviser Brent Scowcroft, Secretary of Housing Jack Kemp and Senators Phil Gramm of Texas and Pete Domenici of New Mexico, ranking Republican on the Senate Budget Committee. Included at a separate session for the Clinton team were campaign chairman Mickey Kantor, former

Chairman of the Joint Chiefs of Staff Admiral William Crowe, Senator David L. Boren of Oklahoma, New York economist Felix Rohatyn and Washington lawyer Vernon Jordan.

The meetings, in which each team tried to make the case that its candidate was closer than the opposition's to Perot on key issues, convinced no one of anything beyond the willingness of both major party campaigns to kowtow to Perot to avoid any appearance of snubbing him or his supporters. Neither the Bush nor the Clinton campaign felt it could chance telling Perot to go to hell, although that distinctly would have been the preference in both camps. Kemp, in fact, appeared miffed at the indignity of it all and walked off early. It was abundantly clear now that Perot was going to reenter the race.

Even before he did, however, negative stories were resuming. CBS News reported and the Perot petition committee confirmed that it had hired a San Francisco law firm specializing in investigations to check into the backgrounds of certain Perot state coordinators and volunteers who did or might handle money for the campaign. Among those checked out was Arnebeck, the "troublemaker" who had been so aggressive in trying to draft Perot right after his July withdrawal.

Perot disclosed that he was having the Perot volunteers polled on whether he should run again, and Swindle subsequently reported that of 150,000 of them contacted, 93 percent wanted him to run. Also, Perot installed an 800 telephone number for the same purpose, but individuals who called got a recording thanking them for registering their desire for him to become a candidate again—whether they wanted him to or not.

By October 1, when Perot announced his reentry, it was hardly an October surprise. In another Dallas news conference, he confessed again that he had "made a mistake" and regretted having hurt his supporters back in July, but said he was now ready "to give it everything I have" in an unconventional one-month sprint for the presidency. Perot insisted that he would not "spend one minute answering questions that are not directly relevant to the issues that concern the people" and walked out, only to come back as reporters demanded that he field their inquiries.

The scene turned raucous, as he complained of news media bias against him. "Everything here is the usual, hostile negative yelling and screaming," he complained before finally walking out—and into the 1992 campaign again.

At this point, he was registering only 14 percent support in the latest *Washington Post*/ABC News poll, compared to 38 percent in early June. A *USA Today*/CNN survey was even more discouraging: Clinton 52 percent, Bush 35, Perot 7.

Perot said his running mate would continue to be Admiral Stockdale, it being too late and politically unlikely that at this juncture he could get anyone of greater public recognition or stature. As for the strategy in the month ahead, Swindle summed it up. "We're going to let Perot be Perot," he said.

By now, it was clear that Perot would not permit it to be otherwise. He revved up another round of television talk show appearances and paid $380,000 for thirty minutes of prime time on the CBS television network to discuss personally, with the use of color charts and a metal pointer, the major problems facing the American economy and how they came to be. He promised solutions in subsequent telecasts.

The presentation was straightforward without frills—the kind of thing the professionals would have scoffed at—and it drew a remarkable audience of 16.5 million viewers, more than watched most regularly scheduled entertainment shows or the National League baseball playoff game.

Maybe Ross Perot knew what he was doing after all with his unconventional methods. He could no longer, however, avoid the conventional. Even before he had reentered the race, Bush and Clinton in agreeing to a series of three presidential debates and one vice presidential debate starting on October 11 had invited him to participate if he became a candidate. Obviously they didn't want his intrusion, but their strategists realized there was no choice, with all those potential millions of Perot voters up for grabs again. And so the stage was set for the debates: George Bush, Bill Clinton and the self-styled 800-pound gorilla.

SQUARING OFF

In an age in which it often seemed the only important things took place before the television cameras, the debate over debates had become one of the familiar rituals of American presidential campaigns. And, like most rituals, this one had become almost totally predictable. The candidate who held the whip hand—that is, the one leading at the time—controlled the terms of the debates.

When the Commission on Presidential Debates was established in 1987, largely on financing from foundations and a few individuals, the hope was that the debates would become institutionalized and routine. That was because so many voters—perhaps too many—had come to depend on them as a prime source of information in deciding which candidate to support. The commission was totally bipartisan; its chairmen were Frank J. Fahrenkopf, a former chairman of the Republican National Committee, and Paul G. Kirk, a former chairman of the Democratic National Committee. So presumably neither campaign had anything to fear from operating under its auspices. Moreover, the political professionals in both parties were delighted with the thought that the commission would free them of the necessity of dealing with the League of Women Voters, whose sponsorship of some debates in earlier years had been contentious, and with whose officials the parties often had little common purpose or cultural affinity.

But in both the 1988 and 1992 campaigns, the George Bush managers were no happier with the commission than with the organization the pols called "the lady voters." James Baker, running the 1988 Bush campaign, insisted the debates could only be negotiated directly with the Michael Dukakis campaign—and confirmed the wisdom of his position by successfully insisting on just two debates, each with a panel of reporters to get in the way of anything that might resemble a genuine exchange between the candidates. There was also that single vice presidential debate between Republican Dan Quayle and Democrat Lloyd Bentsen, friend of Jack Kennedy.

Baker was a firm believer in the idea that the debates, if they were to be held at all, were the "property" of the candidates and of such political significance that the conditions under which they would take place had to be in the hands of the campaign managers, who would be guided by their candidates' best interests. Also, Baker did not want the debates to become "institutionalized"—that is, have them reach the stature that a candidate would be obliged to participate, and under rigid conditions not agreed to by him, when it might not be to his political advantage to do so.

Four years later, the Bush campaign now once again rejected the commission plan, which Clinton had accepted as soon as it was advanced during the summer. It called for three presidential debates and one vice presidential debate, each with a single moderator rather than a panel of reporters. The Democratic debates during the primary season had demonstrated, if further proof were needed, that a single-moderator format produced far more coherent expositions of the differences among candidates than an examining board of posturing reporters.

Under the commission plan, the presidential debates were to be held on September 22 in East Lansing, Michigan, October 4 in San Diego and October 15 in Richmond. The vice presidential debate would be held September 29 in Louisville. Each would last ninety minutes. But on

September 3, with time running out for making the debate arrangements in East Lansing, Bob Teeter told reporters: "I would expect that there would be debates, but we will not accept the commission's proposal as it's outlined now." Campaign officials passed the word that Jim Baker—pulling the strings from behind the curtain—wanted only two presidential debates, each with the panel-of-reporters format. It was good enough last time, the Bush campaign argued, so they were just following that precedent.

"We thought we might could do a little better," Charlie Black said later. With Bush running behind there was the chance the campaign might want "to roll the dice" with more debates or late debates.

But this time the situation was quite different from what it had been in 1988. If one candidate was holding the high cards, it was Bill Clinton, still leading by ten to fifteen percentage points after all the dust from the conventions had settled, and far enough ahead in so many big states—California, New York, Illinois and Pennsylvania—to be in a commanding position. Even with that dominant position, however, Clinton needed the debates to "close the sale" with voters who experienced some feeling of risk in choosing a challenger over an incumbent president.

Mickey Kantor, Clinton's campaign chairman, put it this way: "We were not going to debate under any circumstances, but we wanted debates. We thought debates were important. In a sense, we had a Ronald Reagan 1980 problem; the final sale had to be made that Bill Clinton was credible, so we wanted debates. We knew from the very first that we needed them."

The Bush strategists also understood they needed the debates. They had reached the point that it was essential to change the dynamics of the campaign. "You got to the position," Teeter said later, "where it was clear we weren't moving. From the beginning of the fall until we got to the debates, we didn't move at all." The imperative for the Bush campaign, he said, was "to get people to focus on the choice between Bush and Clinton, not just a referendum on the last three years."

The strategists in each camp also were fully aware of the thinking in the other. "Both sides knew there were going to be debates," Teeter said. "They clearly were in a position where they made enough public statements and were in bed enough with the commission, and I think their natural ideology is they wanted to be pro-debate." Similarly, Kantor said he thought the Republicans "had a sort of theological position" against the commission running the debates but were certain to agree anyway. "They had to have debates, almost regardless," he said.

There were, nonetheless, strategic and tactical considerations for both campaigns. One issue was format. The Bush managers wanted that panel of reporters because it reduced the risk of the kind of freewheeling confrontation in which the president was not at his best. The Clinton managers were equally convinced the less-structured format of a single moderator would allow him to show himself to best advantage.

Bush himself tried to put the most positive face on his resistance to the single moderator. When Bernard Shaw, a CNN anchor who had been one of the panelists in a 1988 debate, asked the president if he would agree to the change, Bush replied: "I don't like that format particularly. I thought when you and others asked tough questions at the 1988 debates, it livened things up. So I don't know. I'm not inclined to say I think that's a brilliant idea. I saw nothing wrong with the former format." Among other things, Bush obviously remembered Bernie Shaw's killer question to Dukakis in 1988 about how he would respond if someone killed his wife, Kitty.

Another question, a more significant one, was the timing of the debates. The Bush camp wanted one as late as possible in the campaign, when voters were paying the closest attention and might be more prepared to see the election more as a choice than the straight referendum on Bush that Teeter feared. The Clinton campaign was adamant that it would agree to no debate later than October 19, two weeks before the election. The key factor here, Kantor said, was the fear that the Bush campaign would inject some late attack to which Clinton, as the lesser-known quantity in the equation, could not react adequately in the last few days before voters made their final decisions.

"We were sure they would," he said later. Even as the debate particulars were being negotiated, he said, "they're out there in Suitland [Maryland] going through boxes." The reference was to the search by Bush administration officials of Bill Clinton's passport files at the National Archives' National Record Center outside Washington, looking for politically damaging information.

But whatever the competing strategies and reasons for Bush to stall, the Bush campaign appeared to underestimate a different element in the political context of 1992. Voters were demanding that the candidates make themselves and their intentions crystal-clear. This was not a year in which the political professionals were going to be able to get away with cute games that denied the electorate full access to the process. On the contrary, the debate-over-debates ritual was entirely too characteristic of politics as usual.

Nonetheless, a letter over Teeter's name finally went to Kantor on September 14 formally rejecting the plan advanced by the commission and adding: "President Bush would welcome an opportunity to debate with Governor Clinton under the same terms and conditions that were agreed upon for the 1988 presidential debates."

Kantor would have none of it. "We plan to sit down with the commission," he said. "We welcome their participation. We've had the same position for ninety-five days"—when the commission first issued its invitation.

Clinton and his strategists clearly understood they held the political high ground. With the whole question of the debates hanging in abeyance, the Democratic nominee pressed his advantage, deriding Bush on the stump for his refusal to participate. Speaking to students at the University of New Mexico in Albuquerque, Clinton said: "I've listened to all their macho talk, but when it comes time to go man to man, plan to plan, where is he? One of the greatest boxers that ever lived, Joe Louis, said, 'You can run but you can't hide.' It's not from me that George Bush is hiding. He's hiding from an honest discussion with follow-ups on a record he wants to hide from, a record that has given this country its worst economic performance in fifty years, the first decline in industrial production in our history, a decline of $1,600 a year in the average family income, 2 million more people in poverty since he's been president."

Bush tried to fight back. Appearing on a radio talk show in New York with Rush Limbaugh, the president protested that he was not "a professional Oxford debater"—unlike Clinton, who was a Rhodes Scholar at Oxford—but was quite prepared to debate. "If people . . . don't think we've got an economic program, I've got a chance for them to compare it eyeball to eyeball with Governor Clinton. If people think that service to country is important, we can talk about that one. If people think that world peace doesn't matter anymore, I'd like to talk about that one with him standing there."

On the other hand, Bush went on, "I'm not going to let this new man dictate the terms" and change a format that had been used regularly since 1976. "Why would I change as the president?" Bush asked. "I'm not going to do it."

But Bush was holding a weak hand. Opinion surveys began showing that voters—63 percent of them in a poll conducted for *The New York Times*—knew it was Bush ducking the debates.

As noted earlier, Clinton turned up in East Lansing on September 22, the day the debate would have been held under the schedule proposed by the commission and rejected by Bush. "I showed up here to debate today," he told several thousand students from Michigan State University, standing before a sign that read BILL CLINTON. THERE'S NO DEBATE ABOUT IT. Bush was not "ducking this debate" because he was a weak debater, Clinton added, but because he couldn't defend his record.

It was an obvious ploy, a version of the empty-chair routine candidates at lower levels of politics had used for years to dramatize their own willingness to debate and their opponents' refusal to do so. Ordinarily, such political stunts don't have any measurable political impact, but this time the situation was quite different. For one thing, there were those hecklers dressed in chicken costumes or holding signs calling him "Chicken George"—a gimmick with irresistible appeal for the television cameras.

The first chicken was a young volunteer who appeared on his own at East Lansing. But the Clinton campaign had a "special projects" or "counterevents" unit working out of an office in the Washington suburb of Arlington, Virginia, that encouraged more chickens to appear at Bush events over the next several days. In Michigan, a critical state for Bush, the damage was particularly telling. "We took a beating up there for a week," Black said, "and even after that there was hangover, all the restaurants with 'Chicken George' on the menu and all." *The Lansing State Journal* gave over its full editorial page the next day to a scathing criticism of Bush as a no-show, accompanied by a large photograph of the empty hall where the debate would have taken place. Editorial comment throughout the state was comparable.

But the Bush strategists were unyielding. When the commission tried to find a way out of the impasse by offering to meet with the two campaigns to discuss a new debate schedule, Kantor quickly accepted but

Teeter continued to insist that the negotiations should be conducted only between the two campaigns, with no intermediaries.

Meanwhile, the pressure continued to build on the president. Although Teeter said there was never any evidence they lost any votes in the end because of the debate strategy, "Bush was beginning to take a hit. We were not losing any votes because of it, [but] our problem was we weren't gaining any votes and we were behind and we needed more people to begin to take a look at it. . . . Hell, we were down to our base at that point."

The Clinton managers were convinced Bush was being hurt by the delay. "The American people wanted engagement," Kantor said later. "They wanted connection to the process, they wanted people to speak directly to them. That's why it hurt. I was surprised it hurt them as much as it did and I think they were surprised it hurt them as much as it did."

The president was also obviously being thrown off his stride by the "Chicken Georges" who showed up in increasing numbers everywhere he went, just as a year earlier he had been spooked by the Democratic National Committee T-shirts poking fun at his foreign travel schedule. Standing on the rear platform of a whistlestop campaign train through the Midwest, Bush spotted one protester in costume holding up a sign that read: CHICKEN GEORGE WON'T DEBATE.

"You talking about the draft-record chicken or are you talking about the chicken in the Arkansas River?" he asked the "Chicken," who remained silent. Bush apparently was referring to reports of extreme pollution in the river resulting from Arkansas's major chicken-processing industry. "Which ones are you talking about? Which one? Get out of here. Maybe it's the draft? Is that what's bothering you?" It was not the kind of serious discussion of the nation's economic problems that the voters of 1992 were seeking.

The Clinton campaign was delighted by Bush's dialogue with the chicken. "He legitimized the chicken," Iris Jacobson Burnett, who worked in the special projects office, said later. "Then everybody wanted to be a chicken."

Bush, far from seeing the political damage the chicken hecklers were inflicting on him, relished the exchanges with them. At campaign stops, Mary Matalin said, "he would ask, 'Where's the chicken?' He would yell at the chicken. He loved it. 'Where's that chicken chicken?' And

30,000 people loved it. I'm supposed to be saying to him, 'Quit talking to the chicken,' and I'm saying, 'That was hilarious!' " When she and others tried to convince the president that not debating was hurting him, he would reply: "You have no data. Get data." So Matalin got it from campaign pollster Fred Steeper and Bush started to listen.

Clinton, meanwhile, continued to pound him on debating. In Louisville, Kentucky, on the day the second debate was to be held there but also had been canceled, Clinton told a midday rally: "Here in Louisville it occurs to me that you can't be a Louisville slugger if you don't stand up to the plate." Around the same time, however, after more than a week of being besieged by chickens, the Bush campaign finally reacted.

Speaking to a rally at Austin Peay State College in Clarksville, Tennessee, where costumed chickens waved signs saying READ MY BEAK: DON'T BE CHICKEN. DEBATE, Bush departed from his text and challenged Clinton to four televised debates on the four Sundays remaining before election day, two with the single-moderator format Clinton preferred and two with a panel of reporters. Bush also called for two vice presidential debates and said Ross Perot, now threatening to reenter the campaign, would be welcome to participate if he reactivated his candidacy.

"Let's get it on," George Bush, hipster, shouted to the Austin Peay students.

The Bush initiative—or, more accurately, strategic retreat—broke the impasse, and the following night negotiators for the two campaigns met in the Washington office of Kantor's law firm to begin ironing out the particulars. The Clinton team included, in addition to Kantor, Democratic National Chairman Ron Brown, television producer and Clinton friend Harry Thomason, Washington lawyer Tom Donilon and Clinton staff aide Bev Lindsey. The Bush negotiators included Teeter, Fred Malek, Dick Darman, campaign counsel Bobby Burchfield, and Robert Goodwin, a veteran of debate negotiations and arrangements in several previous campaigns.

What was most intriguing was the absence of Jim Baker, who had built a reputation of epic proportions for his hard-edged skill in debate negotiations. Stories about him bluffing and bamboozling the Dukakis negotiators four years earlier had become part of political legend. But Baker was a man who understood when he was holding a small pair, and he had a long history of distancing himself from unsuccessful political enterprises. He was, the smart guys in Washington said, "always sick that day" when something went wrong.

Baker was also still stiffly resisting being characterized as a political apparatchik; it was enough of a comedown to leave the portfolio as secretary of state to be White House chief of staff once again. So he maintained the fiction that Teeter was running the campaign. That September 14 letter from Teeter to Kantor, for example, had been drafted in Baker's office by Goodwin for Baker's signature. But when Baker read it, he told Goodwin: "This looks fine, but put Teeter's name in place of mine. I'm not the campaign manager this time." It was done—unknown to Teeter at the time, Goodwin said.

But in the negotiations that opened the night of September 30 and resumed the following day, it soon became apparent that Baker was very much a presence if physically absent. Frequently, the Bush team asked for a recess and left the room to caucus and make telephone calls. "It was clear every time," Kantor said, "that they had to go out and call Baker . . . or call somebody." At one point he needled Teeter, saying: "Do you have authority to make decisions? Because I do."

Goodwin later said that in internal Bush campaign meetings on debate negotiations, Baker was "tolerant" of Teeter's plans, listening to them but then turning them around and redirecting them. Darman was also a kibitzer, sometimes questioning why Bush should debate at all. On those occasions, Teeter would remind him of the reality of the polls showing the president well behind. Baker at one meeting observed, Goodwin said, that "our numbers are at rock-bottom. We can't continue to throw buttonhooks"—in football, a pass thrown to a receiver who goes only a short distance upfield and turns to catch it.

The tone of the debate negotiations with Baker as an invisible hand, several of the participants said, was never rancorous, perhaps because both sides understood from the outset that it was just a question of agreeing on mechanics. The Clinton campaign held the iron side—a CNN poll released during the second day of the bargaining showed him leading by seventeen percentage points. And on more than one occasion, Kantor made a show of throwing his pencil down on the table and saying his candidate was the one who didn't need the debates. Goodwin recalled him telling Teeter at one point: "We've got 330 electoral votes locked up. I don't understand why you're being so obstinate. . . . Don't you realize we're eighteen percent [sic] ahead?'' And Teeter said later it seemed that ''three quarters of the time'' the Clinton negotiators were threatening to walk out. But there never was any serious danger of a breakdown.

When it was all over, it was clear that Kantor and the Clinton campaign had gotten the best of it. ''Bush was behind the eight-ball on the debates,'' Goodwin said. The one nonnegotiable demand from the Clinton side had been that there would be no debate later than October 19, and that was precisely what the final schedule showed. There would be ninety-minute presidential debates on October 11 in St. Louis, October 15 in Richmond and October 19 in East Lansing, with a vice presidential debate on October 13 in Atlanta.

The Clinton campaign, realizing how low the expectations would be for Quayle, and thus easy to surpass, offered at one point to drop the vice presidential debate. But Quayle, hoping to recover from his disastrous 1988 debate showing, wanted to do it. His negotiators proposed that the candidates be permitted to bring notes and props, but the Democrats refused. What Quayle wanted, Goodwin said later, was to bring Gore's new book on the environment onto the set and quote from it.

As matters turned out, the critical debate decision had more to do with format than schedule. From the outset, Teeter had made it plain that the Bush campaign's one nonnegotiable demand was having a three-reporter panel for the first debate. And the implication was that this would be a trade-off for a single-moderator debate and perhaps another divided half and half.

But when Kantor telephoned Clinton during one break in the talks, Clinton suggested his negotiator should, as Kantor recalled it, ''see if they will agree to one of these to be a town meeting. Let real people ask questions.'' Clinton had done many of these during the primaries and had mastered the direct talking to voters.

Kantor was not optimistic that Teeter would accept but promised to give it a try. Bush after all had been doing his ''Ask George Bush'' sessions for years. ''In some ways I think it piqued their interest because they had this incredible anger toward the press,'' Kantor said, and this would be another way to show contempt. Nonetheless, he said, ''My view was they'd never accept this, they'd never give Bill Clinton a chance to deal with real people in an open forum.'' Kantor's fellow negotiators—

Ron Brown, Tom Donilon and Jack Quinn, another Washington lawyer with long political experience—also were dubious. "They all said," Kantor recalled, " 'They'll never agree to that, they'd be crazy to do that.' "

But after another caucus and presumably another telephone call to Jim Baker, the Bush campaign agreed, and the die was cast for that very different—and even pivotal—Richmond debate on October 15.

In the end, all of the alarums and excursions of the debate over debates may have had little direct effect on the election. Teeter was convinced that the back-and-forth thrusts and parries were trivial. "You can add them all up together and put them next to the economy and they're small," he said. "Our objective was to get people to focus on the choice."

Charlie Black, however, was not so sure. He recalled going to dinner in Lansing the night after the final debate there, almost a month since it had originally been scheduled, and opening his menu to find "Chicken George" still among the entrées. He was convinced, he said, that the campaign "waited a little bit too long to roll the proposal [from Bush for four debates] out there. We always knew we would have a proposal, we would go on offense on the issue . . . and we probably should have pulled the trigger a little earlier on the proposal."

The significant thing politically was that the Bush campaign had allowed almost the entire month of September to be frittered away in trying to get off the defensive on the debates issue. It had desperately needed to use that time to build the president's image as a man who could and would deal with the economy more effectively than he had managed in his first four years in the White House.

Beyond that, the final schedule for the four debates over nine days had the effect of freezing the campaign in place for that period. The press focus now was on preparations in both campaigns—both candidates were doing mock debates with stand-ins for their opponents—and on the speculation about what would constitute political success or failure. The consensus among the professionals was obvious: because he was behind, the president needed to make some kind of breakthrough in terms of being convincing on the economy.

Because Clinton was a challenger from Arkansas and still carried relatively heavy negatives, his imperative was to establish himself as properly "presidential." "People were ready to vote against Bush,"

David Wilhelm said later. "They needed to see that Clinton was okay." As for Ross Perot, who by now was back in the race, he would be free once again to play himself, to the hilt, because he was not considered an equally serious competitor. (The Bush and Clinton campaigns, Goodwin said later, held out the option of dropping Perot from further debates if he fizzled in the polls after the first or second one.)

But everyone in the Bush and Clinton campaigns realized that the debates had the potential, even if it seemed remote, for changing the nature and direction of the contest. There was always the possibility of some gaffe that would brand the governor from the baby boom generation as unprepared for the office. There was always the possibility of some dramatic exchange leaving a vivid perception of one candidate or another ascendant. Few in the political community could forget the moment in 1980 when Ronald Reagan, shaking his head more in sorrow than in anger, said to President Jimmy Carter: "There you go again." Nor was it likely anyone would forget Michael Dukakis's dry, legalistic response to Bernie Shaw's "killer question" in 1988.

In the first 1992 confrontation in St. Louis, however, nothing that dramatic happened. Roger Ailes, the hard-nosed and irreverent media consultant who had advised Bush in the 1988 debates, flew in on Air Force One with the president. His assignment was to relax him and get him to focus on the key elements of the debate strategy, one of which obviously was to throw Clinton on the defensive. He loosened Bush up with such things as referring to Perot as "Shrimpo" and describing him as "a hand grenade with a bad haircut."

The most contentious moment of the debate came when, responding to a question about "issues of character," Bush condemned Clinton for participating in demonstrations against the war in Vietnam while he was a Rhodes Scholar in England.

"I think it's wrong to demonstrate against your country or to organize demonstrations against your country on foreign soil," Bush said. "Maybe, they say, well, it was a youthful indiscretion. I was nineteen or twenty flying off an aircraft carrier and that shaped me to be commander in chief of the armed forces. And I'm sorry, but demonstrating—it's not a question of patriotism, it's a question of character and judgment."

Clinton, obviously well prepared for the issue, countered: "You *have* questioned my patriotism. When Joe McCarthy went around this country attacking people's patriotism, he was wrong, and a senator from Connecticut stood up to him named Prescott Bush. Your father was right to stand up to Joe McCarthy. You were wrong to attack my patriotism. I was opposed to the war, but I love my country." (The record on Bush's father had been dug up and printed in a column in *The Boston Globe* that very morning and quickly made its way into Clinton's awareness in St. Louis.)

Bush rather lamely insisted that "I didn't question the man's patriotism. I questioned his judgment and his character. If what he did in Moscow, that's fine. Let him explain it. He did. I accept that." Bush didn't elaborate as to what Clinton "did in Moscow."

Clinton made it clear from the outset that he intended to deal with the stature question—a governor from a small state taking on the president—in the most direct way. Responding to the first question about differences among the candidates, he turned toward Bush and said: "Tonight, I say to the president, Mr. Bush, for twelve years you've had it your way. You've had your chance and it didn't work. It's time for a change."

To which Bush replied: "Change for change's sake isn't enough. We saw that message in the late seventies. We heard a lot about change. And what happened? The misery index [inflation rate plus interest rate] went right through the roof."

But Bush never made a persuasive case on the economy, and seemed to fly in the face of the national consensus of concern by trying to minimize the problem, as he had done all year. "Now I know that the only way he can win," he said of Clinton, "is to make everybody believe the economy is worse than it is, but this country's not coming apart at the seams, for heaven's sake. We're the United States of America."

In what was an attempt to demonstrate he meant business in trying to right the economy, Bush said at one point: "What I'm going to do is say to Jim Baker when this campaign is over, 'All right, let's sit down now. You do in domestic affairs what you've done in foreign affairs, be the kind of economic coordinator of all the domestic side of the house . . . that includes all the economic side, all the training side, and bring this program together.' " In other words, after having called Baker in to save his reelection campaign, he would turn over the domestic challenge to him—an incredible acknowledgment that his chief of staff had more credibility with the American people than he had himself.

For Perot's part, he drew frequent laughter from the studio audience with small jabs at his opponents and the political establishment. Responding to questions about his experience for the presidency, for example, he replied, "Well, they've got a point. I don't have any experience in running up a $4 trillion debt. I don't have any experience in gridlock government. I have experience in not taking ten years in solving a ten-minute problem." And he got the biggest laugh of the night when, defending his call for higher gasoline taxes to cut the deficit, he observed that "if there's a fairer way, I'm all ears."

The instant polls after the debate disagreed narrowly on whether Clinton or Perot was the winner, but they did agree that Bush was the loser. And the same was true of the talking heads on television. Walking back to the president's holding room from her seat in the audience, Barbara Bush told a staff member, "I thought he did really well. I'm really pleased." But after a few minutes of watching the television commentary, she emerged saying: "I can't stand to listen to them." Walking to the presidential limousine, Jim Baker told Bush: "Now we've got to flush him [Clinton] out."

Whatever the validity of the verdicts of polls and pundits, the one thing that was clear was that Bush still "didn't get it" with his continuing attempts to center the debate on character or the "trust issue," as it was usually defined by the Bush campaign. Indeed, the campaign's own focus groups on the night of the first debate found Bush evoked far more doubts about Clinton when he depicted him as another tax-and-spend liberal Democrat than when he talked about trust and character.

Once again, it was a case of a campaign that did not grasp the difference in the electorate of 1992. These voters already had factored into their consideration the history of Bill Clinton dodging the draft and had decided it was not disqualifying. So they were ready to move on to the issues that affected their own lives much more than whether Bill Clinton organized a demonstration in London twenty-three years earlier.

Two nights after that first presidential debate, the confrontation between the three vice presidential nominees gave the Bush campaign an unexpected lift. Vice President Dan Quayle, the goat of the corresponding debate with Lloyd Bentsen four years earlier, came out of his corner attacking Clinton relentlessly on his economic program and personal history, charging that the Democratic nominee "does not have the strength of character to be president." Although Al Gore held his own, repeatedly attacking the Bush administration's record on the economy, the major "story" of the debate was that Dan Quayle had shown Bush the kind of aggressiveness he needed to display to be effective in the two remaining presidential debates.

The clear loser of the night was Ross Perot's running mate, retired Admiral James Stockdale, who demonstrated beyond any doubt that experience counts in big-league politics. Stockdale began by asking rhetorically, "Who am I? Why am I here?" It was a line he had rehearsed in advance, and according to Ed Fouhy, the debate's producer, Stockdale that afternoon had been arresting in practice. But over the ninety minutes of the real thing, he answered the questions with a performance that made it clear he shouldn't have been there, whatever his much-admired qualities of intellect and character. At one point, for example, he cut short his answer on a question about health care by confessing, "I'm out of ammunition." At another, after standing mute as Quayle and Gore argued heatedly, Stockdale confessed, "I feel like I'm a spectator at a Ping-Pong game."

But no one in either the Bush or Clinton campaign expected the vice presidential debate to have any significant effect on the presidential campaign. Even Quayle's weak performance as the nominee in 1988 never showed up in opinion surveys as a factor in the decisions of voters choosing between George Bush and Michael Dukakis.

So the most that could be said was that Quayle had taken at least a small step toward building his own credibility and, more to the point, provided a good example for Bush to follow in the second presidential debate in Richmond two nights later. Unhappily for Bush, however, the "town-meeting" format of that debate and the role of people like Marisa Hall, Kim Usry and Denton Walthall who deplored the spectacle of candidates trashing each other, made it impossible for the president to take that kind of approach.

According to Ed Fouhy, Bush seemed uncomfortable in that setting from the start. For one thing, the Richmond debate started two hours later than first scheduled as a result of a conflict with the baseball playoffs caused when the Oakland Athletics failed to end its series with the Toronto Blue Jays the night before. "That damned Oakland," the president muttered several times. And when Fouhy told him, "Mr. President, you're going to get a much bigger audience," Bush flashed him a disdainful look.

Furthermore, Bush's campaign aides had alerted him by this time to what they saw as the pitfalls of audience participation under Carole Simpson as moderator. In addition, the candidates were fitted with wireless microphones to enable them to move away from the stools on which they would be perched—a gimmick that Clinton duly put to his advantage in the town-meeting format he himself had proposed. When Bush said he was "not sure I get" the gist of Marisa Hall's question about how the "national debt" personally affected him, and Clinton then strode over to her and demonstrated that he did get it, it was what the late Lee Atwater would have called "the defining moment" of the campaign.

Thus, the stakes were sharply raised for the third and final debate in East Lansing four nights later. Bush had been counted as the loser of the first two meetings, and there was no sign in either public or private polling data that he was gaining on Clinton. Nor had he managed to establish his credibility on the economy even with such initiatives as his speech to the Economic Club of Detroit and publication of his new "agenda" for a second-term approach to the economy. "The later and later you got in the campaign," Bob Teeter said, "the more it was perceived as campaign rhetoric."

The importance both campaigns had attached to the final debate was evident in one bizarre episode. Two nights before, Bev Lindsey and Brady Williamson, the Clinton aides overseeing on-site debate preparation, collared Bob Goodwin, their opposite number in the Bush campaign. They needed, they told him, to check out a report—that Gennifer Flowers would be in the audience for the debate and seated with Barbara Bush! The notion was preposterous, as Goodwin quickly assured the Clinton operatives, but the fact the rumor was circulating at all was an indicator of the high stakes in the debate. (A similar rumor had made its way into the Dukakis inner circle before the last presidential debate in 1988—that the Maryland victims of Willie Horton would be planted in the audience by the Bush campaign. That one also was unfounded.)

In the end, the final debate confrontation proved anticlimactic. By virtually all estimates, Bush performed far better than in either of the earlier debates and probably as well as he had all through the campaign, making his points with more visible force than usual and sticking to the story line his campaign had crafted.

Yet for all the admonitions in the Richmond debate against negative campaigning, Bush took a tar brush to Clinton's record in Arkansas, frankly acknowledging he had to, to win. "You haven't heard me mention this before," he said, "but we're getting close now, and I think it's about time I start putting things in perspective. And I'm going to do that. It's not dirty campaigning because he's been talking about my record for a half a year here, eleven months here. So we've got to do that. I gotta get it in perspective." It was as if he were repeating the coaching he had received from his strategists before the debate started.

Clinton, after reminding the audience that "Mr. Bush's Bureau of Labor Statistics says that Arkansas ranks first in the country in the growth of new jobs this year," a few minutes later in a rejoinder to Bush on trickle-down economics recalled that "those 209 Americans last Thursday night in Richmond told us they wanted us to stop talking about each other and start talking about Americans and their problems. . . ."

And when Bush started to talk about "trust" again, Clinton reminded him of "read my lips" and repeated that "the main thing is he still didn't get it, from what he said the other night to that fine woman on our program, the 209 people in Richmond." And at the close of the debate, he told of how he was "especially moved in Richmond a few days ago when 209 of our fellow citizens got to ask us questions. They went a long way," he said, "toward reclaiming this election for the American people and taking their country back." Bill Clinton was not about to let the voters forget that previous debate, and what he was convinced it revealed about George Bush.

Nevertheless, Black said later, "Bush did a good job in that last debate. I don't give a damn what the numbers and the polls said, he got our message out there and got done exactly what he needed to get done, and that helped jump-start us. We were on a pretty good run there for a while."

None of the candidates could complain about not having an ample opportunity to make his case to the widest possible cross-section of the electorate. Contrary to the usual pattern of declining interest in debates, the audience grew over the three debates—just as Clinton adviser Harry Thomason had predicted. The first one attracted more than 80 million viewers despite the competition of a major-league baseball playoff game on CBS; the second more than 84 million and the third 88 million—and those numbers did not include the millions watching CNN and C-SPAN on cable systems or PBS. Indeed, it appeared likely that the audience for the final debate exceeded 90 million viewers.

Taken together, however, the three debates had not accomplished what the Bush campaign needed—a significant change in the dynamics of the entire campaign. The election was now two weeks away and Bill Clinton was still holding a lead in the double digits. And the president was being further compromised by the political stupidity of some of his own supporters at the State Department who had rooted through Clinton's passport files on the same days, as Mickey Kantor noted, that the debates were being negotiated.

The context was that dark suggestion promoted by right-wing Republicans in the House of Representatives, particularly Bob Dornan of California, and later encouraged by Bush himself, that there was something fishy in the trip to Moscow Clinton made while a student at Oxford. At the same time, an implausible rumor began to circulate that when Clinton was at Oxford he also had written letters trying to find out if he could avoid the draft by renouncing his U.S. citizenship or seeking dual citizenship of some other nation. It was an illogical speculation in light of his stated insistence in those days, in the letter to Colonel Holmes, that he wanted to preserve the viability of a future political career.

The State Department acknowledged, however, that the assistant secretary of state for consular affairs, Elizabeth M. Tamposi, a longtime Republican activist from New Hampshire who had been placed in the job by John Sununu, had ordered subordinates to search Clinton's passport files at Suitland after the close of business on September 30 and October 1. The justification was said to be requests from news organizations under the Freedom of Information Act. When the after-hours search was disclosed by *Newsweek* and *The Washington Post*, the department conceded that it was "clearly a mistake" and pointed the finger at Tamposi.

But the notion that she would have ordered such a search on her own was hard to accept. And subsequent departmental investigations established that during this period she had conversations about the matter with Janet Mullins, an aide to Jim Baker who had served in the White House political office, and had tried unsuccessfully to telephone Margaret Tutwiler, Baker's closest White House aide, to report on what was happening. The operative question—never answered during the campaign—obviously was whether Jim Baker had been just a little too clever this time.

For Clinton, the disclosure was a political bonanza, particularly after it was learned that the search had also covered the files of his mother, Virginia Kelley, although no Freedom of Information request had asked that this be done. The Democratic candidate began using in every speech an attack on "political hacks rifling through my mother's files trying to find dirt"—a thrust that invariably evoked boos and hisses from his listeners. And Clinton consistently evoked laughter when he would say, as he did repeatedly, that the Bush administration "was not only rifling through my files but actually investigating my mother, a well-known subversive. It would be funny if it weren't so pathetic."

Bush tried to put some distance between himself and the story, saying that the search into Mrs. Kelley's files was "most reprehensible," while adding that it would be "a stretch" to connect it to his campaign.

The challenger's mother joined the chorus of condemnation. "I'm insulted, I'm indignant," she said. "You know I'm at the age that I lived through Hitler and his Gestapo. I lived through the police state. I do not want this to happen to my country."

Here was another example of the snakebit campaign of George Bush, appearing to be playing the "dirty tricks" politics of the past when the voters were seeking answers to questions about their future that had nothing to do with Bill Clinton's passport. And, with the opportunity of the presidential debates come and gone, time was running out on the beleaguered president.

SHORT-CIRCUITING
A SURGE

With the last of the televised debates behind them, the three candidates had two weeks to make their final pitches to the voters. All the major public opinion surveys continued to show Clinton ahead by various margins in samplings after the third presidential debate. His lead ranged from nineteen percentage points in the *Wall Street Journal*/NBC News poll (47 percent to 28 for Bush and 19 for Perot) down to five in the *New York Times*/CBS News poll, with most of the others somewhere in the middle.

Clinton's pollster, Stan Greenberg, was not worried by the latter survey or any of the others. His own poll had leveled off at a seven-point lead and was staying there. More significant, Greenberg knew that much more important than the national polling numbers were those taken in each of the states, and Clinton was comfortably ahead in more than enough for an electoral college victory. His leads in such large and critical states as California, New York and Illinois were so big that the campaign was able to divert resources and candidate time from them and focus on closer targets, or states where Bush led but would be forced to spend heavy resources of his own if they were contested by Clinton.

Two questions in the *Wall Street Journal*/NBC News poll offered particular comfort for Clinton. In response to one, 54 percent said they were satisfied with his explanation on the draft issue to 38 percent who said they still had doubts. In reply to another, 51 percent said they bought his explanation on the Moscow trip, to 31 percent who said they had doubts. Neither was exactly a ringing exoneraton, but at least he was now getting the benefit of the doubt.

The debates to which Bush had looked forward as a means of closing the gap between himself and Clinton had not achieved that end, and instead had helped propel Perot back into the picture. With his message of better economic times around the corner not credible to most voters, the president was left with the same imperative that confronted him in 1988, in his race against Dukakis. He had to find a way to make the public think less of the opposition. Those questioners in the Richmond debate had let him know they would not look kindly on further personal attacks, but it was too late now to worry about a backlash from going negative.

Complicating the task was the pesky matter of the search for Clinton's passport files. It continued to be an embarrassment to Bush that Clinton exploited on the stump, telling Northern audiences that the Bush administration had sent bureaucrats on an after-hours search through an old, musty file room and even looked into "my mother's" files, which before Southern audiences became "my momma's."

(A week after the election, Bush fired Tamposi after *The Washington Post* reported that the passport files of Ross Perot also had been searched. Tamposi told *Newsweek* that she had acted under indirect orders from the White House; that the assistant secretary for legislative affairs, Steven K. Berry, had told her the search had been requested by Janet Mullins, and that Margaret Tutwiler had known about the search. Berry was demoted and eventually left the department for a job on Capitol Hill.

(A report by the State Department's inspector general, Sherman Funk, held that "there was indeed an attempt to use the Department of State," its records and employees "to influence the outcome of a presidential election," but that there was no evidence of White House involvement. The report was widely criticized as inadequate and Acting Secretary of State Lawrence S. Eagleburger eventually ordered the investigation to be continued. At the same time, the Justice Department and the General Accounting Office both stepped in to investigate as well, the GAO requesting the records not only of Mullins and Tutwiler but of Baker, who had acknowledged he had learned of the search when it was going on. Finally, Bush's attorney general, William P. Barr, appointed an independent prosecutor, Joseph E. diGenova, a former U.S. Attorney, to determine whether crimes had been committed, and if so, by whom.)

Bush undertook a two-day whistlestop train trip through the South coming out of the last debate, and he threw himself with some newfound zest into his task. He seemed never happier than when he was on the attack and playing the underdog, whether it was against Clinton, the pollsters whose numbers showed him facing a severe uphill climb, or the members of the news media, who, he was convinced, never tired of gleefully reporting that fact.

At a rally in Spartanburg, South Carolina, the night after the last debate, he roared: "Don't listen to these pundits telling you how to think. And don't listen to these nutty pollsters. Remember, things are decided in the last couple of weeks in this campaign. And now people are going to decide: who do you trust to be president of the United States?"

It all came down, in this final push, to the issue of trust. All along the route through the Carolinas, Bush hammered at what he called "a pattern of deception" in Clinton's statements, whether about his personal history or his record as governor of Arkansas. In Kannapolis, North Carolina, he reminded the crowd that Clinton had said in the final debate that he wanted "to do for the country what I've done for Arkansas." Bush added: "We cannot let him do that."

In a part of the country dotted with Waffle House restaurants, Bush visited one and made the obvious linkage with what he said was Clinton's manner of slipping off hard questions. Thereafter he took to labeling fuzzy Clinton statements, such as his equivocation on support of Bush in the Persian Gulf, as "a waffle house."

Almost giddy at times with enthusiasm for the fight, he took to ridiculing Al Gore as "the ozone man," eventually shortened to a title, "Ozone Man," and finally simply "Ozone" in allusion to the Democratic vice presidential nominee's expressed concern about the diminishing ozone layer and other environmental fears. If the president of the United States to some ears sounded somewhat silly in this exercise, many in the pro-Bush crowd loved it. At the least, it lent a certain lightness to a campaign that too often had bogged down in whining and bitterness.

Another light touch was added along the way when an unidentified couple and their three children standing along the tracks on signal dropped their trousers and, as Bush's train rolled by, "mooned" the leader of the free world!

In a day or two, the Bush attack on Clinton had settled in to the two words he would pound relentlessly through election day—"character and trust." In Vineland, New Jersey, he said: "My argument with Bill Clinton is he tries to be all things to all people. In the Oval Office you cannot do that. . . . You cannot lie and you can't be all things to all people." But the Clinton campaign, determined never to fall into the turn-the-other-cheek mode that crippled Dukakis in 1988, had its expert rapid-response operation in Little Rock at full throttle. In selected target states, the campaign was running a thirty-second television commercial showing Bush making his now-infamous "read my lips" invitation to voters during the Republican National Convention. The message clearly was, Who is George Bush to be talking about lying?

As the campaign headed into its final full week, and most polls began to indicate that Clinton's lead was shrinking, the Bush campaign began to take heart. Most of the surveys still had the Arkansas governor comfortably ahead, but one, by *The New York Times* and CBS News, had him leading Bush by only five percentage points, 42 to 37, with Perot at 17. And a *Time*/CNN poll, which had Clinton leading by seven among all registered voters surveyed, said the lead shrunk to only three when the sample was confined to "likely voters."

Slowly, cautiously, the Bush operatives began to talk of a late "surge" for the president. Such talk was particularly suspect after the 1988 election, when the strategists for Dukakis excitedly reported a similar phenomenon, but Bush in the end had been elected by a comfortable margin of nearly eight percentage points, winning 426 electoral votes in forty states. In the final stages of that campaign, Dukakis had struck the theme to voters that he was "on your side," a message geared to bring blue-collar Democrats back to the fold, and in the excitement of the final days it seemed to crowd-counters to be working. But large and even enthusiastic crowds were always an unreliable barometer of voting patterns, as Walter Mondale had found out four years earlier.

In the closing days of the 1988 campaign, too, Dukakis had finally stopped turning the other cheek and had generated notable crowd excitement by at last responding to Bush's negative tactics. He took to citing brochures picturing Willie Horton that were being distributed by an allegedly independent group in Illinois, demanding that Bush stop their circulation. "When you throw garbage in the street," he would say, "you've got a responsibility to go out there and clean it up."

But four years later, Bush had no similar wretched excess on the part of the Clinton campaign to cite as a way of rallying wavering Republicans and independents to his side, or to keep the Reagan Democrats aboard. Still, there were signs that Republicans, having had their fling with Perot or loyalty to their party winning out at the end, were coming home.

One who professed to see them was Republican Governor John Engler of Michigan. He was ushered into the press room in Detroit after a Bush speech to report about polls he claimed were showing that Perot was cutting into Clinton's lead and that, when narrowed to "likely" voters, were indicating a surge for the president. Reminded of the Dukakis claim of a surge in 1988, Engler replied: "This is real. His wasn't."

For all that, the dimensions of the task that Bush faced were demonstrated by his campaign schedule. From Michigan he spent most of one day on the next-to-last weekend in the sparsely populated states of South Dakota and Montana, with three electoral votes each, that he should have had in his pocket by now. In poker terms, Bush had to draw to an inside straight in the electoral college to be reelected, and he could not afford to let even these few electoral chips slip away. A few days earlier, a confident Clinton had made a brief raid into Montana as part of a four-state Western swing into what should have been safe country for the heir to the Reagan Revolution.

Another sign that Bush was going all out was the appearance of the heretofore Invisible Campaign Manager, Jim Baker, on Air Force One. Baker not only had been keeping out of the public eye now that he was getting his fingernails dirty in politics again; when he was identified on one occasion as the campaign manager, he corrected the statement, saying he was the White House chief of staff. According to *The New York Times*, although Baker had now surfaced, he "remained camera shy, turning his back and hiding his face this evening to get out of the camera shot" as Bush received a gift from a Montana supporter. Earlier, however, in Sioux Falls, he told reporters that the election was "absolutely doable, and we're going to win."

In all this, both Bush and Clinton competed for the most part in the final days as they did before Ross Perot reentered the race—against each other. Aware that Perot would siphon off a certain number of popular votes, each side was confident that in the real race, for electoral votes, Perot would not make much of a dent, if any. More than any national poll, where the two major candidates were going now was telling the story of the campaign. Both were concentrating on the industrial belt from New Jersey west through eastern Wisconsin, the acknowledged battleground states, in all of which Clinton was running ahead or at worst even. But beyond that, Bush was still occupied shoring up his base in the South and the West, while Clinton was forcing him to defend that base by courting it in selected states where the polls said he was running close.

Much earlier, Clinton campaign manager David Wilhelm in Little Rock had crafted a very specific battle plan that set aside what he called "top end" states—thirteen of them plus the District of Columbia—where, based on polls, past performances, strengths of state tickets and other factors, it was judged Clinton could win without expending major resources. The states were Democratic standbys Massachusetts, Rhode Island, Minnesota, Hawaii and West Virginia (although the latter began to look tougher than expected); plus Arkansas, California, New York, Illinois, Washington, Oregon, Vermont and Connecticut. They were largely bypassed the last week (and he won them all).

The second Wilhelm category was what he called "play hard" states—eighteen that were deemed winnable with an all-out campaign: Maine, New Jersey, Pennsylvania, Delaware and Maryland in the New England and Middle Atlantic regions; North Carolina, Georgia, Louisiana, Kentucky, Tennessee and Missouri among the Southern and border states; Ohio, Michigan, Wisconsin and Iowa in the Midwest; Colorado, Montana and New Mexico in the West. By the last week, Clinton was focusing on the largest of these (and in fact won all but North Carolina, losing there by a single percentage point).

The third category Wilhelm called "big challenge" states, a diplomatic way of saying Clinton's chances were not good in them and would be largely written off. There were ten considered almost sure losers: Alaska, Virginia, Mississippi, Indiana, North Dakota, Nebraska, Oklahoma, Wyoming, Idaho and Utah; and nine more that merited watching only, with a modest effort where warranted: Alabama, Arizona, Florida, Kansas, New Hampshire, Nevada, South Carolina, South Dakota and Texas. (Clinton lost all the "sure losers" and narrowly won two of the nine others—New Hampshire and Nevada.)

Mickey Kantor, the Clinton campaign chairman, told us in an interview in Little Rock shortly after the Republican convention that, for the first time in years, it was going to be the Republican candidate rather than the Democratic who would have to "thread the needle" in the electoral college to eke out a victory, and as November 3 approached, his words, and Wilhelm's calculations, were holding up.

While Clinton and Bush concentrated on each other, Ross Perot at last decided to hit the campaign trail. Since his disastrous appearance before the NAACP in Nashville in July, and his return as an active candidate on October 1, he had confined his political appearances almost exclusively to the television and radio talk shows that had first provided him an entrée onto the national political stage and, along with his healthy bankroll, kept him there. The NAACP experience, however, apparently cured him of venturing into potentially hostile waters, and he chose on Sunday, October 25, to address two crowds of supporters, one in Flemington, New Jersey, and the other in Pittsburgh.

Earlier, Perot had taped an interview for CBS's *60 Minutes*, and he urged his audiences in both places to be sure to watch it. In fact, he gave the faithful a preview—that the real reason he had dropped out of the race in July was that the Bush campaign had threatened to sabotage his daughter's wedding the next month! Offering no proof, he proclaimed that "I could not allow my daughter's happiest day of her life . . . to be ruined because of people who will do anything to win." He said he "realized this was a risk I did not have to take" if he were not a candidate "and I stepped back." Later, he acknowledged that "I cannot prove any of that happened. I just got these reports. But it was a risk I could not take."

This explanation seemed to soothe many in the crowd and it sent reporters scurrying to telephones, and many others to television sets when *60 Minutes* went on the air that night. On the show, Perot said that one of his sources was a former California police officer, Scott Barnes, known to government investigators as a publicity hound given to soliciting news organizations with tales of secret intelligence work involving famous people.

"I received multiple reports that there was a plan to embarrass her [daughter Caroline] before her wedding, and to actually have people in the church at the wedding to disrupt her wedding," Perot said. "I finally concluded that I, as a father who adores his children, could not take that risk. And, since the wedding was on a finite date [August 23], I made the decision that I would step aside." He said two unidentified Republican sources had told him in June that certain Republicans were going to "smear" his daughter by producing a fake photo concocted by computer.

In an interview with the *Boston Herald*, Perot said that while he didn't know how the wedding would be sabotaged, "watch how they disrupt rallies; watch how they tried to disrupt the Democratic convention. . . . They got a bunch of neo-Nazis there that do this kind of stuff." "They" was not specified.

Perot also reported that after he had quit the race in July, he was given a videotape of a park-bench meeting in Dallas between a "very senior person in the Bush campaign" and a contract employee of the CIA at which plans were discussed to wiretap his office. Perot said he had sent the tape to the FBI, which in August had investigated allegations that phones in Perot's Dallas office had been bugged and the tapes had been offered to James Oberwetter, the Texas chairman of the Bush-Quayle campaign.

Barnes had claimed that the Bush campaign had hired him to bug Perot's phones, and CBS reported that the FBI, to check out the claim, had asked Perot to make a recording of his voice, which was then taken by an FBI undercover agent to Oberwetter in a sting operation. The agent, CBS said, told Oberwetter he was working with Barnes and had a Perot tape he could have, but that Oberwetter turned down the offer.

By chance, one of us had lunch with Oberwetter, a business executive, in Dallas after the approach was made. He described how he had refused to allow the contact man who had phoned him to come to his office. Instead, he said, he met him outside the building, quickly realized something was fishy and refused to accept the material. At the time, Oberwetter said, he had no idea who was involved, but he suspected he was being set up, and probably filmed.

All this apparently was what Perot had alluded to in the final presidential debate when he accused "the Republican dirty tricks group" of going to "extraordinary sick lengths" to destroy his family's reputation. In our interview with him in his Dallas office back on May 12, well before the two Republican sources were alleged by him to have told him of the wedding sabotage plans, Perot said:

"I marvel at the stuff they get into, because the first rule of war is don't shoot yourself, right? Remember I said that. . . . Let's assume you bring up an issue that is going to totally embarrass you. That's not too smart, right? Then, if you see me not responding to it, it's probably an issue I would never have brought up, never discussed. They have brought it up. I'll discuss it in October, and they're going to be so sick they brought it up."

Perot declined to be more specific, but added that the Republicans were "down to childhood pranks now. I don't know what else they'll bring up. They're just goofy." Perot observed that when two gorillas fight they throw dust in each other's faces, suggesting this was what the Bush campaign was doing to obscure other issues that might be brought against the president.

"If I had been in charge of deregulation in the eighties," he said in the interview, "and oversaw the savings and loan and banking mess—and the vice president [Bush] had that job, which the press scrupulously never talks about—and if I had been involved in any terrorism all through the eighties, and if my fingerprints were all over Noriega and Saddam Hussein in terms of creating them and supporting them, and if I had been squarely in the middle of letting the national debt go from one trillion [dollars] to four trillion, I would probably spend all my time throwing gorilla dust in the air."

Perot mentioned nothing about his daughter's wedding at the time, but he said he would have more to say "at a time that's appropriate, and they'll be wandering around, whining for mother, because it's the same old story. They can dish it but they can't take it. . . . They think that this is going to cause me to stop doing this. That's their objective. . . . Once that starts, I'm in to the end of the fight."

Yet two months later, he was out of the race, saying nothing about plots against his family. In interviews after the election, Tom Luce, who ran the Perot campaign until his July pullout, and Orson Swindle, who ran it afterward, both said Perot the night before withdrawing had referred to concern over his family's privacy, but without the specifics he was now letting the nation in on through his stump speeches and the *60 Minutes* interview.

The reaction was electric, and if it was Perot's intention to turn the country against Bush, it had another immediate effect—to rekindle all the talk about his own "weirdness," "Inspector Perot" and all the rest. White House press secretary Fitzwater told reporters: "There's simply nothing to it. It never happened. There haven't been any dirty tricks against Ross Perot. This business about his daughter is just crazy, and he's been told that, and he knows that."

(Later that week, in an interview with David Frost, Perot acknowledged that after the third presidential debate Barbara Bush "came up to me and said, 'We didn't investigate your children.' And my reaction was, 'Certainly, I am sure she thinks that. But how does she know what the Republican dirty tricks crowd is doing?' "

(In the same interview, when Frost asked him whether it was true that he had told his supporters back in July, the weekend after getting out of the race, that he had threatened an "October surprise" reentry, Perot replied that "I may have said [it] in that meeting, but never publicly, because they wanted me to stay in the race." He said he told them that if [Bush and Clinton] "don't respond to you, and we're on the ballot in all fifty states, we can come back in." The remark lent credence to the existing speculation that he had dropped out of the campaign in July to avoid further press scrutiny, intending all along to reenter in October when it would be too late for the press to pursue that scrutiny effectively.)

The next day in Dallas, an irate Perot stalked into a press briefing by his son, took the microphone and repeated the charges—but admitted again that he had no proof. He said the Bush campaign and White House never told him that they weren't involved until he went on *60 Minutes*, and did so then "at a time when they were trying to get millions of people who supported me to join them." But, he added, "I accept their word. . . . Let's put it behind us."

At the same time, Perot unloaded on the press as unfair to him, assailing "your bizarre stories and your twisted, slanted stories" and adding: "I am sick and tired of you all questioning my integrity without a basis for it. I am sick and tired of you ignoring the people who can confirm the articles when you run your stories." And he stormed out. Why, if Perot was now so willing to drop the issue, did he choose to air it in the first place over such a high-visibility outlet as the top-rated Sunday television show? The "weird" factor was emerging again. Fitzwater was quick to call on the news media to continue its investigations of him "and prevent us from electing a paranoid person who has delusions."

Perot immediately raised the stakes with an unprecedented paid television blitz, filling the airwaves with a host of new commercials of thirty and sixty seconds' length—full of the sound bites he professed to despise from a narrator—to go with half-hour "infomercials" he was now serving up personally. By now, according to *The Washington Post*, Perot had spent $57.5 million since his initial talk of running, more than half of it—$37 million—in the twenty-six days since his reentry into the race, far more than either Bush or Clinton. Included was a full hour on the ABC network at a cost of $940,000. Back in the early summer, Perot had been a penny-pincher when it came to the expensive television ads his "hired guns" wanted him to buy. But now he was doing it his way, and money seemed to be no object.

Perot's television format was simple and straightforward—the candidate himself on camera with charts and a pointer, explaining, for example, how the federal deficit got to the size it was. He taped a half-hour discussion of his plan to reduce the deficit by raising gasoline and other taxes and ran it twice, both times to surprisingly large audiences.

But buying huge blocks of television time did not seem to make as much sense this time as it might have in the past, what with all the television talk shows and morning and evening news shows all but installing revolving doors in their studios for the candidates to drop by and peddle their political wares. Even Bush, who had denigrated them earlier and vowed he would not demean himself by joining the parade, was now working them as diligently as the others.

On three succeeding nights in the final week, Clinton, Perot and Bush dutifully trooped into television studios to chat with Larry King and his coast-to-coast callers. But the most memorable moment for King, the talk show host said later, was one that demonstrated why Ross Perot had such a hold on so many people in this year of voters who were fed up with politics-as-usual, and the politicians who practiced it.

During his interview with Perot in his Washington studio, King said, a bomb threat had brought about forty police to sweep the building. Afterward, downstairs where Perot's car and driver awaited with no Secret Service or other security, the captain of the detail said, "Mr. Perot, we're going to escort you back to the airport and we're going to see that you get safely on your plane."

Perot balked. As King recalled the conversation, Perot told the officer: "No, I don't want any of that. Listen, I'm a citizen. I'm on the ballot but I'm a citizen." The officer informed him that he had the authority to declare someone a public personality who required police protection, "and I'm not leaving you." But Perot still balked. Turning to the assembled police in uniform, King recalled, "Perot makes a speech. He says, 'I don't want any of you to die for me. You're young men, you have children. I've lived a full life. I don't want anybody here risking himself for me.'"

King continued: "And these guys are staring, like, 'We'll walk through the wall for you, Ross.' One of the cops says [to King], 'I've never had an experience like this.' I thought they were going to applaud. Now they negotiate. Perot says, 'Okay, you've gotta do what you've gotta do. No sirens. If you blare sirens you bring attention to yourself, you get in accidents with sirens.' One cop looks at me and says, 'Yeah, you know, we do have accidents.'"

After further negotiations, King said, Perot finally agreed to having one car in front, other cars in back, but no sirens. "Then when they're leaving," King remembered, "Perot says, 'I want to go to the Vietnam Memorial.' The captain says, 'I don't think that would be wise, Mr. Perot.' Perot says, 'No, I haven't been there in a while, I don't want any fanfare, I just want to go.' So he went off to the memorial and then the airport."

If voters were fed up with politics, they were certainly getting an overdose of bad medicine in these closing days of the campaign. Or was it possible that this forced feeding, with increased opportunity for voters themselves to talk to and question the candidates, was igniting a spark of greater interest in the whole business?

Whatever the voter reaction, it was the strange story about the sabotage of his daughter's wedding as the real reason for his July withdrawal that was providing fodder for the talk show circuit now, not Ross Perot's primer on deficit reduction. Bush on NBC's *Today* called Perot's charges "crazy," adding: "I mean an allegation that we would wittingly or in any other way try to break up a man's daughter's wedding, particularly [when he was] not even in the presidential race at that time—what in the world would be the reason for that?"

Clinton gleefully declared a plague on both opposition houses. "So now we've got this bizarre situation where Bush and Perot have accused each other of investigating each other's children," he told a rally in Saginaw, Michigan. "I want to tell you something, folks. I want to investigate your children—their problems, their promise, their future," and that was what Bush and Perot ought to be talking about.

In a final concentrated swing across the South, Clinton and Gore led the largest bus tour of their campaign through North Carolina on a marathon day that ran from early morning in Winston-Salem eastward across the state until the wee hours of the following day. By now the bus trip phenomenon had become a magnet in itself for curious voters, and the two candidates performed according to the well-established script.

Gore went through his melodramatic warm-up painting Clinton as a log-cabin country boy who rose to be the governor of his state and ending with his question, "What time is it?" Everywhere, the crowds seemed to know the answer as they shouted back: "It's time for them [Bush and Quayle] to go!" Then Clinton would take over, making certain this time to remind his listeners how Bush and Perot were scrapping between themselves while he continued to address the concerns of the middle-class voter.

From North Carolina, Clinton's campaign plane hopscotched into Georgia, Florida, Louisiana, Texas, Mississippi and Kentucky over the next three days, with Clinton insisting he was not merely trying to force the Bush campaign to expend resources there, but was out to win in those states. Along the way, he repeatedly reminded voters of the passport flap, narrating how political agents from the Bush State Department "in $600 suits" had gone rummaging through an old warehouse after-hours looking for dirt in his files.

Clinton also took note of an article in *The New Yorker* magazine quoting former Soviet President Gorbachev as saying Bush once told him "not to pay any attention to what he would say in the presidential campaign" about taking credit for the end of the Cold War. "He's telling foreign leaders the truth," Clinton said, "but he won't tell you the truth." Bush had his nerve, he suggested, making character and trust the centerpieces of his campaign against him.

Bush meanwhile was campaigning through Iowa, Kentucky and Ohio armed with some long-awaited good economic news. He reported that the gross domestic product for the third quarter of 1992 had gone up 2.7 percent, the most encouraging indication that the long recession really was over and the country was on its way to economic recovery. He paired the news with a warning that a Democratic victory would bring a return to "the failed policies that brought us a misery index going right through Gore's ozone layer."

But statistics, the Bush strategists knew, were nothing you could put on the dinner table, and that good economic indicators that came so close to the election were not going to translate into meat and potatoes for average Americans in time to affect many votes.

One statistic did give them hope, however, that things were turning their way. On the next day, October 27, exactly a week before voters would be going to the polls, a new *USA Today*/CNN poll by the Gallup organization proclaimed that the race had become virtually a dead heat, with Clinton leading Bush by a bare percentage point among "likely" voters—41 percent for Clinton, 40 for Bush, 14 for Perot.

The figures were astonishing in their contrast with most other public polls showing the Clinton lead narrowing somewhat but certainly not that much. Talk of a surge rippled anew through the Bush campaign—and from the lips of its designated spin doctors to reporters in the Bush traveling entourage. They insisted that their own polling, by veteran Fred Steeper of Detroit, was confirming the surge. And everywhere Bush hammered at "this pattern of deception" he saw in Clinton—dodging the draft was not the question, but that he was lying about it.

As Bush's adrenaline began to pump, his speech became zanier. At a rally at Macomb County [Michigan] Community College, he said of Gore: "You know why I call him Ozone Man? This guy is so far off in the environmental extreme, we'll be up to our neck in owls and out of work for every American. This guy's crazy. He is way out, far out. Far out, man!" Once again, he was George Bush, hipster. He also took to referring to Clinton and Gore as a couple of "bozos," causing chagrined aides to suggest to him privately that the expression hardly enhanced his "presidential" image.

The next day, in Columbus, Ohio, Bush did some spinning of his own, telling a rally that Clinton supporters "feel it slipping away from them" and continuing his zany patter. "Governor Clinton and Ozone, all they do is talk about change," he said. "If I want foreign policy advice, I'd go to Millie [his dog] before I'd go to Ozone and Governor Clinton." Then he would break into his trademark lopsided grin, to the crowd's cheers. As for Clinton's "waffling" on issues, he said, "You cannot have a lot of buts sitting there in the Oval Office." That one got a lot of howls, too, from some in the audience, if not from his consternated aides.

Clinton down the homestretch sought to keep Bush in his sights, attempting to turn the trust issue back on him, even when asked about Perot's latest charges. "He can't prove what he said and that bothers people," Clinton said on the *Today* show, "but . . . don't forget that Mr. Bush has said himself he would do anything to get reelected. I mean, Mr. Perot may not be able to prove those charges but the Bush campaign has been the most reckless campaign with the truth of any campaign that I've seen in modern American history."

Even when he was asked by a caller about the old Gennifer Flowers charges, after saying that he had told her "to tell the truth," he added: "But if you're concerned about the truth, let's talk about the truth," and he repeated the Gorbachev quotation about what he said Bush had told him concerning what he might say in the campaign.

The Bush entourage was still riding the wave of the perceived surge on the afternoon of Friday, October 30, going into the final weekend of the long campaign, when it hit the shoals. The president had addressed a convention of Kentucky Fried Chicken franchise owners in Nashville and Air Force One had brought him into St. Louis, where he received a surprise eleventh-hour endorsement from a Democratic governor, William Donald Schaefer of Maryland.

Schaefer was at war with his own Democratic Party at home at the time and while he didn't say so, the betting in the press corps was that he was rolling the dice in hopes there would be a place for him in a second Bush administration, if there was one. Maryland by now was rated a shoo-in for Clinton and Schaefer himself could not have delivered it under any circumstances anyway. It was reminiscent of the endorsement in 1972 of presidential candidate Edmund Muskie by an Indiana senator after Muskie had finished fourth in the Florida primary, prompting Democratic veteran Frank Mankiewicz to deem it "the first case in recorded history of a rat jumping aboard a sinking ship."

Bush, however, was taking support from whatever quarter he could get it. He had just joined Schaefer in addressing a relatively modest crowd outside a suburban St. Louis industrial park on the gray, blustery afternoon, and was heading for Milwaukee and yet another talk show appearance that night with Larry King, when word came that the Iran-contra affair and his alleged role in it had suddenly raised its head again.

A federal grand jury had delivered a new indictment against Reagan Secretary of Defense Caspar W. Weinberger, sought by Iran-contra independent counsel Lawrence E. Walsh. It alleged that Weinberger had falsely told the House committee investigating the affair in 1987 that he had not made notes of related meetings in 1985 and 1986, when he had made voluminous notes. A previous indictment had been dismissed by the court as lacking in specificity.

Among the papers released with the indictment was a Weinberger note dated January 7, 1986, describing a White House meeting among Reagan, Bush and senior aides at which a plan was discussed to sell TOW antitank missiles to Iran in return for five American hostages held in Lebanon. The note read: "President [Reagan] decided to go with Israeli-Iranian offer to release our 5 hostages in return for sale of 4000 TOWs to Iran by Israel. . . . George Shultz [the secretary of state] + I opposed. . . . Bill Casey [director of the CIA], Ed Meese [the attorney general] + VP [Bush] favored as did [National Security Adviser John M.] Poindexter."

All through the long investigation of the affair, Bush had said he never realized the deal was a swap of arms for hostages, in contradiction of stated policy, until he learned the findings of a Senate intelligence committee investigation in December 1986 from Republican Senator David Durenberger of Minnesota, the committee chairman. Whenever the issue had come up in his 1988 presidential campaign, Bush insisted that he had answered the question of what he knew and when he knew it many times over. The issue was the subject of his celebrated confrontation with CBS News anchorman Dan Rather during the 1988 Iowa caucuses campaign, in which Bush aggressively stonewalled Rather and in the process did much to counter the so-called wimp image that critics had plastered on him.

Now, however, there appeared to be strong evidence that he knew what was going on long before he said he knew. In an appearance on the *Today* show earlier in the month, he had appeared to backtrack, saying he had known about the arms-for-hostages deal "and I've said so all along, given speeches on it." But when the new indictment came out, including the Weinberger note, White House counsel C. Boyden Gray reverted to Bush's original position, that he left the 1986 meeting considering the missile sales not an arms-for-hostages swap but a scheme for "creating an opening to Iran."

Both Clinton and Gore quickly jumped on the story as evidence that it was Bush, not Clinton, who had a "trust" problem. At an impromptu press conference in Pittsburgh, Clinton charged that the new evidence "not only directly contradicts the president's claims but also diminishes the credibility of the presidency." And Gore, in Bangor, Maine, not hesitant to draw a Watergate parallel, called Weinberger's note a "true smoking gun."

Back at the Bush headquarters, somebody handed Charlie Black the Associated Press story dated 2:34 P.M. about the new indictment. "I guess I didn't verbalize, 'Well, this race is over,' but I knew that was about it," he said later. "I took it home and laid it on my dresser . . . one memento of the campaign." He believed that Steeper's numbers were right and that there had, indeed, been a surge—until then.

Bush, on *Larry King Live* from Racine, Wisconsin, that night, insisted there was "nothing new" to the whole matter, and he used the same circumlocution that had served him well throughout the 1988 campaign—that he did not believe that Reagan ever regarded the arrangement as an arms-for-hostages swap. But that was not the question. The question was what Bush believed and knew, and on that he continued to evade.

Callers pummeled the president with questions, including one from Clinton spokesman Stephanopoulos, which Bush again brushed aside as old stuff, charging the Clinton campaign with "desperation last-minute politics when you feel something slipping away." This campaigning by talk show was getting ridiculous when the mouthpiece for one candidate could call in and grill the opposition candidate—especially when he was the president of the United States. But it made for great show biz.

If there was a feeling of something slipping away now, however, it was within the Bush camp, where others shared Black's reaction that the surge, which they were convinced was real, would be nipped by the resurrection of the old bothersome business of Iran-contra. Steeper had reported just the night before, Black said, that Bush was drawing even nationally, picking up a point or two nightly, and closing Clinton's lead to a few points in such key states as Ohio, Michigan and New Jersey. If the trend line continued at the same rate, Steeper projected, Bush would nudge ahead of him by Election Day.

Stan Greenberg, Clinton's pollster, sharply disagreed, however, that there ever was a surge in this last week of the sort Steeper claimed. On the Tuesday before the election, he said, his own polling saw a temporary drop to five percentage points as the Republican base began to come home to Bush, but nothing like the CNN/*USA Today* survey that suggested that the race was dead even. When Bush spent a full day in Ohio in the final week and seemed in the polling to turn the state around, ''we were scared to death,'' Stephanopoulos recalled. But the nervousness in Little Rock was relieved, he said, as Greenberg's polling shortly found Clinton back up at seven points and steady, where it basically remained, he said, through Election Day. ''Stan was like a great family doctor,'' Stephano-poulos said, telling the often pessimistic young aide and the excitable Carville about the talk of a Bush surge: ''You can say what you want. It's not moving.''

While the fat leads in major states like California and Illinois inevitably came down, reducing the national figures, Greenberg said, there was no danger of losing those states and the electoral vote picture stayed secure. Also, he noted, the Bush campaign was running unanswered television advertising in base Republican states, bringing some of that base home in the last week in states the Clinton campaign never counted on winning.

Steeper's projection of Bush's closing trend, Greenberg argued later, was fine as far as it went, but you couldn't assume that it would continue right through the election absent a negative development like the Weinberger indictment. A true surge, he said, would be the switching of voters from the opposition candidate or the movement of undecided voters, not merely the return of a base the candidate needed to be competitive. Steeper later acknowledged that "you can't assume that a trend will continue" indefinitely, but said his evidence was statistically solid that Bush had been reducing Clinton's lead "by a point a day," until the Weinberger indictment, hard on the heels of Perot's bizarre charges of Bush agents threatening wedding sabotage, killed off the surge.

The problem with the return of the Iran-contra issue, the Bush strategists realized, was not simply or even primarily that Bush would be disbelieved by voters. Rather, the injecting of the story was going to divert public attention from his message—the charge that Clinton could not be trusted with the presidency—and require spending precious time in the closing days on damage control.

"The last four nights," Black said, "two of them, instead of Clinton on defense, Bush on offense, [you had] Bush on defense, and reminding people of something, it wasn't new, but it reminded them of something they didn't like about Bush. It was all the news."

Carville, for his part, shrugged off the Weinberger indictment as a critical factor. " 'Bozos' and that crack about his dog Millie hurt more," he said. And Greenberg said that whatever took Bush off the message voters wanted to hear from him—how he would fix the economy—hurt him, even when he talked about Clinton and the draft or his trip to Moscow. "Once Bush was advancing the story rather than the press advancing the story, it made it political. Bush was not a credible presenter of that argument. Then once Bush took it over the line to the Moscow trip, [going too far by raising] the question of patriotism, he lost the press and lost the public. It just looked whacko."

It was now Saturday, October 31—Halloween—and the Bush campaign had hoped to chase the hobgoblins away with a day-long train trip on an old freight line from southeast to north-central Wisconsin, with all the trappings of an old-fashioned political whistletop. The scheduling was surprising to many in the press corps because Wisconsin, although clearly a state still up for grabs, had only eleven electoral votes and there were many larger states with more that might have commanded a full day of the president's fast-diminishing campaign time.

But Bush strategists reasoned that since their candidate could not afford to lose any battleground states, Wisconsin was as good a place to go as any, especially by train. The planners knew that there are few political events that are better magnets for news and television coverage than a whistlestop train ride, and they scheduled a stream of radio and television interviews by local stations with Bush along the 279-mile route.

"What we were finding this year more than usual," Black said later, "was that stops in the states weren't having that much impact. The half life on them was about two days only; it used to be about a week. So you're really gearing most of it to the news. And because of the change in the way everybody was handling their news, doing a lot of local TV interviews and Larry King and stuff like that, it was more important than doing an extra stop. The best press we got in the whole campaign was those train trips, so we made a calculated decision to do a train trip that Saturday, and there were only a certain number of places you could do them."

Furthermore, the Bush planners understood that an essential ingredient for an effective campaign day was an enthusiastic, upbeat candidate, and they knew that Bush drew strength and optimism from such events, to which big crowds were easy to attract. Even in the television era, small-town America still thrilled at the visit of a president, and the opportunity to bring children down to the depot for a piece of family history that would be long remembered.

The day dawned gray, overcast and windy at the flag-bedecked train station in Burlington, "Chocolate City, U.S.A.," named after a large plant there. A huge crowd packed in around the depot and the glistening Wisconsin Central engine, spit-polished to pull nineteen passenger cars including "The Baltimore," a custom private car at the end, along the long route to the last stop at Chippewa Falls. The mood was cheerful and expectant, despite the intrusion of a single-propeller plane overhead hauling a special message for Bush: IRAN-CONTRA HAUNTS YOU.

The president, suffering from a head cold but clearly buoyed by the turnout, started out using the holiday to accuse Clinton of a campaign of fear-mongering. "Today is Halloween, our opponents' favorite holiday," he said. "They're trying to scare America," he said, by trying to convince voters that the country was "a nation in decline," but the 2.7 percent gross domestic product increase proved otherwise. If Clinton was elected, he warned, "every day is going to be Halloween. Fright and terror!"

As the dark day wore on, Bush seemed to get progressively giddier, until, at Oshkosh, making the same reference, he shouted: "Fright and terror! Witches and devils everywhere!" At the same stop, he finally responded to the latest Iran-contra story, casting it as a desperate Clinton gambit. A "panicked" Clinton, he said, had begun "a series of personal attacks on my character, and he has basically called me a liar" regarding what Bush knew and when he knew it about the arms-for-hostages swap. Clinton, he said, "has now latched on to these silly little charges, accusations, in a desperate attempt to stop his free-fall in the polls," adding that "being attacked on character by Clinton is like being called ugly by a frog."

At Stevens Point, Bush said the latest charges were "part of a Democratic witch hunt," and that the only way Clinton could win was by finding "a last-minute smoking gun" where there was none. It happened that a member of the prosecutorial team that had pressed for the new Weinberger indictment was a Democrat and onetime Clinton contributor, leading some in the Bush entourage to conclude that the whole business was a partisan plot. But the fact remained that Walsh, who approved the seeking of the second indictment, was a Republican.

Nevertheless, inside the Bush campaign, a story circulated of a warning from a Democratic source that a bombshell was about to be dropped on Bush, fueling suspicions of foul play. David Tell, a young Republican in charge of opposition research for the Bush campaign, had become friends with his counterpart at the Democratic National Committee, Dan Carol, who incidentally had produced the T-shirts of Bush's travels that were such a success in 1991. In fact, on occasion the two opponents, Tell said later, swapped information they had on Ross Perot. They would call to tease each other about how the campaign was going, Tell said, and on the day before the Weinberger indictment broke, Carol told him he "had one last bomb to drop," without specifying what it was.

(After the election, Tell said, he phoned Carol to congratulate him on the outcome and asked him directly if the Weinberger indictment was the bomb to which he had referred and, Tell said later, "he did not say no." Carol said he remembered talking to Tell on Tuesday or Wednesday of the final week and being irritated by Tell's needling him about the purported surge. So, Carol said, he told Tell: "Listen, David, we're going to drop a bomb on you Friday, a big bomb." But, Carol insisted in the retelling, "I was completely bluffing." And when Tell called him about the election, Carol said, "I played cute. I said nothing to lead him otherwise." In fact, he told us, he had encountered resistance anytime he had tried to get even information from Walsh's office that was already on the public record.

("I know this," Black said later. "Lawyers and prosecutors in this town [Washington], and especially people who are high-profile like special prosecutors, are very politically sensitive, and very politically smart. I further know that everybody over there [in Walsh's office] is a liberal Democrat, and there were plenty of legal ways not to do that on the Friday before the election. I further believe that some Democrats around town knew on Thursday something big was coming. At least they were bragging about it. It was a hell of a coincidence."

(Black said he had heard about the Carol-Tell conversations. "It's not proof of anything," he said, "but I'd damn sure like to have some investigator put that guy [Carol] under oath and see what he has to say, and where he got it. I'm not accusing anybody of anything, except it's not possible that those Democratic prosecutors didn't fully calculate what they were doing politically. I'm not saying the Clinton people or the DNC were in on it. I don't know. And I'm not saying that alone cost us the race. The momentum might have been tailing off for some other reason or something, but we had a real good race going there.")

In responding to the Weinberger note and the Clinton comments during the Wisconsin whistlestop, the president sought to deflect the issue, but at the same time he was guaranteeing by his remarks that the story would have another day's life in the national news cycle. Fitzwater, standing next to the tracks at one stop in the late afternoon, was peppered with reporters' questions about the impact of the charges. The whole story, he replied, was "only" costing the campaign a day's time—one of the three remaining before election day.

For all that, Mary Matalin said later, the president "was having a whale of a time," as he always did on the train trips. He often sounded mean-spirited, again calling Clinton and Gore "bozos" but quickly apologizing as he remembered the caution from his aides. Then he would flash that somewhat sappy grin and start rambling in choppy Bushspeak— sentences starting with verbs that often went off into the ether.

But above all as a campaigner he understood what it meant to average

Americans to see a president of the United States—not just George Bush—in person, Matalin said, and he reveled in the shouted greetings, waves and other signs of affection along the way. At times he would stand on the rear platform, waving back as the train rolled by, and at others he would send greetings of his own over a public-address system, microphone in hand. When a radio reporter who had been shuttled into his car for a brief interview on the Wisconsin run commented to him about the crowds and asked how he felt about the turnout, Bush beamed and said: "Great! I've only been mooned once!"

The next day, the final Sunday, worse things happened to him. He endured a long CNN interview on which the Iran-contra matter came up again, and although he had said he didn't want to hear any more about polls and state-by-state electoral calculations, he was informed that he had dropped about five percentage points in his own polls in the wake of the Weinberger indictment. "He was cranky, doubly cranky," recalled Matalin.

At one point, when she gave him a sheet of paper with some numbers on it, he threw it across the table, saying, "I don't want to see them anymore." But he snapped out of it, she said, because "he really thought the polls were whacky." So did she, she said, because the election was coming down to a referendum on two men, "and we believed that when people went into the polling booth they would vote on that choice, and we had the superior candidate."

In these final days, Teeter said later, "he knew we were behind . . . we were moving, but we were never at a point where we were close to being ahead, but you didn't know what Perot would do, you had that wild card in there. We knew where we could get our most likely 270 [electoral votes], but we were behind in all of the key states. Our chances of making it were slim. . . . The problem was, we had to have an electoral miracle— we were in the worst of the inside-straight strategies. Not only you had to hit it, you even had to have some breaks. There was never a time where you really felt you ever got a break or a series of breaks that gave you an upper hand for a while."

Still, he said, Bush "was a guy who was working as hard as he could. He was smart enough to know that when you're behind there's only one thing to do—get yourself geared up and go out and campaign as hard as you can and hope it works, hope you get enough breaks or make some to get you going.''

Bush therefore doggedly pressed on, again trying to milk the draft issue against Clinton, this time with a charge that friends of the governor in Arkansas had destroyed his ROTC records, which the Clinton campaign promptly denied.

As a parting shot, Representative Guy Vander Jagt, defeated for reelection in an earlier Republican primary but finishing out his term as chairman of the National Republican Congressional Committee, held an election-eve news conference in Salt Lake City and charged that Clinton was having an affair with a wire-service reporter assigned to his campaign. The charge, also quickly denied, then was faxed to newspaper offices, one of the faxes arriving at the Washington Bureau of *The Baltimore Sun* around 10:30 that night, only shortly before voters in Dixville Notch, New Hampshire, were about to cast the nation's first presidential ballots in the village's quadrennial tradition.

Perot, back on the stump for one last swing that took him to Denver and Long Beach, California, finally turned his sights on Clinton. The target was somewhat surprising after Perot's almost single-minded focus on Bush, but the polls—which he vowed he never bothered with—were indicating that Clinton was the man to beat. Perot lit into him and Gore for acknowledging they had once smoked marijuana. "Do you think the president of the United States and his wife should be good role models for your children?" he asked his cheering supporters. "Do you think it's appropriate to have senior government officials who have used drugs?" The crowd shouted back: "No!"

On a later half-hour paid television appearance, Perot used his charts and pointer to attack Clinton's record as governor in Arkansas. He charged that one in five jobs created in the state during Clinton's nearly twelve-year tenure had been in the poultry industry, adding that "if we decide to take this level of business-creating capability nationwide, we'll all be plucking chickens for a living." Ever ready with the sound bites he disdained, Perot concluded: "So I guess you can just sum it up: the chickens keep on clucking and the people keep on plucking after twelve years of Governor Clinton's leadership."

Meanwhile, Clinton was sprinting to the finish through the industrial belt yet again, his voice so raspy that he winced as he croaked out a few words and then turned the microphone over to his wife. The man well remembered for the speech that never seemed to end at the 1988 Democratic convention spoke for only twenty-one seconds at a stop at a tailgate party outside Riverfront Stadium in Cincinnati, but he told the crowd: "We've fought for a year. We've got two days to go. Fight on!" Although the poll numbers were holding up, there was plenty of nervousness on the Clinton plane about what might yet happen, and it didn't escape the candidate. Paul Begala, as the end approached, told Dee Dee Myers: "I feel like a porcupine in a balloon factory."

The final day was a blur, as both Bush and Clinton raced frenetically by jet around the country, Clinton touching down in nine states in a thirty-hour nonstop marathon, Bush in six and Perot returning to Dallas for one final rally at which he danced with his youngest daughter, Katherine, to Patsy Cline's favorite—"Crazy." It was a fitting theme not simply for his off-again, on-again flirtation with the presidency and the American people, but also for the whole year of ups and downs, of scandalmongering and fearmongering. And it was played out before an electorate that had made clear its distaste for politics as usual, yet engaged itself in the dialogue through the phenomenon of talk-back television as never before.

On Election Day, this involvement manifested itself, after a thirty-two-year trend of steady decline in voter participation in the election of presidents, in an upturn at the polls—55.24 percent of the eligible voting age population, compared to 50.1 in 1988. The decision came early and was unambiguous, if not the blowout that had seemed in the making. Americans gave Bill Clinton 43 percent of their votes and 370 electoral votes in thirty-two states in every region of the country and the District of Columbia, to 38 percent and 168 electoral votes in the remaining eighteen states for Bush and a surprising 19 percent but no electoral votes for Perot.

A survey of 15,490 voters leaving their polling places, conducted by Voter Research and Surveys, a joint operation of the television networks, found a formidable coalition for Clinton. The Democratic nominee reversed the pattern of a generation and won among independent voters, garnering 38 percent of them to 32 for Bush and an impressive 30 for Perot. Clinton won among young voters ages eighteen to twenty-four— 46 percent to 33 for Bush and 21 for Perot—who had flocked to Reagan and Bush in the three previous elections, as well as voters in all other age groups. And he won by two to one over Bush among Reagan Democrats, who had been a prime Clinton target for a year. Among first-time voters, it was Clinton 42 percent, Bush 32, Perot 22.

At the same time, the basic constituencies of Clinton's party held fast. Although the black turnout declined, Clinton captured 83 percent of the black vote to 10 for Bush and 7 for Perot. Among Jewish voters, he won 80 percent to 11 for Bush and 9 for Perot. And in the three-way race his 61 percent among Hispanics to 25 for Bush and 14 for Perot matched Dukakis's share of the same vote in a two-man contest four years earlier.

Bush's best showing was 53 percent among Southern white Protestants, who included many of the religious-right voters who had been so entranced by the emphasis on ''family values'' at the Republican convention. He was held to a virtual tie by Clinton among all white voters (Bush 40 percent, Clinton 39, Perot 20) and trailed him among men and women alike.

For all that, many said it was not much of a mandate for Clinton, only a plurality winner. Still, the overall message was clear enough: 62 percent of the voting American public wanted change from what George Bush had given them the previous four years. And this time they did not say so through the sort of apathy that had marked their turning away from the process since at least 1960. In larger numbers than ever before— 104,423,000—they stood up and were counted. The natural population growth could take part of the credit. But the bottom line was that something happened in 1992 that stirred more Americans to stop running from the political process, and start taking part in it.

CHAPTER 29

VOX POPULI

Why, after more than three decades of steadily increasing apathy and hostility toward the electoral process, did Americans in electing Bill Clinton and denying George Bush a second term post the largest percentage turnout since the election of John F. Kennedy?

Was it in large part simply because they became fed up with politics as usual and punished its most conspicuous practitioner? It was clear that they had had enough of gridlock in Washington, and Clinton as a Democrat offered the hope of working with the Democratic-controlled Congress. Voters wanted no more, either, of the kind of name-calling, personal slander, and negative radio and television advertising that by 1992 had threatened to smother all constructive political dialogue, yet continued to be employed by the Bush campaign. And for all the talk of shared responsibility between the executive and legislative branches in Washington, they continued to believe that the buck stopped where Harry Truman said it did—on the president's desk in the Oval Office, where Bush sat, his critics charged, idly.

Over those three decades since Kennedy's election, the public response to politics as usual had been quite the opposite of the increased turnout of 1992. More and more in those years, voters had shunned both of the great political parties and had opted out of the process, declining to make a choice that with each passing election was labeled the lesser of two evils. Wags reversed it. The evil of two lessers, they called the system that offered them what they saw either as inferior, inadequate choices or tweedledum and tweedledee.

That this disgruntled attitude was not by any means abandoned by the American public in 1992 can be seen in the fact that even the 55.24 percent turnout of the voting age population calculated by the Committee for the Study of the American Electorate for the presidential election paled in comparison with voter turnout in nearly all other Western democracies. The figure in its rawest terms meant that for every eligible voter who went to the polls, roughly one still stayed home. Nevertheless, the trend of recent elections *was* turned around, fueling hope that Americans as a whole saw something in the process or in the candidates that gave them reason for optimism.

Or was it more that their frustration had plunged so low by 1992 and their anger had grown so hot that, like people unable any longer to endure living under an oppressive yoke, they decided they had to take matters in their own hands? This motivation seemed much the more likely one. All of the nine more or less major candidates in the field had identifiable flaws or shortcomings in voters' eyes. Five Democrats—Wilder, Kerrey, Harkin, Tsongas and Brown—and one Republican—Buchanan—fell quickly by the wayside in the primary process, and the major party nominees—Clinton and Bush—survived bearing politically debilitating scars of the battle. The one major independent who did not face the primary voters—Perot—self-immolated at midcourse, only to resurrect himself in similarly scarred condition in the final month of the campaign.

If it was true that American voters were already "mad as hell" for several election cycles, what was it about 1992 that made so many of them decide that they were "not going to take it anymore," to the point of involving themselves in a political process they had shunned in those earlier election cycles?

For one thing, the world had changed in a dramatic fashion since the presidential election of 1988. The Cold War had ended, lifting the international climate of superpower confrontation and easing the threat of nuclear war in a truly significant way for the first time since the end of World War II. Americans were able to focus more of their attention on conditions at home and what their government in Washington was or wasn't doing to improve those conditions.

What they saw was economic decline that hit them not simply at the bottom rungs, with the poor and undereducated bearing the brunt as so often in past recessions. This time the blow was to the nation's solar plexus—the immense middle class that was the legacy of Franklin D. Roosevelt's New Deal, more recently wooed and won by Ronald Reagan—and in a more frightening manner.

Bob Teeter, in analyzing Bush's defeat, called it "a unique recession." Many white-collar, middle-income workers were being laid off or facing layoffs for the first time, Teeter noted, unlike blue-collar workers in the auto and other manufacturing industries who were accustomed to periodic layoffs and rehirings as the cycle of their businesses changed. "In most recessions where you have blue-collar guys laid off," he said, "almost everybody knew they were going to get called back in a couple of months, or six months, or sometime like that. And something like fifteen percent of the people in some worse recessions ended up losing their job and not getting their job back. In this one it was like forty percent who didn't, who were not going to get back to where they were.

"At the same time," he said, "you had real estate deflation, and people with a house that was worth less, and you had people with families who were educating their first generation. . . . So you had a family, the wife had worked, the husband had worked two jobs or something, they had sacrificed for twenty, twenty-five years . . . and the one way you were going to protect your kids from going through the stress and strain that you did was to get them a college education. Then the kids graduated from college and couldn't find a job." With the stories of "huge permanent layoffs" by General Motors, IBM and other giant corporations, Teeter said, "the apprehension and fear that spread way beyond the people who were actually looking for jobs" was what damaged Bush so severely.

Part of the problem was that the whole concept of restructuring of industries that came with the end of the Cold War threatened middle-aged workers with the prospect that the job they were doing would not be there much longer, or that if they were laid off, the job wouldn't be there when there was rehiring. Longer life expectancy confronted these middle-aged workers with greater need for health care insurance and no way to get it through continued employment, and no way to pay the high premiums on their own. And with this apprehension and fear came frustration at a stand-pat president and, in due course, anger.

Bush thought the whole matter of convincing voters that he understood and cared about how people were hurting economically, Jim Lake said afterward, "was election year rhetoric, so he couldn't make the sale. . . . It never was a part of him. He never got it." Teeter said Bush "did get it," but there was too much "disunity" among his economic team to decide on a clear and coherent path to follow.

It was in the context of this inability to address the nation's domestic ills effectively that another Bush insider observed that Bush's success in mobilizing the alliance that drove Saddam Hussein out of Kuwait proved in the end to hurt him politically, by setting "a new standard of performance" for him—"if he could do that, he could fix other problems if he applied himself." And by election time, it was all too clear to these potential voters that Bush was not fixing such problems at home, and couldn't be counted on to do so in a second term. Had the Cold War still been on, Bush White House aide Jim Pinkerton said, the president still would have been able to run on his foreign policy experience. But its end, and then the end of the Gulf War, moved the nation's focus, and inevitably the campaign debate, homeward.

Among staunch old Reaganites, there was a sense that the Reagan Revolution in Bush's hands was already over, with no sense of what would replace it, even if Bush were reelected. By contrast, Clinton offered a clear concept of basic change. As campaign manager David Wilhelm put it after the election, "it was the end of trickle-down economics, it was an economic agenda of putting people first, as we called it. That was a big idea, and unlike 1988 where at the conclusion of the campaign people woke up and said, 'Hey, what was *that* all about?' In 1992, people woke up and said, 'Well, I think I know what that was about.' The Reagan era was over, to the extent that Bush represented the third term of the Reagan era. A new economic philosophy had replaced it, and the election capsulized that, and that was understood . . . by the voter."

In attempting to finesse the economy as the central cause of voter apprehension, frustration, fear and anger by diverting attention to the question of Clinton's character and trustworthiness, the Bush campaign badly miscalculated. The sorts of scare issues that had worked for Bush against Michael Dukakis in 1988, in much better economic times, did not have the same effect against Clinton among voters more concerned about jobs than about such things as pollution in Boston Harbor or some new Willie Horton—or Gennifer Flowers.

Mandy Grunwald put it this way: "There was something unusual about this year that made it possible not to have Gennifer Flowers kill Clinton's candidacy, not to have the draft kill Clinton's candidacy. And that was just how scared people were about the fate of the country. People were engaged in the election in a completely different way than they were in '88 or '84, because the issues were so big and so prescient. It's an odd way to think about it, but there are a lot of issues that I consider 'luxury issues.' I think Boston Harbor and Willie Horton are 'luxury issues.' I think Gennifer Flowers is a 'luxury issue.'

"I mean 'luxury' in the sense that if you can put food on your table and pay your health care bills, and you [aren't] worried about whether you have a job, then you have the luxury to think about whether or not Michael Dukakis furloughed some guy and you can think about whether this guy [Clinton] dodged the draft twenty-three years ago. What was so unusual about this year was that people didn't have that luxury. And they had a very clear sense of how big the problems were, and they were really single-minded about keeping focus on those problems, because it mattered deeply to their lives what the state of the election was. I think that fundamental fact influenced everything, from the viewership of debates . . . to the dismissing of issues like the draft or his [Clinton's] trip to Moscow or any of that."

Charlie Black acknowledged after the election that the Bush campaign in going after Clinton on character and trust had counted on the voters to respond as they had in 1988 to the negative information on the Democratic nominee used against him. "The thing that surprised me about Clinton," he said, "was that he had more Teflon on those things— the lying, flip-flopping, the draft. The guy carried veterans [on Election Day]. I would have been shocked if you told me back in August, 'Hey, this all sounds good [about the Bush attack strategy on the draft issue], but Clinton's going to carry a plurality of veterans.' I would have said,

'Shit, I've got to rethink this whole race,' because I knew we'd play the draft thing.''

The Bush campaign, Black said, tested voter reaction to Clinton's use of the phrase "loathing the military" in his letter to Colonel Holmes, "all kinds of different things. Part of it was public opinion [about the Vietnam War], part of it was he did a pretty good job of spinning it around to, 'Hey, the issue was whether I was for or against the war.' The real issue about the draft was lying. We got that out through the *Time* ad and the other things we did, did get a bunch of people believing he was lying about it. But in the end that didn't matter much to them. We couldn't make it as salient as the economy. That's what it came down to.''

In this context, the Clinton campaign's constant reminder to the country that Bush was again "going negative" as he did against Dukakis in 1988—a reminder reinforced by the news media—instead of talking about the economic plight of people reinforced the notion that the voters didn't have the luxury to dwell on political mud-slinging.

"But you have to understand," Grunwald said. "They reminded *us*. You couldn't go to focus groups much without people using Willie Horton as a frame of reference. And one of the hangovers that I think all of us who've worked in Democratic statewide campaigns since '88 have seen—ask any pollster or media consultant—is that the topic of negative advertising has been a big topic for people. They felt manipulated by Willie Horton—burned by that experience—and they vowed it wasn't going to happen again. They weren't going to be fooled again. They were going to keep their eye on the prize.''

There were other "luxury issues" not mentioned by Grunwald that voters wouldn't or couldn't afford to buy that the Bush campaign tried unsuccessfully to peddle—"family values" and abortion, as best illustrated in Dan Quayle's jab at Murphy Brown and later the whole Hollywood "cultural elite." In better economic times—through most of the Reagan years and Bush's first two—these issues were or would have been golden, nurtured as they were by the Republican right wing.

In one of the great ironies of the 1992 campaign, Bush was obliged to invoke these and other "values" issues repeatedly in his long effort to appease his party's right wing after he had "betrayed" it in breaking his no-new-taxes pledge. That effort not only failed to stem conservative disillusionment with him but also led to a Republican national convention that showcased the party in its least attractive posture—a captive of narrowness, bitterness and exclusivity. Bush needed at that convention to tell voters what he would do to help them. Instead, they heard repackaged old ideas from him and encouragements to division from others, and the voters didn't have the luxury of casting their presidential ballots on the basis of either of them.

Added to this mix was the combustible Ross Perot—a match on dry tinder. He was in a real sense the embodiment of the American voter who was fed up with politics as usual and who felt he did not have the luxury of keeping his mouth shut any longer, or of paying attention to all the personal mud-slinging and diversions from the central issue. That issue, Perot said over and over again, was digging the country out of its economic mess, by taking national power from those who were abusing or squandering it, and giving it back to the people—"the owners" of the country.

Perot sought to mobilize all the apprehension, frustration, fear and anger in the country through the force of his own rather quirky personality and immense wealth, and fashion it into an effective political tool. His effort, though failed, was remarkable considering his inexperience in politics and the dismal history of third-party politics in America. There is no doubt it contributed greatly to shaking the political lethargy and apathy that had captured the country for so long, and to bringing about the demise of the Bush presidency, which he obviously so despised.

In Perot's undertaking, and in Clinton's ability to keep his own focus on the economy in the face of the assault on his character and trustworthiness, another new dimension in presidential politics played a key role. Talk show television to an unprecedented degree enabled the candidates, eventually including Bush as well, to tap directly in to the voters' frustration over having lost an effective voice in the political decisions that affected their lives, and to give it an outlet.

Perot, Clinton and Bush were asked by average voters on the air, and they answered, hundreds of questions, only a handful of which were of a personal nature, or of the "horse race" variety favored by political reporters and hated by most candidates. While a great many were softballs the candidates had heard many times and could knock out of the park with ease, many also went to the heart of the voters' deep concerns about the state of the country, and their own futures in it. Oftentimes the questions were not as smooth as they might have been coming from a professional interviewer or interrogator, but they often were more directly and personally tied to a voter's feelings, and sought to elicit the same kind of response from the candidates. The second presidential debate in Richmond, in the town-meeting or talk show format, was appropriately typical of what such linking of candidate with voter could reveal. When Marisa Hall asked Bush how the "national debt" affected him personally, and he replied that he was "not sure I get" the gist of the question, he left the impression that he simply did not comprehend how public policy affected the lives of average Americans. Clinton stepped forward and did, with his response about the problems of people in Arkansas he knew personally.

After the election, Clinton talked about the impact of greater direct voter involvement in the process. In pressing for the town-meeting format in which voters expressed their displeasure with politics as usual, he said, "I just had this instinctive feeling that this was an election that was terribly important to people and they wanted to lift it up, and sure enough that's what they did. There was a huge turnout, and I think all the stuff we did [to involve voters more directly], I hope we can keep it going."

Larry King, whose CNN call-in show became a regular stopping place on the campaign trail for all three candidates, naturally reveled in the phenomenon, but also underscored its significance to the process. "I think we've never had a year when we knew the candidates better than this year," he said after the election. "I don't think there could have been anybody saying, 'I don't know Bill Clinton' or 'I don't know George Bush' or 'I don't know Ross Perot' by the time they went to vote.

"What showed me the success of it was the audience that the debates had. I think this became a human-interest saga in which these three people and the vice presidential candidates were more than just an election. They were a television series about to end, on November third. It was like the last night of *Cheers*. These guys were going to go away . . . and the public had gotten so absorbed with them that by the time of the debates everyone was watching for something to happen . . . to see the energy."

Also, King noted, it is not so easy for a candidate to slough off a voter who calls in as it is to put aside or put down a celebrity interviewer. "When someone says [on the air], 'I'm out of work, what are you gonna do for me?' it gives a totally different perspective," King said, "than

Larry King or Dan Rather saying, 'What about the people out of work?' You are now hearing a human being out of work talking to a man who can affect his getting work. You can't beat that.''

King predicted that most of the best-known talk shows before long will be taking phone calls as a result of what happened in the 1992 campaign. "The public has become part of the story [of the campaign], and that can't change. It's like showing freedom in the Soviet Union. . . . It is vox populi. It doesn't matter that only twelve calls get in. What does matter is, is you feel, 'I could call this guy.' " (In fact, King's show became a direct line of communication between the campaigns. Republican Party chairman Rich Bond called in to ask Perot to come up with evidence to back his charges of Republican smears; George Stephanopoulos called Bush to tweak him about Iran-contra at the time of the second Weinberger indictment.)

It seemed at times that the whole campaign was taking place on the nation's television screens, but there was nothing new in that. What was new, was the voice of the people speaking out loud and clear, calling directly for answers, over the news medium that had come to dominate presidential campaigns as it had come to dominate the social and cultural life of the country.

As a practical matter, only a handful of Americans actually were able to talk directly to the candidates. But the significant difference to the voters was, as King pointed out, that people just like themselves were questioning the candidates—were in effect surrogates for the average voter. Watching Clinton, Bush and Perot in that Richmond debate, anyone could imagine being the one asking the questions and influencing the process directly. It was no longer the sole province of journalists, whom they saw as part of the distant establishment rather than as their agents.

All these voices, for the first time since the end of World War II and the start of the Cold War, were talking almost exclusively in 1992 about the condition of life on Main Street, U.S.A. They had been quiet long enough. They had turned their backs on the political process long enough. They demanded to be heard—through Ross Perot's ballot petition drive, through Bill Clinton's town meetings, even through the "Ask George Bush" sessions, and through whatever electronic means were available to them. They demanded change, and on November 3, 1992, they forced it—from winter, in Clinton's Inaugural Address words, they "forced the spring."

In many ways, the election of 1992 was a confirmation of the findings of a study in June 1991 for the Kettering Foundation called *Citizens and Politics: A View from Main Street America*. It concluded that Americans, far from being apathetic to the political process, "do care about politics, but they no longer believe they can have an effect." They think, the study went on, "many of the avenues for expressing their views are window dressings, not serious attempts to hear the public," and they "want to know their concerns are understood." These conclusions provide clues to why, with the reach-out candidacies of Clinton and Perot, voter turnout increased in 1992, and why Bush's failure to connect with voter concerns was at the core of his defeat.

The Kettering Foundation study also concluded that Americans "want an ongoing relationship, especially in between elections, in which there is 'straight talk' and give-and-take between public officials and citizens." Almost from the moment William Jefferson Clinton took the oath as the forty-second president of the United States on the West Front steps of the Capitol, he set out to give them that relationship. He resumed the conversation with the American voters that had been a major factor in his election, and in the immediate weeks thereafter, he continued it as he strove aggressively to rally them behind the agenda for change that he had promised them during the campaign.

That agenda was, to be sure, considerably curtailed once Clinton faced the budgetary realities that were waiting for him when he entered the Oval Office. But as he went on television and in person around the country to enlist the people's support, he seemed to treat the presidency he had just assumed as a sort of extension of his successful campaign of going directly to the voters.

Before he held a single formal news conference as president to field questions from the experienced White House press corps, Clinton went to Detroit for a nationally televised "town meeting" with callers from Atlanta, Miami and Seattle linked up by satellite. A few days later, he met with a select group of children, carefully chosen, to take their questions for more than ninety minutes—again on television. And in between he climbed aboard Air Force One for trips to the Midwest and the West

Coast, playing the role of chief salesman for his economic proposals, going right to America's doorstep.

In doing all this, notably, he adopted not only the deficit-cutting emphasis of that other super-salesman, Ross Perot, in his homespun 1992 romance with the "owners" of the country, but his jargon as well. In his Inaugural Address, Clinton cautioned his fellow public servants not to forget "those people whose toil and sweat sends us here and pays our way," and in his enthusiasm he told the voters: "You have raised your voices in an unmistakable chorus, you have cast your votes in historic numbers, and you have changed the face of Congress, the presidency and the political process itself."

In his State of the Union speech, too, Clinton reminded the members of Congress assembled before him that they were the taxpayers' "hired hands" and that "every penny we draw" was "their money." Republicans talked about corraling the Perot voters in advance of 1996; Clinton set out from day one of his White House tenure to do so.

The jury was still out, however, on the new president's contention that the political process had truly been changed. Yet to be determined was whether this bear-hug embrace of the electorate—this new talk show presidency—could be sustained by its creator. Beyond that, the question was whether it could win over not only those mad-as-hell voters who gave the political process one more chance in 1992, but also the millions of Americans still turned away from it. After more than three decades of growing voter alienation, it was now in Bill Clinton's hands to convince them that the great American experiment was still worth the candle.

INDEX